# International Perspectives on Crime and Justice

# International Perspectives on Crime and Justice

Edited by

K. Jaishankar

CAMBRIDGE
SCHOLARS
PUBLISHING

International Perspectives on Crime and Justice, Edited by K. Jaishankar

This book first published 2009

Cambridge Scholars Publishing

12 Back Chapman Street, Newcastle upon Tyne, NE6 2XX, UK

British Library Cataloguing in Publication Data
A catalogue record for this book is available from the British Library



ISBN (10): 1-4438-0198-4, ISBN (13): 978-1-4438-0198-0

*To my Mother, late K. Rukmani,*
*who had a vision for my higher education*
*and my Father, K. Karuppannan,*
*who sacrificed his basic comforts for my education*

# TABLE OF CONTENTS

## Part II. Criminological theory and Research



## Part III. Criminal justice, Prisons and Media, in a Changing World

**Part VI. Globalization and Crime:
Issues of Politics, Prisons, and Terrorism**

# FOREWORD

# KEITH D. HARRIES

I have been fortunate enough to visit India on three occasions, first in 1995, then 1998 and 2008. Each visit has been a learning experience as well as – to some degree – an exercise in culture shock. On each occasion, arrangements were made for me to visit various universities on what might be considered short lecture tours. In the course of these visits, I was fortunate enough to talk to criminology and geography departments, and occasionally other programs such as sociology, policy science, and engineering, the latter owing to my interest in geographic information systems. My visits to India were immeasurably enriched by discussions with scholars in different places and different disciplines and I struggled, at times, to absorb the many collaborative possibilities stimulated by these interactions.

My unforgettable trip in India in 1998 was to *Pondicherry* (now Puducherry), a place of particular interest owing to its French connections, as well as for being the home to the famous *Auroville Ashram*. As a naive foreigner, my principal contact in India, Dr. A. Sivamurthy (who, like me, had a mixed pedigree, with an interest in both criminology and geography), felt that I should be escorted on this trip by a trustworthy graduate student who could steer me away from all hazards. This graduate student was none other than the editor of this book, K. Jaishankar (Jai), who was at that time pursuing a Ph.D. in criminology at the University of Madras. Our visit was interesting, with exciting bus transportation and interesting conversations at the French Institute (where we stayed) as well as an astonishingly good lunch and academic orientation provided by Dr. Christopher Guilmoto, a faculty member at the Institute. Jai and I spent several days' together, visiting Pondicherry University, Pondicherry Law College and went long walks in Pondicherry beach, giving us a good opportunity to get to know each other.

I could immediately see that Jai was a very bright and creative fellow and I had a feeling that he would go on to be a productive scholar. I have not been disappointed. Since 1998, I have followed his professional development with interest. I also had opportunities to see him present at conferences in the U.S., and in January, 2008 (only four months ago at the time of writing) I was able to meet him and his family in Bhopal at the

Annual Conference of the Indian Society of Criminology at the National Law Institute University, and later accompanied them to *Kanyakumari (Cape Comorin)*. This happened in conjunction with a presentation I made at Manonmaniam Sundaranar University in Tirunelveli, where Jai was a faculty member at the Department of Criminology and Criminal Justice. Again, it was clear that Jai's high energy level and creativity were at full throttle. He had already founded two journals (International Journal of Criminal Justice Sciences and International Journal of Cyber Criminology); co-edited a book in Victimology; published several articles in leading journals; developed new classes; and generally done what a university teacher/researcher everywhere are expected to do, but in his case in overdrive.

It came as no surprise to find that he was in the process of editing a book on International Perspectives in Crime and Justice, given his broad range of interests and international experience and contacts. Of course, it's impossible to underestimate the importance of international perspectives in any field. All too often, the experiences of cultures are not shared, even though sharing could be beneficial. As a result, we all tend to reinvent the wheel independently as a result of failures in both communication and the diffusion of information. This can often be attributed to problems of translation – the difficulty of making research findings available in multiple languages. In other cases, there is perhaps a degree of intellectual arrogance based on the implicit assumption that our way is best, perhaps articulated in its most extreme form as: "My way or the highway." We see this expressed, for example, in the evolution of capital punishment at the international level, with some countries in the abolitionist camp (e.g. Canada, the European Community) while others (e.g. U.S., China, Iran) continue to adhere to this form of punishment utterly convinced of its effectiveness, just as the abolitionists are equally convinced that execution is both ineffectual and a violation of human rights.

The comprehensive framework of this book means that it provides a rich variety of international perspectives on an array of crime and justice-related issues. In recent decades, new types of crime have emerged as a result of more or less universal access to the internet. But perhaps an even more far-reaching consequence of the collapse of international boundaries in cyberspace is the staggering availability of instantaneous information on an incomprehensible range of topics, including crime and justice. One obvious point that emerges from this information is that values vary greatly from culture to culture, with acts that may be criminal in one not necessarily so in another. This calls for what might be regarded as a special sensitivity to such cultural variations in a book like this, at more than one level. For example, the chapter authors themselves should incorporate this sensitivity (which they do), but at the next level, assuming that this book is used for instructional purposes, the instructors interpreting the text should also demonstrate similar sensitivity. This is nicely exemplified in the chapter on policing in India, pointing out as it does that the structure in India is a vestige of the British colonial era which saw policing as a tool for control of a large and complex territory. While control in some form is presumably still an objective, the innate purpose of that control is now different. Again, on the subject of policing, we see astonishing international variations in structure and methods. In the U.S., for example, we have what is arguably the most fragmented police structure in the world, with some 17,000 discrete agencies which historically have not been enthusiastic about communicating with each other. In other countries, centralized control is the rule. Does it matter, and if so, why? These are the kinds of questions that an international perspective can at least illuminate if not answer definitively.

The thirty chapters presented here are a treasure trove of insights in terms of both topical variety and approaches within topics, such as the focus of a chapter on eyewitness methodologies or of another on data mining. Dr. Jaishankar has assembled a valuable collection of readings that will find broad acceptance internationally. This book will be useful for criminologists, criminal justice professionals, and graduate students. Also, practitioners and academics of allied fields like sociology, psychology, geography, political science, public administration and forensic sciences whose research interests include either crime/criminal justice system/victim or crime analysis will find this book useful. In short, because this volume touches on so many overlapping fields, a larger-than-normal audience is expected.

Baltimore County, USA, June, 2008
Keith D. Harries
Professor of Geography and Environmental Systems

# EDITOR'S INTRODUCTION

# THINK GLOBAL, ACT LOCAL: EXPANDING THE FRONTIERS OF PERCEPTIONS ON CRIME AND JUSTICE

K. JAISHANKAR

Globalization and the technological advances like wireless communications and Internet have brought countries closer and made business transactions easier than before (Broude & Teichman, 2009). However, globalization has also assisted the cooperation of criminals, internationally (Findlay, 2000). In this globalized era, it is the criminals, who think global, and act local and not the governments. The growth of technology has enriched the knowledge of criminals of any geographical region of the world. Especially the internet has come in handy for the criminals and they use the cyber space to commit crimes and they also have honed up their cultural skills. According to the latest report of McAfee:

> attacks are increasingly being tailored to victims in specific geographical regions. Spam, phishing emails and even malware now address their potential victims in their native tongues, often with flawless grammar. Attackers have also become familiar with local culture, including sports and other pastimes, and often incorporate them into their ploys to further the chances of tricking their Marks (Goodin, 2008, para 2).

Criminals may get easily familiarized with the local culture of a country; however, it may not possible for any law enforcement agency of a country to learn the local culture of another country, until they have good relationship or some treaties with them. If crimes of cyber space are globalized now, crimes of physical space are globalized long back. Crimes are both internationalized as well as localized. Crimes such as drug trade, gambling, money laundering and sex crimes are outsourced as well as in-sourced (Broude & Teichman, 2009). Transnational organized criminals do join hands with local persons to commit transnational crimes and vice versa local persons join hands with international persons to commit local crimes. This kind of collaboration is only feasible for criminals as they do not have restrictions such as bilateral and extradition treaties between two or more countries. Karofi and Mwanza (2006) analyses this situation:

> If we look at drugs, armed conflicts, trafficking and organised crime, local problems may transcend borders. Take for instance armed conflicts have resulted from the commercialisation of armed conflict and the territorialisation of sovereignty around valuable resource areas and trading networks. As such, armed conflict in the post-Cold War period is increasingly characterised by a specific political ecology closely linked to the geography and political economy of natural resources. There are instances of local violence that have had global influences. For instance, the distribution of benefits and externalities has fuelled the Biafra secession and rebellions in the Delta region of Nigeria, near home here, we have Aceh in Indonesia, and the Cabinda enclave in Angola, to name but a few examples of conflicts in oil-rich regions. While many of these secessions have an indigenous political base, domestic or external actors manipulating local political identities for commercial interests also motivate some (Le Billon, 2001). Another example is the drug trade. Not only is the drug trade inherently coupled with a high degree of local and international corruption and violence, which are independent sources of social deterioration, but also its volume worldwide makes it a global phenomena (Eduardo, 2002) (pp. 81-82).

What is happening in the era of Globalization? Can the criminal justice system of any country remain in a closet? How does the world protect itself from the menace of Terrorism which has transcended the borders of every country? Can any country remain aloof without collaborating with other countries to prevent transnational crimes? Attina (1997) argues:

> Contemporary societies suffer from problems which in their origin, evolution and solution exceed national borders. This is true in different fields as the environment (pollution), demography (migrations), health (epidemics) and public security (organized crime, illegal business, people trade, immigrant traffic, etc.). Because of the effects of interconnection that the globalization process has on contemporary societies and states, governments are unable to supply people with personal security, societies with economic growth, groups with social protection and even individuals with rights, unless they turn to international cooperation (para 5).

The solution for the problem of international crimes should be *"Think Global, Act Local"*. If crime is globalized, crime prevention should be glocalized. If criminals can think globally and act locally, why not the governments do the same? *Glocalisation*[1] of criminology/criminal justice is the need of the hour. 'Local crime control policies are not designed and executed in a vacuum. Rather, the policies adopted by one country (be they relatively harsh or relatively lenient) affect the policies adopted by other countries' (Broude & Teichman, 2009, p. 847). Hence, countries should work together to cooperate with each other in trying to solve issues of crime and justice both from national and international perspectives. Governments should think beyond Interpol and Europol to prevent transnational crimes.

As a criminologist, I also am much interested to examine the level of criminological analysis done by criminologists in the area of global criminology. Friedrichs (2007) feels that criminologists involve in a higher level of analysis but they are confused with the myriad use of terminologies related to globalizing criminology:

> First, we have comparative criminology and criminal justice[2] (e.g., Beirne & Nelken, 1997; Dammer & Fairchild, 2006), Second, we have a transnational criminology[3] (e.g., Andreas & Nadelmann, 2006; Sheptycki & Wardak, 2003), Third, we have an international criminology[4] (e.g., Morrison, 2005; Rothe & Mullins, 2006), The term global criminology[5] is

---

[1] Glocalisation (or glocalization) is a portmanteau word of globalization and localization. By definition, the term "glocal" refers to the individual, group, division, unit, organisation, and community which is willing and able to "think globally and act locally." The term has been used to show the human capacity to bridge scales (from local to global) and to help overcome meso-scale, bounded, "little-box" thinking (source: Wikipedia).

[2] "Comparative criminology addresses the nature of the crime problem and the form and character of the criminal justice system in countries around the world." (Fredrichs, 2007, p. 6).

[3] "Transnational criminology is focused principally upon transnational or cross-border forms of crime, and endeavors on various levels to control or respond effectively to such crime (e.g., Edwards and Gill, 2003; Galeottie, 2005). Entities such as Interpol play a significant role in addressing such crime (DeFlem, 2001)" (Fredrichs, 2007, p. 6).

[4] "The focus of international criminology is on international crime—or crime that is specifically recognized widely across nations as a crime against humanity—and international law, as well as on the institutions of international law" (Fredrichs, 2007, p. 7).

[5] "The focus of global criminology is on globalization and its consequences in relation to crime and criminal justice, and the role of the global economy and its regulation in this regard. The harms perpetrated by international financial—and trade—institutions such as the World Bank, the International Monetary Fund, and the World Trade Organization have been little attended to by criminologists, but

> best applied to the study of the evolving societal context within which crime and criminal justice now exist (e.g., Barak, 2000; Findlay, 1999) … Macro-Criminology, for example, is a term applied to the study of large-scale criminological phenomena. To date, however, this term has been applied principally to macro-dimensions of conventional forms of crime and criminal justice. Also, the term Supranational Criminology has been adopted by a group of European criminologists, with a base at the University of Maastricht, who have been interested in large-scale forms of harm such as genocide, and the control of such crime (see Friedrichs, 2007). (pp. 6-7).

Also Friedrichs (2007) questions the balance of criminologists analysing transnational and national issues of crime and justice and also argues about some basic issues in globalizing criminology:

> First, by virtue of their training criminologists do not have the professional competence to address the relevant phenomena on a sophisticated level, and simply become "commentators" in relation to such matters. Then, if criminologists address phenomena outside their traditional areas of competence, the question arises whether this will diminish respect for criminology per se, and even inspire direct attacks from those who believe that criminologists are infringing on their tuff. Furthermore, it could be objected that a shift by criminologists to global concerns would be a counterproductive allocation of finite criminological resources. As suggested earlier, the practical challenges of researching transnational forms of crime and justice are likely to be considerably greater than is the case with conventional, domestic forms of crime and justice (p. 6). ….. If a 21$^{st}$-century criminology is to transcend such parochialism and attend much more fully to transnational forms of crime and their control, and the global context within which such crime and its control occurs, the specific sources of this parochialism must be identified. They surely include: patterns of personal and professional socialization, and a commitment to traditional disciplinary boundaries; the reward structure within the discipline; the higher probability of "successful" outcomes for conventional research projects, relative to those addressing more complex global issues; and a "state of denial" about the complicity of powerful entities and individuals in criminal conduct (p. 5).

Hence, considering the arguments put by Fredrichs (2007), I strongly suggest for *Glocalization* of criminology/criminal justice and the present book is one such model.

---

are part of the subject matter of a global criminology (Friedrichs & Friedrichs, 2002; MacKenzie, 2006) (Fredrichs, 2007, p. 7).

The international criminology division of American society of Criminology showcases George Santayana's (1863-1952) saying *"A man's feet must be planted in his country, but his eyes should survey the world".* This book moves in the direction of the quote of Santayana and it also tries to lay emphasis on the need for the understanding of the philosophy of cultural relativism,[6] and highlight the negative effects of cultural imperialism[7] in criminology.

Current international criminology is seen through the American lens. One British reviewer while reviewing an article for a journal edited by me was annoyed by one American author's feeling that everything is American and international academics will understand that what he is mentioning will be understood by them. The reviewer writes: *"the assumption that the US stands for everywhere, and that no acknowledgement of its specificity needs to be made, is a kind of 'academic nationalism' that might annoy the journal's many readers (like myself) who work outside the US".* However, 'United States is not alone in its academic parochialism' (Barbaret, 2001, p. 3); it has a companion, the Great Britain. If there is a *Blackwell Companion to Criminology* written in US perspective, there is, *Oxford Handbook of Criminology* written in British perspective.

There is a dearth of edited collections purely from an international perspective. Even if there are some, the collections are mostly from two or three countries perspectives. Other contributions from non-english speaking nations such as France, Spain, The Netherlands, China and the Latin American and South Asian countries do not reach the international masses because of the language impediments. This book aims to create a balance among the contributors from various parts of the world bringing forth their national perspectives and placing them in the international arena. The contributors of this book are from: Australia (2), Canada (1), Cyprus (1), Hong Kong (1), India (6), Israel (4), Nigeria (5), Turkey (2),

---

[6] Cultural relativism is the view that no culture is superior to any other culture when comparing systems of morality, law, politics, etc. It's the philosophical notion that all cultural beliefs are equally valid and that truth itself is relative, depending on the cultural environment. Source: http://www.cultural-relativism.com/

[7] Cultural imperialism is the practice of promoting, distinguishing, separating, or artificially injecting the culture of one society into another. It is usually the case that the former belongs to a large, economically or militarily powerful nation and the latter belongs to a smaller, less important one. Cultural imperialism can take the form of an active, formal policy or a general attitude. Source: Wikipedia.

UK (5), and USA (15). This book is one way a book of academic inclusiveness.

This book is not just about 'International' 'Criminal Justice', it is a book on perspectives on crime and justice, where not only comparative perspectives are put forth, but indigenous works of nations which were less focussed earlier are brought to the forefront of international criminology. Barring a few chapters, most of the chapters try to bring in their own country feature and this book will serve as a cultural ambassador to the international academia.

Contemporary works of criminologists are sought from an international perspective and thirty chapters are organised on six themes: Part I. Crime and justice: Towards a global perspective; Part II. Criminological theory and research; Part III. Criminal justice, Prisons and Media, in a changing World; Part IV. Perspectives on Crime Prevention and Victimization; Part V. Technology and Crime: Contemporary Practices and Concerns; Part VI. Globalization and Crime: Issues of Politics, Prisons, and Terrorism.

Part I comprises of chapters which has a comparative aspect of criminological perspectives. In Chapter one, *Henry Pontell* and *Gilbert Geis* deal with issues concerning transnational corporate crimes. The central theme rotates around the notion that while an act may be considered criminal in one country's jurisdiction, it may not be so in another. To deal with this, most often the local authorities have to rely on anachronistic domestic laws and try to reconcile their statutes with those of other involved nations. The authors have taken the approach of putting forth their arguments through analysis of various such acts viz. selling of thalidomide in Japan and Germany; Barings bankruptcy in UK and Singapore; multinational liability through Bhopal and the International Bribery scenario. It is poignant to note how corruption of political leaders and heads of countries encourage the growth of white collar crimes globally. Pontell and Geis have questioned the executing powers of the international conventions, international treaties and international criminal justice system in a very subtle manner. They have rightly pointed out the need for universal definitions for various white collar crimes and the expansion of international laws to tackle them.

Keeping police line-ups at the core, the chapter two by *Avraham Levi* analyzes the eyewitness identification methods in four different countries. The identification system in UK, Canada, Israel and US takes the centre stage for discussion here. Levi points out that UK has a legalized identification system, while countries rely simply on precedents. He makes an exhaustive study of the various practices involved in this practice. The position of witness is also highlighted in the light of improper evidence in identifying the accused. Levi advises that many inferior methods should be rejected by the courts, and the police lineup be strengthened. Levi concludes that lineup and identification system should use more victim focused methods so the innocent (supposed accused) be respited from the grueling court orders.

Human trafficking is a murky area of study in International Criminology. *Lincoln Fry* in chapter three not only employs empirical data to highlight the problem of trafficking across the globe but also highlights the problems involved in gathering such empirical data. Fry's chapter is different from other conventional papers on human trafficking as it attacks the existing conventions, rules and regulations and their loopholes for encouraging human trafficking. Fry has showcased the pattern of human trafficking in the four continents except Australia. However, the usage of the term "global" in the tile could have been justified if he would have discussed some trafficking patterns in Australia also.

In chapter four, *Despina Kyprianou* discusses about the adversarial and inquisitorial prosecution systems in Europe. Despina provides a comparative analysis of prosecution systems in various jurisdictions, including those traditionally associated with the common law tradition, as well as the ones following the continental model. Despina aptly discusses on how prosecution system in Europe can help the criminal justice system and thereby safeguard the rights of the victims as well as the accused. In the conclusion, she argues that a wide scale appraisal of the origins and the primary principles of prosecution systems are prerequisites for any attempt to understand the current situation and discuss any reforms for the future.

The fifth chapter by *Teela Sanders* and *Rosie Campbell* discusses about trends and patterns of global sex trade. Teela and Rosie argue about the distinctions between intentional involvement in the sex trade industry and sex trafficking. What is the role of law and policy guidelines in this aspect? What is the thin line of difference between legality and illegality of sex trade? Teela and Rosie try to analyze these questions in this chapter. They distinguish between the women making women to join the sex industry voluntarily and those organised criminal networks that traffic women against their will into the sex trade.

Part II deals with the criminological theory and research. In chapter six, *Natti Ronel* provides a new criminological theory for understanding criminal and deviant behaviors based on a phenomenological inquiry. Natti deals with criminal spin behavior of individuals as well as groups or community. He advocates using the criminal spin theory to understand the rudiments of criminal behaviour. A basic premise of this thesis is that criminality is subjective by nature, and therefore, any effort to study criminality and its different manifestations as objective entities will inevitably lead to inconsistency. In the conclusion, it is alleged that the theory of the criminal spin may serve as the base for an integrative approach for prevention and intervention of crime. Natti's chapter stands apart from other chapters in its theoretical as well as practical approach towards understanding of criminal behaviors.

*Robert Smith* in chapter seven forges a connection between entrepreneurship and crime. Robert explores the links between crime and learning difficulties and entrepreneurship and learning difficulties. He also examines entrepreneurship as a diversion technique and social entrepreneurship as a positive influence and concludes with the discussion on the scope and shortcoming of using the entrepreneurship theory in the criminal rehabilitation process.

*Arnon Edelstein* (chapter eight) enquires into the attitudes of criminologists towards harmful criminals and particularly focuses on clarifying the area of theoretical thinking to get a better understanding of the phenomena involving crime. He rethinks the concepts related to criminal career, professional crime, habitual offences and seriality, with a critical attitude with respect to the confusion generated over the years. Keeping this critical attitude, he proposes new reformed definitions of various concepts and a model for furthering the research in the definitional aspect of crime.

In chapter nine, *Curtis Fogel* critiques on the ethics review framework in Canada as a major impediment in conducting ethical research in criminology. Curtis has attempted to contribute to the literature pertaining to ethical issues in social science research and strategies to remain ethical without compromising research. He discusses on how ethics is defined and how the ethics review system is structured in Canada and examines the main ethical issues of criminological research and possible strategies for novice researchers to remain ethical in ways that are not detrimental to the research. He also argues on how the current ethics review framework in Canada often acts in contradicting ways making it more difficult to conduct ethical criminological research and concludes with a discussion of the future of criminological research in Canada in the climate of overbearing ethics review boards.

*Sergio Herzog* in the chapter ten tries to gauge the seriousness of crimes by focusing on variance within compared groups. He makes Israel as a base for field study to obtain a different perspective from the Western model of variance. With the help of empirical data collected through a questionnaire, Sergio critiques the existing theories, using group variables for determining the seriousness of a crime.

Part III deals with the theme, Criminal justice, Prisons and Media, in a changing World. In chapter eleven, *Liz Campbell* presents the case-study of using civil forfeiture against serious criminality in Ireland by taking into account the historical setting which influenced this development. She seeks to explain the procedural aspects of civil forfeiture in Ireland in a conventional legal sense, and then seeks to place the process in a theoretical setting, to clarify the development and workings of this innovative approach to tackling organised and serious crime. Liz makes relevant arguments by taking into account the works of Herbert Packer and David Garland. While the former is used for examining the issue of asset forfeiture denoting a shift from due process to crime control imperatives, the latter considers the categorisation of forfeiture as an adaptive response of the State to the phenomenon of crime and the reality of crime control in modern society.

*Tumpa Mukherjee* (chapter twelve) makes an endeavour to explore police and policing practices in post-colonial India at the backdrop of the changing socio-cultural political scenario as well as emerging challenges of the twenty first century. She tries to point out the stagnation within the legal system through the lacunae in the governing archaic legislation, the Police Act of 1861. Tumpa also hints at certain inherent structural problems within the Indian Police System and discusses certain measures adopted by the Indian Government to reform the police system.

In chapter thirteen, *Lee Michael Jhonson* explores the usefulness of art programs in achieving correctional goals. Jhonson takes into account five parameters in highlighting the usefulness of art in correcting an individual viz. educational value, therapeutic, socially productive, improvising environmental quality of life and social reintegration. He also provides guidelines for carrying out art programmes i.e. a) not to be used as an isolated tool, and b) requirement of intelligence, diligence, also honesty while carrying out such programs.

While taking into account the Indian Prison system, *Jeevan Ballav Panda* in chapter fourteen emphasizes on laws which relate to the deplorable condition of prisoners and the legislative and judicial reforms. Jeevan criticizes the present system for being inadequate in addressing the rights of the prisoners while taking into account the measures taken by Judiciary for adopting the reformative and rehabilitative approach. He raises some fundamental questions about the need for change with suggestions about prisoners' rights and the need for a humane approach.

*Akintayo J. Abodunrin, Jimoh Amzat and Rasidi A. Okunola* (chapter fifteen) presents a study of the crime reporting techniques in Nigeria. The authors concentrate on pertinent issues relating to crime reporting like investigation of the sources of crime stories available to the papers; ascertaining the specific part in the layout where crime stories are located; identification of the genre of published crime stories and assessment of the editorial policy of the selected Newspapers on crime. Content analysis, a systematic procedure devised to examine the content of recorded information has been used to examine the contents of the two newspapers selected i.e. *The Guardian and Punch.* The authors' findings demonstrate that violent crimes such as murder and assaults received more coverage in the papers than financial, drug, and property crimes.

Part IV deals with the theme, perspectives on crime prevention and victimization. In chapter sixteen, *Wing Hong Chui* lays down the future policy opportunities to improve legal protection and service provisions for victims. Chui has tried to discuss issues surrounding the protection of victim in the criminal justice system in Queensland, Australia. He attempts to examine victim problems, policies and programmes within the Australian context. He describes different ways of measuring the prevailing rate of crime victimization and explains the importance of studying the topic of 'victim protection' by examining the empirical data about crime victimization in Australia. He also discusses on a wide range of initiatives for victims such as compensation schemes and legal support to the victims of crime and their families.

*P. Madhava Soma Sundaram* and *M. D. Allen Selva Kumar* (chapter seventeen) looks at the ideas on how child trafficking can be combated based on empirical studies conducted in Tamil Nadu, India. The authors are of the opinion, that, while International organizations like the United Nations have taken child trafficking seriously, and developed effective instruments and mechanisms to deal with the problem effectively, but a lot needs to be done at the State level. The authors suggest a need to monitor, review, reform the existing policies and rules related to child trafficking, especially in context to soft trafficking issues in India. They also suggest various ways through which the anti child trafficking scenario in India can be improved.

In chapter eighteen, *Michael L. Pittaro* approaches the concept of childhood bullying from the perspective of both social learning as well as social reaction theory. He tries to bring awareness to the global reader that childhood bullying is a multifaceted social issue that warrants widespread awareness as well as early intervention and prevention. Michael concludes on the note that, it is not only the bully who learns such aggressiveness from observing the behaviours of others, but also the victim, whether real or perceived, learns from repeated acts of aggressive bullying tactics.

*Aiden Sidebottoms'* chapter nineteen concentrates on crime science representing it as a new approach for study of crime and crime prevention predominates. Aiden applies the concepts of numerous fields to further concept of an 'arms race', in which crime prevention is posited as being in a "perpetual struggle to keep up with changing opportunities for crime and adaptable offenders" Aiden also spells the advantages of integrating numerous scientific disciplines in the pursuit of crime reduction.

*Debarati Halder* and *K. Jaishankar* (chapter twenty) analyse the provisions made by Central Adoption Resource Agency in context to inter-country adoption and finds out the various human rights violations in the name of transnational adoption in India. The authors suggest solutions to check the growing violation of human rights involved in this matter.

Part V revolves around the theme, Technology and Crime: Contemporary Practices and Concerns. In chapter twenty one, *Nicolas A. Valcik, Carlos L.V. Aiken, Xueming Xu* and *Mohammed S. Alfarhan,* discuss the acquisition of three dimensional photo-realistic models and technology combined with a software application that can provide data that will create a virtual set of structures cybernetically that could be used for training, crime prevention and homeland security purposes. The authors take into account the theory behind existing technology on the potential uses of these types of technologies and how these types of technologies can be combined for Homeland Security use and also outline the advantages and disadvantages of using such technology for Homeland Security.

*Jhonny Nhan* (chapter twenty two) examines the structural and dynamic variables between organizations and actors that influence prosecutorial decision-making processes in high-tech and computer crimes. Jhonny uses data derived from interviews, observations at state-sponsored and private cyber-security meetings, published literature and survey reports, and relevant documents provided by research participants. He has tried to assess the variables affecting prosecutorial acceptance of cases, how cyber and high-tech cases are processed, and their impact on the overall capacity of California cyber-security network.

In chapter twenty three, *Lynne Roberts* provides an overview of the current state of knowledge on cyber-stalking. Lynne begins with a brief overview of what is known about stalking. Building on this knowledge, the concept of cyber-stalking is explored. Developing typologies of cyber-stalking and current estimates of the prevalence of cyber-stalking are provided. Possible relationships between cyber-stalking and off-line stalking are examined to shed light on whether cyber-stalking is simply an extension of off-line stalking behaviours or whether it is a new form of deviant/criminal behaviour.

*Fatih Ozgul, Julian Bondy* and *Hakan Aksoy* in their chapter (twenty four) demonstrate the utility and value in applying data mining techniques in criminal justice. The authors use a recent police operation in Turkey to illustrate some of the techniques now available to extract and reveal patterns and associations. They demonstrate the application of a Crime Graph Algorithm (CGA) that was developed and trialled in Bursa, Turkey which can reveal previously undetected criminal associations. This case study indicates that criminal justice agencies are able to respond effectively to these new challenges but that new tactics and new skill sets may need to be considered in future police resource planning.

In chapter twenty five, *K. Jaishankar* and *Debarati Halder,* provide a profile of cyber bullying among school students in India. The authors make a case study for distinguishing between ragging and cyber bullying. An analysis of the findings of the Judiciary and various Indian legislations has been presented by the authors. The cases discussed by the authors reveal an astonishing fact, i.e., almost all the cases of cyber bullying in India involving the school children had happened in 2006 - 2007 period. The authors conclude that there is lack of school policy guidelines, law on cyber bullying and weak Information Technology Act, which has paved the way for increasing rate of cyber bullying incidences among the children within a year.

The final part (VI) deals with the theme Globalization and crime: Issues of politics, prisons, and terrorism. *Patrick Webb* (chapter twenty five) seeks to throw light on the issue of media coverage of proceedings on juvenile delinquents. Patrick has tried to expose both sides of the coin by presenting both the pros and cons of publicizing through media. The author argues that presiding judge should grant access only in cases where it is absolutely clear either that no harm will result to the juvenile from the media's presence and subsequent coverage of the proceedings, or that publicity is necessary to prevent a greater harm to the general public.

In chapter twenty six, *Kam C. Wong* deals with the effect of terrorism in China by taking into account its historical context. The author provides a brief review of literature on terrorism in China and informs that there is very little research into the conceptual origin and intellectual history of terrorism in China. He also makes the case that while Western notion of terrorism has no counterpart in China's past, China has treated subversive activities most severely, as challenging to *heavenly mandate* (tianming) and disruption of *cosmic order* (dao).

*Emilio C. Viano* (chapter twenty seven) provides a comprehensive overview of the history and development of terrorism as it is understood at this time. Viano concentrates on the changing meaning of terrorism in light of new technologies; globalization, worldwide news media, and religious fundamentalism have on new forms and expressions of terrorism. He also identifies new areas for research and work and in particular it covers the role that social scientists and criminologists can play in the analysis, investigation and prevention of terrorism.

In chapter twenty nine, *Julie C. Abril* emphasizes to document the power structure in the native Indian Tribal Communities in America. She discusses the transformation of how traditional tribal power has become a hybrid of both traditional and tertiary powers and deplore that the effects of fluidity of power in modern yet traditional tribal societies have not been adequately documented.

In the final chapter (thirty), *Ikuteyijo Lanre Olusegun and Agunbiade Ojo Melvin* discusses the prison reforms in Nigeria. The authors trace the evolution of prisons in Nigeria, examining the social dynamics involved in the transition from the British-inherited system, which still dominates the prison philosophy in Nigeria, to the current reforms influenced by the global events in criminal justice system. The authors concluded that though the prison system in Nigeria is evolving from the retributive to the rehabilitative philosophy of penology, it requires a strong political will to attain the desired change.

Compilation of such a variety of chapters from international contributors was indeed a very exciting task for me. When I let out the call for chapters in late 2006, I was little cynical about the submission of proposals of chapters. Within two months my inbox was flooded with fifty proposals and I was overwhelmed with joy. Finally I received forty chapters in which only thirty was selected by the reviewers. I thank all the contributors for having faith in my editorial acumen. They have stimulated me to achieve my dream of assembling an international volume on crime and justice. Most of the contributors of this edited volume are accomplished academics. I have utilised their services for peer review. In addition, I also sought the professional insights and detailed comments from the following outside reviewers: *Dr Stephen Z Levine*, Bar Illan University, Israel and *Sairam Chinnam*, State University of New York, Albany, USA, to whom I am very much grateful.

Editing such a great volume needs enthusiastic cooperation and I had the support of many individuals in this mammoth task, without them this book would not have been a reality. My mentor *Prof. Keith Harries* was gracious to write the foreword. I sincerely thank him for encouraging me and supporting me in all my efforts. *Megha, Priti, Dhruv, Debarati* and *Sivakumar* assisted me in the editorial process and *Prof. Dipika Haldar* advised me of sections that needed re-writing for clarity. My heartfelt thanks go to the above said individuals for standing with me as a great support in all my editorial and research ventures.

The Editorial staff at Cambridge Scholars Publishing, UK was very much supportive. I sincerely thank *Carol Koulikourdi, Amanda Miller, Nuala Coyle,* and the new member of the Cambridge Scholars publishing team, *Soucin Yip-Sou*. Especially, *Amanda* and *Soucin* need to be appreciated for their patience and for bearing with my weird sense of perfection. My heartfelt thanks are due to *A. Ravishankar* of Sun Graphics, Tirunelveli, India, for bringing out the concept of the book in to an intellectual cover design. My lovely wife *Debarati* was so patient with my late nights, and I specially want to thank her for her intellectual support in editing this book. My daughter *Mriganayani* loves to play with me, however, considering my eccentricity with the book work; she favored teaching talking skills to our feathered friends *Mintu*, the ringnecked parrot and *Tiku*, the cocktail and by playing with our dogs, *Grey, Clippy and Kuttoose*. I heartily thank her for her understanding. I now have finished this colossal work. I hope she will have my company.

## References

Andreas, P., & Nadelmann, E. (2006). *Policing the globe: Criminalization and crime in international relations*. New York: Oxford.

Attina, F. (1997). Globalization and crime. The emerging role of international institutions. *Jean Monnet Working Papers in Comparative and International Politics.* Retrieved on 27th May 2009 from http://www.fscpo.unict.it/EuroMed/jmwp07.htm

Barak, G. (Ed.), (2000). *Crime and crime control: A global view*. Westport, CT: Greenwood Press.

Barbaret, R. (2001). Global competence and American criminology-An expatriate's view. *The Criminologist*, *26*(2), 1-5, March/April, 2001.

Beirne, P., & Nelken, D. (Eds.), (1997). *Issues in comparative criminology*. Dartmouth: Ashgate.

Broude, T., & Teichman, D. (2009). Outsourcing and insourcing crime: The political economy of globalized criminal activity. *Vanderbilt Law Review*, *62*(3), 795-845, April 2009.

Dammer, H. R., & Fairchild, E. (2006). *Comparative criminal justice systems*. Third edition. Belmont, CA: Thomson/ Wadsworth.

Eduardo, F. (2002). Combating money laundering and financing of terrorism. *International Monetary Fund, 39*(3).
Findlay, M. (2000). *The globalisation of crime:* U*nderstanding the transitional relationships of crime in a global context.* London: Cambridge University Press.
Friedrichs, D. O., & Friedrichs, J. (2002). The world bank and crimes of globalization: A Case Study. *Social Justice*, *29*(1), 3-36.
Friedrichs, D. O. (2007). Towards a criminology of international crimes: Producing a conceptual and contextual framework. R. Haveman & A. Smeulers (Eds.), *Towards a criminology of international crimes.* Antwerp: Insentia. Forthcoming.
Goodin, D. (2008). Malware writers think global, act local: Mono-linguists need not apply. Retrieved on 28th May 2009 from http://www.theregister.co.uk/2008/02/22/localized_online_attacks/
Karofi, U.A., & Mwanza, J. (2006). Globalisation and crime. *Bangladesh e-Journal of Sociology, 3*(1), 70-87, January 2006.
Le Billon, P. (2001). Fuelling war or buying peace: The role of corruption in conflicts. *Journal of International Development, 13*, 951-64.
Mackenzie, S. (2006). Systematic crimes of the powerful: Criminal aspects of the global economy. *Social Justice*, *33*(1), 162-182.
Morrison, W. (2005). *Criminology, civilization and the new world order.* London: Cavendish Publishing.
Rock, P. (2007). Sociological theories of crime. In M. Maguire, R. Morgan, & R. Reiner (Eds.), *The Oxford handbook of criminology* (pp. 3-42). Oxford: Oxford University Press.
Rothe, D., & Mullins, C. (2006). *The International criminal court: Symbolic gestures and the generation of global social control.* Lanham, MD: Lexington Books.
Sheptycki, J., & Wardak, A. (Eds.), (2003). *Transnational and comparative criminology*. London: Glasshouse.

# PART I:

# CRIME AND JUSTICE: TOWARDS A GLOBAL PERSPECTIVE

# CHAPTER ONE

# WHITE-COLLAR AND CORPORATE CRIME: A GLOBAL PERSPECTIVE

HENRY PONTELL AND GILBERT GEIS

## Abstract

The global reach of white-collar and corporate crime has become increasingly common, complicated, elusive, and, for its perpetrators, often extremely lucrative. This chapter examines a number of cases that involved criminal offences in one country that were mounted from headquarters in another country. Often these doing cross-national business fail to pay sufficient heed to the fact that what another nation declares to be criminal is not in line with what they are accustomed to do at home. At other times, malefactors take advantage of the distance and differences between where they are operating and another country to carry out illegal schemes that cannot be detected by normal enforcement processes. This chapter highlights the need for cooperation between national jurisdictions and for the development of treaty-brokered standards that apply worldwide.

## Introduction

A major ingredient of white-collar and corporate crime that crosses national borders was pinpointed by a Japanese judge in 1995, when he awarded $US770 million in damages against the Board of Directors of the Daiwa Bank. The judge stressed the failure of bank executives to abandon traditional Japanese customs when operating in a venue with different legal requirements. "The defendants," the judge declared, "had persisted in following informal local rules that apply in Japan despite the fact that [the firm's operation] had expanded on a global scale" (Milhaupt, 2001, p. 2116; see also Misawa, 2005).

The facts were these: The Daiwa Bank branch in the United States had concealed billions of dollars in losses that resulted from a bank official's illegal trading in U.S. Treasury notes over a period of more than eleven years. After the home office in Japan learned of the fraud, the information was concealed from American authorities and from the Japanese public for almost two months (Instefjord et al., 1998). Ultimately, the company pled guilty to 19 criminal counts, was fined $US340 million by an American court, and was barred from doing business in the United States (Hall 1998). In a move unprecedented in Japan shareholders sued the bank's Board of Directors, prompting the judge's statement about the perils of doing international commerce without attending to distinctions between local ways and the law and its enforcement in the place where the business is being conducted.

The Daiwa case is but one of the ever-expanding rosters of white-collar and corporate crimes that play out against a multinational background (see generally Braithwaite & Drahos, 2000). As one writer points out: "Territorial crimes have become increasingly more transboundary and international in character" (Leacock, 2001, p. 263). Testimony to this development can be gleaned from the fact that the ten largest law firms in the world locate more than half of their attorneys at sites other than their home country (Terry, 2004, p. 539).

An earlier case on point also involved a Japanese corporation that became entangled with American law. It testifies to the need to expand domestic statutes or to create overarching international law in order to deal with behaviour that has cross-border implications. The Nippon Paper Industries Company (NPI) had conspired with an unaffiliated company in Japan to fix prices on the sale of thermal facsimile paper. Nippon exported the paper to firms in North America who sold it there at prearranged inflated prices. NPI had committed an act illegal within the boundaries of the United States. Could it be convicted of a criminal violation of America's antitrust law?

A trial court thought not (*United States v. Nippon Paper Industries* 1996), but the first circuit court of appeals overruled that decision. Nippon relied on a view enunciated by Justice Oliver Wendell Holmes almost a century earlier in which he stated: "The general and almost universal rule" holds that whether "the character of an act is lawful or unlawful must be determined wholly by the law of the country where the act is done" (*American Banana Co. v. United Fruit Co.* 1909, p. 356). Thereafter, several decisions by US courts took a more expansive view of extraterritorial wrongdoing, but only in civil suits. Criminal cases such as the NPI charges were uncharted territory. Nippon as well as the Japanese government, the latter in an amicus brief, argued that the appellate court could not create a new precedent by venturing into a juridical wilderness.

The court's response was astringent: "We have reviewed their exhortations and found them rather hollow" (*United States v. Nippon Paper Industries,* 1997, p. 16). Regarding the absence of precedent the court declared: "There is a first time for everything, and the absence of earlier criminal actions is probably more of a demonstration of the increasingly global economy" (*United States v. Nippon Paper Industries,* 1997, p. 16). It avoided the comity issue—that is, whether the law in the United States might differ from that in Japan—by pointing out that neither country allowed antitrust conspiracies. Then the appellate court enunciated the motif that pervades the present chapter. "We live in an age of world commerce, where decisions reached in a corner of the world can reverberate around the globe in less time than it takes to tell the tale" (*United States v. Nippon Paper Industries* 1997 p. 26; see also Everett, Lehmann, & Steil, 2000).

In earlier times, the clash often was between the mores of an immigrant population and the laws and customs in the country where they settled. In a classic criminological contribution, Thorsten Sellin called attention to acts of murderous revenge by Sicilian newcomers to the United States in response to what they saw as violations of the integrity of their family by, for instance, sexual assault of a daughter (Sellin, 1938). Today, traditional or street crimes such as robbery and burglary overwhelmingly are confined to a single political territory, though there are non-white collar crimes that have a strong international component. Trafficking in drugs and women is a prominent example; so too is terrorism, which is coming to be defined as a distinctive crime, as well as money laundering, arms smuggling, espionage, Internet offences, and treason. Piracy, once a major criminal activity, is less common, but still on the scene.

The ubiquity of Internet communications that can move across the globe in seconds often lies at the heart of international white-collar and corporate offences. International financial institutions are common targets for computer fraud and embezzlement. A man who called himself *Vladimir Lenin*, a mathematician, hacked his way into Citibank's computer system from his St. Petersburg apartment and transferred US$10 million to accounts around the world. Efforts to cope with such tactics have led 34 countries to adhere to the Council of Europe's Convention on Cybercrime, adopted in Budapest in 2001, which requires nations to cooperate with each other in the fight against computer-related crimes. By August 2006, 43 countries had ratified the treaty and 16 had obtained the endorsement of their legislative bodies for their participation (Csonka 2005; Goldstone & Shave, 1999).

When cross-border venues become the happy hunting grounds for white-collar and corporate criminals, local authorities often have to rely on anachronistic domestic laws and try to reconcile their statutes with those of other involved nations. The laws against, say, murder, do not differ significantly from country to country, but those regarding commerce and business can vary significantly, and offer opportunities for persons to pursue by illegal means one of the most compelling goals of the human animal—to make money. The attraction is enhanced considerably when both the perpetrator and the authorities in the country where the offence is carried out stand to profit.

Stunning increases in global mobility contribute notably to international episodes of white-collar and corporate crime. These developments led to the establishment of administrative and judicial bodies that seek to impose upon members' consensual standards and penalties for the violation of their regulations. Nevertheless, a core issue is that the disproportionate resources of the more powerful nations can be used to undermine the dictates of such bodies. Besides, nations need not join in these international endeavours and undoubtedly will not do so unless they believe that it is in their best interest; a prime example being the failure of the United States to join in the Kyoto Protocol to control global warming.

We will consider several examples of international white-collar crime in order to establish a base for generalizations about the phenomenon. We apologize beforehand for our over-reliance on materials involving the United States. This bias reflects a condition that ultimately will have to be overcome by many criminologists if we are to develop a truly cosmopolitan understanding of international white-collar and corporate crime that overcomes barriers of language and requires a thorough comprehension of the law and ethos of a variegated cohort of nations.

## Thalidomide: Japan and Germany

The drug thalidomide was introduced into West Germany in October 1957 under the trade name on Contegam. The company Chemie Grüenthal marketed the drug vigorously as an antidote to a considerable variety of human ailments, including morning sickness. By 1959, an estimated one million Germans were using thalidomide on a daily basis. As one doctor observed, the drug had become "West Germany's baby sitter" (Taussig, 1962, p. 1109). It was sold in some parts of West Germany without a prescription. An advertisement by the company indicates what would prove to be an ill-fated claim:

> In pregnancy and during the lactation period, the female organism is under great stress. Sleeplessness, unrest, and tension are constant complaints. The administration of a sedative and hypnotic that will hurt neither the mother nor the child is often necessary (Teff & Munro, 1976, p. 143).

A letter to *Lancet* in 1961 by William McBride, an Australian doctor, reported that he had attended the birth of a number of babies who showed multiple forms of severe abnormalities and whose mothers had taken thalidomide (McBride, 1961). Soon after, *Widikund Lenz,* a German physician, reported that he had observed 52 similar cases, and that when he delivered a lecture on the subject, attending doctors told him of 115 additional cases (Lenz & Knapp, 1962).

The West German government, after considerable delay, filed criminal indictments against 18 persons involved in the distribution of thalidomide, alleging that they had failed to heed warning signs and had tried instead to suppress damaging information. The trial lasted three years, and no decision had been reached when it came to a halt. The West German court declared that the proceedings were being stopped because there no longer was any public interest in the case. All charges were dropped when the manufacturer agreed to establish a fund that would compensate 2,966 thalidomide victims. Nonetheless, despite reform efforts, as Daemnrich (2002, p. 14) points out, "afterward, Germany maintained the system of power division between the medical profession, industry, and the government."

Japan was even tardier than West Germany in stopping the sale of thalidomide. The peak of thalidomide harm in Japan was reached when the drug no longer was being marketed in Germany. "The attitude of the Japanese government in dealing with the [thalidomide] problem was different from that of other countries," Mitsushiro Kida writes. "From the beginning, the government sided with the pharmaceutical companies and took a long time to come to the conclusion that thalidomide was the cause of the various problems involved." He adds: "This attitude prevails to this day." Ultimately, after three years of wrangling, a final settlement compensated approximately 300 Japanese for thalidomide injuries (Kida, 1987, p. 2).

The thalidomide disaster suggests that white-collar pharmaceutical delicts might best be dealt with on an international basis. First-world companies often dump drugs that cannot meet domestic regulatory standards onto third-world countries: the dangerous Dalkon Shield intrauterine device (IUD) was sold overseas for years after it had been withdrawn from the American market (Dowie, 1979), though Braithwaite (1984) points out that higher standards in the manufacturing site sometimes benefits nations with few or no regulations concerning the safety of pharmaceutical products because the companies do not find it cost effective to downgrade safety requirements for offshore sales. However, if an international testing regimen were established, it could operate at the highest level, coordinate information from worldwide sources, and avoid the delays, dangers and deaths such as those that occurred in the thalidomide tragedy.

## Barings Bankruptcy: The United Kingdom and Singapore

*Nicholas William (Nick) Leeson* was at the core of the collapse of Barings Bank. Leeson, in his mid-twenties, was dispatched from London by the bank, an entity that had been founded more than 220 years earlier, first to Jakarta and then to Singapore, where in short order he came to dominate the small branch. He initially earned extraordinary profits by speculating in futures on the Japanese market, which resulted in heady bonuses for Barings employees. But soon Leeson was plunging the company deeper and deeper into debt, and he began to behave like a compulsive gambler, desperately trying to cover losses by higher and higher wagers. When a $US 1.3 billion deficit was finally uncovered, Barings went into bankruptcy (United Kingdom, 1995). Leeson tried to flee to London, but was apprehended in Frankfurt and returned to Singapore, where he was sentenced to six and a half years in a prison that he later described as "gang-ridden" and "marked by conditions beyond belief" (Fay, 1997; Hunt & Heinrich, 1996; Leeson & Whitley, 1996). He survived a bout of colon cancer during his prison stay and when released, moved to Ireland.

The Barings Bank crime offers a simple, almost banal lesson. When young and relatively inexperienced persons are accorded great independence, assigned to sites far from their homeland, and allowed to operate without adequate supervision and accountability, a blueprint for criminal disaster has been put in place. The same sequence of events could have occurred with a trader from Sydney dispatched to Perth or from Mumbai to Goa. A major subtext of international white-collar crime is that, Leeson was speculating from Singapore on the Japanese market, an operation about which the home office apparently had little or no knowledge. Both overseas experience and fluency in the language and customs of the outlying host country would seem to be essential, if international white-collar activities are to be monitored sensibly.

## Bribery

International bribery cases often involve a multinational corporation doing business in a nation where tradition dictates that it is necessary to pay off key politicians and other intermediaries in order to obtain a contract. The Lockheed aircraft corporation, for instance, paid Kakuei Tanaka, the Japanese prime minister, $US 1.7 million to arrange the purchase by his country of 21 Tri-Star airplanes (Hunziker & Kammura, 1994). Lockheed also bribed Prince Bernhard of The Netherlands to facilitate the sale of fighter planes to the Dutch. Bernhard, for his part, had earlier bribed Juan Peron, the dictator in Argentina, to purchase railroad equipment from The Netherlands (Boulton, 1978).

The Lockheed cases challenge the common cliché that bribery will decline when the standard of living in less wealthy countries reaches a satisfactory level so that officials are not dependent upon supplements to their wages to achieve a satisfactory standard of living. The white-collar crime of bribery seems to possess a systemic allure. As far back as the Code of Hammurabi, promulgated in Babylonia about 1770 B.C.E., penalties were specified for accepting bribes, and in ancient Egypt death was decreed for officials or priests who took bribes that related to the performance of their duties (Noonan, 1984).

Yet there is evidence that control measures can have an impact on bribery. Bribery was customary in dealings with customs officers in Mexico. However, the inauguration of the North American Free Trade Agreement (NAFTA) in 1994 led to the appointment of an energetic and scrupulously honest head of the Mexican customs agency. Before that, a mafia-type organization had controlled the Mexico City international airport, where most merchandise from abroad arrived. Now, a registry of imports was established. Earlier, the sixteen steps necessary to get goods through customs provided sixteen opportunities for bribery; otherwise, the clearance process was likely to drag on for at least a month. Reforms reduced the sixteen steps to three and the time involved to about ten minutes. Bribery was significantly reduced (Rosenberg, 2003).

## Bribery: Nigeria and the United States

The case of *W. S. Kirkpatrick v. Environmental Tectonic Corp.*, which in 1990 ended up before the United States Supreme Court, illustrates another element of international bribery. The chair of Kirkpatrick had bid about $US 7 million for a contract to build an aero medical facility at the air force base in Karduna, Nigeria. He was referred to a 'middleman' who said that he could secure the contract but would require a 20 percent "commission" to do so. The bribe money could be added to the bid, and on payment would be deposited to accounts of the intermediary in two Panama banks, and thereafter distributed to a number of Nigerian officials and agencies.

Environmental Tectonics had submitted a significantly lower bid than Kirkpatrick and when it did not receive the contract, it complained of fraud to Nigerian officials and to the American embassy in Nigeria, which referred the case to the Federal Bureau of Investigation (FBI). A grand jury indictment in the U.S. was followed by guilty pleas of the (former) Kirkpatrick chairman and the company itself. The judge fined the company's onetime leader $US 10 million and ordered that he perform 200 hours of community service. The company itself suffered a $US 750,000 fine to be paid over five years. By all accounts, the Nigerian government took no action against any participant in the scheme, though the country since 1975 has had a law against giving or receiving bribes. At the time, Nigeria was regarded as the most corrupt nation in the world, run by persons dubbed "kleptocrats."

One basis for the Environmental Tectonic action, besides it having been unfairly left out in the cold, is that, when a firm shows dazzling earnings from cooking its books or other illegal tactics, officers of competing companies that have been operating honestly come under fire for their failure to match the profits of the law-breakers. Smaller companies also are likely to find themselves at a disadvantage because they do not have the financial wherewithal to compete in the bribery market with the giants (Shichor & Geis, 2006).

## Offshore Financial Shelters

There exists a pattern of employing hospitable (and secretive) sites throughout the world to hide corporate losses and to gain tax exemptions that would not be available domestically. Much attention has been focused on the banking industry in Switzerland which permitted depositors to place money in their vaults without accountability in the site where the money would be taxed and where the manner in which it was gained might come under investigation. Beyond the ethical impropriety of such arrangements, the Swiss took advantage of their situation during World War II. Until relentlessly pressed, they refused to acknowledge that they had accepted millions of dollars from German Jews and others who did not survive the Nazi Holocaust. Investigations disclosed that the Swiss had confiscated some of that money and routed it to the Germans to help finance the war effort (Brailand, 2000; Schapiro, 2003).

## Flags of Convenience

Another international tactic that sets the table for criminal behaviour inheres in the manner in which some countries, most notably Panama and Liberia, register ships – "flags of convenience" the process is called - for lesser sums and impose lower taxes than those available elsewhere (Carlisle, 1981; Metaxas, 1985). They also permit substandard wages to be paid to the crew. Panama maintains the world's largest ship registry with more than 10,000 vessels flying its flag. One such, The *Ocean Glory I,* a ship built in Britain in 1951, was detained in the port of Dover in England in 2001, when it was found to have flagrantly ignored safety regulations and was staffed by a crew that was unable to perform a lifeboat drill. The ship, rechristened *Classica*, was allowed to sail to the Greek port of Piraeus, where it was scrapped. On another front, *Roque Perez*, a maritime lawyer in Panama City, was murdered in broad daylight as he sat drinking coffee in a café, a killing that likely had a connection to the drug traffic that used sea-lanes for smuggling. Again, a central international ship registry would permit oversight that is much more diligent and a standardization of requirements for ocean-going vessels.

## Bhopal: India and the United States

International criminal disputes can involve manoeuvring that pushes the cases into a venue that appears most likely to indulge the multinational corporation. Take but one example: In 1984, the Union Carbide Corporation, an American company, released 40 tons of methyl isocyanate and hydrogen cyanide gas into its plant in Bhopal, India. More than 3,300 people were killed and about 20,000 seriously injured (Dhara & Dhara, 2002). Union Carbide won a judgment in the U.S. declaring that Indian courts had the sole jurisdiction over all civil litigation ensuing from the disaster, a tactic that apparently was chosen because of the company's presumption that it would receive more favourable treatment in India than at home. The case was settled for $US 470 million. The settlement stipulated that criminal charges against Union Carbide officers would be dropped. The Indian Supreme Court subsequently ruled that the criminal charges should stand, and seventeen years after the tragedy an extradition request was made of the United States to turn over *Warren Anderson*, the chief executive of Union Carbide until his 1986 retirement, who had been charged in India with culpable homicide. The U.S. made no effort to do so (Amnesty International, 2004; Kurtzman, 1987; Vivek, 1990).

## International Conventions and Treaties

The proliferation of international business and the accompanying infectious disease of white-collar and corporate crime have led to efforts to put in place overarching regulatory bodies to attempt to control cross-border crimes. Neal Shover and Andy Hochstetler have summarized the nature and difficulties that have accompanied these developments:

> Global oversight develops in dozens of forms and a complex array of institutions. It relies on criminal prosecution primarily in the nations where crimes originate. These nations, however, are reluctant to grant other nations and international bodies, the right to define, and pursue global oversight on their soil (Shover & Hochstetler, 2006, p. 108).

They note that to date most international cooperation has occurred in the areas of war crimes and international organized crime, but, quoting Michael Gilbert and Steve Russell (2002, p. 233), they observe regarding white-collar and corporate crime: "All the while avoidable harms (often of equivalent or greater magnitude) by transnational corporations are ignored."

The international treaties have not been a panacea. It is noted of the World Trade Organization (WTO), for instance, that its dictates often are more in the nature of a verbal exercise than an effective control mechanism. A comprehensive examination of the work of the WTO observes: "A problem with the implementation of WTO dispute settlement recommendations and rules is a lack of guidance over what exactly a losing party must do to comply. The tendency has been for the losing party to take minimal steps and to declare itself in full conformity. The winning party often disagrees." Besides there is evidence that the WTO tends to be partial to the more powerful nations (Matsushita, Schoenbaum, & Mavruidis, 2003, p. 30).

## Japan: Imported White-Collar Crime Techniques

The Livedoor case in Japan epitomizes the complex consequences that can result in the international marketplace when corporate behaviours that violate the law in one country are initiated in another. Such a situation was captured in headlines in two national newspapers in the United States reporting the opening of the trial in a Tokyo district court of *Takfumi Horie*, a 33-year-old Internet entrepreneur. Before his arrest, Horie had parlayed $US 55,000 investments in 1996 in a small Internet consulting company into a network of media firms' worth $US 5 million. The *Los Angeles Times* in large type proclaimed: "Trial Seen as Culture Clash," while the *New York Times* headline declared: "Trial Begins for Icon of the 'New Japan'." The *Wall Street Journal*, in its report, declared Horie to be a person "who came to symbolize a free-wheeling capitalism at odds with Japan's cozy corporate norms" (Onishi, 2006; Wall Street Journal 2006; Wallace, 2006).

Horie was accused of tactics that duplicated those that led to the convictions of the top two Enron executives in the United States. He was charged with inflating the earnings of his company by creating dummy subsidiaries and with misrepresenting the true value of the enterprise. Horie also resorted, albeit unsuccessfully, to after-hours trading, uncommon in Japan, to accomplish a backdoor takeover of Fuji TF. Symbolic of Horie's defiance of Japanese corporate traditions was his wearing of T-shirts to formal meetings, dating fashion models, and driving flashy sports cars. It was notable that for his trial he wore a tie and suit. Horie's arrest in January 2006, led to what was labelled "Livedoor Shock," a development that took $US 327 billion off the total value of shares on the Tokyo Stock Exchange. Livedoor stock dropped $US 5 billion.

## Matters of Definition

When Edwin H. Sutherland coined the term "white-collar crime" in his presidential address in 1939 to the American Sociological Society he meant it to apply to persons who occupied positions of power in the worlds of business, politics, and the professions (Sutherland, 1940). A decade later, Sutherland (1949) expanded on his presidential address in a monograph that concentrated heavily on corporate crime rather than on individual law breaking. Again, the emphasis was on abuse of power by entities that employ their position and resources to the detriment of the general good.

Sutherland's focus on illegal actions by the well-off and well-placed dominated studies of white-collar crime for well over half a century, though his definition was notably tightened by Albert Reiss and Albert Biderman:

> White-collar violations are those violations of the law to which penalties are attached that involve the use of a violator's position of significant

power, influence, or trust in the legitimate economic or political institutional order for personal or organizational gain (Reiss & Biderman, 1980, p. 4).

This definitional approach ultimately drew criticism on both ideological and social scientific grounds. The ideological opposition claimed that the class-based formulation by Sutherland singled out a predetermined segment of the population for an invidious research enterprise. After all, it was argued, what is the difference between a physician who overcharges a medical insurance program and an ambulance driver who does the same thing? Or a fast food employee who steals from his employer compared to a bank president who embezzles funds?

Those devoted to Sutherland's position defended their support of the class-based formulation. Most certainly, they granted, there was an ideological thrust in Sutherland's pioneering approach to white-collar crime, but isn't there an ideological element in all criminology, with its very heavy concentration on traditional offenders, such as burglars and robbers? Their approach, the traditional white-collar scholars said, represents an admirable ideology, placing into the limelight matters that the powerful often manage to camouflage by the very nature of their power. They also pointed out that many wrongs of the powerful are dealt with by responses other than the criminal law, and that a sophisticated scholar should appreciate that it is the nature of the act, the harm it inflicts, that matters, not the statutory provision and not how the criminal justice system reacts to the behaviour. They maintained that objectivity in social science is manifest in the manner in which material is dealt with—honestly and fairly and dispassionately—not in the choice of what is studied.

The revisionist approach to white-collar crime favoured a focus on denoted offences, such as bribery, fraud, antitrust violations, and similar offences (Weisburd et al., 1993). This allowed for the ready accumulation of rosters of persons who had been convicted of the violation of specified statutes, and a determination of their characteristics, both within the particular statutory categories and in comparisons between categories. The makeup of the study groups in terms of such an enterprise often differed greatly from what Sutherland had in mind: considerable portions, for instance, were unemployed, and many of their illegal actions reasonably could be regarded as petty, such as passing small checks at a grocery store on a non-existent account or one with insufficient funds on deposit.

A definition of white-collar crimes that concentrates on violations of specific statutes assuredly simplifies the question of who does and who does not fit within your white-collar crime study sample. At the same time, it bypasses the role of ill-used power and how best to control such power. Besides, law-based definitions represent a default to an enforcement system that has quirks and irregularities. Who gets charged with what statutory crime often is a matter of considerable discretion on the part of the prosecutor and may have no consistent relationship to the essence of the acts that are performed.

In terms of international white-collar and corporate crime, the evidence points to the conclusion that Sutherland's definition is likely to hold sway. For one thing, it usually requires a reasonably high status to commit a white-collar crime that crosses international boundaries. For another, international tribunals are quite unlikely to bother themselves with any but major cases of white-collar law-breaking where the perpetrators typically will be giants of industry or multinational corporations.

## Theoretical Considerations

### *White-Collar Criminals*

White-collar crime typically has been the graveyard—the final resting place—for postulates that set forth general theories to explain all forms of criminal behaviour. Sutherland officiated at the first burial ceremony for general theories when he told his audience that white-collar offences disproved theoretical allegations that all crimes were caused by such considerations as broken homes, immigrant status, defective intelligence, or Oedipus complexes. His suggestion that his own theory of differential association - essentially a series of postulates that maintain that crime is learned from others - could explain all crime would, in its turn, suffer the same fate as the theories he had undermined.

Since legal enactments define crime and since such enactments are the product of a political, not a scientific process, and since the enactments vary in place and time, it appears to be the better part of wisdom to seek theoretical understanding of international white-collar crime and corporate crime by focusing on relatively homogeneous forms of such behaviour and seeking to formulate theoretical postulates that account for these actions. Even so, as Jane Jacobs pointed out, "it can be impossible to take into account every cause, influence, and interrelationship in a complex system, owing to causes being too many, subtle, varied and volatile" (Jacobs. 2000, p. 156). If so, and what Jacobs says is sensible, we must appreciate that our theorizing at best produces pragmatic and partial insights that may put us on the path to increasingly deeper understanding and improved policies. The theories will not, since they concern human behaviour, be the last or the complete word on the issue.

### *Corporate Criminals*

There have been debates concerning whether corporate crime can yield to theoretical understanding in terms of causality. Donald Cressey, a disciple of Sutherland, criticized his mentor for taking an anthropomorphic approach to inanimate entities. He insisted that the proper tactic for theorizing about corporate crime could be achieved only by focusing on individual actors and actions within the transgressing business (Cressey, 1988). John Braithwaite and Brent Fisse (1990) disagreed with Cressey, maintaining that a corporation is more than the sum of the persons who constitute it or those who make its decisions. Often what is done in the name of the corporation represents, they observed, an amalgam of the input of numerous individuals. In Braithwaite and Fisse's view, useful theories can be built around attributes of a corporation, such as its financial condition and its internal ethical climate. In another contribution, Braithwaite maintained "a criminology which remains fixated at the level of individualism is the criminology of a bygone era" (Braithwaite, 1988, p. 148).

In the arena of international corporate crimes, there has been so little accumulation of substantive information that it seems to be premature to seek to achieve more than superficial theoretical understanding. The aim likely should be to undertake a great many detailed case studies that address issues of theoretical importance and that can serve as building blocks to generalized insights.

## Conclusion

White-collar and corporate criminal acts that cross national boundaries are becoming increasingly commonplace, troublesome, and, for the perpetrators, lucrative. Ethnocentric attitudes inhibit sophisticated, encompassing efforts to contain such wrongdoing. For one thing, legal responses tend to lag behind illegal schemes; for another, once such responses appear to be effective, the schemers are likely to be adept at adjusting their tactics in ways that allow them to continue to operate unmolested. Besides, the playing field has been expanded to global proportions so that violators are readily able to launch nefarious operations in a very large number of sites that, directly or implicitly, compete for their business. We now live in a global village, and the need for criminology is to broaden its range and strengthen its commitment to collaborative international research.

## References

Amnesty International. (2004). *Clouds of injustice: Bhopal disaster, 20 years on.* London: Amnesty International.

Boulton, D. (1978). *Lockheed papers.* London: Jonathan Cape.

Brailand, P. (2000). *Switzerland and the crisis of dormant assets and the new gold.* (D. C. de Caprona & A. Lötter, Trans.). London: Kegan Paul International.

Braithwaite, J. (1984). *Corporate crime in the pharmaceutical industry.* London: Routledge & Kegan Paul.

—. (1988). *Crime, shame and reintegration.* Cambridge, UK: Cambridge University Press.

Braithwaite, J., & Drahos, P. (2000). *Global business regulation.* Cambridge, UK: Cambridge University Press.

Braithwaite, J., & Fisse, B. (1990). On the plausibility of corporate crime control. *Advances in Criminological Theory, 2,* 15-37.

Carlisle, R. P. (1981). *Sovereignty for sale: The origin and evolution of the Panamanian and Liberian flags of convenience.* Annapolis, MD: Naval Institute Press.

Cressey, D. (1988). The poverty of theory in corporate crime research. *Advances in Criminological Theory, 1,* 31-56.

Csonka, P. (2005). The council of Europe convention on cybercrime: A response to the challenge of the new age. In R. Broadhurst & P. Grabosky (Eds.), *Cyber-crime: The challenge in Asia* (pp. 303-326). Hong Kong: Hong Kong University Press.

Daemnrich, A. (2002). A tale of two experts: Thalidomide and political engagement in the United States and West Germany. *Social History of Medicine, 15,* 137-158.

Dhara, V. R., & Dhara, R. (2002). The Union Carbide disaster in Bhopal: A review of health effects. *Archives of Environmental Health, 57,* 391-404.

Dowie, M. (1979). The dumping of hazardous products on foreign markets. *Mother Jones, 4,* 23-44.

Everett, S., Lehmann, A., & Steil, B. (2000). *Antitrust goes global: What future for transatlantic cooperation?* London: Royal Institute of International Affairs.

Fay, S. (1997). *Collapse of Barings.* London: Richard Cohen Books.

Gilbert, M. J., & Russell, S. (2002). Globalization of criminal justice in the corporate context. *Crime, Law and Social Change, 38,* 211-238

Goldstone, D., & Shave, B-E. (1999). International dimensions of crimes in cyberspace. *Fordham International Law Journal, 22,* 1924-1971.

Hall, M. J. B. (1998). *Financial reform in Japan: Causes and consequences.* Cheltinham, UK: Edward Elgar.

Hunt, L., & Heinrich, K. (1996). *Barings lost: Nick Leeson and the collapse of Barings.* Singapore: Butterworth-Heinemann Asia.

Hunzinker, S., & Kammura, I. (1994). *Kakeui Tanaka: A political biography.* Los Gatos, CA: Daruma International.

Instefjord, N., Jackson, P., Perraudin, W., Pagona, M., & Röell, A. (1998). Securities fraud. *Economic Policy, 13*, 586-623.

Jacobs, J. (2000). *The nature of economics.* New York: Modern Library.

Kida, M. (Ed.). (1987). *Thalidomide embryopathy in Japan.* Tokyo: Kodansha.

Kutzman, D. (1987). *A killing wind: Inside Union Carbide and the Bhopal catastrophe.* New York: McGraw-Hill.

Leacock, C. C. (2001). The effect of globalization on small states: Internationalization of crime. *New York University Journal of International Law and Politics, 34,* 263-279.

Leeson, N., & Whitley, E. (1996). *Rogue trader: How I brought down Barings Bank and shook the financial world.* Boston: Little Brown.

Lenz, W., & Knapp, K. (1962). Die thalidomide embryopathie. *Deutsche Medinishe Wokenschrift, 87*, 1233-1242.

Matsushita, M., Schoenbaum, T., & Mavroidis, P. C. (2000). *The World Trade Organization: Law, practice, and policy.* Oxford, UK: Oxford University Press.

McBride, W. M. (1961). Thalidomide and congenital abnormalities. *Lancet, ii*, 1358.

Metaxas, B. N. (1985). *Flags of convenience: A study in internationalisation.* Aldershot, UK: Gower.

Milhaupt, C. J. (2001). Creative norm destruction: The evolution of nonlegal rules in Japanese corporate governance. *University of Pennsylvania Law Review, 149,* 2083-2125.

Misawa, M. (2005). Shareholder's action and director's responsibility in Japan. *Penn State International Law Review, 24,* 1-57.

Noonan, John T., Jr. (1984). *Bribes.* Berkeley: University of California Press.

Onishi, N. (2006, September 5). Trial begins for an icon in Japan. *New York Times,* C1, C12.

Reiss, A. J., & Biderman, A. J. (1980). *Data sources on white-collar lawbreaking.* Washington, D.C: U.S. Government Printing Office.

Rosenberg, T. (2003, August 10). The taint of the greased palm. *New York Times, 6*, 28.

Rotman, E. (2000). The globalization of violence. *Cornell Journal of Law and Policy, 10,* 1-41.

Schapiro, J. (2003). *Inside a class action: The Holocaust and the Swiss banks.* Madison: University of Wisconsin Press.

Sellin, T. (1938). *Culture conflict and crime.* New York: Social Science Research Council.

Shichor, D., & Geis, G. (2006). The itching palm: The crimes of bribery and extortion. In H. Pontell & G. Geis (Eds.), *International Handbook of White-Collar and Corporate Crime* (pp. 405-420). New York: Springer.

Shover, N., & Hochstetler, A. (2006). *Choosing white-collar crime.* New York: Cambridge University Press.

Sutherland, E. H. (1949). *White collar crime.* New York: Dryden.

—. (1940). White-collar criminality. *American Sociological Review, 5.* 1-12.

Taussig, H. (1963). A study of the German outbreak of phocomelia. *Journal of the American Medical Association, 180,* 1106-1114.

Teff, H., & Munro, C. R. (1976). *Thalidomide: The legal aftermath.* Farnborough, UK: Saxon House.

Terry, L. S. (2004). Global legal practice symposium: Foreword. *Penn State International Law Review, 22,* 527-539.

United Kingdom, House of Commons (1985, July). *Report of the banking supervision inquiry into the circumstances of the collapse of Barings.* London, UK: Her Majesty's Stationery Office.

Vivek, P. S. (1990). *The struggle of man against power: Revelation of the 1984 Bhopal tragedy.* Bombay: Himalaya Publishing House.

Wallace, B. (2006, September 5). Japanese Internet maverick on trial: Trial seen as culture clash. *Los Angeles Times,* C1, C5.

*Wall Street Journal* (2006, September 5). Securities trial begins in Japan for Livedoor ex-chief Horie, A24.

Weisburd, D., Wheeler, S., Waring, E., & Bode, N. (1993). *Crimes of the middle class: White collar offenders in the federal courts.* New Haven, CT: Yale University Press

## Cases cited

*American Banana Co. v. United Fruit Co.* (1909). 213 U.S. 348.

*United States v. Nippon Paper Industries* (1996). 944 F. Supp. 55 (District Massachusetts).

*United States v. Nippon Paper Industries* (1997). 101 F.3d 1 (1$^{st}$ Circuit).

*W. S. Kirkpatrick v. Environmental Tectonics Corp.* (1990). 499 U.S. 400.

# CHAPTER TWO

# EYEWITNESS IDENTIFICATION METHODS: A COMPARATIVE ANALYSIS OF PRACTICES IN ENGLAND, CANADA, USA AND ISRAEL

AVRAHAM M. LEVI


## Abstract

This chapter compares the eyewitness identification methods of England, Canada, USA, and Israel and the scientific evidence on best practice in obtaining reliable identifications. In general the comparison finds that English practice is most in tune with science, followed by Israel, Canada, and USA. The progression follows the amount of time that has passed since each of the latter countries gained their independence from England. However, even practice in England is far from ideal. The size of the lineup conducted there is still far too small to provide a reliable identification. Research evidence shows that lineups could be far larger without reducing culprit identifications, while decreasing substantially mistaken ones. In addition, suspects can waive their right to the presence of counsel at the lineup, lineups can be held even if the witness has seen a photo of the suspect, witnesses are not routinely requested to state their confidence in their identification, and an inferior method of choosing lineup foils is mandated. Some identification methods far inferior to the lineups are acceptable. The less acceptable practices of the other countries are described in detail. These include failing to have a minimal number of lineup members or the right of counsel at the lineup, or warning the witness that the culprit may not be in the lineup (the US and Canada), or enabling counsel to ensure a fair lineup (Israel). Inferior methods are more acceptable in all three countries, though the situation is worse in the USA.

## Introduction

This chapter defines eyewitness identification evidence as the data that the prosecution gathers from eyewitnesses to a crime and presents in court to prove that the defendant is the culprit. Mistaken identification has consistently been found to be the primary cause of false convictions (Bochard, 1932; Brandon & Davies, 1973). The most recent and widely cited evidence for this has come from the Justice Project in the USA (Conners et al., 1996); Lawyers tracked down DNA samples of rape perpetrators from cases that had been decided before DNA testing had been used to determine the identity of the rapist. Defendants were convicted on the basis of other evidence, usually eyewitness identification. In about 25% of these cases the convicted were found to be innocent.

In addition, preliminary results from an ongoing study examining courtroom outcomes in Israel suggest that in eyewitness cases courts convict the defendant based on insufficient or faulty evidence at about the same 25%. Eyewitness identification evidence is extremely unreliable. A false conviction rate of 25% is clearly unacceptable in the British tradition that requires convictions only when guilt has been proven beyond reasonable doubt. The lesson has been learned for all cases where DNA, or other highly reliable forensic evidence, is available. However, when such data is missing, courts continue to convict using eyewitnesses as they have always done.

Life would be a lot easier for all of us if our eyes, ears and brain worked like a video camera, documenting exactly what is occurring, that could be "played back" whenever we needed the information. Unfortunately this is not the case. Our senses only record some of what is happening, and our brain fills in the rest. When we try to remember something, our brain is then called upon to reconstruct, from incomplete data, what we are trying to remember (Buckhout, 1974). This works fairly well in everyday life. Repetition helps memory a lot, and much of what we are called upon to remember is familiar because we have experienced very similar events quite often. Witnessing a crime, however, is a unique experience. It is a one-time event. Our brain is much more prone to err in filling in the gaps.

Psychologists have been collecting a lot of data on the fallibility of human memory. For example, Allport (reported in Buckhout, 1974) showed a photograph of travellers on a subway to Americans. The photo showed a white man brandishing a type of knife, considered a common weapon of blacks, at a black man. When the witnesses were asked to describe the photo, the knife "miraculously" moved in their descriptions from the hand of the white man to that of the black. A robust body of scientific findings on eyewitness evidence has been developing over more than 100 years. Many recommendations have evolved on the most reliable methods for obtaining such evidence. These proposals have often been honoured in the breach by the very countries in which most of the scientists reside.

This chapter contrasts some of these findings with the practices in England, Canada, USA, and Israel. These countries fall on a continuum relating to when they began developing independent procedures evolving away from the original English model. England itself has of course been developing in its own direction. The USA gained its independence first. Israel is the most recent, having gained its independence with the end of the British Mandate over Palestine less than sixty years ago.

Israel has some other unique qualities. Canada and the USA were colonized largely by Christians from Western Europe, while Jews from Eastern Europe and Jews and Arabs from the Middle East make up the lion's share of the Israeli population. The British mandate existed less than 30 years in Israel, far less than British rule in North America. It can be expected that these factors would result in unique developments in Israel away from the British model. It should be noted that these are actually very rare, and that Israel has remained more true to the British tradition than either the USA or Canada.

## The Police Lineup

The simultaneous police lineup (or parade as coined by England) was invented towards the end of the nineteenth century by Scotland Yard. In England, the suspect is put in a line along with eight people known to be innocent (foils). The witness is then asked whether he can identify the culprit from among the nine persons. This process provides a test of witness memory. When suspects are innocent yet witnesses still choose someone, in most cases they will pick a foil. Each person in an ideal lineup has an equal chance of being chosen, and therefore innocent suspects are only chosen one time out of nine (11%) in a nine-person lineup. When a foil is chosen, the police know that the witness has erred. This is a vast improvement over the previous routine of showing only the suspect to the witness, and therefore has been widely accepted. It became the standard method in most of the Western world. If the witness "identifies" the suspect, the suspect will usually be convicted. However, is this standard lineup good enough? Are we satisfied that 11% of innocent suspects go to jail when witnesses choose someone? Experimental witnesses often compare lineup members and "identify" the person who seems the most similar to the "culprit" (Wells, 1993).

The situation is worse elsewhere, because they allow smaller lineups. Israel requires eight lineup members. Canada and the USA have no minimal requirement. In Canada, Brooks (1983) reports that major police departments range from five to eleven members, with most consisting of six or seven. In the USA, nonbinding guidelines of the Department of Justice (Technical Working Group for Eyewitness Evidence, 1999) recommend five. With this later recommendation, 20% of the innocent suspects will be "identified" when a witness chooses and the suspect is innocent. The situation is worse than the 11% figure, even for England. Courts must decide, on the basis of lineup "identification" and other evidence, whether the defendant is guilty (This is opposite from knowing that the defendant is innocent, and calculating the probability that he will be "identified"). What is the probability that defendants are innocent, even though they have been "identified" in a nine-person lineup?

This is a Bayesian situation (Levi, 1998): In the simplest case, that probability is: (number of innocents chosen)/ (total number of those chosen). The total number of those chosen is: (number of innocents chosen + number of guilty chosen). The defendant is either innocent or guilty. Our formula is then: (number of innocent chosen)/ (number of innocent chosen + number of guilty chosen). We have calculated the number of innocent chosen, 11%. We need still an estimate of the guilty. Three studies in England present data from the police on the rate that suspects have been chosen in lineups. Valentine, Pickering and Darling (2003) found that 41% of the suspects were chosen, Slater (1994) found 36%, and Wright and McDaid (1996) 39%.

These are suspects that were chosen, not necessarily *guilty* suspects. Some of these are innocent, those 11% who are chosen. Moreover, the 11% is based on the assumption that each lineup member has the same chance of being chosen. In real police lineups, innocent suspects are often more likely to be chosen, either because they stand out or because the witness can be discounted as lineup members (Doob & Kirshenbaum, 1973; Malpass & Lindsay, 1999). Valentine and Heaton, (1999) found, using photographs of English police lineups, that "mock witnesses" (research participants asked to guess who the suspect was), chose the suspect 25% of the time. This is significantly higher that the expected 11% if indeed the suspect had no greater chance of being chosen.

In addition, Wright and McDaid (1996) included cases in which the witness claimed to know the perpetrator, and we are interested only in cases of strangers. Perhaps Slater (1994) did the same. Including such cases naturally inflates suspect identifications. Witnesses usually identify suspects that they know personally. Lineups generally are not conducted in such situations because they are deemed unnecessary. The number of guilty who is chosen must be, then, less than the 41%, 36% and 39% of suspects "identified" in English police records. The true number may be half those numbers, and the lower the rate of guilty chosen, the higher the likelihood that a suspect chosen is actually innocent (from our formula we see that the relative number of innocent grows as the number of guilty lessens). Let us however be very conservative, and estimate the number of guilty at a high of 35%.

Putting the 11% innocent and the 35% guilty in our simple formula, we find that the rate of suspects/defendants being actually innocent even if "identified" (chosen in the lineup) is: 11%/ (11% + 35%) = 24%. That is, if in England the court convicts because there is a lineup "identification", which they do, in 24% of the cases they are convicting an innocent person! The situation is worse in countries that allow lineups smaller than nine, since such lineups increase the number of innocent suspects chosen. This is true if the other evidence points to a 50-50 chance of the suspect being guilty. This a-priori probability may be considerably more or less. Suspects are put in lineups sometimes after the stolen goods have been found in their possession. In such cases the a-priori probability of guilt is likely more than 50-50, and the probability that the "identified" defendant is innocent is less.

Sometimes the suspects only fit a general description of the offender common to many. In such cases the a-priori probability of guilt is less than 50-50 and the chance that the suspect is innocent is greater than 24%. The complete Bayesian equation (Levi, 1998) takes this into account. Table 1 gives the probabilities that the defendant is innocent for various a- priori probabilities.

**Table 1:** The probability that the suspect is innocent despite having been "identified" in a nine-person lineup, for various probabilities of being guilty based on other evidence.

| A -priori p guilty | ..10 | ..20 | ..30 | ..40 | ..50 | ..60 | ..70 | ..80 | ..90 |
|---|---|---|---|---|---|---|---|---|---|
| p innocent | ..74 | ..56 | ..42 | ..32 | ..24 | ..17 | ..12 | ..07 | ..03 |

An inspection of Table 1 should be sobering. Courts convicting on the basis of the existing evidence, which includes the lineup "identification", will, unless the other evidence points to about a 90% chance of guilt without the identification, err at a greater rate than the minimum allowed for a psychological experiment, 5%. The consequences of a mistake are much more severe. The liberty, and sometimes even the life of the defendant, hangs in the balance. Courts should convict only if the guilt of the defendant has been proven beyond reasonable doubt. Judges have refrained from putting a precise probability on the somewhat vague "reasonable doubt" criterion. Nonetheless, we might even wonder whether a 3% error rate (when the a-priori probability of guilt is 90%) should be considered acceptable.

In practice, courts convict because of one "identification" without other evidence, or with extremely minimal other support. The gap between their willingness to convict and the actual probative value of the lineups must result in many innocent people being convicted and sent to prison or their death. Why do so many witnesses make so many mistaken choices? If their memory was very good they would not be tempted into choosing anyone. They would be certain that the culprit was missing.

We of course should not be surprised that many witnesses do not have a good memory of the culprits. They are perfect strangers who they have seen just once. Moreover, we have seen familiar people from different angles, with their faces expressing various emotions, over an extended period of time during which their faces may have undergone other changes too. We have learnt to connect John the smiling to John the angry, turning towards us or in another direction. We saw the stranger from a more limited angle, with a particular expression on his face, at a particular moment. When witnesses are standing in front of a lineup, they have to compare a rather hazy memory of the stranger with the lineup members that he may be seeing from a different angle, with a different expression on his or her face, and perhaps other changes that time has caused (the amount of facial hair on men, or the colour and hair style of women) (Levi & Jungman, 1995).

In these conditions a real identification is most likely rare. Wells (1984) has proposed that witnesses, when they choose in this situation, pick the person who seems the most similar to the culprit. This is their best chance of "identifying" the culprit—who, however, is of course missing in culprit-absent lineups. Instead of identifying, witnesses must compare the similarity of the lineup members with their hazy memory. They must decide whether one of them is similar "enough" to the culprit for them to announce that they have "identified" him or her as the culprit.

How much is "enough" for one witness is not necessarily identical to what is "enough" for others. One witness may want to be very careful not to implicate an innocent person, and therefore require a lot more similarity than others who want to catch that scoundrel who robbed them. There are other factors that can affect the threshold that different witnesses set for themselves. It seems that witnesses tend to believe that the culprits are in the lineup even when they are warned, as they were in almost all experimental lineups, that the culprit may actually be missing from the lineup. They want to prove that they are capable of identifying them. If they fail to choose anyone, they are admitting that they cannot.

## *Enlarging the lineup*

One solution is to enlarge the lineup (Levi & Lindsay, 2001). Live lineups would then be impossible. Police often have difficulty finding suitable foils with small lineups. Photo lineups cause somewhat more mistaken identifications (Cutler & Fisher, 1990), and therefore the US guidelines recommend six members for photo lineups, and the Province of Ontario in Canada requires twelve photos. Such adjustments eliminate any concern from that quarter. Larger photo lineups would result in less mistaken identifications than the small live lineup. For example, a 48-person lineup would reduce mistaken identifications to 1/48 = 2% of the mistaken choices.

Photo lineups are the norm in the US, and seem acceptable in Canada too. Israel, on the other hand, requires solid justification for conducting a photo lineup instead of a live one. In England photo lineups are seriously frowned upon, though video lineups have been deemed acceptable. Video-clips of potential foils can be collected almost as easily as photos can, and research has found no difference, in either identifications or mistaken identifications, between live and video lineups (Cutler & Fisher, 1990).The concern about large lineups is that they decrease identifications (Brook, 1983). Levi (2002) found no difference between 10, 20, and 40 person video lineups, but Beaudry, (2004) found a large reduction moving from a 20-person to a 40-person photo lineup.

All those lineups displayed the lineup members one at a time. Levi (2006a; 2007) showed photos in groups. He found in the first experiment that witnesses identified the "culprit" as often in a 42-person lineup consisting of seven groups of six photos as they did in an 18-person lineup of three groups, and made the same number of mistaken choices (71%). Mistaken identifications can be calculated by dividing mistaken choices by lineup size. The rate of mistaken identifications in the 18-person lineups, was 71/18 = 3.9%. That rate in the 42-person lineup was 71/42 = 1.7%. The larger lineup was twice more reliable.

In the second study Levi found no differences in either identifications or mistaken choices between an 84-person and a 24-person lineup with photos in groups of twelve. With 64% mistaken choices, the rate of mistaken identifications in the 84-person lineup was only 64/84 = 0.8%. He concluded that lineups should consist of at least 84 members shown in groups of twelve. There seems to be no loss in correct identifications. The number of mistaken identifications is less than 1% of the mistaken choices.

Making the change in England and Israel would require reconsidering the value of live lineups relative to photo lineups. Regarding video lineups, research has yet to be conducted testing the effects of showing groups of video-clips simultaneously. This can be accomplished easily on standard desk computers. The largest size required that the author have heard of is the photo lineup of twelve in Ontario. The Israeli police adopted on a trial basis a 40-person video lineup based on Levi's, (2002) research. However, before it was implemented the State Prosecutor stopped it.

## *Multiple lineups*

Lindsay (Pryke et al., 2004) has innovated with another approach. He reasoned that while enlarging the lineup from 9 to 36 increases the reliability fourfold, giving witnesses two independent lineups of nine should increase reliability nine times: The chance that a witness would pick the same person in the two lineups by chance is 1/9x1/9 = 1.2%. His solution to finding two independent photo lineups has been, for example, to have the second lineup consisting of the profiles of the people in the first lineup. The only problem with this strategy is that witnesses are used to identifying people from the frontal view of the face normally used in photo lineups. His test of the method was quite successful. However, it may have depended on the exceptionally good viewing conditions afforded to his witnesses that do not conform to real world conditions (Levi, 1998). On the other hand, even if few witnesses in the real world might be able to take advantage of profiles, the method seems quite promising. The only cost is conducting an additional photo lineup.

In all events, Lindsay's approach is compatible with enlarging the lineup. For example, two 42-person lineups would result in a 1/42 x 1/42 = 0.06% chance of a witness choosing the innocent suspect when he/she mistakenly chooses someone in a culprit-absent lineup.

### *The sequential lineup*

The sequential lineup (Lindsay & Wells, 1985) prevents witnesses from comparing lineup members. Witnesses view the members one after the other, and they must decide whether each one is the offender or not before seeing the next person. They are also not told the size of the lineup. This indeed thwarts witnesses from choosing the lineup member most similar to the perpetrator. The sequential lineup has replaced the simultaneous lineup in parts of Ontario (but not Toronto, the major city), and in some states in the US. In Israel its introduction would be retarded by a preference by the courts for simultaneous lineups. In England it is illegal, since the law requires that witnesses view all lineup members before making a decision.

Early research indicated that the sequential lineup resulted in far less mistaken identifications than the simultaneous lineups while paying a smaller price in correct ones (Steblay et al., 2001). However, recent research has cast doubt on this conclusion. Researchers (Levi, 2006b; Memon & Bartlett, 2002, 2003) have found that simultaneous lineups enabled more target identifications relative to sequential lineups than previously found. The theoretical underpinning of this finding is that the sequential lineup benefits far less from choosing foils that fit the description of the perpetrator. The extra advantage to the simultaneous lineup results from the foils being more different from suspects when they are chosen by the fit-to-description method (Luus & Wells, 1991; Wells, Rydell, & Seelau, 1991) and therefore witnesses can more easily discriminate between guilty ones and the foils when they compare lineup members. Since witnesses cannot compare them in the sequential lineup, they benefit less from less similarity between the offender and the foils.

Also, the earlier research exaggerated the number of mistaken identifications in simultaneous lineups. Researchers would designate the person most similar to the target as the "innocent suspect". This led to many "identifications" of the "innocent suspect" in simultaneous lineups, because witnesses choose the person most similar to the target (Wells, 1984). However, in the real world innocent suspects are not always the most similar to the culprit, but rather only 1/9 of the time in ideal nine-person lineups. The sequential lineup suffers far less from the similarity of the innocent suspect to the perpetrator, because, again, witnesses cannot compare lineup members. Thus, the early research found a far greater difference between the two lineups in favour of the sequential lineup than we should expect in real world lineups that are fair. This research underestimated correct identifications of the simultaneous lineup and overestimated its mistaken identifications. With these two factors corrected, Levi (2006b) found no difference in the reliability of the two lineups.

## *The method of choosing foils*

We should note that this lack of difference depends on police choosing lineup foils that fit the description that the witness gave of the culprit, rather than foils that are similar to the suspect. To date this seems a rather rare occurrence. The US Justice Department's guidelines (Technical Working Group for Eyewitness Evidence, 1999) recommend the fit-to-description strategy, but there was no evidence regarding the extent that police have indeed moved there from the older, established similarity-to-suspect method. English Law mandates the older custom and it is by far the most common method in Israel. Brooks (1983) in Canada, generally ahead of his time, recommends that strategy with a proviso that witness description also be taken into consideration. This does not help regarding simultaneous lineup identifications, since the foils will be similar to the culprit, making discrimination difficult. However, it does deal with a more serious problem caused by the similarity-to-suspect method.

The similarity-to-suspect method does not require that foils fit the description of the culprit provided by the witness. Witnesses can often ignore those who do not fit the description they gave. For example, in a case in Israel (The State of Israel vs. Kedoshim, 1999) five of the eight lineup members could thus be discounted by the witness. The real lineup size was thus only three. The witness, when he chose, would "identify" the suspect 33% of the time, even if he was innocent. Such "unfair" lineups are all too common. We have noted that Valentine and Heaton (1999, found, using photographs of English police lineups, that "mock witnesses" chose the suspect 25% of the time, significantly higher that the expected 11% if the suspect had no greater chance of being chosen than any other lineup member.

## *The presence of counsel*

One safeguard to ensure that the foils are appropriate is the presence of the suspect's lawyer at the lineup. In Israel counsel is usually present, yet the police still manage to prevent them from ensuring fair lineups. At the time of the lineup the police usually refuse to provide counsel with the description of the culprit that the witness gave, claiming that it needs to be supplied only after the suspect has been charged. In contrast, English law clearly states that the police must provide counsel with the description.

There is no possible way for counsel to guess which foils are inappropriate without the description. People differ and are the same on so many characteristics. For example, in State of Israel vs. Kedoshim, (1999) the witness described the perpetrator as "the small one". Two lineup members had the same height as the suspect. The suspect did not even stand out on this factor. Yet the lineup was still extremely unfair with the others being so tall as to fail to fit the witness description. This might seem to be but a minor setback. By the time of the trial counsel has been informed of the description, and he or she can then determine how many of the foils were inappropriate. Counsel can argue against the fairness of the lineup in court.

However, in both *The State of Israel vs. Kedoshim*, (1999) and *The State of Israel vs. Nachmias*, (2000) the judges refused to accept counsel's objection to the lineup, arguing that the counsel had forfeited that right by failing to make the objection at the time of the lineup. In *The State of Israel vs. Kedoshim*, (1999) the counsel had actually objected to certain lineup members on various grounds, because of the unusually great height of one foil. That did not satisfy the judge. The counsel did not object specifically to the height of five foils. We have a clear case of Catch 22: judges sometimes demand of counsel exactly what they cannot possibly do without being given at the lineup the description of the culprit, which the police refuse to do! The result is that in Israel the right to counsel at the lineup has been shorn of much of its meaning. The situation is still much worse in the US and Canada. The US Supreme Court determined that the lawyer need be present only if the lineup is being held after the suspect has been charged. A rare event before their ruling that now happens even less often. No lawyer is present.

Canada does not require the presence of the lawyer. Brooks (1983) has noted a small number of cities in Canada where the right to counsel is even denied. The police in all cities report that the counsel is seldom present, and some report that if a lawyer did appear, they would subpoena him or her as a witness! A corollary to the right of having counsel present at the lineup is telling suspects that they have such a right, a practice that Brooks (1983) recommends. He reports that no police force in Canada advises of their right to counsel. This may help to explain why counsel is so rarely present. In England the law requires informing the suspect that he is even entitled to free legal advice. The practice in Israel is similar. Brooks (1983) supports the practice that exists in Israel and England, of allowing suspects to waive their right to counsel at lineups. Such a custom seems to discriminate most against those least likely to be guilty, who have less experience with lineups and do not realize the importance of the presence of a lawyer to protect their rights. Brooks (1983) argues that the budgets are not available to provide public defenders for this purpose. The author fails to understand the logic of this position. Even if we ignored the value of preventing miscarriage of justice in having counsel always present, the position fails to take into account the large economic cost entailed in each innocent defendant being sent to prison. The savings in preventing each such case would provide for many appearances of public defenders at lineups.

The lawyer's presence may also be needed to prevent even worse police behaviour then mentioned so far. This is illustrated in a rare case in which an American photo lineup was taped for research purposes (Lofus & Ketcham, 1991). The police detective is heard subtly directing the witness towards the suspect with his questions, in a way that it is highly unlikely that the witness himself will remember how it happened when he reaches court. The lawyer also serves to provide an additional report of the proceedings for the court (Brooks, 1983).

### *Instructions to the witness*

Another danger to the reliability of the simultaneous lineup lies in the expectation of witnesses that the culprit is in the lineup. They realize that the police would not go to the trouble of organizing a lineup without a suspect, and they may tend to seriously overestimate the evidence that the police have gathered against the suspect. The expectation increases the tendency of witnesses to choose someone, in the hope of picking the culprit. This increases the likelihood that innocent suspects are falsely "identified". Warning witnesses that the suspect may not be in the lineup partially counters this. Research (Malpass & Devine, 1981) indicates that this reduces mistaken identifications. In Israel and England such a warning is mandated. In the US, the warning is recommended both by a committee of expert Psychologists (Wells, et al. 1998) and the US Department of Justice (Technical Working Group for Eyewitness Evidence, 1999). The fact that they found it necessary to mention it suggests that it is far from common practice. Brooks (1983) reports, that, in Canada the warning is never given.

### *Prior to the lineup the witness sees the suspect or a photo of him*

There is widespread recognition outside of the US that if the witness sees the suspect before the lineup the reliability of the lineup is seriously compromised. As Brooks (1983) notes, there are two main reasons for this.

First of all, the witness will have seen the suspect far closer to the time of the lineup than he has seen the culprit, and therefore the witness will remember the suspect better than the culprit. Further, the witness will have had more time, under better conditions, to examine the suspect, and this will also result in better memory. The research evidence validates this (Brigham & Cairns, 1988). When the police fail to adhere to this prohibition, Brooks (1983) claims that courts at least reduce the value of the identification. When in England the police invited a witness, before viewing the lineup, to look through a window at the accused who was sitting alone, the Court of Criminal appeal condemned the practice (R. v. Dickman, 1910).

However, the law in England requires that witnesses be reminded if they have previously made identification by photographs or some other means (Annex A, 13). This is inadequate protection. If the witness' memory has been influenced by, for example, having been shown the photo of the suspect, he will in all likelihood "identify" the suspect. Indeed, there is a provision that an identification procedure be conducted if a witness has made a "positive identification" while viewing photographs (Annex E, 6). Thus, in England they conduct lineups after witnesses have picked the suspect in a mug-shot search. The courts certainly do not object to a practice required by law.

The situation in the US is far worse due to a couple of practices that ignore this principle. There are departments that hold a second lineup for the same suspect with the same witness if the witness fails to identify the suspect in the first one. The only person in both lineups is the suspect. The witness is obviously thus alerted to the fact that indeed that person is the suspect, since they likely remember him or her quite well from the first lineup (Brooks, 1983; Hinz & Pezdek, 2001). Another American procedure is first to hold a photo lineup, and if the witness "identifies" the suspect to hold a live one. Witnesses are more likely to mistakenly identify someone in photo lineups, and courts put more faith in live ones. Once witnesses "identify" a suspect in a photo lineup, it is likely that they will "identify" the same person in the live lineup who they remember from the photo lineup. The court is fooled into believing that the original "identification" was in the live one. In the State of New York it is forbidden to inform the jury that there was a previous photo lineup! In Israel, on the other hand, there is a clear prohibition to conduct a lineup after the witness has seen the suspect or a photo of him or her.

### *The police fail to have the witness report their confidence in their lineup identification*

A grave danger to reliable eyewitness evidence is influences on the witness after the crime and prior to giving testimony (Loftus & Ketcham, 1991). These influences rarely effect eyewitness identification, though we have noted the example of showing witnesses the suspects or their photos prior to lineups. Another example is witness' confidence in their identification. Courts are known to be particularly influenced by highly confident, though perhaps, mistaken witnesses. Yet witness confidence is highly malleable. All that the police have to do is to inform witnesses that they have "identified" the suspect for their confidence to grow (Wells & Bradfield, 1991). The only remedy is to have witnesses report their confidence prior to any feedback from the police, but this rarely happens. Wells et al., 1991) recommend it, and it is included in the US Department of Justice's guidelines (Technical Working Group for Eyewitness Evidence, 1999).

## "Unconscious transference"

The classic case of this phenomenon occurred in England. The clerk at a railway station was robbed, and suspicion fell on a sailor. The clerk "identified" him in a lineup. However, the sailor had an iron- clad alibi. At the time of the crime he had been at a base of His Majesty's navy. The sailor had bought a ticket from the clerk on more than one occasion. It seems that the clerk found the sailor to be the only person in the lineup who looked familiar, and therefore "identified" him. Research indicates that people are far better at recognizing someone as looking familiar than they are at remembering the circumstances around which the person was encountered (Brown, Deffenbacher, & Sturgill, 1977). Furthermore, experiments have been conducted in which an innocent bystander at a crime was later put in the lineup as the suspect and was identified as the culprit by witnesses (Geiselman, MacArthur, & Merrovitch, 1993).

"Unconscious Transference" poses a serious problem for the police lineup. There always is the possibility that the witness "identified" the suspect from some casual previous encounter. It seems incumbent on the police to explore this prospect whenever a suspect is "identified". Clearly the likelihood is greater when there has been a greater chance for previous acquaintanceship, as in a small town (or even neighbourhood) rather than a large city. Police do not seem to be aware of the danger of "Unconscious Transference", and do not raise the issue in their testimony. The author even testified in two cases (*The State of Israel vs. Kedoshim 1999*; *The State of Israel vs. Peri 2002*) in which the victim stated that he did not see who stabbed him in a fight involving multiple participants. In both cases the police nonetheless conducted lineups for the culprit in which the defendant, who was present at the fight, was the suspect.

The victim "identified" the defendant in both cases. In *The State of Israel vs. Peri* (2002) the defendant stood out as the person who had started the fight, and two additional people "identified" him as the stabber. The judge nevertheless acquitted him, understanding that the witnesses could have chosen the defendant simply because he was the only person in the lineup who was at the fight. The victim was even confident that the defendant had stabbed him, even as he continued to maintain that he had not seen who had done it. It seems that aside from recognizing the defendant as the only person familiar from the fight, the victim also deduced incorrectly that the police had other evidence connecting the defendant to the crime.

The defendant need not have been even at the scene of the crime. In a case that also involved a stabbing in the midst of a brawl (*The State of Israel vs. Salman 2006*), the victim was visited by a friend who had not been at the brawl. The victim surmised that the stabber may have been someone with whom they had recently played soccer. The friend then told the victim that it must have been "*Shlomi*", someone who the friend obviously knew personally but the victim did not. Thus *Shlomi* found himself the suspect in a lineup that the victim viewed, and not surprisingly, in light of this section, was "identified".

## Inferior Identification Methods

We have noted that the standard size lineup, simultaneous or sequential, has limited probative value even when conducted under best possible practice. The chance of mistakenly identifying an innocent suspect is too high. We have noted the many pitfalls in the way of best practice that lead to far less reliable "identifications". Yet police often present eyewitness identification evidence far inferior to the lineup. We now turn to these practices.

### *The show-up*

In the show-up, the police present to witnesses a single person, the suspect, and ask them whether that person is the culprit (a "show-up"). This method is clearly very suggestive, and provides no test of witness memory. If the witness "identifies" the person, for example, simply because he or she is wearing a shirt of the same colour as the culprit, the court has no way of discovering this. In the US "field identifications" (show-ups) are very common. This practice was even given the approval of the Department of Justice's guidelines (Technical Working Group for Eyewitness Evidence, 1999). They are termed field identifications because they occur within hours of the crime and usually near the scene of the offence. They also occur in England, where they are termed "confrontations". Wells, (2001) justifies them as a means of quickly exonerating suspects. Brooks (1983) is firm in his rejection. He is particularly concerned about the suggestive nature of the police offering a single person for the witness' judgment. The author would emphasize the lack of any test of the witness' memory. Brooks (1983) notes that there are many possible reasons a witness may have to want to choose someone. Without any foils, all the witness has to do is to choose the only possible person in order to achieve an "identification", which may be mistaken.

Well's (2001) concern for quickly exonerating the innocent seems a dangerous argument given the greater dangers involved in mistakenly "identifying" the innocent. Once a person has been "identified" by a witness in a show-up, a lineup is no longer feasible, since the witness will in all likelihood continue to "identify" the suspect in a lineup. The effect is the same as any case in which witnesses are shown the suspect before the lineup. The research evidence is that even if witnesses choose less often when shown one person rather than a lineup, the absence of foils increases the chances that they will "identify" innocent suspects (Yarmey, Yarmey, & Yarmey, 1996). Every time they choose they "identify" the innocent suspect, while even in the small 6-person US lineup they do so only 1/6$^{th}$ of the time. Technology can cut down on the time required to exonerate the innocent. Suspects and witnesses can be invited to come immediately to a police station where a photo or video-clip of the suspect can be captured on the spot and a lineup conducted. Police departments without the elementary computer equipment are still doing suspects a big favour in inconveniencing them by keeping them in custody a bit longer until a photo can be developed by the old method. The extra waste of time is nothing compared to what they will face if a witness mistakenly identifies them in a show-up.

Brooks (1983) makes two exceptions to his rejection of show-ups. In the first he takes the example of *Stoval v. Denno*, (1967), in which the suspect was brought to the hospital bed of the victim two days after the crime, was identified by her, and was subsequently convicted. The Supreme Court, in upholding the conviction, argued that since the victim could not come to the police station for a lineup, the show-up was the only way of exonerating the suspect by the victim saying "This is not the man". This seems to be a case of Well's (2001) type of reasoning. While theoretically the show-up could have exonerated the suspect, in practice it served to convict him. Again, the danger of identifying the innocent outweighs the potential advantage of exonerating them. There was not even a need for much technology for conducting a photo lineup instead. There was ample time to develop a photo of the suspect.

Brooks' (1984) other exception is even stranger. He recommends conducting a show-up if witnesses fail to identify the suspect in a lineup. He again uses the argument that the show-up may exonerate the suspect. He claims that courts certainly will not convict on the basis of the show-up if the witness failed to identify in a lineup. The author cannot agree. Courts give less weight to non-identifications than they do to "identifications". There remains a real danger that the court will give weight to the "identification" of a defendant in a show-up, as happened in Stoval v. Denno (1967). The lineup, for example, could have been with photos, and the court might consider the live show-up "identification" more reliable. Finally, the need to exonerate the suspect seems exaggerated under the presumption of innocence until proven guilty and the fact that the witness failed to "identify" the suspect in a lineup.

Brooks (1983) claims that Canadian courts are strict in prohibiting show-ups. On the other hand, he notes that there are places even in Canada where the police will frequently have witnesses attempt to identify a suspect at the scene of the crime. This would not happen if the courts did not accept resulting "identifications". In Israel a few cases seem to result from error rather than intention. For example, in *The State of Israel vs. Biton* (2005), a girl who had been touched by a man approached the police van where the defendant was sitting and "identified" him. The police could have removed him sooner from the neighbourhood, to enable a proper lineup later. On the other hand, organizing "confrontations" between witnesses and suspects at the police station is quite common in cases where previous "identifications" have been based on weaker methods than lineups. It is not quite clear what the police expect to gain from a second, even weaker, "identification".

English law, on the other hand, is firm in stating that the "confrontation" may only be used when it is not possible to do anything else. The notion seems to be that it is better than nothing. There are two problems with this reasoning. First of all, the author is not at all sure that it is better than nothing. A very unreliable procedure, we have seen, can easily lead to mistaken convictions. It puts a heavy burden on the sophistication of the court to appropriately discount its probative value. Secondly, it should always be possible to do something else. Since photo lineups are forbidden in England, standard booking of suspects should include taking a video-clip of each suspect. "Confrontations" require that the suspect be in the custody of the police, so such a video-clip should be available Thus, with the aid of a laptop computer if necessary, a video lineup should always be possible.

### *Using the mug-shot album search in place of a lineup*

The mug-shot album search is used by police when they do not have a suspect. Witnesses are invited to view photos of suspects who have been photographed by the police when they were arrested, in the hope that they might "identify" the culprit. While a perfectly acceptable tool of investigation, it is grossly misused when police present mug-shot search "identification" as if the mug-shot search was a photo lineup. While in the lineup the witness must choose the suspect and only the suspect for identification, in the mug-shot search the witnesses can choose anyone. Thus there is again no test of their memory, and no way to know whether they have made a mistake.

Also, since the mug-shot search is not meant to provide identification evidence in court, many precautions required with the lineup are not mandated. For example, the presence of a lawyer is never required, nor need the photos bear any resemblance to each other. The courts are rarely presented with the photos used, so the judges cannot judge whether the defendant stood out among the photos. Some confusion arises because both the photo lineup and the mug-shot search use photos. Until recently mug-shot searches were even termed "photo lineups" in Israel by the forensic technicians who conducted both of them and the same form was used. Brooks (1983) in Canada also makes no distinction regarding reliability between photo lineups and mug-shot searches, and lumps them together as distinct from the live lineup.

In a Supreme Court judgement in Israel a number of reasons were given for limiting the probative value of a particular mug-shot search (for example, dissimilarity between the photos and counsel not being present), but failed to note the critical issue of no memory test. In a more recent case (*Shadid vs. The State of Israel, 2003*), the judges quoted Levi (2005) on the problem of no memory test, but argued that since there was a suspect in the mug-shot search there was no problem. They failed to notice that lineups, not mug-shot searches, should be conducted when there are suspects. Actually there still is no memory test when there is a suspect. In one case the witness "identified" someone other than the suspect. The police simply changed their minds and charged this new person with the crime. He was convicted.

Furthermore, the judges in *Shadid vs. The State of Israel*, (2003) failed to notice that, in contrast to lineups, they were not shown what photos the witness was shown. Were the other photos appropriate enough to be considered fair foils? The simplest solution, of course, would be to make the distinction between photo lineups and mug-shot searches, assigning the latter appropriately to an investigative rather than a probative function. In English law such mug-shot searches are also called a method of identification. This is no problem of confusion in English law, of course, between photo lineups and mug-shots, since they only allow mug-shot searches. The problem with the law is that it mandates conducting a lineup with the same witness who picked the person out of the mug-shots. This is like showing a witness the photo of the suspect before the lineup. A mistaken identification in the mug-shot search will likely be repeated in the lineup.

### *Using a "spontaneous identification" to convict*

Similar problems exist with the "spontaneous identification". The notion of such "identification" is that the witness "spontaneously" "identifies" the "culprit" somewhere. If the police do not rig such an "identification" (which they do sometimes), they have no control over such an occurrence. If they attempt to present it as evidence of identification, however, the court is faced with the same situation as with the "show-up" and the mug-shot search. There is no way of determining whether the witness simply erred. The problem is identical when the police take the witness to search for the culprit in the community, an acceptable procedure in all four countries. As in the previous cases, this procedure can be very useful in finding a suspect. However, it is no more reliable as "identification".

## Towards identification reform

We have noted a sorry state of affairs regarding procedures that are used in order to achieve convictions based on eyewitness identification. The police lineup, by far the most reliable method, is fraught with dangers leading to mistaken identifications of the innocent. Potential improvements, such as an enlarged lineup and multiple lineups, have not been implemented anywhere. All too often, the police get away with dispensing even with the lineup, presenting worthless evidence and achieving convictions nonetheless. We turn now to analyzing the causes of this situation, and discussing potential remedies.

### *The British adversarial system of trials*

All of the countries surveyed in this chapter, along with many others, have maintained the adversarial system of justice, in which the prosecution and defence vie against each other in court to convince the judge or jury that the defendant is guilty (the prosecution) or innocent (the defence). "All is fair in love and war", and the trial is a civilized form of war. The dynamics of conflict push each side to use whatever means are at its disposal in order to win. The system mandates the defence to be loyal to the defendants and therefore do all in its power to bring about their acquittal. The prosecution, on other hand, represents the state. It would seem that it has a responsibility to see that justice is served, which may mean an acquittal. However, the dynamics of conflict are often powerful.

Thus it was the State Prosecutor in Israel who prevented implementation of a superior, larger lineup. The psychologists who sat on the US Justice Department's committee on eyewitness guidelines report that those most opposed to change were the prosecutors. The prosecutor's association even attempted through the courts to prevent publication of the non-binding guidelines. When the author testified under court order for the defence in *The State v. Kedoshim*, (1999) while still a police officer, the district prosecutor complained to his superiors, making totally false allegations regarding his reasons for testifying. Wells ceased appearing as a witness for the defence when he began contacting the prosecution to get them to move to the sequential lineup. Even in England, police officers who perjured themselves to obtain convictions were left unpunished. The atmosphere, then, is not conducive to the introduction of safeguards against the conviction of the innocent. This despite the fact that the prosecution should be interested in making sure the guilty are caught. When an innocent is convicted the guilty party escapes even investigation.

### *Judicial ignorance of research on eyewitness identification*

As the empire in the trial contest, the judge is the last resort to ensuring a fair trial and making sure that defendants will not be convicted by insufficient evidence. However, judges by and large are ignorant of the findings reported in this chapter. Psychologists publish their research in journals of psychology and teach in departments of psychology. Legal scholars read those journals and hire psychologists to teach in their departments as often as psychologists read legal journals and hire legal scholars to teach in their departments, which is a rare phenomenon. Judges realize that they are rather uninformed in other areas of forensic science such as fingerprints and DNA, and rely on the testimony of expert witnesses. Eyewitness identification, on the other hand, has been around long before forensic science, and in the absence of scientific data the legal profession has used common sense to determine the validity of eyewitness evidence. There is a natural reluctance to set aside these precedents in favour of relatively new findings. Of course, there was a time that common sense determined that the world was flat.

## Education vs. Legislation

Of all the countries analysed, England is the only country that has legislated the handling of eyewitness evidence. The others rely on precedent. We have noted that England ranks high among the countries in its practice. However, we have also noted imperfections. The problem with legislation is that law is more difficult to change than practice based on precedent. The alternative seems to be education. Police, despite pressure from the prosecution, have often proven open to change once they were presented with the scientific evidence. They are a critical factor, since the courts usually accept police data.

The other major target audiences are those in the legal profession who are involved in the criminal justice process. Judges are the most important. If judges insist on better evidence and will otherwise acquit, police and prosecution will fall into line. The burden of education must fall on the psychologists who are the experts. This requires uncharacteristic behaviour: giving lectures to police officers and judges and lawyers at every opportunity. If possible, teaching courses in faculties of law is a good investment in the future. Some future judges are likely to be sitting in the class. Publishing in legal journals is another avenue.

Appearing in court as an expert witness for the defence is often a double edged sword. For example, the forensic division of the Israeli police would like to collaborate with the author on a number of mutually beneficial research projects. However, they have set as a condition that the author ceases working with the Public Defenders as an expert witness, something the author loath to do without gaining access to the police division responsible for investigations. The author has been told (Bull, personal communication, July, 2004) that English police do not react that way. However, elsewhere expert psychologists may have to divide themselves into those that appear in court and those who do research with the police.

## Conclusion

The way the criminal justice system of the four relatively advanced countries deals with eyewitnesses who might be able to identify culprits who are strangers leaves much to be desired. Very unreliable "identifications" are accepted by courts as strong proof of guilt. Subsequently many innocents must be serving time in jail. Some have been executed. This chapter advises that many inferior methods should be rejected by the courts, and the police lineup strengthened. This can be done today, for example, by enlarging it and conducting multiple lineups. It turns to those experts in eyewitness identification to engage more the relevant legal community, informing them of the problems and the solutions.

## References

Beaudry, J. L. (2004). *A thorough examination of the multiple-choice, sequential, large lineup.* (Master's thesis, Queen's University, Kingston, Ontario, Canada, 2004).

Borchard, E. (1932). *Convicting the innocent: Errors of criminal justice.* New Haven, CT: Yale University Press.

Brandon, R., & Davies, C. (1973). *Wrongful imprisonment.* London: Allen & Unwin.

Brigham, J. C., & Cairns, D. L. (1988). The effect of mugshot inspections on eyewitness identification accuracy. *Journal of Applied Social Psychology, 18*, 1394-1410.

Brooks, N. (1983). *Pretrial eyewitness identification procedures.* Ottawa: Canada Law Reform Commission of Canada

Brown, E., Deffenbacher, K., & Sturgill, W. (1977). Memory for faces and circumstances of encounter. *Journal of Applied Psychology, 62*, 311-318.

Buckhout, R. (1974). Eyewitness memory. *Scientific American, 231*, 23-31.

Conners, E., Lundregan, T., Miller, N., & McEwen, T. (1996). *Convicted by juries, exonerated by science: Case studies in the use of DNA evidence to establish innocence after trial.* Washington, D.C.: U. S. Department of Justice.

Cutler, B. R., & Fisher, R. P. (1990). Live lineups, videotaped lineups, and photoarrays. *Forensic Reports*, *3*, 439-448.

Doob, A. N., & Kirrshenbaum, H. M. (1973). Bias in police lineups - partial remembering. *Journal of Police Science and Administration*, *1*, 287-293.

Geiselman, R. E., MacArthur, A., & Merrovitch, S. (1993). Transference of perpetrator roles in eyewitness identification from photoarray. *American Journal of Forensic Psychology*, *27*, 71-74.

Hinz, T., & Pezdek, K. (2001). The effect of exposure to multiple lineups on face identification accuracy. *Law and Human Behaviour*, *25*, 185-198.

Levi, A. M. (1998). Are defendants guilty if they were chosen in a lineup? *Law and Human Behaviour*, *22*, 389-407.

—. (2002). Up to forty: Lineup size, the modified sequential lineup, and the sequential lineup. *Cognitive Technology*, *7*, 39-46.

—. (2005). A short and positive response to "Errors in identification..." *Mishpatim*, *35*, 471-488. (In Hebrew)

—. (2006a). A comparison between large simultaneous and MSL lineups, with photos viewed in sets of six. In K. Nixon (Ed.) *Forensic recall and eyewitness testimony* (pp. 26-35). London: IA-IP Publishing.

—. (2006 b). An analysis of multiple choices in MSL lineups, and a comparison with simultaneous and sequential ones. *Psychology, Crime, & Law*, *12*(3), 273-286.

—. (2007) Evidence for Moving to an 84-Person Photo Lineup. *Journal of Experimental Criminology*, *3*(4), 377-391.

Levi, A. M., & Jungman, N. (1995). The police lineup: Basic weaknesses, radical solutions. *Criminal Justice and Behaviour, 22*, 347-372.

Levi, A. M., & Lindsay, R. C. L. (2001). Issues concerning policy recommendations: The example of lineups and photospreads. *Psychology, Public Policy, & Law*, *7*, 776-790.

Loftus, E. F., & Ketcham, K. (1991). *Witness for the defence*. New York: St. Martin's Press.

Luus, C. A. E., & Wells, G. L. (1991). Eyewitness identification and the selection of distracters for lineups. *Law and Human Behaviour*, *15*, 43-57.

Malpass, R. S., & Devine, P. G. (1981). Eyewitness identification: Lineup instructions and the absence of the offender. *Journal of Applied Psychology*, *66*, 482-489.

Malpass, R. S., & Lindsay, R. C. L. (1999). Measuring lineup fairness. *Applied Cognitive Psychology*, *13*, S1-S8.

Memon, A., & Bartlett, J. (2002). The effects of verbalization on face recognition in young and older adults. *Applied Cognitive Psychology*, *16*, 635-650.

Memon, A., & Gabbert, F. (2003). Unravelling the effects of sequential presentation in culprit-present lineups. *Applied Cognitive Psychology*, *17*, 703-714.

Pryke, S., Lindsay, R. C. L., Dysart, J. E., & Dupuis, P. (2004). Multiple independent identification decisions: A method of calibrating eyewitness identifications. *Journal of Applied Psychology*, *89*, 73-84.

Slater, A. (1994). *Identification parades: A scientific evaluation. Police Award Scheme*. London: Police Research Group, Home Office.

Steblay, N., Dysart, J., Fulero, S., & Lindsay, R. C. L. (2001). Eyewitness accuracy rates in sequential and simultaneous lineup presentations: A meta-analytic comparison. *Law and Human Behaviour*, *25*, 459-474.

Technical Working Group for Eyewitness Evidence. (1999). *Eyewitness evidence: A guide for law enforcement*. Washington, DC: U.S. Department of Justice, Office of Justice Programs.

Valentine, T., & Heaton, P. (1999). An evaluation of the fairness of police lineups and video identifications. *Applied Cognitive Psychology*, *13*, S59-S72.

Valentine, T., Pickering, A., & Darling, S. (2003). Characteristics of eyewitness identification that predict the outcome of real lineups. *Applied Cognitive Psychology*, *17*, 969-993.

Wells, G. L. (1984). The psychology of lineup identifications. *Journal of Applied Social Psychology*, *14*, 89-103.

—. (1993). What do we know about eyewitness identification? *American Psychologist*, *48*, 553-571.

—. (2001). Police lineups: Data, theory, and policy. *Psychology, Public Policy, and Law*, *7*, 791-801.

Wells, G. L., & Bradfield, A. L. (1998). "Good, you identified the suspect": Feedback to eyewitnesses distorts their reports of the witnessing experience. *Journal of Applied Psychology*, *83*, 360-376.

Wells, G. L., Rydell, S. M., & Seelau, E. (1993). The selection of distracters for eyewitness lineups. *Journal of Applied Psychology*, *78*, 835-844.

Wells, G. L., Small, M., Penrod, S., Malpass, R. S., Fulero, S. M., & Brimacombe, C. A. E. (1998). Eyewitness identification procedures: Recommendations for lineups and photospreads. *Law and Human Behaviour*, *22*, 603-647.

Wright, D. B., & McDaid, A. T. (1996). Comparing system and estimator variables using data from real lineups. *Applied Cognitive Psychology*, *10*, 75-84.

Yarmey, A. D., Yarmey, M. J., & Yarmey, A. L. (1996). Accuracy of eyewitness identifications in showups and lineups. *Law and Human Behaviour*, *20*, 459-477.

## Cases cited

*R. v. Dickman* (1910) Court of Appeal 135.

*Shadid v. The State of Israel* (2003). Supreme Court 10360

*Stoval v. Denno* (1976). US Supreme Court.

*The State of Israel v. Biton* (2005). Tel Aviv Court 3325.

*The State of Israel v. Kedoshim*, (1999).Tel Aviv District Court 40371.

*The State of Israel v. Peri*. (2002). Nazareth District Court 1079.

*The State of Israel vs. Salman* (2006). Haifa District Court 5015.

# CHAPTER THREE

# GLOBAL HUMAN TRAFFICKING: PATTERNS, INFORMATIONAL NEEDS AND PROSPECTUS

LINCOLN J. FRY

## Abstract

This chapter addresses human trafficking as a global phenomenon, with human trafficking seen as one form of transnational crime. The chapter begins by looking at the issues which surround the definition of human trafficking. International agreements are the next topic, and this section discusses their content and the extent to which they have been ratified. The scope of global human trafficking is assessed, including global estimates, especially the obstacles which impede data collection. The trafficking literature is reviewed, relying on two major sources, the International Organization for Migration's (IOM) data on research on human trafficking: A global survey (2005), and the Global Program Against Trafficking in Human Beings (GPATHB) report entitled trafficking in persons, global patterns (2006); Based on the framework provided by those two reports, especially the distinction between origin, transit and destination countries, trafficking patterns are examined for Africa, Asia, The Middle East, Europe, North America, Oceania, and South America. The discussion section addresses future research needs, policy questions, and then presents a simple prospectus. The conclusion stresses the need to merge existing knowledge, i.e. databases, to concentrate on trafficking hotspots.

## Introduction

Human trafficking has been recognized as a global phenomenon. Governments have made it a political priority and have begun to devote greater resources to the problem. The international community has launched multilateral responses that have been reflected in various protocols. As international awareness of the problem has increased, so has the volume of trafficking literature. This chapter begins by conceptualizing human trafficking as one form of transnational crime and concentrates on global patterns of trafficking, the movement of persons between countries and regions. The chapter continues by addressing problems related to the definition of trafficking, and then turns to the status and content of international trafficking agreements as well as obstacles concerning data collection regarding victims, traffickers, and criminal justice intervention programs. Also included is a discussion of existing sources of information about human trafficking, data sources, special reports, and information about how to locate programs that provide assistance to trafficking victims.

Besides a comprehensive search, the literature review relies heavily on information gathered from two major sources. The first of these is the International Organization for Migration (IOM) publication, "Data on research on human trafficking: A global survey" (2005), which provided overviews of the world's regions as well as bibliographies for each region. This overview includes the characteristics of victims, traffickers, and trafficking routes as they relate to global trafficking patterns. The second major source is based on data collected by the global program against trafficking in human beings (GPATHB), which is sponsored by the United Nations Office on Drugs and Crime (UNODC). This programme's latest report, "Trafficking in persons: Global patterns" (TPGP, 2006) is combined with information gathered from the IOM volume as the framework which guides the literature review.

The purpose of this review will be to present detailed information about global trafficking patterns. This review looks at reported trafficking in persons for various countries by region of the world, especially in terms of whether they are identified as source, transit, or destination countries for trafficking victims. This search is consistent with the suggestion in the literature regarding the need to search for "trafficking hotspots", in this instance, "hotspot countries."

In summary, the objectives of this chapter are two fold: 1) to review the status of knowledge about human trafficking from a global perspective based on the literature review; and 2) to discuss possible solutions and recommendations regarding the problems which plague human trafficking as an area of study in International Criminology.

## Defining Human Trafficking

There has been an ongoing debate about the definition of human trafficking. The most commonly used definition is drawn from a supplemental protocol to the United Nations Convention against Transnational Crime, adopted in December, 2000. In that document, human trafficking is defined as:

> Trafficking in persons shall mean the recruitment, transportation, transfer, harboring or receipt of persons, by the threat or use of force, by abduction, fraud, deception, coercion or the abuse of power or by the giving or receiving of payments or benefits to achieve the consent of a person having control over another person…sexual exploitation, forced labor or services, slavery or practices similar to slavery." (United Nations, 2000, p. 2).

The UN protocol has helped to better define the problem in many ways. This is not to say that there is universal acceptance or endorsement of its content. As Oxman-Martinez, Martinez, and Hanley, (2001) noted, the UN Protocol does not mention borders. They see human trafficking as part of a broader picture which includes the connections of human trafficking to economic globalization and transnational crime. This chapter endorses that position and is concerned with only international trafficking, which by definition includes crossing at least one border. Oxman-Martinez, Martinez and Hanley also state that the concept of "consent" is irrelevant in defining human trafficking. They noted that many individuals consent to being smuggled and end up trafficked. Kelly, (2005) made the same point, stressing that the UN protocols on trafficking and smuggling attempt to make clear, and to an extent, absolute distinctions between the two practices. However, she noted that from the victim's perspective, they may believe that they are making an agreement to be smuggled and exploitation may only be evident at the end point where someone demands payment they think they are owed or discover that promised remittances have not been delivered. Kelly believes that both smuggling and trafficking are best viewed as a continuum, shading into or out of one another across a number of dimensions.

Piper (2005) asked a basic definitional question; "Who is trafficked and for what?" Men are generally absent from official trafficking statistics, which would seem to suggest that women are trafficked and men are smuggled. Piper stressed that more and more studies find that trafficking for labour and sex trade are separate. While more women have been trafficked recently for labour, men represent the majority of those trafficked for labour. The same is true for children where studies also find that more children are trafficked for labour than sexual exploitation.

## International Agreements

The UN General Assembly adopted two international treaties (protocols) to fight international trafficking, which supplement the United Nations Convention against Organized Crime; one protocol dealt with trafficking and the other smuggling. They are part of a package designed to address transnational organized crime. The TPGP Report (2006) offered recommendations that stemmed from those protocols in a number of areas, prevention, prosecution, protection and information. The trafficking protocol is the focus here and it attempts to create a global language as the basis for subsequent legislation to define trafficking, assist victims of trafficking, and prevent trafficking in persons. The protocol also attempts to establish judicial cooperation and information exchange among countries.

As Gallagher (2002) indicated, the trafficking protocol requires countries to: l) criminalize trafficking and related conduct as well as impose appropriate penalties; 2) facilitate and accept the return of their trafficked nationals and permanent residents with due regard for their safety; 3) when returning trafficked persons, to ensure that this happens with due regard both for the safety of the trafficked person and the status of any relevant legal proceedings; 4) exchange information aimed at identifying perpetrators or victims of trafficking, as well as methods and means employed by traffickers; 5) provide or strengthen training for law enforcement, immigration and other relevant personnel aimed at preventing trafficking, and prosecuting traffickers and protecting the rights of victims; 6) strengthen border controls as necessary to detect and prevent trafficking; 7) take legislative or other appropriate measures to prevent commercial transport being used in the trafficking process and to penalize such involvement; and 8) take steps to ensure the integrity of travel documents issued on their behalf and to prevent their fraudulent use.

Gallagher (2002) also notes that the protocol contains victim protection measures. Most of these recommendations are optional but countries are supposed to undertake the following: 1) protect the privacy of trafficking victims and ensure they are given information on legal proceedings and facilities to present their views and concerns during criminal procedures against offenders; 2) consider implementing a range of measures to provide for the physical and psychological recovery of victims of trafficking; 3) endeavour to provide for the physical safety of trafficking victims within their territory; 4) ensure that domestic law provides victims with the possibility of obtaining compensation; 5) consider adopting legislative or other measures permitting victims of trafficking to remain in their territories temporarily or permanently in appropriate cases with consideration being given to humanitarian and compassionate factors; 6) endeavour to establish policies, programmes and other measures aimed at preventing trafficking and protecting trafficked persons from re-victimization; and 7) endeavour to undertake additional measures including information campaigns and social and economic initiatives to prevent trafficking.

It should be noted that not all countries have signed and ratified the UN Trafficking Protocol. Enumeration of the information available in the appendix of the TPGP Report (2006) revealed that about 22 percent of 158 countries with the information available have not signed the protocol and another 21 percent have signed but have not ratified the protocol. One source of criticism of the protocol is the fact that it does not require the introduction of any new laws; the only requirement is that country is obliged to criminalize trafficking in accordance with the protocol's definition. Because of that, some opponents argue that the protocol becomes merely symbolic. The protocol is often criticized as being overly wide and vague. Other criticisms include the fact that trafficking legislation can criminalize the victim, especially by concentrating on prostitution. Often this means that governments will choose to treat victims as criminal illegal migrants, not trafficking victims and subsequently deport them (Oxman-Martinez & Hanley, 2001).

## The Scope of Human Trafficking

Trafficking statistics range from estimates of the total number of victims world-wide to estimates generated from the number of victims rescued or repatriated to their countries of origin. This section begins by presenting the kind of information produced by those estimates.

### *Trafficking population estimates*

The US Department of Justice has produced global estimates of trafficking in persons since 2002. These estimates were as follows: (2002) – 700,000 to 4,000,000; (2003) - 800,000 to 900,000; (2004) – 600,000 to

800,000 (US Department of Justice, 2002, 2003, 2004). The 600,000 to 800,000 estimate appeared in a recent US Department of State Report (2006). Laczko and Gramega (2003) indicated that the Trafficking in persons report is considered to be the most comprehensive anti-trafficking review presented by any government. Clawson, Layne, and Small, (2006) also suggested the report's greatest contribution to trafficking research methods, especially those designed to estimate the magnitude of trafficking.

By way of contrast, "guesstimates" (Kangaspunta, 2003; Laczko, & Elzbieta, Gozdziak, 2005) is used consistently in the literature to describe estimates of the global scale of human trafficking. Kangaspunta (2003) has raised the question as to whether global estimates of trafficking serve any serious policy purposes. She suggests that global estimates are always vague and cannot serve as a reliable knowledge base for policy planning. Kangaspunta (2003) opted for global mapping based on the identification of the main countries involved in trafficking humans as a more useful approach. She indicated that mapping "hot spots" can provide valuable information of the nature and context of trafficking, such as identifying origin, transit, and destination countries, the involvement of organized criminal groups in different countries and the main routes used by traffickers. Kangaspunta (2003) argued that knowledge produced through that approach can be used to develop cooperation between practitioners in fields such as prevention, victim assistance, and criminal justice responses. Monitoring the impact of interventions with data that is carefully collected and analyzed, using national as well as regional data, might yield profiles that can be used for developing regional cooperation in the fight against trafficking.

### *Data collection: Issues and obstacles*

There is general agreement that there is a lack of reliable statistics regarding human trafficking. The literature indicates that this can be traced to a number of factors. According to the TPGP Report (2006), the list begins with the fact that many countries lack anti-trafficking legislation. Even when countries have legislation in place, laws may only define trafficking for certain practices, like sexual exploitation. In some countries trafficking only applies to the exploitation of women and children. Laws are not always enforced and victims may not be seen as crime victims but rather as smuggled migrants. Victims may be afraid to provide information out of fear for themselves or their families.

Countries lack centralized data collection systems. When data is collected, it is often provided by inter-governmental (IGO) or non-governmental agencies (NGO) that assist or repatriate victims. Those numbers only represent a small portion of trafficking victims. As Salt (2001) has suggested, countries experiencing trafficking store data in numerous services and organizations, use diverse terminologies to collect data in different ways and at different times.

## The Trafficking Literature

Perhaps the most recent and comprehensive review of the trafficking literature is the IOM's "Data and research on human trafficking: A global survey" (2005). As Lacyko and Gozdziak (2005) indicated in the introduction to that volume, the rapid rise in the number of publications on trafficking reflects the mounting national and international concern with human trafficking. They point out that since the mid-1990s, a great number of reports covering individual countries and regions have been produced. These studies have typically tried to examine the entire trafficking process, including the causes of trafficking. Studies also have attempted to describe the recruitment process, the transport of victims, as well as the exploitation of victims/survivors. These studies include a description of existing legal and policy frameworks in national case studies. Most reports end with a set of recommendations for further action with the objectives to both inform and contribute to the development of counter-trafficking projects and strategies.

The IOM volume (2005) includes chapters on specific regions of the world and several on issues related to trafficking research methods; the volume also includes a chapter which provides bibliographies for all of the human trafficking literature by region. The following regions are covered in separate chapters: sub-Saharan Africa, North America, Latin America and the Caribbean Region, South Asia, East Asia, South-East Asia and Oceania, Europe and the Middle East. A brief overview of those chapters will be integrated with information available from the TPGP Report (2006).

According to the TPGP Report (2006) the programme was launched in 1999. The purpose was to better enable governments to respond to trafficking in human beings and smuggling of migrants. TPGP aims to shed light on the cause and processes of migrant trafficking and smuggling as well as the promotion of the development of effective responses to those problems. One strategic area of TPGPs functions is the collection and analysis of data in order to increase the global community's knowledge base, raising awareness to prevent human trafficking and migrant smuggling.

### *Database*

According to Kangaspunta (2003), a global database was established in GPATHB designed to collect a wide range of open-source information on trafficking. Information may be qualitative or quantitative and come from official government statistics, reports from research institutes, or from newspaper articles and news agency bulletins.

As the methodology section of the TPGP Report (2006) explains, the database includes publicly available information from 113 different source institutions that provide data on 161 countries. The 113 source institutions produce numerous publications, reports, books, articles, journals, and newspaper articles. Most of the relevant data provides details on human trafficking, routes, victim profiles, and the purposes of trafficking.

There are three different sections in the database: country reports, profiles, and trafficking routes. The country reports include estimates of the volume of human trafficking in a country. This includes trafficking to, within, and through, as well as from the country, trafficking for sexual exploitation or forced labour, and persons encountered and cases dealt with by the criminal justice system. Profiles list characteristics of trafficking victims or traffickers, including nationality, sex, and age distribution. Trafficking routes refers to the list of countries included in the routes used to trafficking humans.

The country profile section includes details about the reported trafficking in countries. Broken down by origin, transit, and destination, the country is ranked from 'very low' (1) to 'very high' (5) on each dimension, origin, transit, destination. The section also provides information about the countries involved in the trafficking process. For instance, if a country is listed as a destination country, the countries of origin, the place where the victim was originally transported from will be noted as will the transit countries, the places the victim passed through on the way to the destination.

## Trafficking Patterns in a Global Context

### *Africa*

As a continent, Africa's 46 countries are broken down into five regions: Western, Eastern, Middle, Northern and Southern. The TPGP Report

(2006) identifies Western Africa as the major centre of human trafficking and both a source and destination sub-region. Eastern and Middle Africa are also reported as origin sub-regions while Southern Africa is identified the primary destination sub-region. Northern Africa was reported as both an origin and transit sub-region but is treated as distinct from the remainder of the continent; the exception is Morocco because of its role in labour trafficking.

The TPGP Report (2006) shows that sex exploitation was the most reported reason for trafficking than forced labour. The trafficking of girls was reported by 18 sources and three reported trafficking of boys. Among origin countries, Nigeria is the only African country ranked 'very high', followed by Benin, Ghana, and Morocco, which are ranked 'high.' Victims are trafficked to other African countries and to Western Europe, the United Kingdom, Italy, and France; Belgium and the Netherlands are reported as destinations. South Africa, Cote d'Ivoire and Nigeria are reported as origin countries. No African nation ranked 'very high' or 'high' on the destination index. A few sources reported trafficking into Africa from other regions, Asia (Thailand), the Commonwealth Independent States, the Russian Federation, and Central and South Eastern Europe.

Adepoju (2005) focused on sub-Saharan Africa. He indicated that this region's human trafficking and smuggling map is complicated, involving diverse origins within and outside the region. He noted that currently, studies are looking into trafficking in children, mainly for farm labour and domestic work and trafficking in women and young persons for sexual exploitation mainly outside the region, as well as for women outside the region for the sex industry in South Africa. In West Africa, source, transit and destination countries for trafficked women and children are Ghana, Nigeria and Senegal. In East Africa, young girls are abducted from war zones and forced to be sex slaves in Sudan and the Gulf States; Ethiopia is also a source country.

Adepoju, (2005) concluded that trafficking in sub-Saharan Africa has reached a crisis proportion and countries need to take timely action to address the deteriorating situation. Governmental action has taken place, namely in the child trafficking area, specifically because of media attention to cases in Gabon and Nigeria. West and Central African countries have agreed to a common platform of laws to protect child workers, improve the system of custody for child trafficking victims, strengthen cooperation among governments, and establish transit and reception centres for repatriated children.

*Asia*

In the TPGP Report (2006) Asia is divided into four sub-regions: South Eastern Asia, South Central and Eastern Asia, Western Asia and Turkey. The IOM volume (2005) has three chapters dealing with Asia, South Asia, East Asia, and South East Asia and Oceania. The IOM's three sub-region chapters provide the framework for this section with information from the TPGP Report integrated into the appropriate geographical section. Western Asia and Turkey will be mentioned later in other regional configurations.

## Overview of Asian Trafficking Patterns

Before specific regions are covered, this section provides an overview of trafficking in Asia. Two Asian countries rank 'very high' on the index for origin countries, the Peoples Republic of China and Thailand. Nine others were rated as 'high': Bangladesh, Cambodia, India, Lao PDR, Myanmar, Nepal, Pakistan, the Philippines and Vietnam. Other countries within the Asian region were reported as destination countries: Thailand, Japan, India, Taiwan, Province of China, and Pakistan. Middle Eastern countries, Saudi Arabia, and the United Arab Emirates were rated 'high' as destination countries. Western Europe and North America are also reported as destination regions.

*South Asia*

India and Pakistan are identified as the major destination countries from Bangladesh to Middle Eastern countries (Masud Ali, 2005). Boys are exploited as camel jockeys and girls and women are trafficked for sexual exploitation. Poor employment prospects and lack of opportunities are seen as the major reasons for men and women to search for better living conditions. External factors that lead to trafficking include the impacts of globalization, which include the loss of traditional sources of income and rural employment. This in turn causes the poor and unskilled to migrate to survive. Competition among countries in South Asia has driven the cost of labour down further, encouraging employers to use illegal practices to access cheaper labor. Conflicts and natural disasters force communities to move, often en masse, to survive. Migration policies frequently exclude the unskilled, especially women, which force them to seek their livelihoods through illegal means (Masud Ali, 2005).

## *East Asia*

Lee, (2005) indicated that migration in Asia has increased dramatically over the decades and is now alarming because 30 to 40 percent of total migration takes place through unregulated channels. Trafficking has not been widely studied in East Asia. Lee finds this curious in the case of Japan which has a large sex industry employing a significant number of non-Japanese women. Asia has experienced rapid growth because of a market-driven intra-regional migration. The end of the cold war, China's economic development and the growing global market has meant the more developed parts of Asia, including Hong Kong, Japan, South Korea and Taiwan have experienced severe labor shortages. None of those governments allow permanent settlement and regional flows of migrant workers have been firmly established in those countries. Earlier studies of labor migration flows in the region revealed that migrants were primarily unskilled men. Starting in the 1990's, a high proportion of women in contract migration became one of the distinctive characteristics of migration in the region. By 2000, it was estimated that the number of female migrants surpassed the number of males; females work mainly in entertainment and domestic services. Source countries include the Philippines, Indonesia, and Sri Lanka. The region has some unusual forms of migration/trafficking including adopted children and brides who have been abducted from their communities.

## *South-East Asia*

According to Piper (2005), South-East Asia has been identified as being of great significance regarding extensive intra-regional trafficking revolving around Thailand. It has been identified as a major source, transit and destination country for trafficking in women and children for the purpose of sexual exploitation.

The Greater Mekong received a great deal of research attention while Indonesia has also emerged as a source, transit and destination country. The Philippines is a source country and Cambodia has begun to receive attention because of sex tourism, particularly child sex tourism.

## *The Middle East*

Calandruccio (2005) indicated that the Middle East in his review includes Bahrain, Egypt, Iraq, Jordan, Kuwait, Lebanon, Oman, the Palestinian Territory, Qatar, Syria, the United Arab Emirates, and Yemen.

Trafficking follows a predominately intra-regional pattern with mainly Palestinian, Egyptian, Lebanese, and Jordanian workers looking for work in the Gulf Cooperation Council countries. The Middle East accounts for ten percent of the world's total migration and the oil-rich countries of the Arab Gulf have the highest concentration of migrant workers in the world. South-East Asian migrants represent almost one-fourth of the total population. It is estimated that there are fourteen million international migrants and six million refugees in the Middle East; Saudi Arabia hosts the largest population, estimated at 6.2 million. Israel is an increasingly popular target for human traffickers and smugglers. Women from countries in the former Soviet Union, Moldova, Russia and the Ukraine, are trafficked into the sex industry. Many low-skilled foreign workers are trafficked into coerced labour and involuntary servitude.

## Europe

This section relies heavily on the TPGP Report (2006) which breaks Europe into two major sub-regions: Western Europe, and Central and South Eastern Europe. The TPGP Report indicated that Western Europe is primarily a destination region and Central and South Eastern Europe serve as origin, transit, and destination regions. Central and South Eastern Europe (CEE) comprises sixteen countries and ranges from the Northern Baltic to the Balkans. Trafficking in persons is reported as primarily as an adult phenomena, though minors are reported to be trafficking victims. Sexual exploitation is reported as the primary purpose of trafficking. Four countries rank as 'very high' in the index of origin countries, Albania, Bulgaria, Lithuania, and Romania. Countries ranked 'high' are the Czech Republic, Estonia, Hungary, Latvia, Poland, and Slovokia.

Victims are trafficked from Central and South Eastern Europe (CEE) countries mainly to Western Europe, Germany, Italy, the Netherlands, Greece, the United Kingdom, Belgium, Austria, France, and Spain. All are reported as frequent destinations. Four countries or territories within CEE are ranked 'high' in the index as destinations: Bosnia and Herzegovina, Czech Republic, Kosovo (Serbia and Montenegro), and Poland. Victims are trafficked into CEE from the Commonwealth of Independent States, especially the Ukraine, Moldova, the Russian Federation, and Belarus.

Western Europe comprises 19 countries. Five of these are ranked 'very high' as destination countries: Belgium, Germany, Greece, Italy, and the Netherlands. Countries ranked 'high' include Austria, Denmark, France, Spain, Switzerland, and the United Kingdom. The majority of reported trafficking was of women and girls. A lesser number reported trafficking of children. The purpose of reported trafficking was sexual exploitation and trafficking for forced labour occurs less frequently. Victims are reported to come from all the major origin regions. South Eastern Europe is reported most often, followed by the Commonwealth of Independent States, specifically the Ukraine. Nigeria, Columbia, and the Dominican Republic are frequently cited as countries of origin for Western Europe.

There are 12 countries in the Commonwealth of Independent States region, countries drawn from either Western Europe or Western Asia. The area is reported as an important origin region with four countries ranked ‘very high’: Belarus, Moldova, the Russian Federation, and the Ukraine. Four others are ranked ‘high’: Armenia, Georgia, Kazakhstan, and Uzbekistan. The majority of reported trafficking victims are women and minors; children (boys and girls) account for 35 percent of 61 reports. The majority of the reported purposes are for sexual exploitation. Western Europe, North America, Western Asia and Turkey are reported as destinations for victims. Other destinations are Israel, Turkey, Canada, and the United States, and other regions include CEE, Asia, and the Middle East.

## North America

In the review of trafficking in North America, Gozdiak, and Collett (2005), stress that the only reliable trafficking statistics are generated from official trafficking victim certification. Canada often combines trafficking victims with illegal migrants. While Mexico is listed as the number one source country, there are no official governmental estimates of trafficking into Mexico. The US Federal Government funds trafficking research but a great deal of attention has been paid to victims, especially the evaluation of services provided to victims of trafficking. Victims have also been a focus of the Canadian literature, especially trafficking in women. Mexico has produced a single report concerned with the national security threat posed by organized crime syndicates using Mexico as a transit country for smuggling and trafficking humans into the United States.

### *Latin America and Caribbean Region*

Langberg (2005) lamented the lack of trafficking data in her review of human trafficking in Latin America and the Caribbean region. She indicated that smuggling has been widely recognized but trafficking is seen as tied or related to prostitution in the region. Langberg (2005) described the roots of trafficking and identified several factors: poverty, police and social violence, gender inequality, and a general indifference towards women, adolescents and children. Globalization, liberalized borders policies, and the ease of movement of people have created what are described as market opportunities for traffickers. The Dominican Republic, El Salvador, Guatemala, Honduras, and Nicaragua were identified as source countries. Transit countries and/or destination countries within the region include Mexico, Belize, Costa Rica, and Panama. There is no chapter in the IOM (2005) volume devoted to South America but Brazil and Argentina do receive some attention in this chapter. However, their role in the trafficking process in the region is not described nor is their role in trafficking in South America addressed in any detail.

## Oceania and South America

Oceania is included in Piper's (2005) chapter on South-East Asia. She indicated that studies on trafficking are most scarce and it is relatively insignificant in terms of trafficking in numerical terms due to its geographic remoteness and inaccessibility. The TPGP Report (2006) divides Oceania into two sub regions, Australia and New Zealand, and Melanesia (Fiji). No country in the region is listed as 'very high' as a destination. Australia is listed as 'high' and New Zealand 'medium'.

Like Oceania, South America is mentioned in Langberg's chapter (2005) on Latin America and the Caribbean. Brazil and Argentina are mentioned in the chapter and Brazil was one of the countries included in a "Trafficking in the America's" study. Langberg stresses that both Brazil and Argentina should receive more attention in terms of internal trafficking, and both countries are concerned with sex tourism and are in the process of designing policies regarding the prevention of trafficking children to satisfy the demand in tourist areas. The TPGP Report (2006) includes South America as a sub region with nine countries. Brazil and Columbia both ranked 'high' as origin countries.

## Discussion

Kelly, (2005) commenting on the growth in the scale of publications on human trafficking has provided a basis for beginning to discuss what has been presented above. She noted that as policy recognition and financial resources were mobilized, many more players entered the increasingly competitive field of non-governmental organizations (NGOs) and international non-governmental organizations (INGOs). While this activity is welcome, including at least five United Nations Agencies, this does not ensure a deepening of the knowledge base regarding human trafficking. Kelly argued that publications may primarily reflect a claims-making process, vying for influence over how the issue is understood and where it is located intellectually, symbolically, and financially. Kelly argued for a much broader approach, interdisciplinary in nature, not only to enhance intellectual understanding but also to provide firmer ground to build and assess counter-trafficking strategies.

## *Research Needs*

Almost all of the literature referenced in this chapter includes a plea for improved research in the human trafficking area. This includes improved data collection, increased governmental support, and increased international information sharing.

These issues have raised some interesting debates in the literature. There are those who stress the need for improved data collection as the basis for the development of comprehensive human trafficking policy. There are also those who argue that it is foolhardy to develop policy based upon what is currently known about human trafficking. Simply, the question is "Where is empirical baseline that can be used to construct current human trafficking policy?"

The literature identifies a number of issues that are roadblocks to improved data collection. One major factor is the lack of agreement about how human trafficking should be defined. The UN Human Trafficking Protocol is a good starting point, but as indicated above, a large number of countries have either not ratified it or have ratified it and have not implemented the protocol. More than that, the protocol merely requires the criminalization of human trafficking but leaves open the kinds of offences that fall under the trafficking heading, and these offences differ from country to country. The second issue concerns identifying those responsible for data collection within countries.

The question is *"What agencies, governmental or private, should be responsible to collect information about human trafficking and how do we standardize that responsibility between and among countries?"* A final factor mentioned here is the fact that even if standardized international data collection systems could be set up, *"How do we keep politics from determining whether individual cases are classified as trafficking or criminal illegal human smuggling?"* It may be politically expedient for governments to classify certain kinds of offences under certain headings.

These are just a few of the issues and the literature does not provide any clear answers to any of them.

## *Policy Questions*

Political concerns are even more important when policy issues are addressed. Before those questions are addressed, it should be noted that there are those who begin to address trafficking policy issues by stressing that we do not know enough about human trafficking to even begin to develop national, let alone international policy. Others indicate that the right questions are not being asked by trafficking researchers. An example is provided by Pattanaik (2006) where she indicated that some authors in the anti-trafficking literature believe that strengthening the criminal justice response and enabling victims to testify against those who exploited them should be priorities. She stated that others in the anti-trafficking community focus only on trafficking for purposes of sexual exploitation and naively believe that criminalization of prostitution would end trafficking. Those who focus on repatriation of trafficked persons or who "rescue" them from brothels or other workplaces often fail to ask 'victims' whether they want to be stopped from working and sent home. Pattanaik (2006) indicated that no one asks if they would like to stay if they could find legal, paid employment.

Pattanaik (2006) addressed several issues that are central to recent trafficking policy debates. One of these is that human trafficking should be cast in much wider frameworks. She opted for what may be called the 'labor- migration' framework. The rationale for this perspective begins by stressing that paid work is necessary for everyone and yet many people either do not receive fair wages or are exploited in their workplaces. Concentrating on trafficked persons means only a small percentage of persons in the migrant worker population become the focus. Pattanaik (2006) argues that there must be a shift in concentration to migration and labour and that the crime of trafficking should be addressed in that context. Another viewpoint suggests that the emphasis on identifying and prosecuting traffickers as well as assisting victims detracts from the core issue, namely the causes of human trafficking. As the literature review indicated a number of reports have dealt with that issue at the country or regional level. This criticism here is not directed towards the literature per se but the fact that policy efforts have not tied human trafficking to factors that are thought to be the causes of trafficking, such as poverty, human development, gender issues and others.

## Prospectus: A Modest Proposal

The question is *"Where do we go from here?"* The lack of reliable information available about human trafficking is the lament of the trafficking literature. The review of the existing literature suggests that the lament should be about the lack of analysis of existing global data bases. Omelaniuk (2005) provided an excellent discussion of the resources currently available regarding human trafficking and discussed ongoing trafficking research projects currently underway. She used IOM's database based on the cases of over 5,000 victims who received assistance from IOM globally to stimulate discussion about data gathering. Omelaniuk (2005) argued trafficking can be seen as a development problem and agencies that support development and poverty reduction should address trafficking. While endorsing that position, it is argued that all of the agencies concerned with factors seen as central to the causes and processes related to trafficking should be integrated into a unified approach to studying trafficking. The literature review suggests that UNODC's TPGP appears to offer the most logical place to begin to centralize trafficking research. There are other global and regional information sources but the TPGP appears to be the most comprehensive database from a global perspective. The literature review indicated that the TPGP Report provides the widest range of coverage regarding human trafficking. Information is available on a country to country basis regarding human trafficking patterns, trafficked victims, apprehension and prosecution of traffickers, and governmental policy regarding trafficking from the victim perspective. Besides the information mentioned above, the TPGP Report (2006) includes a range of data collected at the country level, especially the factors that are thought to be the root causes of trafficking, indexes like the corruption, human development, poverty and other indices. There is the need to examine a whole range of information to determine whether certain factors predict human trafficking activities.

## Conclusion

Human trafficking is a murky area of study in International Criminology. The literature review does suggest that the identification of "trafficking hotspots" is the most promising approach currently available to those who wish to advance the study of human trafficking. The literature review also suggests the need to combine existing knowledge to provide new information regarding human trafficking The TPGP Report (2006) would appear to be a good starting point for that effort because it allows the researcher to easily identify "hotspots" in any part of the world. The report also provides the data that should lend themselves to the identification of the factors that predict how countries evolve into 'hotspots'. The preliminary analysis could concentrate on using the indicators already collected in the database that predict the origin, transit and destination country status.

This would provide direction regarding necessary data integration from other sources. For instance, if corruption and/or the Poverty Index included in the data file predict a county's trafficking status, the World Bank and The UN Global Action against Corruption Program would immediately become potential sources of additional data. Other basic questions that need to be addressed include whether ratification of International Protocols has any relationship to a country's trafficking status. Identifying factors that predict trafficking appears to be the best way to begin to develop trafficking policy. There is no apparent way to deal with the politics and ideology that surround human trafficking. Those who support open immigration for all and those who support tight, limited immigration policies will never find a way to bridge their gap. A comprehensive, data driven analysis of the way countries became 'hotspots", the effects of human trafficking on victims, and the way countries respond to victims, represent a giant leap forward for trafficking research at this point in time.

## References

Adepoju, A. (2005). Review of research and data on human trafficking. In F. Laczko & E. Gozdziak (Eds.), *Data and research on human trafficking: A global survey* (pp.75-98). Geneva Switzerland: International Organization for Migration.

Calandruccio, G. (2005). A Review of Recent Research on Human Trafficking: A Global Survey. In F. Laczko, & E. Gozdziak (Eds.), Data *and research on human trafficking: A global survey* (pp.267-299). Geneva Switzerland: International Organization for Migration.

Clawson, H., Layne, M., & Small, K. (2006). *Estimating human trafficking in to the United States: Development of a methodology.* Rockville, MD: National Institute of Justice.

Gallagher, A. (2002, January). Trafficking, smuggling and human rights: Tricks and treaties. *Forced Migration Review*, 12, 25-29.

Gozdziak, E., & Collett, E. (2005). Research on human trafficking in North America. In F. Laczko & E. Gozdziak (Eds.), *Data and research on human trafficking: A global survey* (pp.99-128). Geneva Switzerland: International Organization for Migration.

Kangaspunta, K. (2003). Mapping the inhuman trade: Preliminary findings of the database on trafficking in human beings. *Forum on Crime and Society*, *3*(1&2), 81-100.

Kelly, L. (2005). You can find anything you want: A critical reflection on research on trafficking in Europe. In F. Laczko & E. Gozdziak (Eds.), *Data and research on human trafficking: A global survey* (pp. 235-265). Geneva Switzerland, International Organization for Migration.

Laczko, F., & Gramegna, M. (2003). Developing better indicators of human trafficking. *Brown Journal of World Affairs*. *X* (1), 179-194.

Langberg, L. (2005). A review of recent OAS Research on human trafficking in Latin America and the Caribbean region. In F. Laczko, & E. Gozdziak (Eds.), *Data and research on human trafficking: A global survey* (pp. 129-139). Geneva Switzerland: International Organization for Migration.

Lee, J. (2005). Human trafficking in East Asia: Current trends, data collection and knowledge gaps. In F. Laczko & E. Gozdziak (Eds.), *Data and research on human trafficking: A global survey* (pp.165-201). Geneva Switzerland: International Organization for Migration.

Masud, Ali, A. (2005). Treading along a treacherous trail: Research on trafficking in persons in South Asia. In F. Laczko & E. Gozdziak (Eds.), *Data and research on human trafficking: A global survey* (pp. 141-164). Geneva Switzerland: International Organization for Migration.

Omelaniuk, I. (2005). *Trafficking in human beings*. United Nations Expert Group Meeting on International Migration and Development: United Nations Secretariat, New York.

Oxman-Martinez, A., Martinez, A., & J. Hanley. (2001). Human trafficking: Canadian government policy and practice. *Refuge*, *19*(4), 14-23.

Pattanaik, B. (2006). Reflections on initiatives to address human trafficking. *Forced Migration*, *25*, 4-5.

Piper, N. (2005). A problem by a different name? A review of research and trafficking in South East Asia and Oceania. In F. Laczko & E. Gozdziak (Eds.), *Data and research on human trafficking: A global survey* (pp. 203-233). Geneva Switzerland: International Organization for Migration.

United Nations (2000). Protocol to Prevent, Suppress and Punish Trafficking in Persons, especially Women and Children, supplementing the United Nations Convention against Transnational organized Crime. Retrieved on May 21, 2008 from http://www.uncjin.org/Documents/Conventions/dcatoc/final_documents_2/convention_%20traff_eng.pdf

United Nations Office on Drugs and Crime (UNODC). (2006). *Trafficking in persons: Global patterns*. Vienna, Austria.

United States Department of Justice. (2002). *Assessment of US activities to combat trafficking in persons*. Washington, DC.

—. (2003). *Assessment of US activities to combat trafficking in persons*. Washington, DC

—. (2004). *Assessment of US activities to combat trafficking in persons*. Washington, DC.

United States Department of State. (2006). *Trafficking in persons report*. Office to Monitor and Combat Trafficking in Persons. Washington, DC.

# CHAPTER FOUR

# ADVERSARIAL VS. INQUISITORIAL PROSECUTION SYSTEMS IN EUROPE: COMMONALITIES AND DIVERSITIES

DESPINA KYPRIANOU

## Abstract

This chapter will provide a comparative analysis of prosecution systems in various jurisdictions, including some of those traditionally associated with the common law tradition, as well as some associated with the continental one. The distinct choices and paths that different legal systems have followed as well as the common trends that can be observed nowadays (both in theory and in practice) will be explored. It will be remarked that the main questions that have troubled most prosecution systems over time centred on three crucial dichotomies: a) Systematic v. unsystematic approach to prosecutions; b) Prosecutors' power to direct investigations v. complete separation of the investigative and the prosecutorial stages; and c) Legality v. expediency principle. Nowadays, all jurisdictions are confronted with the need to adapt the structures and the functioning of their prosecution services to the requirements of the 21st century and the new challenges that the criminal justice system faces. It is argued that a wide scale appraisal of the origins and the primary principles of prosecution systems are prerequisites for any attempt to understand the current situation and discuss any reforms for the future.

## Introduction

In all countries there is a state agency entrusted with the power and the responsibility for all, or a significant part, of criminal prosecutions; especially with the crucial decision whether criminal cases should be forwarded or not to courts. Naturally, the prosecuting authorities' specific structures, additional functions and powers differ from country to country as they are rooted in the history and the legal culture of the jurisdictions where they are found. The description of prosecution systems in various jurisdictions used to be characterized by dichotomies: on the one hand, there were adversarial prosecution systems and on the other, inquisitorial ones; there were systems where prosecutors were also responsible for the investigative stage, and others where there was a complete division of responsibility regarding the prosecution and the investigative stage; finally, there were systems which adhered to the opportunity principle, and others which adhered to the mandatory one.

However, both adversarial and inquisitorial systems either in theory or in practice have been moved away from their traditional models and at the present time no prosecution system can be characterized as coming under one particular model. *Inter alia*, practical inefficiencies of the previous structures and the appearance of new forms of criminality urged the search for novel solutions and the approach of traditional prosecutorial dilemmas with a new perspective. Nowadays, it can be said that there are as many variations in prosecution systems as the number of the countries involved. However, some common trends have been observed – encouraged also by the guidance of supranational institutions such as the Council of Europe[1] and the European Court of Human Rights – that argue towards the adoption of some common principles regarding prosecutions. At the same time, a number of remaining differences can still be detected among prosecution systems which can be traced back to their different origins and convey their different philosophies.

This chapter will provide a comparative analysis of prosecution systems in various (mainly European) jurisdictions, including some of those traditionally associated with the common law tradition, as well as some associated with the continental one. The distinct choices and paths that different legal systems have followed as well as the common trends that can be observed nowadays (both in theory and in practice) will be explored. In the *second section* of this chapter, the origins, constitutional position and organisation of prosecution services in a common law country (England and Wales), a mixed jurisdiction (Scotland), as well as a number of inquisitorial jurisdictions (mainly France, Germany and the Netherlands) will be described. The *third section* will deal with the role of the prosecuting authorities in investigations and the *fourth one* with the way different prosecution systems approach the issues of prosecutorial

[1] See a series of Recommendations issued by the Council of Europe relating to prosecutions: Rec (2000) 19, Rec (97) 13, Rec (92) 17, Rec (95) 12, etc.

discretion, diversion from prosecution and the formulation of prosecution criteria and policies.

This review is necessarily selective, as it is impossible for a single chapter to cover all the issues related to prosecutorial arrangements in a number of countries. The main focus will be on the aforementioned areas, for two reasons: firstly, these concern characteristics that distinguish one jurisdiction from another and, therefore, illuminate both the different choices adopted by various legal systems and also their implications; and secondly, they have represented controversial topics of discussion among academics and practitioners, and at times have been included in the agenda of various Commissions vested with the duty to examine reforms in various jurisdictions.

## Origins, Constitutional Position and Organisation of Prosecution Services

If we consider the development of the prosecution arrangements in various countries, it is evident that many jurisdictions have always been grappling with the question of the position of the prosecution service within the state structure and its relationship with the police. There is a long tradition in civil law systems of public prosecutors taking responsibility for prosecutions in the public interest, which pre-dates the creation of police forces. In the common law tradition, by contrast, as Stenning (1986) describes, 'the system of criminal prosecutions…relied heavily upon the initiative of private individuals, rather than being exclusively controlled by public authorities' (p. 17). In most common law countries the notion of a separate prosecution agency emerged after police forces had already been established.[2] During the course of the last century, however, independent prosecution services established themselves and took responsibility for prosecutions.

### *England and Wales*

The history of the prosecutorial arrangements in England and Wales charts a progression from a clearly private activity to a half-hearted introduction of a public prosecution service in the mid 1980s, and then, after a series of piecemeal reforms, to the more recent changes that may

[2] See Langbein (1973), Hay (1983) and Hetherington (1989) for a comprehensive account of the origins and the history of public prosecutions in common law.

potentially alter the whole philosophy of public prosecutions in that country.

Until the nineteenth century, in England and Wales, there was no public official responsible for ensuring that crimes were prosecuted. Emphasis was placed upon the concept of individual responsibility in the administration of criminal justice and, thus, the responsibility for prosecuting the perpetrators of crimes lay predominantly with private individuals. Since the early part of the nineteenth century, as the police developed and their powers increased, they progressively replaced the old system of law enforcement. As a result of evolution rather than of any deliberate decision, the police had become convenient substitutes for private prosecutors. However, no specific prosecution powers or responsibilities were conferred on the police and private prosecutions remained the model on which police prosecutions were based.[3] Eventually, many police forces set up their own in-house departments of prosecuting solicitors or employed local firms of solicitors to act on their behalf. Thus, throughout the nineteenth and twentieth centuries (until, 1986), the police controlled the vast majority of prosecutions, with the exception of a small minority of the most complex and serious cases which were prosecuted by the Director of Public Prosecutions (DPP). The Office of the DPP was established in 1879 and was characterised as a 'compromise between those who wanted to retain England's unsystematic approach to prosecution and those who wanted prosecutions in general to be structured and controlled as was believed to happen in most of Europe' (Sanders, 1996 p. xii).

During the 1980s, complaints and opposition to the system of police prosecutions increased. In 1970 the Committee of JUSTICE[4] published a report in which they highlighted the danger to public perception and the quality of justice when the same police officer decides on whether to charge a suspect, selects the charge, acts as prosecutor, and also takes the stand as his or her own chief witness. This report, as well as a report by Sir Henry Fisher in 1977 after the *Confait* Case[5] and growing public concern, led to the appointment of a Royal Commission on Criminal Procedure under the chairmanship of Sir Cyril Philips. They reported in 1981, recommending the establishment of a separate service responsible for the prosecution of all offences.

The government, acting on the recommendation of the Commission, enacted the Prosecution of Offences Act, 1985, which created the Crown

---

[3] This legal form of police prosecutions with all its accompaniments survived the mid-1980s changes to the system. See Sanders (1996) and Bennion (1986, p. 3-4).
[4] The British Section of the International Commission of Jurists.
[5] R v. Leighton, Lattimore and Salih (1975) 62 Crim. App. R. 53.

Prosecution Service (CPS). The CPS was a national service headed by the DPP and formally accountable to the Attorney General. The new service had a duty to take over the conduct of all criminal prosecutions instituted by the police and advise the police forces on matters relating to criminal offences. It was also empowered to discontinue prosecutions or drop and amend specific charges when they disagreed with initial police decisions. The CPS was not given any role concerning prosecutions brought by a series of other organisations, such as the Serious Fraud Office, the Environment Agency, etc. Neither was it given any powers to institute proceedings itself, nor a role regarding the investigative stage of a case, contrary to some suggestions heard for the adoption of a public prosecution system similar to the Scottish one.

Even since its creation, the CPS has been the subject of considerable adverse publicity and criticism. Belloni and Hodgson (2000) report that the CPS was criticised 'for the very weaknesses which it was set up to remedy: a lack of objectivity and legal scrutiny in the decision to prosecute; inconsistency in the decision to prosecute and in the choice of offence; and an inability or disinclination to weed out even obviously weak cases at an early stage in the process' (p. 106). Fionda (1995) reports that the CPS, in the early days of its creation, experienced criticism from various groups from all branches of the criminal justice process.

A series of research studies revealed deficiencies in the CPS performance but at the same time commented on inherent structural problems of the system that could not be easily overcome, and also pointed at the conflicting expectations that the service was called to fulfil. Ashworth (2000) pointed out: 'On the one hand there has been criticism of the CPS for discontinuing too many cases; on the other hand there has been criticism that too many Crown Court cases end in acquittal, suggesting that the CPS is not fulfilling its function of weeding out weak cases' (p. 274).

Research studies (e.g. Crisp & Moxon, 1994), as well as the CPS's own surveys, found that discontinuance rates have been rising in the years since the introduction of the CPS. This could have been seen as a positive trend and as an indication that the CPS was actively screening cases but some commentators were critical that too many cases were dropped on efficiency grounds. Closely related to these criticisms were accusations that too many cases used to be downgraded by the CPS, either by amending the charges preferred by the police or by accepting a plea of guilty to a lesser offence.

Nevertheless, a decline in the number of convictions for indictable offences, as well as a rise in the number of non-jury acquittals, was observed since the introduction of the CPS, which suggested that prosecutors allowed too many weak cases to be forwarded to courts. A study by Block, Corbett and Peay (1993) and a similar one by Baldwin (1997) found that a great proportion of non-jury acquittals were foreseeable. Prosecutors failed to discontinue weak cases due to lack of experience or self-confidence and tended simply to endorse the initial police decision. Although in some cases it was very obvious that the chances of acquittal were very high, Baldwin (1997) reported that it appeared easier for the prosecutors 'to pass the buck to the courts' (p. 542) than to discontinue. As Ashworth (2000) points out, the most worrying finding of Baldwin's research was that some prosecutors shared a common value system with the police.[6]

Furthermore, research by McConville, Sanders and Leng (1991) found that prosecutors, constrained by police-generated information, most of the time, used to endorse the initial police view of a case. Cases were constructed by the police presenting evidence in a way which pointed to the disposal that they preferred. That research confirmed previous arguments by Sanders (1986b) that the CPS could not be independent of the police, partly because they relied on the police for information; the police had the power to construct cases for prosecutions and made weak cases appear strong.[7] Moreover, McConville *et al.* (1991) pointed out that prosecutors also lacked the incentive to weed out weak cases as, in an adversarial system, the goal of the CPS was to assist the police in achieving a maximum conviction rate. Therefore, a half-hearted attempt to graft an inquisitorial element on to an adversarial system was destined to fail.

Many academics argued that the failure of the CPS to live up to their promises was inevitable precisely because deeper changes in the system were not introduced. Prosecution practices were not altered dramatically because the structural relationship between the CPS and the police

---

[6] Baldwin (1997) reported that 'some prosecutors remain stubbornly of the view that the defendant may do the decent thing and plead guilty' (p. 548) even in apparently weak cases and they also believed that serious cases ought to be prosecuted 'almost irrespective of considerations as to the evidential strength' (p. 551). See also a similar finding of the research by Hoyano et al. (1997). They found that in some cases prosecutors felt under pressure to continue a prosecution in serious cases even when the case was weak, especially where a decision not to prosecute may have resulted in public or press criticism.

[7] This is more problematic due to the prosecutors' practice when reviewing the cases to rely mostly on police summaries, which proved to be very selective and sometimes misleading (Baldwin & Bedward, 1991).

remained problematic and ill defined.[8] The police retained their power to charge and make the initial decision of instituting a prosecution and the CPS was given only a reactive role, namely to review a police decision to prosecute based only on evidence collected by the police themselves.

Over the years, there has been a series of attempts to clarify the relationship between the CPS and the police, and efforts made to establish closer cooperation between the two services during the stage prior to charge. With the Criminal Justice Act, 2003 (CJA 2003), however, more radical changes have been introduced which 'mark a significant reorientation of the English prosecution system' (Ashworth & Redmayne, 2005, p. 173). The CJA 2003 implements many of the changes suggested by Lord Justice Auld (2001) in order to improve the effectiveness and efficiency of the criminal justice system in England and Wales. As far as prosecutions were concerned, Auld concluded that one contributor to the high level of discontinuances was the 'overcharging' by the police and the failure of the CPS to remedy it at an early stage. He identified one of the causes of this to be the fact that it was the police who initiated prosecutions. To resolve these problems, Auld suggested that the CPS should become involved earlier in the process and be given the power to determine the charge and initiate the prosecution.

Therefore, with the CJA 2003 the responsibility for charging suspects and, thus, initiating criminal proceedings in all but very minor offences is transferred from the police to the CPS. The new legislation provides for new, extensive powers allocated to the CPS and the DPP[9] to enable them to discharge their new functions. It also emphasises and facilitates the early consultations between the police investigators and 'duty prosecutors' before a charge is preferred.[10] Since the provisions of the CJA 2003 involve considerable resource and organisational implications, the new system will come into being gradually. It remains to be seen whether in practice it will achieve its objectives.

## *Scotland*

The Scottish prosecution system has long been considered as a possible model to be adopted by various English and Irish committees when

---

[8] See *inter alia* Ashworth (2000), Belloni and Hodgson (2000), Leng et al. (1996), Fionda (1995, Chapter 2).

[9] E.g. the power of the DPP to issue guidance to custody officers as to how detained persons should be dealt with and as to what the police ought to do to facilitate the decisions on charge by prosecutors.

[10] For a detailed analysis of the new legislation, see Brownlee (2004).

discussing the reform of their prosecution systems. Fionda (1995) remarks that '(t)he Scottish criminal justice system has enjoyed the advantages of a public prosecution system, with independent prosecutors working in the public interest, for a good deal longer than England and Wales' (p. 65). The Scottish prosecution system has many characteristics which resemble those of its counterparts in continental jurisdictions and, therefore, it has been characterised as a quasi-inquisitorial prosecution system.

The Office of the *Procurator Fiscal* emerged during the late sixteenth to eighteenth centuries, when it took over the investigative and prosecutorial functions of the medieval sheriff who was left primarily with a judicial function. The police forces, on the other hand, came into being during the nineteenth century, being formed in a 'piecemeal and largely unstructured way' (Gordon, 1980, p. 21). The Fiscal in Scotland, therefore, pre-dates the police and has developed as an integral part of the Scottish system and culture over the centuries.[11]

The Lord Advocate, assisted in his functions by the Solicitor General, is the Government Minister responsible for the prosecution of crime in Scotland. Although a member of the Scottish Executive, as the head of the prosecution system, he is said by convention to be independent in making decisions concerning prosecution. Under the authority of the Lord Advocate, the Crown Office and the Procurator Fiscal Service provide the sole public prosecution service in Scotland. Officers known as Procurators Fiscal undertake prosecutions in the Sheriff or District Courts. In addition, there is a number of Advocates who are practicing members of the Bar and hold a commission to prosecute in the High Court, where the most serious cases are heard. The Crown Agent, who is the permanent civil service head of the fiscal service, has responsibility for the management of the prosecution service but the Lord Advocate is politically accountable for acts and decisions taken by the prosecution service. Directions and guidance on policy and practice are issued to prosecutors on his authority and with his approval.

In Scotland all criminal prosecutions are conducted by a single service (the Fiscal Service). As Duff (1999) reports, '(i)n Scotland, a few statutory offences may be prosecuted by a public body…but, in practice, such proceedings are normally undertaken by the public prosecutor' (p. 117). Furthermore, the right of private prosecutions was abolished for summary cases with the Criminal Justice (Scotland) Act, 1995 and in solemn cases

---

[11] See Moody and Tombs (1982, Chapter 2) for an historical account of the development of the Office of Procurator Fiscal.

such proceedings require the concurrence of the Lord Advocate or the High Court.

The police and other reporting agencies send reports of crimes to the Procurator Fiscal. The Procurator Fiscal then decides whether to begin criminal proceedings and, if he decides positively, he determines the forum and the procedure (summary or solemn) as well as the charges to be brought; otherwise, he decides whether to take alternative action or no action at all. Depending on the nature of the offence, the decision to prosecute may be made by a more senior officer on behalf of the Lord Advocate, instead of the Procurator Fiscal.

What has been characterised as the most significant aspect of the Scottish system of Public Prosecutors is the hierarchical position of the Procurators Fiscal in relation to the police and their complete independence (Duff, 1999). The hierarchical position of the Procurators Fiscals is also connected with their supervisory role over the investigation of crimes. Fionda (1995) points out that 'since the office of fiscal was created early in the nineteenth century before permanent police forces were set up, the police remain in law subordinate to the prosecutor in the investigation of crime, a position now embedded in statute…' (p. 66).

However, although in theory Procurator Fiscals' decisions are entirely independent, in practice they are heavily and often exclusively based on information collected by the police. Research by Moody and Tombs (1982) concluded that the role of the police in the supply of information to fiscals was crucial.[12] Nevertheless, Fionda (1995) during her research observed a very good relationship between police officers and Procurator Fiscals: 'There are close links between senior fiscals and Chief Constables who have regular meetings to discuss policy. Hostilities rarely arise, and the tensions that exist in England and Wales are not present in Scotland' (p. 93). Therefore, the same writer concludes, this good cooperation between the two services surely contributes to the dissemination of the information needed to make well-informed decisions.

## *Inquisitorial Jurisdictions*

There is a long tradition in civil law systems that pre-date the creation of police forces, of public prosecutors taking responsibility for prosecutions in the public interest. Although the inquisitorial process

[12] See also research by Stedward and Millar (1989), Duff and Burman (1994) and Duff (1997) confirming that fiscals are heavily influenced by the information contained in the police report when deciding whether to divert an offender to social work or psychiatric treatment.

originated in an inquiry by a judge, specialised officials acting on behalf of the court later became charged with building the case against the defendant, long before police forces came into existence. In this section some of the broad characteristics of jurisdictions belonging to the continental tradition regarding the origins, constitutional position and organisation of their prosecution services will be examined.

First, it has to be said that it would be wrong to assume that there is only one model of prosecution service in the civil law family of countries. Leigh and Hall Williams (1981), after conducting their research on the prosecution systems of Denmark, Sweden and the Netherlands, concluded that '(i)t became clear that Continental institutions differ markedly from jurisdiction to jurisdiction…There is no single Continental approach to this matter of the management of prosecutions' (p. 1). Nevertheless, there are still some characteristics in the prosecution system of these jurisdictions which are commonly associated with the inquisitorial model of criminal justice and prevail in the majority of these countries.

The origins of prosecutorial arrangements in most civil law jurisdictions can be traced back to the French *Code d'Instruction Criminelle* of 1808, which created the *ministère public*, the French Public Prosecution Service. In the years following the creation of the *ministère public*, other European countries, which were under French rule at that time, saw the creation of their own equivalents of the *ministère public*. After regaining independence, the Public Prosecution Service was maintained in these countries; until quite recently, Belgian and Dutch Public Prosecution Services were still very similar to the French *ministère public*. In Germany, the Office of the Public Prosecutor (*Staatsanwalthschaft*) was created in the middle of the nineteenth century by splitting the investigative and judicial functions of the inquisitorial judge.[13]

These days, prosecutors in civil law systems, as a rule, function in a *hierarchical structure* with strong internal guidelines controlling the use of discretionary prosecutorial powers. For example, the organisation of the *ministère public* is based on French judicial organisation, and it is structured in two layers corresponding with the District Tribunals and the Courts of Appeal.[14] The *ministère public*'s office at each of the 181 District Tribunals constitutes its basic working level. It is directed by a public prosecutor, the *procureur de la République,* who assures the investigation and prosecution of criminal offences in the district of the tribunal. Other magistrates of the *ministère public*, called *substitutes*, assist

---

[13] See, including others, Fionda (1995, Chapter 5), Albrecht (2000), Jehle (2003) and Weigend (2004) for more information on the German prosecution system.
[14] See Verrest (2000, pp. 212-13) for a more detailed description.

the public prosecutor. At the 35 Courts of Appeal in France the *ministère public*'s office is directed by a *procureur général*, who has authority over the public prosecutors in the district of the Court of Appeal and is responsible for the application of the government's criminal policy. The French Judicial Organisation Act, 1958, states that the members of the *ministère public* are subordinated to the Minister of Justice. The latter can give formal instructions to the procurators general and is politically accountable for the functioning of the Public Prosecution Service. A similar hierarchical structure of the prosecution system exists in Belgium, the Netherlands[15] and Germany.[16]

As a rule, in the continental tradition the state *monopolises the right to prosecute* and vests it in the public prosecution services, which represent the public interest. This is in contrast to the common law tradition where even these days the prosecutorial power is granted to both the state prosecution service and the individuals. As Tak (2004a) reports, however, the general rule of state's monopoly in civil law countries has been somewhat compromised. In some countries there is a right to private prosecution restricted to certain crimes, mainly those which constitute a violation of private legal rights, and in others (e.g. Denmark, Finland and Sweden) this right can only be exercised when the public prosecutor decides not to prosecute. There are, however, a few countries (e.g. France and Belgium) where 'the public and private rights to prosecute co-exist in a unique fashion' (Tak, 2004a, p. 7).

Public prosecutors in continental jurisdictions normally belong to the *judicial branch* (e.g. in France and the Netherlands) or they are considered as quasi-judicial officers (e.g. in Germany). This is in accordance with the inquisitorial tradition in which the prosecutor is seen as a neutral and impartial party. Fionda (1995) reports that '(i)n the Netherlands and Germany judges and prosecutors usually train together on the same postgraduate training course, with some law graduates opting to enter the judicial branch of the legal profession and others the prosecution and defence branches' (p. 7). The relationship between judges and prosecutors in France is even tighter. The *procureur*, the *juge d'instruction* and the trial *juge,* after following the same education program at the *Ecole nationale de la Magistrature*, become members of the same body, the

---

[15] See Leigh and Hall Williams (1981), Fionda (1995, Chapter 4), and Tak (2004b) for detailed descriptions of the Dutch Prosecution Service.

[16] However, in Germany the criminal justice system is organised on a federal basis and, thus, each of the twelve German States operates its own justice system headed by a different Minister of Justice.

*magistrature,* and it is not uncommon for them to change from *ministère public* to the bench or vice versa during their career.

As a rule, in the continental tradition, the police have never had a prosecutorial role.[17] This has always been the responsibility of prosecution services, which were created before the establishment of organised police forces. Furthermore, police are regarded as coming under the command of and being controlled by the public prosecution services[18] as far as all the functions related to prosecutions are concerned. The police must report to the prosecutors all offences known to them and the prosecutors take the decision on prosecuting criminal offences. Therefore, the responsibility for the decision to prosecute or not lies exclusively with the public prosecutors. Thus, even in countries where the opportunity principle applies, the police theoretically are not allowed to end cases but instead are obliged to pass them on to prosecutors to decide. The Netherlands appears to be an exception to this rule: a clear legal framework is in place which allows the police to end cases by imposing a condition in accordance with general guidelines of the prosecutor-generals.[19] It has to be noted that in the other countries as well, in practice, police also enjoy some discretion regarding their reporting requirements. Verrest (2000), for example, reports of the situation in France: 'In a certain sense, the police do settle some criminal offences themselves. The police do not forward all the information they have on criminal offences to the *ministère public* – even though they are supposed to' (p. 243).[20]

## The Role of Prosecution Services in Investigation

While the decision as to whether a case should be prosecuted or not is undoubtedly regarded as the central function of every prosecuting authority, the role and the powers that a prosecuting agency acquires

---

[17] See, however, an exception to this rule in the case of Norway, where in some particular minor cases the police have the responsibility for prosecutions (Jehle, 2000).

[18] See, for example, Article 13 of the Dutch Police Act of 1993 which states that the police functions under the command of the public prosecution service and a prosecutor is entitled to give orders to the police in criminal matters that they are obliged to obey.

[19] This is the so-called *transactie* system, which also applies to the prosecution level.

[20] There are very few empirical studies in continental jurisdictions with which to draw a better picture of the situation that exists in practice. See, however, Hodgson (2005) for a valuable contribution.

during the investigation of a case is a matter of great variation across different prosecution systems. It is, furthermore, a controversial issue in the discussions about the relationship between police and prosecutors. In theory, it can be stated that in common law jurisdictions, investigations have been traditionally regarded as the preserve of the police, contrary to the pure continental tradition which places prosecutors in charge of the investigatory as well as the post-investigatory stage. In practice, and as time passed, there have been developments that have caused adjustments in this crude statement.

### *Common law tradition*

As was shown earlier, in most common law countries there is no a direct line of authority between the police and the prosecution service and the police enjoy a considerable independence in the execution of their duties. Related to this, it has been declared that the responsibility for investigations lies exclusively in the hands of the police. After the creation of modern public prosecution services, the police may have been released from their responsibilities in prosecutions,[21] but they remained the institution responsible for the investigatory stage. Indeed, the main reason behind establishing the CPS in England and Wales and the DPP Offices in Ireland and Northern Ireland was the desire to draw a clear line between functional responsibility for investigation and for prosecution.

The maintenance of an investigator-prosecutor divide was central to the report which led to the establishment of the CPS. The Philips Royal Commission recommended that the CPS should not have a role in supervising police investigations apart from giving advice to the police, which the Royal Commission encouraged.[22] The investigator-prosecutor divide was premised on the belief that if the prosecutor becomes involved in the investigation of a case, then the prosecutor may become committed to a particular line of inquiry and lose objectivity in assessing that case. Therefore, even after the creation of the CPS, the police retained the power to investigate and to decide what charge to bring without the interference of the CPS.

In the early 1990s, a series of miscarriages of justice led to the appointment of another Royal Commission on Criminal Justice which examined once again the possibility of giving the CPS a role in

---

[21] However, not entirely as in many common law countries, including Ireland (and until very recently Northern Ireland) police still have a role in the prosecution of minor cases.

[22] Royal Commission on Criminal Procedure (1981, pp. 71-73).

investigations. The role of the *juge d'instruction* in France was particularly discussed as a possible model but, in the end, it was rejected along with any other proposal which went against the strict separation of the roles of investigator and prosecutor. Field (1994), as well as other commentators, criticised the Commission for not giving proper and creative thought to the possibility of introducing some inquisitorial elements in the pre-trial stage, adapting them to the English system of criminal justice. Instead, they were seeking to 'take a pre-existing system and implant it in its entirety' (p. 121) and, naturally, this approach was destined to fail.

A similar reasoning to that of the two Royal Commissions of Criminal Justice was followed in other common law countries when discussing the possible involvement of prosecutors in the investigative stage.[23] Thus in Ireland,[24] Australia, New Zealand, Canada[25] and other common law countries, prosecutors have no formal role in the pre-trial stage apart from that of advising the police whenever the latter wish to consult them.

## *Problems and inefficiencies*

The division between investigation and prosecution proved to be problematic in practice and researchers were critical of the absence of a prosecutor's power to exert a form of control in the investigative stage. They argued that the failure to give the prosecutor control over investigations meant that the control over prosecutions actually stayed with the police.[26]

Much research evidence concluded that prosecutors could not effectively monitor police investigations via police-constructed files,[27] that many police files contained insufficient and sometimes misleading evidence with the result that weaknesses often came out only in or after the trial,[28] and that the police investigation focused prematurely upon a police suspect, sometimes overlooking other crucial evidence.

---

[23] See Hunt Report (1969) and Bryett and Osborne (2000) in Northern Ireland and Public Prosecution Study Group (1999) in Ireland.

[24] In Northern Ireland, the DPP had some indirect investigatory powers. See Articles 6(3) and 5(1)(b) of the Prosecution of Offences Order.

[25] See Law Reform Commission of Canada (1990) and Stenning (1986).

[26] See *inter alia* Lidstone (1987) and Fionda (1995, Chapter 2).

[27] E.g. McConville *et al.* (1991)

[28] Ashworth (1998, Chapter 6), Sanders (1988), McConville et al. (1991). See also Baldwin and Bedward (1991) who found that the police summaries, on which most of the time prosecutors based their prosecution decisions, were even more selective.

Furthermore, research studies revealed that there had been reluctance from the police to use the possibility available to them of seeking prosecutors' advice during investigations. McConville et al. (1991), based on their research undertaken in the early days of the CPS, reported that police asked for prior advice in only 51 out of 711 cases. Later research by Moxon and Crisp (reported in RCCJ Report, 1993) found that police asked for the CPS's prior advice in four per cent of cases, mainly in order to resolve doubts about the sufficiency of the evidence.

## *Change of thinking and practice*

All the problems mentioned above caused a gradual change of thinking regarding the prosecutors' involvement in investigations. Before reflecting on this, it should be mentioned that the police themselves were gradually forced to seek prosecutors' advice more often. The appearance of new forms of criminality (organised crime, especially money-laundering and drug-trafficking) and the ever-increasing complexities of substantive and procedural law made the police more dependent on the prosecutors for legal advice. In many common law jurisdictions this has evolved into forms of cooperation that provide the prosecutor with some influence in the investigation process. In most jurisdictions, though, this form of cooperation has remained on an informal and usually *ad hoc* level, without changing the constitutional relationship between the two institutions.[29]

In England and Wales more formal responses started to emerge in order to face the inefficiencies observed in practice as far as investigations were concerned. The thrust of the new thinking, evidenced in such reviews as the Narey Report in 1997 and the Glidewell Report in 1998, has been to place the emphasis on co-ordination, partnership and integrated working between the police and CPS, with the prosecutor being fully involved from the point of charge. The Narey Report (1997), stating that they did 'not consider that working with the police in this way would necessarily impinge on the proper independence of the prosecutor' (p. 11), recommended that prosecutors should be placed permanently in police stations as a means of ensuring that appropriate decisions are made for the prosecution of cases from the start. However, in reporting on a review of the 'Lawyers at Police Stations' (LAPS) scheme which was introduced as

[29] However, in many jurisdictions special offices were created long ago which were dealing mainly with economic crime and combined the roles of investigator and prosecutor. See, for example, the Serious Fraud Office in the UK, the Criminal Assets Bureau in the Republic of Ireland and the Integrated Proceeds of Crime (IPOC) Units in the Canadian Federal jurisdiction.

a result of these recommendations, Baldwin and Hunt (1998) concluded that CPS lawyers were being used inefficiently to provide oversight and guidance to police officers. The fact that the police retained control of the decision to charge was arguably a factor that prevented a change in the balance of powers between prosecutors and the police.

The Glidewell Committee (1998) recommended the creation of Criminal Justice Units (CJU) in each major police station where CPS case workers and police civilian staff were able to work together on some cases. It was believed that through co-location the relationship between the prosecutor and the police would improve and cases would be prepared earlier and more efficiently. A first review of the CJU scheme was generally positive. However, again, this scheme was criticised as being based on police control of the charging process and as creating a danger that the CPS officers would lose a degree of their independence and objectivity by being co-opted into the rubber-stamping of police decision-making.[30]

With the CJA 2003 however, as was shown above, the responsibility for deciding whether to lay a charge is transferred from the police to the CPS. Once the prosecutor has charge responsibility, the prosecutor can require the police to investigate further before agreeing to the commencement of criminal proceedings. In the guidance issued by the DPP according to the Act, 'custody officers are expressly required to direct investigating officers to consult a duty prosecutor as soon as practicable after a suspect is detained in custody. During these consultations the lawyer is expected to identify whether a case is likely to proceed and to advise on lines of inquiry and evidential requirements' (Brownlee, 2004, pp. 902-903). It is, therefore, evident that with the new law prosecutors are given a more powerful role regarding investigations. It remains now to be seen how they will discharge it in practice.

## *Continental tradition*

In the inquisitorial environment the distinction between investigation and prosecution is more blurred than in common law systems. As Ambos (2000) remarks, '(t)he French distinction between *poursuite* and *instruction* refers to different phases of the proceedings and thereby distinguishes between the competences of *procureur* and *juge d'instructio*n' (pp. 513-514). Generally, prosecutors are responsible for the

---

[30] See Baldwin and Hunt (1998), Sanders and Young (2000, Chapter 6) and Sanders (2004).

whole pre-trial stage, including investigations, although there are a number of variations among different inquisitorial systems as far as the extent of prosecutors' powers are concerned.

In France, the Code of Criminal Procedure states that the *procureur* has formal authority over the police services when they investigate criminal offences. In order to facilitate the execution of their duties, the Code provides that prosecutors can issue general instructions (apart from the specific instructions they give in individual cases) to investigators in which they explain the choices in the crime policy and the priorities in the detection of particular categories of crimes. The police must report to prosecutors all offences known to them and seek instructions as to the lines of investigations. They also have the formal obligation to inform the public prosecutors of all arrests they make and of the decision to put a suspect in police custody, as well as to seek their authorisation for the use of undercover investigation techniques. The prosecutors may, if they think proper, take over the investigation themselves.

In the case of serious offences and complex investigations the public prosecutors can request that a judicial inquiry be opened. The case is then brought to the *juge d'instruction*, who opens the judicial inquiry. It is estimated that only seven per cent of all cases are the subject of judicial inquiries despite 'the image of an omnipresent examining judge, sometimes imagined by foreign academics' (Verrest, 2000, p. 215).

The German Criminal Procedure Law provides that the prosecution service is legally and functionally responsible for the pre-trial stage and it is referred to as 'the ruler of the investigative stage' (Elsner, 2005). It authorises prosecutors to perform acts of investigation themselves or to request the police to do so. They can also give general instructions to the police regarding how particular cases are to be handled and can set areas of priority of investigation.

The police are obliged to inform the prosecution service of their actions and to provide them with information in order to facilitate their decisions for further investigatory actions. In practice, there are only a few areas where the prosecutor's office is involved from the very beginning in investigations. Weigend (2004) refers to homicide cases, serious white-collar cases and cases where significant publicity is expected. Furthermore, when there is a need of search and seizure, pre-trial detention, telephone tapping, deploying an undercover agent or DNA-analysis, in principle a court has to authorise these actions[31] and, therefore,

[31] See, however, the Law on Control of Organised Crime of 1992 by which the police have been authorised to initiate deployment of undercover agents and have also been authorised to make independent decisions in emergency cases.

the public prosecutors must serve as an interface in terms of moving a corresponding motion. In the rest of the cases the police can complete the investigation on their own and pass on the complete file to the prosecution service. Nevertheless, as Weigend (2004) remarks, '(n)otwithstanding the practical domination of the investigation process by the police, the prosecutor's office remains ultimately responsible...' (p. 208).

In Scotland, Procurators Fiscal has similar powers to their counterparts in continental jurisdictions. They have a common law duty to investigate crime and Chief Constables are under a statutory duty to comply with the lawful instructions of the fiscal. In practice, it is only in the more serious or complex cases that the fiscal would become heavily involved at the investigative stage, for example through attendance at the scene of a murder to take charge of the evidential aspects of the investigation and autopsy arrangements.

Some limited empirical research in continental jurisdictions revealed a number of inefficiencies[32] which do not match up to the ideal picture of the system that some common law commentators have in their minds. During the RCCJ, 1993, discussions, there were allegations by some researchers of a lack of cultural commitment to impartiality amongst some prosecutors and *juges d'instruction* in France but Field (1994) claims that these general assessments were not empirically founded and that 'there does seem to be an impressionistic case of thinking that processes of training do not seem to shape cultural attitudes in quite the same way in France as they do in Germany and the Netherlands' (pp. 128-9) (where there was evidence that prosecutors do appear neutral and impartial). Hodgson (2001), however, based on her research, also expressed doubts about the neutral stand of the *magistrats* in France, stating that 'in practice independence does not guarantee neutrality and in particular, the stance of the *procureur* in representing the public interest is predominately one of crime control' (p. 357).

Related to this, concerns are expressed that the regular involvement of prosecutors with the police in an investigation might compromise their ability to make dispassionate judgments.[33] However, there is evidence that

---

[32] Apart from the mentioned inefficiencies, see also criticisms of the limited defence rights during investigations (Hodgson, 2004). However, in an attempt to demonstrate conformity with the ECHR and under the influence of the Recommendations of the Council of Europe (e.g. Rec 97(13)), there are a series of reforms in inquisitorial countries aiming to strengthen the defence's position. See Field and West (2003) and Hodgson (2005) for a review of relevant reforms introduced in France.

[33] See evidence presented in Bryett and Osborne (2000).

prosecutors are involved in investigations on an everyday basis only in very serious cases and for the rest they only exercise overall control and supervision.[34] This evidence leads to a contrary argument that the involvement of prosecutors in the investigative stage is largely rhetorical and not effective[35] and 'a dangerous disguise for untramelled police control of investigations' (Field, 1994, p. 126). This argument, though, does not take into consideration the fact that prosecution services in civil law countries make a great use of their power to issue guidelines and directives to the police on how to investigate particular cases and what kind of methods they can use. They also require the police to keep them informed of the most crucial investigative actions.[36] Furthermore, prosecutors in their relationship with the police place a great importance on trust and mutual understanding (Hodgson, 2001). Leigh and Zedner (1992) report:

> A striking feature of the French and German systems which we might further emulate is the readiness of the police to request advice from prosecution. The foreign observer cannot but be struck by the harmonious working relationships in Germany between prosecutors and police which exist notwithstanding the independence and superior status of the prosecutor in the procedure (p. 69).

This is in contrast to the tension that has always characterised the relationship between police and prosecutors in England and Wales.

Leigh and Zedner (1992) confirm that prosecutors' monitoring generally starts after preliminary police investigations. But, as Field (1994) points out, these authors 'do not conclude from this that prosecutors always become prisoners of a police-constructed file and their supervision meaningless' (p. 127). This is prevented partly by the defence actions which provide the prosecutor with additional information that challenges the police view of the case. It is argued (Field, Alldridge, & Jorg, 1995) that when prosecutors are alerted to ambiguities or impropriety in investigations, they are often decisive in response. Field (1994) claims that especially the German and the Dutch systems 'seem to depend on the development of a particular kind of relationship between the defence lawyer, the prosecutor and (in the Netherlands) the investigative judge in the development of the dossier' (p. 127).

---

[34] See Elsner (2005), Weigent (2004), Falletti (2004), Hodgson (2001).

[35] See Goldstein and Marcus (1977) and the discussions in the RCCJ 1993.

[36] See Weigent (2004), Jehle (2000).

## Prosecution Principles and Policies

The power to decide whether a particular case should be forwarded to courts or filtered out of the system is regarded as the central function of every prosecuting authority. In this section, a comparative analysis will be attempted of the way different prosecution systems approach the issues of prosecutorial discretion, diversion from prosecution and the formulation of prosecution criteria and policies.

### *Theoretical background: Mandatory v. opportunity principle*

Prosecution systems have traditionally been characterised as adhering or coming closer to either the legality or the opportunity principle. This depends on the extent of the discretion that the prosecuting authorities are allowed over the decision to prosecute and the permission to take into account factors other than evidence in making this decision.

The *legality principle* commands that every case in which there is enough evidence and in which no legal hindrances prohibit prosecution has to be brought to court. Adherence to the legality principle means that the prosecution service cannot exercise any discretion over the prosecutorial decision.[37] Its role is limited to the legal assessment of the sufficiency of the evidence against the suspect. Other considerations – what are known as public interest factors in opportunity systems – are not considered as factors that prosecutors are allowed to deploy in their decisions. Rather, the public interest is regarded as a consideration for the court that might be reflected in the verdict or the penalty imposed.

The adoption of the legality principle is usually connected with the continental tradition in which enforcement agencies are, at least theoretically, denied any discretion and primacy is given to the legislative power of the state. In these systems (e.g. Germany, Italy, Spain) '(t)he Penal Code is the foundation of legal authority: judges and prosecutors have no "inherent" power to take positions that modify or nullify the Code's requirements' (Goldstein & Marcus, 1977, pp. 246-7). As Ashworth and Redmayne (2005) remark, '(i)f the administration of the criminal law produces unjust results, it is for the legislature to amend it and not for prosecutors to make their own policies' (p. 147).

---

[37] Langbein (1974) remarks that '(t)he prosecutor's power of non-prosecution becomes controversial when it extends beyond the power to discard hopeless cases. Prosecutorial discretion...means the power to decline to prosecute in cases of provable criminal liability' (p. 440).

Tak (2004a) refers to two principal reasons usually given for the mandatory prosecution of all offences as prescribed by the law. The first is the safeguard of the principle of equality before the law and the second is the upholding of the concept of general deterrence: 'The guarantee that all offenders will be tried and that no offence will remain unpunished would be an important means by which to uphold the trust of the population in law enforcement, and in the proper administration of justice' (Tak, 2004a, p. 9). Furthermore, the dispensation of justice in open court is seen as essential in ensuring that the law is impartially upheld and that undue influences by the executive are prevented (Ashworth & Redmayne, 2005 p. 165).

Prosecution systems that adhere to the *opportunity principle* (e.g. England and Wales, Ireland, Canada and Australia ) 'allow enforcement agencies almost unfettered discretion over whether or not to prosecute, which allows prosecutors to take account of factors other than evidence in making their decisions' (Sanders, 1996, p. xi). These factors are normally classified as exigencies of the public interest and cover a wide range of issues that entail consideration of factors associated with the accused, the victim, the gravity of the offence, the availability of resources, etc.

This high level of discretion with which the enforcement agencies are entrusted is mostly associated with the common law tradition. Unlike codified systems that aspire to provide in advance for all eventualities, the common law tradition admits the impossibility of pre-determined answers to all future questions and recognises the need for flexibility in the law, so that it can be adapted to every variation in circumstances.[38] Furthermore, the permission that is given to prosecutors to apply extra-legal considerations to prosecution decisions is a recognition that within a society there are competing interests and values which must be reconciled (Mansfield & Peay, 1987) and a realisation that prosecutors are possibly in the best position to pursue a cost benefit analysis.

Finally, it is advocated that the adoption of the opportunity principle has three main advantages: (a) it prevents 'the negative counter-effects of the strict application of the legality principle which, under circumstances, could lead to injustice' (Tak, 2004a, p. 9); (b) it enables the individualisation of criminal justice; and (c) it prevents 'delays and backlogs in the court and prison system, which may in turn jeopardise the overall aim of protecting the rights and interests of the accused' (Fionda, 1995, p. 10).

[38] See McConville and Wilson (2002) and Mansfield and Peay (1987, pp. 26-29).

### *Changes in practice and remaining differences*

Despite the doctrinal contrast between the principle of legality and the principle of opportunity, the differences between the systems that were originally used to adopt either principle are increasingly eroded in practice. These days, most of those traditionally regarded as legality systems,[39] especially due to rising caseloads and scarce resources,[40] allow the prosecutors to also take into account other reasons apart form the evidential ones when deciding to prosecute or drop a case. Wade (2005) reports that 'in systems which do not explicitly allow this, practices achieving the same effect can be found' (p. 2).

In Germany, which used to be considered one of the strong representatives of the mandatory prosecution philosophy, as early as the 1960s, a statutory basis for discretionary non-prosecution was introduced in order to cope with the rising caseloads. Since then, a number of exceptions from the mandatory prosecution rule have been enacted. Therefore, currently, prosecutors can refrain from or dismiss a prosecution in the following cases: (a) for minor criminal offences with low guilt and no public interest in prosecuting and (b) for less important criminal offences where the penalty would be insignificant alongside the punishment for some other crime committed by the same offender. In these cases there can be a dismissal without consequences but also a conditional dismissal by which prosecutors impose upon the offender certain obligations. It is worth noting that the court's consent is necessary for the dismissal of cases concerning certain kinds of offences. For more serious offences (felonies) only the Federal Prosecutor General is empowered to refrain from prosecutions in very specific circumstances.[41]

In France the expediency principle also applies currently in a number of cases and there also a number of options available for prosecutors when

---

[39] With the exception of Italy, this theoretically still adopts the principle of strict legality. See, however, Di Federico (1998): 'The first clear element that emerges from our research is that, in spite of the constitutional provisions that require our magistrates to prosecute all criminal violations, penal action in Italy is de facto just as discretionary as in other countries, and perhaps more' (p. 378).

[40] Ashworth and Redmayne (2005) mention another important reason for this trend, naming the 'increasing realisation that prosecution and sentence in court are stressful for all participants and are not necessarily more effective (in terms of reconviction rates) than forms of diversion' (p. 147).

[41] See Weigend (2004) for more information on the diversionary options in Germany.

they decide to divert a case out of the courts (e.g. *mediation penale*, *composition penale*, etc).

However, although there is a good deal of convergence between opportunity and legality-based systems in practice, commentators draw attention to some important differences that still exist: 'Because diversion in a legality system is an exception to a general rule, non-prosecution decisions are relatively strictly controlled even if they are greater in number than in systems like that in England and Wales' (Sanders & Young, 1994, p. 209). As the examples of Germany and France indicate, the conditions under which those exceptions can be made, are stipulated and diversion decisions are usually reserved for the prosecutors to make. Furthermore, in order to encourage consistency and adherence to official policy, only a relatively small number of senior decision-makers are empowered to take the most serious diversionary decisions.[42]

On the contrary, in opportunity-based systems such as that in England and Wales, 'neither the basis for the exercise of discretion nor the level of decision-maker is consistent throughout the system' (Sanders & Young, 1994, p. 209).[43] Diversionary decisions are not the exclusive responsibility of prosecutors. Most non-prosecution decisions are still made by a relatively large number of police officers and, thus, are difficult to control. Police are empowered to take no further action, give an informal warning, or administer a caution without notifying the CPS. Furthermore, until recently, prosecutors had no power to impose any diversionary measures instead of prosecution. Their only option was to recommend to the police – but not require – the administration of a caution.[44]

Prosecutors could, of course, discontinue a case for public interest reasons but research revealed that they were not very successful in doing so. McConville et al. (1991) found that the CPS rarely dropped cases on public interest grounds alone and although later on discontinuances of this kind were increased, most of the time, these occurred in trivial cases and mainly on cost grounds (Sanders & Young, 2002). It was argued, that

---

[42] See Sanders (1986a), Leigh and Zedner (1992), Sanders and Young (1994, Chapter 6).

[43] This is not necessarily the same in all expedience-based systems. See, for example, the situation in the Netherlands where prosecution policy is 'strikingly organised and determinate, implementing a carefully considered and coherent working philosophy' (Fionda, 1995, p. 63).

[44] Contrary to the situation in Scotland, where for a long time now there has been a sophisticated diversionary package available to the procurators fiscal, including fiscal warnings, conditional offers of fixed penalties, fiscal fines and diversionary schemes.

police control of information and case construction used to make it extremely difficult for prosecutors to identify cautionable cases.[45] The experiment with 'Public Interest Case Assessment' (PICA) schemes, where the CPS was provided with information from other than the police sources (e.g. Social Services), proved that far more cases could be diverted provided that the right information was available (Crisp et al., 1995).

The introduction of the Criminal Justice Act, 2003, confers a greater role on the CPS in relation to diversion. It gives them the power to offer conditional cautions to offenders and requires them to propose the conditions. However, the police seem to retain the power to offer a police caution or otherwise to divert the case. Therefore, even after the introduction of the new legislation, it appears that in England and Wales's diversionary decisions will still not be centrally controlled by a single agency acting on explicitly pronounced policies and common starting points for all cases.

### *Formulation of prosecutorial policy*

Once it is admitted that a certain amount of discretion should be allowed to prosecuting agencies over the decision to prosecute or divert a case from the courts, a number of issues arise to which different jurisdictions have not responded in a similar manner.

*First*, should prosecutors act on a predefined policy, publicly announced or does this negate the very need for individualised decision-making? In England and Wales the CPS are obliged by law to issue a code setting out their policies and criteria according to which prosecution decisions should be made.[46] This is a public document formulated by the DPP and revised periodically. Moreover, recently, as Ashworth and Redmayne (2005) remark, 'there has been a welcome step towards openness, with the publication on the CPS website of considerable amounts of prosecutorial guidance previously confidential to Crown prosecutors' (p. 176). Prosecutors are, theoretically at least, obliged to follow all these guidelines, although practice showed that there has been a considerable degree of variation regarding their approaches and their understanding of the code (Hoyano et al., 1997).

---

[45] However, McConville et al. (1991) and Gelsthorpe and Giller (1990) report that, even when cautionable cases could be identified, the CPS was reluctant to drop them, especially where police working rules pointed to prosecution.

[46] In Scotland there is also a Prosecution Code which sets out the criteria for decision-making and the range of options available to prosecutors dealing with reports of crime.

Other jurisdictions have adopted a different approach to the one mentioned above, which allows prosecutors a broader discretion regarding the creation of predefined policies, while at the same time significantly limiting the number of decision-makers. For example, in Germany there are no published documents specifying the conditions under which a prosecution is dismissed or reflecting on the proper conduct of criminal prosecutions. There are some internal guidelines issued by the Federal Chief Prosecutor that are not published. It is argued that the strong hierarchical structure that exists, as well as the concentration of the most crucial decisions in the senior prosecutors, makes up for the lack of detailed and published guidelines.[47]

The *second issue* concerns the question of who should formulate prosecution policies. The most important issue in this context is the relationship between the Executive and the prosecution services. Ashworth (2000, p. 282) argues that the quasi-judicial role that prosecutors play suggests that they should enjoy certain independence in matters of policy-making. In England and Wales the DPP formulates the CPS policies on prosecution and the Attorney General is constitutionally answerable for these policies to Parliament. In practice, Parliament never debates the principles or the contents of the code (Sanders, 2004). The relationship between the Attorney General and the DPP is in practice primarily consultative in nature, enabling the Attorney General to retain a general overview of prosecution policy; also, the DPP is expected to provide sufficient information to the Attorney General to enable him to answer to Parliament for the performance of the CPS. In theory, both the Attorney General and the DPP are independent of the Executive. However, as Ashworth (2000, p. 262) remarks, the CPS in the past failed to act in an independent way from the Executive and his policies have been highly influenced by the Home Secretary's policies for prosecution and diversion.[48]

In other countries, such as France, Belgium, Germany, and the Netherlands, the prosecution services act under the supervision of the Minister of Justice who can issue directives to his subordinates concerning prosecutorial decisions to be made. The instructions of the minister can relate to a specific case or be of a general nature and thus concern general prosecution policies. For example, Article 5 of the French Judicial Organisation Act, 1958, states that the members of the *ministère public* are

---

[47] Furthermore, the law on which prosecutors base the exercise of their discretion is also relatively detailed.

[48] See also Ashworth and Fionda (1994) and a response to this criticism by Daw (1994).

subordinated to the Minister of Justice. The Minister of Justice is politically accountable for the functioning of the Public Prosecution Service and thus can issue general instructions 'so that criminal politics of the government can be put in practice.' Verrest (2000) argues that:

> the more ideological ground behind the criminal policy entirely led by the government, is the deep fear in France of "judicial corporatism". The belief is high that if the Minister of Justice would cede any of his prerogatives in the field of criminal policy, the government would rapidly lose control over legal practice. (pp. 223-4)

In Germany there is a similar situation to the French one regarding the formulation of prosecutorial policies. Nevertheless, it has been argued that although general rules for the proper conduct of criminal prosecutions are defined by the Minister of Justice, more specific prosecution policies are not usually determined at the level of the Ministry of Justice but at that of the Federal Chief Prosecutor (Weigend, 2004).

## Conclusion

Concluding this chapter, it can be remarked that the main questions that have troubled most prosecution systems over time centred on three crucial dichotomies:

- Systematic v. unsystematic approach to prosecutions
- Prosecutors' power to direct investigations v. complete separation of the investigative and the prosecutorial stages
- Legality v. expediency principle.

Furthermore, questions concerning the desirability of prosecutors and police having a more clearly hierarchical constitutional relationship; the retention by the police of the power to filter cases out of the system without any control from the prosecuting authorities; and the institution responsible for formulating the prosecution policy in the jurisdiction have constituted the most controversial topics of discussion among academics and practitioners and are still included in the reform agenda of various commissions.

The choices that prosecution systems have adopted regarding these issues have traditionally and at large defined their characterisation as adversarial or inquisitorial systems. However, as was demonstrated in this chapter, these dichotomies have progressively eroded not only in practice but also in the legislations providing for prosecutorial arrangements. Nevertheless, even today, certain existing characteristics of prosecution systems can be traced back to their different origins and convey their different philosophies.

In the *second section* of this chapter, the origins, constitutional position and organisation of prosecution services in a number of jurisdictions were analysed. There is a long tradition in civil law systems of public authorities taking responsibility for prosecutions in the public interest, which pre-dates the creation of police forces. By contrast, in the common law tradition, prosecution services are a relatively new feature, the responsibility for prosecutions having previously been left to private individuals and mainly to the police. However, although in some common law countries (e.g. Ireland, Australia and Canada) the police still retain significant prosecutorial functions, the trend has been towards giving responsibility for prosecutions to a prosecution agency independent of the police. Even now, the specific characteristics of the modern prosecution services, their structures as well as their constitutional relationship with the police vary from jurisdiction to jurisdiction and point to their different law tradition. In common law countries, there is still a *right to private prosecution*, a number of other agencies apart for the main prosecution service carry out a significant number of prosecutions, and the *police enjoy a strong independence* not coming under the control of the prosecution service. In inquisitorial jurisdictions, as a rule, the state *monopolises the right to prosecute* and prosecution services function in a *hierarchical structure* with strong internal guidelines. Public prosecutors normally belong to the *judicial branch* or they are considered as quasi-judicial officers. The police have never had a prosecutorial role and are regarded as coming under the command of, and being controlled by, the public prosecution services.

The *third section* dealt with the role of the prosecuting authorities in investigations. It is widely accepted that whatever takes place during this phase exerts considerable influence on the later decision of prosecution, but also on the progress of the case overall. The classical divide between the prosecutor and the investigator, which is often seen as a distinguishing characteristic of common law systems, in some countries tends to dissolve. This either takes the form of informal arrangements between police and prosecutors without changing the constitutional relationship between the two services or, as in the case of England and Wales, a statutory reform. In inquisitorial systems, prosecutors have always been regarded as responsible for the investigatory as well as the prosecuting stage. Although, in practice, the police are left to investigate alone the majority of – especially less serious – crimes, prosecutors still retain overall control and responsibility for the regulation of the investigative stage.

The *fourth section* dealt with the way different prosecution systems approach the issues of prosecutorial discretion, diversion from prosecution and the formulation of prosecution criteria and policies. Prosecution systems have traditionally been characterised as adhering to either the *legality* or the *opportunity principle* depending on the extent of the discretion that prosecutors are allowed over the decision to prosecute and the permission to take into account factors other than evidence in making this decision. Most of those traditionally regarded as legality systems, due to rising caseloads, currently provide for exceptions in the legality principle. However, although there is a good deal of convergence between opportunity and legality-based systems in practice, it is important to draw attention to some important differences that still exist. Because diversion in a legality system is an exception to a general rule, usually the conditions under which those exceptions can be made are stipulated and diversion decisions are usually reserved for the prosecutors to make. There are also relatively small numbers of senior decision-makers and a more centralised approach regarding diversion from prosecution. In opportunity-based systems, on the contrary, diversionary decisions are not the exclusive responsibility of prosecutors. Most non-prosecution decisions are still made by a relatively large number of police officers and, thus, are difficult to control.

As far as the formulation of prosecutorial policies is concerned, in some countries prosecutors are obliged to issue a code stating their policy and criteria according to which prosecution decisions should be made. In other jurisdictions, however, a different approach has been adopted, which allows a broader discretion while at the same time significantly limiting the number of decision-makers. Furthermore, the formulation of prosecutorial policies, in some countries is the responsibility of the prosecution service itself, while in others it belongs to the control of the Executive (usually the Ministry of Justice) which also defines the government's criminal policy.

In this chapter, the distinct choices and paths that different legal systems have followed, their underlying philosophy, as well as the implications of these choices as documented by empirical studies, has been explored. Nowadays, all jurisdictions are confronted with the need to adapt the structures and the functioning of their prosecution services to the requirements of the 21st century and the new challenges that the criminal justice system faces. It is argued that a wide scale appraisal of the origins and the primary principles of prosecution systems are prerequisites for any attempt to understand the current situation and discuss any reforms for the future. It is hoped that this chapter has contributed towards this direction.

## References

Albrecht Hans-Jörg. (2000). Criminal prosecution: Developments, trends and open questions in the Federal Republic of Germany. *European Journal of Crime, Criminal Law and Criminal Justice*, *8*(3), 245.

Ambos, K. (2000). The status, role and accountability of the prosecutor of the international criminal court: A comparative overview on the basis of 33 National reports. *European Journal of Crime, Criminal Law and Criminal Justice*, *8*(2), 89.

Ashworth, A. (1998). *The criminal process: An evaluative study* (2nd edn). Oxford: Oxford University Press.

—. (2000). Developments in the Public Prosecutor's Office in England and Wales. *European Journal of Crime, Criminal Law and Criminal Justice*, *8*(3), 257.

Ashworth, A., & Fionda, J. (1994). The new code for crown prosecutors: (1) Prosecution, accountability and the public interest. *Criminal Law Review*, 894-903.

Ashworth, A., & Redmayne, M. (2005). *The criminal process* (3rd edn). Oxford: Oxford University Press.

Auld, R. E. (2001). *Review of the criminal courts of England and Wales*; *report*. London: The Lord Chancellor's Department.

Baldwin, J. (1997). Understanding judge ordered and directed acquittals in the crown court. *Criminal Law Review*, 536.

Baldwin, J., & Bedward, J. (1991). Summarising tape recordings of police interviews. *Criminal Law Review*, 671.

Baldwin, J., & Hunt, A. (1998). Prosecutors advising in police stations. *Criminal Law Review*, 521.

Belloni, F., & Hodgson, J. (2000). *Criminal injustice: An evaluation of the criminal justice process in Britain*. London: Macmillan.

Bennion, F. (1986). The new prosecution arrangements: (1) The crown prosecution service. *Criminal Law Review*, 3-15.

Block, B., Corbett, C., & Peay, J. (1993). Ordered and directed acquittals in the crown court: A time of change? *Criminal Law Review*, 95.

Brownlee, I. D. (2004). The statutory charging scheme in England and Wales: Towards a unified prosecution system. *Criminal Law Review*, *869*, 902-903.

Bryett, K., & Osborne, P. (2000). *Criminal prosecution procedure and practice: International perspectives*. Northern Ireland, Criminal Justice Review Group Research Report 16. Belfast: Stationery Office.

Council of Europe (2000). *The role of the public prosecution office in the criminal justice system, Recommendation Rec. (2000) 19 and explanatory memorandum,* Strasbourg.

Crisp, D., & Moxon, D. (1994). *Case screening by the Crown Prosecution Service: How and why cases are terminated.* Research Study No 137. London: HMSO.

Crisp, D., Whittaker, C. & Harris, J. (1995). *Public interest case assessment schemes.* Home Office Research Study 138. London: HMSO.

Daw, K. R. (1994). The new code for crown prosecutors: A response. *Criminal Law Review*, 904.

Di Federico, G. (1998). Prosecutorial independence and the democratic requirement of accountability in Italy: Analysis of a deviant case in a comparative perspective. *British Journal of Criminology, 38*(3), 371-387.

Duff, P. (1997). Diversion from prosecution into psychiatric care: Who controls the gates? *British Journal of Criminology*, *37*(1), 15-34.

—. (1999). The prosecution service: Independence and accountability. In P. Duff, and N. Hutton (Eds.), *Criminal justice in Scotland* (pp. 115-130). Aldershot: Ashgate.

Duff, P., & Burman, M. (1994). *Diversion from prosecution to psychiatric care.* Edinburgh: Scottish Office Central Research Unit.

Edwards, J. L. (1964). *Law Officers of the Crown: A study of the Offices of Attorney- General and Solicitor-General of England with an account of the Office of the Director of Public Prosecutions of England.* London: Sweet and Maxwell.

Elsner, B. (2005). Police function within the Criminal Justice System - talk at the Conference '*The growing importance of the public prosecution service: best European practices in the face of heightened crime rates'* organised by the Georg-August University Gottingen (6-8 October 2005), Germany.

Falletti, F. (2004). The French Prosecution Service. In P. J. P. Tak (Ed.), *Tasks and powers of the prosecution services in the EU member States* (pp.176–201). Volume. I. Nijmegen: Wolf Legal Publishers.

Field, S. (1994). Judicial Supervision and the Pre-Trial Process. *Journal of Law and Society*, *21*(1), 119.

Field, S., Alldridge, P., & Jorg, N. (1995). Prosecutors, examining judges, and control of police investigations. In C. Harding, P. Fennel, N. Jorg, & B. Swart (Eds.), *Criminal justice in Europe: A Comparative study* (pp.227-250). Oxford: Clarendon Press.

Field, S., & West, A. (2003). Dialogue and the Inquisitorial Tradition: French Defence Lawyers in the Pre-Trial Criminal Process. *Criminal Law Forum*, *14*, 261.

Fionda, J. (1995). *Public Prosecutors and Discretion: A Comparative Study*. Oxford, Clarendon Press.

Gelsthorpe, L., & Giller, H. (1990). More justice for juveniles: Does more mean better? *Criminal Law Review*, 153-164, March.

Glidewell, I. (1998). *Review of the crown prosecution service: A report*. Cmnd. 3960. London: The Stationery Office.

Goldstein, A., & Marcus, M. (1977). The myth of judicial supervision in three "inquisitorial" systems: France, Italy and Germany. *Yale Law Journal*, 87, 240.

Gordon, P. (1980). *Policing in Scotland*. Glasgow: SCCL.

Hay, D. (1983). Controlling the English Prosecutor. *Osgoode Hall Law Journal*, *21*(2), 175.

Hetherington, T. (1989). *Prosecution and the public interest*. London: Waterlow Publishers.

Hodgson, J. (2001). The Police, the Prosecutor and the Juge D'Instruction: Judicial supervision in France, theory and practice. *British Journal of Criminology*, *41*(2), 342-361.

—. (2004). The detention and interrogation of suspects in police custody in France. *European Journal of Criminology*, *1*(2), 163-199.

—. (2005). *French criminal justice: A comparative account of the investigation and prosecution of crime in France*. Oxford: Hart Publishing.

House of Commons (1989). *Crown Prosecution Service: Fourth report of the Home Affairs Committee*. London: H.M.S.O.

Hoyano, A., Hoyano, L., Davis, G., & Goldie, S. (1997). A study of the impact of the Revised Code for the Crown Prosecutors. *Criminal Law Review*, 556-564.

Jehle, J. (2000). Prosecution in Europe: Varying structures, convergent trends. *European Journal on Criminal Policy and Research*, *8*, 27.

—. (2003). *Criminal Justice in Germany, 2003*. Berlin: Federal Ministry of Justice.

Langbein, J. H. (1973). The origins of public prosecution at common law. *The American Journal of Legal History*, *27*, 313.

Law Reform Commission of Canada (1990). *Controlling criminal prosecutions: The attorney general and the crown prosecutor*. Working Paper 62. Ottowa: The Commission.

Leigh, L., & Zedner, L. (1992). *A Report on the administration of justice in the pre-trial phase in France and Germany*. Royal Commission on Criminal Justice Research Study No. 1. London: HMSO.

Leigh, L. H., & Hall Williams, J. E. (1981). *The management of the prosecution process in Denmark, Sweden and the Netherlands*. Leamington Spa: James Hall.

Leng, R., McConville, M., & Sanders, A. (1996). Researching the discretion to charge and to prosecute. In Sanders, A. (Ed.), *Prosecution in common law jurisdictions*. Dartmouth: Aldershot.

Lidstone, K., (1987). The reformed prosecution process in England: A radical reform? *Criminal Law Journal*, 296.

Mansfield, G., & Peay, J. (1987). *The director of public prosecutions: principles and practices for the crown prosecutor*. London: Tavistock Publications.

McConville, M., Sanders., A. & Leng, R. (1991). *The case for the prosecution*. London: Routledge.

McConville, M., & Wilson, G. (Eds.). (2002). *The handbook of the criminal justice process*. Oxford: Oxford University Press.

Moody, S. R., & Tombs, J. (1982). *Prosecution in the public interest*. Edinburgh: Scottish Academic Press.

Narey, M. (1997). *Review of delay in the criminal justice system: A Report*. London: Home Office.

Royal Commission on Criminal Justice. (1993). (Chair: Viscount Runciman). *Report*. Cmnd. 2263. London: HMSO.

Royal Commission on Criminal Procedure (1981). *The investigation and prosecution of criminal offences in England and Wales: The law and procedure*. Cmnd 8092-1. London: HMSO.

Sanders, A. (1986a). Diverting cases from prosecution: Can we learn from other countries? *Justice of the Peace*, *150*, 614-617.

—. (1986b). The new prosecution arrangements [2] An independent crown prosecution service? *Criminal Law Review*, 16.

—. (1988). Incorporating the "public interest" element in the decision to prosecute. In J. E. Hall Williams, (Ed.), *The role of the prosecutor*. Aldershot: Gower.

—. (1996). Introduction. In A. Sanders (Ed.), *Prosecution in common law jurisdictions* (pp.1-7). Aldershot and Brookfield, USA: Dartmouth.

—. (2004). 2004). Prosecutions in England and Wales. In P. J. P. Tak (Ed.), *Tasks and powers of the prosecution services in the EU member states* (pp.45-56). Volume I. Nijmegen: Wolf Legal Publishers.

Sanders, A., & Young, R. (1994). The rule of law, due process and pre-trial criminal justice. *Current Legal Problems*, *47*, 125.

—. (2000). *Criminal Justice*. London: Butterworths.

Stedward, G. & Millar, A. (1989). *Diversion from prosecution* (Central Research Unit Papers). Edinburgh: The Stationery Office Books.

Stenning, P. C. (1986). *Appearing for the Crown: A legal and historical review of criminal prosecutorial authority in Canada*. Cowansville, Qué.: Brown Legal Publications.

Tak, P. J. P (2004a). Introduction. In P. J. P. Tak (Ed.), *Tasks and powers of the prosecution services in the EU member states* (pp.1-6). *Volume I*. Nijmegen: Wolf Legal Publishers.

—. (2004b). The Dutch prosecution service. In P. J. P. Tak (Ed.), *Tasks and powers of the prosecution services in the EU member states* (pp.16-26). *Volume I*. Nijmegen: Wolf Legal Publishers.

—. (2005). The prosecution service in control of police investigation policy? A European comparison'- unpublished talk at the Conference *'The growing importance of the public prosecution service: Best European practices in the face of heightened crime rates'* organised by the Georg-August University Gottingen (6-8 October 2005), Germany.

Verrest, P. (2000). The French public prosecution service. *European Journal of Crime, Criminal Law and Criminal Justice*, *8*(3), 210-244.

Wade, M. (2005). The changing role of european prosecution. *European Society of Criminology (ESC) Newsletter*, *4*(2), 3.

Walther, S. (2000). The position and structure of the prosecutor's office in the United States'. *European Journal of Crime, Criminal Law and Criminal Justice*, *8*(3), 283-295.

Weigend, T. (2004). The prosecution service in the German administration of criminal justice. In P. J. P. Tak (Ed.), *Tasks and powers of the prosecution services in the EU member states* (pp.153-165). *Volume I*. Nijmegen: Wolf Legal Publishers.

# CHAPTER FIVE

# GLOBAL SEX WORK REGIMES, POLITICS AND POLICY

TEELA SANDERS AND ROSIE CAMPBELL

## Abstract

This chapter sets out the complex relationships between the sex industry, organised crime and illegal economies by examining different regulatory regimes, legal frameworks and current policy debates through an international perspective. The relationships between women involved in the sex industry, organised crime, migrant labour, trafficking and coercion, as well as women moving to work in the legal and illegal sex markets are situated across national and international borders. This chapter will be based on a review of the literature as well as our own empirical observations of the sex industry accumulated through 11 years of research (Sanders, 2004, 2005, 2007a; Campbell, 1996, 1998 with Pitcher et al., 2006; Sanders & Campbell, 2007). The core aims of the chapter are to explore the inter-relationships between the sale of female adult sexual services, the polar arguments that define prostitution as either exploitation or work, and the relationships between the sex industry, migrancy, 'trafficking' and different forms of organised crime.

## Introduction

In this chapter nuances will be demonstrated between differences in organised crimes that assist women voluntarily to move into sex markets and those organised criminal networks that traffic women against their will into the sex trade. Myths and stereotypes around the 'trafficking' discourse will be highlighted. In addition, the reality of women making choices to sell sexual labour will be discussed by referring to systems across the world, the labour rights movement and narratives that frame sex work as labour. These aims will be achieved by examining the following issues: the spectrum of regimes that regulate the sex industry; trafficking and prostitution; voluntary migrant labour; sex as 'work' and the legal sex industry. The conclusions to the chapter will examine how international policy is tackling the sex industry and whether women are protected or increasingly facing danger because of the regulatory regime.

It is important to make a note about language and terminology at this point. The word 'prostitute' is avoided because of the derogatory, insensitive and objectifying way the term has been utilised. The word 'prostitute' is considered judgemental by many of those who support the rights of women to be involved in the sex industry at their choice, because the word is associated with the negative stereotypes such as 'vice', 'criminality' and ' immorality'. In order to recognise the spectrum of debates; the diversity of women's experiences of selling sex and the agency of women, the term 'sex work' and 'sex industry' will be used. The term 'sex industry' is preferable to prostitution because it encompasses the wide range of activities that involve sex work. The term 'sex industry' in this chapter will refer mainly to the street sex market and indoor sex markets which incorporate brothels. This chapter is focused on adult female sex work and does not specifically speak of male or transgendered sex work or the sexual exploitation of children involved in the sex industry.

## Feminist Politics, Prostitution and Sex Work

Practical and legal theories that govern the sex industry are shaped by philosophical positions regarding the rights and wrongs of prostitution. Different theoretical positions on the ability of women to make decisions to work in the sex industry create divisions between feminists and other writers on the legitimacy of the sex industry (Kesler, 2002; Peach, 2005). In short, the perspectives on prostitution fall into the abolitionists and the sex-worker rights debates. The former contends that prostitution is always oppressive, perpetuating male patriarchal privilege and subjugating women to suffering and victimization (Dworkin, 1996; Pateman, 1988; Raymond, 1999). Amongst the abolitionists, zero tolerance solutions which aim to eradicate prostitution are favoured. Some abolitionists, in recognition of what is seen as the "victimhood" of all women involved in sex work, support removing laws which criminalise women who sell sex but advocate the criminalisation of men who pay for sex, focusing on demand as the exploitative force fuelling the sex industry. Within this position there is much focus on the "trafficking" of women and children into sex industries, demonstrating for such theorists the global linkages between gender subordination and the sex industry (Kelly & Regan, 2000;

Munro, 2005). There is within this position little discussion of women who migrate to work in both legal and illegal sex markets abroad (Agustin, 2007).

In contrast, other scholars have moved beyond regarding all women involved in the sex industry as only victims but instead argue that abolitionism denies the agency that women have to make choices about entering the sex industry and any notion of 'rights' once working. Building on this, activists and academics have argued that selling sex can be considered as work in certain circumstances (Brewis & Linstead, 2000; Chapkis, 1997). As detailed below, the sex worker rights movement (Gall, 2006) has campaigned for labour and human rights frameworks to be applied to the sex industry arguing that they provide the best way for improving working conditions for those in the sex industry and reduce opportunities for exploitation within the industry and unequal and unfair treatment outside the industry (by the courts, banks, marriage, law for instance). Such frameworks would enable women to work legitimately as a sex worker (Lopes, 2006; West, 2000) and establish clearer boundaries between legitimate sex work activity/business and criminal activity such as forced labour. This would enable governments to both regulate the legitimate sex industries and focus criminal justice resources on criminal activity. Within the sex worker rights movement trafficking is recognised a serious crime and human rights violation but there is acknowledgement of the wider issue of migrant sex work - women and men who travel from their own countries and work in sex industries abroad within a range of conditions. Sex worker rights activists argue for migrant sex work to be located in wider debates about migrant workers generally, and particularly those working in informal and illegal economies.

The stigma surrounding women involved in the sex industry continues, fuelled by media campaigns that continually reinforce the 'Madonna/whore' dichotomy. Popular culture and consumerism inflates these dichotomies by the visibility and prevalence of many aspect of the sex trade in the night time economies (Bernstein, 2001). Yet despite the prevalence of the sex industries as a visible and accepted aspect of many night time economies and leisure industries, prostitution is considered to be an activity that signals a failure in individual morality, a breakdown of cohesive institutions such as marriage and the family and an indictment on female gender expectations and appropriate behaviour. This perspective fuels the belief that because prostitution symbolises a transgression of acceptability then the relationships that facilitate the sale of sex must also be chaotic and nefarious without internal coherence or structure. Images of the coercive 'pimp' and the sex worker as victim, alongside that of drug addiction and hopelessness are manoeuvred by the media to paint a simple picture of what is in reality a complex phenomenon where women enter, experience and leave the sex industry in complex social, economic, and political contexts (McNaughton & Sanders, 2007).

Against this backdrop of feminist ideological theory there is a range of legal positioning on the place of sex work in a society, and the laws that govern the sale of sex, by whom and under what conditions. Not only does the legal framework draw from the cultural context of the given country, but the laws that govern prostitution contribute to the cultural understanding and value placed on sex workers, and to a lesser extent, men who buy sex. These different legal regimes have different consequences for the control of sexuality, safety and security.

## The Spectrum of Regulatory Systems

The regulatory systems that attempt to control the sex industry highlight the complexity of the legal frameworks and the 'place' of prostitution in different cultural contexts. This section will examine the varied regimes across the globe, identifying how the sex industry is managed, the main philosophical arguments that underpin the regimes, and exactly how the regimes manifest as management systems.

### *Prohibition*

Within prohibition or abolition approaches there are legal and policy approaches premised on notions that sex work should not be encouraged, not be tolerated and indeed a policy goal should be eradication. Within abolitionist regimes different methods are favoured for achieving the eradication of prostitution. Some focus on criminalising men who pay for sex and managers but not sex workers (see Swedish example in Ekberg 2004), others focus laws on sex workers (see UK example in Hubbard 1997; Sanders, 2007) and some criminalise all parties (such as Scotland). The severity of sanctions and penalties can vary a great deal across regimes. The UK system that aims to eradicate prostitution (particularly street prostitution) have introduced a welfare approach to prohibition that encourages street sex workers to 'exit' the sex industry, through various sanctions offered through the criminal justice system. This 'regulatory therapy' approach (see Harrison & Sanders, 2006) is based on the premise of individual responsibilization through the parallel systems of the criminal justice and welfare system (Scoular & O'Neill, 2007). As Scoular and O'Neill argue, sex workers have been criminalised through the compulsory rehabilitation through 'exiting' with the aim of increasing social control and punitive governance of marginalised people. Amongst the sanctions of prohibition, stigma and shame can be incorporated into such polices making them a structural and permanent features of the culture. This leads to structural discrimination aimed at vulnerable women whose status is subject to targeting by policing agencies. Indeed the public naming and shaming of men who pay for sex is something that appears in a number of countries and is gathering pace in the UK (see Brooks Gordon, 2005; Kulick 2005; Sanders, 2007).

Across the world, amidst varied cultures and religions, there are examples of prohibition. Iran provides one example of a prohibitionist regime with severe punitive penalties for women caught selling sexual services. Women who are known to have been involved in prostitution are charged with 'moral crimes' and are subject to stoning and the death penalty, even when it is clear that human rights have been breached and that the women are extreme victims of brutality and violence (Telegraph, 19/12/2004). As some government policies have incorporated notions that all women involved in sex work are victims some may not punish sex workers but offer; "routes out", re-education and re-integration. Such interventions can be on a spectrum from voluntary engagement with support services to compulsory re-integration which begins to share some of the same features of custodial punishment and limits to freedom.

Chinese policy illustrates a model where it is a crime to pay for sex and men face considerable penalties which make shaming inevitable if not a desired outcome of compulsory rehabilitation programmes. Ren (1999) describes how sex workers are subject to mandatory rehabilitation and men who pay for sex can be arrested and sent to labour camps for re-education. Ren (1999) states that by 1993 there were 145 rehabilitation centres open for women detained for prostitution. 24% of 56,351 women arrested for prostitution were detained between 6 months and 2 years in the centres. 13,454 men were arrested for patronizing prostitutes with 10% ending up in jails or rehabilitation centres. Ren (1999, p. 1432) argues that 'the corrections and public health authorities along with women's rights agencies have mobilized to work together against the sex trade in China'.

Some regulatory regimes that have generally favoured a system that does not tolerate prostitution have adopted laws that prohibit relationships that surround the buying and selling of direct sexual services. In the UK domestic regulation of prostitution is influenced by the ideological constructions around the 'choice/agency' versus 'exploitation/victim' models (Edwards, 1997). Contradictions surround the regulatory laws because the act of two consenting adults exchanging sex for cash or commodities is in itself not illegal. Instead the exploitative nature of prostitution under certain circumstances and the nuisance factor of publicly negotiating commercial sex was historically considered unacceptable (Self, 2003) and more recently has been seen as a social activity to be reduced and eradicated because of its distastefulness (Soothill & Sanders, 2004) and incivility (Scoular, et al., 2007). Therefore, in the UK the law criminalises the organising, soliciting and procuring of people into prostitution that renders it 'legal to *be*, but not to *work* as a prostitute' (Day, 1996, p. 75).

The prohibition model in the UK is an example of many complex systems whereby the purchase of sex between consenting adults is legal, but the relationships around the commercial transaction are illegal. In the UK, since the 1950s, there are laws against brothel keeping, procuring individuals into prostitution, advertising, living off the earning of commercial sex, soliciting and loitering, and kerb-crawling. Brooks Gordon (2006, p. 30) describes how street prostitution is heavily legislated against compared with the indoor sex markets, with more control mechanisms introduced for street sex workers through Anti Social Behaviour Orders, since 2001. Such control mechanisms have seen sex workers returning to prison for breaching the Order which disqualifies them from entering certain streets (Clark, 2006; Jones & Sagar, 2001; Sagar, 2007). Over the past two decades, men who buy sex have been the focus of increased legislation with the police receiving powers of arrest in 2001 (Brooks Gordon, 2005). Such an approach was more clearly enshrined in the recent strategy on prostitution for England and Wales (Home Office, 2006) which identified as an objective the eradication of street prostitution, prioritising 'tackling demand' through kerb-crawler operations, heavy fines and naming and shaming tactics (Phoenix, 2007), providing "routes out for sex workers and "ensuring justice" in terms of addressing violent and sexual crimes committed against sex workers and trafficking.

Similar to the UK regime, Canadian laws since 1972, have 'the dubious distinction of making it legal to 'be' a prostitute but next to impossible to actually engage in prostitution-related activity' (Jeffery, 2004, p. 83). Anti-brothel laws and laws that outlaw prostitution on the streets have been dealt within criminal law. The political power to criminalise prostitution came from local resident groups who were disturbed by prostitution in their neighbourhoods. Representing the nexus between political and moral entrepreneurs, street prostitution became framed as public nuisance by neighbourhoods, local police and local government (Lowman, 2000). As a result the prohibition stance has criminalised both the female sex worker and the male client – exactly what the women's movement hoped to avoid (Jeffery, 2004, p. 100). Most notably, Canadians have been world leaders in rehabilitation programmes for men who kerb-crawl (known as Johns School's) (Van Brunschot, 2003). This form of court diversion scheme has been heavily criticised for penalising male sexuality, having little impact on re-offending and recidivism rates and is solely motivated by shaming men rather than protecting women (Campbell & Storr, 2001; Monto & Garcia, 2001). Equally, since new laws were introduced in the 1980s to further criminalise street prostitution, there has been little impact on the levels of street prostitution (Lowman, 2000) and the issue has disappeared from the agenda's of political parties.

Introduced in 1999, Sweden became unique in Europe as it made the purchase of sexual services a criminal offence under the 1998 Violence Against Women Act, carrying a fine or six month prison sentence. Pushed through by the radical feminist movement who favoured a prohibition stance, Swedish social policy decided to criminalise the men while decriminalise the selling of sex. This was largely due to arguments, and unanimous thinking from political parties, that prostitution was considered violence against all women and children (Svanstrom, 2004). This regime is built on the belief that prostitution is an extension of patriarchy and not something that a gender equal society should tolerate (Gould, 2001). Supporters of the law state that this is the first country to make a stand against the oppression of women and children through prostitution: 'This groundbreaking law is a cornerstone of Swedish efforts to create a contemporary, democratic society where women and girls can live lives free of all forms of male violence' (Ekberg, 2004, p. 1187). Immediately such a statement suggests that in Swedish law there is no room for women to have agency in this debate and that a woman's right to have autonomy over her body are eroded by not allowing men to purchase sex. Although officially framed in the language of gender equality, Kulick (2003) highlights that Sweden's stance, which was in the opposite direction to the majority of European countries that have opted for more liberal means of managing prostitution, had other international and national concerns at heart, namely its own national identity. There is little concrete evidence that the extreme case in Sweden has been successful, with few men prosecuted and only one man sent to prison, the street prostitution markets, and others based on the Internet, are a consistent feature of Swedish society (McDonald 2004; Ostergren, 2004).

### *Consequences of Prohibition*

Regimes that are punitive in their outlook, with the aim of criminalising either sex workers, men who buy sex (or both) and those who are involved in organising the sex industry, produce serious consequences. Regarding the organisation of prostitution, there are two significant consequences of the legal constraints. Prohibition prevents women legally working together otherwise they risk the charge of brothel keeping, and a male-female partnership cannot legally operate without the risk of procuring or living off immoral earnings. Thinking about the wider relationships within the sex work community, prohibition disallows commercial sex, making it difficult for relationships to form between sex business owners, organisers and workers, leaving limited opportunity to collaborate on ethical business, safety or good working conditions. The second consequence is related to violence against sex workers. In December 2006, five women were found murdered in rural East England within a week: they were all working in street prostitution (Goodyear & Cusick, 2007). The prohibition of prostitution essentially exacerbates violence against sex workers, forcing them to work in dangerous environments, denying them protection and maintaining their vulnerable status (Sanders & Campbell, 2007). What Lowman (1998) calls a 'discourse of disposability' is maintained whereby women involved in prostitution are considered worthless, without rights and outside the realms of protection and citizenship.

The prohibition models, ranging from the extreme outlawing of commercial sex in Sweden, to the complicated and grey legal situation in the UK (Phoenix, 2007) have similarities. The principles driving these regimes are that women who sell sex are victims and that the State should be there to protect them from harm, and punish those who harm them through organising or buying sexual services. Phoenix and Oerton (2005) explain the framework of 'moral authoritarianism', as a mechanism for understanding how sexual behaviour is at the centre of social policy and law enforcement. They document how the 'problem of sex' over the past two decades has become the 'problem of men', resulting in social and criminal justice policy focusing on male sexual behaviour as the culprit of harm. The emphasis on eradication, intolerance, protecting women and gender equality has not reduced prostitution in any of these states. There is little evidence to support that the regimes of prohibition and criminalisation have any effect on the levels of prostitution, the safety of sex workers or is a feasible management option.

### *Decriminalised and Legalised Prostitution*

There are countries that adopt regimes to take the sex trade out of the illegal and informal economy by legislating for a formal commercial sex industry. These regimes adopt systems of zoning on the streets and registration and licensing systems for indoor sex markets, namely brothels (Van Doornick & Campbell, 2006). There are other examples of regulatory regimes built on what are often seen as "liberal" management styles across the world. Legalisation can take many forms: the model of legalisation in a particular country is shaped by the ideology and objectives of different governments. There are a number of recurrent ideologies including; moral conservatism, overt concerns for public health, harm minimisation or a labour rights discourse in which sex work is considered work (this will be discussed below). Hence some models aim to control and contain sex workers and sex work. Some legalised systems may include policies of mandatory registration (such as New Zealand) and or screening for sexually transmitted infections (such as Nevada, USA) and may impose measures that restrict the rights of sex workers in a way other workers rights would not be. Other models are developed with the intention of legitimising sex work, encouraging owners of sex work businesses to operate within professional standards improving conditions and rights for sex workers be they employees or self employed entrepreneurs (such as Germany).

One of the most famous legalised regimes is the legalised brothel regime in Nevada, USA. In general, the USA has a prohibition stance on all forms of adult sex work, preventing adult sexual rights and criminalising all relationships that involve commerce and sex, except in the legalised system of Nevada, Las Vegas. This system is regulated by the local sheriff and the area has become a hot spot for commercial sex as a leisure industry. Sex workers can legally work in the brothels that are highly regulated, state controlled, and training is compulsory and official (Campbell, 1991, p. 1371). Hausbeck and Brents (2000) provide an insight into the Nevada brothels. The state where sex work is legalised in a strictly regulated system provides one model that upholds the safety, security and good working conditions for women. Brents and Hausbeck (2005) interviewed sex workers, brothel owners and policy makers in the legalized brothels of Nevada to examine the relationship between violence, prostitution policy and safety. They found that only 1 of the 40 sex workers interviewed reported violence at work, concluding that 'the legalisation of prostitution brings a level of public scrutiny, official regulation and bureaucratization to brothels that decrease violence' (Brents & Hausbeck, 2005, p. 270).

The Netherlands distinguished between voluntary and forced prostitution in policy (Outshoorn, 2004). Sex work was legalised in The Netherlands in 2001. This process of legalisation dealt with the off street brothel industry and window sex work. To address street sex work The Netherlands has taken another route. Van Doornick and Campbell (2006) reflect on the tipple zones of The Netherlands which are appointed designated areas where street prostitution can take place between certain hours. This management solution is informed by a harm minimisation approach, providing a safe location for women to work and reduce nuisance for residents. The zones are managed and funded by local authorities and the police are key stakeholders as they are responsible for controlling the zone, send messages to clients and drug dealers that a strong monitoring force is present. Some zones are heavily regulated: sex workers require a license to work in the zone which makes it less likely for drug using sex workers to engage in complex bureaucracy (ibid: 70).

Germany has legalised both indoor and outdoor sex work. Sex work is legal but within a regulatory framework with a range of prohibitions in law (European Parliament, 2005). The 2002 prostitution act in Germany gave sex workers rights to social security benefits and health insurance and pension insurance. The act aimed to allow sex workers to enter into these social security schemes via their sex working profession. The act also served to decriminalise the management of indoor establishments which provided good working conditions and legal recourse for independent sex workers under contract law (Laskowski, 2002). Sex workers can work on a self employed basis or as an employee. Independent sex workers now work under law which allows them to work within legally enforceable contracts with clients, so if a client does not pay for services the sex worker has the right to legal recourse.

Some municipalities in Germany have established managed areas for street sex work, where sex workers can work without criminalisation within a specified area at certain times and with health, social care and drug services on site. For example in the city of Cologne, where a managed area was opened in 2001, the key aims were to; reduce violence against sex workers, reduce street sex work in other areas of the city, enable more effective criminal prevention and investigation regarding “pimping” and drugs markets and access sex workers more effectively to street sex workers (Kerschl, 2004). The first phase of evaluation found that; violence against sex workers had reduced dramatically, sex workers were more rapidly accessing on site support services and referral to drug treatment and that the zones had been accepted by both sex workers and their clients, with a reduction in street sex work outside of the area (Kerschl, 2004).

Many eyes are on the changes that have happened in New Zealand, which introduced the Prostitution Reform Act, 2003, after a fifteen year campaign. The law did not take any moral position on prostitution but included clauses to ensure criminalisation of some activities. The minimum age of working in prostitution is 18 which protected those underage and a new crime of coercing someone to provide sexual services holds a maximum penalty of 7 years. Soliciting in New Zealand is no longer a crime. Specific legal obligations were placed on operators, clients and sex workers to ensure condom use and the provision of information on safer sex. There have been reports that sex workers have used the new law as an opportunity to force clients to recognise their obligations. The NZ Prostitutes Collective has questioned the wisdom of the provisions placing legal obligations regarding safer sex on sex workers. Occupational Health and Safety are now the body responsible for 'policing' the brothels. The new law means that a contract could be formed, both between operator and sex worker, and between client and sex worker.

The Bill gives sex workers a specific right to withdraw from a contract with a client (with appropriate reimbursement) if they want to, therefore providing protection against threatening behaviours. Operators and sex workers were also able to take legal proceedings against non-paying clients, therefore moving structural powers in favour of the sex workers position. The Bill was also aware of the need to prevent organised criminal involvement in prostitution as a money making activity. The Bill encouraged the development of smaller, prostitution operations in which gang involvement would be much more difficult to sustain. The removal of the essential criminality from prostitution and the stronger penalties against coercion were intended to reduce the opportunity for gang involvement (see www.sexwork.com)

## *Consequences of Legalisation*

Evidence from studies of violence against sex workers in different regulatory regimes suggests that the method of regulation has a significant impact on the levels of violence that sex workers experience. Where there are state controlled or regulated sex markets there is evidence of less violence. Although there is minimal evidence that compares the effects of legalisation on the levels of violence, there has been some muted attempts to equate the global changes in the sex industry (the expansion of erotica industries, the increase in demand for paid sex, trafficking of women and children, child exploitation, migrant women independently moving to work in the industry) with legalisation (see Sullivan & Jeffreys, 2002). The claims of Sullivan and Jeffreys (2006) that 'sex industrialists' have over taken the Victoria brothel scene and are not providing empowering working conditions for women, is by their own admission a failure in the bureaucratic administration system to monitor licensed premises, and not a failure of the system of legalisation.

There is strong evidence from European systems of managed street sex work zones that such regulatory provision reduces violence and insecurity. Kershl (2004) reports that in Cologne, Germany, the zone system has produced a near total reduction of violence against sex workers by pimps or clients (also see Laskowski, 2002). Similarly, the managed zone in Utretch, The Netherlands, has an exemplary safety record: there have been no murders of sex workers whilst working in the zones. In addition the zones enable the police to target exploitation in the street sex work scene (Schumacher, 2004). Although there have been some problems in the Dutch zones, these are attributable to wider changes in the sex industry, such as global migration and do not justify a call to abandon the zone as safety continues to be maintained.

## *Informal Regimes*

In a number of countries regimes of sex work occur which are at odds with national law and policy. These informal regimes often transcend the national policy and instead reflect local agreements and partnerships between police, health authorities and sex work communities. In England and Wales whilst the official regime is one of prohibition, informal practices are tolerated in some areas. May et al. (2000) in a government funded study found that many off street sex work establishments managed sex workers in relatively benign ways. They found that many off street establishments were ignored by the police unless a complaint was made. They recommended a pragmatic approach in which outreach projects work with indoor establishments to provide support and advice and the police monitor parlours to ensure "unwritten rules" were observed and to be aware of the extent of indoor markets. So the approach advocated was that the police and other responsible authorities encourage responsible "risk adverse management" of indoor premises, allowing the police to focus criminal enforcement on disreputable owners and managers involved in coercing and controlling under 18's, trafficking, drug dealing and other forms of exploitation. They warned against no regulation of indoor markets but recommended an approach which involved regulation and promoting good management. Ideally with commitment from councils who licence premises and the police systems could develop to ensure vulnerable individuals are protected and criminal activities are not allowed to flourish. May et al. (2000) argue that, this would reduce the opportunity for indoor markets to be colonised by criminal operators who may manage sex workers via coercion and violence and have less considerations to conditions of working.

## Voluntary Migrant Labour

Concentrating on women who voluntarily agree to be trafficked to other countries (generally from developing countries to the West), this section highlights the complexities of women who migrate across borders to work in the sex industry. Non-nationals who end up working as sex workers are the end result of a complex set of national and international forces. Agustin (2006, 2007) explains how there has been turmoil and confusion over the use of the work 'migrant', particularly in relation to those working in the sex industry. How and why women come to work in the sex industry from other countries has begun to be documented. Agustin (2006) describes how the global structural inequalities that create distinct 'push-pull' factors in the country of origin and the host country that result in female migration. Agustin (2006, p. 120) points to the feminisation of migration generated by the service industry as one reason for a steady flow of women moving from poorer southern countries to Western countries to work in the unregulated and poorly paid economies. Alongside agriculture, domestic labour and child care, and sweatshop manufacturing, sex work is one unregulated industry that provides economic opportunities for migrant women.

With significant changes in the border controls and freedom to move across Europe, including the expansion of the European Union to 27 member states, the number of women moving across borders to work in sex industries in different countries has increased. The Netherlands has seen women from Russia, Poland, Hungary, Ukraine and the Baltic States, who have travelled both legally and illegally to work (Bruinsma & Meershoek, 1999). Legal migrants can legitimately move across borders, obtain the correct papers and work in official labour markets. But these legal opportunities can be very difficult, with complex bureaucracy around working visas and tax, making the informal economy a preferred option for some women. The cases of The Netherlands where the sex industry has semi-legal status and enforcement is low are attractive for illegal migrants because business relationships are non-transparent and unregulated. There are no checks on who works in a brothel or the status of individuals, allowing those without correct documents to work.

There is clear evidence that some women migrate to voluntarily work in the sex industry (see Agustin, 2005; Buzsa, 2004; Doezema, 2000). Advocating for the role of the migrant voice to be heard above that of the policy makers and moral entrepreneurs, Agustin (2007) describe how women recount their journey to host countries: they use their own informal networks to find passages and contacts in an unregulated market, paying arrangers for introductions. Sometimes, deceit, control and intimidation are part of these relationships but usually women are aware of the move they are making and the type of work they are signing up to. Agustin points out that the diversity of migration is important to qualify as there is no 'one type fits all' which categories all migrant sex workers as victims. There are a vast range of experiences of migration into the sex industry.

The case of whether a woman is a legal or illegal migrant does not determine whether the woman was trafficked or forced into prostitution. Outshoorn (2004, p. 194) fleshes out the differences between voluntary and forced prostitution as experienced in The Netherlands. Concerns about trafficking and migrancy in The Netherlands during the 1990s lead the government to reduce its full support for the ideology that prostitution was sex work in order to encompass a new law, and heavy penalties, on forced prostitution as illegal (Outshoorn, 2004). There is evidence that the policies on sex work in various countries have been influenced by wider panics about immigration, population change, and organised crime. Kantola and Squires (2004) note that the debates in the UK parliament in the 1990s had an undertone that suggested greater fears about the migrant worker that were masked by moral anxiety about prostitution. Kulick (2003), commenting on the changes to Swedish prostitution law, identifies how the policy responses encompass a whole range of wider moral panics about the status of Sweden, the internal stability in light of their recent entry into the European Union and a concern that they will see an influx of women from Eastern Europe. In the Swedish instance, such inflated concerns gave rise to a forceful policy against all forms of sex work but was framed to be against the 'demand' rather than criminalising the women.

An equally misguided understanding of the 'demand' side of the sex trade results in the debate about migrant or forced sex workers moving to other parts of the world simply because there are men who want to buy sex. Making strong links between the 'demand' side of the sex industry and migrant women moving to work in known 'hot spots' around the world, blurs the reasons why some women opt to migrate and work in informal and illegal economies. Phongpaichit (1999, p. 99) advocates that in a country like Thailand which is both a receiver and sender country of migrant female labour, decriminalization of adult prostitution would reduce the vulnerability of migrant sex service workers to exploitation by agents. Further, labour laws would prevent extensive amounts of organised crime connected to prostitution as official regulation would make the sex industry less attractive to crime syndicates.

Butcher (2003), puts forward a powerful argument that explains how sex work is often conflated with sex trafficking, which results in confused policy and mistreatment of women. These conflations between sex work, trafficking and violence persist: the United Nations Commission on the Status of Women that met in New York in 2007 maintain that involvement in prostitution is an expression of violence and subordination. The absence of the sex worker rights and labour rights perspective is a sad indication of the lack of understanding of the complexities of migrancy, trafficking and voluntary sex work.

## The Moral Panic of 'Trafficking' and Organised Crime

This section is not intending to be in any way a detailed or comprehensive assessment of debates and research concerning the nature and extent of 'trafficking' for purposes of the sex industry (see Goodey 2004; Willams, 1999). We accept that trafficking is a serious crime and a violation of human rights. Yet there has to be space in policy debates to acknowledge both voluntary migrant sex work and voluntary sex work without dismissing the existence or seriousness of trafficking, or conflating the two separate phenomena (see Outshoorn, 2005).

Organized crime networks aim to make illegal profits through crime, and hide their activities through physical violence, intimidation and sometimes terrorization. Ruggerio (1997) describes how the smuggling of people, contemporary slavery, creates profits for official and semi-official agencies, organized criminal gangs and the hidden economies the trafficked work in. Equally, he argues that the sectors (such as servants, domestic labour, mail-order brides) are not sharply distinguished from mainstream industries and institutions and at the same time are facilitated by entrepreneurs from conventional, official and criminal fraternities. Schloenhardt (1999) provides a network model of the complex and dynamic illegal markets that include amateur traffickers; small groups of organised criminals; international trafficking networks; corrupt public officials; informers; and recruitment specialists.

The criminal relationships between those who are considered to be involved in 'trafficking' are not always connected to sophisticated criminal groups. Bruinsma and Meershoek (1999) note from the police files of trafficking operations in The Netherlands that traffickers range from loosely organized professionals to organised criminal networks that link together the recruiter, the trafficker and the recipient in the host country. These authors highlight two main categories of criminal groups. First, the 'cliques of professionals' consist of two or three working together, forging traditional sexual relationships with women, and then use their international acquaintances to introduce women to other countries. Second, the organized crime groups are larger (up to 12 men) whom all have definite roles and tasks in the 'trafficking' process. Members of these groups own or work in brothels, clubs, bars and use violence to control the workers. The criminals work with travel and mediation agencies for false passports and documents for trafficking women. What is known of the trafficking rings suggests that they do not specialise in finding women just for prostitution. Of 161 people suspected of trafficking women in 1997 in the Netherlands, the majority were Dutch and also involved in other criminal activities such as smuggling arms, drugs or stolen cars, money laundering schemes and racketeering (see Shannon, 1999). Diversification has long been a trademark of organized crime as crime syndicates look for illegal profit making activities within their transnational networks.

The kind of criminal groups that are involved in trafficking of women from places such as Eastern Europe to Western European countries is still not understood. Using police files and police organizations, Bruinsma and Meershoek (1999) set out three phases of the trafficking process: the recruitment of women from home countries; the trafficking of the women from their home country to the new country; and social control of employment in the sex industry. These organised phases can be interlinked and controlled by one group of criminals, but equally, these organised phases can be separate, unrelated and within the control of individual women who want to make moves to other countries. In each of the recruitment, moving and working phase the complexities of the relationships and processes between the women and the 'traffickers' are simplified, diluted and wrongly merged by discourses, promoted by the media and some radical charities, that conflate voluntary migrancy with forced trafficking. The media simplifies the discourse on trafficking by rendering all immigrant women working in the sex trade as trafficked victims.

The movement of female labour from one country to another does not necessarily equate with trafficking. Busza (2006) highlights the example of Vietnamese sex workers who paid recruiters to introduce them to brothels in neighbouring Cambodia where they knowingly came to work as voluntary sex workers. The women paid off their debt to the recruiters and mediators over a period of up to two years and voluntarily worked in the sex industry or took up other opportunities. Although there are international organised crime issues where women are kidnapped, sold by families and given false promises of work in the trafficking process (ibid), women who voluntarily migrate and find themselves in the sex industry, can be wrongly categorised as victims of trafficking. Connecting all women who work in the sex industry who are not nationals of the host country as simply 'trafficked' is misleading. Most women do not work under duress but make economic decisions about how to earn money, to support themselves, their immediate and distant family. For example, in China, the majority (90%) of 4,235 women arrested for prostitution worked alone without any connection to organised crime (see Ren 1999, p. 1415).

The exaggerations of the extent of 'trafficking' and 'forced prostitution' in some countries have lead to an unbalanced policy approach to the sex industry as a whole (Weitzer, 2007). For instance, much of current UK policing policy in 2006 on indoor sex markets appears to be shaped by concerns about the 'trafficking' of girls and women for sexual exploitation (see Sanders & Campbell, 2007). This was clear in the wake of "Operation Pentameter" launched in February 2006 and heralded as the first ever national campaign against trafficking for sexual exploitation. The key objectives of Pentameter were to recover victims and reduce harm caused to the individual and the UK; raise national awareness of the issue of trafficking and operationally focus on the organised crime groups. There are concerns that anti-trafficking measures are not appropriately separated from immigration service actions with implications for trafficked and non trafficked migrant women (Taylor, 2006). The UK, until 2007, resisted becoming a signatory to the Council of Europe Convention on action against trafficking in human beings, under which trafficked women are automatically granted residency in the country they have been trafficked into. In the UK there is a slow recognition that the human rights of women who are involved in sex work for whatever reason involves a complex interplay between immigration status, global poverty and the feminisation of labour movement across the world.

## Sex as Work, Labour Rights and Unionisation

The mobilisation and organisation of sex workers, activists, academics and in some countries, policy makers that seek to promote the human, social and citizenship rights of sex workers has gathered support across Europe in the last decade (see Gall, 2006 for a review). 'The Declaration of the Rights of Sex Workers in Europe' was endorsed by 120 sex workers and 80 allies from 30 countries at the European Conference on Sex Work, Human Rights, Labour and Migration 15 - 17 October 2005, Brussels, Belgium (see www.sexworkeurope.org). 'The Declaration of the Rights of Sex Workers' in Europe identifies human, labour and migrant's rights that sex workers should be entitled to under international law. It is a synthesis of all the rights that have been agreed in international treaties and covenants, to uphold for all citizens, together with proposals to ensure the protection of those rights for sex workers. In addition, the Declaration of the Rights of Sex Workers in Europe will highlight current violations of the rights of sex workers in Europe which occur across health and social care, housing, employment, education, administrative law and criminal justice systems; highlight actions required to ensure that the rights of sex workers are respected in Europe'.

The International Union of Sex Workers (www.iusw.org) campaign for 'the decriminalisation of all aspects of sex work involving consenting adults; The right to form and join professional associations or unions; Zero tolerance of coercion, violence, sexual abuse, child labour, rape and racism; Clean and safe places to work'. There are also country specific organisations that campaign for the civil and human rights of sex workers. For example in Australia the Scarlet Alliance organisation 'actively work towards guaranteeing the right of all sex workers to optimum occupational health and safety provisions and to promote conditions where safe sex and general health knowledge can be converted to safe work practices. Furthermore, they challenge any legislation, policy or process which does not so promote the rights of the worker' (www.scarletalliance.org.au). The sex work movement is strongly supported by the increase in unionisation and joint collaboration at a national level between sex providers, establishments and formal representative bodies (Lopes, 2001-2006).

There is evidence across the world that a global sex worker rights movement is gathering momentum. Since 1993 in India, the health project Durbar (www.durbar.org) has supported 65,000 sex workers and campaigned for sex work to be recognised as labour in the face of stigmatisation, marginalised and religious persecution (Gooptu, 2002). The organisation promotes self-reliance, and alongside health services, provides a savings credit and co-operative system. One of their significant achievements came in 2001 (and subsequent years since) when they held a Global Millennium Meet to protest against anti-prostitution laws.

Prostitution has been a contentious issue within the international framework, but the United Nations formally agreed that if commercial sexual relations are consensual then prostitution should not be condemned as a human wrong but as a human right, especially to economic survival and as a plight out of dire poverty (Raymond, 2002). Mathieu (2003, p. 30) describes how there has been a global and especially European development in the politics of prostitution over the last decade with the resurgence of a prostitutes rights movement. Although prostitution activists have previously been criticised for a 'failure in the movement' (Weitzer, 1996), the European movement holds more promise as a political movement that is taken seriously and has the capital to make an impact. For example, organisations like the 'Red Thread' Amsterdam based group were initiated by sex workers and receives funding from the Dutch Ministry of Social Affairs and Employment. TAMPEP (Transnational AIDS/STD Prevention amongst Migrant Prostitutes in Europe) receives European Community funding to provide active intervention with sex workers across Europe and favour peer educators and cultural mediators as distinct methods of communication (see Wallman, 2001).

Multi-agency communication and policy initiatives between government and voluntary organisations offer models and guidelines to help improve the services for women in prostitution. Although in its infancy, the collaboration between projects and cross-cultural research is set to expand to reflect the growing international flavour of the sex trade (O'Neill & Barbaret, 2000). Other forms of collaboration are noted in Europe where laws, although growing increasingly conservative (see Kilvington, Day & Ward 2001), enable prostitution to be offered as a legitimate job. For example, the 'Prostitution Information Centre' in Amsterdam offer a six day training workshop in sex work techniques, fieldtrips to establishments, role plays with actors posing as customers and legal and tax information. Although there are distinct barriers to mobilising women involved in prostitution (see Mathieu, 2003, p. 33), key activists have been at the forefront of collective organisations that aim to establish prostitution as valid work.

There is evidence that a range of political influences have, to greater or lesser extent, forced prostitution politics onto the policy agenda in many countries across Western Europe, Australia and North America. Outshoorn's (2004) edited collection reflects on how the women's movement in several countries have affected policies on prostitution and trafficking of women and children since the 1970's. In addition, countries that have increasingly experienced a conservative attitude towards the sex industry through criminalised control mechanisms have also experienced upset and outrage from communities who campaign against the negative impact of street prostitution in the neighbourhood. For example, Kantola and Squires (2004) demonstrate from verbatim reports of the parliamentary discussions, that in the UK, the dominant discourses related to the fear from local residents who were disgruntled at the street prostitution affecting their quality of life (see Pitcher et al., 2006). Van Brunschot (2003) equally demonstrates the power of the community discourses in Canadian cities where the community voice influenced campaigns to remove street prostitution.

## International Directions in Sex Work Policy

This final section examines the international responses to prostitution, namely relating to trafficking of women, coercion and exploitation. The final section of the chapter will review the international response to prostitution, trafficking and both legal and illegal sex markets. The dominant conservative politics that govern the most powerful states in the world have significant influence over the narratives that dominate prostitution politics and regulatory management systems. This is no where as visible as in the United States where the election of George Bush in 2000 saw the 'global gag rule' implemented through the Global Aids Act (2003). This legislation stated that US government funds could not be allocated to organizations that 'promote or advocate' legalization and the practice of prostitution. Radical sexual politics promoted abstinence, anti-abortion and anti-sex work and refused to view harm reduction work as anything other than supporting prostitution. Busza (2006) sets out how the US government policy, advocating the religious right and the abolitionist feminist perspective, took a moral stance that had significant implications for international projects, support services and health education programmes that received US funding. Busza (2006) documents how a HIV prevention project for sex workers in Cambodia was closed due to lack of funding, only to be replaced by 'forced rescue interventions' to 'save' women who were suspected of being trafficked or coerced. As Busza (2004) identifies amongst Vietnamese women who work in the sex industry in Cambodia, that the relationship between sex work and crossing borders is not simply about forced trafficking and that women involved in the sex industry do not always need 'rescuing'.

The practical implications of conservative moral perspectives that make sweeping generalisations about all sex workers as victims have serious consequences for the health and safety of women. By defining all sex work through trafficking discourses or exploitation, and avoiding any understanding of the diversity in sex work, may harm reduction work. There is evidence prostitution is on international policy agendas. The Platform for Action, adopted by the Fourth World Conference on Women held in Beijing in 1995 and the United Nations Convention against Transnational Organized Crime, 2000, are examples of the international efforts to protect women abused in prostitution and tackle the complexities of organised crime surrounding trafficking of women into prostitution. Yet there are dangers that only one side of the debate is finding its way onto the international agenda. International policy and protocol needs to condemn any systems that support violence, danger and poor working conditions, while at the same time recognising the labour rights and voluntary involvement in sex work by some women across the globe. Policy that understands the diversity in sex work can provide solutions that reduce organised crime, victimisation and exploitation.

We see no uni-directional movement in sex work policy globally and across continents. Some national frameworks are embracing sex work as labour and developing law to enhance the rights of sex workers as labourers yet maintain or strengthen prohibitions re involuntary sex work and exploitation in sex work. The Netherlands, New Zealand and Australia serve as examples here. Others, such as Sweden, are more informed by a discourse of sex work as violence against women and hence have focused on criminalising men who pay for sex and providing support and routes out for sex workers. Such nations tend to conflate sex work and trafficking and have anti-trafficking law and measures to the fore in their approach to all sex work. Other nations still define sex work as immoral and retain laws which criminalise all forms of sex work, with little awareness of the safety implications for women who experience these ideological systems.

## References

Agustin, L. (2005). Migrants in the Mistress's House: Other Voices in the "Trafficking" Debate. *Social Politics, 12*(1), 96-117.

—. (2006). Migrant Sex Work and Trafficking. In R. Campbell & M. O'Neill (Eds.), *Sex Work Now* (pp.116-140). Cullumpton: Willan.

—. (2007). *Sex at the Margins: Migration, Labour Markets and the Rescue Industry*. London: Zed Books.

Bernstein, E. (2001). The meaning of the purchase: Desire, demand and the commerce of sex. *Ethnography, 2*(3), 389-420.

Brents, B., & Hausbeck, K. (2005). Violence and legalized brothel prostitution in Nevada: Examining safety, risk and prostitution policy. *Journal of Interpersonal Violence, 20*(3), 270-295.

Brewis, J., & Linstead, S. (2000c). The worst thing is the screwing' (1): Consumption and the management of identity in sex work. *Gender, Work and Organization, 7*(2), 84-97.

Brooks-Gordon, B. (2005). Clients and commercial sex: Reflections on paying the price: A consultation paper on prostitution. *Criminal Law Review*, 425-443.

Bruinsma, G., & Meershoek, G. (1999). Organized crime and trafficking in women from Eastern Europe in the Netherlands. In P. Williams (Ed.), *Illegal Immigration and Commercial Sex* (pp.105-117). London: Frank Cass.

Busza, J. (2004). Sex work and Migration: The dangers of over simplification. A case study of Vietnamese women in Cambodia. *Health and Human Rights, 7*, 231-49.

—. (2006). Having the rug pulled from under your feet: one project's experience of the US policy reversal on sex work. *Health Policy and Planning, 21*(4), 329-332.

Butcher, K. (2003). Confusion between prostitution and sex trafficking. *The Lancet 361*(June 7), 1983.

Campbell, C. (1991). Prostitution, AIDS, and preventive health behaviour. *Social Science and Medicine, 32*(12), 1367-1378.

Campbell, R. (1998). Invisible Men: Making visible male clients of female prostitutes in Merseyside. In J. Elias, V. Bullough, V. Elias & G. Brewer (Eds.), *Prostitution: On whores* (pp.155-171). Hustlers and Johns, New York: Prometheus Books.

Campbell, R., Coleman, S., & Torkington, P. (1996). *Street Prostitution in inner City Liverpool.* Liverpool: Liverpool Hope University College.

Campbell, R., & Storr, M. (2001). Challenging the Kerb Crawler Rehabilitation Programme. *Feminist Review, 67* (Spring), 94-108.

Chapkis, W. (1997). *Live sex acts: Women performing erotic labour*. New York: Routledge.

Clark, L. (2006). *Provision of support for imprisoned adult female street-based sex workers*. The Griffins Society.

Day, S. (1996). The law and the market. In O. Harris (Ed.), *Inside and outside the law* (pp.75-98). London: Routledge.

Doezema, J. (2000). 'Loose women or lost women': The re-emergence of the myth of white slavery in contemporary discourses of trafficking women. *Gender Studies, 18*(1), 23-50.
Dworkin, A. (1996). Pornography. In S. Jackson & S. Scott (Eds.), *Feminism and Sexuality* (pp.297-99). Edinburgh: Edinburgh University Press.
Edwards, S. (1997). The legal relation of prostitution: A human rights issue. In G. Scambler & A. Scambler (Eds.), *Rethinking Prostitution* (pp.57-82). London: Routledge.
Ekberg, G. (2004). The Swedish law that prohibits the purchase of sexual services: Best practices for prevention of prostitution and trafficking in human beings. *Violence against Women, 10*(10), 1187-1218.
European Parliament (2005) *Study on legalisation on prostitution and the trafficking in women and children.* European Parliament: Brussels.
Gall, G. (2006*). Sex worker union organising: An international study.* London: Palgrave Macmillan.
Goodey, J. (2004). Sex Trafficking in Women from Central and East European countries: promoting a 'victim-centred' and 'woman-centred' approach to criminal justice intervention. *Feminist Review,* 76, 26-47.
Goodyear, M., & Cusick, L. (2007). Protection for Sex Workers. *British Medical Journal,* 334.
Gooptu, N. (2002). Sex workers in Calcutta and the dynamics of collective action: Political activism, community identity and group behaviour. In J. Heyer, F. Stewart, & R. Thorp (Eds.), *Group Behaviour and Development: Is the Market Destroying the Cooperation?* (pp.227-251). Oxford: Oxford University Press.
Gould, A. (2001). The criminalisation of buying sex: The politics of prostitution in Sweden. *Journal of Social Policy*, 30(3), 437-456.
Harrison, M., & Sanders, T. (2006) Vulnerable people and the development of 'regulatory therapy'. In T. Newburn, A. Dearling, & P. Somerville (Eds.), *Supporting safe communities: Housing, crime and communities.* (pp.155-168) London: Chartered Institute of Housing.
Hausbeck, K., & Brents, B. (2000). Inside Nevada's Brothel Industry. In R. Weitzer (Ed.), *Sex for Sale* (pp217-243). London: Routledge.
Home Office, (2006). *Coordinated Prostitution Strategy*. London: HMSO.
Hubbard, P. (1997). Red-light districts and Toleration Zones: Geographies of female street prostitution in England and Wales. *Area, 29*(2), 129-140.
Jeffrey, L. (2004). Prostitution as public nuisance: Prostitution policy in Canada. In J. Outshoorn (Ed.), *The politics of prostitution* (pp.83-102). Cambridge: Cambridge University Press.

Jones, H., & Sager, T. (2001). Crime and disorder act 1998: Prostitution and the anti social behaviour order. *Criminal Law Review,* Nov: 873-885.

Kantola, J., & Squires, J. (2004). Discourses surrounding prostitution policies in the UK. *European Journal of Women's Studies, 11*(1), 77-101.

Kelly, L., & Regan, L. (2000). Stopping Traffic: Exploring the extent of, and responses to, trafficking in women for sexual exploitation in the UK. London, *Home Office Policing and Reducing Crime Unit*. Police Research Series Paper 125.

Kershl, A. V. (2004). The dislocation process of the illegal street prostitution scene in cologne: Results of the scientific evaluation of the pilot project, Presented at *Drugs and Mobility in Europe AMOC Conference*, Prague, 3rd-5th June.

Kesler, K. (2002). Is a feminist stance in support of prostitution possible? An exploration of current trends. *Sexualities, 5* (2), 219-235.

Kilvington, J., Day, S., & Ward, H. (2001). Prostitution policy in Europe: A time for change? *Feminist Review, 67* (Spring), 78-93.

Kulick, D. (2003). Sex in the New Europe. *Anthropological Theory, 3*(2), 199-218.

—. (2004). Sex in the new Europe: The criminalization of clients and Swedish fear of prostitution. In S. Day & H. Ward (Eds.), *Sex Work, Mobility and Health in Europe* (pp.215-240). London: Kegan Paul.

—. (2005). Four Hundred Thousand Swedish Perverts. GLQ: A *Journal of Lesbian and Gay Studies, 11*(2), 205-235.

Laskowski, S. (2002). The new German prostitution act - an important step to a more rational view of prostitution as an ordinary profession in accordance with European community law. *The International Journal of Comparative Labour Law and Industrial Relations 18*(4), 479-491.

Lopes, A. (2001). Sex Workers of the World Unite. *Feminist Review, 67*, 151-153.

—. (2006). Sex Workers and the Labour Movement in the UK. In R. Campbell & M. O'Neill (Eds.), *Sex Work Now* (pp.263-290). Cullompton: Willan.

Lowman, J. (2000). Violence and the outlaw status of (street) prostitution in Canada. *Violence Against Women, 6*(9), 987-1011.

Mathieu, L. (2003). The emergence and uncertain outcomes of prostitutes' social movements. *The European Journal of Women's Studies, 10*(1), 29-50.

May, T., Harocopos, A., & Hough, M. (2000). For Love or Money: Pimps and the management of sex work. London, *Home Office Policing and Reducing Crime Unit*. Police Research Series Paper 134.

McDonald, I. (2004). Criminalising 'Punters': Evaluating the Swedish position on prostitution. *Journal of Social Welfare and Family Law, 26*(2), 195-210.

McNaughton, C., & Sanders, T. (2007). 'Housing and Transitional Phases out of 'Disordered' Lives: A case of leaving homelessness and street sex work', *Housing Studies, 22*(6), 885-900.

Monto, M. A., & Garcia, S. (2001). Recidivism among the customers of female street prostitutes: Do intervention programs help? *Western Criminology Review, 3*(2). Retrieved on 25th June 2008 from http://wcr.sonoma.edu/v3n2/monto.html

Munro, V. (2005). A tale of two servitudes: Defining and implementing a domestic response to trafficking of women for prostitution in the UK and Australia. *Social & Legal Studies, 14*(1), 91-114.

O'Neill, M., & Barbaret, R. (2000). Victimisation and the social organisation of prostitution in England and Spain. In R. Weitzer (Ed.), *Sex for Sale* (pp.123-137). London: Routledge.

Ostergren, P. (2004). Sex workers critique of Swedish prostitution policy. March 2004. Retrieved on 25th June 2008 from http://www.petraostergren.com/content/view/44/38/

Outshoorn, J., (Ed.). (2004). *The politics of prostitution: Women's movements, democratic states, and the globalisation of sex commerce.* Cambridge: Cambridge University Press.

—. (2005). The political debates on prostitution and trafficking of women. *Social Politics,* (Spring), 141-155.

Pateman, C. (1988). *The sexual contract.* Oxford: Blackwells.

Peach, L. J. (2005). 'Sex slaves' or 'sex workers'? Cross- cultural and comparative religious perspectives on sexuality, subjectivity and moral identity in anti-sex trafficking discourse. *Culture and Religion, 6*(1), 107-134.

Phoenix, J. (2007). Regulating prostitution: Different problems different solutions, same old story. *Community Safety Journal 6*(1), 7-10.

Phoenix, J., & Oerton, S. (2005). *Illicit and Illegal: Sex, regulation and social control.* Cullompton: Willan.

Phongpaichit, P. (1999). Trafficking in Thailand. In P. Williams (Ed.), *Illegal Immigration and Commercial Sex* (pp.73-103). London: Frank Cass:

Pitcher, J., Campbell, R., Hubbard, P., O'Neill, M., & Scoular, J. (2006). *Living and working in areas of street sex work: From conflict to coexistence*. Abingdon: The Policy Press.
Raymond, J. (2002). The UN Trafficking Protocol. *Women's Studies International Forum, 25*(5), 491-502.
—. (1999). Prostitution as violence against women. *Women's International Forum, 21*(1), 1-9.
Ren, X. (1999). Prostitution and Economic Modernization in China. *Violence Against Women, 5*(12), 1411-1436.
Sagar, T. (2007). Tackling on-street sex work: Anti social behaviour orders, sex workers and inclusive inter-agency initiatives. *Criminology and Criminal Justice,* 7(2), 153-168.
Sanders, T. (2004). The risks of street prostitution: Punters, police and protesters. *Urban Studies, 41*(8), 1703-1717.
—. (2005). *Sex work: A risky business*. Cullompton: Willan.
—. (2007). No room for a regulated market? The implications of the co-ordinated prostitution strategy for indoor sex industries. *Community Safety Journal, 6*(1), 34-44.
—. (2008). *Paying for pleasure: Men who buy sex*. Cullompton, Devon: Willan.
Sanders, T., & Campbell, R. (2007). Designing out violence, building in respect: Violence, safety and sex work policy. *British Journal of Sociology, 58*(1), 1-18.
Schloenhardt, A. (1999). Organised crime and the business of migrant trafficking. *Crime, Law and Social Change, 32*(2), 203-233.
Schumacher, J. (2004). *Policing the zone for street walking in Utrecht*, presentation for Liverpool City Council, John Moores University, February, Avril Robarts Building, Liverpool.
Scoular, J., Pitcher, J., Campbell, R., Hubbard, P., & O'Neill, M. (2007). What's anti-social about sex work? The changing representation of prostitution's incivility. *Community Safety Journal, 6*(1), 11-17.
Scoular, J., & O'Neill, M. (2007). Regulating prostitution: Social inclusion, responsibilization and the politics of prostitution reform. *British Journal of Criminology, 47*(3), 764-778.
Self, H. (2003). *Prostitution, women and misuse of the law: The fallen daughters of eve*. London: Frank Cass.
Shannon, S. (1999). Prostitution and the mafia: The involvement of organized crime in the global sex trade. In P. Williams (Eds.), *Illegal Immigration and Commercial Sex* (pp.119-144). London: Frank Cass.

Soothill, K., & Sanders, T. (2004). Calling the Tune? Some observations on Paying the Price: A consultation paper on prostitution. *Journal of Forensic Psychiatry and Psychology, 15*(4), 642-659.

Sullivan, M., & Jefferys, S. (2002). Legalization. The Australian Experience. *Violence Against Women, 8*(9), 1140-1148.

Svanstrom, Y. (2004). Criminalising the John - a Swedish gender model? In J. Outshoorn (Ed.), *The Politics of Prostitution* (pp.225-244). Cambridge: Cambridge University Press.

Taylor, D. (2006, June 22). Sex workers are a soft target in the asylum figures battle. *Guardian*, London. Retrieved on 24th May 2008 from http://www.guardian.co.uk/commentisfree/2006/jun/22/comment.immigrationandpublicservices

Van Brunschot, E. G. (2003). Community policing and John schools. *Canadian Review of Sociology and Anthropology, 40*, 215-232.

Van Doorninck, M., & Campbell. R. (2006). 'Zoning' street sex work: The way forward? In R. Campbell & M. O'Neill (Eds.), *Sex Work Now* (pp 62-91). Cullumpton: Willan.

Wallman, S. (2001). Global threats, local options, personal risk: Dimensions of migrant sex work in Europe. *Health, Risk & Society, 3*(1), 75-88.

Weitzer, R. (1996). Prostitutes' rights in the United States: The failure of a movement. *Sociological Quarterly, 32*(1), 23-41.

—. (2007). The social construction of sex trafficking: Ideology and institutionalization of a moral crusade. *Politics & Society, 35*(3), 447-475.

West, J. (2000). Prostitution: Collectives and the politics of regulation. *Gender, Work and Organisation, 7*(2), 106-118.

Williams, P. (Ed.). (1999). *Illegal Immigration and Commercial Sex.* London: Frank Cass.

# PART II.

# CRIMINOLOGICAL THEORY AND RESEARCH

# CHAPTER SIX

# THE CRIMINAL SPIN: TOWARDS AN ALTERNATIVE CRIMINOLOGICAL THEORY

NATTI RONEL

## Abstract

The theory of the criminal spin offers a new understanding of criminal and deviant behaviors based on a phenomenological inquiry. The theory describes and interprets the criminal spin as a common characteristic of different criminal and related behaviors. It also provides an interpretive description of the states of consciousness that accompany diverse behaviors considered as criminal, regardless of their causes. Criminal spins are states in which individuals behave more extremely or in greater frequency than they did initially, and sometimes contrary to their wishes, norms, or decisions. Individuals in a criminal spin may rapidly or gradually lose control over their behavior, emotions, or cognition, while sensing both the ability and an existential need to commit offenses. The criminal spin is manifested in acute or chronic phases and is found in individuals, groups, communities, and cultures. When a spin is recognized, it is possible to identify individual "gateways" and to construct the intervention accordingly. In any direction of intervention, its perceived power must be greater than that of the spin.

## Introduction

What is the nature of deviant and criminal behavior? Early and modern criminologists have provided a wide variety of theories that attempt to answer this and related questions (Goode, 2002; Hagan, 1988; Shoam, Adad, & Rahav, 2004). As might be expected, the different theories are based on diverse, sometimes contradictory assumptions (Young, 1981). Most theories are at least partially confirmed by research, although the same findings may be claimed to support different or even opposing theories. Some theories have good explanatory and even predictive ability for some phenomena, while others may fit other cases and circumstances. For example, in his observation of street gangs, Klein (1998) concluded that three different theories of delinquency could account for three different aspects of the observed phenomenon. Against this background, there seems to be a need for a new perspective for understanding criminal phenomena that transcends these contradictions and theoretical incongruities.

The theory of the "criminal spin," which describes the evolution of diverse, though not all, manifestations of criminality, attempts to address this need. The theory offers an alternative perspective on criminality that may be used in conjunction with other theories. A basic premise of this thesis is that criminality is subjective by nature, and therefore, any effort to study criminality and its different manifestations as objective entities will inevitably lead to inconsistency. This subjectivity refers to the culture and society that define behaviors and situations as criminal, and as well the individuals involved, both offenders and their victims. Accordingly, the perspective presented here is based on this subjective nature, and an attempt to represent the perspective of the offending person "from within."

Thus far the field of criminology has offered several insights into the subjective nature of criminality, several of which support the author's view. For example, Matza (1969) describes the process of becoming a criminal as a "criminal drift," a term that can be linked to the criminal spin. Additionally, Matza emphasizes the holistic nature of the criminal phenomenon while viewing it from within, a perspective also followed here. The present phenomenological inquiry of the criminal consciousness is also consistent with Denzin's analysis of emotions, violence, and addictive behaviors (1984; 1987), as well as the existential account of the offender's experience of inner emptiness (Shoham & Addad, 2004). Timor's (2001) innovative description of the narrative of Balagan – the lack of a solid behavioral or personality center among offenders – follows a path parallel to the present one. Finally, Ben David (2000) introduces the concept of "victim's victimology," stressing the subjective nature of victimology, while the criminal spin is a "criminal's criminology," which stresses the subjective nature of criminology.

The theory of the criminal spin describes a common characteristic of different criminal and other behaviors, namely, the behavioral spin. It also provides an interpretive description of the states of consciousness that accompany diverse behaviors that are considered to be criminal, regardless of their cause. This inquiry and the resulting description of the criminal spin may enable us to understand criminal processes of individuals, groups, or societies and to analyze which interventions are required in different cases. It is important to note that this description is phenomenological, focusing on the process rather than on its etiology and causality.

Most criminological models, such as the general theory of deviance (Gottfredson & Hirschi, 1990) or the study of the criminal career (Farrington, 1995), seek common factors within a wide range of criminal activities. The notion of the criminal spin follows a parallel line. It describes and interprets the criminal spin as a common feature in the outbreak of some forms of acute criminality and in the development of chronic delinquency at the individual, group, community, and cultural level. It is argued that, it is possible to evaluate the existence and strength of the criminal spin within these levels. Thus the theory is intended to provide a conceptual framework that characterizes criminal phenomena and to indicate relevant interventions at each level or stage.

## The Varieties of the Criminal Spin

It is relatively easy to recall situations in which a person decided upon a behavior that led to another one, triggering a process or recurrence to the point of reduced self-control, undesired consequences, or some degree of crisis. Almost everyone has experienced this process many times. The reduced self-control may be temporary and does not necessarily indicate weak self-control as a fixed trait.

A common example is eating: one chooses a certain diet, then "just tastes" a "forbidden" food, and subsequently eats more and more, despite the undesired consequences, sensing a loss of self-control. Another typical example is of the expression of anger – a minor aversive behavior may develop into a more serious one, reaching a peak of personal aggression, despite an initial peaceful intention. The same thing may happen in any life domain: one begins a behavior that leads to more of the same with a reduced sense of control, regardless of the initial intention and planning and despite the displeasing consequences. Human relationships are full of similar experiences: intimate partners who fight recurrently regardless of their strong emotional bond, to the point of mutual bitterness and alienation, or parents who, in the name of love and caring, push their growing children away with insistent yet fruitless attempts to control their behaviors are just two examples.

This chain of behaviors is accompanied by chains of emotion and cognition, as well. At these moments, or even seconds, our emotions and thinking develop in the same line, supporting and responding to our behavioral spin. An extreme manifestation of this process is known as "the addiction disease," a metaphorical term that represents the tendency of addicted people to exacerbate their addictive behavior after its initial appearance, and to experience a general deterioration of their lives (Kurtz, 1982; Ronel & Humphreys, 1999-2000). Still another extreme manifestation of the same process, which is found among male batterers, is known as "the violent circle", where attitudes, emotions, and behaviors are interwoven into recurrent outbursts of domestic violence (Barnett Miller-Perrin & Perrin, 1997; Denzin, 1984; Ronel & Tim, 2003). A similar process underlies the criminal spin.

The criminal spin is a process where there is an aggravation – sudden, rapid, or gradual – of behaviors considered as deviant or criminal, along with a marked diminishment of the sense of personal control. An initial behavior, be it deviant or normative on its own, accompanied by relevant cognition and emotions, leads to another behavior, more distinctively deviant or criminal, and is then repeated to the point of an inevitable crisis or even a criminal career. This process operates as though it is beyond one's control. The aggravation seems to get out of control and assume its own "life cycle". Rarely does this cycle subside by itself. Usually it either ends with a peak and crisis, or it leads into a continuation of criminality; it may seem to possess its own power of self-preservation. The individual, trapped in the process, is directed by the chain of behaviors, cognitions, desires, and emotions, which work together to increase the process itself, up to a "spinning" experience – the criminal spin.

Although not every form of criminality is the result of a criminal spin, it is possible to identify traces of spin within most known manifestations of criminality, deviance, and related behaviors. It is possible to detect a spin in most expressive offenses, such as sexual abuse or domestic violence. In instrumental, planned crimes, it is also possible to detect a cognitive criminal spin that leads to the crime. In *Crime and Punishment,* Dostoevsky (1961) demonstrates artistic insight in his description of the cognitive, instrumental spin of *Raskolnikov*, the protagonist, who was trapped in mistaken, spinning ideas about the privileges of the elite. Eventually this spin ended with a cold-blooded planned murder while robbing an old lady. In such an instrumental spin, the individual may experience a sense of self-control, but external analysis may detect a spin of cognitions, emotions, and behaviors that indicates developing or continuous criminality.

The criminal spin is usually a chain of behaviors, but it may also represent a similar chain of avoidance. For example, a father may neglect the needs of his child in a spiraling, spinning manner, or an employee may criminally neglect her duties at work. In any case, such a "passive" manifestation of the spin operates in a similar manner to the more "active" form.

The criminal spin operates in different phases and levels. First, we can detect a spin at the individual level, within the person who is trapped in a criminal spin. Many individuals experience such a spin once or more during their lives. Even "holy" individuals may experience such a spin. For example, in his well-known "Confessions," St. Augustine (2004) describes how as an adolescent he drifted, spun, and participated in theft, despite his moral inclination. Such cases represent a one-time or acute individual spin, where a single spin develops, progresses to a peak or crisis, and ends. Usually, spins of this type within an individual's life are weakly connected and each of them represents a discrete event.

However, when recurrent individual spins become associated in an ongoing process, a chronic individual spin is indicated. In this phase, there is a developmental process of certain criminal behaviors (such as battering) or a wide range of criminal activities and a criminal lifestyle. Chronic individual spins correspond to the development of an individual criminal career, as well as the description of career criminals (Blumstein, Cohen, & Farrington, 1988; DeLisi, 2005). While an acute individual spin is rather common, especially in cases of relatively minor criminality or deviance, the chronic spin is less common and typifies the criminal population.

During a criminal spin process, individuals may join and participate in a criminal or deviant group activity, thus creating a group criminal spin. A group spin may be acute or chronic, parallel to the phases of the individual level. When several individuals join once only to perform a deviant or criminal group behavior that has the characteristic of a spin, it is an acute group spin. For example, a group of non-criminal adolescents may spin together in one spree of vandalism. However, if the members of a group recurrently join in deviant activities, so that they may be considered, for instance, a criminal gang, then it is a chronic group spin phase. Acute or chronic, a group criminal spin, like the individual one, also includes cases of neglect and avoidance of necessary behaviors.

The criminal spin of a small group of participants (such as a gang) represents the ability of the criminal spin to "infect" others, as described by different criminological theories, such as differential association (Sutherland & Cressey, 1974). The process of neighborhood deterioration (Schuerman & Kobrin, 1986) demonstrates the infectious ability of the spin beyond the small group level and the existence of a community criminal spin. To some extent, the influential and controversial "broken windows" theory (Harcourt & Ludwig, 2006) describes this process, as well.

However, the spin may go further. History has shown us time and again how relatively easy it is for a large number of people to criminally spin together in a cultural spin, sometimes almost whole-community spinning. Racism, racial prejudice, ethnic discrimination and oppression, religious repression, and extreme nationalism are just a few examples. In such cases, a whole culture, or sometimes even a whole society spins criminally, defining itself by hate, negation, and aversive activities. Examples include Germany in the 1930s or the period of African slavery in the Americas. A cultural or societal spin is usually detected in a developing chronic phase. Like any other criminal spin, it has its own "life cycle" and self-preserving power and may include passive forms of neglect, such as a spin into neglect of minority rights.

Cultures, communities, and small groups are constructed by individuals who join together. In the same manner, a criminal spin of communities, cultures, neighborhoods, or groups always consists of individual criminal spins. The individual level provides the foundation for other levels. Within the individual level of the criminal spin, the acute phase is the most basic one, which may or may not develop into a chronic spin. Hence, an understanding of the acute individual criminal spin provides the basis for understanding any other form of the spin.

### *The Individual in an Acute Criminal Spin*

Under normal circumstances, most individuals do not engage in criminal behavior. However, as already mentioned, most individuals can identify a few occurrences (at least minor ones) of deviant or criminal spin in their lifetime. The understanding of these events may support the description of the criminal spin. Looking deeper into these incidents, one may identify "a moment of choice," when the behavior was chosen. The decision may be a product of personal, external, or situational influences. During this moment of decision, one is able to choose from different alternatives. One of these alternatives, however, has the power to trigger the spin. Once the spin is in motion, the primary behavior is strongly linked to a second and following one, which continue in a direction that may contradict the initial decision, to the point of behavior that this individual would never have chosen intentionally. Although the same process may occur in the case of a wide range of behaviors, the deviant or criminal spin has specific phenomenological characteristics.

A common feature that accompanies various criminal activities is the self-interest of the person involved (Elkind, 1967; Gibbs, 1991). The initial motivation and goals, the means to achieve them, the choice of behaviors, and the related emotions and cognition all represent the self-interest, egoism, or self-centeredness of the performing individuals (Ronel, 2000a). Although it is natural for human beings to demonstrate self-interest, during criminal activities the self-interest or self-centeredness reaches an extreme. Increased self-centeredness is common during the first choice of the criminal spin. From several alternatives, the individual chooses the one that meets his or her own desires, wishes, or sense of strength and safety. However, in a vicious circle, this alternative usually increases one's sense of self-centeredness (Denzin, 1984). In other words, while the criminal spin develops out of an initial self-centered decision, there is a corresponding development of this self-centeredness, manifested in the feelings and thinking of the individual. This is a typical characteristic of the criminal spin. For example, an adolescent boy enters a bookstore and examines various books. Although not intending to buy, he focuses on a particular book, absorbed in a growing self-centered wish to take it. When he eventually slips the book into his coat, this adolescent begins a set of behaviors that will end when he walks safely outside the store with the desired stolen book. Since it is an acute criminal spin, this behavior is not typical for this youngster and may contrast his everyday norms. However, during his criminal spin, this young person focuses increasingly on his self-interest – at first, the wish to have the book or to show his ability and courage, and afterwards, how to survive it safely, to succeed, and so forth. Although he may feel in control of himself, this process is guided by his self-centeredness. Correspondingly, the youngster may feel intense fear, tension, excitement, or even some pride – all feelings that represent a growing self-centeredness.

The criminal spin is typically accompanied by a narrowing of perceptions and feelings, leaving only those directed at oneself – personal needs, threats, desires, and aims. As a result, the individual's sense of empathy for others declines as the criminal spin develops. For example, a man who argues with his wife and loses his empathy for her while falling into a growing self-centeredness spins into a violent outburst that could not have taken place previously (Ronel & Tim, 2003). The lack of empathy enables a process of neutralization (Agnew, 1994; Sykes & Matza, 1957) that supports the criminal spin by self-justification of the spin behaviors.

Another major attribute of the criminal spin is that the self-centered person may increasingly feel either a survival need or a growing power to act according to his or her wishes. During the spin, the consciousness is increasingly occupied with a sense of either "I must" or "I can," and sometimes both. The self of the individual in spin is narrowly directed towards expected outcomes – to regain safety or achieve satisfaction – while minimizing or ignoring other possible consequences. In the above example of the adolescent who stole a book, after the initial desire to have it, he may have experienced an "I can" feeling that overpowered his moral restraint or fear of being caught. Similarly, drivers who run red lights may feel a sense of "I can," which represents and supports their criminal spin. "I can" means that, at least momentarily, they accept this behavior and give themselves permission to act, while sensing an increasing ability to continue. Simultaneously, they reject any message of "no" and external limitations. For these people, the state of "I can" means the ability to continue the self-centered activities regardless of external or internal boundaries. This may lead to a behavioral spin and may, in turn, be further encouraged during the spin. This is demonstrated by Gottfredson et al.'s (2001) finding of elevated juvenile delinquency when there is lack of adult supervision. There are several possible explanations for this, including the relative ease of committing an offence in the absence of supervision, or the tendency of those prone to delinquency to reject adult care. In both these cases, the "I can" spin may be present.

Another common attitude preceding or during a spin is that of the need to survive. This is exemplified by a man who feels existentially threatened by his partner (Ferraro, 1988), where the threat presents itself in his consciousness as a need for appropriate action in order to survive – "I must." In this example, the man seeks existential safety but ignores other predictable outcomes, such as his violent outburst and the ensuing price he will have to pay. When it occurs, the consciousness is trapped, sensing an existential call for behavior – usually fight or flight. Since this is perceived as an existential need, which may be intrinsic as well as situational, it may overpower the individual's moral values, norms, or intention. A prominent example is that of Zidane, the French soccer player who responded violently to a provocation by an Italian player during the final match of the 2006 World Cup. As he explained later, the provocation was such a threat that he felt an insurmountable urge to respond. Consequently, he spun violently, despite the exceptional circumstances and the eyes of millions of spectators worldwide.

During a criminal spin, the heightened self-centeredness increases and the "I can" or "I must" consciousness shapes one's perception of reality. The situation becomes one-dimensional in accordance with the content of the spin controlling the individual's behavior. Although such people may be at least partially aware of the situation, this awareness is also influenced by the distorted, one-dimensional consideration. Usually, the distorted perception overcomes the sense of personal responsibility and shifts the burden to others or to situational causes, as described in the neutralization theory (Minor, 1984). For example, a mother may get angry with her child and fall into a violent spin, while blaming the child for both her anger and the subsequent violence. In her experience, at least during the spin, this justifies her aggressive behavior. Sometimes such distortion and denial of responsibility are experienced as temporary powerlessness – such individuals feel they can not control events. For instance, such an angry mother may feel unable to control her behavior, while at the same time, paradoxically; she blames the child for not doing so.

An acute criminal spin is a distinct event in an individual's life. When this event is repeated and there is a developmental series of related incident, it is no longer an acute instance, and becomes a chronic criminal spin.

### *A Chronic Individual Criminal Spin*

In its chronic phase, the criminal spin represents a chronic recurrence of criminal acts and sometimes the development of a criminal career (Ulmer & Spencer, 1999). The chronic spin has two aspects. The first is the individual's progression from a non-criminal to a criminal life. The second is the tendency of individuals in a chronic spin to repeatedly fall into acute spins.

The process of deterioration to deviance, abusive behavior, and crime may begin at any age. There are reports of individuals whose violence was present and predictable even when they were young children (Loeber & Hay, 1997). In any case, people in chronic criminal spins first experienced an acute criminal spin, which they then repeated, in the same or different forms (for example, they may begin with drinking binges and continue with violent spins). In a study of 380 married men who reported some violence in their marriage, Feld and Straus (1989) found that minor assaults tend to encourage major assaults. While many reasons and associated factors may be involved, there is a typical pattern of repetition of the initial manifestation of criminal or deviant behavior, which appears to have a life of its own, a force of self-preservation. The field of developmental criminology has focused extensively on this aspect of the chronic criminal spin (Farabee, Joshi, & Anglin, 2001; Nagin, Farrington, & Moffitt, 1995), although the term itself is innovative.

Analysis of the life stories of different offenders enables us to understand the development of the chronic spin as a manifestation of a central narrative that increasingly shapes the individual consciousness. The existence of such a narrative typifies the chronic spin, as it links separate spins into a distinct pattern of behavior. For example, Timor (2001), who studied the life stories of convicted prisoners, identified a general narrative in their lives, namely, a growing chaos and lack of personality center that recurrently resulted in criminal activities. Topalli's (2005) study of hardcore street criminals reveals a chronic criminal narrative typified by the street ethic of violence, hedonism, opportunism, and self-sufficiency. This narrative is central to the people involved; any retreat from it, such as contact with the police, is followed by a process that neutralizes this deviation from the street code. In another example, Yassour-Borochowitz's (2003) phenomenological study of male batterers shows how their violence developed to meet a central narrative in each man's life. The development of each personal narrative is associated with the deterioration into a chronic violent criminal spin. Such narratives can be found accompanying every chronic criminal spin. A break in such a narrative denotes recovery (Maruna, 1997), that is, the end of the criminal spin.

The second aspect of the chronic criminal spin is the existence of recurrent and aggravating acute criminal or deviant spins during the life of the offender. These acute spins may be specific to certain situations, as in the case of a male batterer who is non-violent outside the home, but has recurrent domestic outbursts. However, such spins may also be broad, spanning different aspects of the individual's life, as in the case of a recidivist property offender who also behaves violently with others, including his partner. More often than not, the person in the chronic criminal spin is expected to display acute criminal spins in most situations. The outburst of the different acute spins is so frequent that they become the expected norm for that individual.

Since the chronic criminal spin is comprised of numerous acute ones, its phenomenology is a development of the acute spin described earlier. As such, it manifests similar attributes, although they cover a larger portion of the individual's life. The first such trait is self-centeredness, which becomes a central motivation in many moments of the chronic phase, sometimes becoming a major theme in the person's worldview. People in a chronic spin are increasingly occupied with internal issues of desire, fantasy, fears, power, self-denial, and the like. The "I can" and "I must" consciousness become the primary narrative of the self. Motivation develops accordingly and the self is caught in an endless existential struggle with its surroundings, while facing a continuous threat and a growing need to get as much gratification as possible.

The phenomenology of the chronic criminal spin leads to diminished ability to empathize, because of the emphasis on self-occupation. With little empathy and a dominant self-interest, criminal behavior becomes a commonplace option. Life becomes one-dimensional, controlled by the self-centered consciousness and situational factors that frequently trigger acute spins. An expected outcome is a sense of powerlessness, in which the person feels trapped in a chronic process and forced to perform a continuous series of behaviors with limited ability to break out of the pattern. The sense of powerlessness is usually translated into lack of accountability and denial of responsibility. In the absence of a crisis or external intervention, continued criminal behavior is perceived as the only option. The chronic spin preserves itself – it remains in motion. *Junebug*, a persistent violent offender on the St. Louis street scene, summarizes this succinctly: "I don't think that I will ever stop doing these robberies until the day that somebody kills me. There is nothing in the world that would stop me from doing it" (Topalli, 2005, p. 806).

### *The Criminal Spin of Groups*

Since its early days, the field of criminology has paid special attention to the fact that criminal behavior is socially transmitted among individuals (e.g. Sutherland & Cressey, 1974). Researchers often focus on individuals who develop criminal behaviors within groups or become socialized into the criminal sub-culture. In comparison, the concept of a group criminal spin focuses on the activity of the group as a whole. A group of individuals may perform an activity in a criminal spin, analogous to the individual level. In these cases, an initial group behavior may start a spin and deteriorate in a criminal direction, reaching far beyond the early intention of its members. A tragically common example is group rape. Each member of the group plays an important role – even the passive members support the criminal spin by their silent participation in the activities. In group rape, according to Porter and Alison (2006):

> The presence of another might also provide an individual with ideas that s/he would not have alone, or provide the opportunity for committing acts that an individual may not think possible alone. … The presence of a majority can both help to legitimize acts to convince others to follow and also provide peer pressure upon the minority to conform (p. 306).

Similar to the individual spin, the criminal group spin operates in two phases: acute and chronic. The most common incident is when non-delinquent individuals join in a one-time criminal activity. Coming together in this acute group spin, each of the group members may exhibit an acute individual spin.

Another case is when some members of such a group go into a chronic spin while the group as a whole is still in an acute spin. In this case, one or more delinquents and non-delinquents engage in a criminal spin, such as, for example, a rape performed by a group of adolescents only one of whom has been involved in rape previously. On their own, the others would never initiate a rape. However, encountering an unexpected opportunity together, they co-spin, reinforcing and neutralizing each other, ending with a violent rape. The distinct nature of this case is that individuals who would not choose criminal behavior on their own either influence one another or are influenced by another member of the group to perform a criminal group behavior. In this acute group criminal spin, they each go through an individual criminal spin – for some it may be an acute spin while for those more experienced it may be a chronic one. Whichever the case, the group becomes a whole that is more than the sum of its parts, that is, more criminal as a whole than its individual participants are. Since the group is in a criminal spin, its members engage in a criminal behavior that it is far beyond the norm for several of them.

In another type of case, most or all members of a group are in a chronic criminal spin. A group of delinquents may cooperate in joint criminal activity. However, as a group, they might spin together in an unplanned direction. For example, based on former studies, Porter and Alison (2006) claim that about one-fifth of the cases of group rape are unplanned and occur while performing another criminal activity, such as robbery. In such cases, although the group may consist of recidivist offenders, they all enter into an acute criminal group spin that increases the extent and magnitude of their criminal activity. Again, the criminality of the group as a whole exceeds that of some of its members.

Yet another type of group spin occurs when a group of individuals, each in an individual chronic spin, habitually joins to perform criminal activities. In this case, the group activity is influenced by, but also reinforces and increases, each member's criminal involvement. The group frequently spins together as a whole, thus intensifying the chronic spin of each participant. An obvious example of the above is the street gang (Huff, 1998; Klein, 1998). A comparative study of the delinquency of youth gang members and non-gang youth who associate with delinquent friends revealed that gang membership intensifies delinquent behavior beyond the expected effect of having delinquent friends (Battin-Pearson et al., 1998; Battin et al., 1998). A longitudinal study of 1203 young adolescents in Norway verified these results and showed that during active gang periods, the criminal activity of the members increased (Bendixen, Endresen, & Olweus, 2006). Gatti et al (2005) obtained similar results, and concluded that "the higher delinquency rates among gang members are largely linked to the experience of the gang itself" (p. 1188). This is consistent with the theory of the group criminal spin. When a group is in a chronic spin, each of its members is in a chronic spin as well, since a primary narrative of the group is the criminal activity.

One may hypothesize that the phenomenology and common consciousness of the group in a chronic spin, as manifested in its values, norms, language, motivation, and expectations, corresponds with that of an individual in a chronic spin, that is, they represent the self-centered consciousness; however this requires further examination.

### *The Criminal Spin of Community and Culture*

The prevalence of individual and group spins does not increase in a social vacuum, but develops in dynamic relations with its surroundings. Such an increase may appear in waves of amplified criminality during specific periods (Kilias, 2006). It may also appear in particular areas. According to various studies and theories (Bursnik, 1988; Hagan, 1988), high crime rates in a given community are connected to "social disorganization." Schuerman and Kobrin (1986) assert that at first, the neighborhood goes through ecological changes to a point that the social and cultural characters of that neighborhood are transformed. Then, the increase in criminality exceeds that of other changes within the community. The social interactions inside that local community seem to be infected with criminal behavior (Fagan, Wilkinson, & Davies, 2007). When the criminal spin of individuals or groups within a community exceeds an upper limit, the entire community enters into a criminal spin. In that case, delinquency and behaviors considered as deviant elsewhere are established as norms. The legitimization and normalization of criminal or behaviors that are considered deviant elsewhere is a marked sign of the existence of a criminal spin of a local community.

The criminal spin of a community indicates a developmental process that requires "a critical mass"; hence it appears only in the chronic phase. In such a case, even non-deviant members of the community may allow themselves to behave according to the new norms. For example, within the limits of such a neighborhood, otherwise law-abiding local residents sometimes disregard traffic laws that they obey elsewhere. Since criminal behavior is legitimized in the local community, a growing number of local individuals and groups adopt these norms, turning to criminality and experiencing a criminal spin. As more members of the community discover that they can transgress the law, and as their transgressions increase, the magnitude of the community spin, as well as its ability to affect other members of the community, grows. An example of this is the acceptance of white-collar crimes within a given community. For instance, in societies or subgroups where baksheesh and bribes are an expected norm, the criminal spin reaches a peak. The more widespread the criminal spin in the given community and the more it reaches "normative" members, the deeper the distress of the community as a whole.

Another case is when an entire society is in a spin that would be considered as criminal in other societies. In these cases, the cultural system of values, norms, language, and social roles may reflect the spin. For example, during Nazi rule of Germany, the culture as a whole was Nazi, as mirrored in the extremely racial value system adopted by individuals who belonged to the mainstream. In this case, the main targets were Jews; anti-Semitic prejudice and harm to Jews became normative, accepted behavior. As the spin increased, even mass killing became "normative." Another example is the prejudice and discrimination against African-Americans that took place in certain areas in the USA. Since it was considered as normative, even individuals who might consider themselves as relatively liberal participated in the cultural racism while ignoring the incongruity. In such cases, the cultural spin has the power to direct the choices taken by individuals in that culture, who consequently may increase their participation in that spin.

A cultural criminal spin of a whole society is typically based on ethnic or religious grounds. When it exists, there is a growing, spinning division of people to "us" and "them," with identification and belonging to any given group bearing profound significance. Fear of "the others," a sense of religious sanctification through a struggle, resentment, hate, or contempt may lead to violence, abuse, and exploitation. The emotional spin rules cognition in a process that creates double standards for one's culture or nation and for "the others." A subsequent rationalization and neutralization process supports the normalization of the abusive behaviors towards "the others," while the same behaviors are not legitimized when turned upon those who belong to "the right" group. Unfortunately, this narrative can be traced through the history of most regions of the world during most periods. The cultural, societal, or religious spin, which is criminal by nature (that is, which leads to violence and abuse while representing cultural self-centeredness), is one of the greatest sources of harm that we face today in the form of wars, terrorism, suppression, and discrimination.

## Conclusions and Implications

The innovative theory of the criminal spin presented here describes a well-known, longstanding, and widespread human tendency to do "more of the same" and to deteriorate. Sometimes it is referred to as "a slippery slope," meaning that after one has set out on a path, an uncontrollable downfall is almost inescapable. Similarly, it may be termed "a broken dam," meaning that when there is a small crack, a growing flow of water is virtually unavoidable, culminating in a flood. This decline or flood begins with an initial choice of the certain "slope," regardless of the risk of slippage or overflow. However, the notion of a criminal spin supplements these descriptive terms, as it is the first theory that describes the phenomenology of the spin in detail, from the level of an individual in a temporary moment of spin to an ongoing spin of a society.

The theory of the criminal spin is by no means an all-inclusive, universal one. Its phenomenology, however, covers a wide variety of distinct phenomena. This phenomenology indicates two complementary motives that may exist separately or simultaneously within an individual criminal consciousness: "I can" and "I must." While the first denotes a perceived ability and opportunity to deviate, the second reflects the perception of an existential threat and the belief that it can be best removed by a deviant act. The more advanced and intense the criminal spin the stronger the effect of these motives on the consciousness. Traces of these motives, in varying intensity, can be detected in most criminal and deviant behaviors, at any level – individual, group, or society. The sources, causes, and development of such motives may be subject to different explanations, based on different perspectives. The phenomenological interpretation, however, links diverse perceptions about the causal sources of criminality, as well as enabling several pragmatic implications.

First, the criminal spin, as presented here, is a detectable and predictable phenomenon – at the individual, group, community, or societal level. Future studies may enable definition of its stages and the relative magnitude of its different components. Second, detection of such a spin indicates the relative intensity and level of intervention required. Usually, external intervention is necessary, since the spin seems to be driven by inertia. In order to induce a behavioral transformation, an immediate, intensive, noticeable intervention that is experienced as stronger than the spin itself is needed. When a spin is in motion, the transformative power of a less distinct intervention is questionable. Third, it is worthwhile and less difficult to disrupt the cycle of the spin life as early as possible, before it reaches its self-preservation stage. Otherwise, the consequences may be inescapable.

In known occurrences of criminal spin, it is possible to identify individual "gateways" of the spin, and to construct the intervention accordingly. The suggestion of Alcoholics Anonymous that its members abstain from alcohol, as well as other pragmatic recommendations that target the declared limitation of alcoholics (Kurtz, 1982) exemplify the usefulness of avoiding the gateways of the spin.

The phenomenology of the criminal spin indicates an enhanced self-centeredness, with a mixture of the major "I can" and "I must" motives. Therefore, efforts for prevention and intervention should target these two motives. These efforts should reduce and prevent the sense of ability to engage in deviant behavior, while responding to the existential needs and threats of individuals that may lead to frustration and deviance. Research in criminology, as well as any other human sciences, generally oscillates between a humanistic-liberal approach and a more conservative one (Etzioni, 1997). While the first emphasizes the rehabilitative benefit of reducing existential needs, the second indicates law enforcement as a means for reducing the "I can" motive. The theory of the criminal spin may serve as the base for an integrative approach to intervention.

The theory of the spin involves a defined notion about determinism vs. free will underlying human nature (Young, 1981). While the theory emphasizes the first choice of individuals to act of free will, it also describes the spin as a diminution of the ability to choose freely, to the point of a sense of determinism (Agnew, 1995). Before an individual enters the spin process, there are several possibilities to choose from; however, while proceeding along the spin route, a person experiences increasingly less freedom to choose and finally acts as though governed by the inertia of the process itself. The individual increasingly abandons the initial ability of free choice, and faces deterministic outcomes. When the process is repeated numerous times in a chronic spin, the whole life experience of the individual becomes deterministic, shallow, and non-rewarding. A sense of existential emptiness may arise (Frankl, 1982; Ronel, 2000b; Shoham & Addad, 2004). In turn, this sense of existential emptiness and the wish to release it drive the individual into "more of the same," setting the deterministic cycle in full motion. At any moment, however, a break in the spin may foster a renewed sense of free will. The deterministic process is a product of choice, and it can be reversed.

The criminal spin is only one behavior pattern, part of a larger general behavioral spin that may be a widespread human tendency. It seems that most behavioral disorders involve a spin. Groups and individuals may display this tendency to get into a spin in any domain of life. Furthermore, any behavioral spin is accompanied by emotional and cognitive ones. Sometimes the behavioral spin precedes corresponding mental and affective processes; at other times the emotional or cognitive spin leads the process. In any case, a spin process suggests a known phenomenological scenario. One may assume that the phenomenological process of the criminal spin resembles that of other behavioral spins. This assumption, as others taken here, warrants further study.

## References

Agnew, R. (1994). The techniques of neutralization and violence. *Criminology, 32*(4), 555-580.

—. (1995). Determinism, indeterminism, and crime: An empirical exploration. *Criminology, 33*(1), 83-109.

Augustine, S. (2004). *Confessions* (Hebrew ed.). Tel Aviv: Miscal.

Barnett, O. W., Miller-Perrin, C. L., & Perrin, R. D. (1997). *Family violence across the lifespan*. Thousand Oaks, CA: Sage.

Battin-Pearson, S. R., Thornberry, T. P., Hawkins, D. J., & Krohn, M. D. (1998). *Gang membership, delinquent peers, and delinquent behavior*: U.S. Department of Justice: Office of Justice Programs.

Battin, S. R., Hill, K. G., Abbott, R. D., Catalano, R. F., & Hawkins, D. J. (1998). The contribution of gang membership to delinquency beyond delinquent friends. *Criminology, 36*(1), 93-115.

Ben-David, S. (2000). Needed: Victim's victimology. In P. C. Friday & G. F. Kirchhoff (Eds.), *Victimology at the transition from the 20th to the 21st century* (pp. 55-72). Monchengladbach: Shaker Verlag & WSVP.

Bendixen, M., Endresen, I. M., & Olweus, D. (2006). Joining and leaving gangs: Selection and facilitation effects on self-reported antisocial behaviour in early adolescence. *European Journal of Criminology, 3*(1), 85-114.

Blumstein, A., Cohen, J., & Farrington, D. P. (1988). Criminal career research: Its value for criminology. *Criminology, 26*(1), 1-35.

Bursnik, R. J. J. (1988). Social disorganization and theories of crime and delinquency: Problems and prospects. *Criminology, 26*(4), 519-551.

DeLisi, M. (2005). *Career criminals in society*. Thousand Oaks, CA: Sage.

Denzin, N. K. (1984). *On understanding emotions*. San Francisco: Jossey-Bass.

—. (1987). *Treating Alcoholism*. Newbury Park, CA: Sage.
Dostoevsky, F. M. (1961). *Crime and Punishment* (Hebrew ed.). Tel Aviv: Hakkibutz Hameuchad.
Elkind, D. (1967). Egocentrism in adolescence. *Child Development, 38*, 1025-1034.
Etzioni, A. (1997). *The New Golden Rule*. London: Profile Books.
Fagan, J., Wilkinson, D. L., & Davies, G. (2007). Social contagion of violence. In D. A. Flannery & V. I. Waldman (Eds.), *The Cambridge handbook of violent behavior* (pp. 688-723). Cambridge: Cambridge University Press.
Farabee, D., Joshi, V., & Anglin, D. M. (2001). Addiction careers and criminal specialization. *Crime & Delinquency, 47*(2), 196-220.
Farrington, D. P. (1995). The development of offending and antisocial behavior from childhood: Key findings from the Cambridge Study in Delinquent Development. *Journal of Child Psychology and Psychiatry, 36*, 929-964.
Ferraro, K. J. (1988). An existential approach to battering. In G. T. Hotaling, D. Finkelhor, J. T. Kirkpatrick & M. A. Straus (Eds.), *Family Abuse and Its Consequences* (pp. 126-138). Newburu Park, CA: Sage.
Frankl, V. (1982). *The unheard cry for meaning* (Hebrew ed.). Tel Aviv: Dvir.
Gatti, U., Tremblay, R. E., Vitaro, F., & McDuff, P. (2005). Youth gangs, delinquency and drug use: A test of the selection, facilitation, and enhancement hypotheses. *Journal of Child Psychology and Psychiatry, 46*(11), 1178-1190.
Gibbs, J. C. (1991). Sociomoral developmental delay and cognitive distortion: Implications for the treatment of antisocial youth. In W. M. Kurtines & J. L. Gewirtz (Eds.), *Handbook of Moral Behavior and Development* (Vol. 3: Application, pp. 95-110). Hillsdale, New Jersey: Earlbaum.
Goode, E. (2002). *Deviant behavior* (Hebrew ed.). Tel Aviv: The Open University of Israel.
Gottfredson, D. C., Gottfredson, G. D., & Weisman, S. A. (2001). The Timing of Delinquent Behavior and Its Implications for After-School Programs. *Criminology and Public Policy, 1*(1), 61-80.
Gottfredson, M. A., & Hirschi, T. (1990). *General theory of crime*. Stanford, CA: Stanford University Press.
Hagan, J. (1988). *Modern criminology*. Singapore: McGraw Hill.
Harcourt, B. E., & Ludwig, J. (2006). Broken windows: New evidence from New York city and a five-city social experiment. *The University of Chicago Law Review, 73*, 271-320.

Huff, R. C. (1998). *Comparing the criminal behavior of youth gangs and at-risk youths*: Research in Brief. U.S. Department of Justice, Office of Justice Programs, National Institute of Justice.
Kilias, M. (2006). The opening and closing of breaches: a theory of crime waves, law creation and crime prevention. *European Journal of Criminology, 3*(1), 11-31.
Klein, M. W. (1998). Street gangs. In M. Tonry (Ed.), *Crime and punishment* (pp. 111-132). Oxford: Oxford University Press.
Kurtz, E. (1982). Why AA works. *Journal of Studies on Alcohol, 43*(1), 38-80.
Loeber, R., & Hay, D. (1997). Key issues in the development of aggression and violence from childhood to early adulthood. *Annual Review of Psychology, 48*, 371-410.
Maruna, S. (1997). *Desistance and development: The psychosocial process of 'Going Straight.'* Paper presented at the British Criminology Conference, Queens University, Belfast.
Matza, D. (1969). *Becoming deviant*. Englewood Cliffs, NJ: Prentice-Hall.
Minor, W. (1984). Neutralization as a Hardening Process: Considerations in the Modeling of Change. *Social Forces, 62*(4), 995-1019.
Nagin, D. S., Farrington, D. P., & Moffitt, T. E. (1995). Life-course trajectories of different types of offenders. *Criminology, 33*(1), 11-138.
Porter, L. E., & Alison, L. J. (2006). Examining group rape: A descriptive analysis of offender and victim behaviour. *European Journal of Criminology, 3*(3), 357-381.
Ronel, N. (2000a). From self-help to professional care: An expansion and an application of the 12-Step Program. *Journal of Applied Behavioral Science, 36*(1), 108-122.
—. (2000b). Perception of addiction as a disease: A metaphoric approach to encourage recovery (Hebrew, English abstract). *Society and Welfare, 20*(1), 83-98.
Ronel, N., & Humphreys, K. (1999-2000). World-views transformations of Narcotics Anonymous members in Israel. *International Journal of Self-Help and Self-Care, 1*(1), 101- 127.
Ronel, N., & Tim, R. (2003). Grace Therapy: Meeting the challenge of group therapy for male batterers. *Clinical Social Work Journal, 31*(1), 63-80.
Schuerman, L., & Kobrin, S. (1986). Community careers in crime. *Crime and Justice, 8* (Communities and Crime), 67-100.
Shoam, S. G., Adad, M., & Rahav, G. (2004). *Criminology* (Hebrew ed.). Tel Aviv: Schocken.

Shoham, S. G., & Addad, M. (2004). *The insatiable gorge* (Hebrew ed.). Tel Aviv: Babel.
Sutherland, E. R., & Cressey, D. R. (1974). *Criminology* (9'th ed.). Philadelphia, PA: J.B. Lippincot.
Sykes, G. M., & Matza, D. (1957). Techniques of neutralization: A theory of delinquency. *American Journal of Sociology, 22*, 664-670.
Timor, U. (2001). Balagan: Delinquency as a result of the lack of a center of norms and consciousness. *International Journal of Offender Therapy and Comparative Criminology, 45*(6), 730-748.
Topalli, V. (2005). When being good is bad: An expansion of neutralization theory. *Criminology, 43*(3), 797-835.
Ulmer, J. T., & Spencer, W. J. (1999). The contributions of an interactionist approach to research and theory on criminal careers. *Theoretical Criminology, 3*(1), 95-124.
Yassour-Borochowitz, D. (2003). *Intimate violence - the emotional world of batterers* (Hebrew ed.). Tel Aviv: Resling.
Young, J. (1981). Thinking seriously about crime: Some models of criminology. In M. Fitzgerald, G. McLennan & J. Pawson (Eds.), *Crime and Society: Readings in history and society* (pp. 248-309). London: Routledge and Kegan Paul.

# CHAPTER SEVEN

# ENTREPRENEURSHIP: A DIVERGENT PATHWAY OUT OF CRIME?

ROBERT SMITH

## Abstract

This chapter illustrates how knowledge of entrepreneurship can be used as a diversionary mechanism to divert and lead offenders out of crime. Indeed, entrepreneurship offers such a divergent pathway but paradoxically entrepreneurship being amoral can be used to achieve both good and bad ends. Nevertheless, entrepreneurship as a life theme pervades society and the actions of individuals within them. The chapter begins by discussing the links between entrepreneurship and crime and in particular the hidden links between crime – dyslexia – and entrepreneurship. Building upon this theoretical foundation by using examples and case studies from across the globe, this chapter demonstrates how social entrepreneurship and entrepreneurship education is already making a contribution to the criminal justice systems in their respective countries. These examples and other themes developed within the chapter are worked into a tentative model which can be used by those in such criminal justice systems to divert even more offenders away from a debilitating life of crime.

## Introduction

Traditionally for the working classes, crime and entrepreneurship are often divergent pathways for the acquisition of wealth, status and power. This exploratory theoretical/conceptual contribution illustrates how knowledge of entrepreneurship can be used by society and by individuals as a 'divergent pathway out of crime'. This approach is international in perspective because crime and entrepreneurship are international and indeed global in nature. Moreover, the social problems faced by different countries are often generic in nature - therefore a model which works in one country may work in another. In addition, the notion of criminal-entrepreneurship is a recurrent international/global phenomenon of interest.

As a theory entrepreneurship has been portrayed in criminology in a variety of ways in the past. For example crime has been considered as a career and in particular the professional thief has been considered an entrepreneur (Sutherland, 1937); Anomie (Merton, 1938); and Opportunity Theory (Cloward & Ohlin, 1960) played a part in the generation of the Poverty Program in the United States. Moreover, Bell (1953, 1960) wrote of the 'Crooked Ladder of Crime' as an alternative avenue of entrepreneurial advancement. This emphasis led to entrepreneurship generated programs which failed and, like rehabilitation, these efforts have been generally abandoned. Nevertheless, there is a residual interest in entrepreneurship which refuses to dissipate and the notion of the Crime-entrepreneur (Van Duyne, 2000) is very much in vogue.

Of necessity this chapter must gloss over much of the relevant crimino-entrepreneurial theory as it concentrates upon issues of entrepreneurship and rehabilitation. The collective consensus is that entrepreneurial propensity appears to provide the criminal with an alternative legitimacy. Nevertheless, the idea of the criminal as entrepreneur no longer holds the criminological imagination. Indeed, academic writings on the crime-entrepreneurship nexus tend to be firmly rooted in one domain or the other – that is either in Criminology or Entrepreneurship studies. As such the knowledge base is generally confined within the particular discipline. This acts as a constraining mechanism hindering the development of cross-disciplinary theories. However, of late, entrepreneurship scholars such as Baumol (1990) have argued that the paucity of genuine entrepreneurial opportunities can act as a pathway into crime; and Williams (2006) that often criminals and entrepreneurs come from the same societal pool. Clearly, there may be merits in forming hybrid theories of criminal entrepreneurship.

As a general rule, the focus of research into how entrepreneurship influences crime and criminality is on the individual and their traits as opposed to the crimino-entrepreneurial system in which both entrepreneurial genres are nurtured. Incisively, Baumol (1990) posited the notion of entrepreneurship as productive, unproductive and destructive. Baumol (1990) classified criminal entrepreneurship as destructive blaming the system / establishment for the lack of genuine opportunity. This chapter argues for the need to take a more holistic approach. This is important because systemic artefacts can be applied in a global perspective. Accordingly, this chapter takes a different stance by examining selected theories of crime and entrepreneurship in conjunction. This highlights points of convergence in relation to marginality thesis; class based theories of crime and enterprise; push versus pull theories of crime and enterprise; trait and personality theories and in particular the significance of dyslexia and other learning difficulties as a pathway to direct those who are 'differently abled' into the virtuous path of enterprise. The alternative is to do nothing and see disaffected youth spiralling out of control along the pathway to crime. Bolton and Thompson (2000) suggest that entrepreneurial life themes permeate the rhetoric of crime. Indeed, the two socially constructed entities share so much in common that it is surprising that no one has to date attempted to combine the knowledge base which comprises of the theories of both crime and entrepreneurship. This chapter makes an attempt to do just this by creating a theoretical model to underpin the practical models discussed below. Nevertheless, the focus of this chapter is very much upon using entrepreneurship as a diversionary mechanism to reduce the social effects of crime. In particular, dyslexia is an example of a social malady that cuts across crime, entrepreneurship and rehabilitation. Developing an appreciation of the destructive and constructive power of dyslexia is the first step towards building a theoretical bridge between crime and entrepreneurship which one day may provide a solution to the complex problem of crime.

The approach taken in the chapter is inductive as opposed to deductive. Although it is based upon phenomena observed by the author, it is grounded in a body of research forming a model. The chapter is structured as follows. Section one explores the divergent pathways of crime and entrepreneurship concentrating upon the links between crime and learning difficulties and entrepreneurship and learning difficulties. This section also looks at prison entrepreneurship. Section two examines entrepreneurship as a diversion technique and social entrepreneurship as a positive influence. This section posits a model for using entrepreneurship as a diversion out of crime. The final section assesses the contribution of the chapter. Using the inspirational narratives of a new breed of social entrepreneurs to illustrate the achievability of pursuing an alternative pathway mid trajectory this chapter makes a significant contribution in highlighting the possible.

## Exploring the divergent pathway

In traditional criminology much is made of the subjects of criminal families and criminal areas. In such families, crime is viewed as being almost hereditary and influenced by exposure to the criminogenic area

(See Morris, 2003 for a discussion of criminal areas). In such areas poverty, deprivation, poor housing, ill health and lack of educational opportunities are often a feature of everyday life. Such areas nevertheless appear to be a breeding ground for what have become regarded as the criminal classes. Indeed, the link between social class, education, crime and one's eventual life chances is a fruitful field requiring further research. As criminologists we are familiar with the myth of the stereotypical working class male criminal. Although we appreciate that criminal propensity crosses all barriers of social class and gender it appears that when one factors in issues such as learning difficulties that those from the lower social classes do not get the same life chances as the more prosperous middle and upper classes. Entrepreneurship, in its many forms, provides one achievable route to improve life chances. Indeed, Fiet et al. (2006) have researched ways of training the economically vulnerable, working poor of inner cities to make entrepreneurial discoveries. Fiet et al. argue that in doing so one has to overcome the challenges inherent in training the economically disadvantaged and that it is necessary to build bridges to gain trust.

### *Exploring the link between learning difficulties and crime*

Learning difficulties such as dyslexia, Attention Deficit Disorder (ADD) and Attention Hyperactivity Attention Disorder (ADHD) are believed to be hereditary in nature and are most frequently encountered in areas of social deprivation. These can be argued to correspond roughly to criminal areas. An appreciation of the role of such learning difficulties is increasing. Kerr (1973) and Morgan (1998) have highlighted the links between dyslexia and crime. Kirk and Reid (1999) conducted research at a Young Offenders Institution, testing a random sample of 50 young offenders for signs of dyslexia, using an accepted computer program. Prior to the research they had expected to confirm the accepted national average of between 5-10% of the population who suffer from varying degrees of dyslexia. They hoped to prove that the prison population might contain a slightly higher than average number of dyslexics. When the test results were analysed it was established that 50% of the respondents had tested positive for dyslexia and corresponding educational problems. Eighty two % of their respondents had a record of truancy; 83 % had been suspended and 50 % plus expelled. The respondents expressed bitter disappointment and a sense of feeling cheated by society for not having been diagnosed as dyslexic earlier. Many interviewees stated they knew deep down that something was wrong. Having been labeled as 'thick' by their peers and by the educational establishment they rebelled.

Similarly, Yates (2006) explored the links between dyslexia and drug dependency noting that four times more boys than girls are dyslexic and that 40% of his respondents amongst a community of persistent offenders were dyslexic. Although there were no significant differences between dyslexics and non dyslexics in the number of crimes they committed the dyslexic respondents were more prone to excessive drug consumption and therefore to becoming repeat offenders. Dyslexia is an example of a malady that cuts across crime, entrepreneurship and rehabilitation and is but one example of a social ill which could provide a bridge between crime, entrepreneurship and a solution.

### *Exploring the link between learning difficulties and entrepreneurship*

According the acknowledged expert in Dyslexia and entrepreneurship Julie Logan, entrepreneurs are five times more likely to have dyslexia than the average UK citizens and that as much as 20% of entrepreneurs are dyslexic (Logan, 2001). Seventy per cent of the entrepreneurs studied did not succeed at school. Conversely, managers reflected the UK national average of 4%. Smith (2008) conducted a study of the link between dyslexia and entrepreneurship and identified over 50 Entrepreneurs, CEO's and Inventors who are 'differently abled'. Some entrepreneurs such as Richard Branson from Britain and Kjell Inge Rokke from Norway had brushes with the law straying onto the path of crime. Richard Branson had a brush with HM Customs for importing records without paying the resulting duties, whilst Kjell Rokke was allegedly involved in the theft of a car.

Entrepreneurship scholar and psychologist Kathy Marshack (2007) heads up a research project into ADD, ADHD and Entrepreneurship devoted to turning the disorders into an asset for entrepreneurs. Marshak links the following entrepreneurial characteristics to ADD/ADHD - Someone who has a lot of great ideas, but not too many are successfully implemented; Great at delegating, but often oversimplifying the task; Full of energy, but saps everyone else's energy; Possess a sense of urgency about the latest project, but forgets about the 10 other projects they gave someone else yesterday? Marshack stresses that some experts estimate that as many as half of all entrepreneurs have ADD (either the hyperactive type or the inattentive type). Coincidentally, more and more youths are being identified with ADD as diagnosis of the disorder becomes more refined. Marshack asks if these are future entrepreneurs struggling to express their talents and comments upon the number of gifted children who drop out of high school and the high incidence of prison inmates who suffer from ADD.

Logan (2001) incisively points out that traditional classroom method of teaching entrepreneurship do not work with dyslexics. She also acknowledges the high incidence of dyslexics in prison. With this in mind it is telling that Logan's research revealed that 87% of dyslexic entrepreneurs were from middle class backgrounds. This suggests that there may be an unintentional class biased system and that remedial work at lower levels of society may well 'pay dividends' to use a financial metaphor.

### *The link between learning difficulties and the pathway to prison*

A study by the National Probation Service in 1996 found that 52% of prisoners in London may be dyslexic. A similar study by the British Dyslexia Association in conjunction with the Bradford Youth Team suggests that more than 50% of their young offenders were dyslexic. Snowling et al. (2000) and Svensson et al. (2001) highlight poor literacy, spelling and reading levels among juvenile offenders. The combined effect of this research has undoubtedly influenced Prison Service Policy. However, not all scholars agree that dyslexia is linked to crime and that dyslexics form a disproportionate part of the prison population. Michael Rice challenges the popular belief that as many as one in two prisoners is dyslexic, indicating that his research offers no support for this belief asserting that the reading problems he encountered could be ascribed to social disadvantage. He is concerned that other researchers are using false assumptions and flawed methods – namely that 1) dyslexia is the unique cause of low reading attainment; 2) low attainment necessarily indicates a learning difficulty, rather than adverse environmental circumstances such as low levels of literacy in the childhood home and unstructured, inexplicit alphabetic skills teaching in the primary school; 3) that 'signs of dyslexia', such as difficulty in reading non-words and difficulty in sustaining attention, are specific to dyslexia; and 4) that, apart from offending, prisoners form a representative sample of the general population. Thus exposing inmates with dyslexia to entrepreneurship theory may not offer a universal panacea which sets them on the path to legitimacy but it is certainly a valid option.

### *Prisons, inmates and entrepreneurship*

In Britain, Rieple (1998) surveyed/mapped numerous small business training and support programmes in prisons and the probation services. Fletcher (2004) built upon this researching the provision of enterprise initiatives in English prisons from the perspective that encouraging self-employment addresses issues of high unemployment and social exclusion amongst the offending population. Fletcher reported upon a plethora of such initiatives in British prisons. Fletcher based his study on his (2004) report for the Small Business Service and concludes that such initiatives are characterized by a number of fundamental weaknesses. Also, Fletcher (2004) established that there is a paucity of such research. The literature can conveniently be divided into American and British contributions. See table 1 below – A literature review of entrepreneurship diversion in prisons.

**Table 1- A literature review of entrepreneurship diversion in prisons**

| School | Researchers | Contribution |
|---|---|---|
| American | Jansy et al. (1969) | Posited the notion of ex-offenders as businessmen |
| | Price (1973) | Considered private enterprise in a prison as a free market economy |
| | Goodman (1982) | Researched prison industries and the prisoner as entrepreneur |
| | Washburn (1987) | Examined the case for prisoner entrepreneurship |
| | Sonfield (1992) | Analysed the inmate as an entrepreneur |
| | Sonfield & Barbato (1994) | Tested prison inmates for entrepreneurial attitude |
| | Sonfield et al. (2001) | Built upon the previous study concentrating upon the potential benefits of self-employment training programmmes |
| | Fairlie (2002) | Researched drug dealing and legitimate self-employment |

| | | |
|---|---|---|
| British | Rieple (1998) | Researched the potential which offenders have for entrepreneurial activity and in particular training of ex prisoners and offenders in small business skills. |
| | Fletcher et al. (2001) | Investigated recruiting and employment of offenders |
| | Social Enquiry Unit (2002) | Conducted a survey on re-offending by ex-prisoners concluding that entrepreneurship was a viable option. |
| | Fletcher (2004) | Surveyed entrepreneurship initiatives in English prisons |

Another good example from Britain is the 'Offenders in Employment Project' in Lancashire, by University of Central Lancashire in conjunction with the National Probation Service, Lancashire, and Morecambe College, and H.M. Prison Service to address the problems of ex-offenders gaining useful employment on being released from prison. This was set up in response to research which indicated that there are a variety of issues including a lack of cohesiveness and collaboration across the agencies, both statutory and voluntary and a lack of sharing of information. This project involves a mapping process to identify providers of a range of interventions across the region. One problem identified was the discrimination ex-offenders face in seeking employment. Entrepreneurship and self-employment is one distinct possibility open to ex-offenders to overcome this ingrained discriminatory social process.

Notwithstanding this, the most advanced model of prison entrepreneurship appears to be the American 'Prison Entrepreneurship Program'. See Case study 1 below for details.

### Case Study 1 - The Prison Entrepreneurship Program[1]

The Prison Entrepreneurship Program was conceived in May, 2004 in Houston, Texas on the basis that a large percentage of inmates came to prison as seasoned entrepreneurs who had ran successful drugs rings and gangs. As such they had a proven track record of managing others and getting things done and above all are risk takers. Many inherently understand business concepts, so it would be possible to teach them how to run legitimate companies. The mission statement of the PEP is to "*stimulate positive life transformation for executives and inmates, uniting them through entrepreneurial passion, education and mentoring*". The progam engages top business and academic talent to redirect inmates' talents via "values-based entrepreneurial training". The aim is to return them to society as productive citizens. It is a nonprofit organization providing post-release entrepreneurial assistance to parolees. PEP positions itself as the only entrepreneurship program in the U.S., targeted at inmates / former inmates. PEP provides an In-Prison Business Plan Competition, access to financing and a Reintegration Service. The latter includes work readiness programs, Executive Mentoring and Entrepreneurship school.

The list of achievements on the 'PEP' website is impressive:-
- The Business Plan Competition culminates in a formal graduation ceremony.
- In excess of 200 business executives participate in events such as venture capital panels.
- PEP has established partnerships with MBA programs at leading US Universities including Harvard.
- PEP has recruited Executive Mentors.
- Two inmates have filed patents.
- A significant number of inmates (approximately 15%) have set up their own business.
- Participant employment rates are 93% within 1 month of release.
- The recidivism rate is less than 3%.

The program is partially funded by appeals for donations to business community and has plans to deliver a service nationwide.

[1] The case study is based on information posted on the website www.prisonentrepreneurship.org

This is not the only example of successful state intervention using entrepreneurship as a route out of crime. Fernández-Stembridge and Badell (2003) comment that in Shanghai, China, authorities there ran a successful programme turning ex-criminals into self-employed criminals into entrepreneurs and that as many as 4% of new entrepreneurs/self-employed were ex-prisoners. Such programmes, if properly evaluated, clearly have the potential to be replicated globally.

However, in reality there is a gap between good practice and what is achievable. Offender assessment takes place on a massive scale once offenders are sent to correctional institutions. It is of course necessary to highlight that some of the assessment may, or may not be appropriate, like omitting testing for dyslexia, but as highlighted above, the number of illiterate/learning disabled inmates is well known. The deficit between what could or should be done in theory may arise from a lack of resources to address remedial learning difficulties. Often the mentality of offenders is that they are here to do time, not go to school or learn trades. This requires to be changed for progress to be made. The purpose of this discussion is not to disparage the prison systems in individual countries but it is necessary to highlight the failure of many prison vocational training programmes. Another problem to be overcome is the opposition of labour unions to the implementation of competitive/useful vocational programmes. Entrepreneurship education should therefore always be optional and never compulsory or seen as a threat to the inmates or to the prison system. As previously highlighted, by Bolton and Thompson (2000) entrepreneurship is a life theme and as such spans many spheres of society thus individual social institutions cannot be held accountable for ingrained behavioral practices beyond their control.

The notion of productive entrepreneurship discussed above, provides an individual with a career trajectory in which they are very much in control of their own destiny. With this in mind, the remainder of the chapter highlights some examples of how entrepreneurship can be channelled into effective diversionary mechanisms.

## Entrepreneurship as a diversion technique

This section examines entrepreneurship as a diversionary strategy. It is divided into two parts. The first looks at social entrepreneurship and encouraging the proliferation of life enhancing social enterprises. Social entrepreneurship, as a paradigm for change, allows committed individuals to give back to their communities because it reverses the orientation of traditional entrepreneurship which is about 'taking between'. Social entrepreneurship is about ‘giving’. Accordingly this section discusses some possible diversion strategies and highlights some case studies where social enterprises are diverting criminals onto a divergent pathway.

### *Social Entrepreneurship in action*

The accepted paradigm of the entrepreneur has become somewhat stereotyped as if stuck in a time warp. Nevertheless, the image of the entrepreneur as a male person located primarily in the business sector is changing rapidly. Another entrepreneurial type worthy of consideration is the Social Entrepreneur. Established social enterprises such as the “*The Kids Company*” have already made a significant impact on the lives of the communities they service. One of the fundamental strengths of a social entrepreneur is that they go beyond the immediate problem to instigate fundamental change within their communities of practice.

Social entrepreneurship as a remedy for the causes of crime is not a modern phenomenon, only the concept is. For example consider the work of the Philanthropic Society of London founded in 1788 to divert the children of recidivist criminal families away from crime. Moreover, Robb (1996) describes the anti mafia work carried out by the Paleremian photographer, and tireless net-worker, Letizia Bataglia whom can only be described as a ‘social entrepreneur’. She operates a social intervention squad of volunteers who nightly clean up the drug squalor and also campaigns in schools against the Mafia by showing photographs of the Mafia’s victims to children in order to break the romance and myth of the mafia. In giving back to her community, Bataglia is obviously placing her self in danger and taking risks. In his discussion of the work of Bataglia, Robb does not indicate whether Batagalia is dyslexic or not – however, her tireless behaviour is typical of that associated with entrepreneurs.

The entrepreneurial spirit is central to the success of all such entrepreneurial social ventures. Boschee (1995) a pioneer of social entrepreneurship discusses nonprofit organizations and in particular the phenomenon of affirmative business. These facilitate social changes for the economically or educationally disadvantaged; the mentally ill; potential high school drop outs; recovering addicts; present or former convicts, all of whom feature heavily in the criminal statistics of any given locality. The following case studies from England and America illustrate the type and scale of initiatives which are out there and succeeding.

## Case Study 2 – 'Kids Company', London, U.K.[2]

Kids Company is an outstanding charitable organization founded in December 1996 by psychotherapist and serial social entrepreneur Camila Batmanghelidjh. Camila was born in Tehran into a wealthy professional family. Aged 13 she was sent to a boarding school in England during a period of unrest in Iran. She went to university and became a psychotherapist. The Kids Company offers values based practical, emotional and educational support to profoundly vulnerable 'hard to reach' children and young people in inner London. The philosophy of the company is based upon the concept of emotional well-being and grounded in attachment theory. The services offered are holistic, child-centered and multi-disciplinary. It supports a paid staff of 180 and 1,500 volunteers. The staff are internationally and culturally diverse (40 different languages are spoken). It now supports over 11,000 children and young people. Many of the youths suffer mental health and emotional difficulties arising from neglect and abuse. This impinges upon their ability to become functioning adults, access education, health, housing and meaningful employment. The organization utilises multi-disciplinary teams working at street level adapting neurophysiological thinking in order to deliver a preventative and reparative therapeutic service. Ninety five per cent of the children self refer themselves to the company which delivers services across London in 33 schools; a Children's Centre 'The Arches II' and an 'Urban Academy'. Many of the children and young persons at the Arches have been drug couriers, gang members or in prostitution. The majority are users of hard drugs. 57% arrive homeless. 85% have identifiable mental health problems. Sport is also an integral part of the program because it promotes self-confidence, unity, tolerance, teamwork, youth leadership and coaching. The Urban Academy caters for the needs of young people who reject or have been rejected from other educational facilities because of their complex emotional or behavioural needs. The Urban Academy provides tailor made teaching packages to students and encourage them to succeed via skills based literacy and numeracy programmes. The aim of the Academy is to prepare and divert students for other establishments including university. The Company survives by support from charitable trusts, businesses and individual donations. To continue operating Kids Company raises approximately £5 million per annum. On two occasions Camila has re-mortgaged her own flat to bridge funding gaps. Camila who is known as 'The Angel of Peckham' who won the Ernst and Young Social Entrepreneur of the year award for 2005 is severely dyslexic. Interestingly she does not concentrate upon dyslexia per se.

---

[2] This case study is based upon internet research and the book *'Shattered Lives: Children living with Courage and Dignity'*.

## Case Study 3 – The Delancey Street Foundation.[3]

This case study describes the actions of Social Entrepreneur/Criminal Psychologist Mimi Silbert who in 1972 along with a prison parolee John Maher opened a drug rehabilitation house for counselling ex-offenders. They named the house after New York's famous Delancey Street where Jewish Immigrants such as Mimi's parents lived. It was initially devised as being a recycling centre for those defined by society and themselves as rejects. Maher borrowed the start up capital of $1000 from a loan shark. The Delancey Street business Empire now has a £20 million per annum turn over. It has businesses in New York, New Mexico, North Carolina and Los Angeles. The organization is undergoing a period of expansion. Silbert prides herself that it has been achieved without public funding. She firmly believes that a spirit of independence is essential to business survival. Silbert does however accept donations. The success of the organization is that it is run solely by its residents. The work of Mimi Silbert and Delancey Street has been recognised by Journalist John Glionna of the Los Angeles Times as a 'University of the Streets' (a Harvard for losers) where the students include former pimps and prostitutes, junkies and drug dealers, armed robbers and the homeless (Glionna, 2006). Many are illiterate and unskilled. The programme has turned out 15,000 social outcasts into law abiding, self-respecting working people. Silbert rejects the conventional 'hold your hand' style of counselling in favour of active participation in the Delancey businesses which include a gourmet waterfront restaurant, a bookstore café, a health club, a cinema, a moving company and a catering company. The aim is to encourage offenders to go into business themselves, turning convicts into entrepreneurs but all employees are also ex offenders. Glionna states that employees' suits are donated by businesses such as Brook Brothers and Gap. There is a feeling of belonging amongst employees who were formerly often from opposing factions. Sex Offenders and Psychiatric patients are not eligible for the programme. There is a strict no violence, no drugs and no alcohol policy. Employees receive on the job training and general education classes and are encouraged to seek employment elsewhere. The Foundation is an example of what Boschee (1995) describes as an Affirmative Business Venture.

---

[3] This case study was put together from internet research and from readings of Boschee (1995).

There are numerous other examples of entrepreneurship education in action. Boschee (1995) discusses another Affirmative Business, namely 'Cooperative Home Care Associates' founded by Rick Surpin to create permanent employment for hard to employ Black and Latino women in the Bronx community in New York. It is now a business with a $5 million turnover employing 300 women, providing home-health care facilities. Its employees have above average pay and benefits, career mobility, profit sharing and annual bonuses. It is a truly entrepreneurial company as evidenced by the fact that six of the ten seats on the board of directors are occupied by elected employees. The company won the national Business Enterprise Trust Award in 1992 and is expanding to cover other cities. Boschee (1995) also discusses a direct services business venture 'Ombudsman Educational Services' founded by Jim Boyle and Lori Sweeney in Illinois. The venture is an alternative learning centre for potential school dropouts. To stay in the programme the students must undertake to demonstrate mastery in the following subjects – maths, reading, social studies and science. They have an 85% success rate. It is not a drain on public expense because it tackles the students before they drop out of the school system. It now has 37 centres operating in seven states. The company revenue exceeded $4 million last year.

In addition the Canadian based Second Chance Employment Counselling provides access to a variety of resources and services to assist such youths to conduct successful career and job searches. Another service is the After School Program available for youth aged 13 to 24 through a variety of information and skill building workshops. Interestingly, a report (NWT Youth Business Conference, 2006) on the programme talks of addressing roadblocks to youth wanting to get into business and encourage them to pursue their ideas if they have what it takes to be an entrepreneur. The Second Chance Entrepreneurship programme aims to assist 'Street Involved Youth', in starting their own business.

What the above case studies and examples have in common is that they were initiated by dynamic, motivated, enterprising individuals who used their combined social capital and life experiences to help other less advantaged people. This independence from authority is a key part of their success. In the next section, we will consider examples of initiatives instigated by authority figures. These case studies and examples also provide evidence that entrepreneurship can be utilised by society to instigate beneficial changes to the social system, and as a method for alleviating social problems and distress which occur as a result of crime. Social entrepreneurship can thus be used as a mechanism to achieve a paradigm change. It is significant that social entrepreneurship is very much in vogue in the United Kingdom with Conservative Party Leader David Cameron in a talk to the Centre for Social Justice recently called for voluntary sector entrepreneurs to help assist with problems caused by crime and drugs. Cameron called for greater flexibility in the voluntary sector to encourage visionary leaders to get involved in community work. Cameron envisaged the establishment of areas similar to the 'enterprise zones' set up to promote regeneration in deprived locations where a new breed of social entrepreneurs could make a difference.

These examples discussed above highlight the various roles government and social entrepreneurs play. Social entrepreneurs such as *Letizia Batagalia, Camila Batmanghhelidjh, Mimi Silbert, Rich Surpin* and *Jim Boyle* are positive entrepreneurial role models for disadvantaged communities. However, it is ironic that a common, almost universal, theme of the successful role models discussed above is that of their refusal to accept governmental funding. Entrepreneurial propensity must germinate from within an individual. If this spark is not present then the offender is unlikely to buy into the ideology. Likewise, there is a tension between those who have the ability to become social entrepreneurs, government departments and Non Governmental Organizations (NGO's). Whilst independence of mind and operation is laudable each sector has a role to play and they need to be cooperative and not competitive. This is clearly a major problem to be overcome at present.

### *Entrepreneurship education as a diversion technique*

In the previous section we discussed the contribution of social entrepreneurs. However, there is a place for intrapreneurs within a variety of organisations connected to criminal justice systems or the voluntary sector to use diversionary techniques. Marshack (2007) cites an example of a Superior Court Judge in Seattle, Washington who instituted a program to test all first time offenders appearing before him. If they were diagnosed with ADD and qualified for probation part of their sentence was to participate in an outpatient treatment program. The program taught them about the disorder and how to utilize their strengths to learn and work more productively. The programme has had a 90% success rate. Marshak (2007) believes that if criminals with ADD/ADHD can be rehabilitated then entrepreneurs with similar issues can accomplish even greater contributions to society, if they are shown how to utilize their strengths and avoid their weaknesses. This example is unusual in that it has court sanctions attached to it.

Entrepreneurship has considerable potential as a diversion technique to wean a proportion of recidivist criminals away from a life of crime. If the entrepreneurial process were more widely understood by society, especially the marginalized; and access to it made more accessible - then perhaps the necessity to commit crime could be reduced. The author envisages that in addition to encouraging social entrepreneurs to do their own thing there is room for a planned system of inter-agency diversionary educational strategies can be used individually or together as a package to change social expectations and divert children away from the path to criminality. It could also be used to educate criminal recidivists, into reforming their former criminal behaviour. Table 2 below demonstrates the range of interagency intervention programmes using entrepreneurship education open to the authorities.

**Table 2 - Interagency intervention programmes using entrepreneurship education**

| Interventions | Details of intervention |
|---|---|
| **Entrepreneurial Awareness Training** | Pitched at a very basic level in Primary and Secondary Schools, as a part of the learning for life curriculum in a similar manner as existing Police School Liaison lessons that teach social inclusion, social responsibility and anti-drugs messages. The child will be exposed to a very basic level to the message that entrepreneurship is a good for society. The method of delivery would utilise storytelling and case study methodologies. The case studies will consist of inspirational stories about entrepreneurs as compared to stories about criminals. As is already common practice the message could be facilitated via CD Rom and interactive learning packages. The moral entrepreneur would be presented as a socially beneficial character. By this method children will be introduced to the entrepreneurial paradigm at an earlier age, than is traditionally the case. |

| | |
|---|---|
| **Screening for Communicational Deficits** | Children who are susceptible to communicational learning difficulties such as ADD, ADHD, Dyslexia etc. would benefit from screening at an earlier age and provided with the relevant learning packages in order to maximise their learning potential. In this manner disruptive behaviour will be channelled appropriately thus preventing the children presently at risk from being pushed into escalating patterns of anti-social behaviour and eventually criminality. The positive and negative aspects of their communicational deficit will be explained to them properly and the positive aspects accentuated. The children should be encouraged to achieve career paths (including entrepreneurial careers) that are suitable to their abilities. Again the case study method and inspirational story telling will be a feature of the training. |
| **Entrepreneurial Awareness Training for Young Offenders** | Taking the format discussed at point one, but operating at a higher and more specialised level. The Case Study Method and Story Telling Methods will be utilised as before. Training could take place on a one to one basis or in small groups. The Young Offenders could be introduced to the power of the "*Entrepreneurial Dream*". The benefits of entrepreneurial lifestyles would be compared to the vagaries of a criminal lifestyle. The lesson materials will include CD Rom exercises, videos, and selected passages from criminal biographies highlighting the strong entrepreneurial life themes present in the narratives. Perhaps talks from entrepreneurs and reformed criminals could also be a feature. The main aim of the programme would be to introduce the offender to the possibilities of achieving success via legitimate self-employment. |
| **Basic Entrepreneurial Awareness Training for Adult Offenders** | This would take a similar format to the scheme described above using a similar training package. The main aim this scheme would be to orientate the offender towards considering the alternative of legitimate entrepreneurial behaviour. It is appreciated that this may inadvertently improve the sophistication of the criminal's modus operandi. This could be followed up by teaching interested students how to set up a business. |

| | |
|---|---|
| **Advanced Entrepreneurial Learning for Adult Offenders** | This is envisaged as a voluntary educational activity for those who show a genuine propensity and willingness to learn. This could include a correspondence course in entrepreneurial studies; aspects of business management; and in some instances full degrees in Entrepreneurship. If it were linked to training for freedom courses etc it would provide an incentive to learn. |
| **Entrepreneurial Learning for Reformed Criminals** | This is envisaged as a series of talks to non – institutionalised criminals living in the community and supported by Offender Organizations and Enterprise Agencies etc. The desire to be educated is what separates the concept of self-education from enforced education. If even a few seized the opportunity and volunteer to study entrepreneurship and other related courses taught by individuals whom they could relate to - they would benefit from it. It could compliment existing training for freedom programmes. |

Reiple (1998) and Fletcher (2004) have both commented upon the fragmentary nature of the provision of entrepreneurship education in Britain and also the range of partner agencies involved. This need not be problematic (or anti-entrepreneurial) if the disparate service providers used a common model such as the tentative model outlined above at table 2. If such a coherent strategy was followed nationally then the possibility of those involved in such criminal justice systems to divert even more offenders away from a debilitating life of crime would undoubtedly increase.

Nevertheless, entrepreneurs and entrepreneurial ability by its very nature emerges from societies and societal systems. Therefore, policy makers and officials involved in the criminal justice system cannot afford to be dogmatic and prescriptive in the provision of entrepreneurship interventions because intrapreneurs, social entrepreneurs and offenders with an entrepreneurial bent must be allowed to instigate and initiate their own diversification schemes no matter how these differ in philosophy from the officially sanctioned model. This necessitates consideration of another model. See figure 1 – An ideational map of how entrepreneurship theory can be used to divert persistent offenders away from crime. This model allows all parties involved directly and indirectly criminal justice system to play a part in the process. Thus central and local government, funding bodies, Non Government Organisations (NGO's) and other bodies all contribute to creating a positive entrepreneurial climate. In this model,

**Figure 1**

**AN IDEATIONAL MAP OF HOW ENTREPRENEURSHIP THEORY CAN BE USED TO DIVERT PERSISTENT OFFENDERS AWAY FROM CRIME**

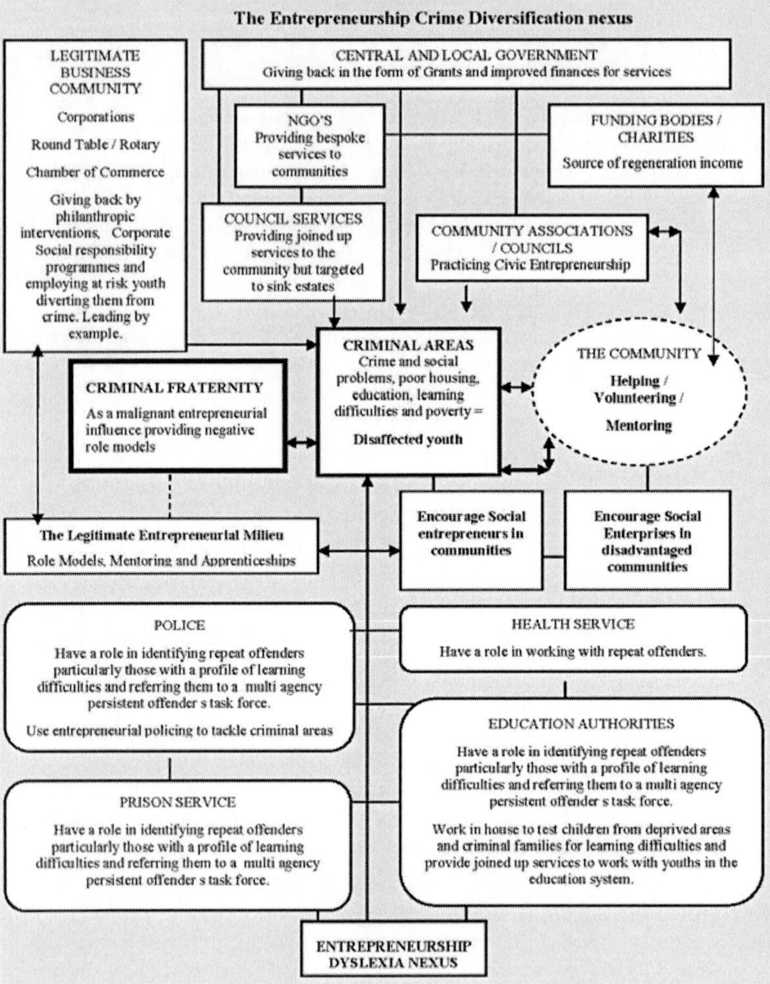

legitimate entrepreneurs and social entrepreneurs stand together as achievable role models. However, it is also necessary to highlight that there may be possible links between the criminal fraternity and the entrepreneurial community. These links may not always be visible but may have a malignant influence in the form of providing negative role models. In this model central government play a key role in coordinating and financing efforts. Individual NGO's have a significant role in that they could provide bespoke services such as drug counseling. Local Councillors and Community Councils can help by canvassing local businesses and the local community to help, volunteer and mentor. Autonomous Social entrepreneurs should be positively encouraged as should the generation of social enterprises. The Police, Prison Service, Health Service and Education Departments could all problem solve together.

## Conclusion

This chapter has the potential to act as an inspirational template for those working in the criminal justice system by making policy makers and practitioners aware of the possibilities for using entrepreneurship as a mechanism for facilitating positive change. It has the potential to influence offenders themselves because the information and ideas presented in the chapter are life changing scenarios which enable them to retain their identities and dignity by increasing their life chances. The life lessons illustrated in the chapter are not examples of entrepreneurial evangelism but real life success stories which can be replicated wherever there is a crime problem.

One drawback of the application of entrepreneurship theory as a diversion out of crime is that offenders are often entrepreneurial criminals and therefore it could prove problematic in getting some of them to pursue legitimate as opposed to illegal ventures. Indeed, entrepreneurship theory is amoral and its tenets also cover criminal activities such as drug dealing, money laundering and other acquisitive crime. Thus many offenders may need to be convinced of the virtue and practicality of legitimate enterprises. It may well be that they are not at the correct life stage or mindset to make the switch to legitimate entrepreneurial activity. It is the case that as a general rule the offender population itself and society values white collar criminals as opposed to petty thieves. Changing this mindset requires to be addressed as part of any education package.

This chapter has modest implications for both the educational and criminal justice systems. One of the important messages of this chapter is that it suggests a biological basis for the criminal predisposition of the respondent's criminality. If a progressive policy of testing every person in the penal system for such disorders was instigated a definitive statistical portrait of the problem would emerge. Remedial action could ensue. It is probably too late for the majority of those trapped in the vicious spiraling social system that is criminality. However, if lessons are learned and the tests extended to everyone entering the education system then those diagnosed early can be helped. Learning is an addictive process. It is a method of diverting criminal energy into "Doing the business" legitimately, instead of wasting it on socially divisive and personally destructive criminal activities. Although not all of those in the criminal / prison population diagnosed as dyslexic could be diverted onto the pathway of enterprise the author believes that a significant proportion could benefit from such an opportunity. In dealing with young people in conflict with the law, the key to success appears to lie in facilitating a multi agency approach. Working together, holistically individuals acting entrepreneurially within the system have the power to make significant and lasting changes.

## References

Batmanghelidjh, C. (2006). *Shattered lives: Children living with courage and dignity*. London: Jessica Kingsley Publishers.

Baumol, W. J. (1990). Entrepreneurship: Productive, unproductive, and destructive. *Journal of Business Venturing*, *11*, 3-22.

Bell, D. (1953). Crime as an American way of life. *Antioch Review*, 13, 131-154.

—. (1960). *Crime as an American way of life: A queer ladder of social mobility in the end of ideology*. New York: Free Press.

Bolton, B., & Thompson, J. (2000). *Entrepreneurs: Talent, temperament, technique.* London: Butterworth, Heineman.

Boschee, J. (1995). Social Entrepreneurship. *Across the Board*, *32*(3), 20-27.

Cloward, R., & Ohlin, L. (1960). *Delinquency and Opportunity*. NY: Free Press.

van Duyne, P. (2000). Mobsters are human too: Behavioural science and organized crime investigation. *Crime Law and Social Change 34*(4, December), 369-90.

Fairlie, R. W. (2002). Drug dealing and legitimate self-employment. *Journal of Labor Economics*, *20*(3), 538-563.

Fernández-Stembridge, L., & Badell, T. F. (2003). *China Today: Economic Reforms, Social Cohesion and Collective Identities*. London:

Routledge.

Fiet, J. O., Nixon, R. D., Gupta, M., & Patel, P. C. (2006). Entrepreneurial discovery by the working poor. *Journal of Developmental Entrepreneurship*, *11*(3), 255-273.

Fletcher, D., Taylor, A., Hughes, S., & Breeze, J. (2001). *Recruiting and employing offenders*. York: Joseph Rowntree Foundation.

Fletcher, D. R. (2004). *Reducing re-offending the enterprise option: A report for the small business service,* Small Business Service – available online at www.sbs.gov.uk/Research.

—. (2005). Providing enterprise support for offenders: realising new opportunities or reinforcing old inequalities? *Environment and Planning: Government and Policy, 23*(5) 715 – 731.

Goodman, S. (1982). Prisoners as entrepreneurs, developing a model for prisoner-run industry. *Boston University Law Review*, *62*, 1163-1195.

Glionna, J. M. (2002, March 29). Making Rehabilitation into a Serious Business Programs: Psychologist has built a small empire by empowering thousands of ex-cons. *The Los Angeles Times,*

Jansy, L., Kohlhof, E., Sadowski, C., & Toby, J. (1969). Ex-offenders as small businessmen: Opportunities and obstacles. New Brunswick, New Jersey: Rutgers University.

Kerr, J. (1973). Crime and Dyslexia. *Criminologist*, *8*(29), 29-32.

Kirk, J., & Reid, G. (2001). An examination of the relationship between dyslexia and offending in young people and the implications for the training system. *Dyslexia*, *7*(2), 77-84.

Logan, J. (2001). *Entrepreneurial success: A study of the incidence of dyslexia in the entrepreneurial population and the influence of dyslexia on success*. Unpublished Ph.D. Dissertation submitted to Bristol University.

Marshak, K. (2007). ADD & ADHD. Retrieved on 29/9/2007 from http://www.kmarshack.com/therapy/add/add_research_project.html

Merton, R. K. (1938). Social Structure and Anomie. *American Sociological Review*, *3*, 672-82.

Morris, T. (2003). *The criminal area: A study in social ecology*. London: Routledge.

Morgan, W. (1998). Dyslexia and Crime: Innovation and Insights. *Dyslexia*, 3 (4), 247 – 248.

NWT Youth Business Conference. (2006). A Report on the NWT Youth Business Conference, Second Chance Programme", Retrieved on 25.09.2007 from http://www.dehchobdc.ca/Main/Resources/Reports/Final%20Report%20Youth%20Conf.pdf

Price, J. A. (1973). Private enterprise in a prison - the free market economy of La Mesa Penitenciara. *Crime and Delinquency*, *19*(2), 18-27.

Reiple, A. (1998). Offenders and Entrepreneurship. *European Journal on Criminal Policy and Research*, *6*(2), 235-256.

Robb, P. (1996). *Midnight in Sicily*. London: Harvill Press.

Sonfield, M. (1992). From inmate to entrepreneur: A preliminary analysis. Retrieved on 28/9/2007 from www.sbaer.uca.edu/Research/1992/SBIDA/92sbi039.htm.

Sonfield, M., & Barbato, R. (1994). Testing prison inmates for entrepreneurial aptitude. *Journal of Small Business Strategy*, *5*(2), 45-51.

Sonfield, M., Lussier, R. & Barbato, R. (2001). The entrepreneurial aptitude of prison inmates and the potential benefit of self-employment training programs. *Academy of Entrepreneurship Journal*, *17*(2), 85-94.

Smith, R. (2008). Re-reading criminal biographies as entrepreneur stories. Unpublished working paper Robert Gordon University, Aberdeen.

—. (2008). Being differently abled: Learning lessons from dyslexic entrepreneurs. In R. T. Harrison & C. M. Leitch (Eds.), *Entrepreneurial Learning in Conceptual Frameworks and Applications* (pp. 219-312). Routledge: London.

Snowling, M. J., Adams, J. W., Bowyer-Crane, C., & Tobin, V. (2000). Levels of literacy among juvenile offenders: The incidence of specific reading difficulties. *Criminal Behaviour and Mental Health*, *10*(4), November 2000, 229-241.

Social Exclusion Unit. (2002). *Reducing re-offending by ex-prisoners*. London: Office of the Deputy Prime Minister.

Svensson, I., Lundberg, I., & Jacobson, C. (2001). The prevalence of reading and spelling difficulties among inmates of institutions for compulsory care of juvenile delinquents. *Dyslexia*, *7*(2), 62-76.

Sutherland. E. (1937). *The professional thief*. Chicago: The University of Chicago.

Yates, P. R. (2006). *Bad mouthing, bad habits and bad, bad boys: An exploration of the link between dyslexia and drug dependence*. MSc. Dissertation submitted at Department of Applied Social Science, University of Stirling.

Washburn, J. J. (1987). Business behind bars: The case for prisoner entrepreneurship. *New England Journal on Criminal and Civil Confinement*, *13*(1), 117-144.

Williams, C. C. (2006). *The hidden enterprise culture: Entrepreneurship in the underground economy*. Edward Elgar: Cheltenham.

# CHAPTER EIGHT

# CRIMINAL CAREER AND SERIAL CRIMINALITY: RE-THINKING THE CONCEPTUAL DEFINITIONS

ARNON EDELSTEIN


## Abstract

Since Lombroso's days (1911), criminology, the "science of crime," seeks to define, explain and categorize the various types of criminals, their behaviors and motives. This aim has theoretical as well as policy-related implications. One of the important areas in criminology thinking focuses primarily on recidivist criminals, who perform large numbers of crimes and/ or commit the most dangerous crimes in society (rapists, killers, arsonists, arm robbers). These criminals have been defined as: "habitual offenders", "professional criminals", "career criminals", and "serial offenders". The interest in these criminals is a rational one, given the perception that they present a severe threat to society. A better understanding of these criminals' social and psychological background, motives and behaviors, will enable criminologists and law enforcement agencies to act more effectively against criminality, by way of punishment and/ or rehabilitation. The main challenge in this area of research is a conceptual problem, which has significant effects across the field. To this day, scholars have reused and misused titles to define and explain different concepts. The aim of this chapter is three-fold[1]: Firstly, to review the concepts of criminal career, professional crime, habitual offences and seriality, with a critical attitude with respect to the confusion generated over the years. Secondly, to propose a re-definition of the concepts mentioned above, mainly with regards to the criminal career. Thirdly, to propose a theoretical model that will enable a better understanding of and serve as a basis for further research in this important area of criminology.


---

[1] Some of the ideas in this chapter are based on the author's book on the subject (2006)

## Introduction

It is only natural that criminology, as other sciences, should strive to study and fight crimes and criminals that are the most harmful to society. Medical researchers have been researching cancer, heart problems and AIDS for many years but to this day, they have been unable to find a cure for the flu. Likewise, criminology tries to fight murderers and rapists, by building typologies, studying these behaviors in relation to many independent variables, but it still does not have the answer or the solution for shoplifting and other minor crimes. Our aim is to enquire into the attitudes of criminologists towards these harmful criminals, as well as the research carried out so far, in order to clarify the area of theoretical thinking and to get a better understanding of these phenomena.

### *Brief review of the historical development of the main concepts*

Professional crime as an occupation in Western societies was documented as early as the 15th century. There are numerous descriptions of professional criminals in London in the 19th century, including prostitutes, thieves, robbers, gamblers and shoplifters (Inciardi, 1975). The development of criminology's theoretical approach to this phenomenon can be linked to five main events:

First of all, Sutherland's essay from the late 1930s, on the "professional thief" is, to this day, the best known reference to concepts such as professional crime and professional criminals (Sutherland, 1939). His important insights formed the basis for later concerns regarding distinctions between professional and non-professional criminals, and between those with and those without a criminal career.

Secondly, Becker's essays on occupations and careers (Becker & Carper, 1956; Becker & Straus, 1956) provided another theoretical basis for exploring similarities between criminal and legitimate careers. As a result, scholars started to consider and explore criminality as a form of "work", "occupation" or "profession" (Gould et al., 1966; Letkemann, 1973; Klockars, 1974; Inciardi, 1975; Klein & Montague, 1975; Prus & Sharper, 1977; Miller, 1978; Walsh, 1980, 1986).

Thirdly, Wolfgang's famous research on birth cohort and criminality (Wolfgang, Figlio, & Sellin, 1972), found that a small percentage of criminals were responsible for most of the offences. These findings gave rise to the demand that criminologists, as well as the authorities, focus their attention on these hard-core or "career" criminals. The assumption was that this would lead to a drop in crime rates throughout society (Blumstein & Cohen, 1986).

Fourthly, the rise of the neo-classic theory in criminology introduced the viewpoint that the criminal had the ability, the will and the cognitive abilities to choose whether to be a chronic, a professional or a career criminal (Cornish & Clarke, 1986).

Finally, the rise of the notion of "serial offenders" in the 80's was another innovation, linked to more serious criminals, such as rapists, killers etc, although its definition is problematic at various levels (See also Roebuck & Windham, 1983).

As a result of these innovations in criminology theory, the literature became flooded with concepts, such as professional criminal, serial criminal, chronic/ habitual criminal and career criminal. Since no clear distinction was drawn between these concepts, however, a conceptual confusion ensued. For example, De Lisi (2005) argues that career criminals are habitual criminals - in other words, both concepts share the same meaning.

## *Criminal career, career and professional criminals: Definitions and conflicts*

One of the reasons for the conceptual confusion lies in the various definitions of the concept of "criminal career." One set of definitions emphasizes the different phases of the criminal career, including learning and specialization (Farrington, 1997; Smith & Smith, 1996); another emphasizes the connection between professional criminals and career criminals (Clinard & Quinney, 1967; Holmes & Holmes, 1998); others link careers and recidivism in crime (Blumstein et al., 1986; DeLisi, 2005); while others refer to the motive of material gains in criminal career (Inciardi, 1975). In addition, most scholars emphasize the fact that legitimate careers, as well as criminal careers, can only occur in an organizational setting (Hassin, 1987).

These various definitions initiated the confusion and gave rise to some difficult questions. For example, is a habitual offender a career criminal? (DeLisi, (2005) claims that they are the same). Is it possible for a career criminal not to be a professional criminal? Is every professional criminal necessarily a career criminal? First of all, not every professional criminal is a career criminal, but all career criminals must be professional criminals.[2] Secondly, a habitual or chronic offender who is not a professional is not a

[2] The re-definition will be presented later

career criminal. Finally, two conditions are necessary in order to identify a career criminal: material motives and professionalism. However, most writers have overlooked these conditions in compiling their definitions.

Based on the definitions and typologies suggested by various scholars (Inciardi, 1975; Chaiken & Chaiken, 1982; Clinard & Quinney, 1967) it was possible to compare professional and non-professional criminals (in the literature, they are labelled chronic, habitual, and even prone) as a first stage towards a better understanding of the various concepts.

Table 1: A comparison between professional and non-professional criminals

| **Criteria** | **Professional criminal** | **Un-professional criminal** |
|---|---|---|
| Nicknames | "Heavy", "professional" | "Semi-professional", "prone", "conventional", "lifestyle criminal", "chronic offender"[3], "moonlighter", "drift." |
| Professional skills | Highly developed, including professional development and specialization in specific crimes, well-defined plan. | Limited or no skills, type of crimes may be fixed or varied, no preliminary plan, moonlighting. |
| Monetary gains | High and stable. | Low, cut off because of detentions. |
| Interactions with other criminal | Membership in organized crime, working as part of ad-hoc work teams, or acting alone. | Membership in a gang or alternatively, acting alone. |
| Professional obligations | A single full time job. | A part time job, "moonlighting" |
| Self image | In most cases: professional pride, self esteem as a professional. | In most cases: lack of professional pride, a sense of victimization of personal or social circumstances. |
| Career development | Professional development and progress by learning techniques from other professionals. | Fixture of professional development without any specialization because of detentions and differential association with non-professional criminals. |

[3] These titles are sometimes mistakenly attributed to the professional criminal

## A Comparison between Criminal and Legitimate Careers

Over the years, different scholars used the concept of criminal career in different ways and given it various meanings. Some, according to the literature, have used the concept as referring to a legitimate career, hence emphasizing the professional element, (Blumstein et al., 1986; Blumstein et al., 1996; Farrington, 1997; Levi, 1995), while others have seen the criminal career as "a way of life", devoid of professional aspects (Diton, 1977), or as David (1974) called it: "a life in crime". Many scholars since Sutherland have tried to compare legitimate and criminal careers. Roebuck and Windham (1983) claimed that a criminal career is a type of work or profession involving qualifications, tools and time spent, in order to make money. From these scholars' point of view, we can analyze criminal careers in the same way that we analyze legitimate careers.

In these comparisons, a criminal career mainly refers to a specified set of people: drug dealers, thieves, robbers, pickpockets, prostitutes, burglars, and white collar criminals (Coombs, 1996; Adler & Adler, 1996; West, 1996; Shover, 1996; Weisburd & Waring, 2001; Mawby, 2001). These comparisons include six common elements: hard work; career rewards; status quest; a commitment to a common role and status; a distinction between specialization and professionalism vs. non-professionalism and non-specialization; and common values and similar behavioral standards. These comparisons contributed some important insights on the similar characteristics and phases of recruitment, training, specialization and commitment, as crucial phases towards professionalism and a career (Gould, 1966; Inciardi, 1975; Smith & Smith, 1996; Greenberg, 1996; Farrington, 1997; Gadd & Farrall, 2004). For example, scholars have gained a better understanding of organized crime and its developments.

On the other hand, the idea of comparing legitimate and criminal careers generated a lot of criticism. For example, Greenberg (1996) claims that a reference to continuity of crimes does not imply that all [serial] criminals have careers. Conklin (1986) claims similarly, that a criminal career is a series of crimes committed over a long period of time, rather than an occupation. Another criticism is that while the two careers may begin similarly, their development and completion (retirement) are very different (West, 1996) mainly because the legitimate career takes place within stable, organized surroundings with clear rules that define the different positions along the career, ways of mobility and rewards (Best & Luckenbill, 1996). However, the question of stability and security in the legitimate career vs. the criminal career, which these writers raise, is inaccurate: insecurity and instability are likely to occur in both types of career. For example: Will the medical student have a job within his area of specialization? Will a hi-tech engineer always have a secure job?

However, the debate on the possibility of comparing legitimate and criminal careers does not end here. It can be minimized by considering two issues. First of all, various scholars mistakenly assume that criminal careers can and must exist only within organizations. In addition, current definitions of the two careers in the literature do not address criminals or legitimate professionals outside organizational settings, and thus do not enable a true comparison between the careers. We see many professional criminals who are highly qualified and cause significant damage, although they are working alone or in ad-hoc teams. These criminals do have criminal career, according to the definition proposed in this chapter. The same is true of legitimate professionals, such as physicians or lawyers, who do not work in a formal organization, but still have a legitimate career within the social system that validates their professions, supervises them etc.

Secondly, the existing definitions for legitimate and criminal careers suffer from ambiguity and contradictions. Hence, we should re-define these concepts, before attempting an improved comparison between them.[4] In spite of these criticisms, the same literature claims there are some similarities between the two types of careers, although they are not identical: both careers include professionals who are working with the primary motivation of achieving material gains. In both cases, there are phases of recruitment, learning and training, acceptance of values and norms which characterize the profession and its practitioners, development of self-esteem, and building a reputation and achieving recognition by colleagues. The final phase in particular – building a reputation and achieving recognition - confirms that the individual is a "professional", a "specialist" etc.[5]

## *Re-Definition of the Concepts of "Career" and "Criminal Career"*

As mentioned earlier, some of the confusion that arose when linking career-related concepts to different kinds of offenders results from problematic definitions of the concepts of "career", in general, and of "criminal career", in particular. A conceptual definition is operationalized for career and criminal career.

---

[4] Even serial killers are looking for fame in the media and in the public.
[5] For example, see Sutherland, 1939

## *Career*

A career is the main occupation of an individual. This occupation is of a professional nature, its goal being more than sustenance and its motivation above momentary satisfaction. The appeal of the occupation can stem from various personal, physiological, psychological and social factors. A career involves learning the occupation, or specialization, in other words, the passage from one professional stage to another along a hierarchy of knowledge, qualifications and understanding. The qualifications and talents needed for a career are either innate or acquired. The perception of a career includes a long-term commitment and a way of life, with the aim of achieving the highest level of specialization and professionalism. The specialization scale can be determined formally by governmental supervision systems, by professional organizations; or by the individual who sets targets or chooses role models for himself. This characteristic requires a socialization process that includes technical as well as normative and ethical learning within the occupation.[6] This process may be formal or informal, and takes place in an organizational setting or in an individual-social setting. A career must have a social recognition - this recognition can be either formal (diploma, license) or informal, and come from professional authorities or from colleagues. In addition, it is expressed by public recognition via the media, gossip and rumors. A person's career is designed to supply him with material rewards, while it can also supply some by-products of a social, emotional, or physical nature. The sum of the rewards can be derived from the individual's location on the career scale, his reputation, the scarcity of his professional qualifications and the strictness of his adherence to the ethical code. This broad definition enables us to propose a new definition for the concept of criminal career.

## *Criminal Career*

"A criminal career is a career of "serial criminality",[7] designed to gain material rewards, which can also provide the actor with psychological, physical, social and other rewards. The main characteristics of serial criminality are professionalism and specialization, which requires continued learning and the perfecting of skills throughout the career. The career criminal is obligated to this professional way of life and he views it

[6] A broad reference to this concept will follow the discussion

[7] It will be expanded further on.

as a destination (from a rational or pathological point of view). Some career criminals - mainly those focused on achieving material gains - may wish for a normal life after getting the "big amount". The career of the professional serial offender can gain formal or informal recognition, public or secret, and be known to the law enforcement agencies or only by his colleagues.

The above definition contrasts with earlier definitions of criminal career in a number of ways:

1. Not every serial criminal has a criminal career, but a criminal career must involve serial criminality (Becker, 1963),

2. Not every professional criminal has a criminal career, but a criminal career must involve professional criminality (Roebuck & Windham, 1983).

3. A criminal career is designed for material rather than pathological-psychological gains, as its preliminary motive.[8]

Jackson, et al. (1987) argued that career criminals are directed toward crime as providing their main and primary source of income. The same claim was made by Roebuck & Windham (1983), Inciardi (1975), Gould (1966), Messinger (1966) and Letkemann (1973).

From the new definition, we can infer the kinds of crimes that can be regarded as reflecting criminal careers: serial murder for material profit, serial arson for material profit, serial professional crimes of fraud, forgery, robbery, theft, breaking in and entering, membership in organized crime, and prostitution, whose purpose is not limited to funding drug use. In contrast, crimes such as psychologically (and sexually) motivated serial murders, serial arsons perpetrated out of revenge, curiosity or for any other mental reason, as well as serial rapes, should not be regarded as examples of a criminal career. This narrow definition argues that criminals, who act on the basis of psychological-pathologic motives, cannot be regarded as career criminals - although they may be professional criminals - precisely because their motives are pathological rather than rational.

## Lifestyle criminals vs. career criminals

Before proceeding with our discussion, we need to deal with another confusion of concepts that appears in the literature, which stems from equating "career criminals" with "lifestyle criminals". Walters (1990) deals with the thought process and choices that criminals make when entering the criminal world and when embarking on a criminal career. In his

[8] For example, see Cornish & Clarke, 1986

opinion, both concepts overlap. Walters also mentions that these criminals are irrational because they are unrealistic about their future success in the criminal world.

However, Walters does not differentiate between these criminals and other kinds of criminals mentioned before. Walters treats them as career criminals although they are not even professional criminals. This is another example of the misleading confusion between the concepts. For him, career criminals are irrational, un-professionals and chronic offenders. In other words, for Walters, the career criminal is a serial or habitual offender who lacks rationality and professionalism. The question is: What turns him into a career criminal? Is it the serial aspect of his crimes? In addition, the fact that he is not a professional offender denies him the title of career criminal. We can now turn to a revised view of the different definitions mentioned above and summarize the various kinds of criminals described in the literature under one main conceptual title: "serial offender." The different subtypes of criminals under this title all share one main characteristic, i.e. they all act in a serial manner in the crime world, until they retire freely or forcibly.

## Serial criminality

The concepts of "serial offenders," or "serial crimes," appeared in the 80's and added to the conceptual-theoretical confusion. These concepts related primarily to such specific severe criminals as the serial killer, the serial rapist and the serial arsonist (Holmes & Holmes, 1998; Davis, 2001; Egger, 1985; Hale, 1998, Hickey, 1992; Holmes & DeBurger, 1988; Kocsis & Cooksey, 2002; Leyton, 2000).[9] The concept of "serial crimes" seems compatible with the criminal career, in which one component is the continued committing of crimes. Hence, the notions of serial crimes and continuity of crimes seem to be identical. In this context, Becker (1963), for example, claimed that we can look at a "criminal career" as constant involvement in crime. This added confusion, since, scholars tended to attribute criminal careers to serial offenders even when they were not professional criminals. This misattribution reinforces the argument raised earlier, according to which a criminal career must include serial aspects of crime, while every serial crime need not be the outcome of a criminal career.

---

[9] For more reading, there is a large body of literature on serial crimes and profiling, some of which appear in the reference list below.

Scholars who address the concept of serial crimes (Holmes & Holmes, 1996; Best & Luckenebill, 1996; Egger, 1985; Holmes & DeBurger, 1988; Mitchell, 1997), define the notion of serial crimes on the basis of two conditions: first, there must be a minimal time range of three days between one crime and the next - this is most important in defining serial murders (Holmes & Holmes, 1998), - and secondly, a serial offender must be a criminal who has carried out at least three crimes of the same type. The author would like to raise at least two objections to this definition and to the conditions they require. First of all, according to the current definition, we can ask the following question: Should a killer who kills three times at twenty-year intervals be regarded as a serial killer? If the answer is negative, because there is no real continuity in his behavior, then the definition is illogical. On the other hand, if the answer is positive, simply because the scenario fits the two conditions, then the definition suffers from arbitrariness. Hence, we should add a third condition to the current definition, which will specify a reasonable maximum range of time between the three crimes required.

Secondly, the second condition (a minimum of three crimes) is even more arbitrary than the first one. Indeed, one crime may represent a one-time phenomenon; by definition, serial crimes cannot occur at once. Moreover, this condition lacks an argument for the determination of the minimum of three crimes. On the same weak basis, we could suggest as a condition that four or even five crimes are required in order to qualify an offender as a serial criminal.

## Serial offenders: Professional vs. Un-Professional

In this section, the differences between the two kinds of serial offenders are described. It is important to recall that there are various kinds of serial offenders. One subtype is the professional serial offender. These criminals acquire skills and expertise over the years, so that the chances of finding them are slim. As a result, they can act uninterruptedly in furthering their criminal career. As an example, most female serial offenders who killed their husbands in order to collect life insurance (the “black widows") were caught years after the killings, as were nurses who killed old people in their custody and collected the social security money monthly ("angels of death").

In contrast, there is a second subtype of serial offenders - the non-professional serial offenders. Their life can be described as a circle in which they alternately and repeatedly commit crimes and are arrested. These criminals are not professional, nor do they specialize in crime. Their criminal behavior lacks careful planning, they leave many pieces of evidences at the crime scenes and, as a result, they are more easily captured, so that the concept of career does not apply to them. For them, criminality is more of a "moonlighting" type of activity (Holzman, 1995), or a way of life. Thus, in the literature, they are called "habitual" or "chronic" offenders. While the professional criminal may live a double life in order to conceal his criminal career, the non-professional criminal essentially lacks a double life. These criminals commit crimes for extra earnings, or to finance an addiction such as drug abuse or gambling.

One can object to this by arguing that a habitual or chronic offender can be a professional or even a career criminal. This is true but incomplete and should be properly argued. These careful distinctions and differentiations could have prevented much of the confusion that appears in the literature. Moreover, we can see how criminologists use the same label in order to describe different types of criminals. The title of "habitual/ chronic offender," is used by criminologist to describe a whole range of serial criminals, without relating to the fundamental differences between them.

## *Preliminary motives in serial offenders*

The distinction between professional and non-professional serial criminals is a necessary one. However, it is not sufficient; it is also necessary to distinguish between pathological vs. material gains as a preliminary motive among serial professional criminals. Although some scholars will argue that this distinction in not necessarily a dichotomous one, it is irrelevant at this stage, as long as we can point out to the main motive. Moreover, this distinction is a critical one for understanding serial criminality as a criminal career, following our theoretical model.

As we have seen, the work of professional serial offenders reflects specialization and professionalism. These criminals may act, among others, following a rational professional choice, or because of some pathological or mental disorder.[10] The latter motivates the criminals to obtain psychological gain (e.g. relief and satisfaction) by committing their crimes. In such cases, the criminals are aware that their behavior is wrong and they do not have the legal defense of insanity (Holmes & DeBurger, 1988; Holmes & Holmes, 1998; Vronsky, 2004). In the authors' opinion, some or most of these criminals use techniques of "neutralization" (Sykes & Matza, 1957) in order to deny blame or shame.

---

[10] The discussion here does not deal with insane serial criminals

The main distinction emphasized here is that, although the two types of serial professional offenders may act out of different motives (material vs. psychological), they will pursue a life of serial criminality, as long as these motives are met. In this point, it is important to make yet another distinction between primary and secondary motives. A criminal may have material and pathological motives - one of them is viewed as the primary and the other as secondary (Doley, 2003). For example, a prostitute who kills her clients because of a pathological hatred of men (primary, pathological motive) may also rob her victims in order to gain material profit (secondary, material motive), although it is not always easy to differentiate between them. Furthermore, either motive may be present in serial professional offenders who are members of an organization or who act outside of an organization, alone or in teams. However, such motives do not constitute sufficient grounds for categorizing either of them as career criminals.

Earlier, it is argued that a criminal career must involve serial criminality, but not all serial criminality constitutes a criminal career. The same logic holds for the definition of professionalism. Moreover, the professional serial offender can be considered as having a criminal career only if his preliminary motive is material or financial, and not psychological or pathological. Notably, one of the historical difficulties when comparing legitimate and criminal careers was that the comparisons were sometimes made in relation to career criminals who acted for gain, and sometimes in relation to professional criminals motivated by pathological reasons. Since this argument or condition with respect to primary motive may be regarded, prima facie, as arbitrary, it demands further clarification. Maslow (1943) defined the hierarchy of human needs as follows: The primary needs that must be met in order to survive are physiological and security needs. Only after these needs are met is the person free to obtain higher needs in the hierarchy, such as social belonging, social status and other self-fulfillment needs.

Based on this theory, the professional workers in the legitimate and in the criminal spheres (whether in an organizational or private setting), aspire preeminently to attain the conditions that will guarantee that their survival and security needs are met. This is only possible by having a high and steady income. For some people with mental problems, a psychological threat may be an existential one, which gives more credibility to the view that career criminals mainly act for material gains, rather than for psychological relief or satisfaction. Only after these needs are met, can a person aspire to fulfill other needs such as social recognition, belonging and self-fulfillment. The serial professional criminal, as well as the legitimate professional worker, aspire to maximize the material benefits that their profession can provide. These professionals wish to specialize and to continue with their work in order to increase these material benefits. In the process, people make rationalizations in order to justify their growing aspirations and to maximize their material benefits on behalf of their deeds. For example, a professional call girl will claim that she helps men who have difficulty in entertaining emotional relations with women.

Alternatively, their professionalism gratifies them with psychological and social needs that accompany their professional position (honor, reputation, power). Thus, by embarking on a professional career, be it in the legitimate or in the criminal sphere, professionals are given social recognition as such (whether formally or informally). In contrast, the professional serial offender and the legitimate professional worker, who are motivated by pathological motives,[11] cannot be compared to the career owners even if they succeed in camouflaging their deeds. Indeed, they can specialize as time goes by and refine their work methods, but their core pathological motives distinguish them from the career criminals and from legitimate workers.

Their psychological gains are neither permanent nor high. The actor feels disappointed and frustrated with respect to the expectations he developed during the fantasy phase, which occurs before his act. The continuity of the acts these offenders perform does not raise their gains; on the contrary, they get "burnt out" over time, until they eventually retire. In addition, the satisfaction the criminals receive is of relatively short duration (even for serial killers who abuse the corpses); and the positive recognition they receive is minimal, even from other criminals - the number of "copycat" incidents is relatively small. This type of criminal reaches a peak or plateau in his professional life, beyond which he cannot refine his criminal skills or career. For example, the professional pathological serial killer ("the hedonist") does not refine the selection of his victims because his pathology causes him to repeatedly look for the "ideal victim" (Holmes & DeBurger, 1988; Hickey, 1992; Holmes & Holmes, 1998; Leyton, 2000).

In contrast, the professional serial offender acting in order to achieve material gains, who is actually a career criminal, is constantly searching for "bigger" targets. For example, the "hit man" who dares to choose his targets (victims), increases his material gains and his reputation. In turn,

[11] There are cases of sadistic workers with sexual pathology who used their job to gain psychological gains (working with children, prisoners and insane patients).

this reputation will increase his fees in the future. Another example is the "black widow," who carefully chooses her husbands to gain increasing material benefits once she has murdered them. Hence, the relatively constant pattern exhibited by the pathological professional serial criminal limits his ability to progressively aspire to stable and higher psychological gains. In contrast, the career criminal is freer and more creative in his search for higher material gains. This non-binding pattern enables him to perfect and develop his actions and career in different directions, without limitations.

However, a problem arises since professional and career criminals' share many features, which has lead to the confusion discussed earlier. As we have seen, a close analysis of the primary motive may help clarify this confusion. Examining the concept of "serial crimes" enables us to move forward towards our final goal. We will define and clarify the different kinds of serial criminals, in relation to criminal careers. This will enable us to determine which kinds of serial criminals should be called career criminals and which should not.

## Serial criminality and its relation to criminal career

A criminal career is, by definition, a series of criminal acts that are characterized by specialization and professionalism, its primary motive being material gains. The distinction made above has helped to lay the theoretical foundations necessary for a conclusive description of the connections between a criminal career and serial criminality, two important concepts included in this chapter. In order to reach this conclusion, a typology summarizing the insights gained so far is presented.

Serial criminality may manifest itself in three kinds of criminals (according to the current definition of seriality). Each of them are addressed with its relation to criminal career.

### *1. Unprofessional serial criminal activity*

This type of criminal activity is performed by criminals who have low or nonexistent obligations to crime. They may commit crimes and then withdraw to a legitimate occupation, or they may be arrested repeatedly. While in jail, their criminal activity is halted. These criminals lack professionalism and /or specialization in crime, which is why they are arrested repeatedly. In addition, even if they want to become law-abiding citizens, they are already labeled as criminals and their chances of finding a legitimate employment are very low. Their obligation to crime is low because crime does not serve as a significant means of sustenance or family support for them – which is why it is defined as a form of moonlighting. It is a convenient way of maintaining their standard of living, or pursuing their habits or addictions. In other words, this kind of serial criminality is not a criminal career but a "lifestyle." The crimes these criminals commit are not much different from crimes of professional criminals, but they lack the trait of professionalism. These serial criminals fit the notions mentioned in the literature as "chronic offender" or "habitual offender." Because the existing definition of serial offenders does not define a maximum range of time between crimes, these criminals are still regarded as serial criminals, although they can be in jail for long periods of time between their criminal acts.

### *2. Professional-pathological serial criminal activity*

This type of criminal activity is carried out by serial criminals who are motivated by a pathological urge, and whose purpose is some kind of psychological reward. For example, the visionary and hedonist serial killers, serial rapists and pyromaniacs generally perform criminal acts for pathological motives. Although they may perform their acts in a professional way, since their primary motive is psychological rather than material, they cannot be regarded as being career criminals.

### *3. Professional serial criminal activity - criminal career*

This type of criminal activity is performed by professional serial offenders who are driven towards constantly higher material gains. In addition, secondary motives, such as a desire for psychological, social and other secondary rewards, may also exist. Their professionalism manifests itself in the development of a criminal career, in which they acquire and improve professional skills that will enable them to chase after ever-growing material profits. Their commitment to their occupation and career in crime is very high. Theses career criminals may commit the same kind of crimes as those committed by serial criminals, but the main motives are different. Therefore, they will not rape their victims, nor will they set anything on fire in order to obtain psychological satisfaction. In addition, they will plan their acts very carefully and perform their crimes in a professional way, so that they will avoid being caught. Examples include serial killers for material profit ("the hit man" - Levi 1995 - or the "contract murderer" - Schlesinger 2001); serial thieves; merchants in stolen property; robbers; burglars; forgers; money launderers; professional call girls; and high level drug dealers who also import drugs.

The following discussion presents a model based on the idea that serial crimes is a common or mutual element shared by different types of criminals, namely: habitual, professional and career criminals. For this reason, the serial aspect of their activity should be the point of departure of the model. On the other hand, the model also enables us to distinguish between these different criminals. In order to do so, we must add two other elements to the model: professionalism and primary motives. This extension enables us to demonstrate the relationship between the type of criminal and the presence and absence of a criminal career.

The model shows three crucial distinctions between the various serial offenders. First of all, habitual or chronic offenders must fulfill only one element or condition – they carry out their activities in a serial way. These criminals are not professionals and therefore cannot be regarded as career criminals, regardless of their primary motive. Moreover, it is doubtful whether these criminals are even serial offenders at all. Their non-professionalism means they do not pursue carrying out criminal activities. Secondly, professional criminals must fulfill two elements or conditions - acting in a serial way and professionalism. In addition, if their primary motive is a pathological one, they are not career criminals (serial rapists, sadistic serial killers). On the other hand, if their primary motive is a material one, they should be labeled career criminals. Thirdly, career criminals must fulfill three elements or conditions: serial crimes, professionalism and a primary material motive ("the hit man", "the black widow", people setting buildings on fire in order to collect insurance).

Table 2: comparison of the three kinds of serial criminals

| Kind/ element | Seriality | Professionalism | Primary motive: material gains | Primary motive: other |
|---|---|---|---|---|
| Habitual | + | - | + usually | + addiction |
| Professional | + | + | +(career criminal) , - | +, - |
| Career | + | + | + | - |

Table 3: Serial criminality and criminal career- the model

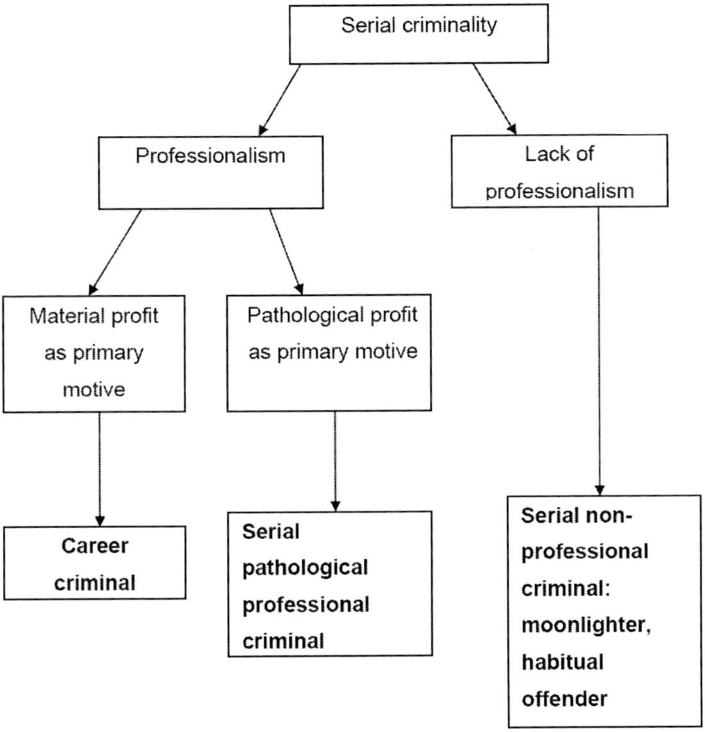


Source: Edelstein (2006).

# Summary and conclusions

Crime and criminals threaten the peaceful and secure lives of citizens. Fear of crime harms many people's well-being and causes them to change their lifestyle. This is primarily due to professional and career criminals, who are responsible for most serious criminal activities. For these reasons, criminology seeks to understand and explain these types of behavior. However, the relevant research in criminology has suffered from confusion since scholars have been using different titles to explain the same concepts, while others have been using the same titles to explain different concepts. This confusion hindered the possibility of reaching a common theoretical basis for further research.

This chapter focuses on the conceptual confusion described in order to clarify some of the confusion in this important area of criminological thinking and revises some of the main concepts in this area: "criminal career", "professional crime", "habitual/ chronic crime" and "serial crime". The point of departure of this reevaluation is that committing serial crimes is a characteristic shared by the three types of criminals - non-professionals, professionals and career criminals. In fact, these common traits, which formerly caused confusion, now enable us to differentiate these three types of criminals.

The analysis of these concepts suggests several contributions to the current literature. First of all, this chapter proposes a new definition of the concept of "career criminal", in order to differentiate it from other kinds of criminals such as “professional criminals” and “chronic offenders”. In addition, this redefinition will enable a more appropriate comparison between legitimate vs. criminal careers. Secondly, this chapter proposes two criteria to distinguish between different kinds of criminals: professionalism and primary motive.

From this point of view, it is easier to differentiate the chronic/ habitual offenders who are not professional criminals, from other kinds of criminals, such as career criminals. This differentiation will prevent further confusion between the concepts. Thirdly, this chapter proposes to distinguish between two sub-categories of professional criminals, according to their primary motive. From this point of view, there are professional criminals whose primary motive is pathological, and who should not be considered as career criminals. On the other hand, those who act for material motives are career criminals. Fourthly, a hierarchical model is proposed, that distinguishes between the three kinds of serial criminals mentioned above, thus preventing further confusion between them. Finally, the theoretical discussion, as well as the model, shows us that professional crime and criminal career may occur in organizational, team or individual settings. This argument contradicts previous assumptions in this field and broadens this theoretical and empirical area for future research.

However, this chapter does not resolve all the theoretical problems in this field, and at least two issues require further research. First of all, the proposed model does not resolve the problems stemming from the current definition of serial criminality, which suffers from two main shortcomings:

1. It lacks clear guidelines regarding the maximum time range between crimes performed by the same criminal. For example, should a criminal who performs three crimes at intervals of twenty years, be regarded as a serial criminal? This question still remains unanswered.

2. It lacks a reasoned argument for the number of crimes required to determine the presence of serial criminality. The current definition calls for three crimes of the same kind being perpetrated by the same criminal. While it is clear that more than one crime is needed to talk about a series of crime, the requirement of at least three crimes seems arbitrary and calls for further support.

In the future, scholars should consider re-defining the concept of "serial criminality," while taking into account the shortcomings mentioned above. Secondly, criminologists, like other scientists, seek to categorize crimes and criminals in order to understand and explain these phenomena. Clusters of crimes, such as violence, sex, drugs, and crimes against property help them in this mission. Clusters of criminals, as we have seen throughout this chapter, represent another important area, although they are more difficult to categorize. One in-depth way of categorizing criminals is by profiling their behaviors, background, family status and other characteristics and traits.[12] For example, the literature shows that serial killers and serial arsonists share some common traits and motives. This type of categorization may provide a valuable contribution to law enforcement personnel.

On the other hand, aspiring towards making generalizations may harm our ability to identify differences that exist between various types of criminals. For example, although prima facie, there may be some similarity in traits and motives between a serial killer and a serial arsonist, there must be fundamental differences between them that manifest themselves substantially through the type of crime they perform. It is concluded by stating that over-generalizations may conceal these fundamental differences.

## References

Adler, P. A., & Adler, P. (1996). Shifts and oscillations in deviant careers: the case of upper-level drug dealers and smugglers. In D. F. Greenberg (Ed.), *Criminal Careers* (pp.192-205). Dartmouth, U.S.A: Washington News Books.

---

[12] See, for example: Weisburd & Waring, 2001; Holmes & Holmes, 1996; and Kocsis & Cooksey, 2002

Becker, H. (1963). *Outsiders: Studies in the Sociology of deviance*. N.Y: Free Press.

Becker, H., & Carper, J. (1956). The Elements of identification with an occupation. *American Sociological Review*, *21*(1), 341-348.

Becker, H., & Strauss, A.L. (1956). Careers' personality and adult socialization. *The American Journal of Sociology*, *62*(3) 253-263.

Best, J., & Luckenebill, D. F. (1996). Careers in deviance and respectability. In D. F. Greenberg (Ed.), *Criminal Careers* (pp. 3-14). Dartmouth, U.S.A: Washington News Books.

Blumstein, A., Cohen, J., Roth, J. A., & Vishers, C. A., (Eds.), (1986). *Criminal careers and career criminals.* Vol. 1. Washington, DC: National Academy Press.

Blumstein, A., Cohen, J., & Moitra, S. D. (1996) Specialization and Seriousness during adult criminal careers. In D. F. Greenberg (Ed.), *Criminal careers* (pp.135-178). Dartmouth, U.S.A: Washington News Books.

Chaiken, J. M., & Chaiken, M. R. (1982). *Varieties of criminal behavior*. Santa Monica, CA: The Rand Corporation.

Clinard, M. B., & Quinney, R. (1967). *Criminal behavior systems: A typology*. N.Y: Rinehart & Winston.

Conklin, J. E. (1986). *Criminology*. New York: Macmillan Publishing.

Coombs, R. H. (1996). Drugs abuse as Career. In D. F. Greenberg (Ed.), *Criminal careers* (pp. 369-374). Dartmouth, U.S.A: Washington News Books.

Cornish, D., & Clarke, R. V. (1986). *The reasoning criminal*. N.Y: Springer- Verlag.

David, P.R. (Ed.), (1974). *The world of the burglar*. Albuquerque: University of New Mexico Press.

Davis, C.A. (2001). *Women who kill: Profiles of female serial killers*. London: Alison and Busby.

De Lisi, M. (2005). *Career criminals in society*. Thousand Oaks, CA: Sage Publications Inc.

Ditton, J. (1977). *Part-time Crime*: *An ethnography of fiddling and pilferage*. London: Macmillan.

Doley, R. (2003). Making Sense of Arson through Classification. *Psychiatry, Psychology and Law*, *10*(2), 346-352.

Edelstein, A. (2006). *Criminal career and serial criminality.* Ben- Gurion University of the Negev Press, Israel (in Hebrew).

Egger, A. S. (1985). A working definition of serial murder and the reduction of linkage blindness. *Journal of Police Science and Administration, 12*(3), 348-357

Farrington, D. P. (1997). Human development and criminal careers. In M. Maguire, R. Morgan, & R. Reiner (Eds.), *The Oxford handbook of criminology* (2nd ed., pp. 361-408). Oxford: Clarendon Press.

Gadd, D., & Farrall, S. (2004). Criminal Careers, desistance and Subjectivity. *Theoretical Criminology*, *8*(2), 123-156.

Gould, L.C. et al. (1966). *Crime as a profession*. Washington, D.C.: Government.

Greenberg, D. F. (Ed.), (1996). *Criminal careers*. Dartmouth, U.S.A: Washington News Books.

Hale, R. (1998). The application of learning theory to the serial murder. In R. M. Holmes, & S. T. Holmes (Eds.), *Contemporary perspective on serial murder* (pp.75-84). Thousand Oaks, CA: Sage.

Hasin, Y. (1987) The prone offender, the dangerous offender and the career criminal. *Crime and Social Deviance*, *15*(1-2), 5-18 (in Hebrew).

Hickey, E. W. (1992). *Serial murderers and their victims*. Belmont, California: Wadsworth Publishing Company.

Holmes, R. M., & DeBurger, J. D. (1988). *Serial murder*. London: Sage Publications.

Holmes, R. M., & Holmes, S. T. (1996). *Profiling violent crimes*. London: Sage Publications.

Holmes, R. M., & Holmes, S. T. (1998). *Serial Murder*. London: Sage Publications.

Holzman, H. R. (1995). The serious habitual property offender as "Moonlighter". In D. Hobbs (Ed.), *Professional criminals*. Dartmouth, U.S.A: Washington News Books.

Inciardi, J. A. (1975). *Careers in crime*. Chicago: Rand McNally.

Jackson, H. F., Glass, C., & Hope, S. (1987). A functional analysis of recidivistic arson. *British Journal of Clinical Psychology*, *26*(3), 175-185.

Klein, J. F., & Montague, A. (1975). *Check forgers*. Lexington, MA: D.C. Heath and Co.

Klockars, C. B. (1974). *The professional fence*. New York: The Free Press.

Kocsis, R. N., & Cooksey, R. W. (2002). Criminal psychological profiling of serial arson crimes. *International Journal of Offender Therapy and Comparative Criminology*, *46*(3), 631- 656.

Letkemann, P. (1973). *Crime as work*. Englewood Cliffs: Prentice-Hall, Inc.

Levi, K. (1995). Becoming a hit man. In D. Hobbs (Ed.), *Professional criminals* (pp.197-214). Dartmouth, U.S.A: Washington News Books.

Leyton, E. H. (Ed.). (2000). *Serial murder: Modern scientific perspectives*. Aldershot, UK: Dartmouth/Ashgate.

Lombroso, C. (1911). *Criminal man*. New York: Putnam.
Maslow, A. (1943). A theory of human motivation. *Psychological Review, 50,* 370-396.
Mawby, R. I. (2001). *Burglary*. Willan Publishing: Cullompton.
Messinger, S. L. (1966). *Some reflections on professional crime in west city*, Mimeographed Personal to Author.
Miller, G. (1978). *Odd Jobs: The world of deviant work*. Englewood Cliffs: Prentice-Hall, Inc.
Mitchell, B. A. (1997). *The aetiology of serial murder: Towards an integrated model.* Cambridge, UK: University of Cambridge.
Prus, R. C., & Sharper, C. R. D. (*1977*). *Road hustler: The career contingencies of professional card and dice hustlers.* Toronto: Lexington Books.
Roebuck, J. B., & Windham, G. O. (1983). Professional theft. In G. P. Waldo (Ed.), *Career criminals* (pp.13-29). Beverley Hills, CA: Sage Publications.
Schlesinger, L. B. (2001). The contract murderer: Patterns, characteristics, and dynamics. *Journal Forensic Sciences, 46*(5), 1119-1123.
Shover, N. (1996). *Great Pretenders: Pursuits and careers of persistent thieves.* Boulder, CO: Westview Press.
Smith, D. R., & Smith, W. R. (1996). Patterns of delinquency careers: An assessment of three perspectives. In D. F. Greenberg (Ed.), *Criminal careers* (pp.215-242). Dartmouth, U.S.A: Washington News Books.
Sutherland, E. H. (1939). *The professional thief.* Chicago: University of Chicago Press.
Sykes, G., & Matza, D. (1957). Techniques of neutralization: A theory of delinquency. *American Journal of Sociology*, *22*, 664-670.
Vronsky, P. (2004). *Serial killers*. New York: Berkley Books.
Walsh, D. (1980). *Break-Ins: Burglary from private houses*. London: Constable.
—. (1986). *Heavy business: Commercial burglary and robbery*. London: Routledge & Kegan Paul.
Walters, G. D. (1990). *The criminal lifestyle*. Beverley Hills, CA: Sage Publications.
Weisburd, D., & Waring, E. (2001). *White-Collar crime and criminal careers*. Cambridge, UK: Cambridge University Press.
West, W. G. (1996). The short term careers of serious thieves. In D. F. Greenberg (Ed.), *Criminal careers* (pp.169-187). Dartmouth, U.S.A: Washington News Books.
Wolfgang, M. E., Figlio, R. M., & Sellin, T. (1972). *Delinquency in a birth cohort*. Chicago: University of Chicago Press.

# CHAPTER NINE

# ETHICAL CONSIDERATIONS FOR FIELD-BASED CRIMINOLOGY: A CANADIAN PERSPECTIVE

CURTIS FOGEL

## Abstract

In Canada, all research involving human subjects requires approval from a formal ethics review board before it can be conducted. Despite this, the body of literature relating to ethics in social science research is marginal, particularly in relation to research on crime and deviance. This chapter contributes to this void in the literature by exploring the ethical issues presented by field-based criminological research. The issues examined include: eliciting sensitive information, coercive potentials, and the consequences of knowing, conflicts of interest, and confidentiality and the possibility of subpoena. This chapter argues that the current ethics review framework in Canada often acts in contradicting ways making it more difficult to conduct ethical criminological research.

## Introduction

Considering that all social science research with Canadian university affiliation that involves contact with humans requires formal ethics review by an approved Research Ethics Board (REB), the contemporary published literature pertaining to ethical issues in social science research is meagre. The literature on strategies to remain ethical without compromising research is even sparser. This chapter seeks to contribute to the literature in both of these areas as it relates to field-based criminological research. It examines the main ethical issues of criminological research and possible strategies for novice researchers to remain ethical in ways that are not detrimental to the research. Further to this, this chapter will briefly discuss how the ethics review framework in Canada has added further complications to researchers, rather than ameliorating these issues and strategies.

The first section of this chapter will discuss how ethics is defined, why we have ethics review boards, and how the ethics review system is structured in Canada. The second section will examine five main ethical issues involved in field-based criminological research, and when pertinent, simple strategies to possibly address these issues. The ethical issues that will be examined include: 1) eliciting sensitive information, 2) coercive potentials, 3) the consequences of knowing, 4) conflicts of interest, and 5) confidentiality and the possibility of subpoena. The third section will briefly discuss how the framework of ethics review in Canada has done little to curb these issues, and in some cases have unethically placed researchers and research participants at further risk of harm. This chapter will then conclude with a discussion of the future of criminological research in Canada in the climate of overbearing ethics review boards.

## The Importance of Ethics

The Canadian *Tri-Council Policy Statement: Ethical Conduct for Research Involving Humans* states that ethical research includes two fundamental components: 1) "the selection and achievement of morally acceptable ends", and 2) "the morally acceptable means to those ends" (Sec. B, i.4). Ethics, as defined in relation to human research, is a moral standard of conduct to ensure that risks of harm are minimized to those who participate in research (Berg, 2004). When one is wrapped up in the sometimes difficult and lengthy ethics application process, it can be easy to think that the process is, as Mueller (2007, p. 1) suggests, just a "tool for harassment in the academic workplace." However, that is more a testament of how the ethics review process is organized in Canada, rather than a suggestion that ethics are not needed in social science research.

Some, such as Barber (1973), have cited the rise of the civil rights movement in the 1950s and 1960s as having raised the awareness of ethics in human research. Whereas, scholars such as Babbie (2001) suggest that this concern has arisen from questionable studies such as those conducted by Milgram (1973), Humphreys (1970), and Zimbardo (1973). However, before these studies there were numerous atrocities committed in the name of science during the Second World War by a group of German physicians that included "immersing [concentration camp subjects] in freezing water, and injecting them with poison, diseases, and even gasoline- in an effort to learn how the body responds to such extreme manipulations" (Haggerty, 2004, p. 403 cited in Annas & Grodin, 1992).

These atrocities were later tried in the Nuremberg War Crimes Tribunal in 1946, which led to the subsequent indoctrination of the

Nuremberg Code (Haggerty, 2004). It is here that the concern for ethics in human research first began to take on its contemporary form. The principles of the Nuremberg Code of 1947 include:

*1) To obtain voluntary consent of the persons involved as subjects.*

*2) To allow persons to end their participation in a study at any time.*

*3) To ensure the research is needed to obtain the information sought (i.e. it could not be obtained in any other way) and that the research is expected to be beneficial to society.*

*4) To minimize the risk to the subjects and the suffering they are likely to experience*

*5) To ensure the expected benefits outweigh the risks* (Itlas, 2006).

These guidelines have become the foundation of the Canadian *Tri-Council Policy*. This is not to say, however, that the authors who have suggested different origins of ethical concern are wrong. Milgram (1974), Zimbardo (1973), and Humphreys (1970), among countless others, have certainly added increased concern to how we conduct human research in contemporary academics, but it has really been questionable practices by biomedical researchers, such as the Nazi doctors that have led to the contemporary ethics review mandate.

While the *Tri-Council Policy* guidelines are not set out to eliminate harm to participants, they do aim to strike a balance between benefit and harm. Such a balance is, however, the ideal for human research; harm to participants and researchers, should be minimized. Many scholars have raised questions about REBs in Canada overstepping their bounds (Haggarty, 2004; Adler & Adler, 2002; Mueller, 2004, 2007; Palys & Lowman, 2000, 2002, 2006) however; this does not negate the importance of ethics in social science research. The concerns raised by these researchers are not on the importance of ethics but rather, that the ethics review framework in Canadian universities is inadequate in ensuring ethical research.

While some variations of the ethics review process likely exist across Canadian universities, they are all governed by the mandate laid out in the *Tri-Council Policy Statement*. In general, each REB requires that researchers submit an application of their proposed project before conducting any research involving human subjects. This application includes, but is not limited to, an overview or discussion of the proposed project, the methodology, the possible harms, and the procedures taken to minimize these harms (Haggarty, 2004). Research that does not involve human subjects does not require ethics review; although, it is not uncommon practice for contemporary Canadian researchers to error on the side of caution and submit an ethics application even if they are relying strictly on secondary data. The penalties for not adhering to this mandate is that no federal research funds will be released, and those found to act in non-compliance can be fined, fired or suspended (Haggarty, 2004).

## Ethical Issues

There are number of ethical issues that must be addressed in most research projects involving human subjects such as: voluntary participation, informed consent, privacy of personal information, and the potential harms and benefits of the research (Berg, 2004). Criminological researchers must negotiate through these concerns, as well as a number of other issues that are heightened or more specific to the nature of the research. This chapter will focus on these specific ethical issues of field-based criminological research. The ethical issues that will be examined include: i) eliciting sensitive information, ii) coercive potentials, iii) the consequences of knowing, iv) conflicts of interest, v) confidentiality and the possibility of subpoena, and vi) researcher risks.

### *i) Eliciting Sensitive Information*

While criminological research is not the only research that touches on potentially sensitive topics, it is most commonly found within such research (Renzetti & Lee, 1993). Two main forms of sensitive information that are often elicited during field-based criminological research include: information that could potentially disturb the participant, and information pertaining to illegal activities. Renzetti and Lee (1993) suggest that the eliciting of information that might disturb the participant is an ethical issue of all research projects involving human subjects, regardless of substantive focus. One can never know if something in the interview process will strike a negative cord with the respondent. The second sensitivity issue, eliciting information on illegal activities is possible in all studies as well, but is certainly most common in research that is specifically geared towards discussing criminal behaviours, e.g. Osborne and Fogel's (2008) qualitative research of illicit drug use. While all efforts should be made to minimize the emotional distress of participants, the elicitation of sensitive information type is not necessarily problematic. In some instances, particularly in criminological research, the research is intended to gain further understanding of a sensitive topic. Uncovering sensitive information, particularly of illegal activities, is however, the starting point for the next three ethical issues that will be discussed.

### *ii) Coercive Potentials*

Researching a group or population, regardless of the study being conducted, requires a measure of invasiveness that might expose individuals to a higher risk of harm than they would assume in their everyday life (Palys & Lowman, 2006). As such, researchers are required to present the possibility of these risks to participants to ensure their free and informed consent. A participant can potentially be coerced into participating in a study, that is, not to have free and informed consent, if a) their consent is not completely voluntary or b) if they have received misleading or inadequate information about the purposes of a study (Berg, 2004).

To ensure voluntary participation, participants must not perceive any coercive potential. A good example of a coercive potential is a professor asking his or her students to take part in a study. The students might feel that participating, or not participating, will have an influence on the grade they receive in this professor's course (Berg, 2004). There is a clear power differential here that could have the effect of coercing the students into participating. In criminological research, this issue is most clearly illustrated by studies on prison populations (Arboleda-Florez, 1991). If the study appears sanctioned by anyone with administrative authority, then the participants might think that they will get points for good behaviour for participating, which would subsequently lead to their early release. Participation, under these conditions, would be considered to be coerced participation.

To avoid this form of coercive potential, researchers should avoid sampling approaches that clearly identify who provided their contact information for participation, or who the gatekeeper to access the population was. By providing this information, the participant might feel that the study is being sanctioned by the contact information source, e.g. if researching juvenile delinquents, to say that their social worker provided their contact information might coerce them to participate, much like inmates in a prison study, because of the award they might hope to receive for good behaviour (Arboleda-Florez, 1991). One strategy to avoid this problem, then, is to avoid identifying contact information sources when contacting potential participants. Or alternatively, recruitment posters and websites could be used to allow potential participants to voluntarily contact the researcher, thereby allowing for a more indirect sampling approach (Im & Chee, 2004).

Not providing the name of those who provided contact information should not be confused with providing misleading information to participants. To confuse the two would negate the informed consent of study participation (Berg, 2004). Since criminological research deals with topics of a sensitive nature, participants must be informed of these risks. To not to do this would be an exploitation of the research participant; the researcher and their institution would profit from the potential uninformed harms to the research subject. This is what caused such ethical alarm in the studies conducted by Milgram (1974), Humphries (1970), and Zimbardo (1973) that were mentioned previously in this chapter.

### *iii) The Consequences of Knowing*

Being privy to sensitive information has the further issue that the researcher might be faced with difficult ethical decisions of what to do with the information. Three problems could arise in field-based criminological research in this regard, including: a) the participant has revealed a need for help or counsel, b) the participant has admitted to something that might require reporting to legal officials, c) there are conflicts of interest between researchers, subjects and funding agencies, or d) legal officials want to know confidential information that the researcher may know, i.e. the possibility of subpoena.

The first two ethical issues surround if and when researchers should interfere. One research stance is to enter the fields of research with as little invasiveness in the lives of those being studied as possible, i.e. the fly on the wall (Savage, 2000). However, some complications could arise that make this approach difficult. For example, common topics of criminological research include drug abuse, gambling, and pornography. In any of these types of studies the researcher could perceive that a participant is suffering from a serious addiction. This issue can be dealt with by a) securing counselling services that might seem plausible before beginning a research project, listing the details on the participant consent form, and ensuring that the services will be at no financial cost to the participant, and b) providing this information to the participant in a debriefing at the end of the participation (Berg, 2004). The researcher should plan ahead for such occurrences, and avoid trying to act as counsellor to the participant.

The researcher might also be faced with the ethical dilemma of whether or not to interfere in the lives of participants if they become privy to information about illegal behaviours that could be useful to legal authorities. The issue here pertains to what that privileged information is. To ensure that participants provide honest answers, participants must be given the privilege of confidentiality; this is essential for valid and reliable research (Palys & Lowman, 2000, 2002, 2006). Thus, just as a psychiatrist would not report the confessions of a client, neither should a researcher. Palys and Lowman (2000, p. 75) do suggest that researchers should, however, report what they term "heinous discoveries". They suggest that these discoveries could fall under two conditions including: a) public safety, e.g. knowledge of child abuse, or b) innocence at stake, e.g. knowledge of a wrongly accused.

This is only to say that researchers *should* report heinous discoveries, but is not always that they must. For example, in Smith v. Jones (1999) the Canadian Supreme Court delved over whether or not to employ the public safety clause to allow a psychiatrist to break confidential doctor-client privilege. The court considered three public safety factors:

- *Is there a clear risk to an identifiable person or group of persons?*
- *Is there a risk of serious bodily harm or death?*
- *Is the danger imminent?*

The court ruled that the psychiatrist could not reveal specific details of his interactions with the client, but could only express his opinion on the danger he felt the client posed to a specific population, in this case towards prostitutes. The rationale behind this decision was to "foster a climate in which dangerous individuals are more likely to disclose their disorders, seek treatment and pose less danger to the public" (Smith v. Jones, 1999).

## *iv) Conflicts of Interest*

Gaining detailed sensitive information can lead to conflicts of interest for researchers conducting criminological research. For criminological researchers, a definite ethical dilemma is presented when the data one collects is in fundamental opposition to the values and objectives of his or her funding agency. This is becoming an increasingly important ethical issue to consider as more criminological research projects are being funded by various external sources ranging from private enterprises to government initiatives. When confronted with such a conflict of interest, researchers are faced with the decision of whether to censor certain information to protect the mission of their funding agency, or alternatively to go against this mission in the interest of academic integrity.

Geis, Mobley and Shichor, (1999) suggest that criminologists have an ethical obligation to report their findings, even if it means going against the desires of their funding agency. To not do so would be a major compromise to social science research. To illustrate their contention, Geis, Mobley and Shichor, (1999) look specifically at the case study of Professor Charles W. Thomas at the University of Florida. Professor

Thomas, a major supporter of the privatization of prisons, authored work exaggerating the positive impact and reduced recidivism rates of juveniles leaving private prison facilities compared to those in the public system. Geis, Mobley and Shichor, (1999) did some digging and discovered that Thomas had received $50 an hour by the Florida Correctional Privatization Commission for the research he conducted. As a result of this funding, Thomas's results have been viewed as tainted amongst other criminologists. How could he conduct unbiased research for an agency that was paying him his livelihood? The Florida Commission on Ethics had similar concerns ruling that by receiving funding from the company that he was researching Thomas had acted unethically, regardless of what merit his research might have, and he was subsequently fined and forced to leave his funded position.

Another researcher, Jeff Benedict (1997), faced a similar conflict of interest while researching instances of violence perpetrated by collegiate athletes but took an alternate route. At the time of the research, Benedict was serving as the Research Director of the Centre for the Study of Sport in Society at North Eastern University. The Centre was materially dependent on the sports world and as such, had a vested interest in portraying athletes as healthy role models. Through his research, however, Benedict uncovered a litany of stories of physical and sexual assaults disproportionately committed by university athletes, as well as numerous cover-ups of these occurrences. Benedict refused to stay silent, which led him to part ways with the research centre, his course of funding, for the sake of academic honesty.

As research funding increasingly becomes external and privatized, ethical conflicts of interest such as these have become pivotal ethical issues in conducting criminological research. To ensure that academic integrity is not violated through conflicts of interests, criminological researchers should: a) avoid directly researching an organization in which they are receiving funding from, b) explicitly acknowledge their funding sources in all publications, as well as any biases that may have been formed as a result and c) hold higher ideals of valid research, even if that means a reduction in funding sources.

### *v) Confidentiality and the Possibility of Subpoena*

A central concern of researchers writing on ethical issues of criminological research appears to be the concern for insuring confidentiality of research participation, particularly in light of the possibility of subpoena (see Palys & Lowman, 2000, 2002, 2006; Lowman

& Palys, 2004; Israel, 2004; Roberts & Indermaur, 2003). The incident that spurred this debate involves a graduate student at Simon Fraser University named Russell Ogden who was subpoenaed to turn over his research materials on assisted suicide to a Vancouver coroner (Palys & Lowman, 2000). After a lengthy legal debate, the coroner finally agreed that the costs of disrupting the researcher-participant privilege did not outweigh the benefits of knowing the privileged information. A lengthy legal battle was fought between Ogden and Simon Fraser University (SFU) regarding Ogden's contention that SFU failed to support his refusal to turn over the subpoenaed material. SFU was subsequently not held liable for Ogden's legal fees, but the judge presiding over the case did suggest that SFU had acted inappropriately in failing to support Ogden.

Palys and Lowman, (2000) suggest two strategies for criminological researchers to use in dealing with the possibility of subpoena including: a) methodological precautions, and b) legal strategy. The use of a methodological strategy entails confusing ones research materials in such a way that even if materials are subpoenaed they will be meaningless as no participants could be identified. One example of this approach is provided by Roberts and Indermaur, (2003) who suggest that researchers in criminology do not used signed consent forms because this will provide concrete evidence of who participated in a study. Instead, participants can read the consent form and then check a box stating that they voluntarily consent to participate.

In terms of legal strategy, Palys and Lowman, (2000, 2002, 2004, 2006), suggest that researchers plan their consent forms in a manner that appeals to the Wigmore test. The test is used in common law to determine case-by-case confidential privilege. The four tenets of the test include (Palys & Lowman, 2000, p. 51):

1) *The communications must originate in a confidence that they will not be disclosed.*

2) *This element of confidentiality must be essential to the full and satisfactory maintenance of the relation between the parties.*

3) *The relation must be one which in the opinion of the community ought to be sedulously fostered.*

4) *The injury that would inure to the relation by the disclosure of the communications must be greater than the benefit thereby gained for the correct disposal of litigation.*

Russel Ogden was able to convince a coroner to negate his Coroner's Court subpoena for his research materials by successfully appealing to these Wigmore criteria. Palys and Lowman, (2000) suggest that researchers can plan ahead by using Wigmore criteria to guide their research practices, so as to ensure that their research materials are not subpoenaed. For example, a statement in the consent form along the lines of "your right to privacy is ensured and will not be waived under any conditions" would provide a legal contract of privilege the courts would likely acknowledge.

## The Role of Canadian REBs

While research ethics boards in Canada have been created to ameliorate the issues previously discussed, as well as many others, it could be argued that they have in fact done the opposite, making ethical research more difficult to conduct for field-based criminologists. This is most evident in the failure to resolve the issue of confidentiality and the possibility of subpoena. For example, when Russell Ogden was subpoenaed by a coroner to turn over his research materials, Simon Fraser University unethically failed to stand behind their graduate student who was acting in accordance with his ethical provisions (Palys & Lowman, 2000). Further to this, some REBs in Canada will not allow researchers to assume the risk when it comes to the subpoena, instead, through the provision of limited confidentiality, they place the burden of risk on the research participants who have volunteered their time and efforts and little to no direct benefit to themselves (Palys & Lowman, 2006). While a series of reports by the federally-appointed Social Sciences and Humanities Research Ethics Working Committee has specifically addressed the issue of confidentiality suggesting that full or limited confidentiality should be at the discretion of the researcher, this does not appear to be the practice at all Canadian universities.

As such, many scholars have suggested that REBS are overstepping their bounds and legislating on research projects in ways that they do not have the authority (Haggarty, 2004; Adler & Adler, 2002; Mueller, 2004, 2007; Palys & Lowman, 2000, 2002, 2006). Haggarty, (2004, p. 392) terms this an "ethics creep" whereby "REBs have unintentionally expanded their mandate to include a host of groups and practices that were undoubtedly not anticipated in the original research ethics formulations." He equates this creep to the problem of bureaucratization, where new regulatory structures are continuously developed and intensified to the point that they are out of control. And yet, there are few checks and balances of the ethics review process; there is nothing to ensure they are acting ethically. American researchers Adler and Adler (2002) as well as Australian researchers Lucas and Lidstone (2000) attribute this encroachment on social science research to a fear of litigation against universities. Similarly, it is likely the case that Canadian ethics boards are becoming less concerned with minimizing harm to researchers and participants, and more concerned with protecting the university from litigation and poor publicity.

To an extent, one could argue that this is legitimate. If researchers are failing to provide adequate ethical standards in their research projects they can, and should, be held liable. However, the manner in which REBs are approaching their duties is in effect making it more difficult for researchers to ensure adequate ethical standards. At some universities in Canada, researchers are not supported in guaranteeing anything beyond limited confidentiality to their participants. This allows for a much weaker appeal to the Wigmore criteria, as it would be more difficult to prove that a contract of privilege was formed between the researcher and the participant. In this regard, Canadian ethics boards are, in effect, making it more difficult to conduct ethical field-based research on criminological topics and settings.

## Conclusion

This ethics creep, which has amounted to placing research participants at further risk of harm, has and will continue to have some devastating effects on the future of criminological research in Canada. One possibility is that researchers will take what Haggerty (2004, p. 412) terms "the path of least institutional resistance." Similarly, both Christopher Shea (2000) and Bruce Berg (2004, p. 56) suggest that this crackdown on human research has and will continue to lead researchers to conduct "vanilla research or the research of the sterile and mundane." Within the competitive and productivity-centered academic world, social science researchers simply do not want to waste months of time trying to push their projects through a lengthy ethics review process, when, there is the definite possibility that the REB will kill their project anyways. That is, by not allowing researchers to guarantee confidentiality, the validity and reliability of the participants' claims becomes questionable (Palys & Lowman, 2000).

A second negative consequence, beyond forcing researchers to study the mundane, is an increasing disjuncture between the academic world and that which it is situated within. There is now a censorship barrier that makes researchers reluctant to conduct research outside the privacy of their office. Research is becoming increasingly devoid of contact with the world it seeks to explore, understand and explain. This does, of course, only have an effect those who stay in academics. A third possible effect, as

John Mueller (2007) suggests, is that people are leaving academic jobs and graduate students are either dropping out because they cannot do the projects they planned or they are not entering at all. To paraphrase Mueller (2007), *Zimbardo knew enough to stop his experiment, the question is, when will Canadian REBs have such insight?*

## References

Adler, P. A., & Adler, P. (2002). Do university lawyers and the police define research values? In W. C. Van den Hoonard (Ed.), *Walking the tightrope: Ethical issues for qualitative researchers* (pp.34-42). Toronto: University of Toronto Press.

Annas, G., & Grodin, M. (Eds.), (1992). *The Nazi doctors and the Nuremberg Code: Human rights in human experimentation.* New York: Oxford.

Babbie, E. (2001). *The practice of social research.* Belmont, CA: Wadsworth Publishing.

Barber, B. (1973). *Prepared statements to the House Subcommittee on Health Hearing, Protection of Human Subjects Act.* Washington, DC: U.S. Congress.

Benedict, J. (1997). *Public heroes, private felons: Athletes and crimes against women.* Boston, MA: North Eastern University Press.

Berg, B. L. (2004). *Qualitative research methods for the social sciences.* Toronto: Pearson Education.

Fitzgerald, J., & Hamilton, M. (1996). The consequences of knowing: Ethical and legal liabilities in illicit drug research. *Social Science and Medicine, 43*(11), 1591-1600.

Geis, G., Mobley, A., & Schichor, D. (1999). Private prisons, criminological research, and conflict of interest: A case study. *Crime and Delinquency, 45*, 372-390.

Lucas, K. B., & Lidstone, J. G. (2000). Ethical issues in teaching about research ethics. *Evaluation and Research in Ethics, 14*, 53-64.

Haggerty, K. (2004). Ethics creep: Governing social science research in the name of ethics. *Qualitative Sociology, 27*(4), 391-414.

Humphreys, L. (1970). *Tearoom trade: Impersonal sex in public places.* Chicago: Aldine.

Im, E. O., & Chee, W. (2004). Recruitment of research participants through the internet. *Computers, Informatics, Nursing, 22*(5), 289-297.

Israel, M. (2004). Strictly confidential? Integrity and the disclosure of criminological and socio-legal research. *British Journal of Criminology, 44*, 715-740.

Itlas, A. S. (2006). Human subjects research: Ethics and compliance. In A. S. Itlas (Ed.), *Research ethics* (pp.1-21). New York: Routledge.

Lowman, J., & Palys, T. (2004). Ethics and institutional conflict of interest: The research confidentiality controversy at Simon Fraser University. *Sociological Practice*, *2*(4), 245-264.

Milgram, S. (1974). *Obedience to authority*. New York: Harper & Row.

Mueller, J. (2007). Ignorance is neither bliss nor ethical. *Northwestern University Law Review, 101*(2), 809-836.

—. (2004). Research ethics: A tool for harassment in the academic workplace. In K. Westhues (Ed.), *Workplace mobbing in academe* (pp. 1-24). Lewiston, NY: E. Mellen Press.

Osborne, G., & Fogel, C. (2008). Understanding the motivations for recreational marijuana use among adult Canadians. *Substance Use and Misuse, 43*(3), 539-572.

Palys, T., & Lowman, J. (2006). Protecting research confidentiality: Towards a research-participant shield law. *Canadian Journal of Law and Society, 21*(1), 163-185.

Palys, T., & Lowman, J. (2002). Anticipating law: Research methods, ethics, and the law of privilege. *Sociological Methodology, 32*, 1-17.

Palys, T., & Lowman, J. (2000). Ethical and legal strategies for protecting confidential research information. *Canadian Journal of Law and Society, 15*(1), 39-80.

Roberts, L., & Indermaur, D. (2003). Signed consent forms in criminological research: Protection for researchers and ethics committees but a threat to research participants? Presented at the *Evaluation in Crime and Justice: Trends and Methods Conference,* Canberra AU. March 24-25, 2003.

Savage, J. (2000). Participant observation: Standing in the shoes of others? *Qualitative Health Research, 10*(3), 324-339.

Scarce, R. (2005). *Contempt of court: A scholar's battle for free speech behind bars*. Lanham, MD: Altamira press.

Shea, C. (2000). Don't talk to humans: The crackdown in social science research. *Lingua Franca, 10*(6), 26-34

*Tri-Council Policy Statement: Ethical Conduct for Research Involving Humans*. Retrieved on 28th December 2007 from http://www.pre.ethics.gc.ca/english/pdf/TCPS%20October%202005_E.pdf

Zimbardo, P. G. (1973). On the ethics of intervention in human psychological research: With special reference to the Stanford prison experiment. *Cognition*, *2*, 243-256.

# CHAPTER TEN

# PUBLIC PERCEPTIONS OF CRIME SERIOUSNESS IN ISRAEL: AN EMPIRICAL STUDY OF VARIANCE WITHIN COMPARED GROUPS

SERGIO HERZOG

## Abstract

The most consistent finding of studies on public perceptions of the seriousness of criminal offenses has been apparently extensive consensus among many different and varied respondents, within and between cultures. However, many of these studies have been criticized, mainly on the basis of their disregard for, ignorance of, and even masking of two important kinds of variance. This study focused on the empirical analysis of a third overlooked source of variance, namely, within compared groups, which would also call in question this apparently wide consensus. The analysis of this variance was based on the successive partition of an Israeli sample into groups and subgroups. The findings reveal similar (although not identical) rankings of crime scenarios after successive partitions of the sample, but also many significant differences between the seriousness values given to the scenarios by different respondents. These findings do not contradict the similarity previously found in public's perceptions on crime seriousness, but rather add understanding of the subtle distinctions within this wide consensus.

## Introduction

Social scientists have long been interested in the public's perceptions of seriousness as an important topic in social science research for the last forty years. Among its main contributions, this area of research helps to understand both individual, group, and societal reactions to and evaluations of crime, culture or subculture's most basic belief systems, the role of law in the society, and the relationship between perceptions about seriousness and punishment attitudes (see Blumstein & Cohen, 1980; Hawkins, 1980; Herzog, 2006; O'Connell & Whelan, 1996). This is evident in the growing body of research on the effect of public opinion regarding crime seriousness on general criminal justice policy, and particularly on sentencing (Golash & Lynch, 1995; Heller & McEwen, 1975; Levi & Jones, 1985; Roth, 1978; Wolfgang, 1976).

The systematic evaluation of subjective seriousness perceptions relating to crime through surveys has become a particularly common and legitimate research area since the publication of the influential (and often replicated) work by Sellin and Wolfgang (1964), *The Measurement of Delinquency*, in which samples of students, police officers, and judges were requested to evaluate the seriousness of 141 criminal offenses. That research has been successfully replicated regardless of scaling method used (e.g., Levi & Jones, 1985; O'Connell & Whelan, 1996; Walker, 1978), research period (Cullen et al., 1982), and type of respondent, from different countries or cultures (e.g., Akman et al., 1967; Evans & Scott, 1984; Hsu, 1973; Levi & Jones, 1985; Newman, 1976; Rossi et al., 1974; Scott & Al-Thakeb, 1977; van Dijk & van Kesteren, 1996; Wolfgang et al., 1985) and from various social sectors (e.g., Corbett & Simon, 1991; Figlio, 1975; Levi & Jones, 1985; McCleary et al., 1981), and grouping according to personal variables within a given research sample (e.g., Cullen et al., 1982; Levi & Jones, 1985; Rossi et al., 1974; Sparks et al., 1977; Thomas et al., 1976).

Despite the wide diversity of the studies in this area, most of their research findings indicate close agreement (i.e., consensus) in seriousness perceptions across respondents both within and between cultures, with violent offenses (i.e., homicide, rape, and interpersonal violence) graded as the most serious offenses, followed (often in much the same order) by property, white-collar, and victimless (vice) offenses. Moreover, when a certain offense is perceived as relatively more serious, its high seriousness mean is usually accompanied by low standard deviations; hence the high consensus regarding the perceived high seriousness of violent offenses (see Cullen et al., 1985; Levi & Jones, 1985; O'Connell & Whelan, 1996).

These consensual findings have many implications (see Herzog, 2006). On a theoretical level, they are often cited in support of the *consensus model* (as opposed to the more politically oriented *conflict model*) of the criminal law. Briefly, the consensus model postulates a close match between the attitudes of various social groups toward both the definition of certain acts as criminal offenses, their perceived seriousness, their appropriate punishments, and their expression in the formal criminal law (e.g., Rossi & Henry, 1980; Thomas et al., 1976; Warr et al., 1982). In this regard, if different social groups, both within a given society and cross-culturally, reach very similar rankings of offenses based on their seriousness, this finding tend to show modern societies as functional units, in which their parts, despite some cultural differences, share important perspectives (Hansel, 1987).

In the context of public policy, these apparently common public preferences concerning the seriousness of offenses have led in some situations to political justification both of differential levels of punishment for different offenses and of unequal distribution of resources by the criminal justice system. In this way, the redefinition of priorities, the greater punishments, and transfer of resources determined, for example, for the investigation and prosecution of murder and other violent offenses, and on the contrary, the lesser investment of human and economic resources on the police investigation, and also on the prosecution of victimless and moral offenses, have been justified based on consensually common opinion (e.g., Blumstein & Cohen, 1980; Carlson & Williams, 1993; Cullen et al., 1985; Heller & McEwen, 1975; Levi & Jones, 1985; O'Connell & Whelan, 1996; Roth, 1978).

However, despite its robustness, the consensus finding has been criticized on methodological and theoretical grounds. According to some critics (e.g., Cullen et al. 1985; Herzog, 2006; Miethe, 1982; 1984; O'Connell & Whelan, 1996; Rossi & Henry, 1980), agreement among respondents is in fact a methodological artifact by which actual variability both *between scenarios* (offenses) and *compared groups of respondents* is usually ignored. On the one hand, it has been argued that many of these studies over-emphasize violent offenses for evaluation. As already noted, these offenses give rise to relatively slight variation in perceptions of seriousness. On the other hand, it has also been argued that crime seriousness studies have mostly succeeded in demonstrating consistent relative *rankings* of offenses, but simultaneously produce a much smaller degree of agreement concerning their *rating*, namely obtaining similar numerical values for the evaluated offenses by different kinds of respondents. Hence, differences in average seriousness scores between respondents from different groups are often reported (e.g., O'Connell & Whelan, 1996; Rossi et al., 1974; Walker, 1978). For example, Evans and Scott (1984) reported that despite the similarity in the ranking of offenses by respondents with various degrees of religiosity, highly religious respondents provided absolute seriousness scores significantly higher than other respondents. According to these critics, the lack of reference to these variances artificially raises the degree of consensus in such studies. In a similar vein, the present study attempts also to analyze this consensus finding more precisely. However, unlike the aforementioned studies, this research focused on an additional source of variance, namely, *variance within compared groups*. This study is the first made in this direction.

## Background: The two identified sources of variance

With regard to *between-scenarios variance*, it has been consistently shown that consensus increases when a common, unique indicator of all offenses is employed – "global consensus" – rather than referring separately to specific offenses – "local consensus" (Miethe, 1982, 1984; Rossi & Henry, 1980). As a result, it has been argued that apparent consensus among respondents is in fact a methodological artifact resulting from the use of a mean score across all offenses, while variance among them is ignored and masked (see also Lesieur & Lehman, 1975). It has also been argued that the finding of consensus is directly influenced by the types of offenses included in the survey questionnaires (Miethe, 1982). In most studies, violent offenses (especially those in which victims died or were seriously injured) are overrepresented, and less obviously grave offenses are underrepresented. Findings show high consensus regarding the high seriousness of violent offenses (see Carlson & Williams, 1993; Cullen et al., 1982, 1985; Levi & Jones, 1985; O'Connell & Whelan, 1996). Accordingly, the predominance of violent offenses resulted in significantly reduced between-scenario variance, artificially raising the degree of consensus when all offenses were taken into account (see also Chilton & DeAmicis, 1975; Cullen et al., 1985; Rossi & Henry, 1980).

With regard to criticism based on disregard of *between-group variance*, it has also been argued that although the studies succeeded in demonstrating a high level of "consistency" - i.e., similar relative rankings of offenses by respondents of different groups -, such findings masked the much lower level of "absolute agreement" - i.e., the rating of the same scenarios by respondents from different groups with identical numerical values (Corbett & Simon, 1991; Cullen et al., 1985; Miethe, 1984; Rossi & Henry, 1980; see also Cohen, 1988; O'Connell & Whelan, 1996; Rauma, 1991). In this case, the impression of absolute consensus among respondents of different kinds is often a statistical artifact of high Pearson (correlational) coefficients resulting from the comparison of mean group values. The correlations do not discern identical, similar, or different values assigned to individual scenarios and, therefore, they do not reveal between-group variance. The correlations may be very high even when there is no absolute agreement, that is, there are significant differences between the means of seriousness values of compared groups (Cullen et al., 1985).

This typical disregard for between-group variance which, in turn, creates a discrepancy between absolute and relative agreement, is a common feature of cross-cultural and between-sample comparisons, especially among subgroups within the same sample (Rossi & Henry, 1980). As a result, despite similarity in relative rankings, significant differences in mean scores in different groups are often reported. For example, women, blacks, less educated people, and/or those from lower socioeconomic status tend to treat crime in general and/or specific types of offense as significantly more serious than men, whites, better educated people, and/or those from higher status (e.g., Levi & Jones, 1985; O'Connell & Whelan, 1996; Rauma, 1991; Rossi et al., 1974; Sparks et al., 1977; Walker, 1978). Similar findings emerge from multivariate regression analyses, in which seriousness values (from an index of all scenarios or types of offense, or each scenario taken separately) serve as dependent variables, and the respondents' personal characteristics serve as independent variables. A high degree of consensus among respondents would require the coefficients of these independent variables to be non-significant but empirical reality often demonstrates precisely the opposite (Cullen et al., 1985).

## Variance within compared groups

It appears that many of the crime seriousness studies overlooked two important sources of variance, which, when taken into account, decrease the consensus in public perceptions of crime seriousness significantly. However, beyond these masked variances, research on crime seriousness has not focused specifically on an additional source of variance, namely, *variance within compared groups.* Like the other aforementioned variances, if this particular variance were to be demonstrated empirically, it too would call into question the apparent high degree of consensus on crime seriousness.

Defining *within-groups variance* generally as variation in individual respondents' observations from the means of their own group, it may be argued that most crime seriousness studies have already referred to this kind of variance: it is traditionally expressed as standard deviations from the mean seriousness scores. Moreover, taking these standard deviations into account, as previously cited there was consistent relatively high agreement (low standard deviations) between respondents regarding the seriousness of violent offenses, and standard deviations increased with decreasing crime seriousness (see Carlson & Williams, 1993; Cullen et al., 1982, 1985; Levi & Jones, 1985; O'Connell & Whelan, 1996). However, the use of standard deviations as a measure of disagreement within given groups is limited. By definition, they only show a *general* situation of dispersion around the means of given statistical series. In contrast, this study focuses on whether different subgroups in a given group of respondents rank or rate various offenses differently, and whether any of these differences are significant.

## Data analysis

Traditionally, within-group variance is perceived as a methodological indicator of the degree of error in the research. In general, researchers strive to attain large differences *between* the means of the compared groups (due to treatments or explained variance), and small differences *within* each of the compared groups (due to chance or unexplained variance). Thus, researchers have greater confidence in the data when the within-group variance is as small (homogeneous) as possible (for example, ANOVA).[1]

However, this typical reference to variances between and within groups as respectively desirable and undesirable is not appropriate in studies attempting to demonstrate or refute consensus in respondents' perceptions of crime seriousness. In such studies, within-group variance does not necessarily constitute error in the data; it may reflect disagreement among the respondents within the group. Therefore, consensus has to be expressed by the absence of both these variances. In other words, the seriousness values given by respondents from a certain group to different crime scenarios should not be significantly different from parallel values given to the same scenarios by other respondents from their own group (within-group variance) or by respondents from other groups (between-group variance).

After rejecting the simple use of standard deviations and ANOVA, the two components of disagreement and possible error were empirically differentiated in the present study by basing the analysis of *within-group* variance on the transformation of each such variance into *between-subgroup* variance. In other words, given a sample of respondents, if distinct groups could be differentiated within it, the variance could be

---

[1] In this way, the likelihood of methodological error in the data collection, measurement and analysis stages is minimized, thus indicating that the choice of the sample was sound and that the respondents' answers were not false or biased.

analyzed by subdivision into subgroups. Accordingly, *within-group* variance was seen as explained variance (disagreement within the group, i.e., between subgroups), and *within-subgroup* variance included the error component. Similarly, further subdivisions of the primary subgroups into secondary and even tertiary subgroups could differentiate additional corresponding components of disagreement and error, until the size of the new subdivisions disallowed the use of parametric tests for analyzing differences in their means (based on the central limit theorem).

Based on the above review, it is predicted that empirical analysis of successive divisions of groups of respondents from the same sample will yield similar relative rankings for various crime scenarios but significant differences will appear between their mean values. However, due to the gradually decreasing size and heterogeneity of the successive subgroups, it may also be hypothesized that the number of these significant differences will gradually decrease.

## Method

The present study was conducted in Israel. It may be considered a good choice for the analysis of personal perceptions of crime seriousness, and this choice for the analysis of within-group variance of personal perceptions of crime seriousness was considered appropriate, mainly in view of the demographic and social heterogeneity of its population. The variance generally found in Western countries on characteristics, such as gender, age, education and income, is augmented in Israel by additional categorizing variables, such as the division between its Jewish majority and Arab minority, between secular and religious sectors, and between Israel-born and immigrant citizens (see Goldscheider, 1996).

In this regard, it should be added here that studies on perceptions of crime seriousness such as the present one, are very relevant to our times, especially in multi-cultural and divided societies, such as Israel. Important differences among social groups, whereby at least one of them ranks offenses differently from the others or treats them permissively and/or condones them, may indicate the existence of contradictory crime perceptions in the same society. This situation may well be criminogenic, in that some of these groups may refer to certain prohibitions, and even to the entire criminal law, as not reflecting their values and attitudes (see Herzog, 2006). Such anomie may be followed by acquiescence in crime expressions and even active crime involvement. Moreover, relatively little research has been done on public perceptions of seriousness in countries outside the U.S. and England. Due to these reasons, Israel can be seen as a natural laboratory for the analysis of differences in the perceptions of various subgroups taken from the same national sample.

Unlike other studies based on the selective sampling of certain groups of the public (e.g., Corbett & Simon, 1991; Figlio, 1975; Sellin & Wolfgang, 1964), this study was based on a relatively wide, random sample of the adult Israeli respondents (over 16 years old: n = 987). The most recent Israeli telephone directories provided the sampling framework, using a systematic random sampling method assuring identical probability of inclusion of all persons listed. Overall, the distribution of the sample's characteristics showed a very close fit with official national data (CBS, 2006), although compared with the general population, there is a bias in the direction of older and consequently more educated respondents due to the preclusion of very young respondents. Hebrew-, Arabic- and Russian- (these are the most common languages in Israel) speaking interviewers were used to conduct this study.

Personal perceptions of the relative seriousness of various criminal offenses were collected by personal, anonymous questionnaires administered by means of a telephone survey. Data collection took place between December, 2000 and February, 2001. In light of the research goals, it was felt that the main drawbacks of this method (low response rate, inability to include a large number of items in the questionnaire, and limited ability of the researcher to clarify and explain the survey to respondents) were outweighed by its advantages, namely: access to a large number of respondents in a relatively short period of time (as noted, the sample size constituted a decisive aspect of the study, allowing successive partition into subgroups); enhancement of external validity by the relative ease of obtaining a nationally representative sample; relatively low cost; standardized answers; minimal risk of the researcher biasing respondents, and high level of anonymity.[2] To reinforce these advantages, efforts were also made to overcome some of the disadvantages of the method. Many additional re-calls were made to increase the response rate (to a high level of 76%); the content of the questionnaire were checked by means of a pre-test; the language was kept as simple as possible; and the student-surveyors were carefully trained to prevent bias.

---

[2] Respondent anonymity was considered important in this research because of the sensitive content of the questionnaire (permissiveness to criminal acts). Accordingly, at the beginning of the interview, respondents were assured complete anonymity, that their inclusion in the sample was random, and that their answers would serve only for statistical analysis.

## *Questionnaire and Dependent Variables*

The questionnaire included 18 crime scenarios (see the details of these scenarios and the offenses they represent in Appendix 1) based on the method developed by Sellin and Wolfgang, (1964). Respondents' perceptions of the relative seriousness of the various scenarios presented to them constituted the dependent variables of the research. However, due to the criticism of the analysis of a global index of offenses or scenarios (Miethe, 1982; 1984; Rossi & Henry, 1980), which, as noted earlier, artificially raises the degree of consensus, each scenario was also analyzed as a separate dependent variable.

Respondents were requested to evaluate the 18 scenarios by choosing one value on a Likert scale from 1 = "Not serious at all" to 11 = "Very serious."[3] This categorical scale, because it is essentially a wide-order scale, was used as an interval scale (O'Connell & Whelan, 1996). As indicated in the theoretical review above, the seriousness values were analyzed on two levels: firstly, as means and standard deviations for each scenario (rating) and, secondly, based on the means, as measures of the relative seriousness of the offenses (ranking). Accordingly, it should be stressed that although respondents have typically been reported as "ranking" the seriousness of the offenses, these rankings had in fact been assessed by the ordering of the seriousness scores they gave to the scenarios.

Regarding the order of the scenarios in the questionnaire, the pre-test supported Sheley's (1980) finding that order had no significant effect on perception of offense seriousness. The first two scenarios, chosen from the extreme high and low ends of the scale (according to pre-test data and data of other studies), were placed at the beginning of the questionnaire to give the respondents an immediate sense of the scale range and thus increase the possibility of variance across scenarios (see Warr, 1989). The order of the remaining scenarios was determined randomly (see also Cullen et al., 1985; O'Connell & Whelan, 1996). Respondents were told at the beginning of the interview that all of the scenarios referred to acts defined as criminal offenses in Israel and their responses should be based on their personal evaluation of the seriousness of the offense and not their knowledge of the legal situation in the country (see Carlson & Williams, 1993; Miethe, 1984; Rossi et al., 1974; Sellin & Wolfgang, 1964; Travis et al., 1986; Warr, 1989). Finally, in addition to the offense, and to enhance specificity, the crime scenarios also included background information on

[3] For criticism against the magnitude estimation method for measuring seriousness see Collins (1988), Levi and Jones (1985), Miethe (1986), and Parton et al. (1991).

the offenders and their victims - additional details were randomly provided on ethnic affiliation and age (see Blum-West, 1985; Walker, 1978).

### *Independent and control variables*

As stated, for the analysis of within-group/subgroup variances, the general sample was successively divided into two main groups and then into smaller primary, secondary, and tertiary subgroups. As in other studies of crime seriousness (e.g., Cullen et al., 1985; Levi & Jones, 1985; O'Connell & Whelan, 1996; Rossi et al., 1974; Walker, 1978), here too, respondents' personal characteristics served as independent variables - respondents provided their personal details after evaluating all the crime scenarios, at the end of the questionnaire -, and they include: *gender* (0 = female; 1 = male); *age* (in years); *education* (in years); *monthly familial income* (0 = over NIS 5,000; 1 = under NIS 5,000); *ethnicity* (0 = Jew; 1 = Arab); *religiosity* (0 = secular; 1 = non-secular, i.e., traditional and religious); and *country of birth* (0 = Israel; 1 = other).[4]

Based on the research question and design, it should be noted that the choice of the independent variables for the successive division of the sample into groups was not based on theoretical justifications; it was based on a multivariate ordinary least squares (OLS) path analysis performed on the whole sample. This regression analysis enabled for the identification of the most influential independent variables (significant standardized coefficients), by which the sample was successively divided.

Based on the aforementioned criticism about overrepresentation of violent offenses in some seriousness studies, which according to some researchers were responsible for artificially augmenting consensus in them (Cullen et al., 1985; Miethe, 1982; 1984), care was taken to avoid the overrepresentation of violent offenses (main control variable in this study); thus the offenses described in the scenarios were highly diverse, from very grave (e.g., domestic murder) to very minor (theft of a watch), and included offenses of many kinds – violent, property, economic, white-collar, judicial, and victimless.[5] Unlike other studies in which offenses

---

[4] Due to the nature of the present survey, other independent variables that might be relevant for their influence on public perceptions of crime seriousness were not included in the regression models. As will be seen, this produced specification errors and low $R^2$ coefficients (see Babbie, 1992; Blalock, 1979).

[5] As seen, due to the controversy around the definition of "victimless" offenses, they were defined in this study in a broad way, including all such definitions, in order to juxtapose them to crimes in which there are concrete, personal victims suffering direct harm.

were selected from lengthy existing lists (e.g., Sellin & Wolfgang, 1964; Rossi et al., 1974; Wolfgang et al., 1985), this study chose offenses randomly from a larger pool of offenses representing the population of criminal offenses in Israel. To minimize prejudice and stereotyping in evaluating the criminal acts (see Blum-West, 1985; Parton et al., 1991; Sebba, 1980; Walker, 1978), all of the evaluated offenses involved criminal intent, were committed by adult men, and included background information on the offenders and their victims. In addition, the scenarios were also highly varied with regard to victim type, harm inflicted, and the victim's personal and ethnic relationship with the offender.

## Results

Table 1 presents the standardized regression coefficients of the personal characteristics of all of the respondents in the sample (independent variables) for each of the crime scenarios (dependent variables), analyzed together and separately.

From Table 1, we see that the relative influencing importance of the various personal characteristics changes, taken under a unique global index or separately. The coefficient obtained for the *ethnicity* variable was significant for 12 of the 18 scenarios and the most influential variable in seven of them and under the unified index, compared to the other independent variables. *Religiosity* was the second most influential variable in the global scenario index. The coefficients of this variable were significant in 10 scenarios, and it was the most influential variable in six of them. *Gender* and *country of birth* (significant in 10 and 7 scenarios, respectively) were the third most influential variables in the global index. The coefficients of these two variables were found to be the most influential variable in one scenario (for gender, scenario 7 – *threat to witness*, for country of birth, scenario 14 – *ideological murder*) and the second most influential variable in (for gender) four and (for country of origin) five additional scenarios.

**Table 1: Standardized Regression Coefficients for the Seriousness of 18 Offenses in the Total Sample (n = 987) by Personal Details.**

| Independent variables Scenario | Gender | Age | Educ. | Income | Ethnic. | Religion | Country of birth | Valid N | $R^2$ |
|---|---|---|---|---|---|---|---|---|---|
| 1. Wife murder | -.095* | .001 | .043 | .071* | -.250* | .023 | .000 | 932 | .075* |
| 2. Low tax declaration | -.060 | .075* | -.006 | -.051 | -.133* | .034 | -.047 | 932 | .033* |
| 3. Apartment burglary | -.101* | -.016 | .001 | -.013 | -.032 | .106* | -.040 | 930 | .023* |
| 4. Wife assault | -.156* | -.042 | .118* | .021 | -.331* | -.089* | -.046 | 932 | .196* |
| 5. False testimony | -.098* | .018 | .008 | -.123* | -.072 | .058 | -.053 | 932 | .034* |
| 6. Girl rape | -.065* | .038 | .040 | -.033 | -.221* | .014 | -.092* | 932 | .063* |
| 7. Threat to witness | -.129* | .025 | .054 | -.029 | .026 | .055 | -.125* | 932 | .036* |
| 8. Shop arson | -.037 | -.111* | .008 | .089* | -.365* | .071* | -.030 | 932 | .102* |
| 9. Drug selling | -.093* | -.009 | -.089* | .021 | .100* | .133* | -.050 | 932 | .078* |
| 10. Street murder | .001 | -.025 | .042 | -.065 | -.056 | .017 | .003 | 932 | .013 |
| 11. Shop robbery | -.060 | -.051 | -.029 | .015 | -.109* | .089* | -.043 | 932 | .019* |
| 12. Illegal sexual relations | -.086* | .120* | .030 | -.033 | .039 | .147* | -.118* | 932 | .050* |
| 13. Illegal abortion | -.114* | .084* | -.099* | -.012 | .114* | .205* | -.125* | 929 | .134* |
| 14. Ideological murder | -.042 | .030 | .023 | -.079* | .069 | -.017 | -.129* | 932 | .024* |
| 15. Watch theft | -.069* | .043 | -.006 | -.047 | -.102* | .141* | -.105* | 931 | .035* |
| 16. Inflated bill | -.058 | -.038 | -.056 | .072* | -.184* | .197* | -.069 | 932 | .060* |
| 17. Clerk bribe | .014 | .099* | .014 | -.033 | -.117* | .079* | -.106* | 932 | .029* |
| 18. Concealing evidence | -.005 | -.071 | .004 | .045 | -.268* | .041 | -.032 | 932 | .053* |
| All the 18 offenses | -.129* | .027 | .008 | -.022 | -.179* | .139* | -.129* | 926 | .062* |

* $p < 0.05$

This relative order of importance of the independent variables determined the successive partition of the general sample into two main groups, and then into primary, secondary and tertiary subgroups. Tables 2 to 5 present the means, standard deviations and, accordingly, the relative rankings of the 18 scenarios, taken separately and as a global index, for the different levels of sample division. For ease of understanding, the scenarios appear in the tables as ranked by the whole sample; the most remarkable offenses discussed are printed in bold type. These tables also show the statistical comparisons (t-tests) between the seriousness scores of the compared sample divisions at each partition level.

Table 2 presents the rankings and ratings of the whole sample and the two main groups (by ethnic affiliation; *Jews, Arabs*). From this table, it is clear that, in general, violent offenses (various types of *murder* and *rape*) received the highest means (and in most cases the smallest standard deviations); thus ranking them as the most serious offenses. However, their relative ranking was not identical in the two groups: *Wife murder* was perceived as the most serious offense by the whole sample and the *Jewish* respondents, whereas the *Arab* respondents perceived *ideological murder* as the most serious. In contrast, victimless offenses (*low tax declaration, illegal abortions* and *sexual relations with a minor*) received the lowest means (and in most cases the largest standard deviations) in the whole sample and among the *Jewish* respondents and, accordingly, they were ranked as the least serious offenses. Among the *Arab* respondents, in addition to the *tax* offense, *wife assault* and *clerk bribe* were ranked as the least serious offenses. Between these extremes, the relative rankings by *Jewish* and *Arab* respondents varied in some of the offenses. Note the large gap in the ranking of *wife assault* (ranked in seventh place by *Jews* and almost last by *Arabs*) and *drug selling* (ranked fourteenth and fifth, respectively). This considerable gap in relative rankings between *Jewish* and *Arab* respondents was also expressed by the Spearman's Rho index for the measurement of rank order association ($r^s = .653$, $p < 0.01$). Table 2 shows significant differences in 12 of the 18 scenarios taken separately and also when computed globally: compared to the *Jewish* respondents, the *Arab* respondents assigned significantly lower seriousness values to most of these scenarios.

**Table 2: Mean Rankings and Ratings of the Seriousness of 18 Offenses by Ethnic Affiliation (Jewish, Arab).**

| **Respondents** | **Whole sample (n = 987)** | | | **Jews (n = 635)** | | | **Arabs (n = 352)** | | | **t** |
|---|---|---|---|---|---|---|---|---|---|---|
| **Scenario** | *Mean* | *SD* | *Rank* | *Mean* | **SD** | **Rank** | **Mean** | **SD** | **Rank** | |
| **Wife murder** | 10.37 | 1.67 | 1 | 10.69 | 1.04 | 1 | 9.81 | 2.31 | 3 | * |
| **Street murder** | 10.24 | 1.88 | 2 | 10.36 | 1.83 | 2 | 10.02 | 1.94 | 2 | * |
| **Girl rape** | 9.89 | 2.06 | 3 | 10.25 | 1.40 | 3 | 9.23 | 2.77 | 4 | * |
| **Ideological murder** | 9.88 | 2.24 | 4 | 9.78 | 2.40 | 6 | 10.07 | 1.90 | 1 | * |
| Concealing evidence | 9.49 | 2.15 | 5 | 9.82 | 1.63 | 4 | 8.88 | 2.75 | 8 | * |
| Shop arson | 9.31 | 2.40 | 6 | 9.79 | 1.57 | 5 | 8.45 | 3.25 | 10 | * |
| Shop robbery | 9.26 | 2.11 | 7 | 9.33 | 1.77 | 8 | 9.14 | 2.62 | 6 | |
| Apartment burglary | 8.91 | 2.29 | 8 | 8.90 | 2.18 | 9 | 8.92 | 2.48 | 7 | |
| Threat to witness | 8.76 | 2.20 | 9 | 8.71 | 2.18 | 10 | 8.84 | 2.28 | 9 | |
| **Wife assault** | 8.50 | 3.12 | 10 | 9.40 | 2.18 | 7 | 6.88 | 3.84 | 17 | * |
| **Drug selling** | 8.41 | 2.75 | 11 | 7.99 | 2.71 | 14 | 9.15 | 2.66 | 5 | * |
| Inflated bill | 8.04 | 2.56 | 12 | 8.10 | 2.42 | 13 | 7.92 | 2.80 | 12 | |
| False testimony | 8.04 | 2.68 | 13 | 8.23 | 2.58 | 11 | 7.71 | 2.83 | 13 | * |
| **Clerk bribe** | 7.92 | 2.72 | 14 | 8.13 | 2.51 | 12 | 7.53 | 3.03 | 16 | * |
| Watch theft | 7.82 | 2.66 | 15 | 7.91 | 2.61 | 15 | 7.65 | 2.75 | 15 | |
| **Illegal sexual relations** | 7.48 | 3.16 | 16 | 7.35 | 2.95 | 16 | 7.71 | 3.51 | 14 | |
| **Illegal abortions** | 7.01 | 3.32 | 17 | 6.42 | 3.33 | 18 | 8.07 | 3.01 | 11 | * |
| **Low tax declaration** | 6.18 | 2.97 | 18 | 6.54 | 2.71 | 17 | 5.53 | 3.30 | 18 | * |
| All the offenses | 8.64 | 1.38 | | 8.76 | 1.37 | | 8.41 | 1.37 | | * |

* $p < 0.05$

**Table 3: Mean Rankings and Ratings of the Seriousness of 18 Offenses by Religiosity (Secular, Non-secular: Traditional/Religious) and Ethnic Affiliation (Jewish, Arab).** * $p < 0.05$

| **Groups** | *Jews (n = 635)* | | | | | | | **Arabs (n = 352)** | | | | | | |
|---|---|---|---|---|---|---|---|---|---|---|---|---|---|---|
| **Subgroups** | **Secular (n = 457)** | | | **Non-secular (n = 176)** | | | *t* | **Secular (n = 122)** | | | **Non-secular (n = 230)** | | | **t** |
| **Scenario** | *Mean* | **SD** | **Rank** | *Mean* | **SD** | **Rank** | | *Mean* | **SD** | **Rank** | **Mean** | **SD** | **Rank** | |
| Wife murder | 10.73 | 0.88 | 1 | 10.57 | 1.38 | 1 | | 9.54 | 2.73 | 3 | 9.96 | 2.05 | 3 | |
| Street murder | 10.42 | 1.79 | 2 | 10.21 | 1.94 | 3 | | 9.77 | 2.13 | 2 | 10.15 | 1.82 | 2 | |
| Girl rape | 10.22 | 1.43 | 3 | 10.34 | 1.28 | 2 | | 9.24 | 2.49 | 4 | 9.23 | 2.92 | 6 | |
| Ideological murder | 9.91 | 2.24 | 4 | 9.43 | 2.76 | 7 | * | 9.80 | 2.00 | 1 | 10.21 | 1.83 | 1 | |
| Concealing evidence | 9.80 | 1.61 | 5 | 9.88 | 1.67 | 5 | | 8.67 | 2.90 | 7 | 8.99 | 2.68 | 9 | |
| Shop arson | 9.65 | 1.62 | 6 | 10.14 | 1.38 | 4 | * | 8.24 | 3.26 | 10 | 8.56 | 3.25 | 10 | |
| Shop robbery | 9.20 | 1.79 | 8 | 9.66 | 1.67 | 6 | * | 8.86 | 2.94 | 5 | 9.29 | 2.42 | 5 | |
| Apartment burglary | 8.75 | 2.17 | 9 | 9.27 | 2.16 | 8 | * | 8.47 | 2.70 | 9 | 9.16 | 2.33 | 7 | * |
| Threat to witness | 8.65 | 2.17 | 10 | 8.85 | 2.19 | 10 | | 8.52 | 2.25 | 8 | 9.01 | 2.29 | 8 | |
| **Wife assault** | 9.50 | 2.06 | 7 | 9.11 | 2.46 | 9 | * | 7.40 | 3.52 | 12 | 6.60 | 3.98 | 17 | |
| **Drug selling** | 7.66 | 2.70 | 15 | 8.81 | 2.58 | 11 | * | 8.85 | 2.67 | 6 | 9.32 | 2.65 | 4 | |
| **Inflated bill** | 7.84 | 2.41 | 13 | 8.78 | 2.31 | 12 | * | 6.95 | 3.10 | 17 | 8.44 | 2.48 | 12 | * |
| False testimony | 8.10 | 2.56 | 11 | 8.53 | 2.59 | 14 | | 7.59 | 3.02 | 11 | 7.77 | 2.73 | 15 | |
| Clerk bribe | 7.97 | 2.44 | 12 | 8.54 | 2.65 | 13 | * | 7.36 | 3.11 | 13 | 7.63 | 2.99 | 16 | |
| Watch theft | 7.67 | 2.62 | 14 | 8.50 | 2.49 | 15 | * | 7.06 | 2.68 | 16 | 7.97 | 2.74 | 14 | * |
| Illegal sexual relations | 7.03 | 2.96 | 16 | 8.17 | 2.80 | 16 | * | 7.11 | 3.73 | 15 | 8.02 | 3.34 | 13 | * |
| Illegal abortions | 5.94 | 3.26 | 18 | 7.66 | 3.20 | 17 | * | 7.33 | 3.23 | 14 | 8.46 | 2.82 | 11 | * |
| Low tax declaration | 6.35 | 2.69 | 17 | 7.00 | 2.69 | 18 | * | 5.81 | 3.21 | 18 | 5.38 | 3.35 | 18 | |
| All the offenses | 8.63 | 1.39 | | 9.08 | 1.28 | | * | 8.14 | 1.45 | | 8.56 | 1.31 | | * |

Table 3 compares the seriousness scores and the relative rankings of two pairs of subgroups: *secular/non-secular, Jewish/Arab*. In general, the relative rankings obtained for *Jewish* and *Arab* respondents (Table 2) were replicated by their corresponding subgroups ($r^s$ = .944, $r^s$ = .889, respectively, $p < 0.01$). The largest between-subgroup differences were found among the *Jews* for *drug selling* (placed 15$^{th}$ and 11$^{th}$ by *secular* and *non-secular Jews*, respectively), and among the *Arabs*, for *wife assault* (placed 12$^{th}$ and 17$^{th}$ by *secular* and *non-secular Arabs*, respectively) and *inflated bill* (17$^{th}$ and 12$^{th}$, respectively). In addition, significant between-subgroup differences in the seriousness scores were found both for the global index and the separate analysis of the scenarios (12 for *Jews* and 5 for *Arabs*). Non-secular respondents, *Jews* and *Arabs*, assigning significantly higher seriousness scores, compared to *secular* respondents.

Table 4 presents the comparison of the secondary subgroups obtained by dividing the primary subgroups into *Jewish, secular/non-secular*, *male/female* respondents. (The parallel table for Arab respondents is not included because the relatively small size of one of its secondary subgroups prevented the operation of valid parametric tests). Like Table 3, Table 4 shows that the relative rankings in these secondary subgroups are very similar to those described for the foregoing subgroups ($r^s$ = .981, $r^s$ = .874, respectively, $p < 0.01$). Among *secular Jewish* respondents, the largest gap was obtained for *wife assault* (placed 8$^{th}$ by *men* and 5$^{th}$ by *women*) and among *non-secular Jewish* respondents for the same scenario (placed 13$^{th}$ by *men* and 7$^{th}$ by *women*); and for *clerk bribe* (*men* 9$^{th}$ and *women* 16$^{th}$). With regard to significant differences between the secondary subgroups in the seriousness scores assigned to these scenarios, there were four differences between *male* and *female secular Jewish* respondents, and three between *non-secular Jewish* respondents. Compared to *men, women, secular and non-secular,* tended to assign significantly higher seriousness scores to the scenarios. With regard to the global index of scenarios, a significant difference between *men* and *women* was found among *secular Jewish* respondents, but not among *non-secular Jews*.

**Table 4: Mean Rankings and Ratings of the Seriousness of 18 Offenses by Gender (Male, Female), Religiosity (Secular, Non-secular), among Jewish Respondents.**

| **Group** | **Jews (n = 635)** | | | | | | | | | | | | | |
|---|---|---|---|---|---|---|---|---|---|---|---|---|---|---|
| **Subgroups** | *Secular (n = 457)* | | | | | | | **Non-secular (n = 176)** | | | | | | |
| **Secondary subgroups** | **Men (n = 218)** | | | **Women (n = 239)** | | | *t* | **Men (n = 74)** | | | **Women (n = 102)** | | | **t** |
| **Scenario** | *Mean* | **SD** | **Rank** | *Mean* | **SD** | **Rank** | | *Mean* | **SD** | **Rank** | **Mean** | **SD** | **Rank** | |
| Wife murder | 10.53 | 1.21 | 1 | 10.92 | 0.30 | 1 | * | 10.64 | 0.74 | 1 | 10.51 | 1.70 | 1 | |
| Street murder | 10.32 | 1.88 | 2 | 10.50 | 1.70 | 2 | | 10.52 | 1.02 | 2 | 9.99 | 2.37 | 4 | |
| Girl rape | 10.07 | 1.46 | 3 | 10.36 | 1.40 | 3 | * | 10.31 | 1.03 | 3 | 10.36 | 1.44 | 2 | |
| Ideological murder | 9.73 | 2.39 | 5 | 10.07 | 2.08 | 4 | | 9.51 | 2.39 | 7 | 9.37 | 3.01 | 8 | |
| Concealing evidence | 9.78 | 1.47 | 4 | 9.81 | 1.74 | 6 | | 9.94 | 1.29 | 5 | 9.84 | 1.91 | 5 | |
| Shop arson | 9.64 | 1.52 | 6 | 9.66 | 1.71 | 7 | | 10.05 | 1.53 | 4 | 10.21 | 1.26 | 3 | |
| Shop robbery | 9.11 | 1.81 | 7 | 9.28 | 1.77 | 8 | | 9.58 | 1.71 | 6 | 9.72 | 1.66 | 6 | |
| Apartment burglary | 8.55 | 2.20 | 9 | 8.93 | 2.14 | 9 | | 9.17 | 2.08 | 8 | 9.35 | 2.22 | 9 | |
| Threat to witness | 8.51 | 2.12 | 10 | 8.77 | 2.22 | 10 | | 8.54 | 2.10 | 11 | 9.08 | 2.23 | 11 | |
| **Wife assault** | 8.96 | 2.33 | 8 | 10.00 | 1.63 | 5 | * | 8.44 | 2.61 | 13 | 9.60 | 2.23 | 7 | * |
| Drug selling | 7.55 | 2.74 | 15 | 7.76 | 2.66 | 15 | | 8.39 | 2.77 | 14 | 9.11 | 2.40 | 10 | |
| Inflated bill | 7.67 | 2.40 | 13 | 7.99 | 2.42 | 13 | | 8.78 | 2.19 | 10 | 8.78 | 2.40 | 12 | |
| False testimony | 7.73 | 2.72 | 12 | 8.45 | 2.36 | 11 | * | 8.24 | 2.51 | 15 | 8.74 | 2.65 | 13 | |
| **Clerk bribe** | 7.91 | 2.42 | 11 | 8.02 | 2.45 | 12 | | 8.81 | 2.35 | 9 | 8.35 | 2.84 | 16 | |
| Watch theft | 7.55 | 2.61 | 14 | 7.79 | 2.63 | 14 | | 8.45 | 2.34 | 12 | 8.52 | 2.61 | 14 | |
| Illegal sexual relations | 6.86 | 3.04 | 16 | 7.18 | 2.87 | 16 | | 7.77 | 3.02 | 16 | 8.46 | 2.61 | 15 | |

| | | | | | | | | | | | | | | |
|---|---|---|---|---|---|---|---|---|---|---|---|---|---|---|
| Illegal abortions | 5.88 | 3.08 | 18 | 6.00 | 3.42 | 18 | | 6.98 | 3.57 | 17 | 8.15 | 2.81 | 17 | * |
| Low tax declaration | 6.35 | 2.81 | 17 | 6.35 | 2.57 | 17 | | 6.43 | 2.35 | 18 | 7.42 | 2.86 | 18 | * |
| All the offenses | 8.48 | 1.41 | | 8.77 | 1.36 | | * | 8.92 | 1.20 | | 9.20 | 1.33 | | |

* $p < 0.05$

**Table 5: Mean Rankings and Ratings of the Seriousness of 18 Offenses by Country of Birth (Israeli-Born, Immigrant), Gender (Men, Women), among Secular Jewish Respondents.**

| Subgroup | **Secular Jews (n = 457)** | | | | | | | | | | | | | |
|---|---|---|---|---|---|---|---|---|---|---|---|---|---|---|
| **Secondary subgroups** | *Men (n = 218)* | | | | | | | **Women (n = 239)** | | | | | | |
| **Tertiary subgroups** | **Israel-born (n = 151)** | | | **Immigrants (n = 67)** | | | *t* | **Israel-born (n = 165)** | | | **Immigrants (n = 74)** | | | **t** |
| **Scenario** | *Mean* | **SD** | **Rank** | *Mean* | **SD** | **Rank** | | *Mean* | **SD** | **Rank** | **Mean** | **SD** | **Rank** | |
| Wife murder | 10.51 | 1.12 | 1 | 10.56 | 1.40 | 1 | | 10.92 | 0.29 | 1 | 10.91 | 0.32 | 1 | |
| Street murder | 10.30 | 2.01 | 2 | 10.37 | 1.59 | 2 | | 10.61 | 1.44 | 2 | 10.25 | 2.16 | 2 | |
| Girl rape | 10.19 | 1.41 | 3 | 9.80 | 1.52 | 3 | | 10.55 | 1.13 | 3 | 9.94 | 1.80 | 3 | * |
| **Ideological murder** | 9.95 | 2.30 | 4 | 9.23 | 2.52 | 6 | * | 10.32 | 1.77 | 4 | 9.51 | 2.57 | 5 | * |
| **Concealing evidence** | 9.93 | 1.39 | 5 | 9.44 | 1.58 | 4 | * | 10.07 | 1.50 | 6 | 9.24 | 2.07 | 6 | * |
| Shop arson | 9.76 | 1.40 | 6 | 9.37 | 1.73 | 5 | | 9.94 | 1.50 | 7 | 9.05 | 1.99 | 7 | * |
| Shop robbery | 9.13 | 1.92 | 7 | 9.05 | 1.55 | 7 | | 9.40 | 1.71 | 8 | 9.01 | 1.88 | 8 | |
| Apartment burglary | 8.57 | 2.21 | 9 | 8.49 | 2.19 | 9 | | 9.15 | 2.09 | 10 | 8.45 | 2.18 | 9 | * |

| | | | | | | | | | | | | | | |
|---|---|---|---|---|---|---|---|---|---|---|---|---|---|---|
| Threat to witness | 8.56 | 2.13 | 10 | 8.40 | 2.11 | 10 | | 9.16 | 1.96 | 9 | 7.90 | 2.50 | 10 | * |
| Wife assault | 9.03 | 2.31 | 8 | 8.79 | 2.39 | 8 | | 10.14 | 1.33 | 5 | 9.70 | 2.15 | 4 | |
| **Drug selling** | 7.53 | 2.79 | 15 | 7.61 | 2.63 | 12 | | 8.04 | 2.48 | 15 | 7.13 | 2.94 | 14 | * |
| Inflated bill | 7.78 | 2.37 | 13 | 7.43 | 2.45 | 14 | | 8.35 | 2.16 | 13 | 7.18 | 2.78 | 13 | * |
| False testimony | 7.84 | 2.72 | 12 | 7.49 | 2.75 | 13 | | 8.73 | 2.26 | 11 | 7.81 | 2.45 | 11 | * |
| Clerk bribe | 8.04 | 2.46 | 11 | 7.61 | 2.33 | 11 | | 8.40 | 2.26 | 12 | 7.20 | 2.68 | 12 | * |
| Watch theft | 7.64 | 2.60 | 14 | 7.34 | 2.62 | 15 | | 8.13 | 2.49 | 14 | 7.04 | 2.78 | 15 | * |
| Illegal sexual relations | 6.87 | 3.03 | 16 | 6.85 | 3.09 | 16 | | 7.61 | 2.76 | 16 | 6.22 | 2.92 | 16 | * |
| Illegal abortions | 6.03 | 3.15 | 18 | 5.56 | 2.92 | 18 | | 6.30 | 3.36 | 18 | 5.31 | 3.47 | 18 | * |
| Low tax declaration | 6.31 | 2.91 | 17 | 6.44 | 2.60 | 17 | | 6.68 | 2.42 | 17 | 5.63 | 2.76 | 17 | * |
| All the offenses | 8.56 | 1.44 | | 8.32 | 1.34 | | | 9.03 | 1.24 | | 8.18 | 1.45 | | * |

* $p < 0.05$

Table 5 presents the partition of secondary subgroups (*male/female, secular, Jewish*) into tertiary subgroups (*Israeli-born/immigrant*). Like Table 4, Table 5 refers only to *secular Jewish* respondents due to the relatively small size of one *non-secular Jewish* tertiary subgroup. As in the previous tables, the relative rankings of the higher partition level (in this case, *male/female, secular, Jewish*) were generally maintained in the successive subdivisions (*Israeli-born and immigrants*, $r^s = .981$, $r^s = .994$, respectively, $p < 0.01$). There were few gaps in the rankings of these tertiary subgroups: among *men*, the gap in the ranking of *drug selling* (15$^{th}$ position for *Israeli-born* vs. 12$^{th}$ for *immigrants*), with no notable gaps among women. However, despite the similar rankings provided by *Israeli-born* respondents and *immigrants*, significant differences between them were found in seriousness values, especially among *women* – in 14 out of the 18 scenarios taken separately and also in the global index. By contrast, few significant differences were found among *men* – only for two scenarios (*ideological murder* and *concealing evidence*, scenarios 14 and 18, respectively). *Immigrants*, both *men* and *women*, tended to give these scenarios significantly lower seriousness scores than *Israeli-born* respondents.

## Discussion

As stated earlier, the goal of the present study was to examine the generally accepted finding of high consensus around public perceptions of crime seriousness by examining a large sample of respondents for the existence of within-group variance. Based on previous studies, the main research hypothesis was that even with repeated partition of the whole sample, similar relative rankings would be obtained at each division level: violent offenses would be seen as most serious and victimless or vice offenses as least serious. On the other hand, it was also hypothesized that significant differences would be found in the mean seriousness scores assigned by different kinds of respondents to the same crime scenarios in the successive sample subdivisions. The expectation was that such differences (disagreement) would tend to appear for offenses ranked as non-serious (expressed in wider standard deviations). However, due to the successive division of the sample into subgroups, with corresponding reduction in both their relative size and heterogeneity, it was also hypothesized that as the fractioning of the groups continued, less significant differences would be found. From the research findings, it may be concluded that these hypotheses were basically supported, albeit not completely.

## *Relative rankings*

In general, the relative rankings of the 18 offenses included in the questionnaires in each of the four successive subdivisions of the whole sample proved relatively stable. At each level (within-group variance), violent offenses (*murder, rape*) received the highest means (and usually the smallest standard deviations) and, accordingly, they were ranked as the most serious offenses. At the other extreme, victimless and vice offenses (*tax offenses, illegal abortions, sexual relations with a minor,* and *bribery*) received the smallest means (and usually the largest standard deviations); hence, they were ranked as the least serious offenses. It can therefore be concluded that within-group variances were not reflected in the seriousness rankings across the successive divisions of the whole sample into smaller subgroups based on personal characteristics. Generally, these rankings were similar to those found in other studies of crime seriousness (e.g., Blum-West, 1985; Cullen et al., 1982, 1985; Herzog, 2006; Levi & Jones, 1985; O'Connell & Whelan, 1996; Rossi et al., 1974; Warr, 1989).

Nevertheless, this apparently high consensus was far from perfect: Lack of absolute consensus in the relative rankings of criminal offenses was expressed on two levels. On the one hand, the relative rankings were similar, mainly at the extremes, with regard to the kind of offenses ranked but not with regard to the absolute ranking of the offenses themselves. For example, the same violent offenses placed in the highest positions by all respondents at every level of division exchanged alternatively the first, second, and third highest positions in every ranking. This situation is seen across all rankings, offense types, and respondent-types in the research. On the other hand, despite the great similarity between the relative rankings in each subgroup partition, important gaps in certain offenses were found between the compared subgroups. A notable (and not unique) example was found for *wife assault*: *Jewish* respondents ranked it in 7$^{th}$ place and *Arab* respondents placed it 17$^{th}$; *male secular Jewish* respondents ranked it 13$^{th}$ whereas *secular Jewish women* ranked it 7$^{th}$. This finding means that important gaps in the ranking of specific offenses did not appear only in the comparison between the primary groups at the beginning of the partition procedure (between-group variance); they were also evident in the comparison of secondary subgroups (within-subgroup variance). These findings point to the existence of within-group disagreement (variance) regarding the relative rankings of specific criminal offenses.

## *Significant differences in seriousness scores*

As predicted by the research hypotheses, despite the similarity in relative rankings, the absolute seriousness values assigned to the scenarios appearing in the questionnaire showed variation, often reaching statistical significance. These significant differences were directly expressed by t-tests, comparing between-subgroup score means (Tables 2 to 5), but also by the regression analysis carried out on the whole sample, which showed significant, standardized coefficients of their personal characteristics (Table 1). Hence, the research findings show that personal characteristics significantly influence individual perceptions of crime seriousness. These findings indicate that even if the various relative rankings of the offenses are similar (albeit not identical), a certain degree of disagreement still exists in the values assigned by various kinds of respondents to each scenario (Corbett & Simon, 1991; Cullen et al., 1985; Miethe, 1982, 1984; Rossi & Henry, 1980).

The research findings attest to some variation in perceptions of crime seriousness between parallel groups (between-group variance), and in particular, with respect to the perceptions of respondents within the same groups and subgroups (within-group variance). Individual perceptions of crime seriousness were not homogeneous within groups and subgroups of respondents. Instead, significant differences between them are likely to be found in successive fractioning of the whole sample. Note that the direction of such significant differences remained stable along the subdivisions: In general, *Arab, secular, male*, and *immigrant* respondents tended to evaluate the scenarios as significantly less serious than *Jewish, non-secular, female, Israeli*-born respondents. Yet, in contrast to the research hypothesis, these significant differences at all subdivision levels were not found mainly for the least serious offenses; significant differences were found for many of the scenarios, serious and non-serious.[6] Therefore, it may be concluded that these significant differences in respondents' perceptions support the existence of within-group variances. These indicate heterogeneity in these perceptions among respondents within different groups as to the seriousness values they assigned to various criminal offenses.

This conclusion raises questions about the wide consensus in seriousness perceptions. However, despite the existence of heterogeneity in both between- and within-group perceptions, expressed by significant

---

[6] See the significant differences for wife murder, ranked as the most serious offense, in the comparisons of Jewish and Arab respondents (Table 2) and male and female secular Jewish respondents (Table 4).

differences between groups and subgroups in the successive partitions of the sample, it should be noted that many of them seem not to be substantively important. Although most of these differences were statistically significant, their absolute size (on a scale of 1-11) is often too small to reach the conclusion that these findings disconfirm the consensus hypothesis.

### *Significant differences and partitions of the sample*

Generally, the extent of these significant differences at each new level of division decreased gradually. In the first comparison of the two main groups (*Jewish/Arab*, Table 2), significant differences were found for 12 of the 18 scenarios; in the second comparison of four primary subgroups (Table 3), this figure fell to five among the *Arabs*; in the third division (Table 4), only four and three significant differences were found in the various comparisons; and in the last (tertiary) subdivision (Table 5), only two significant differences were found, among the men. Moreover, significant differences in the global index of all the 18 offenses were found in the first divisions of the sample (Tables 2 and 3); in the last subdivisions such differences were not found in any of the comparisons (Tables 4 and 5). Thus, it may be concluded that these findings support the research hypotheses. At each new subdivision level, both the extent of heterogeneity within the groups and subgroups and their relative size gradually decrease; as a result, despite the possibility of finding significant differences in respondents' perceptions within the groups, this likelihood gradually decreases.

Note, however, that this conclusion is supported by most but not all the research findings: The highest number of significant differences in crime seriousness scores was found (14 of 18 scenarios) precisely in the last subdivision of the sample into tertiary subgroups (*Israeli-born* vs. *immigrant female secular Jewish* respondents). These differences were not confined to specific offense types; on the contrary, they were found for a great variety of scenarios, across the seriousness span. This finding also attests to the heterogeneity found between these subgroups of *female secular Jewish* respondents, despite their relatively small number (n = 165 and 74, respectively), and personal heterogeneity (all *secular Jewish women*). In other words, this finding also supports the existence of within-group variance and, accordingly, lack of complete consensus in the sample.

## Conclusions

Previous findings pointing to widespread consensus regarding public perceptions of the seriousness of criminal offenses suggest that cultural, socioeconomic and personal heterogeneity do not influence seriousness evaluations. However, such findings have been criticized for their methodological disregard for, and masking of, two very important sources of variance: variance among crime scenarios, and variance among respondents. Indeed, critics have argued that if these sources of variance had been taken into account, such consensus would have decreased considerably (e.g., Cullen et al., 1985; Miethe, 1982, 1984).

The present study, while considering these two types of variances, analyzed a third type of variance, previously overlooked, namely within-group variance. Operationally, these variances were translated into the successive fractioning of compared main groups into compared subgroups. Repeated divisions of the sample into small units of analysis produced similar relative rankings of criminal offenses by different kinds of respondents. However, these rankings were not identical; important gaps in the offense rankings were evident. Moreover, many significant differences between seriousness scores were found in the successive subdivisions of the sample, even when the sizes of the compared units and the extent of heterogeneity in them were relatively small. Although many of these significant differences were in fact small in their absolute size, these results thus support the criticism that complete consensus may be partially a methodological artifact stemming from disregard for, or masking of important sources of variance. In sum, although the similarity in both relative ranking and absolute seriousness scores, between and within compared groups should be recognized, it still seems premature to speak of absolute consensus regarding public perceptions of crime seriousness (Blum-West, 1985; Cullen et al., 1985; Hansel, 1987; Miethe, 1984). To cite Hansel (1987, p. 456) (see also Miethe, 1982, p. 516), "…Social groups differ about education, religion, and a wide variety of social objects. Thus, they 'of course' should also differ in their views on crime seriousness."

## References

Akman, D., Normandeau, A., & Turner, S. (1967). The measurement of delinquency in Canada. *Journal of Law, Criminology and Police Science*, *39*, 330-337.

Babbie, E. (1992). *The practice of social research.* Belmont, CA: Wadsworth.

Blalock, H. (1979). *Social statistics*. New York: McGraw-Hill.

Blumstein, A., & Cohen, J. (1980). Sentencing of convicted offenders: An analysis of the public's view. *Law and Society Review*, *14,* 233-261.

Blum-West, S. (1985). The seriousness of crime: A study of popular morality. *Deviant Behavior*, *6*(1), 83-98.

Carlson, J., & Williams, T. (1993). Perspectives on the seriousness of crimes. *Social Science Research*, *22,* 190-207.

CBS - Central Bureau of Statistics (2006). *Statistical Abstract of Israel.* Jerusalem: Central Bureau of Statistics.

Chilton, R., & DeAmicis, J. (1975). Overcriminalization and the measurement of consensus. *Sociology and Social Research*, *59*, 318-329.

Cohen, M. (1988). Some new evidence on the seriousness of crime. *Criminology*, *26*(2), 343-353.

Collins, M. (1988). Some cautionary notes on the use of the Sellin-Wolfgang index of crime seriousness. *Journal of Quantitative Criminology*, *4*(1), 61-70.

Corbett, C., & Simon, F. (1991). Police and public perceptions of the seriousness of traffic offenses. *British Journal of Criminology*, *31*(2), 153-164.

Cullen, F., Clark, G. & Polanzi, C. (1982). The seriousness of crime revisited. *Criminology*, *20* (1), 83-102.

Cullen, F., Link, B., Travis, L., & Wozniak, J. (1985). Consensus in crime seriousness: Empirical reality or methodological artifact? *Criminology*, *23*(1), 99-118.

Evans, S., & Scott, J. (1984). The seriousness of crime cross-culturally: The impact of religiosity. *Criminology*, *22*(1), 39-59.

Figlio, R. (1975). The seriousness of offenses: An evaluation by offenders and non offenders. *The Journal of Criminal Law & Criminology*, *66*(2), 189-200.

Golash, D., & Lynch, J. (1995). Public opinion, crime seriousness, and sentencing policy. *American Journal of Criminal Law*, *22*(3), 703-732.

Goldscheider, C. (1996). *Israel's changing society: Population, ethnicity, and development*. New York: Westview Press.

Hansel, M. (1987). Citizen crime stereotypes – normative consensus revisited. *Criminology*, *25*(3), 455-485.

Hawkins, D. (1980). Perceptions of punishment for crime. *Deviant Behavior*, *1*(2), 193-215.

Heller, N., & McEwen, T. (1975). Applications of crime seriousness information in a police department. *Journal of Research in Crime and Delinquency*, *12*, 44-50.

Herzog, S. (2006). Public perceptions of crime seriousness: A comparison of social divisions in Israel. *Israel Law Review*, *39*(1), 57-80.

Hsu, M. (1973). Cultural and sexual differences on the judgment of criminal offenses: A replication study of the measurement of delinquency. *Journal of Criminal Law and Criminology*, *64*(3), 348-353.

Kvalseth, T. (1980). Seriousness of offenses: An experimental study based on a psychological scaling technique. *Criminology*, *18*(2), 237-244.

Lesieur, H., & Lehman, P. (1975). Remeasuring delinquency: A replication and a critique. *British Journal of Criminology*, *15*, 69-80.

Levi, M., & Jones, S. (1985). Public and police perceptions of crime seriousness in England and Wales. *British Journal of Criminology*, *25* (3), 234-250.

McCleary, R., O'Neil, M., Epperlein, T., Jones, C., & Gray, R. (1981). Effects of legal education and work experience on perceptions of crime seriousness. *Social Problems*, *28*(3), 276-289.

Miethe, T. (1982). Public consensus on crime seriousness: Normative structure or methodological artifact? *Criminology*, *20*, 515-526.

—. (1984). Types of consensus in public evaluations of crime: An illustration of strategies for measuring consensus. *Journal of Criminal Law and Criminology*, *75*, 459-473.

—. (1986). Social psychophysical measurement: A comparison of the measurement properties of magnitude and categorical scaling of social perceptions. *Social Science Quarterly*, *67*(1), 195-204.

Newman, G. (1976). *Comparative deviance: Perception and law in six cultures*. New York: Elsevier.

O'Connell, M., & Whelan, A. (1996). Taking wrongs seriously: Public perceptions of crime seriousness. *British Journal of Criminology*, *36*(2), 299-318.

Parton, D., Hansel, M., & Stratton, J. (1991). Measuring crime seriousness: Lessons from the National survey of crime severity. *British Journal of Criminology*, *31*(1), 72-85.

Rauma, D. (1991). The context of normative consensus: An expansion of the Rossi/Berk Consensus Model, with an application to crime seriousness. *Social Science Research*, *20*, 1-28.
Rossi, P., & Henry, P. (1980). Seriousness: A measure for all purposes? In M. Klein & K. Teilmann (Eds.), *Handbook of criminal justice evaluation* (pp.489-505). Beverly Hills, CA: Sage.
Rossi, P., Waite, E., Bose, C., & Berk, R. (1974). The seriousness of crimes: Normative structure and individual differences. *American Sociological Review*, *39* (2), 224-237.
Roth, J. (1978). Prosecutor perceptions of crime seriousness. *Journal of Criminal Law and Criminology*, *66*(2), 175-188.
Scott, J., & Al-Thakeb, F. (1977). The public's perception of crime: Scandinavia, Western Europe, the Middle East, and the United States. In C. Huff (Ed.), *Contemporary corrections* (pp.78–88). Beverly Hills, CA: Sage.
Sebba, L. (1980). Is Mens Rea a component of perceived offense seriousness? *Journal of Criminal Law and Criminology*, *71*(2), 124-135.
Sellin, T., & Wolfgang, M. (1964). *The Measurement of delinquency*. New York: Wiley.
Sheley, J. (1980). Crime seriousness ratings: The impact of survey questionnaire form and item context. *British Journal of Criminology*, *20*(2), 123-135.
Sparks, R., Genn, H., & Dodd, D. (1977). *Surveying victims*. London: Wiley.
Thomas, C., Cage, R., & Foster, S. (1976). Public opinion on criminal law and legal sanctions: An examination of two conceptual models. *Journal of Criminal Law and Criminology*, *67*, 110-116.
Travis, L., Cullen, F., Link, B., & Wozniak, J. (1986). The impact of instructions on seriousness ratings. *Journal of Criminal Justice*, *14*, 433-440.
van Dijk, J., & van Kesteren, J. (1996). The prevalence and perceived seriousness of victimization by crime: Some results of the International Crime Victims Survey. *European Journal of Crime, Criminal Law and Criminal Justice*, *4*(1), 48-70.
Velez-Diaz, A., & Megargee, E. (1970). An investigation of differences in value judgments between youthful offenders and non-offenders in Puerto Rico. *Journal of Law and Criminology*, *61*, 549-553.
Walker, M. (1978). Measuring the seriousness of crimes. *British Journal of Criminology*, *18*(4), 348-364.

—. (1989). What is the perceived seriousness of crimes? *Criminology*, *27*(4), 795-821.

Warr, M., Gibbs, J., & Erickson, M. (1982). Contending theories of criminal law: Statutory penalties versus public preferences. *Journal of Research in Crime and Delinquency*, *19*(1), 25-46.

Wolfgang, M. (1976). Seriousness of crime and a policy of juvenile justice. In J. Short (Ed.), *Delinquency, crime and society* (pp.225-244). Chicago: University of Chicago Press.

Wolfgang, M., Figlio., R., Tracy, P., & Singer., S. (1985). *The National survey of crime severity*. Washington DC: U.S. Government Printing Office.

# PART III.

# CRIMINAL JUSTICE, PRISONS AND MEDIA, IN A CHANGING WORLD

# CHAPTER ELEVEN

# ASSET FORFEITURE IN IRELAND: CONCERNS OF CRIMINAL ADMINISTRATION AND JURISPRUDENCE

LIZ CAMPBELL

## Abstract

This chapter seeks to explain and contextualise the introduction and implementation of civil forfeiture by reference to a number of theoretical insights. While the situation in the Irish State is the particular case-study emphasised in this chapter, the conceptual interpretations presented are relevant to comparable international provisions. First, the issue of whether asset forfeiture denotes a shift from due process to crime control imperatives will be examined, using the work of Herbert Packer. Next, the possibility that this approach represents a move away from criminal justice *per se* to what may be described as "criminal administration" will be explored. Finally, the categorisation of forfeiture as an adaptive response of the State to the phenomenon of crime and the reality of crime control in late-modern society will be considered, drawing on David Garland's work.

## Introduction

Since the 1970s in the United States, and more recently in countries as diverse as South Africa, Albania, Serbia, the United Kingdom, Ireland and the Philippines, a civil means of asset forfeiture has been used to counter and undermine serious and organised criminality, such as drug trafficking and money laundering. The seizure and forfeiture of assets believed to be the proceeds of crime, or of property relating to the commission of an offence, is increasingly employed in a bid to remove the resources and profits of criminals. The very nature of organised crime, with its secrecy and violence, appeared to necessitate alternative law enforcement measures to the traditional prosecutorial approach which is often stymied by witness intimidation and which moreover may fail to diminish the wealth of criminal gangs and their leaders. Moreover, the perception that, criminals could accrue and enjoy sizeable profits without fear of confiscation, thereby facilitating and encouraging future criminality, provided the rationale for the widespread adoption of such a legal tactic.

While numerous jurisdictions now use civil forfeiture against serious criminality, this chapter presents the case-study of the tactic in Ireland, given that it was the first European Union (EU) State to utilise such a measure in the 1990s, and also given the unique historical setting which influenced this development. This chapter explains the procedural aspects of civil forfeiture in Ireland in a conventional legal sense, and then seeks to place the process in a theoretical setting, to clarify the development and workings of this innovative approach to tackling organised and serious crime. As Garland notes, "theoretical argument enables us to think about that real world of practice with a clarity and a breadth of perspective often unavailable to the hard-pressed practitioner" (Garland, 1990, p. 277).

After describing the forerunners of civil forfeiture in Ireland, the various types of confiscation and forfeiture orders which may be granted under the relevant legislation, namely the Proceeds of Crime Act, 1996, and the 2003 Amendment Act, will be considered. While forfeiture under the 1996 Act is not conditional on a conviction in a criminal court, and the standard of proof which the State must satisfy is the civil standard, it is arguable that the true nature of asset forfeiture is criminal. In determining whether the means of asset forfeiture authorised by the Proceeds of Crime Act, 1996, merits its title of a civil process, or is truly criminal in nature, jurisprudence from the superior courts of Ireland will be considered, in addition to that of the US Supreme Court.

## The Situation in Ireland

The burgeoning of organised crime in Ireland in the 1990s precipitated a surge of legislative action which sought to strengthen the State's abilities to counter such criminality. There was a notable rise in "gangland" killings in that decade, and the low conviction rate for such crimes prompted the belief that organised criminals were evading justice (Dooley, 1995, p. 26; Dooley, 2001, pp. 15-17). Political will was fomented in 1996 as a result of the murders of police officer Jerry McCabe and of investigative journalist Veronica Guerin. These murders expedited the introduction of a number of legislative measures that significantly enhanced the capabilities of the Irish State in tackling organised criminality, including extended detention periods, and the drawing of inferences from the silence of the accused. In particular, the Proceeds of Crime Act 1996, which establishes a means of civil asset forfeiture, was introduced, and an agency called the Criminal Assets Bureau (CAB), which has the ability to seize assets, was established.

## Historical Templates for Asset Forfeiture in Ireland

The current model of asset forfeiture in Ireland is grounded on two prototypes: the approach adopted in the United States from the 1970s onwards, and an Irish tactic which was employed only against subversive and paramilitary criminals. In the US, asset forfeiture was provided for in a number of legislative measures, such as the Racketeering Influenced Corrupt Organisations (RICO) provision (Racketeering Influenced Corrupt Organisations, Title IX to the Organised Crime Control Act 1970, 18 USC 1961 § *et seq.*). While RICO requires a conviction before asset forfeiture, the Comprehensive Drug Abuse Prevention and Control Act 1970 (21 USC § 848) allows property to be forfeited after civil proceedings (Jaipaul 1999, p. 191). RICO served as an important precursor to the present Irish approach, and indeed was explicitly mentioned in the Irish legislature as a model for future legal measures (*Dáil Debates*, 2 July, 1996, Vol. 467, Cols. 2372-2373 *per* Mr Ahern; Col. 2444 *per* Mr Shatter; and Col. 2473 *per* Mr O'Dea).

In addition to this American example, the current forfeiture scheme is influenced by an older Irish provision used against subversive criminality, which authorised the forfeiture of the assets of an illegal organisation. Under section 2 of the Offences Against The State (Amendment) Act 1985, the Minister for Justice could freeze monies held by a bank which he believed to be the property of an unlawful organisation, and cause the monies to be paid to the High Court. The person claiming to be the owner of the property could also within six months apply to have the monies paid to him, but the onus of proof was on him to establish ownership (section 3). Once six months had elapsed, the Minister could make an *ex parte* application to the High Court directing that the monies be paid to him. A challenge to the constitutionality of the Act was rejected by the Supreme Court in *Clancy* v *Ireland* [1988] IR 326, which regarded the measure as a permissible delimitation of property rights in the interests of the common good.

The Offences against the State (Amendment) Act, 1985, was limited in its life span and therefore in its effect, as it was brought in on a temporary basis and operated for a mere three months unless renewed by Government order, and was only implemented in one particular instance. Nevertheless, it provided a useful example for the mechanism under the

1996 Act, and indeed the 1985 Act was described as a "clear and direct precedent" for the Proceeds of Crime Act 1996 (*Dáil Debates*, 2 July 1996, Vol. 467, Col. 2409). Moreover, judicial approval of the 1985 Act in *Clancy* paved the way for the subsequent upholding of the constitutionality of the 1996 Act in the Irish courts.

## Procedural Aspects of Asset Forfeiture in Ireland

Civil forfeiture represents a radical alteration to the tactics traditionally adopted by the Irish State in tackling serious crime. While the Criminal Justice Act, 1994, facilitates the confiscation of a convicted offender's property, the Proceeds of Crime Act, 1996, permits the seizure and forfeiture of the "proceeds of crime" in the absence of a criminal conviction.

Upon application by CAB, the High Court may issue an interim order under section 2 of the Act prohibiting any person from disposing of or "dealing with" property worth at least €13,000, which is believed to be the proceeds of crime, for 21 days. Section 3 provides that this interim order lapses after 21 days unless an application for an interlocutory order is made, and an interlocutory order must be granted unless the respondent refutes the contention that the property is the proceeds of crime, or if there would be a serious risk of injustice. Finally, where an interlocutory order has been in force for not less than seven years, the High Court may make a disposal order under section 4, depriving the respondent of his rights in the property and transferring it to the Minister for Finance. Section 7 of the Proceeds of Crime (Amendment) Act, 2005, allows a disposal order to be made where an interlocutory order has been in force for a period of less than seven years with the consent of all the parties concerned.

Significantly, the standard of proof required in an application for an order under the Proceeds of Crime legislation is the civil burden of proof, and hearsay evidence is admissible in an application for an order under the Act if the court is satisfied that there are reasonable grounds for that belief (section 8).

A number of challenges to the constitutionality of the forfeiture process have failed in the Irish courts. The constitutionality of the Proceeds of Crime Act, 1996, was unsuccessfully questioned on three main grounds: firstly, that the Act breaches the right against self-incrimination; secondly, that it infringes the constitutionally protected right to private property; and thirdly, that it is in fact a criminal process which merely purports to be civil in nature. This upholding of the procedure's constitutionality has permitted the circumscription or evasion of the rights which would usually accrue to an individual in a criminal trial.

## A Criminal Sanction in a Civil Context?

Asset forfeiture may be justified on the basis that an individual should not be allowed to profit from his crime. However, in the context of such forfeiture in Ireland, the criminality of the person has not been established on foot of a hearing to the criminal standard of proof, and so it is questionable whether this equitable maxim is applicable. This chapter will next seek to determine if the forfeiture mechanism is "an ersatz civil proceeding" which is "really a disguise for what [is] truly an attempt by the Oireachtas [legislature] to impose a criminal sanction in a civil context" (*O'Keeffe* v *Ferris* [1997] 3 IR 463 at 470 *per* O'Flaherty J., referring to a submission by counsel for the plaintiff). To this end, Irish jurisprudence will be considered, in addition to that of the US Supreme Court.

### *Irish Jurisprudence*

The Irish courts have concluded that the forfeiture proceedings under the Proceeds of Crime Act, 1996, do not have "all the features of a criminal prosecution", on the basis that the respondent cannot be arrested, remanded in custody or on bail, and because there is no specific penalty or fine (*Murphy* v *GM* [2001] 4 IR 113, p. 417; *Gilligan* v *Criminal Assets Bureau* [1998] 3 IR 185, p. 217). In other words, a procedure is not a criminal process if it does not involve features likes arrest and detention. However, it is arguable that the lack of these characteristics facilitates the depiction of forfeiture as civil in nature. While the lack of detention under the Proceeds of Crime Act, 1996, may be cited as evidence that the proceedings are not criminal in nature, it is arguable that the classification of the process as civil in nature by the legislature has resulted in the fact that an individual may not be detained.

In addition, the Irish courts relied on previous cases which regarded forfeiture in the context of other statutory proceedings as civil (*Gilligan* v *Criminal Assets Bureau*, p. 223; *Murphy* v *GM,* p. 153). Furthermore, asset forfeiture was interpreted as an *in rem*, rather than *in personam*, action, following the decision of the US Supreme Court in *Various Items of Personal Property* v *United States* (1931) 282 US 577, p. 581. Notwithstanding these conclusions of the Irish courts, it is arguable that asset forfeiture may be interpreted as a criminal sanction which should operate in the criminal realm with its concomitant due process rights and protections. To determine its true nature, this chapter will adopt tests outlined by the US Supreme Court.

## *US Jurisprudence: The Ward and Mendoza Tests*

A two-part test which establishes whether a legislative measure is criminal or civil in nature was described and applied by the US Supreme Court in *United States* v *Ward* (1980, 448 US 242, pp. 248-249), and this is a fruitful approach in determining the status of asset forfeiture in Ireland. First, the court must establish whether the legislature "indicated either expressly or impliedly a preference" for the label of civil or criminal when introducing the measure. Second, if the legislature intended to introduce a civil penalty, the court must determine if the statutory scheme was as punitive either in purpose or effect as to negate that intention.

Applying part one of the *Ward* test to the Proceeds of Crime Act, 1996, does not reveal an explicitly punitive intent on the part of the Irish legislature. As noted in *Enright* v *Ireland* [2003] 2 IR 321, the legislature's intention may be gleaned from the long title of a statute. The long title of the Proceeds of Crime Act, 1996, describes the Act as enabling the High Court to make orders for the preservation and the disposal of the proceeds of crime and to provide for related matters, and so does not include any punitive intention. In addition, no punitive intent may be detected in the language of the legislation itself, given that there is no use of terminology such as "guilty", "offence" or "conviction".[1] While it is conceivable that the legislature had an implicit punitive intent when drafting the legislation, as is evidenced in comments such as this: the "ultimate aim is not to seize the profits of drug trafficking: it is to put drug traffickers out of business altogether" (*Dáil Debates*, 9 July, 1997, Vol. 480, Col. 166), this does not conclusively establish that the legislature intended to accord a criminal label to asset forfeiture.

As the application of part one of the *Ward* test does not reveal that the Irish legislature "indicated either expressly or impliedly a preference" for a

---

[1] The absence of terminology such as "guilty" and "conviction on indictment" was seen as significant in *Downes* v *DPP* [1987] IR 139 where Barr J found that a statutory provision concerning revenue matters was coercive rather than punitive. He noted that such concepts were used in other provisions which created revenue offences. Moreover, in *DPP* v *Boyle* [1994] 2 IR 221 the High Court relied on the presence of the words "an offence" and "on summary conviction" in sections 24 and 25 of the Finance Act 1926 to determine that the wrongdoing referred to constituted a criminal matter.

civil or criminal label, the second aspect of this test, which centres on the purpose and effect of the measure and seeks to determine if it is so punitive as to negate the civil intentions of the legislature, must be applied. This second branch is grounded on the more detailed test elaborated in *Kennedy* v *Mendoza* (1963) 372 US 144, pp. 168-169, where the US Supreme Court specified various factors which denote whether legislation is penal or regulatory in character: whether the sanction involves an affirmative disability or restraint; whether it has historically been regarded as a punishment; whether it comes into play only on a finding of *scienter*; whether its operation will promote the traditional aims of punishment, namely retribution and deterrence; whether the behaviour to which it applies is already a crime; whether an alternative purpose for it exists to which it may be rationally connected; and whether it appears excessive in relation to the alternative purpose.

### *Affirmative Disability or Restraint*

The first factor of the *Mendoza* test, which considers whether the sanction involves an affirmative disability or restraint, has been compared to Hart's depiction of punishment as involving "pain or some consequence normally considered unpleasant" (Hart, 1968, pp. 4-5; Clark, 1976, p. 455). This criterion is satisfied by the Proceeds of Crime Act, 1996, on the basis that asset confiscation and forfeiture may be seen as involving a disability or restraint, as it prevents a person from dealing with his assets and eventually erases his interest in them.

### *Historical Approach*

While historically forfeiture has been characterised as a civil remedy rather than a criminal punishment in Ireland, as outlined above, a more ambiguous approach has recently been evidenced in the US, a development which may be pertinent to the approach adopted by the Irish courts. While the US Supreme Court initially interpreted forfeiture as a remedial rather than a punitive sanction,[2] in *Austin* v *United States* (1993, 509 US 602, p. 618-619), the court determined that forfeiture was punitive in nature, because of the existence of an "innocent owner" defence. The

[2] *Helvering* v *Mitchell* (1938) 303 US 391, p. 401; *United States ex rel. Marcus* v *Hess* (1943) 317 US 537, pp. 549-550; *Rex Trailer Co* v *United States* (1956) 350 US 148, p. 151-154; and *One Lot Emerald Cut Stones and One Ring* v *United States* (1972) 409 US 232, p. 237.

availability of such a defence which emphasises the culpability of the owner was seen to reveal an intent on the part of the legislature to punish only those involved in drug trafficking.

Similarly, orders under section 3 and 4 of the Proceeds of Crime Act, 1996, in Ireland may not be imposed or may be overturned if there is a serious risk of injustice. This is comparable to an innocent owner defence, given that an innocent person may retain the assets and have the order lifted if he proves that he was unaware of the property's criminal origins or connections. Moreover, the seven-year waiting period before a section 4 disposal order is granted seeks to ensure that any person who jointly owns property with an individual who is allegedly involved in criminal activity could claim ownership of the property (see Comment of Minister for Justice, Equality and Law Reform to the Select Committee on Justice, Equality, Defence and Women's Rights, 30 June 2004, Vol. 37). This implies that orders under the 1996 Act are not aimed at the property, but rather the allegedly culpable individual, thereby refuting the contention that the orders are *in rem*. Guilt seems to be an important issue in the context of asset forfeiture in Ireland, given that individuals who are perceived to be guilty are treated differently to innocent people.

While historically forfeiture has been regarded as remedial rather than punitive in Ireland, the decision of the US Supreme Court in *Austin* may suggest that the innocent owner defence in Ireland denotes that forfeiture is punitive in nature. Although this facet of the *Mendoza* test is not strictly satisfied, it is arguable that the change in emphasis in the US is of considerable persuasive value.

## *Finding of Scienter*

This element pertains to the respondent's intention, and is comparable to the requirement of *mens rea* for a criminal offence. As Bishop observed in 1858:

> [D]isguise the matter as we may, under whatever form of words, if the intent which the owner of the property carries in his bosom is the gist of the thing on which the forfeiture turns, then the question is one of the criminal law, and forfeiture is a penalty imposed for crime (Bishop, 1858, as cited in Piety, 1991, p. 942).

It appears that this criterion is satisfied by the Proceeds of Crime Act, 1996, given that the alleged criminal behaviour of the respondent is at the core of the matter. The High Court cannot make an order under the Act without evidence that the assets were attained as a result of criminal activity or conduct, and while the criminal standard of proof need not be satisfied, the blameworthiness of the respondent remains central. The moral responsibility and social blame that accrue as a result of a determination by the High Court that property represents the proceeds of crime indicates that the culpability of the respondent is of import in this regard, thus arguably satisfying the third requirement (Stahl, 1992, text accompanying, n. 176).

### *Promotion of Punishment's Traditional Aims*

The application of this aspect of the test examines if the forfeiture process in Ireland promotes the traditional aims of punishment, such as retribution or deterrence. Neither the statutorily defined objectives of CAB, as outlined in section 4 of the Criminal Assets Bureau Act, 1996, nor the long title of the Proceeds of Crime Act, 1996, reveal such aims. Moreover, the legislation may be interpreted as regulatory, as it redresses the imbalance caused by the generation of funds by means of criminal activity. As McGuinness J observed in *Gilligan* v *Criminal Assets Bureau* (p. 218), the removal of property that represented the proceeds of crime "could well be viewed in the light of reparation rather than punishment or penalty". However, the definition of "proceeds of crime" in section 1 of the Proceeds of Crime Act 1996 is not limited to profits of crime but incorporates any property received at any time as a result of or in connection with the commission of an offence. This suggests that the process moves beyond a purely remedial or reparative approach into the retributive realm (Meade, 2000, p. 17).

Forfeiture also seems to display deterrent effects, thus fulfilling another traditional aim of punishment. While it may be claimed that as forfeiture simply recoups what was not legitimately owned, it does not act as a deterrent because it does not render the individual worse off than before the criminal conduct (Fried, 1988, pp. 371-372), it is more persuasive to interpret the seizure of earnings of alleged criminal activities as a general deterrent, on the basis that it negates the incentive to commit crime. The potential seizure of one's assets because of a suspicion of criminal behaviour represents an effective deterrent. Moreover, asset forfeiture may act as a specific or individual deterrent to any individual whose property has been seized by CAB.

In addition to the traditional objectives of retribution and deterrence, asset forfeiture serves punishment's aims of censure and incapacitation. As Hart (1958) argued, criminal sanctions "take their character as punishment from the condemnation which precedes them and serves as the warrant for their infliction" (p. 405). Steiker (1997) reiterated this, and distinguished criminal from civil measures by the features of "blaming" in the former (p. 804). Asset forfeiture in Ireland derives from, and encapsulates, the popular and political censure of the targeted individual's suspected actions. Furthermore, although the process does not incapacitate offenders in the sense of removing them from society, it does aim to incapacitate criminal organisations and "reduce their power and influence" by "divesting major criminals of their ill-gotten gains" (*Gilligan* v *Criminal Assets Bureau*, p. 217; Meade, 2001, p. 17).

These conclusions suggest that the fourth element of the *Mendoza* test is satisfied, given that asset forfeiture in Ireland promotes punishment's traditional aims of retribution and deterrence, and that it demonstrates censure and serves incapacitative ends.

## *Process Applies to Criminal Behaviour*

Although forfeiture proceedings in Ireland do not require a conviction, it must be established that the property is the proceeds of crime, thereby requiring proof of criminality, albeit on the lower civil burden of proof. This suggests that the behaviour to which forfeiture proceedings pertain must be a crime. However, the courts have held that it is not necessary for particular assets to be related to a particular crime, as this would make the Act "useless and unworkable" (*McK* v *F* and *McK* v *H* [2005] 2 IR 163, para. 15 *per* Geoghegan J.) Nevertheless, the activities which the Act seeks to combat are primarily the sale and trafficking of drugs, and money laundering, which are on the Irish statute book as criminal offences (see section 15 of the Misuse of Drugs Act 1977 (as amended); and Part IV of the Criminal Justice Act 1994 respectively). It is therefore suggested that the fifth element of the test is satisfied in the context of the Proceeds of Crime Act, 1996.

## *Alternative Non-Punitive Purpose*

The final two elements of the *Mendoza* test consider whether there is a non-punitive purpose that can rationally be connected to the measure, and whether the measure appears excessive in relation to this alternative purpose. Forfeiture serves significant non-punitive aims, by seeking to recover assets unjustifiably and illegally acquired as a result of criminal activity. Whether the forfeiture process is excessive in relation to this objective will now be examined.

When applying these final criteria to a forfeiture provision in the US, Stahl (1992) noted that for a measure to be seen as remedial or regulatory, it must not burden property owners any more than is reasonably necessary to achieve regulatory ends (text accompanying n. 185). It is arguable that in the Irish context the infringements on the respondent's rights to private property are not justifiable, given that his interest in the property may be completely erased by means of a disposal order under section 4 of the Proceeds of Crime Act, 1996, after seven years, without a hearing to the standard required by the criminal law. However, the Irish courts have held that forfeiture does not breach the constitutional right to private property, because of the public interest inherent in the legislation (see *M* v *D* [1998] 3 IR 175, p. 184). The Act was not seen to unjustly attack property rights, given that the State must first demonstrate that the property is the proceeds of crime and that an order shall not be made if there is a serious risk of injustice (*Gilligan* v *Criminal Assets Bureau*, p. 237).

It is questionable whether the infringement on the right to private property by asset forfeiture is justified, given that such a determination is made on foot of a civil hearing. Moreover, the "serious risk of injustice" caveat, which was described as a "vague and intangible yardstick" (O'Higgins, 1996, p. 12), may not effectively protect the rights of the individual, given its imprecise and malleable nature. Therefore, it is arguable that the forfeiture process is excessive, having regard to its aims, as it does not afford the respondent the rights which accrue in the context of a criminal trial.

The tests delineated by the US Supreme Court in *Ward* and *Mendoza* are valuable in analysing the Proceeds of Crime legislation, and suggest that the forfeiture process is in fact a criminal rather than a civil or regulatory mechanism, which should therefore attract due process rights. Indeed, "civil labels and good intentions do not themselves obviate the need" for criminal procedural protections (*In Re Winship* (1970) 397 US 358, pp. 365-366), and so such protections must be accorded to all respondents in asset forfeiture proceedings.

## Theorising Asset Forfeiture

This chapter next places asset forfeiture in Ireland in a theoretical context, so as to clarify the tactic's underlying rationales and aims. Three particular concepts will be considered, to explain and contextualise the introduction and implementation of forfeiture. Firstly, the work of Herbert Packer will be used to determine the extent to which asset forfeiture denotes a shift from due process to crime control imperatives. Secondly, asset forfeiture will be interpreted as representing a shift away from criminal justice *per se* to "criminal administration". Finally, forfeiture will be categorised as an adaptive response of the State to the phenomenon of crime and the reality of crime control in late-modern society, drawing on the work of David Garland. While this chapter relates these insights to the Irish situation, they are germane and useful in explaining comparable tactics in other jurisdictions.

## *From Due Process to Crime Control?*

Civil forfeiture may be classified as favouring crime control to the detriment of due process. In *The Limits of the Criminal Sanction* (1968), Herbert Packer presents two normative models of the criminal process, the crime control model and the due process model, which represent two separate value systems in the criminal process (p. 153). These normative models provide a useful framework on which an analysis of civil forfeiture may be grounded.

For the crime control model, the suppression of criminal conduct is the most significant function of the criminal process, and efficiency, speed and finality are of primary importance: therefore the criminal process should not involve "ceremonious rituals" that delay the progress of a case (ibid, p. 158). This model of criminal justice regards expert administrative fact-finding as more reliable than formal adjudicatory processes, and so favours minimum restrictions on extrajudicial, informal processes (ibid, pp. 160-162).

In contrast, the due process model resembles an obstacle course which hinders the progress of the accused through the criminal process (ibid, p. 164). While accepting the need to prevent crime, this model sees the protection of the innocent in the criminal process as of equal importance as the conviction of the guilty, and so favours formal, adversary adjudication. More emphasis is placed on reliability than on efficiency. Furthermore, an individual is guilty only if he is found to be likely on the basis of reliable evidence to have committed the crime; and that determination must be made in a procedurally regular fashion by competent authorities (ibid, p. 167).

Packer's crime control and due process models are valuable interpretive devices which allow civil forfeiture to be conceptualised and analysed. Nevertheless, a number of problematic issues must be noted. Firstly, it may be argued that his approach is superficial and skims over the key characteristics of the models. Moreover, he fails explain why aspects of one model would be favoured over the other in any given jurisdiction.

Although Packer's thesis may be lacking in depth, this does not undermine the analytical value of his models, as they provide a clear means of assessing the tactics employed by the state in the criminal justice system, as they may clarify the underlying rationale for the introduction and implementation of a particular mechanism.

It has also been claimed that Packer's models should not be compared, given that crime control is the central aim of the criminal process, while due process values are simply procedures which temper that objective (Goldstein 1974, p. 1016; Arenella, 1983 p. 211). As Smith (1997) argues, due process is not a goal in itself, and only acquires a meaning in the context of the pursuit of other goals, such as crime control (pp. 335-336). Ashworth (1994) proposes a reconstruction of Packer's models so as to articulate that crime control is the underlying purpose of the system, the pursuit of which is qualified by respect for due process (p. 28), while Duff (1998) suggests that the crime control model should be renamed the efficiency model, given that crime control may refer to both the goal of the system and a set of values underpinning that goal (p. 614). Although the claim that the due process model is not a true procedural model has merit, it is submitted that the usefulness of Packer's depiction of the overarching ideologies in the criminal justice system surmounts this shortcoming. Notwithstanding the aforementioned criticisms, Packer's normative models provide a useful framework on which an assessment of asset forfeiture may be grounded. As Henham (1998) notes, Packer's approach is theoretically deficient but heuristically valuable as an empirical tool (p. 593).

It is arguable that the enactment of the Criminal Assets Bureau Act, 1996 and the Proceeds of Crime Act, 1996, signified a move away from due process towards the imperatives of crime control. Asset forfeiture in Ireland occurs in the civil realm with the associated lower burden of proof, and so involves a realignment of the approach adopted by the State in the fight against organised crime, demonstrating a preference for the needs of the State over due process rights. By adopting a civil process to tackle criminal matters, the Irish State evaded the need for and demands of due process rights.

Packer (1968) argues that while the validating authority of the crime control model is ultimately legislative, the due process model's validating authority is judicial (p. 173). Such a division between the arms of the State is evident in Ireland, with much legislative action being driven by crime control demands while the judiciary are more often guided by due process norms. Recent legislative enactments and political discourse in Ireland indicates the strength of the crime control model in an ideological sense, and judicial decisions are generally more protective of due process.[3] However, as the Irish courts have sanctioned the use of civil asset forfeiture, a technique which erodes due process values, this denotes the favouring of the imperatives of crime control.

The Irish courts have characterised asset forfeiture as civil in nature and have rejected challenges to its constitutionality, thereby indicating a clear preference for crime control over the due process rights of the accused. This is part of a growing trend which involves a reconfiguration of the role and power of the State: no longer is the State the entity from which individuals must be protected, rather it is the State that must protect us from each other. While due process safeguards aim to defend the individual from the might of the State, civil forfeiture circumvents these protections and thereby implies a benign view of state power.

The application of Packer's thesis to the tactic of civil forfeiture indicates that due process values are being subsumed by crime control demands. In addition, the forfeiture mechanism may be explored by reference to the concept of criminal administration.

## *Criminal Administration*

The method of civil forfeiture in the Proceeds of Crime Act, 1996, may be described as "criminal administration" (Dubber, 2001, p. 93) rather than criminal justice, in which the concept of *mens rea* is circumvented in the drive to tackle crime (Kilcommins, forthcoming, 2007). In 1933 Sayre claimed that the modern conception of criminality was moving from a focus on individual culpability to social danger, and questioned whether this signified the abandonment of *mens rea* as an essential element of criminality (Sayre, 1933, p. 35). It is arguable that similar developments are evident in the use of civil forfeiture, where harm as opposed to culpability appears to be central. Civil forfeiture, which purports to be an *in rem* action by focusing on the property rather than on individual intent,

---

[3] The upholding of the due process model by the Irish courts is evident in the exclusion of evidence obtained in breach of constitutional rights (*People (AG)* v *O'Brien* [1965] IR 142; *People (DPP)* v *Kenny* [1990] 2 IR 110); the strict rules governing the admissibility of confession evidence (*People (AG)* v *Cummins* [1972] IR 312); the exclusion of compelled statements in later criminal trials (*Re National Irish Bank Ltd and the Companies Act 1990* [1999] 3 IR 145); and the avoidance of presumptive sentences for drug trafficking under section 5 of the Criminal Justice Act 1999 (*People (DPP)* v *Botha* [2004] 2 IR 375; *People (DPP)* v *Vardacardis,* Court of Criminal Appeal, unreported, 20 January 2003).

may indicate a move towards "a day when criminality will be based upon external behaviour alone irrespective of intent" (ibid).

Civil forfeiture may be characterised as an impersonal means of tackling crime, in which emphasis is laid on the non-moral and regulatory aspect of the law, rather than on the individual. This mechanism does not focus on individual rights or behaviour, but rather on the societal interest in recouping illegally acquired assets and thereby countering the threat of organised crime. The fundamental aim of the forfeiture process is to neutralise the threat posed to society by organised criminals, rather than seeking to rehabilitate or reintegrate them according to the traditional aims and means of criminal justice. While this interpretation of civil forfeiture seems convincing at first, it is questionable whether the concept of intention or the significance of the individual is as marginal as such an understanding would have us believe. As was noted previously, an individual's culpability is of relevance to asset forfeiture in Ireland, given that orders under the Proceeds of Crime Act, 1996, may not be imposed or may be lifted if there is a serious risk of injustice. Moreover, while forfeiture does not aim to rehabilitate, its objectives are not limited to risk neutralisation, given that, as previously argued, it may embody traditional objectives of punishment such as deterrence and censure. Therefore, it seems that construing asset forfeiture as a shift away from personal guilt or notions of intent towards criminal administration overlooks the tactic's expressive aspects which centre on perceived culpability.

A further way of conceptualising civil forfeiture is to regard it as an adaptation by the Irish State to the reality of crime control in late-modern Western societies.

### *Adaptation to Reality*

In *The Culture of Control*, David Garland (2001) argued that criminal justice authorities are now facing a criminological predicament which influences all policy decisions, namely that high crime rates have become a normal social fact and the criminal justice state is seen as limited and ineffective (p. 105 *et seq.*) The inability of the State to deliver law and order and control crime on its own results in a predicament for government authorities: while there is a need reassess the claim that the state is the primary provider of security and crime control, doing so could be disastrous politically (ibid p. 110). Garland characterises the responses to this predicament as "volatile and ambivalent" policies, which may be subdivided into adaptations to reality and denials.

Adaptive responses include the professionalisation and rationalisation of justice, systematic information gathering and better caseload management (ibid, p. 113 *et seq.*). In adapting to the predicament, the State may privatise and commercialise criminal justice, and criminal justice agencies may develop a managerialist ethos with new incentives and interests. Moreover, the ultimate aims of the criminal process may be altered, so that incapacitation rather than rehabilitation is emphasised. In contrast, non-adaptive responses are evident in the denial of the predicament facing the State, with a reassertion of the State's power to punish (ibid, pp. 131-132). Reasoned action is abandoned, and the State withdraws into expressive mode in a bid to re-establish public confidence.

The introduction and implementation of asset forfeiture in Ireland may be classified as an adaptive response to the phenomenon of organised criminality.[4] This radical tactic was introduced because of the feeling that powerful organised criminals were able to protect themselves from prosecution or conviction in the criminal process by allocating responsibility for criminal acts to lower-level associates. Furthermore, organised criminals were seen to have adopted advanced and increasingly impenetrable methods of communication and concealing criminality, thereby requiring a "radically new and thorough approach" on the part of the State (*Seanad Debates*, 27 June 1996, Vol. 148, Col. 420). As Keane J emphasised in *Murphy* v *GM* (p. 136):

> this unquestionably draconian legislation was enacted…because professional criminals had developed sophisticated and elaborate forms of what had become known as "money laundering" in order to conceal from the authorities the proceeds of their criminal activities.

Asset forfeiture in Ireland requires evidence on the civil burden of proof, thereby mitigating the difficulty of achieving a successful conviction against an organised criminal. As was stated in the Irish legislature:

> [i]f traditional methods fail we must devise new ones. If we cannot punish, deter or reform these people we must set a new aim, to stop them from operating their evil trade….If we cannot arrest the criminals, why not confiscate their assets? (*Dáil Debates*, 2 July 1996, Vol. 467, Col. 2435).

[4] The introduction of extended detention periods for suspected drug traffickers under section 2 of the Criminal Justice (Drug Trafficking) Act 1996 and presumptive sentences of ten years for convicted drug traffickers under section 5 of the Criminal Justice Act 1999 may be classified as non-adaptive responses, or forms of "acting out".

The conventional means of criminal prosecution was deemed to be ineffective in the face of organised criminality, and so a new adaptive mechanism was devised which eased the burden on the State, and which facilitated the control of organised crime in a novel sense.

Asset forfeiture holds the potential to usurp ordinary police investigation regarding organised criminality. The approach espoused by the Criminal Assets Bureau represents a softer option to traditional investigative and prosecutorial approaches, due to the lower standard of proof, and the admissibility of hearsay evidence (Lea, 2004, p. 81). The Deputy Commissioner of An Gardaí Síochána (Irish police force) has stressed that the work of the Criminal Assets Bureau operates in parallel to the normal investigating procedures of the police, rather than replacing them, and that the need to gather evidence to support prosecutions in order to obtain convictions for criminal activity must remain the first priority of the Gardaí (*Gilligan* v *Criminal Assets Bureau,* p. 205). Despite these intentions, it is conceivable that, in time, the preferred tactic will come to be the civil seizure of assets and the gathering of taxes by CAB, given the relative ease with which such orders and assessments may be granted. As Pound (1921) observed:

> [t]he function of securing social interest through punitive justice seems to be insensibly slipping away from courts and hence from law and in substance, if not in form, to be coming more and more into the hands of administrative agencies (p. 1).

## Conclusion

While this chapter presented a black-letter and theoretical consideration of civil asset forfeiture in Ireland, the analysis is applicable to equivalent tactics in other jurisdictions. Similar forfeiture processes have been established in other states, such as South Africa, the US, the Philippines, and numerous European countries, and so the conceptual considerations in this chapter are pertinent to many jurisdictions. Indeed, in contrast to the typical practice of policy-transfer in which the Irish legislature adopts the developments of other jurisdictions, the Irish civil forfeiture mechanism has been heralded as a prototype for other states. CAB's structure and *modus operandi* has served as a model for other jurisdictions, with its multi-agency approach in particular attracting considerable international attention (Criminal Assets Bureau, 2000, p. 5).

Asset forfeiture in Ireland, which is based on comparable provisions in the US and on an anti-subversive Irish tactic, was described in this chapter as a *de facto* criminal tactic, on the basis of its satisfaction of the *Ward* and

*Mendoza* tests. This approach embodies a move away from due process to crime control, with a diminution of concern for individual liberties so as to recover illegally acquired assets. While asset forfeiture may be further construed as a representing a shift from criminal justice to criminal administration, the persuasiveness of this interpretation was challenged, given that culpability still plays a central role in the process. Furthermore, forfeiture may be classified as an adaptation to reality, in which the State seeks to overcome its shortcomings by adopting an innovative technique which functions in the civil arena to combat crime.

Notwithstanding the potential infringements on the rights of the individual, and the imposition of a punitive measure in the guise of a civil process, asset forfeiture holds a secure status in the Irish legal system. Civil forfeiture is seen as the most effective means of tackling the problem of organised crime in Ireland. The Minister for Justice, Equality and Law Reform has spoken of "the outstanding performance and success of the Criminal Assets Bureau" in hitting "serious criminals where it hurts most – in their pockets, bank accounts, fancy houses and fast cars" (*Dáil Debates*, 19 November 1998, Vol. 497, Col. 122). Similarly, it was claimed in the legislature that

> [t]he establishment of the Criminal Assets Bureau has been one of our success stories in tackling crime. ...We have for the first time ever, a mass exodus of criminals from this jurisdiction. Criminals are on the run as never before. They have gone to ground overseas and elsewhere because their assets are being seized and their ill gotten gains, their motivation for committing crime, are being taken from them (*Dáil Debates*, 8 October 1997, Vol. 481, Col. 276).

The resounding popular and political support for civil forfeiture, which has also received judicial approval in the face of constitutional challenges, indicates that this process will continue to be a key weapon in the State's arsenal against organised crime.

## References

Arenella, P. (1983). Rethinking the functions of criminal procedure. *Georgetown Law Journal, 72,* 185.

Ashworth, A. (1994). *The criminal process: An evaluative study.* Oxford: Clarendon Press.

*Bunreacht na hÉireann* (Constitution of Ireland).

Clark, J. (1976). Civil and criminal penalties and forfeitures: A framework for constitutional analysis. *Minnesota Law Review, 60*, 379-500.

*Dáil Debates*, 2 July 1996, Vol. 467.
—. 9 July 1997, Vol. 480.
—. 8 October 1997, Vol. 481.
—. 19 November 1998, Vol. 497.
Dooley, E. (1995). *Homicide in Ireland, 1972-1991.* Dublin: Stationery Office.
—. (2001). *Homicide in Ireland, 1992-1996.* Dublin: Stationery Office.
Dubber, M. D. (2001). Policing possession: The war on crime and the end of the criminal law. *Journal of Criminal Law and Criminology, 91*(4), 829-996.
Duff, P. (1998). Crime control, due process and 'The Case for the Prosecution. *British Journal of Criminology, 38*(4), 611-615.
Fried, D. (1988) Rationalizing criminal forfeiture. *Journal of Criminal Law and Criminology, 79,* 328.
Garland, D. (1990). *Punishment and modern society: A study in social theory.* Clarendon Press: Oxford
—. (2001). *The culture of control: Crime and social order in contemporary society.* Oxford: Oxford University Press.
Goldstein, A. S. (1974). Reflections on two models: Inquisitorial themes in American criminal procedure. *Stanford Law Review, 26*(5), 1009-1025.
Hart, H. L. A. (1958). The aims of the criminal law. *Law and Contemporary Problems, 23,* 401-441.
—. (1968). *Punishment and responsibility.* Oxford: Clarendon Press.
Henham, R. (1998). Human rights, due process and sentencing. *British Journal of Criminology, 38*(4), 592-610.
Jaipaul, S. (1999). Asset forfeiture in the United States. *Irish Criminal Law Journal, 9,* 191.
Kilcommins, S. (2007, forthcoming). The primacy of crime control in Ireland. *Irish Jurist.*
Lea, J. (2004) Hitting criminals where it hurts: Organised crime and the erosion of due process. *Cambrian Law Review, 35,* 81-86.
Meade, J. (2000). The disguise of civility – Civil forfeiture of the proceeds of crime and the presumption of innocence in Irish law. *Hibernian Law Journal, 1,* 1.
O'Higgins, M. (1996). The proceeds of crime Act 1996. *Bar Review, 2*(1), 12.
Packer, H. (1968). *The Limits of the criminal sanction.* California: Stanford University Press.
Piety, T. (1991). Scorched earth: How the expansion of civil forfeiture doctrine has laid waste to due process. *University of Miami Law Review, 45,* 911, 916-918.

Sayre, F. B. (1933). Public welfare offences. 35 *Columbia Law Review, 55*, 78-79.

*Seanad Debates*, 27 June 1996, Vol. 148.

*Select Committee on Justice, Equality, Defence and Women's Rights*, 30 June 2004, *37*.

Smith, D. (1997). Case construction and the goals of criminal process. *British Journal of Criminology, 37*(3), 319-346.

Stahl, M. (1992). Asset forfeiture, burdens of proof and the war on drugs. *Journal of Criminal Law and Criminology, 83,* 274.

Steiker, C. S. (1997). Twenty-sixth annual review of criminal procedure: Foreword: Punishment and procedure: Punishment theory and the criminal-civil procedural divide. *Georgetown Law Journal, 85*, 775.

## Cases cited

*Austin* v *United States* (1993) 509 US 602.

*Clancy* v *Ireland*[1988] IR 326.

*Downes* v *DPP* [1987] IR 139.

*DPP* v *Boyle* [1994] 2 IR 221.

*Gilligan* v *Criminal Assets Bureau* [1998] 3 IR 185.

*Helvering* v *Mitchell* (1938) 303 US 391.

*In Re Winship* (1970) 397 US 358.

*Kennedy* v *Mendoza* (1963) 372 US 144.

*M* v *D* [1998] 3 IR 175.

*McK* v *F* and *McK* v *H* [2005] 2 IR 163.

*Murphy* v *GM* [2001] 4 IR 113.

*O'Keeffe* v *Ferris* [1997] 3 IR 463.

*One Lot Emerald Cut Stones and One Ring* v *United States* (1972) 409 US 232.

*People (AG)* v *Cummins* [1972] IR 312.

*People (AG)* v *O'Brien* [1965] IR 142.

*People (DPP)* v *Botha* [2004] 2 IR 375.

*People (DPP)* v *Kenny* [1990] 2 IR 110.

*People (DPP)* v *Vardacardis,* Court of Criminal Appeal, unreported, 20 January 2003.

*Re National Irish Bank Ltd and the Companies Act 1990* [1999] 3 IR 145.

*Rex Trailer Co* v *United States* (1956) 350 US 148.

*United States ex rel. Marcus* v *Hess* (1943) 317 US 537.

*United States* v *Ward* ((1980) 448 US 242.

*Various Items of Personal Property* v *United States* (1931) 282 US 577.

## Statutes

Comprehensive Drug Abuse Prevention and Control Act, 1970 (21 USC § 848).
Criminal Justice Act, 1994.
Criminal Justice Act, 1999.
Criminal Justice (Drug Trafficking) Act, 1996.
Misuse of Drugs Act, 1977.
Offences against the State (Amendment) Act, 1985.
Proceeds of Crime Act, 1996.
Proceeds of Crime (Amendment) Act, 2005.
Racketeering Influenced Corrupt Organisations, Title IX to the Organised Crime Control Act 1970, 18 USC 1961 § *et seq*.

# CHAPTER TWELVE

# POLICING IN INDIA: CONTEMPORARY ISSUES AND INTROSPECTIONS

TUMPA MUKHERJEE

## Abstract

This chapter depicts how the colonial legacy of policing is followed and practiced in post –colonial India. The institution of police in India was created by the 'alien' British colonial power to maintain hegemony over its colonial subjects. However, even after independence and at the dawn of the millennium, the police is still governed by the archaic, repressive Police Act of 1861. The chapter points out lacunae within certain sections of the Police Act and in certain legislations. This chapter points out certain vices which have emerged within the Indian society, which has affected the Indian Police System. The chapter also hints at certain inherent structural problems within the Indian Police System and discusses certain measures adopted by the Indian Government to reform the police system. The chapter concludes with certain suggestions to improve the police services in India.

## Introduction

This chapter explores police and policing practices in post-colonial India at the backdrop of the changing socio-cultural political scenario as well as emerging challenges of the twenty first century. It tries to point out the stagnation within the legal system that governs the institution of police as well as uncovers the vices prevalent. It is an endeavour to find out the possibilities of police reforms in India. This chapter is based upon case studies, derived as extracts from Indian newspapers.

On $26^{th}$ January 1950, India became a sovereign, socialist, secular, democratic, republic with an aim to ensure justice, liberty, equality and fraternity to all its citizens. The political leaders had a vision to establish a Welfare State where democratic policing would be practiced. In such a welfare state police and policing practices would be 'of the people, by the people, for the people'. Under the Indian Constitution police and policing is a state subject under list II of the Seventh Schedule, with the Central Government having no say whatsoever in the operation of the State Police force. In India the formal institution of police was formulated by the 'alien' British colonial power, following the pattern of the Royal Irish Constabulary. The model proved successful in protecting the British commercial interest by providing security and order (Das & Verma, 2003) and for maintaining hegemony over the colonial subjects. The structure of the colonial police force resembled the officer corps structure of the army. Centralization of command and hierarchy in the police structure were the two important features of the 'colonial' police.

Following the military ethos, the police force was housed in barracks, cantonment, an effort which would help to create and sustain social distance between the rulers and the ruled. From its inception such an act was reactive, repressive in nature and was never accountable to the masses.

## Lacunae within the Police Act of 1861

The legal framework which governs the Indian Police has many loopholes and contradicts the mission of democratic functioning of the government. Section 3 of the Police Act of 1861 states that the Superintendence of the Police throughout a general police district shall vest in and be exercised by the State Government to which such district is subordinate and except as authorized under the provisions of this Act, no person, officer or court shall be empowered by the State Government to supersede or control and police functionary (Police Acts). Thus this section lays down the Superintendence of the Police shall be authorized by the State Government. However, in the name of 'Superintendence' the elected representatives of the people constituting the government often control the police. As elected representatives of the people of a democratic country, the government has a duty to monitor and evaluate the functioning and performance of police. However, the reality is that the ruling party, whichever ideology they profess, cannot afford the police to be functioning impartially. They need an edge over other rival political parties and they also have an imperative need to protect the interest of the criminal element in their own party who have attained legitimacy by winning elections or still continue to support it with their money or muscle power (Senthilathiban, 1993).

As per Section 23 of the Police Act of 1861, it is the duty of every police officer to promptly obey and execute all orders and warrants lawfully issued to them by any competent authority. The insistence on prompt obedience and execution of all orders lawfully issued by any competent authority underlies the total submission of police to executive authority.

Section 4 of the Police Act of 1861 states that the administration of the police throughout a general police district shall be vested in an officer to be styled the Inspector General of Police and in such Deputy Inspector General and Assistant Inspector General as the (State Government) shall deem fit (Police Act). According to this act the administration of the police throughout the local jurisdiction of the Magistrate of the district shall, under the general control and direction of such Magistrate, be vested in a District Superintendent and Assistant District Superintendent as the State Government shall consider necessary (Police Act). As a result of this decision, the district police have been closely associated with the District Magistrate, who functions as the Chief Executive in the district (Police Act).This has resulted in the exercise of dual control over the performance of the police personnel.

The State Governments of the different states in India have enacted new legislations since independence to govern the functioning of their respective police forces. For instance, the police forces in the states of Maharashtra & Gujarat are governed by thc Bombay Police Act of 1951, in Kerala by the Kerala Police Act of 1960, in Karnataka by the Karnataka Police Act of 1963 and in Delhi by the Delhi Police Act of 1978. However these new laws are also patterned on the model of the old 1861 legislation.

## Lacunae within the legal codes that the police follows…

At the same time certain provisions in Indian criminal law leaves a mark of distrust in the functioning of the police. For example under Section 162 of the Code of the Criminal Procedure the statement of witness recorded by the police during an investigation is not to be signed by the person making the statement and it cannot be used during the trial for any purpose other than to contradict the witness if they differ from it. The Indian Evidence Act (Section 25 to 26) lays down that no confession made to a police officer or while a person is in police custody, unless recorded by a Magistrate shall be proved against an accused. It implies the reports submitted by the police officers have to be authenticated by an independent agency. However confessions made before other enforcement agencies like Income Tax, Central Excise, Enforcement Directorate even Railway Protection Force are admissible. Thus such legal provisions generate a complete distrust for the police in our minds.

## Post Independent Socio-Political Scenario

In these last six decades the population explosion was not simultaneously marked by the growth in industry and national income. The economy's failure to create enough employment avenues for the masses created an acute scarcity of jobs and led to immense competition for availability of jobs during the sixties and seventies. Mass discontentment led to agrarian struggles like Naxalite movement in Bengal as well as anti-migrant 'Sons of Soil' movement. During the post independent era India faced four types of terrorism– Khalistan[1] oriented terrorism in Punjab, militant terrorism in Kashmir,[2] Naxalite[3] terrorism in Bengal, Bihar, Andhra Pradesh and the United Liberation Front of Asom

---

[1] Terrorism in Punjab (hereafter called Khalistani terrorism) was an imported phenomenon, born out of an identity crisis within the Sikh Diaspora in the West. Migrants to Canada, the UK, the US and West Germany grew increasingly conscious of their ethnicity once abroad. Rediscovering religion, they began to fund religious militants in Punjab from the late 1970s. Among the Sikhs who remained in India, the concept of a separate Sikh homeland had practically no grassroots-level support. The biggest impetus for Khalistan only occurred in 1984. Reacting to a wave of violence by Sikh extremists in Punjab, on June 5, 1984, the Indian Government sent the Army into the Golden Temple, the Sikh faith's holiest shrine. The Temple had long been used as a headquarters complex by the terrorists, who had fortified it heavily. A bitter battle followed, during which the Temple suffered extensive damage. In retaliation, two Sikh Policemen assassinated India's Prime Minister, Indira Gandhi.

[2] Insurgency in Kashmir has existed in various forms, mainly on the Indian administrated side of the disputed territory of Jammu and Kashmir. Kashmir has been the target of a campaign of militancy by all sides in the conflict. Thousands of lives have been lost since 1989 due to the intensified insurgency. Casualties include civilians, Indian Armed Forces, and Kashmiri and foreign militants.

[3] Naxalite or Naxalism is an informal name given to communist groups that were born out of the Sino-Soviet split in the communist movement in India. Ideologically they belong to various trends of Maoism. Initially the movement had its centre in West Bengal. In recent years, they have spread into less developed areas of rural central and eastern India, such as Chhattisgarh and Andhra Pradesh through the activities of underground groups like the Communist Party of India (Maoist). They are conducting an insurgency, typically called the Naxalite-Maoist insurgency.

(ULFA)[4] terrorism in Assam (Ahuja, 2003). The citadel of Indian Democracy-the Parliament, has also not been spared by the terrorists. In the last few years religious sites like Jama Masjid in Delhi, Swami Narayan temple in Gujarat and many more have witnessed terrorist attacks. Apart from terrorism, ethnic violence, communalism, fundamentalism have marred the Indian society. In the last few decades communal riots in different parts of the country like Meerut, Vadodara, and Gujarat have tried to destroy the secularism in India.

India is a developing country and like most countries worldwide has opened its doors to globalization for an increasingly steady growth in economy. However, the process of globalization has been opposed by the localized indigenous culture. On 2nd January, 2006, nearly eight hundred tribal members from nearby villages in Orissa protested against the construction of a boundary wall for a proposed mega steel plant by the corporate giant Tata Steel. The threat of displacement without an alternative livelihood had stemmed the tribal resentment (Communist Party of India (Marxist-Leninist) Liberation, 2007). Similarly few months back (Nov–Dec, 2006, March, 2007) the police had to resort to violence against those who raised their voice against the Government of West Bengal's agricultural land acquisition policy for industrialization in the Singur and Nandigram region of West Bengal.

Thus, instead of following 'consensus' politics the government has time and again opted for 'confrontation' by deploying police forces who had to resort to using violent tactics to curb disturbances. It is a shame that, instead of using police services for the betterment of the society it is evidently being used to curb socio-political and economic discontentment faced by the masses.

## Enactment of Draconian Laws and Police – Custodial Torture

To curb socio–political turmoil in India in the decades following independence, the Indian Government has enacted laws which violate human rights and civil liberties. They include draconian laws like Preventive Detention Act of 1950, Disturbed Area Act, Maintenance of

---

[4] United Liberation Front of Asom (ULFA) was formed on April 7, 1979 by Bhimakanta Buragohain, Rajiv Rajkonwar alias Arabinda Rajkhowa, Golap Baruah alias Anup Chetia, Samiran Gogoi alias Pradip Gogoi, Bhadreshwar Gohain and Paresh Baruah at the Rang Ghar in Sibsagar to establish a "sovereign socialist Assam" through an armed struggle.

Internal Security Act of 1980 & the Terrorist & Disruptive Activities (Prevention) Act (TADA) of 1985. From 1985 to 1995, TADA was extensively used for suppressing the secessionist struggles in Punjab, Kashmir, North Eastern regions. Due to mounting public pressure against TADA, the act was finally withdrawn in the year 1995. The Prevention of Terrorism Act (POTA) has been used extensively to detain political opponents, especially in the State of Jammu and Kashmir and was implemented in other states including Andhra Pradesh, Bihar, Jharkhand, Tamil Nadu, Uttar Pradesh and New Delhi. In the year 1995–96 and 1996–97 around 136 and 188 custodial deaths were reported respectively to the National Human Rights Commission (Ghosh, 2002). Between April 1998 & March 1999, the National Human Rights Commission received 1297 complaints of custodial deaths (Sen, 2001).

In the year 1999–2000, the National Human Rights Commission received reports of 117 deaths in police custody, 1157, 1647, 5783 incidents of illegal detention and arrest, false implication and other police excesses (National Human Rights Commission, 2002). In 2003–04 instances of 167 deaths in police custody and in 2004–05 (till January) 112 cases have been reported (Sen, 2005). 791 police shootouts took place in the year 2004, an average of more than 2 per day. 51,060 complaints against the police took place in the year 2004 (Sharma, 2006). Around 3,362 cases were registered against the police in the year 2004. 22,389 departmental proceedings were pending against policemen until January 2005. And yet convictions of policemen are very rare. In the year 2004, only 55 policemen were convicted (Sharma, 2006). According to Article 3 of the Code of Conduct for Law Enforcement (adopted by the United Nations General Assembly on 17th December 1979), law enforcement officials may use force only when strictly necessary and to the extent required for the performance of their duty. The Code of Conduct for the police in India adopted at the Conference of the Inspector Generals of Police in 1960 and circulated to all the state governments clearly stated that in securing the observance of law or in maintaining order, the police should use the method of persuasion, advice and warning. Should these fail and the application of force becomes inevitable, only the absolute minimum required in the circumstances should be used.

Under Section 197 of the Code of Criminal Procedure, 1973, a public servant cannot be prosecuted without the sanctions of the appropriate authorities for acts done while acting or purporting to act in the discharge of his official duties. The purpose of this provision is to ensure that fabricated complaints are not filed against police officers to demoralize them from performing their duties. However, this legal provision has been misused to provide protection to police officers even in serious cases of violation of human rights by the police. This occurs due to widespread nexus between the Criminals - Politicians - Bureaucrats.

## Criminals - Politicians - Bureaucrats Nexus

Vices in the form of criminalization of politics and politicization of criminals have plagued the Indian society. Being aware of this issue the Government of India in 1993 constituted a Committee with the then Union Home Secretary N.N. Vohra as Chairman, popularly known as Vohra Committee to find out about the Crime Syndicates/Mafia Organizations that have developed links and were being shielded by Government functionaries and political personalities. The committee reported that Crime Syndicates have become a 'law unto themselves'. It is according to Vohra Committee running a 'parallel' government and pushing the state apparatus into irrelevance. Below are some high profile cases that expose extreme levels of corruption and inefficiency within the police department.

### *Nithari Case*

The 2006 incident of serial killing of children in Noida once again proved the unhealthy connivance of the police force with the powerful, as Noida police refused to register cases when the children of the migrant workers started disappearing. An unholy alliance between the police and the criminals has been suspected for long, but here's clear evidence. A Tehelka magazine string operation, carried out over four weeks, tells a frightening tale of police corruption.

The men in uniform beat up the relatives of those killed in Nithari, made merry on the main accused Moninder Singh Pandher's money and stayed in touch with the high and mighty Uttar Pradesh politicians. The spy cam probe shows that circle officer Dinesh Yadav, who was in charge of Nithari investigation called up Shimpal Singh Yadav, Chief Minister (CM) Mulayam Singh's brother and Uttar Pradesh Public Works Department Minister at his residence at 7, Kalidas Marg, three times from his mobile phones. This happened just before Shivpal visited Nithari to describe the serial killings, as 'small, routine incidents'. While six Noida police officers have been dismissed, three have been suspended for negligence. Dinesh Yadav appears to be a man with considerable political connections. Apart from ringing up the CM's brother, he also received a call from Ravi Prakash Verma, Samajwadi Party Member of Parliament's (M.P.) residence on January 5, when the police officer was in Gujarat, for the narco-analysis test of Pandher and Surinder Koli (Times News Network, 2007, Feb 2, p.1).

All this while Dinesh Yadav and his police colleagues were happily spending Pandher's money to carry out their duties in style. The investigation shows the officers travelled first class Air conditioned (A.C) berths in train, all at Pandher's expense-to appear for hearings on anticipatory bail application of the accused before Allahabad High Court. This happened not once but three times. According to the sting operation, police officer Simranjit Kaur went to the Allahabad High Court twice in November: once with a constable and then again with station officer S.P. Singh. The third time she went with Dinesh Yadav in December. The three trips were made on Prayagraj Express, the travel vouchers were recovered by Central Bureau of Investigation (CBI) from Pandher's factory. It has also been reported that Pandher had paid off Kaur. The spy cam shows sub-inspector Vinod Pandey, unaware that he was being recorded, saying "S.K. Sharma (Pandher's manager) paid money on Pandher's behalf………….. Simranjit Kaur (Nithari Chowki –in-charge since November) was paid 2.5 Lakh (One Hundred Thousand)to cover up the matter" (Times News Network 2007, Feb 2, p. 1).

## *Telgi Scam*

Few years back the Telgi scam also opened a can of worms. Abdul Karim Telgi was arrested in 1991 by the Mumbai Police for fraud. He was released and in 1994 he acquired a stamp paper license from the Government of India. He began printing fake stamp papers and appointed 300 people as agents who sold fake stamp papers to bulk purchasers including banks, financial institutions, and insurance companies. Telgi scam brought corruption within the police force to light, causing a national scandal in India. The investigations were carried out by a Special Investigation Team (SIT), which is linked with the Mumbai Police, both at the senior and junior levels. However, SIT had a linkage with the criminals as well- a discovery that has sullied the reputation of the police force beyond repair. So far, the SIT has done painstaking investigations and unravelled omissions and commissions of the Commissioner of Police and other police personnel who have amassed huge properties and shielded Abdul Karim Telgi and his gang (Sen, 2003, p. 15).

The Telgi scam undoubtedly had other dimensions. It had interstate ramifications and there is also a possibility that politicians who favoured Telgi also instructed police officers to shield them. However, on 17th

January, 2006, Telgi and his associates were sentenced to 10 years of rigorous imprisonment (Sen, 2003, p. 15).

### *Political Drama*

Indian Police Service (IPS) officer Gyanwant Singh, former Deputy Commissioner (Head Quarter) of Kolkata Police, always favoured the ruling Communist Party (Marxist) (CPM) in West Bengal. As observed by Afzal Amanullah who served as an Election Commissioner during the 2004, Lok Sabha[5] had criticized Gyanwant Singh's behaviour many a times. According to Amanullah, Gyanwant Singh, the then Murshidabad's Superintendent of Police (SP) had asked his men to help the CPM rig the vote and "cooked up" cases against a Congress candidate. The officer worked like the CPM's hatchet man rather than (the) Murshidabad Superintendent of Police (SP) and a man in uniform is supposed to work as the upholder of law. He was close to political leaders like former CPM state secretary Anil Biswas and former party Member of Legislative Assembly (MLA) Rabin Deb. Because of his close associations with the bosses of the ruling party and his nepotism with the ruling party made him to win the coveted post of Deputy Commissioner of the Detective Department and Headquarters of Kolkata Police in 2005 and 2006 respectively (Verma & Bureau, 2007, October 10, p. 6).

### *Jessica Lall Murder Case*

On April 29, 1999, Jessica Lall an upcoming model in New Delhi was working as a celebrity barmaid at a crowded socialite party when she was shot dead. Dozens of witnesses pointed to Manu Sharma, son of Vinod Sharma, a wealthy powerful Congress politician in Haryana as the murderer. The trial went on for over 7 years and due to inadequacies in the investigation and possible judicial lapses Manu Sharma and number of others were acquitted on 21st February, 2006. Following intense media pressure, the prosecution appealed and Delhi High Court conducted proceedings on a fast track with daily hearing over 25 days. The lower court judgment was found faulty in law and Manu Sharma was found guilty of having murdered Jessica Lall. He was sentenced to life imprisonment on December 20, 2006 (Singh, 2006).

---

[5] The Lok Sabha (also titled the House of the People, by the Constitution) is the directly elected lower house of the Parliament of India.

### *Mattoo Rape and Murder Case*

Priyadarshini Mattoo was a 22 year old law student when she was found raped and murdered at her house in New Delhi on 23rd January, 1996. On October 17th 2006, the Delhi High Court found Santosh Kumar Singh guilty of committing rape and murder and on October 30th, 2006 the Court awarded him Capital Punishment. Santosh Kumar Singh, son of an Inspector General of Police had earlier been acquitted by a trial court in 1999 and the High Court decision was widely perceived in India as a landmark reversal and a measure of the power media holds in a democratic setup. The intense media spotlight also led to an accelerated trial, unprecedented in the tangled Indian court system (Staff Reporter, The Hindu, 2006).

### *Rizwanur Case*

David Arnold had pointed out that the colonial police acted in defence of the interests of Indian propertied classes. This feature has continued even in the twenty first century, when police personnel are found to favour the rich and influential and have a callous and indifferent attitude towards weaker sections. One of its blatant manifestation which had raised hue and cry among not only the intelligentsia, human rights organization but also among the common masses in Kolkata is the recent incident (2007) of some top brass of Lalbazar (Kolkata Police Headquarters) interfering into the 'personal' 'married' life of *Rizwanur Rehman* and *Priyanka Todi.*

Rizwanur Rehman, a young man belonging to a middle class Muslim family in Kolkata fell in love with Priyanka Todi, daughter of a rich influential Hindu businessman. They got legally married under the Special Marriage Act on 18$^{th}$ August 2007 and both decided to lead conjugal life from 31$^{st}$ August 2007. However due to differences in religion and socio-economic status between the two families, the bride's family refused to accept this relationship as well as the legality of the marriage. The bride's father utilized his police connections at Lalbazar, to harass and separate the couple.

In India the Supreme Court guidelines clearly states that the government officials should protect and safeguard couples, who have inter-religious marriage. But unfortunately the law enforcement officials deliberately took the side of the rich businessman. They flouted the apex court guidelines and went beyond their jurisdiction to threaten, harass, mentally torture and separate the couple. Priyanka was informed of her father's sickness and was forced to separate on 8$^{th}$ September 2007.

According to media reports her family took her to Tirupati in South India. On 21st September 2007, Rizwanur Rehman's dead body was found along the rail track near Patipukur.

Mr. Prasun Mukherjee, the then Police Commissioner of Kolkata Police at a press conference defined this act as a suicide, even before the post-mortem report came out. The brazen remarks of the senior cop while justifying the action of his force gives us an impression of how the institution of police, an important state apparatus, acts on behalf of the influential section of society in a Marxist state (Times News Network, 2007, September 24, p. 1).

Thus in Indian context Lord Acton's dictum that 'power corrupts and absolute power corrupts absolutely' is a reality. Another serious vice that has plagued the Indian Police system is that the government and political parties have often used the institution of police for serving their own vested political ends.

The brazen manner in which the police were misused during the Emergency period (1975–77) to subvert lawful procedures and serve purely political ends is brought out in Chapter XV of the Interim Report II dated 26th April 1978, given by the Shah Commission of Inquiry which is as follows:

The Commission invites the Government's attention pointed to the manner in which the police was used and allowed themselves to be used for purposes some of which were to say the best questionable. Some police officers behaved as though they are not accountable to any public authority. The decision to arrest and release certain persons were entirely on political considerations which were intended to be favourable to the ruling party. Employing the police to the advantage of any political party is a sure source of subverting the rule of law. The Government must seriously consider the feasibility and the desirability of insulating the police from the politics of the country and employing it scrupulously on duties for which alone it is by law intended. The policemen must also be made to realize that politicking by them is outside the sphere of their domain and the government would take a very serious view of it'. Not only in the operational functioning of police but also in the posting and transfer of senior police officers, political leaders play an important part which is best illustrated in the following table (Bureau Report 2006, September 25, The Times of India, p. 8).

**Table 1. Transfer of Police officers**

| State | Name of the Officer | Posting (date of Posting) Transferred | Transferred | Reason |
|---|---|---|---|---|
| Bihar | Satyendar Prasad Singh | SP, Chhapra on Dec 24, 2005 | July 14, 2006 | Fall out with local JD(U)MLA |
| Bihar | D.P. Ojha | DGP on June, 2003 | December 2003 | Had sanctioned re – opening of cases against Siwan M.P. Md. Shahabuddin |
| Gujarat | Rahul Sharma | DSP, Bhavnagar on Feb 16, 2002 | a) March 26,2002 b) June 2002, (14 transfers in six years) | Fall out with Narendra Modi, the Chief Minister of Gujarat |
| Maharashtra | Arvind Inamdar | DGP, Maharashtra | Removed in 2002, after a 36 year career | Refused to heed the instructions of the then Home Minister Chhagan Bhujbal |
| Mumbai | Sanjeev Dayal | Joint Commissioner in – charge of administration in Mumbai | Transferred in 2002 | Had resisted Bhujbal's interference in police recruitment. |

However, even though atrocities committed by the police and police bashing by the media, human rights activists, academicians and intelligentsia makes regular news headlines, their sacrifices often remain unheard. In the year 2004-2005, 885 police personnel were killed on duty (BPR & D, 2007). Lay persons often fail to comprehend the difficulties police personnel confront. Police forces are most often required to operate under harsh condition with minimum resources. The population of India has increased from 107.3 crores (1crore = 10,000,000) in 2004 to 109.0 crores in 2005, showing the growth of about 1.58% (BPR & D, 2007). At an all India level the number of people per policemen was 712 on 01.01.2005 as compared to 717 on 01.01.2004 showing a slightly decrease in population per policeman (BPR & D, 2007). The ratio is 11.2 policemen for every 1000 people (Baruah, 2006, May 21). The all India average workload per investigating officer is 42.6 cases per year (Debroy, 2004, January 15). An area looked after by a policeman is about 2.07 sq. km on 01.01.2005 whereas it was 2.12 sq. km on 01.01.2004 showing a slight increase in police force (BPR & D, 2007). The ratio of transport facility available /'00' policeman remains almost same during the year 2003 & 2004 which is 6.0 vehicles/'00' policeman (BPR & D, 2007). The number of Mobile Forensic Science vans available at an all India level were 258 on 01.01.2004. The number increased to 313 on 01.01.2005, an increase of 55 mobile vans during the year. At an all India level the number of computers available on 01.01.2005 was 15351 (BPR & D, 2007). The man in uniform use outdated 303's (Calibre rifle), while terrorist use sophisticated AK–47s (Raaj 2006, August 6). Of the Rs.19,000 crores of police expenditure in 2004 – 05, only Rs.1.7 crore was spent on training (Raaj, 2006, August 6). Often the training police personnel receive is inadequate in nature.

## Police Reforms initiatives undertaken by the Government

A number of committees and commissions were formed after independence with the aim to reform the police system of the country. However the most important has been National Police Commission, formed by the Janata party (which came to power after the revocation of the Emergency in 1977) to make a comprehensive review of the police system in India.

One of the most important recommendations of the National Police Commission to isolate the functioning of police from illegitimate political and bureaucratic interference is the establishment of the Statutory State Security Commission. The functions of the State Security Commission included:

1. Laying down broad policy guidelines and directions for the performance of preventive tasks and service oriented functions by the police.
2. Evaluation of the performance of the state police every year and presenting a report to the state legislative,
3. Functioning as a forum of appeal for disposing off representatives from any police officer of the rank of Superintendent of Police and above regarding his being subject to illegal or irregular orders in the performance of his duties,

4. Functioning as a forum of appeal for disposing of representatives from police officers regarding promotion to the rank of Superintendent of Police and above generally keeping in review the functioning of the police in the state (National Police Commission Reports, hence forth NPC Report).

The State Security Commission shall have the State Minister in charge of Police as the ex-officio Chairman, two members chosen from the State Legislative (one from the ruling party and another from the opposition parties.) They shall be appointed to this Commission on the advice of the Speaker of the State Legislative. The remaining four members of the commission shall be appointed by the Chief Minister, subject to approval by the State Legislature, from retired judges of the High Court, retired Government Servants who had functioned in senior positions in the Government while in service, social scientists or academicians of public standing and eminence (NPC Report). The posting of the Chief of Police in a State should be from a panel of Indian Police Service (IPS) officers of that State cadre prepared by a committee of which the Chairman of the Union Public Service Commission will be the Chairman and the Union Home Secretary, the senior most among the Heads of the Central Police Organization the Chief Secretary of the State and the existing Chief of Police in the State as members (NPC Report). Other important recommendations are as follows (NPC Report) –

- Appointment of Criminal Justice Commission which would comprehensively monitor the performance of all agencies of Criminal Justice system and apply corrective measures from time to time.
- Police performance should not be evaluated on the basis of crime statistics or number of cases solved.
- Training institutions should develop scientific interrogation techniques and impart effective instruction to trainees in this regard.
- All police activities to the extent possible should be open except in four areas which are as follows- (i) operation (ii) intelligence on the basis of which operations are planned and conducted (iii) privacy of the individual citizens (iv) judicial requirement.
- Separation of investigating staff from law and order.
- There should be a continuous monitoring of the performance of the police force in the country. The State Security Commission should have an independent cell to evaluate police performance.
- Enactment of a Model Police Act.

Sadly, the noble recommendations of the National Police Commission finds place only in archives and libraries.

In the year 1996 a Civil Writ petition was filed in the Supreme Court by two retired IPS Officers praying for the issue of orders to the Government to implement the recommendations of the National Police Commission in pursuance of the directions imposed by the Court. The Union Government then had set up a committee on police reforms under the chairmanship of Mr. J. F. Riberio, a retired IPS Officer to review actions taken to implement the recommendations of the above commission. However, the State governments were not willing to implement the National Police Commission recommendations. In April 1997, Mr. Indrajit Gupta, the then Union Home Minister wrote a letter to the Chief Minister of all states, exhorting them to introduce police reforms by following the path as recommended by the National Police Commission. However, the letter failed to produce a single response.

Some of the recommendations of the Riberio Committee included:

- Establishment of the Police Performance and Accountability Commission (PPAC) to oversee the performance of the police and ensure that it is accountable to the law of land.
- Establishment of a District Police Complaints Authority in each police district as a non–statutory body to examine complaints from the public of police excesses, arbitrary arrests detention, false implications in criminal cases, custodial violence etc. and to make appropriate recommendations to the Police Performance and Accountability Commission as well as to the Government and to the State or National Human Rights Commission.
- In every state a Police Establishment Board should be constituted with the Director General of Police (DGP) and his four senior officers, borne on the IPS cadre of the state but who are immediately junior to the DGP, as members to monitor all transfers, promotions, rewards and punishment as well as other service related issues. The old Police Act of 1861 needs to be replaced by a new Police Act.

In the year 2000 the Ministry of Home Affairs, Government of India had set up another committee under the Chairmanship of Mr. K. Padmanabhiah, popularly known as the Padmanabhiah Committee on Police Reforms. Some of the important recommendations of the Committee are as follows-

- A Police Establishment Board consisting of Director General of Police three other members of police force selected, by him, should be constituted to decide transfers of all officers of the rank of Deputy Superintendent of Police and above.

- A body headed by the Chief Justice of the State High Court as Chairman, State Chief Secretary and an eminent public person as members should be constituted to recommend a panel of two names for appointment to the post of the Director General of Police.
- The Government of India should establish a permanent National Commission for Policing standards to lay down norms and standards for all police forces on matters of common concern and to see that the State government set up mechanism to enforce such standards. The Police Act of 1861 should be replaced by a new act.

In December 2004, the Ministry of Home Affairs, the Government of India had set up a committee headed by Mr. Kamal Kumar, the then Director of Sardar Vallabhbhai Patel National Police Academy to review all the recommendations made so far by different national level committee on the issue of police reforms. The committee selected some of the most relevant recommendations made by different committee and submitted its report to the Ministry for immediate action. The United Progressive Alliance Government headed by Dr. Manmohan Singh has set up yet another committee which includes jurists, academicians, representatives of police organization in September 2005 to draft new police legislation. The Committee (popularly known as Soli Sorabjee Committee) has been tasked to draft a new Police Act in view of the changing role/responsibility of the police and challenges before it especially on account of the growth and spread of insurgence/militancy/naxalism etc. The new act will include measures for attitudinal changes of police including working methodology to elicit cooperation and assistant of the community.

Some of the features of this Model Police Act 2006 (PADC) include the following –

- There shall be one police service for each state.
- The composition of police station shall as far as possible reflect adequate representation of all sections of society including gender representation.
- Police personnel shall at all time remain accountable to the law and responsive to the lawful needs of the people and shall observe codes of ethical conduct and integrity, as prescribed.
- The post of Director General of Police shall be the senior most position in the hierarchy of the Police Service of the state and no other officer senior or equivalent in rank to the

incumbent DGP shall be posted to any position within the police organization to ensure that the unity of command is maintained at all times.

- Director General shall have a minimum tenure of 2 years irrespective of his normal date of superannuation
- State Government shall establish full fledged Police Training Academy at the State level. The State Government may set up such bodies to take up such other steps as considered necessary or expedient for the purpose of undertaking research into matters related to the efficiency of Police Service.
- It emphasizes on the concept of community participation in policing.

However the committee set up by the Central Government has no representatives of the civil society. Although police and policing fall under the jurisdiction of the State in the Constitution of India, there is no indication that the different states have been consulted before setting up the committee. Neither are there any representatives of the state government in the committee.

The Supreme Court has directed states to implement directions on setting up of State Security Commission, separation of police force for maintaining law and order and investigation and setting up of police complaint authority. The court had asked states to implement police reforms by December 31, 2006. It has extended the deadline till March 31, 2007 (Times News Network, 2007, January 12).

## Suggestions and Conclusion

Mere enactment of laws and new Police Act cannot make the police accountable for their deeds. The Human Rights Commission established under the Protection of Human Right Act of 1993 can function as an independent agency in making the police accountable in cases of misconduct. For Human Rights Commission to function effectively along with advisory function, power to pressurize government to enforce decisions should be bestowed upon it. The non–governmental organization and media can also act as watchdogs over the operational functioning of the police. To curb social problems of child abuse, sexual harassment, domestic violence etc, a social policing system may be formed under the Ministry of Social Welfare, Justice and Empowerment, Government of India. Community policing schemes may be brought under the purview of Social Policing System. The Police organization can collaborate with private security agencies to ensure community safety. The areas of collaboration range from detection of crime to prevention of crime. It is necessary to look after the well being of the middle or lower level police personnel and provide them with necessary requisites which would help them to deliver services. It is necessary to upgrade the content of police training for middle or lower level police personnel. Inter–state training on different aspects of policing should be organized frequently for middle level officers.

Police Science is a specialized branch of knowledge. In countries like the United States of America, United Kingdom, the Department of Criminal Justice exists in universities where applied research on policing is conducted. In the Department of Police Science at the Korean National Police University police studies are taught and research projects are undertaken. But unfortunately in India very few academic research centres exists (except Bureau of Police Research and Development, and few universities) where research studies on issues related to police and policing receive priority. Universities should set up research institutes where issues on different dimensions of police and policing like community policing, cyber policing, traffic management etc may be intensively probed and researched. Such researches help in effective policy formulations and its implementation by the police personnel.

Public Opinion surveys may be conducted by the police personnel after every three months. Such opinion surveys help the general public to evaluate the delivery of police services. Police personnel can find out the level of citizen satisfaction. After finding their lacunae, if any, the police personnel can revamp their operational functions. There is an urgent need to draft a National Police policy as a part of social planning at the national level.

## References

Ahuja, R. (2003). *Social problems in India*. Jaipur: Rawat Publication.

Baruah, B. (2006, May 21). Bitter truth behind the brutality. *The Times of India,* p.12.

Bureau of Police Research and Development. (2007). Basic police data from the data on police organization from the reports of 2004-05. Bureau of Police Research and Development, New Delhi. Retrieved May 6, 2007 from http://www.bprd.gov.in

Bureau Report. (2006, September 25). Cop story. *The Times of India,* p.8.

Communist Party of India (Marxist-Leninist) Liberation (2007). Orissa: Killing fields of corporate loot. Retrieved May 6, 2007, from http://www.cpiml.org/liberation/year_2006/February/Orissa_killing.htm.

Das, D., & Verma, A. (2003). *Police mission: Challenges & responses,* Maryland: The Scarecrow Press Inc.

Debroy, B. (2004, January 15). Crimes unnumbered. *The Telegraph,* p.10.

Ghosh, A. (2002, November 10). Dead terrorist tell no tale. The *Telegraph*, p.9.

Government of India. (1981). Ministry of Home Affairs, National Police Commission Report (First-Eighth)

National Human Rights Commission. (2002). Annual Report. Government of India.

Police Acts. (2004). Delhi: Universal Law Publishing Co.

Police Act Drafting Committee. (2006). Model Police Act 2006. Government of India.

Raaj, N. (2006, August 6). Policeman defend thyself. *The Times of India,* p.11.

Rebeiro Committee on Police Reform. (1998). Government of India

Sen, S. (2001). Summing up. *The Indian Police Journal, XLVIII*(4), 49-58.

—. (2003, December 23). The rot within. *The Telegraph*, p.15

—. (2005, May 24). Custodial deaths: Lasting changes can only come from within. *The Statesman.*

Senthilathiban, K. (1993). Controlling political interference in policing - A case of community based policing. *Indian Journal of Criminology, 21*(1).

Sharma, S. (2006, May 21). Cops on the beat. *The Times of India*, p.12.

Singh, S. (2006, December 18). Manu sharma convicted in Jessica lal murder case. *Daily News and Analysis.* Retrieved October 14, 2007 from http://www.dnaindia.com/report.asp?NewsID=1069899

Staff Reporter. (2006, October 31). Priyadarshini mattoo Case: Death for Santosh singh. *The Hindu,* Retrieved October 14, 2006 from, http://www.hindu.com/2006/10/31/stories/2006103105981000.htm

The Padmanabhiah Committee on Police Reports. (2000-01). Government of India

Times News Network. (2007, January 12). SC: No review of police reforms. *The Times of India,* p.8.

—. (2007, September 24). Cops ignored Rizwanur plea for protection. *The Times of India,* p.1

Verma, N., & Bureau. (2007, October 10). Blot on cop, before Rizwanur, SP Gyanwant worked as CPM 'hatchet man' said poll observer. *The Telegraph*, p.6.

# CHAPTER THIRTEEN

# UTILITY OF ARTS IN CORRECTIONS

LEE MICHAEL JOHNSON

## Abstract

The objective of this chapter is to explore the usefulness of art programs in achieving correctional goals. Kornfeld (1997) argues that the value of art programs in corrections is multi-dimensional—they offer simultaneous opportunities for therapy, education, vocation, and recreation. Despite the need to explore alternative approaches to corrections, and the well-established functions of art programs, support for the arts in corrections (especially financial) has severely declined (Kornfeld, 1997). Perhaps artistic activities in corrections are too often thought of as being merely recreational—a privilege to be earned with good behaviour, a non-essential amenity, a way for the incarcerated to just pass the time. With this view, it may seem that art programs in corrections are dispensable. A well-made argument can be made to the contrary. Plenty of evidence suggests that the arts perform an effective role in offender rehabilitation and improve the quality of life in correctional environments; it has been shown that art programs can be useful in prison, jail, and community correctional settings (Johnson, 2007a, 2007b, and 2008).

## Introduction

When considering high recidivism rates, it does not appear that correctional strategies are very effective in reducing re-offending (Newbold, 2003). Since it does not respond to individuals' criminogenic needs, criminal sanctioning (punishment) itself does nothing to reduce tendencies toward re-offending (Bonta, 1996). Also, popular conventional approaches to offender rehabilitation do not seem to work very well (Palmer, 1994). However, it is far too pessimistic to believe that "nothing works." Some correctional rehabilitation programs show successful outcomes while others show promise (Gendreau, 1996; Palmer, 1994; MacKenzie, 2006), such as those geared toward cognitive-behavioural change (Elliott-Marshall, Ramsay, & Stewart, 2005). Rehabilitation programs may also work in that they improve the quality of life of the correctional setting (Newbold, 2003) and therefore institutional management. One study of an in-prison therapeutic community treatment program in Delaware reported lower levels of institutional disorder (grievances filed and rule violations by prisoners) compared to non-treatment units, while controlling for the severity of prisoners' anti-social behavioural histories (Dietz, O'Connell, & Scarpitti, 2003). Further, the failures of correctional programs appear to be exaggerated. Some states recently experienced reductions in re-incarceration rates (Austin, 2001), and crude recidivism rates can be deceptive in that they include re-arrests for less serious offences and technical violations (Newbold, 2003).

In short, there are plenty of reasons to be optimistic about our ability to develop more effective rehabilitation programs in corrections, as long as our efforts are well-conceived, diligent, and innovative. Rehabilitation strategies that show promise need to be refined and instituted, not abandoned. Currently, integrated (multi-modal) programs that address a variety of offender needs, including personal development, are being targeted as promising approaches (Harper et al., 2005; MacKenzie, 2006).

The objective of this chapter is to explore the usefulness of art programs in achieving correctional goals. Kornfeld (1997) argues that the value of art programs in corrections is multi-dimensional—they offer simultaneous opportunities for therapy, education, vocation, and recreation. Despite the need to explore alternative approaches to corrections, and the well-established functions of art programs, support for the arts in corrections (especially financial) has severely declined (Kornfeld, 1997). Perhaps artistic activities in corrections are too often thought of as being merely recreational—a privilege to be earned with good behaviour, a non-essential amenity, a way for the incarcerated to just pass the time. With this view, it may seem that art programs in corrections are dispensable. A well-made argument can be made to the contrary. Plenty of evidence suggests that the arts perform an effective role in offender rehabilitation and improve the quality of life in correctional environments; it has been shown that art programs can be useful in prison, jail, and community correctional settings (Johnson, 2007a, 2007b, and 2008).

## Prison Art Programs

Art has a long, well established tradition in prison (Gussak Ploumis-Devick, 2004; Ursprung, 1997). In the past, arts and crafts were a normal part of prison work, vocation, education, and therapy programs (Cardinal 1997; van der Hoeven, 1988). During the 1980s, the thought that prisoners were receiving undeserved privileges and amenities—that prisons were becoming more comfortable, less punitive places—became a popular view in the United States. The reduction of prison amenities became a prominent political issue and soon, prison art programs declined sharply (Hillman, 2003). Prison art programs seem to be more highly regarded in England (Schoonover, 1986), but programs there too experienced sharp cuts in the late 1990s (Clements, 2004). This decline in support occurred despite a lack of evidence that prison art programs failed in achieving important correctional goals and the presence of evidence that they have several uses (Hillman, 2003). In various forms, prison art programs have received a great deal of validation from researchers, teachers, artists, therapists and counsellors, and administrators; this community of scholars report several benefits of prison art programs (Johnson, 2008a). Art serves to rehabilitate prisoners through its educational and therapeutic properties, and by fostering productive relationships with the outside community. Also, art improves the quality of life for prisoners and staff by humanizing the prison environment and improving institutional management.

### *Education*

Providing artistic activities in prison is not simply a matter of allowing recreational privileges. Art is regarded by many as a valuable part of the prison education curriculum (Billington, 2002; Williams, 2003). Learning art involves acquiring the kinds of new, creative ways of thinking needed for rehabilitation to occur (Clements, 2004). Art encourages students to examine and learn about the world in a fresh way—by creating artwork and analyzing the work of others (Edwards, 1994). Engaging in art offers prisoners' opportunities to explore their inner potential and alternative interests, improve their communication abilities, become active citizens, and develop the critical attitude necessary to examine lifestyle (Clements, 2004). Because art exposes one to diverse perspectives, it can be used to develop multicultural awareness and appreciation among prisoners (Carlyle, 2000; Gussak & Ploumis-Devick, 2004), as well as help them further explore and appreciate their own culture (Clements, 2004).

Well implemented education programs that meet prisoners' multiple educational needs are shown to improve employment capabilities and reduce re-incarceration; these effective programs will likely include academic, vocational, social skill, emotional self-management, *and artistic* instruction (Vacca, 2004). Programs that focus narrowly on basic, key, and cognitive skill sets are expected to be much less rehabilitative than those that incorporate the arts and humanities. Arts and humanities offer the creativity and heuristic learning, and encourage the self-discipline and autonomy, that enables the profound personal transformation demanded by true rehabilitation (Clements, 2004). To provide an example, one arts-based educational program for women in a Florida prison integrated art and health education as a successful way to promote students' wellness and global self-development (Mullen, 1999).

Art education fosters student self-directedness (Clements, 2004). To undergo personal transformation and change their circumstances for the better—to make the changes needed to desist in offending—prisoners need to be enabled by self-direction. Self-direction, though, stems from high degrees of freedom and autonomy. The freedom of exploration and expression offered through the arts is empowering, not just liberating. If education is to truly rehabilitate prisoners, it must not only empower them through the acquisition of human and social capital; it must at the same time emancipate them from the confines of social psychological institutionalization. Art, as part of a more creative and expressive curriculum that encourages spontaneous and participatory learning, gives incarcerated students the ability and freedom to self-direct their personal transformations, and thus become more involved in the rehabilitative process (Clements, 2004).

It is important that curricula contain elements that draw prisoners into being personally invested in programs—in their own education. Educational programs are more effective when instruction engages topics that motivate and sustain students' interests (Vacca, 2004). Art serves to attract and enable incarcerated students who have experienced little academic success and may be reluctant to participate in educational programs (Clements, 2004; Gussak & Ploumis-Devick, 2004; Leach, 2002; Riches, 1994a; Schoonover, 1986). Making art is a hands-on approach to learning that offers the opportunity to do well at another important type of study (Riches, 1994a). One county prison art project in Pennsylvania incorporated art-making and creative writing into a basic general education (adult education/GED) and computer skill program. The project led to a publication outlet for students' works--an *Anthology of Inmate Art*--which increased enrolment in the overall program, created camaraderie among students, and made a favourable impression on guards, members of the community, and other prisoners (Hawk et al., 1993).

It can be seen, then, that the arts are more than supplementary to prison education—they are integral to achieving its primary goals (Graef, 2002). Further, since education creates individual growth and contributes to one's well-being, many aspects of art education are closely linked, and overlap, with those of therapy (Edwards, 1994; Riches, 1994a).

## *Therapy*

Works of art and the process of creating works them itself are both therapeutically valuable (Riches, 1994a). The following are some of art's key therapeutic benefits (see Gussak 1997a & Liebmann, 1994). First, clients with poor literacy and verbal skills may communicate meaningful nonverbal messages through their artwork. Communicating through art removes the vulnerability associated with verbal expression and yields concrete objects to be used to initiate discussion and note developments over time. Next, art can bridge the space between therapist and client when dealing with issues that make clients feel uncomfortable. Artistic expression bypasses clients' reluctance to genuinely explore treatment issues and increases their active involvement in therapeutic processes. Next, art provides a non-destructive way to express, release, and deal with distressful feelings like anger, anxiety, and hostility; statements based on these kinds of feelings are made more socially acceptable through artistic expression. Finally, art is a means of self-expression and self-exploration that allows clients be creative and enjoy themselves in the face of adversity; it taps into the creative impulse that stems from the intense need for diversion and escape from stressful circumstances (Gussak, 1997a; Liebmann, 1994). While much of art therapy's benefits to incarcerated clients have to do with the benefits of art therapy in general, they take on a particular meaning and importance in the prison environment.

Art therapy is an important part of treating prisoners with issues of substance abuse, traumatic childhood experiences (Williams, 2003), mental disorder (Cheney, 1997; Day & Onorato, 1989; Delshadian, 2003; Edwards, 1994; Karban & West, 1994; Sundaram, 1997; Teasdale, 1997; Woodall, Diamond, & Howe 1997), and physical impairment (Sundaram 1997; Taylor, 1997). Art therapy can even help identify those at high risk of committing self-harmful acts, including suicide (Cheney, 1997; Day & Onorato, 1989). The main objective of art therapy is healing. Making visual images generates self-insights, brings suppressed feelings to the surface, and helps one cope with the stress of prison life (Hall, 1997;

Merriam, 1998; Riches, 1994a; Schoonover, 1986; Teasdale, 1995). Art offers prisoners a non-destructive release of distressful feelings stemming from the deprivation of prison life as well as mental health issues that extend beyond the experience of imprisonment (Day & Onorato, 1989; Hall, 1997; Williams, 2003).

Examples of prison art therapy in action are easy to find. Day and Onorato (1997) have used art therapy with incarcerated females with histories of sexual, physical, and emotional abuse; their work with survivors led them to view art therapy as an effective way to treat prisoners and propose that it be more widely used. Using quasi-experimental designs, Gussak (2006 and 2007) found that art group therapy significantly reduced depressive symptoms and improved mood in prisoners. In case analyses conducted by Merriam (1998), art images enabled incarcerated female survivors of abuse to safely process potentially destructive thoughts and feelings associated with traumatic experiences. One pilot program used visual art, storytelling, music and journaling to heal and empower female prisoners with histories of abuse, largely through self-concept change and an identity reconstruction as "survivor" (in contrast to "victim"). This program established a model that could be applied to other populations, including male prisoners, as well as other treatment issues (Williams & Taylor, 2004). Also, another pilot study program showed favourable outcomes in using art therapy to treat incarcerated women who were grieving the death of a loved one (Ferszt et al., 2004).

By focusing on an artistic image that is separate from the person, art therapy gives clients a comfortable distance with which to discuss disowned thoughts and feelings (Merriam, 1998). It is uncomfortable to express certain feelings outward, or they are simply difficult to put into words; these feelings can be more easily externalized through visual images (Day & Onorato, 1989; Cronin, 1994; Gussak & Ploumis-Devick, 2004; Merriam, 1998; Teasdale, 1995). A visual activity framework allows prisoners to appropriately express pent-up feelings—"to be able to see what one feels and thinks" (Teasdale, 1995, p. 9). As a safer form of ventilation, art teaches an alternative outlet for feelings of aggression and anger that one may otherwise be inclined to project outward as destructive behaviour (Cronin, 1994; Graef, 2002; Gussak, 1997a; Hall, 1997; McCourt, 1994; Merriam, 1998). Things that one cannot, or should not, say "out loud" be said more safely with colours, lines, shapes, etc. (Hall, 1997). Gussak (1997b p. 61) calls art "the ultimate hidden weapon" because of its ability to "hide" the therapeutic process—to allow clients to express themselves without fear of retaliation (from other prisoners as well as authorities). Further, Teasdale (1997, p. 215) points out that in contrast to verbal therapy, art therapy "allows for a physical record of thoughts and ideas to be kept and matured. The storing of images enables a visual diary to be maintained for future reference and feedback."

Creating works of art helps prisoners gain self confidence "by making them feel productive, normal, and human" (Williams, 2003 p. 3). Learning and creating art builds self-esteem (Clements, 2004; Merriam 1998; Riches, 1994a; Schoonover, 1986), instils a feeling of self-worth (Grace, 1993; Karban & West, 1994), and helps one create and maintain a favourable social identity in spite of the stigmatizing, identity-stripping environment of prison (Hall, 1997; Williams, 2003). The compassion and individualized attention given by teachers and counsellors sends messages to prisoners that they are valuable and important (Day & Onorato, 1989), as does the admiration and respect they receive for creating good work (Baroody-Hart & Farrell, 1987; Gussak & Ploumis-Devick, 2004; Kornfeld, 1997). Further, the self-confidence gained from improving art skills helps them achieve in other areas of their lives (Edwards, 1994).

In addition to one-on-one therapy, art is also highly effective in prison group therapy and therapeutic community (TC) programs. Therapeutic communities require its members to be open and honest with one another about their emotions and treatment issues—something that group art therapy specializes in accomplishing (Teasdale, 1997). Also, art therapy allows group members to carry over and further explore issues that arise in other group therapeutic venues (Teasdale, 1997). Group collaborative activities such as theatrical and musical productions require cooperation, discipline, dedication, and commitment to mutual goals; they therefore promote the kinds of transformations expected of offenders, even when addressing offending is not the primary concern of an art program. As Aylott (2002, p. 5) put it, "The experience of working as part of a team, recognising and fulfilling your responsibilities, being valued for your contribution, and depending on and valuing the contribution of others, are part of the experience required to become a responsible citizen."

Finally, intrinsic to the goals of corrections is the assumption that a truly rehabilitated offender is one who has taken responsibility for his or her offences. However, accepting accountability for offences, which often involves realizing that one has caused harm to others, is an uncomfortable, perhaps even frightening, process. Art therapy helps offenders confront their behaviour (McCourt, 1994; Teasdale, 1997), break the cycle of violence and fear that threatens to capture them (Graef 2002), and explore desistance strategies (Grace, 1993). Through art, clients can emerge from avoidance and denial (Graef, 2002; Murphy, 1994), come to terms with the realization that they have hurt others, and cope with shame (Murphy, 1994).

## *Community Involvement*

Art programs help incarcerated artists make valuable contributions to their communities. To begin, their work can be put on display to the public. "Inside Out," a partnership program between Frackville Prison and the Philadelphia Museum of Art, produced exhibitions of prisoner art showcasing several hundred paintings and drawings that earned favourable public response (Wisker, 1997). Exposure to the outside raises the relevance and value of prisoners' involvement with the arts and, potentially, increases involvement with and appreciation by the outer community (Aylott, 2002; Wisker, 1997). The artists and craft makers can sell their work on the outside (Baroody-Hart & Farrell, 1987) to earn legitimate income (Riches, 1994b; Williams, 2003), engage in productive continuous exchanges with the community, and help fund the art programs (Williams, 2003). With enough guidance, education, and training, some prisoners could even develop artistic or vocational careers (Schoonover, 1986).

Partnerships between the prison and community can generate several different kinds of creative projects. The Summit Group is a program in the United Kingdom that engages prisoners in a variety of artistic collaborations with schools, businesses, industries, and other community organizations. The group's projects included writing music for an original piece of drama performed at a local school (Aylott, 2002). Similarly, another prison in the UK collaborated with a local theatre company on several projects including one that produced a video and resource pack on drugs for social workers and educators (Carlyle, 2000). In the United States, the Prison Creative Arts Project (PCAP) is a collaborative program based at the University of Michigan (Alexander & Gothard, 2006). It's partnerships with prisoners and correctional facilities generated several projects. Alexander and Gothard (2006) maintain that these projects provide "creative spaces" inside of the harsh environment of prison that extend into the outer community. The following are some examples of PCAP projects. *The Sisters Within Theater Troupe* performed over twenty plays and held several workshops in prisons, juvenile facilities, and high schools. *The Sisters of Unique Lyrics (SOUL)* contributes readings and anthologies to prison workshops. There is an Annual Exhibition of Art by Michigan Prisoners and the Portfolio Project helps incarcerated youth present their work to judges, employers, and teachers. Finally, the

Speakers Bureau brings the voices of the incarcerated to the public and the Linkage Project connects formerly incarcerated with community arts mentors (Alexander & Gothard, 2006).

Art programs can help improve relationships between prisoners and their families in particular (Murphy, 1994; Riches, 1994a; Schoonover 1986). Just as in therapy, art increases one's abilities to communicate important messages to one's family—works presented or given to family members convey thoughts and feelings that are difficult for prisoners to express verbally, even to close family members. Also, creative works give family members something concrete to enjoy and be proud of, which will likely improve the incarcerated family member's sense of self-worth (Murphy, 1994; Riches, 1994a; Schoonover, 1986).

Art programs may better prepare prisoners for community re-entry and aftercare. Efforts to integrate released prisoners may begin during incarceration--rehabilitation programs can be designed to help prepare them to return to the community (Elliott-Marshall, Ramsay, & Stewart, 2005). A study of over 4,000 male and female prisoners in California showed that time spent in prison-based therapeutic community treatment was positively related to participation in aftercare and negatively related to return to custody (in the next twelve months), while time in aftercare was also negatively related to return to custody (Burdon, Messina, & Prendergast, 2004). Also, the "Life Skills Project," a multi-agency project in Florida that works with participants from jail to aftercare/re-entry, showed some reduced recidivism as well as favourable cognitive, emotional, and behavioural outcomes. The program included many curricular areas including self-development, communication skills, interpersonal relationship development, stress management, and accessing community resources (Jalazo, 2005). The arts could be included in any of these areas.

## *Quality of Life*

The arts are beneficial to prison staff and administrators as well as prisoners (Grace, 1993; Graef, 2002; Riches, 1994b; Schoonover, 1986). Art programs help build peaceful, cooperative relationships among prisoners, among staff, and between prisoners and staff (Day & Onorato, 1989; Hall, 1997; van der Hoeven, 1988) and therefore contribute to the security and overall quality of life of the prison (Clements, 2004; Gussak & Ploumis-Devick, 2004; Schoonover, 1986). Arts and crafts may even improve the behaviour of highly disruptive prisoners who are reluctant to participate in rehabilitation programs (Leach, 2002).

Evidence exists that art programs reduce prisoners' disruptive behaviour (Gussak & Ploumis-Devick, 2004; Riches, 1994b; Schoonover, 1986). For example, an evaluation of an art and wellness education program in a Florida women's prison associated it with outcomes favourable to interpersonal safety and fewer disciplinary actions, in addition to improvements in students' self-esteem, self-concept, and interpersonal relationships (Mullen, 1999). The necessity for disciplinary control measures such as restraints and isolation may be reduced when artistic activities are available as options for emotional ventilation (Day & Onorato, 1989). Creating art serves as an alternative way to vent frustration and aggression—art is a distraction from acting out (Clements 2004; Day & Onorato, 1989; Hall, 1997; Riches, 1994a). Further, the availability of art programs offers prisoners a practical stake in conformity. For example, prisoners who take art seriously depend on guards for some of the resources and privileges needed to create art—they must conform to rules in order to develop mutually beneficial relationships with the guards (Baroody-Hart & Farrell, 1987). As a management tool then, art programs can reduce stress, violent behaviour, and the financial costs of responding to health, behavioural problems, and physical damages (Schoonover, 1986; Williams, 2003).

Art programs humanize the prison environment, and subsequently, the persons who reside (and work) in it. Art helps some survive prison by making "doing time" less burdensome (Baroody-Hart & Farrell, 1987; Schoonover, 1986). Prison life is harsh, tedious, controlling, regimented, and lonely; artistic activities provide prisoners with a little respite and escape from these conditions (Day & Onorato, 1989; Gussak & Ploumis-Devick, 2004; Hall, 1997; Riches, 1994a; Schoonover, 1986) and are a good way to deal with boredom (Baroody-Hart & Farrell, 1987; Clements, 2004; Gussak, 1997a; Williams, 2003). For instance, Baroody-Hart and Farrell (1987) identified a subculture of prisoners highly committed to their artwork. By integrating into the safer artist subculture, these "serious artists" distance themselves from the violence, exploitation, and lack of freedom emanating from the general prison population and prison bureaucracy (Baroody-Hart & Farrell, 1987). Creating artwork can improve prisoners' attitudes in spite of the pains of imprisonment and, subsequently, their behaviour (Graef, 2002). Over time, prisons erode prisoners' relationships with the outside world. Art provides a connection to the outside world--recreation, decoration, and the opportunity to make gifts may somewhat normalize prisoners' lives (Hall, 1997; Williams, 2003).

Prison is a controlled environment that deprives its residents' of liberty, power and individuality; it allows prisoners few outlets for creative expression, stimulation, and self-development (Williams, 2003). Art programs help meet "the need for constructive, creative, and purposeful activities to offset the deleterious and dehumanising effects of prisons life" and encourage "personal development, self-esteem, and a small degree of autonomy" (Riches, 1994a, p. 79). Art involves acts of creation that are inherently liberating and exploratory, even inside the restrictive space of prison (Grace, 1993). It "offers the possibility of self-empowerment… because art making is such a highly personal and self-directed activity" (Merriam, 1998, p. 158). (Perhaps art then plays a special role in directing the energies of prisoners with long-term and life sentences.) Art may be one of the few opportunities that prisoners get to live creatively within the boundaries of social acceptability and develop as decent humans while in prison (McCourt, 1994; Murphy, 1994).

## Art in Jail

While there is a great deal of literature on art in prison, very little is written on art in jail specifically, which may suggest that formal art programs are infrequently used in jails (Johnson, 2007b). A few programs have been mentioned however. Overhultz (2001) reported on an annual exhibit/sale of artwork created by inmates in the Broward County, Florida jail system that raises money for local charities, and Day and Onorato (1989) wrote about an art therapy provided to patients incarcerated in the psychiatric wing of a large metropolitan jail.

Jails are more temporary holding facilities and typically do not have as many amenities and programs as prisons. Still, work favouring prison art programs imply that the potential to nurture constructive creativity also exists in jails. Both incarcerate, so many of the uses of art programs in prisons would apply to jails as well (Johnson, 2007b). While the shorter stays in jail are still enough time to participate in rehabilitative activities, stays in jail are not necessarily very short. One can spend a significant amount of time in jail awaiting trial or transfer, or serve a short sentence in jail instead of prison. Some jail stays amount to a year or more—plenty of time to participate in an art program. Perhaps jail art programs can give detainees a good start in orienting themselves to art programs in other settings (in the community, or in prison). While shorter stays and limited resources may render elaborate, costly jail art programs unfeasible, modest programs could be sufficient to provide constructive activities. For instance, a program does not necessarily need elaborate art supplies to offer creative activities that are therapeutically beneficial and enjoyable (Day & Onorato, 1989).

Hanes (2005) identified several functions of creating art in jail that resemble some of the important functions of formal prison art programs: fulfilling the need for self-directed expression, adapting to and enduring the circumstances of incarceration, filling idle time and dealing with boredom, providing a temporary escape or imaginary retreat, and providing a safer and more benign outlet for expressing thoughts, feelings, and aggressive impulses. As with prisons, art programs could be used as an effective jail management tool, promoting the safety and quality of life for both inmates and staff. Jail conditions are often harsher than those of prison, and can therefore be more physically and psychologically stressful (Irwin, 1985). These harsh conditions are counter-rehabilitative. Individuals distressed by this environment, especially those who adapt to it, are much less able to achieve personal growth and develop cooperative relationships during incarceration, and are not being prepared for community re-entry and re-integration.

One county jail in Indiana provides an example of how artistic activities can be incorporated into jail treatment programs. As a therapeutic tool, participants in its drug treatment program are routinely asked to write letters saying "goodbye to their drug of choice" upon graduating from the program (Johnson, 2007b). Figures 1-3 display one of these letters and its accompanying drawing, taken from a summer 2004 cohort. It is interesting that the author took it upon himself to include a drawing—he did not simply complete the assignment as directed by the counsellor. Apparently, he had a great deal to say and felt a desire to express his hopes and fears visually. The author may have received a greater therapeutic release by going beyond the assignment and creating the drawing. Perhaps he was seeking autonomy, a more active role, and a broader outlet for expression—a kind of involvement in one's treatment that should be encouraged.

Figure 1: First Page

## GOOD BYE MR ALCOHOL

SAYING GOOD-BYE TO MY DRUG OF CHOICE IS LIKE SAYING AN EULOGY AT A FUNERAL. ALCOHOL WAS SUCH A GOOD FRIEND OF MINE. I CAN REMEMBER ALL THE GOOD TIMES WE HAD TOGETHER AND TRIED TO FORGET MOST OF THE BAD ONES. THE BALLGAMES, PINICS, CAMPING TRIPS, EVERYTHING I DID CENTERED AROUND YOU. IF THERE WASN'T ALCOHOL THERE I WOULDNT GO OR BROUGHT MY OWN.

THEN WHY AM I SO HAPPY TO SAY GOOD-BYE TO ONE OF MY CLOSEST AND DEAREST FRIEND? WHY HAS IT CAUSED SO MUCH PAIN AND SORROW IN MY LIFE? I WOULDNT OR COULDNT DO ANYTHING WITHOUT YOU. I EVEN WOULD TAKE SHOWERS WITH YOU.

NOW THAT YOU ARE GONE OUT OF MY LIFE. I FEEL LIKE PARTYING AGAIN. BUT WILL I KNOW HOW TO PARTY WITH OUT YOU BY MY SIDE? THIS IS THE QUESTION.! CAN I FUNCTION WITHOUT YOU THERE? YES I CAN!! YOU HAVE DESTROYED SO MANY THINGS IN MY LIFE. I TAKE THAT BACK. WE HAVE DESTROYED SO MUCH BECAUSE ALCOHOL CANT DO IT ALONE WITH OUT MY HELP. EACH TIME I TRIED TO KICK YOU OUT OF LIFE, YOU JUST CAME BACK AGAIN AND AGAIN.

YOU HAVE BEEN MY DOWN FALL SINCE THAT FIRST TIME WHEN I WAS A TEEN-AGER. I SHOULD OF LEARNED WHEN I GOT IN TROUBLE WAY BACK THEN. BUT NO, SOME OF US JUST NEVER SEEM TO CATCH ON. ONE

Figure 2: Second Page

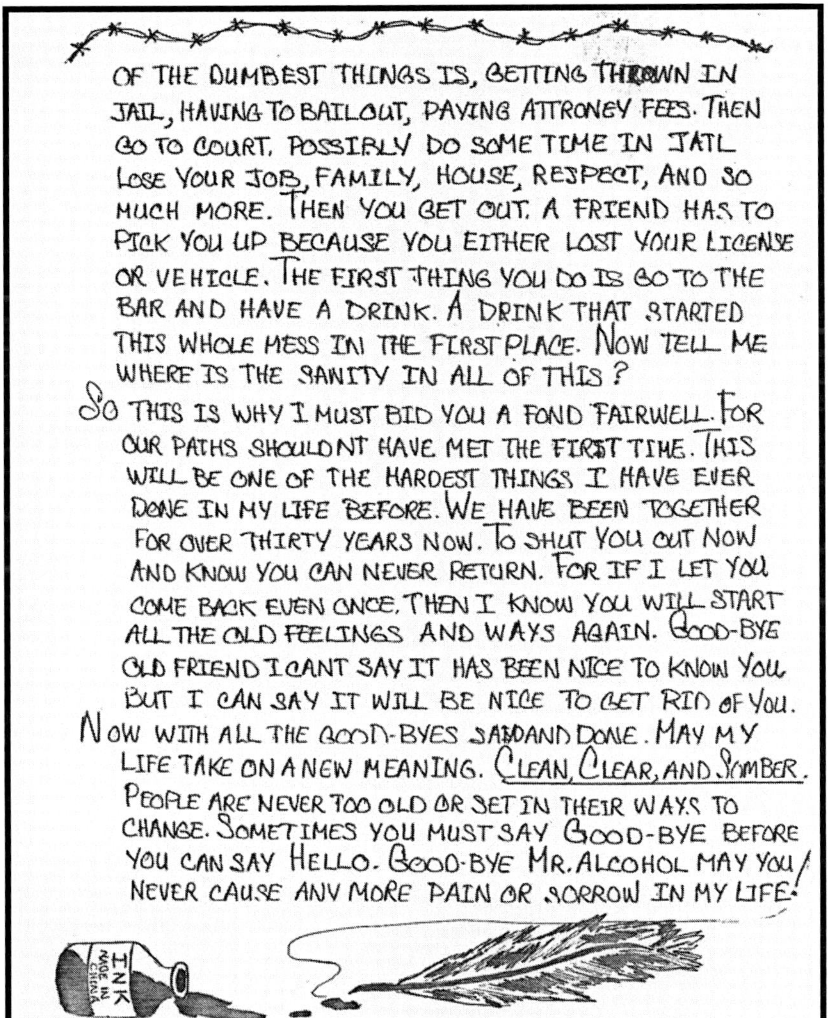

OF THE DUMBEST THINGS IS, GETTING THROWN IN JAIL, HAVING TO BAILOUT, PAYING ATTRONEY FEES. THEN GO TO COURT. POSSIBLY DO SOME TIME IN JAIL LOSE YOUR JOB, FAMILY, HOUSE, RESPECT, AND SO MUCH MORE. THEN YOU GET OUT. A FRIEND HAS TO PICK YOU UP BECAUSE YOU EITHER LOST YOUR LICENSE OR VEHICLE. THE FIRST THING YOU DO IS GO TO THE BAR AND HAVE A DRINK. A DRINK THAT STARTED THIS WHOLE MESS IN THE FIRST PLACE. NOW TELL ME WHERE IS THE SANITY IN ALL OF THIS?

SO THIS IS WHY I MUST BID YOU A FOND FAIRWELL. FOR OUR PATHS SHOULDNT HAVE MET THE FIRST TIME. THIS WILL BE ONE OF THE HARDEST THINGS I HAVE EVER DONE IN MY LIFE BEFORE. WE HAVE BEEN TOGETHER FOR OVER THIRTY YEARS NOW. TO SHUT YOU OUT NOW AND KNOW YOU CAN NEVER RETURN. FOR IF I LET YOU COME BACK EVEN ONCE, THEN I KNOW YOU WILL START ALL THE OLD FEELINGS AND WAYS AGAIN. GOOD-BYE OLD FRIEND I CANT SAY IT HAS BEEN NICE TO KNOW YOU BUT I CAN SAY IT WILL BE NICE TO GET RID OF YOU.

NOW WITH ALL THE GOOD-BYES SAIDAND DONE. MAY MY LIFE TAKE ON A NEW MEANING. CLEAN, CLEAR, AND SOMBER. PEOPLE ARE NEVER TOO OLD OR SET IN THEIR WAYS TO CHANGE. SOMETIMES YOU MUST SAY GOOD-BYE BEFORE YOU CAN SAY HELLO. GOOD-BYE MR. ALCOHOL MAY YOU NEVER CAUSE ANY MORE PAIN OR SORROW IN MY LIFE!

Figure 3: Third Page—Drawing

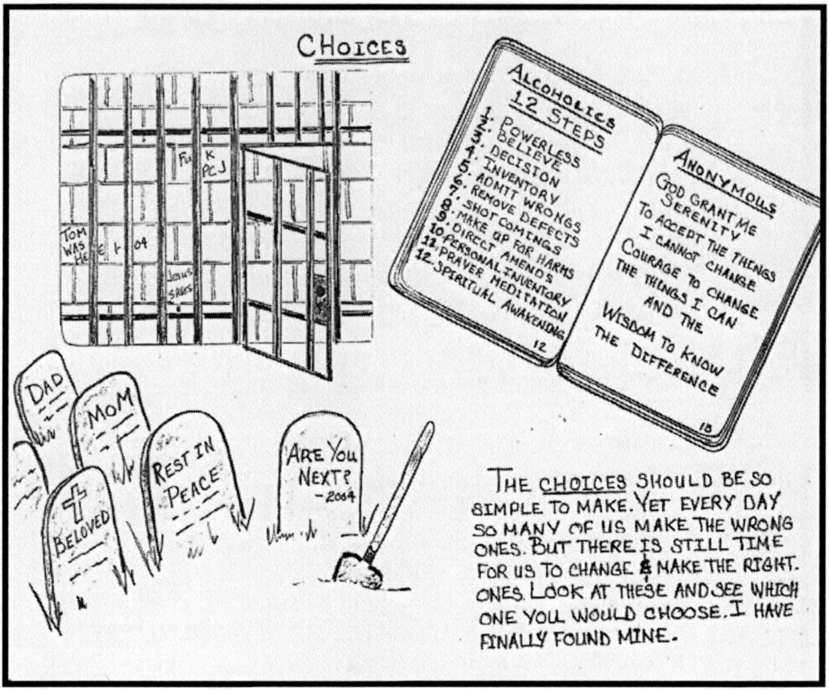


## *Jail Wall Drawings*

Many persons in jail, or prison for that matter, will seek outlets for creative expression whether authorities offer artistic activities or not. Various forms of "jailhouse art" have existed since the creation of jails and prisons (Ursprung, 1997). Further, artwork created spontaneously under detainment—such as wall drawings and carvings, small handmade items, and tattoos--existed long before the creation of formal penal systems in other prison-like environments like gladiator barracks, medieval dungeons and oubliettes, prisoner of war/internment camps, concentration camps, and insane asylums (Cardinal, 1997). Throughout history, captives have proven to be quite resourceful in creating artwork (Cardinal, 1997; Riches 1994b; Ursprung, 1997). Alternative drawing materials like pen ink and makeshift carving tools were used to create wall art and tattoos, and objects—symbols, sculptures, toys, replicas, etc.—were crafted from materials like clothing and other fabrics, meat bones, wood, matchsticks, straw, paper, playing cards, and even bread dough (Cardinal, 1997). It should be apparent then that "creativity and artistic expression are naturally inherent in correctional settings" (Gussak & Ploumis-Devick, 2004, p. 35).

Illicit jail wall drawings illustrate the creativity that exists even in the confines of jail. The drawings soon to follow are examples of several created on cell walls and ceilings inside of a county jail in Indiana (Johnson, 2007b). They were photographed in October 2002 soon after the jail was vacated (a new jail was built). The drawings greatly varied in size and were made with pencil, pen ink, scratching devices, and other sources of removable colour. They addressed a wide variety of subjects, including more "pleasant" ones such as Christianity, pop culture, humour, and love as well as more controversial ones such as violence, horror, doom, fantasy, mystery, evil, death, and drugs. The period over which the drawings accumulated is unknown, but most appeared to have been drawn in recent years.

The artists created the drawings with few resources. Virtually everything they could have used would have been contraband, and their artwork of course violated jail rules. They were considered minor infractions instead of formal crimes--vandalism or destruction of property. The chief explained that controlling graffiti was very difficult. First, it was difficult to administer sanctions, mostly because there was no separate disciplinary area in which to place detainees. Limiting visitation and privileges such as television and microwaves were punishment options but were seldom feasible. Usually, the most that could be done was to document the action on the detainee's conduct record. Second, acts of graffiti were nearly impossible to detect. The jail was very overcrowded, making it hard to monitor such behaviour. Officers could not enter cells often enough to catch someone drawing on the walls. Also, the transient nature of the jail population made it difficult to determine who, exactly, was responsible for the drawings. Therefore, one very rarely got caught for making graffiti.

Virtually nothing is known about the artists who created the drawings, other than their gender. Diligent efforts failed to locate them for interviews. The drawings presented in Figures 4 through 13 were in men's cells. Drawings by women were scarce, mostly because only about twelve women (out of a total of approximately 250 inmates) were held there at any given time. Also, the female cells contained fewer drawings than male cells. The result is that only a handful of photographed female drawings were obtained. (To view work created by the female artists, see Yogan and Johnson's 2006 analysis of gender differences in the art.)

Figure 4: Celtic Cross

(The pages on the left contained some bible passages.)

Figure 5: Cross & Heart

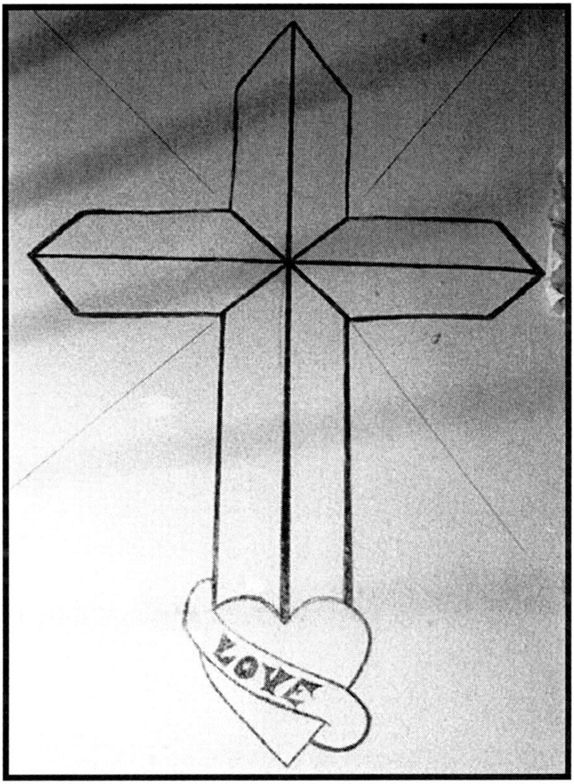


The Cross was a frequently used symbol among the jail's many Christian drawings; they could represent the artists' feelings of redemption and atonement (Hanes, 2005).

Figure 6: Dragon & Skulls

Figure 7: Skull

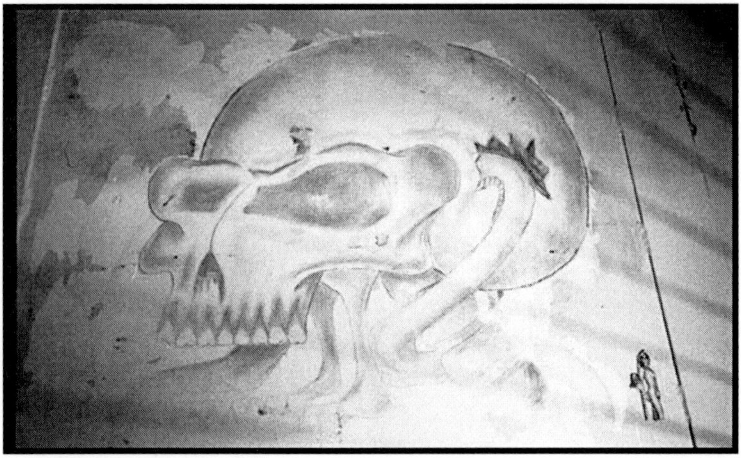

"Scary" images were also popular, especially skulls.

Figure 8:

Figure 9:

Figure 10: "Pandy"

Figure 11: Snake

The symbolism of the pencil-dagger impaling the snake provokes curiosity.

Figure 12: 3D

Figure 13: CRIMINAL

These drawings speak to the ability of human creativity to resist strong suppressive conditions and reveal the creative potential that exists behind bars. Art therapist Ursprung (1997, p. 13) writes, "The incarcerated artist's need to synthesize 'new' artistic materials in response to a desolate, restrictive and often debilitating environment speaks to the wonders of creative expression and the resiliency of the human spirit against major odds." It seems then that constructive creative activities should be offered in jail (Johnson, 2007b). While the drawings are technically graffiti, perhaps it is more important to recognize them as artwork, than that they were drawn on inappropriate spaces. "Graffiti" carries a connotation of illegitimacy and implies the inconsideration of or intent to destroy property (to vandalize) as a major motive and/or way to aggressively communicate (such as representing gang affiliation or making political statements). However, the motives of the jails artists are not known, so destructive or hostile intentions on their part cannot be inferred. The artists very well may have been driven by creative desire rather than aggression or defiance; the interior of the jail may have been the only "canvas" available to them at the time. Their artwork shows that incarcerated artists can be quite talented, their work can be fascinating and worthy of broad appreciation and support, they have a strong desire to express themselves, and they can spend their time in incarceration productively.

In his rare and interesting analysis of jail wall artwork, art therapist Michael Hanes (2005) determined that wall art is a form of creative expression that helps inmates endure the harsh conditions of incarceration and maintain their sense of humanity. Hanes (2005) pointed out the self-directedness, resourcefulness, and adaptability evident in jail wall art. The same is evident in the preceding artwork. The artists produced it on their own terms, without instruction or assistance from a formal art program, and against jail rules. This kind of "will" signify an opportunity to rehabilitate more than a breakdown in control. The work of jail wall artists suggests that they want to be productive and have a strong desire for creative autonomy and outlets for expression. An art-enhanced rehabilitation program would provide such outlets for creative expression in jails (Johnson, 2007b).

By creating their work, the jail wall artists revealed their desire and ability to engage in a conventional, widely respected and appreciated human activity—*art*. The talent exhibited in their work shows that the artists can make valuable aesthetic contributions to the community, even if simply through appreciation, patronage, and hobbies. (It is likely that many do not have an interest in being a highly skilled artist.) Their artistic interests tie them to the community outside of jail, and as such, incline them more toward its conventional norms, values, and systems of support and control. Herein lies great potential for rehabilitation—a chance to build and strengthen community-sanctioned or re-entering persons' relationships with the community through involvement in creative activities. It can be recommended then that artistic activities be incorporated into correctional programs aimed at community reintegration (Johnson, 2007).

## Art in Community Corrections

The correctional utility of artistic activities is not limited to jail and prison; art is also useful in community corrections (Johnson, 2007). Art in corrections can help meet the needs of parolees and other released prisoners in need of aftercare, probationers and other community-sentenced offenders, and the communities in which they live. Concerning the general public, communities have a vested interest in the successful (re)integration of released prisoners and community-sanctioned individuals. Avoiding acts harmful to others is obviously an important part of one's harmonious fit with the community. Currently there is a need to find and develop innovative integration strategies and techniques in corrections. More attention is being given to alternative approaches to integrating offenders into the community (Elliott-Marshall, Ramsay, & Stewart, 2005). The possibility that creative activities can be used to build ties to the community deserves further exploration. If art can boost programs' abilities to facilitate re-entry and community integration, it can help reduce re-offending.

Conventional approaches to ex-prisoner reintegration are not very effective. Soon-to-be released prisoners receive little preparation for re-entry—programs during incarceration are either absent or ineffective in promoting successful transitions to the community (Austin, 2001). Those that exist may be ill-conceived, under-supported, and do not get prisoners actively involved in the programs or the transitional process in general (Lanier, 2003; Richards & Jones, 2003; Ross & Richards, 2002). Next, released prisoners receive little preparation and assistance *during* re-entry (Austin, 2001). They receive little to no assistance in overcoming the many obstacles that they face: the "shock" of suddenly going from a routine controlled environment to the "streets," lack of money, finding a job, the lure of drugs, and the tight restrictions of parole and intensive supervision programs (Austin & Irwin, 2001). An ex-prisoner has several needs for successful re-entry, including health care, shelter, and moral support (Ross & Richards, 2003). Programs that address a variety of re-entry needs will be more effective. For example, a parolee crime prevention program in California that provided literacy training, employment services, housing assistance, and substance abuse treatment resulted in reduced re-incarceration and parole absconding (Zhang, Roberts, & Callanan, 2006). In trying to develop new, more effective correctional practices, it is important to locate and meet needs that are being overlooked. One such need is to be able to live creatively—to experience aesthetic enjoyment.

Conventional community sanctions appear to lack effectiveness in preserving and strengthening community integration. In fact, it is apparent that some are not even aimed at community integration. Ill-conceived attempts at community correction may be nothing more than "community punishments" (Richards, 1998) that actually facilitate an offender's (re)incarceration (Richards & Jones, 1997, 2003). The burdens of parole, probation, and restitution can be so extreme that they inhibit ex-prisoners and probationers in their efforts to negotiate reintegration and refrain from re-offending (Richards, 1998; Richards & Jones, 1997, 2003). Halfway houses are often guarded correctional institutions instead of community homes, and they may take most of the ex-prisoner's income in charging for housing and mandatory services (Ross & Richards, 2002). Further, intermediate sanctions such as intensive supervision, house arrest, and electronic monitoring do not appear to reduce recidivism; they may simply be less expensive ways to control and punish (Dean-Myrda & Cullen, 1998; MacKenzie, 2006). These problems seem contradictory to the logic of community sanctions. Guiding offenders toward peaceful, cooperative relationships with the community, and toward "making the right choices," requires a certain kind of empowerment. After all, they are the key players in meeting the expectations of community corrections—to repair/form bonds with the community and find and choose behavioural alternatives to offending. As argued earlier, creative autonomy and freedom of expression are empowering. Perhaps involvement in the arts, then, can help empower community sanctioned persons to maintain and strengthen their bonds with the community, and thus increase their stake in conformity.

If aesthetic expression and enjoyment are part of human nature, it can be assumed that system-involved persons, like anyone else, have the need to creatively interact with and contribute to the community (Johnson, 2007). Of course, activities such as education and employment are of tremendous, perhaps primary, importance to community (re)integration, as they greatly determine access to legitimate opportunities. Being well educated/trained and gainfully employed characterize a productive member of society. However, a productive member of society does not merely work and reside in a community, and obey laws. One is integrated into the community in several ways, not just economically and legally. Members are also aesthetically tied to the community through involvement in visual arts, crafts, music, karaoke, writing and literature, spoken word and poetry slams, museums, dance and "dancing," film and theatre, street performance art, antiquing, custom autos and motorcycles, landscaping, cooking, and so on. These activities promote community connectedness in addition to personal enjoyment. They form and result from communal ties and stand as pro-social alternatives to illegal behaviour expected of ex-offenders (Johnson, 2007). Those lacking experience engaging in creative activities may be missing an opportunity to form an important kind of bond with the community—an aesthetic bond. As a part of needs assessment then, in-depth interviews could be conducted to determine how released and community-sanctioned individuals can pursue their creative interests and become more aesthetically engaged with the community.

As with art in jail, art in community corrections does not receive a great deal of coverage in the literature. However, while it does not appear to be an instituted practice, the use of artistic activities in community corrections is not being proposed herein as a brand new idea. Art and craft activities have been included in education and therapy services offered in some correctional day treatment programs (Mackie, 1994). Also, prison art therapists Eileen McCourt (1994) and Marian Liebmann (1994) incorporated art therapy into their work as probation officers in the United Kingdom. Many of art therapy's benefits to the incarcerated apply to community sanctioned persons as well. For example, Liebmann (1994) used art to help some probationers confront their problems—they were allowed to draw out what they were unable, unwilling, or too afraid to say verbally. The probationers used visual images to give accounts of their offences, the consequences of these offences, and how they have been harmed in their lives.

Artistic components can easily be built into existing alternative community correction models. Holistic, multi-systemic models designed to create individualized support—such as a "wraparound" approach—are well prepared to cultivate the aesthetic interests of clients (these models approach a community-sanctioned person as a "client" more than an "offender"). Wraparound models are individualized comprehensive plans that integrate multiple treatment approaches and recognize the interactive, interdependent nature of social systems and resources. They treat the client as a partner in identifying and activating individual strengths, determining needs and directions, drawing from familial and community resources, and achieving treatment goals (Reed & Leavitt, 2000). For example, Reed and Leavitt (2000) identify "organizations that provide leisure options" as a community resource and mention enjoyment of leisure time as an important long-term goal for women in community corrections. They point out: "Many have no leisure activities that do not expose them to environments that trigger behaviours that got them into trouble with the criminal justice system" (p. 84) and argue:

> Engaging in one or more of the arts is especially useful for many women—both in terms of satisfaction and also as an aid for surfacing and expressing long-buried memories and feelings. These include poetry reading and writing, journaling, and participating in drama clubs (which can do community presentations to raise awareness), various forms of arts and crafts, and music or dancing. Food preparation and sewing classes can meet women's needs to be creative and to acquire new skills. Creative individuals, working alone or as parts of arts or music associations, may be willing to sponsor or provide some activities, sometimes as an integral component of wraparound services (p. 84-85).

Some clients will have creative abilities as strengths to be employed in treatment, while appreciation and patronage too may be included in clients' sets of needs and directions. Exploring and encouraging client interests in aesthetic activities can easily be considered part of the duties of a case manager. Reed and Leavitt (2000) also state:

> They [case managers] must broker services and differences across corrections and community settings and between service sectors in the community. They often advocate for the client's best interests, and act as counselors, teachers/consultants, service providers, and cheerleaders (p. 18).

Due to a variety of possible barriers, persons deeply involved with the criminal justice system have difficulty living successfully in mainstream social institutional settings. Many released prisoners, for instance, are under-educated, stigmatized, and unaccustomed to living on the outside. Therefore, they have trouble finding good jobs and functioning in a variety of social settings (Austin & Irwin, 2001; Pollock, 2004). With disrupted ties to the community, ex-prisoners and anyone else experiencing severe community sanctions might not find much to look forward to when trying to reintegrate, at least at first. But it is important that they remain optimistic about establishing a fruitful life outside of prison or jail—to not give up. Engaging in aesthetically pleasing activities is something that they can immediately look forward to, especially during hard times

(Johnson, 2007). Everyone needs to be able to make creative contributions to the community in order to feel like a part of the community. Creative activity, such as art, is one avenue through which communities can reach out to members experiencing marginalization (Johnson, 2007).

## Conclusion

Generally speaking, people desire to be creative and active and will search for outlets for expression, even when confined to environments that highly restrict freedom. Those in trouble with the law, like anyone else, desire to be creative and autonomous and need outlets for expression. Rehabilitation programs—in prison, jail, and community settings—that provide opportunities for creative expression, then, may draw their participants into becoming more personally invested in the program. This in turn would boost programs' ability to enable intrapersonal transformation and community reintegration, and thus reduce re-offending.

To be clear, "artistic" herein does not just reference visual art such as painting, drawing, sculpture, acting, dance, etc., nor is it limited to any mainstream forms, genres, or definitions. Art in corrections may address a wide variety of creative interests including poetry, personal narratives and short stories, spoken word, music, crafts, topiary, horticulture, landscaping, culinary arts, and many other possibilities (Johnson, 2007). Also to be clear, the rehabilitative value of art is not restricted to highly skilled and sophisticated artistic production—that which may meet professional or advanced amateur standards. The artistic activity of less serious or less skilled individuals ("dabblers" perhaps) and the appreciation of art—observing, enjoying, and supporting it—are also important forms of artistic involvement. In fact, basing the value artistic involvement on the perceived level and/or quality of work can be detrimental to treatment, especially for persons experiencing low self-esteem, poor self-concept, and social alienation. That being said, some system involved artists may become highly skilled and can make a financial living with their type of art. Some prisoners and ex-prisoners have even been able to achieve mainstream popularity and historical recognition (Cardinal, 1997). Therefore, aesthetic life need not be separate from economic and educational domains. With guidance, education, and training, some formally sanctioned individuals could put their creative talents to use in vocational and artistic careers. Both the production and appreciation of aesthetically appealing stimuli, done professionally or passively, constitute mainstream activity that connects individuals with others through common interests and goals (Johnson, 2007).

Ultimately, the many specific functions of correctional art programs may combine to help achieve the primary goal of corrections—to reduce re-offending. The effectiveness of art programs in reducing recidivism is not yet known, partly because they have not been tried enough (Gussak & Ploumis-Devick, 2004; Schoonover, 1986; Williams, 2003). So then, can art be used to prevent or reduce crime? Teasdale (1995) proposed that art therapy be included in treatment services to counter criminality, and that the effectiveness of these services be assessed in terms of recidivism. Teasdale believes that opportunities to engage in artistic activities may motivate offenders to purposely engage in programs that assist them in changing their attitudes and circumstances in favour of desistance.

Art programs in corrections are strongly supported by theoretical arguments, anecdotal testimony from practitioners, and some empirical research (Johnson, 2007b, 2008). However, while there are plenty of reasons to believe in the potential of such programs, few thorough tests of their effectiveness have been done (Gussak, 2006, 2007; Gussak & Ploumis-Devick, 2004). While a few published studies evaluating art programs have reporting favourable outcomes (see Gussak, 2006, 2007; Hawk et al., 1993; Merriam, 1998; Mullen, 1999), much more research needs to be done to judge art's effectiveness in achieving various goals in corrections. For the moment however, it seems that art programs have many uses in corrections and are helpful in achieving the goals of rehabilitation and institutional management.

To be effective, art rehabilitation, like any other correctional strategy, must be applied properly. Two important points need to be made here. First, art in corrections will generally lack potency if used as an isolated tool. Obviously, art by itself cannot be expected to transform individuals and steer them away from offending (although this is not impossible—art can certainly touch one's life profoundly). Artistic activities must be part of treatment packages containing several components tailored to individuals' needs. Multi-modal programs addressing the multiple needs of offenders are shown to be more effective rehabilitation strategies in corrections (Harper et al., 2005; MacKenzie, 2006). Second, art programs must be carried out with intelligence, diligence, and honesty. Many correctional programs fail because they are not properly implemented, not necessarily because they are based on weak theories (Bonta, 1996; Gendreau, 1996; Harper et al., 2005; Palmer, 1994; MacKenzie, 2006). To be properly implemented, art programs need cooperation from everyone working in the correctional setting (Day & Onorato, 1989; Grace, 1993; Riches, 1994a; Mackie, 1994), and art professionals need proper training and support (Schoonover, 1986).

One potential obstacle to the proper application of art rehabilitation strategies is censorship. Censorship suppresses creative expression, and in doing so, interferes in the therapeutic, educational, and socially interactive processes that lead to rehabilitation (Mullen, 1999). Artistic censorship in corrections stem from rules, political ideology, and employees' personal opinions, as well as from the sanctioned population itself (Kornfeld, 1997; Mullen, 1999). For example, the prison subculture of toughness pressures prisoners to contain expressions of feelings that could be perceived as weakness and the reluctance by prisoners to explore and expose inner thoughts and feelings can lead to self-censorship (Kornfeld, 1997).

It is easy to misinterpret the artistic activity of convicted offenders, especially if their work deals with controversial themes. Without careful consideration, art in corrections may appear to threaten the goals of rehabilitation and institutional control. Prison art, for instance, is inherently contradictory—the prison is punitive, but creative activities are enjoyable (Gussak, 1997b). The purpose of incarceration is to strip power and deliver pain, while the purpose of art is to empower and create happiness. However, art's benefits for rehabilitation and institutional management lie within this contradiction. Authorities who adhere strongly to a punitive ideology tend to be suspicious of creative activities and may view prisoner art as a threat or problem (Gussak, 1997b), but cooperation from authorities is needed for art programs to work. Hopefully then, correctional administrators and staff can be assured that artistic activities and their products do not pose a threat to security or offender accountability (Gussak, 1997b) and will support art programs that grant high degrees of freedom of expression.

To summarize, art in corrections has the following general uses. First, art is educational. Art education is an important part of global personal development. Learning art not only improves specific artistic knowledge and abilities; it also builds cognitive and social skills in general—skills applicable in a variety of social settings including work. Second, art is therapeutic. Art is a form of communication that can be used to treat a variety of mental health problems that may underlie offending, such as emotional distress, post-traumatic stress, and substance abuse. Also, engaging in art helps one cope with imprisonment and other forms of correctional confinement. Third, art is socially productive. System-involved artists can produce objects and performances for significant others and the general public to enjoy. Fourth, art improves environmental quality of life. Artistic activities humanize correctional environments; they promote peaceful, cooperative relationships among those being sanctioned and those working in the correctional setting, creating a safer environment for all. And fifth, art socially (re)integrates. Involvement in the arts is productive, pro-social activity that bonds released prisoners and community-sanctioned individuals with the community. In conclusion then, because involvement in the arts is educational, therapeutic, socially productive, humanizing, and socially integrative, art in corrections is a valuable tool for helping formally sanctioned individuals transform their lives.

## References

Alexander, B., & Gothard, S. (2006). Poetry in Michigan prisons: Urgency of the incarcerated. *New Politics, 10*(4), 36-38.

Austin, J. (2001). Prisoner re-entry: Current trends, practices, and issues. *Crime and Delinquency, 47*(3), 314-334.

Austin, J., & Irwin, J. (2001). *In it's about time: America's imprisonment binge, 3rd ed.* Belmont, CA: Wadsworth/Thomson Learning.

Aylott, M. (2002). Taking arts forward. *Prison Service Journal, 139*, 3-5.

Baroody-Hart, C., & Farrell, M. P. (1987). The subculture of serious artists in a maximum security prison. *Urban Life, 15*(3-4), 421-448.

Billington, B. (2002). Making good—a special place for art in prison education. *Prison Service Journal, 141*, 41-46.

Bonta, J. (1996). Risk-needs assessment and treatment. In A. T. Harland (Ed.), *Choosing correctional options that work* (pp.18-32). Thousand Oaks, CA: Sage.

Burdon, W. M., Messina, N. P., & Prendergast, M. L. (2004). The California treatment expansion initiative: Aftercare participation, recidivism, and predictors of outcomes. *The Prison Journal, 84*(1), 61-80.

Cardinal, R. (1997). A brief history of prison art. In P. Kornfeld (Ed.), *Cellblock visions: Prison art in America* (foreword). Princeton, NJ: Princeton University Press.

Carlyle, T. (2000). Love United at HM Community Prison Bullingdon: A multicultural arts project. *Prison Service Journal, 159*, 34-36.

Cheney, J. (1997). Suspending normal prison taboos through the arts in a prison psychiatric setting. In D. Gussak & E. Virshup (Eds.), *Drawing time: Art therapy in prisons and other correctional settings* (pp.87-98). Chicago: Magnolia Street Publishers.

Clements, P. (2004). The rehabilitative role of arts education in prison: Accommodation or enlightenment? *International Journal of Art Design Education, 23*(2), 169-178.

Cronin, P. (1994). Ways of working: Art therapy with women in Holloway Prison. In M. Liebmann (Ed.), *Art therapy with offenders* (pp.102-120). Bristol, PA: Jessica Kingsley Publishers Ltd.
Day, E. S., & Onorato, G. T. (1997). Surviving one's sentence: Art therapy with incarcerated trauma survivors. In D. Gussak & E. Virshup (Eds.), *Drawing time: art therapy in prisons and other correctional settings* (pp.127-152). Chicago: Magnolia Street Publishers.
—. (1989). Making art in a jail setting. In H. Wadeson, J. Durkin, & D. Perach (Eds.), *Advances in art therapy* (pp. 126-147). New York: John Wiley & Sons, Inc.
Dean-Myrda, M. C., & Cullen, F. T. (1998). The panacea pendulum: An account of community as a response to crime. In J. Petersilia (Ed.), *Community corrections: Probation, parole, and intermediate sanctions* (pp. 3-18). New York, NY: Oxford University Press.
Delshadian, S. (2003). Playing with fire: Art therapy in a prison setting. *Psychoanalytic Psychotherapy, 17*(1), 68-84.
Dietz, E. F., O'Connell, D. J., & Scarpitti, F. R. (2003). Therapeutic communities and prison management: An examination of the effects of operating an in-prison therapeutic community on levels of institutional disorder. *International Journal of Offender Therapy and Comparative Criminology, 47*(2), 210-223.
Edwards, S. (1994). Out of line: Art therapy with vulnerable prisoners. In M. Liebmann (Ed.) *Art therapy with offenders* (pp. 121-143). Bristol, PA: Jessica Kingsley Publishers Ltd.
Elliott-Marshall, R., Ramsay, M., & Stewart, D. (2005). Alternative approaches to integrating offenders into the community. In G. Harper & C. Chitty (Eds.), *The impact of corrections on re-offending: A review of "what works," 3rd ed.* (pp. 57-74). London: Home Office Research, Development and Statistics Directorate.
Ferszt, G. G., Hayes, P. M., DeFedele, S., & Horn, L. (2004). Art therapy with incarcerated women who have experienced the death of a loved one. *Art Therapy: Journal of the American Art Therapy Association, 21*(4), 191-199.
Gendreau, P. (1996). The principles of effective intervention with offenders. In A. T. Harland (Ed.), *Choosing correctional options that work* (pp. 117-130). Thousand Oaks, CA: Sage.
Grace, N. (1993). Arts-related activities in prisons. *Convergence,* 26 (3), 65-71.
Graef, R. (2002). The value of arts in prison: Breaking the cycle. *Prison Service Journal, 139*, 2-3.

Gussak, D. (2007). The effectiveness of art therapy in reducing depression in prison populations. *International Journal of Offender Therapy and Comparative Criminology, 51*(4), 444-460.

—. (2006). Effects of art therapy with prison inmates: A follow-up study. *The Arts in Psychotherapy, 33*, 188-198.

Gussak, D., & Ploumis-Devick, E. (2004). Creating wellness in correctional populations through the arts: an interdisciplinary model. *Visual Arts Research, 29*(1), 35-43.

—. (1997a). Breaking through barriers: Advantages of art therapy in prison. In D. Gussak and E. Virshup (Eds.), *Drawing time: art therapy in prisons and other correctional settings* (pp.1-11). Chicago: Magnolia Street Publishers.

—. (1997b). The ultimate hidden weapon: Art therapy and the compromise option. In D. Gussak & E. Virshup (Eds.), *Drawing time: Art therapy in prisons and other correctional settings* (pp.59-74). Chicago: Magnolia Street Publishers.

Gussak, D. & Virshup, E. (Eds.) (1997). *Drawing time: Art therapy in prisons and other correctional settings*. Chicago: Magnolia Street Publishers.

Hall, N. (1997). Creativity and incarceration: The purpose of art in a prison culture. In D. Gussak and E. Virshup (Eds.), *Drawing time: Art therapy in prisons and other correctional settings* (pp.25-41). Chicago: Magnolia Street Publishers.

Hanes, M. J. (2005). Behind steel doors: Images from the walls of a county jail. *Art Therapy: Journal of the American Art Therapy Association, 22*(1), 44-48.

Harper, G., Man, L-H., Taylor, S., & Niven, S. (2005). Factors associated with offending. In G. Harper and C. Chitty (Eds.), *The impact of corrections on re-offending: A review of "what works," 3rd ed.* (pp.17-29). London: Home Office Research, Development and Statistics Directorate.

Hawk, K., Bohna Jr., E. A., Riddell, K., & Stark, J. M. (1993). *Special demonstration project: Anthology of inmate art, a report*. Uniontown, PA: Fayette County Community Action Agency, Inc.

Hillman, G. (2003). The mythology of the corrections community. In R. M. Williams (Ed.), *Teaching the arts behind bars* (pp. 14-27). Boston, MA: Northeastern University Press.

Irwin, J. (1985). *The Jail*. Berkeley and Los Angeles, CA: University of California Press.

Jalazo, M. D. (2005). Life skills project. *The Journal of Correctional Education, 56*(2), 108-114.

Johnson, L.M. (2007a). Jail wall drawings and the role of artistic creativity in community reintegration. *Justice Policy Journal, 4*(2).
—. (2007b). Jail wall drawings and the potential of jail art programs. *International Journal of Criminal Justice Sciences*, *2*(2), 66–84.
—. (2008a). A place for art in prison: Art as a tool for rehabilitation and management." *Southwest Journal of Criminal Justice, 5*(2), 100-120. Retrieved on 4th November 2008 from http://swjcj.cjcenter.org/archives/5.2/3%20Art%20in%20Prison.pdf
Karban, B., & West, A. (1994). Working as an art therapist in a regional secure unit. In M. Liebmann (Ed.), *Art therapy with offenders* (pp.135-164). Bristol, PA: Jessica Kingsley Publishers Ltd.
Kornfeld, P. (1997). *Cellblock visions: Prison art in America*. Princeton, NJ: Princeton University Press.
Lanier, C. S. (2003). Who's doing time here, me or my children? In J. I. Ross & S. C. Richards (Eds.), *Convict criminology* (pp.247-266). Belmont, CA: Wadsworth/Thomson Learning.
Leach, A. (2002). "Even Idiots Can Paint, Can't They?" *Prison Service Journal,* 139, 20-21.
Liebmann, M. (1994). Introduction. In M. Liebmann (Ed.), *Art therapy with offenders* (pp. 1-13). Bristol, PA: Jessica Kingsley Publishers Ltd.
MacKenzie, D. L. (2006). *What works in corrections: Reducing the criminal activities of offenders and delinquents*. New York: Cambridge University Press.
Mackie, B. (1994). Art therapy—an alternative to prison. In M. Liebmann (Ed.), *Art therapy with offenders* (pp.220-249). Bristol, PA: Jessica Kingsley Publishers Ltd.
McCourt, E. (1994). Building up to a sunset. In M. Liebmann (Ed.) *Art therapy with offenders* (pp. 39-56). Bristol, PA: Jessica Kingsley Publishers Ltd.
Merriam, B. (1998). To find a voice: art therapy in a women's prison. *Women & Therapy, 21*(1), 157-171.
Mullen, C. A. (1999). Reaching inside out: Arts-based educational programming for incarcerated women. *Studies in Art Education, 40*(2), 143-161.
Murphy, J. (1994). "Mists in the darkness": Art therapy with long-term prisoners in a high security prison—a therapeutic paradox. In M. Liebmann (Ed.), *Art therapy with offenders* (pp. 14-38). Bristol, PA: Jessica Kingsley Publishers Ltd.
Newbold, G. (2003). Rehabilitating criminals: it ain't that easy. In J. I. Ross & S. C. Richards (Eds.), *Convict criminology* (pp. 247-266). Belmont, CA: Wadsworth/Thomson Learning.

Overhultz, E. (2001). The Broward County Sheriff's office inmate art exhibit and sale: Bringing art from the jailhouse to the community. *American Jails, 15*(1), 43.

Palmer, T. (1994). *A profile of correctional effectiveness and new directions for research.* Albany, NY: SUNY Press.

Pollock, J. M. (2004). *Prisons and prison life: Costs and consequences.* Los Angeles, CA: Roxbury.

Reed, B. G., & Leavitt, M. E. (2000). Modified wraparound and women offenders in community corrections: Strategies, opportunities, and tensions. In M. McMahon (Ed.), *Assessment to assistance: Programs for women in community corrections* (pp.1-106). Lanham, MD: American Correctional Association.

Richards, S. C. (1998). Critical and radical perspectives on community punishment: Lessons from the darkness. In J. I. Ross (Ed.), *Cutting the edge: Current perspectives in radical/critical criminology and criminal justice* (pp.123-144). Westport, CT: Praeger.

Richards, S. C., & Jones, R. S. (1997). Perpetual incarceration machine: Structural impediments to post prison success. *Journal of Contemporary Criminal Justice, 13*(1), 4-22.

Richards, S. C., & Jones, R. S. (2003). Beating the perpetual incarceration machine: Overcoming structural impediments to re-entry. In S. Maruna & R. Immarigeon (Eds.), *After crime and punishment: Pathways to offender reintegration* (pp.201-232). Cullompton, Scotland: Willan.

Riches, C. (1994a). The hidden therapy of a prison art education programme. In M. Liebmann (Ed.), *Art therapy with offenders* (pp.77-101). Bristol, PA: Jessica Kingsley Publishers Ltd.

—. (1994b). "It's the only thing keeping me going in this place": Art in prison—a resource for prisons and prisoner. *Prison Service Journal, 92*, 68-71.

Ross, J. I., & Richards, S. C. (2002). *Behind bars: Surviving prison.* Indianapolis, IN: Alpha.

Ross, J. I., & Richards, S. C. (2003). Introduction: What is the new school of convict criminology? In J. I. Ross and S. C. Richards (Eds.) *Convict criminology* (pp. 1-14). Belmont, CA: Wadsworth/Thomson Learning.

Schoonover, B. (1986). The captive audience. *Art Education, 39*(3), 33-35.

Sundaram, R. (1997). Helping criminally insane men who are hearing-impaired through art therapy. In D. Gussak & E. Virshup (Eds.), *Drawing time: Art therapy in prisons and other correctional settings* (pp.187-196). Chicago: Magnolia Street Publishers.

Taylor, M. (1997). Growing old, the hard time way: Art therapy as an intervention in gerontology and criminology. In D. Gussak & E.

Virshup (Eds.), *Drawing time: Art therapy in prisons and other correctional settings* (pp.197-209). Chicago: Magnolia Street Publishers.

Teasdale, C. (1997). Art therapy as part of a group therapy programme for personality disordered offenders. *Therapeutic Communities, 18*(3), 209-221.

—. (1995). Creating change: Art therapy as part of a treatment service to counter criminality. *Prison Service Journal, 99*, 6-12.

Tumim, S. (1994). Foreword. In M. Liebmann (Ed.) *Art therapy with offenders*. Bristol, PA: Jessica Kingsley Publishers Ltd.

U.S. Census Bureau. *Indiana quick facts*. (2004). Retrieved on 5th November, 2008 from http://www.quickfacts.census.gov/indiana.html

Ursprung, W. A. (1997). Insider art: The creative ingenuity of the incarcerated artist. In D. Gussak & E. Virshup (Eds.), *Drawing time: Art therapy in prisons and other correctional settings* (pp.13-24). Chicago: Magnolia Street Publishers.

Vacca, J. S. (2004). Educated prisoners are less likely to return to prison. *The Journal of Correctional Education, 55*(4), 297-305.

van der Hoeven, T. F. M. (1988). Dutch prisons and education through art: a new offshoot. *Prison Service Journal,* January: 2-3, 8.

Williams, R. M. (2003). Introduction. In R. M. Williams (Ed.), *Teaching the arts behind bars* (pp.3-13). Boston, MA: Northeastern University Press.

Williams, R. & Taylor, J. Y. (2004). Narrative art and incarcerated abused women. *Art Education, 57*(2), 46-52.

Wisker, C. (1997). What one museum does for prison art. In D. Gussak & E. Virshup (Eds.), *Drawing time: art therapy in prisons and other correctional settings* (pp.231-239). Chicago: Magnolia Street Publishers.

Woodall, J., Diamond, P. W., & Howe, A. H. (1997). In D. Gussak & E. Virshup (Eds.), *Drawing time: art therapy in prisons and other correctional settings* (pp.99-125). Chicago: Magnolia Street Publishers.

Yogan, L. & Johnson, L. M. (2006). Gender differences in jail art and graffiti. *South Shore Journal, 1*, 31-52. Retrieved on 5th November, 2008 from http://www.nwiqlc.org/ssj/.

Zhang, S. X., Roberts, R. E. L., & Callanan, V. J. (2006). Preventing parolees from returning to prison through community-based reintegration. *Crime and Delinquency, 52*(4), 551-571.

# CHAPTER FOURTEEN

# PRISONER'S RIGHTS IN INDIA: TIME FOR A HUMANE APPROACH?

JEEVAN BALLAV PANDA


## Abstract

Prison as a penal institution and a formal agency of control has a significant role to play in the criminal justice administration. This chapter explores those aspects of criminal law in India which relates to the deplorable condition of prisoners and the legislative and judicial reforms which have been taken, with suitable suggestions for improving their status in this era of human rights. The chapter also aims at identifying challenges posed by the criminal justice system and to find out ways and means for addressing these challenges through suitable mechanism. Furthermore, it concentrates on the recent developments which have taken place through judicial approach by making a transition from an obsolete retributive or deterrent approach towards punishment to a modern reformative or rehabilitative approach. In the absence of a specific legislation emphasizing the rights of a prisoner and very few outdated legislations addressing the issue indirectly, the primary focus of the chapter is to create awareness among the readers by emphasizing the existence of prisoners' rights and their importance through various judicial pronouncements. This chapter suggests that the present (emerging) system of criminal justice does not adequately accommodate such concerns. Accordingly, it considers and analyses the adequacy of the criminal justice system and the need for a transformation in our approach in order to accommodate the range of concerns. The chapter concludes by raising some fundamental questions about the need for change of course to a new direction with appropriate recommendations and suggestions about prisoners' rights and the need for a humane approach.

## Introduction

Right from the inception of the society, criminal law occupies a predominant place among the agencies of social control and is regarded as a formidable weapon that society has forged to protect itself against anti-social behaviour. Whatever views one holds about the penal law, no one will question its importance to society. This is the law on which men place their ultimate reliance for protection against all the deepest injuries that human conduct can inflict on individuals and institutions. By the same token, penal law governs the strongest force that we permit official agencies to bring to bear on individuals. Its promise as an instrument of safety is matched only by its power to destroy. Nowhere in the entire legal field, is more at stake for the community or for the individual (Government of India, 2003).

The oldest penal institution in India is actually the 'Jail' which is also commonly called a 'Prison' in many countries (Chakraborti, 1997). Prisons, as a formal agency of control, have a unique role especially in a democratic society. As a vital agency of criminal justice administration they perform the twin role of incarcerating the convicts as well as providing custodial care for the under trials and detained. Thus, contrary to the common belief, prisons come into picture not only after trial and conviction but also right from the stage of investigation and the commitment of the accused to judicial remand or in the course of preventive detention. Such overbearing roles of prisons become almost a routine in cases of poor, ignorant and helpless accused who are not in a position to secure release on bail. They remain under trials for long periods and are subjected to varied forms of discriminations within prisons (Vibhute, 2004).

Imprisonment as a mode of punishment started in the 16$^{th}$ century, but spread widely as the main punishment for crime only in the 19$^{th}$ century. Before then the few prisons that existed were used mainly to hold those destined for some other punishment such as execution or to contain people unable to pay their debts (Vibhute, 2004). From 19$^{th}$ century onwards and following in to the 20$^{th}$ century, certain individualized measures of offenders were introduced into prison sentences. Thus began the concept of institutional correction (Chakraborti, 1997). By the end of the 20$^{th}$ century imprisonment was part of the penal code of every country and those countries too small to maintain a prison system sent their prisoners to neighbouring States for incarceration (Stern, 1998). The process of replacing physical punishments with imprisonment continues even today as more countries remove the death penalty from their statute books and substitute life imprisonment as the punishment for the most serious crimes (Amnesty International, 2002).

## Indian Prison System: A Critical Appraisal

The Indian prison system, just like the other agencies of the criminal justice administration can be described to exist perpetually in a state of crisis. The reasons for such deplorable state of affairs are: *First*, antiquated and over-worked nature of prison institution. *Secondly*, lack of proper training, skills and motivation of the prison staff. *Thirdly*, policy-level ideological conflicts brought about by the modern ideas of prisoners rights and egalitarianism.

The aforesaid reasons manifest in several specific problems that may assume different forms in the vast network of prisons. However, some of the notable problems that afflict and substantially determine the very character of the system itself that needs immediate attention can be described as follows:

1. Overcrowding.
2. Inadequate provision for basic needs.
3. Torture, ill-treatment and repressive control.
4. Unequal treatment and privileges.

### *Overcrowding*

Imprisonment as a mode of punishment has increased surprisingly when its drawbacks in social policy and human rights terms are considered. Overcrowding has almost become a hallmark of most of the prisons and its intensity can be estimated from Tihar prison itself, which started with an average prison population of 900 inmates in 1958 and has reached 9000 by 1996 (almost ten times in four decades). During this period the Tihar complex from one Prison in 1958, opened in 1996 the $5^{th}$ Jail to house mainly adolescent category prisoners (16-21 age group) (Ministry of Home Affairs, 1977).

In some countries overcrowding reaches levels where it can be described as ‘cruel, inhuman, degrading treatment or punishment’. For example, the Special Rapporteur on Prisons and Conditions of Detention in Africa found on a visit to Mozambique in 1997 that the overcrowding was so acute that the inmates did not have sufficient space even to sit down comfortably although 96 of them had been transferred the previous day’ (African Commission on Human and Peoples Rights, 1999). In Brazil, prisoners tied themselves to the window bars so as to be able to sleep standing up (Human Rights Watch, 2006); prisoners taking it in turns to use the beds or bunks and suffocating from shortage of air (Radio Free Europe, 1996).

The main reason for prison overcrowding is that over seventy-six percent inmates are under trials, which are a composite outcome of powers of arrest and remand under the Indian law, delay in investigation, and trial and unequal administration of right to bail. Subsequently, it may be a cause for many other prison problems such as greater risk of disease, higher noise levels, denial of conservancy facilities, difficulties in surveillance, consequent danger levels, etc. This issue was recently raised before the Supreme Court by public interest litigation in *Rama Murthy v. State of Karnataka*[1], seeking wide ranging reforms in prison conditions. The Supreme Court did not consider overcrowding *per se* as unconstitutional, but held that:

> [T]here is no doubt that the same does affect the health of prisoners...The same also adversely affects hygienic conditions...[2] There is yet another baneful effect of overcrowding. The same is that it does not permit segregation among convicts. Those punished for serious offences and for minor. The result may be that hardened criminals spread their influence over others. Then juvenile offenders kept in jails (because of inadequacy of alternative places where they are required to be confined) get mixed up with others and they are likely to get spoiled further... So, the problem of overcrowding is required to be tackled in right earnest for a better future.[3]

The Seventy-Eighth Report of the Law Commission of India on 'Congestion of Under trial Prisoners in Jails' under Chapter 9, made some recommendations acceptance of which would relieve congestion in jails. These suggestions include liberalization of conditions of release on bail or by taking recourse to alternatives to incarceration (Ministry of Home Affairs, 1983). These being:

- Fine;
- Civil commitment; and
- Probation

As to release on *probation*, it may be stated that it really results in suspension of required to execute bond under the provisions of the Probation of Offenders Act, 1958, requiring maintenance of good conduct during the probationary period, the failure to do which finds the concerned persons in prison again. That Act has provision of varying conditions of

---

[1] (1997) 2 SCC 642.
[2] *Ibid.* at 654.
[3] *Ibid.* at 655.

probation and has also set down the procedure to be followed in case of the offenders failing to observe conditions. Overcrowding is reduced by releases on *parole* as well, which is a conditional release of an individual from prison after serving the imposed sentence he has served part of the sentence imposed upon him. Chapter 20 of the Report of All India Committee on Jail Reforms, 1980-83 makes recommendations to streamline the system of remission, leave and premature release. As to premature release, which is the effect of parole, the Committee has stated that this is an accepted mode of incentive to a prisoner, as it saves the prisoner from the extra period of incarceration; it also helps in reformation and rehabilitation (Ministry of Home Affairs, 1983). Building more prisons is one obvious solution to overcrowding and indeed the number of prison places available in the world has increased over the past decade.

The recent amendment to the Criminal Procedure Code, 1973 (Cr.P.C.) is indeed commendable. Section 436-A of the Criminal Procedure Code is good news for under trials languishing in prisons. The law states that if a person has been detained in prison for a specified period and if that period extends the period for which he can be sentenced then he cannot be imprisoned any longer. However this amendment shall not be fruitful for those accused of an offence, which carries death penalty. This amendment also states that even if the accused does not have sufficient money to pay off the bail bond then also he can be released on the furnishing of a personal bond. This amendment is indeed a boon for several under trials languishing in prisons since for a long period of time.

### *Inadequate Provision for Basic Needs*

There is not much to doubt that though the Jail Manuals do provide rules and standards for food, clothing and other basic needs to be given to prisoners, they are rarely complied with.[4] This puts the prison inmate in a specially disadvantaged position, because his incarceration places limitations on his ability to organize any kind of basic needs on his own, while the prison system ties him up with sub-standard need satisfaction. The All India Committee on Jail Reforms, 1980-83, has observed:

> The Committee recognized that the Central Jail, Tihar had been widely criticized on account of maltreatment of, and indiscipline amongst prisoners on the one hand and improper attitudes, incompetence, corruption and abuse of power by the staff on the other (Ministry of Home Affairs, 1983).

---

[4] *Rama Murthy v. State of Karnataka*, (1997) 2 SCC 642

Furthermore, prisons being places with concentrations of poor people, overcrowding and poor food, it is not therefore surprising to find neglect of health and hygiene leading to infections and diseases. The society has an obligation towards prisoners' health for two reasons. First, the prisoners do not enjoy the access to medical expertise that free citizens have. Their incarceration places limitations on such access; no physician of choice, no second opinions, and few if any specialists. Secondly, because of the conditions of their incarceration, inmates are exposed to more health hazards than free citizens. Prisoners therefore, suffer from a double handicap.

### *Torture, Ill-Treatment and Repressive Control*

As a custodial institution prisons have a basic responsibility for protecting the inmates from being subjected to any harm or suffering. But in actual practice the absolute dependence and powerlessness makes an accused or under trial an ideal target for torture, ill-treatment and repression. Prison torture and repression emanates from three distinct sources, *namely* (a) Prison officials who recognize torture and repression as the best means of control, if not the most satisfying form of sadism, (b) 'Convict officers' who are pressed into prison services mostly on account of their past repressive experience,[5] and (c) 'Prison mafia' which is making its presence felt in most of the prisons as an extra-legal source of control.

### *Unequal Treatment and Privileges*

Prison society is inherently unequal. There exist within the prison several hierarchies, most of which have no formal or legal recognition. The vast bulk of resource less, lower-class, inmates invariably occupy the lowest position in the hierarchy. They are not only subject to the lawful and legitimate commands of prison officials but are also treated as subjects by the influential 'convict officers' and the mafia under trials. The issue of perpetuating the outside class and status hierarchies within the prison was examined by the Jail Manual Committee and the All-India Committee on Jail Reforms which recommended for doing away with the issue of classification based on social status, education and mode of living. In 1997, the issue of classification of prisoners into B and C classes on the basis of social status, education and mode of living under Rule 34(1) (b)

[5] *Watchdogs International v. Union of India*, (1998) 7 SCC 338

and Rule 38 of the Delhi Prison (Admission, Classification, Separation, Remission, Reward and Release of Prisoners) Rules, 1988 was examined by the Justice Duggal Committee in terms of the equality guarantee under the Constitution of India. The Committee recommended the striking down on constitutional grounds the classification into 'B' and 'C' class prisoners in vogue in Delhi prisons.

The prison system both at the Central as well as the State levels has been trying to resolve these basic problems through short-term and long-term measure. The State has only partially succeeded in resolving some of the problems, but like any other human rights institution the resolution of one sets off the generation of new sorts of problems.

## Prisoners' Rights: A Global Perspective

The mood and temper of the public in regard to the treatment of crime and criminals is one of the most unfailing tests of the civilization of any country (Carney, 1979). A prisoner, be he a convict or under trial or a detainee, does not cease to be a human being, and hence continues to enjoy all his basic human rights. On being convicted of crime and deprived of their liberty in accordance with the procedure established by law, prisoners shall retain the residue of the human rights. The Universal Declaration of Human Rights, 1948, under Article 5 stipulates that *"No one shall be subjected to torture or to cruel, inhuman or degrading treatment or punishment"*. Thus, a prison atmosphere can be accepted as civilized only if it recognizes the basic human rights of the prisoners and makes efforts for the effective and meaningful enjoyment of the same by means of prison reforms.

These abuses and injustices continue in spite of an international and regional framework of human rights conventions, treaties and instruments. The United Nation's conventions and standards on the treatment of all detained persons constitute the reference point for all States that have signed up to the International Covenant on Civil and Political Rights (ICCPR). Article 10 of the Covenant requires that people in any form of detention should be treated *'with humanity and with respect for the inherent dignity of the human person'*. Similar expressions of this message can be found in the European Charter on Human Rights (Article 3), African Charter on Human and People's Right (Article 5) and the American Convention on Human Rights (Article 5).

However, the first document exclusively dealing with prisoners was the United Nations Standard Minimum Rules for the Treatment of Prisoners. This document is concerned not only with the rights of prisoners, but with the proper management of a penal institution, with a view to avoiding indiscipline, disease, and the induction of inmates into lives of crime; these objectives can be derived from the nature of the recommendations, particularly under Rules 57 and 58. These include the separation of different classes of prisoners, individual sleeping accommodation (except where the system deliberately embraces dormitories), decent sanitation, food, clothing and exercise, medical services, fair and not excessive punishment regime for disciplinary offences, complaint procedures, contact with family and 'reputable friends', access to general news, to reading materials, to respect and facilities for religious observance, respect for property, protection from unnecessary exposure to public insult and curiosity, general respect for dignity, freedom from discrimination, and a regime designed to reintegrate the prisoner into the society, with appropriate education and rehabilitative measures.

But these rules are not law, and the only treaty obligations which touch on the rights of prisoners are the ICCPR and the Declaration against Torture and other Cruel, Inhuman or Degrading Treatment or Punishment (1975) and the Convention against Torture and other Cruel, Inhuman or Degrading Treatment or Punishment (1985). These instruments clarify that torture and ill-treatment of prisoners is outlawed (Article 10, ICCPR). Clearly, some rights are lost when a person is incarcerated, but basic human rights remain. The rights accorded to all human beings, the right to life (Article 6, ICCPR), to justice and redress in all proceedings (Article 9, ICCPR) and to family life (Article 23, ICCPR), remain.

Prison should be places where justice reigns. The noted jurist, Lord Woolf, now Chief Justice of England, said that *'the system of justice which has put a person in prison cannot end at the prison doors. It must accompany the prisoner into the prison...'* (Home Office Prison Disturbances, 1990). When considered as a whole, the international instruments about the treatment of detained people put certain obligations on all prison administrations. First, it is clear that the purpose of prison is, as the American Convention on Human Rights says, the 'reform and social re-adaptation' of the prisoners. When prisoners are accused of offences against prison rules they should be dealt with according to the principles of natural justice. They should be able to appeal against decisions made against them (Article 2, ICCPR). Pre-trial prisoners are accorded special protection and must be presumed innocent until found guilty (Article 14(2), ICCPR). Their access to their legal advisers must be assured and they should be held separately from convicted prisoners (Article 10(2a), ICCPR).

In UK, the House of Lords has said, *'a convicted prisoner, in spite of his imprisonment, retains all civil rights which are not taken away expressly or by necessary implication'*,[6] Similarly, US Courts have established that prisoners do not lose all their rights: *'there is no iron curtain drawn between the Constitution and the prisons of this country'*.[7] The same view has been reiterated and reaffirmed by the Constitutional Court of South Africa.[8] Furthermore, as Penal Reform International says, the human rights of prisoners with which it is concerned are derived from '*universal general human rights*' and are applicable to every individual (Penal Reform International, 2001). One might argue that it would be enough to do as the recently adopted Constitution of East Timor does and provide that prisoners remain entitled to the fundamental rights except to the extent that these are inherently incompatible with the situation of being a prisoner (Article 32, Constitution of East Timor). However, prisoners are not adequately protected by the inclusion in national Constitutions of human rights provisions found in the ICCPR and the International Covenant on Economic, Social and Cultural Rights (ICESCR).

## Prison Reforms in India: A Legislative and Judicial Appraisal

One of the significant post-independence developments in the field of prisons has been the emergence of the prisoners' right touchstone, which has been responsible both for the demystification of prisons, as well as the movement towards standardization. Though the rights discourse has its roots in the United Nations initiatives concerning civil and political rights at the international level, and the enactment of the Fundamental Rights by the Constitution of India at the national level, the real impetus came from the activist appellate court rulings, particularly in the post-emergency era.

Legislative enactments regarding prisoners are obsolete and are not comprehensive, to address the issue of protection of prisoners' rights. The first legislation regarding prisons regulation in India was The Prisons Act of 1894, which was largely based on deterrent principles reflected mainly from the British policies. The legislators took little pains to look into the other side of the problem. They were concerned more with the prison

---

[6] *Raymond v. Honey*, (1983) AC 1 (10) quoted from *Secretary of State for the Home Department, ex parte Simms ex parte O' Brien, R*, (1999) UKHL 33: (2000) 2 AC 115.

[7] *Wolff v. McDonell*, 418 US 539 (555-556) (1974)

[8] *August v. Electoral Commission*, CCT 8/99 Judgment April 1, 1999, para 18

working than with treatment of the prisoners. This Prison Act has remained unchanged for the last one hundred years except for some very minor changes (Mohanty, 1997). The Prisoners Act, 1900, referred to appropriate places for confinement of prisoners and also included reformatory schools within the meaning of confinement and detention.[9] The Transfer of Prisoners Act, 1950, was enacted to provide for removal of prisoners from one state to another. The Prisoners (Attendance in Courts) Act, 1955, contains provisions authorizing the removal of prisoners to a civil or criminal court for giving evidence or for answering to the charge of an offence.

The Indian Constitution is also silent on the issue of prisoners' rights and there are no specific provisions as such, yet certain rights, particularly under Part III of our Constitution have been interpreted and extended through some landmark judicial pronouncements. Article 14 of the Constitution of India contemplated that like should be treated alike, and also provided the concept of reasonable classification. This Article is an essential guide and basis for the prison authorities to determine various categories of prisoners and their classifications with the object of reformation. Moreover, Article 19 of the Indian Constitution guarantees six freedoms to all the citizens of India. Amongst those freedoms there are certain freedoms which the prisoners cannot enjoy because of the very nature of these freedoms, such as, "freedom of movement" [Article 19(1) (d)], "freedom to residence and to settle" [Article 19(1) (e)] and "freedom of profession" [Article 19(1) (g)]. But there are other freedoms which can be enjoyed by the prisoners also behind the bars and his imprisonment and sentence has nothing to do with these freedoms, such as, "freedom of speech and expression" [Article 19(1) (a)], "freedom to become a member of an association" [Article 19(1) (b)], etc. These freedoms are very much related to the concept of reformation of prisoners.[10]

The other provisions of the Constitution though directly cannot be called as prisoners' rights but may be relevant are Article 20 (1 and 2), Article 21, and Article 22 (4 to 7) which deals with the rights of any persons. The occasions for judicial intervention in prison matters is so varied and the range of interest covered so vast that, at times, the outcome is rhetorically described as the *"prisoners' rights jurisprudence"*. In no other country of the world has the judiciary played such a key role in evolving a rights touchstone and ultimately contributing to the movement for prison reform itself.

---

[9] *Communist Party of India, Nagpur v. State of Maharashtra*, AIR 1989 Bom. 29

[10] *Sunil Batra (II) v. Delhi Administration*, AIR 1980 SC 1579

The trend of judicial activism in this field since the late seventies, was initiated by the series of judicial decisions that ruled out not only what the prisons ought not to do, but also what they ought to do and how they ought to do things. The rationale for such an interventionist approach, a contrast to the 'hands-off' approach adopted by the judiciary till the decision as late as early 1977, in *Bhanudas v. Union of India*[11], was that a prisoner is sent to prison as a consequence of a judicial decision, therefore, the judiciary is concerned with how and for what purpose he is imprisoned right till the last day.[12] This was reaffirmed in the landmark case of *Charles Sobraj v. Union of India*[13], where it was held that, this Court would intervene even in prison administration when constitutional rights or statutory prescriptions are transgressed to the injury of a prisoner.

Broadly, the judicial control of prisons has arisen from two streams of cases. First, those that focuses on the constitutional rights and human rights of prisoners. Second, those that relate to a wide range of prison conditions and standards of prisonisation. Other significant areas of extension were right not to be handcuffed or leg-fettered unless absolutely necessary, speedy trial, right to counsel, proper condition of detention,[14] dignified prisonisation, under trials' right to favourable bail release.[15]

The beginning of prisoners' rights can be traced back to the *State of Maharashtra v. Prabhakar Pandering*[16], where the Supreme Court ruled against extinguishing other rights not consistent with the fact of detention. The court included within the purview of prisoners' rights, his freedom to dispatch for publication a manuscript prepared by him while in detention, particularly in the absence of any rules that bar pursuit of such activities. In *D.B.M. Patnaik v. State of A.P.*[17], the Apex Court asserted even more emphatically that by mere reason of their detention the convicts do not become 'denuded of all the fundamental rights' which they possess. In the case of *Francis Coraile v. Union Territory of Delhi,*[18] a challenge was made to a prison rule which permitted only one interview in a month with the members of the family or legal advisor, and was held to be violative of

---

[11] AIR 1977 SC 1027

[12] *Giasuddin v. State*, AIR 1977 SC 1936

[13] AIR 1978 SC 1514

[14] *Sunil Batra (I) v. Delhi Administration*, (1978) 4 SCC 494: 1979 SCC (Cri) 155: AIR 1978 SC 1675

[15] *Prem Shankar v. Delhi Administration*, AIR 1980 SC 1535: (1980) 3 SCC 526 and *Citizens for Democracy v. State*, (1995) 3 SCC 743

[16] AIR 1966 SC 424

[17] (1975) 3 SCC 185: 1974 SCC (Cri) 803: AIR 1974 SC 2092

[18] AIR 1981 SC 746

Article 21 of the Constitution. Recently, the Supreme Court in *State of A.P. v. Challa Ramkrishna Reddy*[19] speaking through S. SAGHIR AHMAD (for self and D.P. Wadhwa, J.,) reiterated that, 'a prisoner, being a convict or under trial or a detainee, does not cease to be a human being.'

In *Hussainara Khatoon v. State of Bihar,*[20] the court was appalled at the plight of thousands of under trials languishing in the jails in Bihar for years on end without ever being represented by a lawyer. The court declared that "there can be no doubt that speedy trial, and by speedy trial, we mean reasonably expeditious trial, is an integral and essential part of the fundamental right to life and liberty enshrined in Article 21." The court pointed out that Article 39-A emphasized that free legal service was an inalienable element of 'reasonable, fair and just' procedure and that the right to free legal services was implicit in the guarantee of Article 21.

The recent Supreme Court decision in *State of Gujarat v. High Court of Gujarat*[21] represents the high watermark in prisoners' rights field, in as much as the Court in this case for the first time extended Article 23 of the Constitution to prisoners, and created a right not to be put or forced to work unless work is a part of the sentence or with the authority of law. Thus, this view can really constitute the basis for new thinking about prisoners' rights and would mean the end of the prison administration's blanket power over the prisoner. Further, the Supreme Court in *Pathak v. State of Andhra Pradesh*[22] held that the benefit of provision of Article 42 of the Constitution is also applicable to prisoners and extended the dimensions of prisoners' rights making basis for prison reforms.

In the *Sunil Batra (II)* case[23] the court laid down that prisoners cannot be subjected to deprivations not necessitated except incarceration and sentence of the court, all other freedoms to read and write to exercise and recreation, to meditate and chant, protection from extreme heat and cold, protection against indignities like compulsory nudity, forced sodomy and other forms of vulgarity, joys of self-expression and to acquire skills and techniques are still open to him. In addition visits to prisoners by family members and friends are also to be ensured. In the *Vikram Deo Singh* case[24] the Court ruled that inhuman living conditions in old dilapidated buildings, ill-treatment, insufficient and poor quality food and little medical attention were in derogation of the rights of a detained person. In

[19] (2000) 5 SCC 712
[20] (1980) 1 SCC 81
[21] (1998) 7 SCC 392
[22] AIR 1994 SC 2092
[23] *Sunil Batra (II) v. Delhi Administration*, AIR 1980 SC 1579.
[24] *Vikram Deo Singh v. State of Bihar*, (1988) Supp. SCC 734.

the *Gurudev Singh* case[25] the Court cast a duty on the State to guarantee basic needs of food, rest, recreation and work and health facilities inside the prison. Finally, in the *Rama Murthy* case[26] the Court considered the issue of standard of prisonisation in the context of overcrowding, delay in trial, torture and ill-treatment, health and hygiene, food and clothing, deficiencies in communication, jail visits and open-air prisons.

Though in the past decades we have witnessed growing control exercised by the judiciary on prison administration, but only a few cases that have contained specific directions such as directions against solitary confinement within prison, bar on minors being detained in adult prisons, etc. have had greater impact on prison administration. However, the growing control of the judiciary has been contested by those who favour prison autonomy. They blame judicial interference both for demotivation of the prison officials as well as the trend of indiscipline among prison inmates. Has the judicial activism done enough to ensure that in future none suffers total denial of fundamental rights and basic human rights, is the question that we need to answer?

## Conclusion

Prisons have never been an effective way of responding to serious crimes and or of protecting the public from crime. Imprisonment is expensive in terms of financial cost and also in terms of the social damage it can cause. It can allow criminal networks to be formed and strengthened, break up families and disrupt prisoners' ties to society such as a home and work. And as such, there is no evidence that the fear of prison as such deters offenders from committing crime.

On the other hand, the open-air prison system has evolved as a very modern and effective alternative to the closed imprisonment system. It plays an important role in the scheme of reformation of a prisoner, which has to be one of the desiderata of prison management. This is in consonance with the reformatory theory of punishment which is essentially the base for the Indian Penal System and more importantly the Criminal Justice Administration. It also represents one of the most successful applications of the principle of individualization of penalties with a view to social re-adjustment. It has been said so because release of offenders on probation, home leave to prisoners, introduction of wage

---

[25] *Gurudev Singh v. State of Punjab*, (1992) Supp. (2) SCC 551: (1992) SCC (Cri.) 834.

[26] *Rama Murthy v. State of Karnataka*, (1997) 2 SCC 642.

system, release on parole, educational, moral and vocational training of prisoners are some of the features of the Open-air prison (camp) system. Furthermore, it is less costly than a closed establishment and also provides employment benefit to the Government for the benefit of the public at large, which would have otherwise remained unproductive. The monetary returns are positive, and once put into operation the camps pay for it. For the greater good of the society, which consists in seeing that the inmates of a jail come out, not as a hardened criminal but as a reformed person, no managerial problem is insurmountable.

Centralization of prison administration is one of the important aspects, which needs immediate attention. The prison administration is only under the state list of the respective states' as specified in Schedule VII of the Indian Constitution, which leads to decentralization. The Central Government has been providing financial assistance to State Governments, through the Finance Commission's awards as well as under the Central Scheme for Modernization of Prison Administration, for strengthening their prison infrastructure. In the gravity of the situation of several thousands languishing and in the wake of deplorable conditions of prisons, the administration of prisons should be entrusted to the Central Government. This shall lead to effective centralization of prisons and a setting up of uniform standards to be maintained in all the states. Setting up of a statutory body specifically at the centre for the monitoring of the prisons as well as for allocation of resources or funds for the better upkeep and maintenance of prisons in the states shall be very effective.

One important aspect, which should not be disregarded, is the sympathetic approach and attitude of the prison staff and officers towards the prisoners. Effective and adequate training must be provided to prison officers regarding human rights so as to imbibe in them professional competence and a feeling of social purpose of their activity. The modern theory of prison reformation should focus on the scientific methods of treatment of prisoners like looking into the psychology of the prisoners, being responsive to the need of the prisoners when first offenders are committed to jails and ensuring basic human rights to them. With greater liberties being conferred upon the jail personnel, particularly in a country like India where a bewildering variety of processes goes on; there is ample of scope for abuse of power. Hence, there must be adequate control mechanisms and public accountability so that they are subjected to internal departmental evaluations and control, external monitoring and media scrutiny.

Section 12(c) of the Protection of Human Rights Act 1993, authorizes the National Human Rights Commission (NHRC) to visit, under intimation to the State Government, any jail or any other institution under the control of the State Government, where persons are detained or lodged for purposes of treatment, reformation or protection to study the living conditions of the inmates and make recommendations thereon. Members of State Human Rights Commissions and the National Human Rights Commission being in permanent liaison with the prison administration can have an appropriate external monitoring on prisons and shall be very effective to curb the problem of violation of human rights in prisons. In addition, regular feedback of the prisoners through complaint and feedback boxes in every prison cell, beyond the scrutiny of the prison authorities but under the direct scrutiny of the State Human Rights Commission shall be very effective indeed. This practice shall remove any sort of bias and neglect on behalf of the prison authorities regarding the complaints of prisoners.

Although much has been debated about the reformation of prison system in the country and ensuring basic human rights to prisoners, but practical reality speak otherwise. The legislative, executive and the judiciary have to go hand in hand so as to secure the rights of prisoners through necessary amendments in the existing laws, legislative enactments securing their rights, proper administration of the prison system with proper training and accountability of prison staff and officials and lastly, by appropriate judicial interpretation through judicial activism. At last, emphasizing the exigent need for a humane approach, it is essential that we should create a legal framework so as to ensure legal awareness and change our mindset towards prisoners and take their rights seriously so as to attain our objective of becoming a welfare state in its true sense.

## References

African Commission on Human & Peoples Rights. (1999). *Prisons in Mozambique: Report of the special rapporteur on prisons and conditions of detention in Africa* (Series IV, No. 3, p. 26). Paris

Amnesty International. (2002). *Annual Report 2002* (p. 21), London: International Secretariat. Retrieved September 6, 2005 from *http://web.amnesty.org/library/Index/ENGACT530032000?open&of=ENG-MLT*

Carney, L. P. (1979). *Introduction to correctional science*. Dallas, USA: McGraw- Hill Inc.

Chakraborti, N. K. (1997). *Administration of criminal justice: The correctional services*. New Delhi: Deep & Deep Publications.

Government of India. (2003). *Report of the committee on reforms of criminal justice system. pp. 1-298.*

Home Office, Prison Disturbances. (1990). *Report of an inquiry by the Rt. Hon. Lord Justice Woolf (Parts I and II) and his Honour Judge Stephen Tumim (Part II)* (p. 273). London: HMSO. 1991, p. 273

Human Rights Watch. (2006). *Human Rights abuses against prisoners*, Retrieved October 3, 2006 from http://www.hrw.org/prisons/abuses.html.

Iyer, K. V. R. Justice. (2004). *Legally speaking.* Delhi: Universal Law Publishing Co. Pvt. Ltd.

Ministry of Home Affairs. (1977). *Committee on rationalization of prisoners classification*. Delhi: Government of India

—. (1983). *Report of the All-India committee on jail reforms* (1980-83, Vol. 1, Chap. 9). New Delhi: Government of India

Mohanty, A. (1997). Correction under prisons act: Theory and practice. In N. K. Chakraborty (Ed.), *Administration of criminal justice: The correctional services* (Vol. II, p.35-40). New Delhi: Deep and Deep Publications.

Penal Reform International. (2001). *Making standards work: An International handbook on good prison practice*. London: Penal Reform International.

Radio Free Europe. (1996). *In search of a solution - Crime, criminal policy and prison facilities in the former Soviet Union*. Moscow: Centre for Prison Reform, Human Rights Publishers.

Stern, V. (1998). *A sin against the future: Imprisonment in the World.* England: Penguin Books

Vibhute, K. I. (2004). *Criminal Justice (1st Edition).* Lucknow: Eastern Book Company.

## Cases cited

*August v. Electoral Commission*, CCT 8/99 Judgment April 1, 1999, para 18

*Bhanudas v. Union of India,* AIR 1977 SC 1027

*Charles Sobraj v. Union of India,* AIR 1978 SC 1514

*Citizens for Democracy v. State*, (1995) 3 SCC 743

*Communist Party of India, Nagpur v. State of Maharashtra*, AIR 1989 Bom. 29

*D.B.M. Patnaik v. State of A.P.,* (1975) 3 SCC 185: 1974 SCC (Cri) 803: AIR 1974 SC 2092

*Francis Coraile v. Union Territory of Delhi,* AIR 1981 SC 746

*Giasuddin v. State*, AIR 1977 SC 1936
*Gurudev Singh v. State of Punjab*, (1992) Supp. (2) SCC 551: (1992) SCC (Cri.) 834
*Hussainara Khatoon v. State of Bihar,* (1980) 1 SCC 81
*Jennison v. Baker,* (1972) 1 All ER 997
*Pathak v. State of A.P.,* AIR 1994 SC 2092
*Prem Shankar v. Delhi Administration*, AIR 1980 SC 1535: (1980) 3 SCC 526
*Rama Murthy v. State of Karnataka*, (1997) 2 SCC 642
*Raymond v. Honey*, (1983) AC 1 (10)
*Secretary of State for the Home Department, ex parte Simms ex parte O' Brien, R*, (1999) UKHL 33: (2000) 2 AC 115
*State of A.P. v. Challa Ramkrishna Reddy,* (2000) 5 SCC 712
*State of Gujarat v. High Court of Gujarat,* (1998) 7 SCC 392
*State of Maharashtra v. Prabhakar Pandurang,* AIR 1966 SC 424
*Sunil Batra (I) v. Delhi Administration*, (1978) 4 SCC 494: 1979 SCC (Cri) 155: AIR 1978 SC 1675
*Sunil Batra (II) v. Delhi Administration*, AIR 1980 SC 1579
*Sunil Batra (II) v. Delhi Administration*, AIR 1980 SC 1579
*Vikram Deo Singh v. State of Bihar*, (1988) Supp. SCC 734
*Watchdogs International v. Union of India*, (1998) 7 SCC 338
*Wolff v. McDonell*, 418 US 539 (555-556) (1974)

# CHAPTER FIFTEEN

# THE PRESENTATION AND REPRESENTATION OF CRIME IN NIGERIAN MEDIA

AKINTAYO J. ABODUNRIN, JIMOH AMZAT AND RASIDI A. OKUNOLA

## Abstract

Despite the volume of research crime reporting has generated globally, it has received little attention in Nigeria, making the need for an appraisal of crime in Nigerian newspapers imperative. The study addresses various issues in crime reporting: identifying the crime that gets most reported in Nigerian newspapers; investigation of the sources of crime stories available to the papers; ascertaining the specific part in the layout where crime stories are located; identification of the genre of published crime stories and assessment of the editorial policy of the selected Newspapers on crime. Content analysis was used to examine the contents of two purposively selected Newspapers, the Guardian and Punch over a three-year period covering January 2001 to December 2003. Interviews were also conducted with crime reporters and editors of the selected newspapers. Ethnographic summary and content analysis were also used in analysing the data gathered from the interviews. The findings showed that violent crimes such as murder and assaults received more coverage in the papers than other categories of crime such a financial, drug, and property crimes. Official sources i.e. police and courts are the major source of crime stories available to the press. The chapter concludes that, there is need for print media to have official editorial policy and to report crime as epidemics.

## Introduction

Crime is a major social problem in Nigeria like any other countries of the world, though there might be differential patterns and social context in predisposition to criminality. Crime is one of the greatest threats to human security and attracts concerted efforts in its control especially through designated agencies like the police and so on. Aside the social concern of feeding, clothing and shelter, crime is a major concern of the Nigerian public. Concern and fear of crime among Nigerians is reflected in coping strategies such as living in houses with high walls similar to those of prisons, (Dambazau, 1994, Nwosu, 2001), formation of neighbourhood security association (vigilante), engaging private security guards and purchasing electronic security gadgets among other strategies to protect themselves from falling victim of crime. Fear of crime is influenced by many different sources, including the news media. Newspapers, television stations and radios are among the most influential sources used by the public to develop opinions about crime and the criminal justice system (Chermak, 1995).

In spite of informing the public about criminal activities going on in the society, studies have shown that the press over-reports violent crimes like homicide, assault, rape etc, and gives them more prominence in the layout in comparison with non-violent crime stories like property and environment crime (Cohen, 1972; Chiricos et al., 1997; Beckett & Sasson 2000; Reiner et al., 2000; Dubois, 2002). Some of the studies further contend that such violent crimes are featured disproportionately compared to their incidence in official crime statistics or victim surveys, thereby contributing to concern over crime among the public (Davis, 1952; Sheley, & Ashkins, 1981; Marsh, 1991; Kirby et al., 1997; Westfeldt & Wicker 1998). The agenda-setting perspective has stipulated that audiences not only learn about public issues and other matters through the media, they also learn how much importance to attach to an issue or topic from the emphasis placed on it by the media (Folarin, 1998). The mass media play important role in the construction of criminality and criminal justice system as the public perception of crime, criminals and criminal justice system is largely determined by their portrayal in the mass media (Dowler, 2003). The press role and functions in the society aids in identifying and setting the tone of public debate on issues. By its agenda-setting activities, the press may consequently influence public perception on crime, create new categories of crime and influence the criminal justice system by the way it reports criminalities.

But despite the volume of research and attention crime reporting has generated and received globally, the nature of crime news, which also forms part of the content of Nigerian newspapers still needs to be situated and examined. In Nigeria, like in other countries, crime reporting is also institutionalised as almost all the newspapers have crime/police affairs correspondents. The national dailies, news magazines and tabloids all feature stories of one crime or the other in their editions. Reporting crime in Nigeria, more than ever before is being approached differently with a penchant for shocking and human interest in crime news in recent years. Consequently, Nigerians now daily read, see and hear stories of people's homes being attacked, the owners injured or killed, of people being abducted for ritual purpose; of underage girls being sexually assaulted; and of public officials being involved in corrupt practices. It is in this light that the need for an appraisal of crime news, vis-à-vis type, location, prominence and sources in Nigerian newspapers becomes imperative. This would form part of the efforts in analysing the incidence of crime in the society with a focus of print media. Generally, crime reporting is one of the mechanisms of raising the alertness of the public about the patterns and dynamics of criminality in the society. It is pertinent to stimulate discussions on patterns of crime reporting in more dynamic ways that would stimulate the concern of the public. The main objective of the study is to examine the presentation and representation of crime in Nigerian print media. This objective is simplified by analysing which crime gets most reported, investigate the sources of crime stories available to the papers, ascertain the specific part in the layout of the papers where crime stories are located most, identify the genre of published crime stories in the papers, assess the editorial policy of the selected newspapers on crime and identify who is focussed on most between offenders and victims.

Crimes were categorized using the format below:

1. Crime against persons/violent crimes: Murder, Manslaughter, Attempted Murder, Suicide, Rape and indecent assault, Child trafficking, Human trafficking, Grievous bodily harm, Child abuse, Sexual offences, and unnatural offences.
2. Property crime: Stealing, robbery, extortion, bunkering, forgery, vandalisation, burglary, and arson.
3. Economic/Financial crime: fraud/false pretence and cheating, corruption, graft, embezzlement, fake currency, impersonation, smuggling, and illegal mining.
4. Drug offences.
5. Local acts: Traffic Acts, offences against township Acts, liquor Acts, dog Acts and other related offences.
6. Other offences: perjury, coining offences, demand and menace and related offences.

Due to the nature of this study, content analysis, a systematic procedure devised to examine the content of recorded information was used to examine the contents of the two newspapers selected. The content analytic method was particularly useful because it afforded a high degree of precision, accuracy and objectivity, which were required in the results of the study. To further gain insight into the process of crime news production and make the research findings robust and detailed, structured interviews were also conducted with crime reporters and editors of the selected papers while data on the incidence of reported was also obtained from the police. Data were analysed using a systematic, objective, and quantitative descriptions of the manifest content of the papers. Ethnographic summary and content analysis were used to analyse the qualitative data gathered from interviews.

Two newspapers, The *Guardian* and *Punch*, provided materials for this study. Although both are privately owned, the decision to use the two was informed by the fact that both papers have well-established crime/police desks coupled with their national character and respective peculiarities. *The Guardian* often referred to as ‘Flagship’ of Nigerian journalism is regarded as an ‘elitist’ newspaper catering to the needs of intellectuals in the society while *Punch* is ‘populist’. The period of study covered is January 2001 to December 2003, a three-year period. This was divided into three parts of 12-month duration each for a detailed and easy analysis of data.

Data for the study was sourced primarily and secondarily. The primary source was the interviews with the crime reporters and editors, while the secondary source was the newspapers that, contents were examined and analysed. A total 1,095 issues of the *Guardian* and *Punch* published during the study scope was used. A coding scheme containing lists of categories to look for in the papers was developed. After the extraction of the items/data from the newspapers, the frequency of occurrences of the items were taken and presented in tables. Verbatim-transcribed responses of the interviews were also done and used to corroborate the content analysis findings. Statistical tools (mainly frequencies and percentages) were utilised in analysing specific items gathered from the papers. The data were then presented in tabular form. The tables were merged because it was found out that the result for each year exhibited similar patterns, thereby making presentation and discussion individually repetitious. This study did not test the relationship between crime reporting and fear of crime among the people. Finally, efforts were made to be completely objective and scientific in examining and analysing crime news from the papers selected, thereby making a replication of the study possible.

## The Content of Media Crime

Table 1 shows the kind of crime reported by the press from the two papers. Crime against person (usually violent) overrides other forms of crime in the three years with 50%, 51% and 47% in 2001, 2002 and 2003 respectively. This indicates that the newspapers are fascinated more by violent crimes, i.e. murder, assault, grievous bodily harm, and consequently report crimes against persons more than other categories of crime, Nigerian newspapers, true to form, did not deviate from the norm by reporting crimes against persons more than other categories of crime.

**Table 1: Crimes Reported Jan 2001 – Dec 2003.**

| Type of crime story | Guardian | Punch | Jan-Dec 01 Total |
|---|---|---|---|
| Persons | 346 (52%) | 281 (49%) | 627 (50%) |
| Property | 168 (26%) | 137 (24°) | 305 (24%) |
| Financial | 103 (16%) | 101 (18%) | 204 (16%) |
| Drug | 14 (2%) | 19 (3%) | 42 (3%) |
| Local acts | 6 (1%) | 22 (4%) | 28 (2%) |
| Total | 660 | 572 | 1260 |

| Type of Crime story | Guardian | Punch | Jan-Dec 02 Total |
|---|---|---|---|
| Persons | 392 (59%) | 369 (45%) | 761 (51%) |
| Property | 121 (18%) | 239 (29%) | 360 (24%) |
| Financial | 103 (15%) | 150 (18%) | 253 (17%) |
| Drug | 29 (4%) | 17 (3%) | 46 (3%) |
| Local acts | 31 (5%) | 19 (2%) | 50 (3°) |
| Others | 9 (1%) | 24 (3%) | 33 (2%) |
| Total | 685 | 818 | 1503 |

| Type of crime story | Guardian | Punch | Jan-Dec 03 |
|---|---|---|---|
| Persons | 264 (44%) | 441 (50%) | 705(47%) |
| Property | 104 (18%) | 233 (26%) | 337(23%) |
| Financial | 151 (25%) | I27 (14%) | 278 (19%) |
| Drug | 20 (3%) | 28 (3%) | 48(3%) |
| Local Acts | 45 (8%) | 38 (4%) | 83 (6%) |
| Others | 12 (2%) | 23 (3%) | 35 (2%) |
| Total | 596 | 890 | 1486 |

**Table 2: Crime Rate in Nigeria, 2001 – 2003[1]**

| Crime categories | 2001 | 2002 | 2003 |
|---|---|---|---|
| Crime against Persons | 58655 | 52257 | 52420 |
| Crime against Property | 58269 | 50224 | 46886 |
| Financial Crimes | 11127 | 9933 | 10268 |
| Crime against Local Acts | 7844 | 7553 | 7568 |
| Other offences | 599 | 111 | 146 |

Source: CLEEN, 2007.

Invariably, crimes against persons are the most important to the Nigerian press going by its frequency of reportage compared to other categories of crime. In further corroboration of the findings, the reporters confirmed their fascination with crimes against persons or incidence of robbery in which violence occurred, because according to them, it is such stories that interest the public most.

---

[1] Statistics on drug offences not available.

A correspondent *of Punch* asserted:

> Crime stories that touch the heart, anybody that is reading it will feel touched. You'll want to read it; you will want to learn from it. That's the kind of stories I go for. Like somebody being raped: A 50-year-old man raping a two-year-old girl; murder; robberies; in short, stories that would fascinate the readers.

That of the *Guardian*'s view is similar as he revealed:

> Stories that concern young people in armed robbery... May be the police arrest offenders with ammunition and they kill two or three people or they robbed a bank and they were caught, stories of murder.

The statements confirm the press' fascination with violent crime stories and also portray that the public could also be more interested in such crimes. This signifies that the public gets what it wants because it is enamoured with violent crime. Property, financial and drug crimes also received some significant coverage in the papers during the study scope. The table also shows an increase in the number of financial crimes reported in 2003 compared to the previous two years. Drug crimes also received some attention in the papers, although one would have expected that the figures would be higher than the obtained figures because increasing activities of the government against drug peddling.

A comparison of the findings from the newspapers in Table 1 and the incidence of reported crimes at the national level in Table 2 show a marked variation between the amount of crimes reported by the press and the police. Crime against persons featured most in the incidence reported by the Police and the press but with remarkable proportion compared to that of crime against property. It also becomes clear that the proportion of crime the press reports is insignificant compared to the incidence reported by the police. Although the element of news worthiness might have come into play here, the press might be giving an inaccurate and distorted picture of the crime situation in the country. What this implies then is that the press is not a reliable means of getting a good picture of the incidence of crime in Nigeria (see table 2). This is not based on the authenticity of the reports but on the news worthiness-value attached to different reports. The press' propensity to report crimes against persons (in relative large proportion) more than other categories of crimes in effect can also contribute to fear of crime as the public only get to read stories that involve violence such as murder, rape, and assault etc.

The foregoing discussion underscores the agenda-setting function of the press and gives an insight into how, by focusing on specific news themes, the press can begin to draw people's awareness to such an issue that violent crimes against persons predominate in the society. Beyond this however, the trends reported by the press and the police does not take cognizance of the *Dark Figures,* i.e. unknown crime, the undetected offender and offenders who, though detected were declared free because of lack of evidence. This makes both sources unreliable for estimating or ascertaining the extent of crime in the Nigerian society. Ultimately, this means that until self-report studies and victim surveys are introduced in the country, the real extent of crime would remain obscure.

## Extraction of Crime News: Official versus Unofficial Sources

The table 3 confirms Chibnal, (1977), Schlesinger and Tumber, (1991) and Amari's, (1999) finding that crime stories reported by newspapers most often originate from official sources (the police and criminal justice system), which control much of the information on which crime reporters rely. Table 3 shows that official sources account for 53%, 49% and 40% of all the sources of crime news in 2001, 2002 and 2003 respectively.

**Table 3: Sources of Published Crime Report Jan 2001 - Dec 2003.**

| Source | Guardian | Punch | Jan-Dec 01 (Total) |
|---|---|---|---|
| Official | 373 (59%) | 248 (46%) | 621 (53%) |
| Eye witness | 40 (6%) | 31 (6%) | 71(6%) |
| Victim | 54 (9%) | 15 (3%) | 69 (6%) |
| Reporter | 166 (26%) | 245 (45%) | 411 (35%) |
| Total | 633 | 539 | 1172 |
| | | | Jan-Dec 02 |
| Official | 302 (52%) | 361 (47%) | 663 (49%) |
| Eye witness | 40 (7%) | 22 (3%) | 62 (5%) |
| Victim | 52 (9%) | 19 (2%) | 71 (5%) |
| Reporter | 188 (32%) | 364 (48%) | 552 (41%) |
| Total | 582 | 766 | 1348 |

| Source | Guardian | Punch | Jan-Dec 03 |
|---|---|---|---|
| Official | 185 (41%) | 301 (39%) | 486 (40%) |
| Eyewitness | 22 (5%) | 37 (5%) | 59 (5%) |
| Victim | 37 (8%) | 30 (4%) | 67 (5%) |
| Reporter | 207 (46%) | 407 (52%) | 614 (50%) |
| Total | 451 | 775 | 1226 |

The journalists, who revealed the police as the major source of their crime stories, also corroborated the finding. A Punch reporter observed:

> Majority of reporters daily go out but basically, they source their stories from the police... Because the police gets return from all their stations on what is happening, we sometimes go to the Police Public Relations Officer's (PPRO's) office: Some of us also have networks and sources in police stations who are able to tell us things, even when it is not official.

What this signifies is that there is a close relationship between the press and official sources i.e. criminal justice system. Without the official sources, especially the police which is the body saddled with the responsibility of maintaining law and order, crime prevention and detection among other functions, the press would have little knowledge of crime incidents in the society to report. This also buttresses the indispensability of official sources to the press in sourcing for crime stories.

The comments of the journalists who expressed reservations about police sources, citing as example the tendency of the Nigerian police to implicate innocent persons as offenders' tallies with the position of Sandman, et al (1976). A Guardian reporter submits:

> I don't often rely on the police. Normally, if you rely on the police, you'll not get the truth and you may not get the true position of issues. Some of the suspects the police tell you they arrest may be innocent and you may ignorantly publish the name of an innocent person as an armed robbery suspect. You don't rely on the police to supply you information. They'll only supply you what they want you to publish to the public.

Head of Crime news, *Guardian* holds the same view:

> If police claim they've arrested a person, that the person is an armed robber, I'll still interview the person. There are cases where the police have paraded some supposed armed robbers whom when I interviewed told me they are not robbery suspects, that the police just picked them on the way and forced guns into their hands.

The inference from this is that the Nigerian Press recognizes attempts by the police and criminal justice system to manipulate crime stories from an angle that favours official viewpoints. The press on the other hand strives to be objective by guiding against being influenced by the police and other official sources to the detriment of the accused.

Stories sourced by the reporters independently come next after stories from official sources with 35%, 41% and 50% in 2001, 2002 and 2003 respectively. But in spite of sourcing the stories themselves, analysis of the various news items showed that even when the reporters sourced their stories independently, from eyewitnesses or victims, they still confirm the veracity of such stories with the police. Advancing reasons for the practice unravelled by the finding, the reporters and editors explained it as a fundamental law of journalism practice which stipulates that it behoves the reporter to confirm stories from the police, lest the media become a tool in the hands of people seeking vendetta against perceived foes through the press. This is also necessary in order to be objective and fair to all parties involved.

*Punch* Editor's response, reflective of the journalist's position captures it best:

> In journalism, the cardinal principle is that there is always more than a side to a story; sometime three sides to a story. So for any paper worth the newsprint on which it publishes its materials, you have to double-check because you have to protect your credibility, and the only way to protect your credibility is to ensure that all the facts that you are giving the public are facts that could hardly be under controversy. There are times people will give you reports just for personal aggrandizement or for their own benefit. It's possible someone would tell you that a gang of armed robbers came to my house to rob me. He could even say I suspect this person. Maybe he has some scores to settle with that person but when you confirm from the police, the police are supposed to be neutral, so to say, so you expect that they are going to give you an unbiased account of the situation. Moreover, by double-checking, you would be able to check the loopholes in the report given by the eyewitness or even by the source. Confirming that way will help you know what to leave in your report and what to remove.

The practice of confirming stories sourced independently from the police is a further testimony to the relationship explicated by Schlesinger and Tumber (1991) as existing between the press and criminal justice system. Neither the press nor the criminal justice system can afford to do without the other in the discharge of their duties. There is a symbiotic relationship between them. However, the only way the press can be objective and fair to the accused is to hear his/her side of the story, which the Nigerian press is doing and upholding. Aside the ideals of fairness, objectivity, and credibility, the press also confirms stories from the police to ensure internal checks, i.e. guiding against the unsavoury practice of reporters concocting fictitious crime stories in order to meet deadlines.

Overall, what emerges from the finding is the dependence of the press on official sources, not only as major sources of their stories, but also to lend credibility to such stories.

## Captivating the Readers: Positioning of Crime Stories in Nigerian Print Media

Majority of crime stories published in the papers was tucked away in the inside pages, as seen from the table 4. Location inside the pages accounts for 70%, 74% and 81% in 2001, 2002 and 2003 respectively. The implication is that the papers do not consider most crime as serious enough to be given prominence in the layout of the papers. However, it is important to note that crime stories that constituted lead stories during the study period were highly violent crime or general financial crime which involved a popular figure in the society.

**Table 4: Positioning of Crime Stories. Jan 2001 - Dec 2003.**

| Location | Guardian | Punch | Jan-Dec 01Total |
|---|---|---|---|
| Front page lead | 30 (4%) | 32 (5%) | 62 (5%) |
| Front page | 99 (15%) | 67 (11%) | 166 (13%) |
| Inside | 456 (68%) | 452 (74%) | 884 (70%) |
| Back page lead | 16 (2%) | 21 (4%) | 37 (3%) |
| Back page | 74 (11%) | 37 (6%) | 111 (9%) |
| Total | 675 | 609 | 1260 |

| Location | Guardian | Punch | Jan-Dec 02 |
|---|---|---|---|
| Front page lead | 25 (4%) | 36 (4%) | 61 (4%) |
| Front page | 88 (12%) | 55 (7%) | 143 (9%) |
| Inside | 504 (73%) | 608 (73%) | 1108 (74%) |
| Back page lead | 25 (4%) | 17 (2%) | 42 (3%) |
| Back page | 46 (7%) | 113 (14%) | 159 (10%) |
| Total | 688 | 829 | 1503 |

| Location | Guardian | Punch | Jan-Dec 03 |
|---|---|---|---|
| Front page lead | 17 (3%) | 27 (3%) | 44 (3%) |
| Front page | 52 (8%) | 61 (7%) | 113 (8%) |
| Inside | 481 (78%) | 735 (84%) | 1205 (81%) |
| Back page lead | 15 (2%) | 6 (1%) | 21 (1%) |
| Back page | 58 (9%) | 45 (5%) | 103 (7%) |
| Total | 623 | 874 | 1486 |

The total number of stories that were the lead stories in the papers and the total of ordinary front-page crime stories during the study scope further reinforce this fact. The analysis of stories that were the lead stories gives an insight into the category of crimes most attractive to the Nigerian press. These in order of importance as observed from the frequency of reportage are crimes against persons, property crimes and financial crimes.

Examples of front-page lead stories in The *Guardian* for the period under study include:

> Teenage Nigerian Rapist on the Prowl in London (28/01/01); Students Protest Shooting of Colleague (10/03/01); Government Probes N50 billion Fail Contract (19/03/01); Child Trafficking Syndicate Smashed: 28 Victims Rescued (02/06/01); Reps Panel Alleges N250 Billion Scam in NNPC: Accuses NMA, NPA of Collusion (02/08/01); Terror in America: WTC Twin Towers in Rubbles. Pentagon, Defence Hqtrs on Fire. White House, U.N, Federal Buildings Evacuated. All Airports Closed, Flights Cancelled (12/09/01); He Was Shot Close to The Lower rib with a Special Bullet...Which dissolves in the Body (26/12/01); Gunmen kill Marshall Harry, ANPP leader. Fed. Govt., Rivers Deplore Killing. Obj Plans Political Summit on Violence. (06/03/03);

Examples of Front- page lead stories in the *Punch* for the period under study include:

> N23 million Fraud: Commissioner kicked out... to face trial. (13/08/01); Obj's staff, Others Rob Ota Farms. OPC arrests them (18/08/01); Terrorists attack U.S. Hundreds killed. Pentagon, WTC Hit. Bush vows to Retaliate (12/09/01); Man Arrested With Fresh Human Heads: Three beheaded in Lagos (10/11/01); Ritualists kill Chief of Air Staff's aide (18/11/01); Landlord Throws 5-Month Old Baby into Well... Over rent palaver (17/11/01). Anti-graft Panel Probes Anyim (17/3/02); Bank's Frauds hit N15bn in Four Months: Surpass Last Year's Mark. (9/12/02); Police Halt Printing of 5 million Fake Voter's Card: Three suspects arrested, Rtd. Colonel on the Run (17/01/03); Marshall Harry, ANPP Chieftain Shot Dead 06/03/03); Policemen Abduct Anambra Gov.: I've taken over, Deputy. Gov in Protective Custody (11/06/03).

Some of the above listed examples of front page lead headlines in the papers reinforce the fact that the Nigerian press favours crimes against persons i.e. murder, assault etc, property crimes and financial crimes, especially those involving huge sums of money and highly placed individuals in the society. The strength of a particular crime stories i.e. its attractiveness and appeal to members of the public is also a major determinant of where it is located in the layout of a paper.

According to *Punch* Editor,

> When we get a story, we look at it and consider its strategic importance to the readership. Its only stories that you feel majority of your readers will like to read that you put on the front page. But if you know it's a story that may not interest everybody, you put it inside... It's a competition and it all depends on the strength of the story.

That of *The Guardian* also submits that:

> Crime reports and news stories are allocated based on the strength. There is no columnization of crime reports in The Guardian. Stories on crime compete for space on the news pages like any other stories depending on their strength.

From their statements, some elements of the Agenda-setting theory become obvious. The theory stipulates that the public can learn how much importance to attach to an issue or topic from the emphasis placed on it by the media. And going by the emphasis placed on crimes against persons, property crime and financial crime by the papers through their prominence on the front pages as lead stories, the implication is that the papers would enamour the public to attach more importance to crimes against persons, property crimes and financial crime than other categories of crime.

Meanwhile, the noticeable increase in the number of ordinary back page stories on the back page of *Punch* in 2002 and 2003 compared with what obtained in 2001 can be attributed to the existence of a special column, *City Update* which featured mainly crime stories. The examination of the newspapers content also showed that there were specialized inside pages, apart from the news pages where crime stories were featured. *The Guardian* has The Metro Section, where crime stories were published in the daily paper, and another column, *Crime Note* in the *Guardian* on Sunday. *Punch* also had its crime page which featured different crime and security stories indicating that the papers consider crime an issue but only that they don't give it prominence on the front page (except violent and financial crimes) like they do to governance, political and economic stories.

## Genre of Crime Stories

Table 5 shows that genre of crime stories with news taking 86%, 83% and 78% in 2001, 2002 and 2003 respectively. News ranked highest in the genre of published stories in the papers for the three years studied and the reason is not far fetched. Unlike writing a features story which requires in-depth analysis and follow-ups like interviewing offenders/victims of crime incidents and confirming with the police to include facts that news by its terse nature would not allow, writing an ordinary news story is relatively easier and less tasking since it does not require the depth and background of a feature story.

**Table 5: Genre of published crime stories. Jan 2001 – Dec 2003**

| Genre | Guardian | Punch | Jan-Dec 01 Total |
|---|---|---|---|
| News | 570 (83%) | 538 (89%) | 1080 (86%) |
| Features | 72 (11%) | 19 (3%) | 91 (7%) |
| Editorial | 12 (2%) | 8 (1%) | 20 (2%) |
| Letter to Editor | 5 (1%) | 6 (1%) | 11 (1%) |
| Opinion | 8 (1%) | 9 (2%) | 17 (1%) |
| Illustrations | 18 (2%) | 23 (4%) | 41 (3%) |
| Total | 685 | 603 | 1288 |

| Genre | Guardian | Punch | Jan-Dec 02 |
|---|---|---|---|
| News | 519 (74%) | 764 (92%) | 1252 (83%) |
| Features | 68 (10%) | 20 (2%) | 88 (6%) |
| Editorial | 20 (3%) | 7 (1%) | 27 (2%) |
| Letter to Editor | 21 (3%) | 13 (2%) | 34 (2%) |
| Opinion | 23 (3%) | 5 (1%) | 28 (2%) |
| Illustrations | 50 (7%) | 24(%) | 74 (5%) |
| Total | 701 | 833 | 1534 |

| Genre | Guardian | Punch | Jan-Dec 03 |
|---|---|---|---|
| News | 463 (75%) | 722 (81%) | 1155 (78%) |
| Features | 41 (6%) | 72 (8%) | 113 (8%) |
| Editorial | 20 (3%) | 30 (3%) | 50 (3%) |
| Letter to Editor | 17 (3%) | 10 (1%) | 27 (2%) |
| Opinion | 19 (3%) | 13 (2%) | 32 (2%) |
| Illustration | 60 (10%) | 49 (6%) | 109 (7%) |
| Total | 620 | 896 | 1516. |

Features stories, which Amari (1999), argues should contain perspective, identified risk factors, and consequences and costs of crime to enrich people's information on crime patterns and trends comes a distant second in the papers with 7% in 2001, 6% in 2002 and 8% in 2003. This translates that Nigerians only read brief accounts of crime that offer no context or useful information in the papers contrary to what Stevens (1998) proposed that context and other useful information on crime incidents should be included in newspaper reports of crime as part of efforts towards reporting crime as a public health issue.

In effect, the papers contribute little to the readers' knowledge giving them terse news items when ideally good features stories would benefit the Nigerian public more and enrich their knowledge on crime substantially. But rationalizing why there is less feature stories on crime in the papers compared to news, the reporters and editors interviewed justified it on the basis of the feedback they get from the public to stories they publish on particular crime incidents.

To the journalists, only stories that generate public interest from the public that they write features stories on. Reporter of the *Guardian* sums it thus:

> It is a feature story that generates public interest, like when policemen who are supposed to arrest and parade armed robbers are themselves arrested for robbery. That will generate public interest. We get many responses on such stories on our website and to satisfy the interest, we write features on such stories. When we do that, there are lots and lots of accolades.

A comparison of the two papers showed that in 2001 and 2002, *The Guardian* published more feature crime stories than *Punch* while 2003 proved the exception with *Punch* having more features stories. However, the existence of The Metro Section page in *The Guardian* which has more feature stories on crime could be advanced as reason for the 2001-2002 situation, while conversely, it could be that the number of crime stories published on the page reduced in 2003 as a result of the papers pre-occupation with other social issues other than crime. The analysis also revealed that the weekend editions of *Punch* had more feature stories on crime than the daily edition, but perhaps, the general character of weekend editions of Nigerian newspapers, which are magazine like in outlook account for this. Also, the assumption that people have more time to read and relax with papers on weekends than on week days when they are pressed by the demands of work probably made the *Punch* publish more feature stories on crime on weekends.

Contrary to expectations that concern and fear of crime would make the public make more inputs to the papers in the form of letters and opinion articles expressing their concern on crime and security issues, letters and opinion articles on crime are the least featured after illustrations in the papers during the study scope. This may not suggest that the public is not worried or concerned about crime. However, the analysis of the two papers showed that little space is reserved for letters and opinion articles from the public. Both papers for instance have only one page for opinion articles from outsiders other than their regular columnists and a half page for letters, thus making any attempt to assess the public fear of crime from the public input in these papers becomes meaningless, since the public is not given enough space in the first instance to express such fears.

Illustrations, comprising cartoons, pictures etc also did not feature prominently in the papers during the period studied as it was 3% in 2001, 5% in 2002 and 7% in 2003 thus making it the least featured genre in the papers. What this means is that unlike the old practice of splashing pictures of criminals in the papers, Nigerian papers no longer favours this practice. The inference then is that the papers have gone beyond the stage of publishing pictures of offenders and criminal incidents like they used to in the past, and that they no longer consider including such pictures in the papers necessary and useful. The press might have realized that rather than deter crime, such pictures end up portraying the criminals as martyrs to some young impressionable minds in the society. But whatever their reason for reducing the amount of illustrations in the papers, the practice conforms with some of the suggestions made by Seymour and Lowrance (1988) that photographing and filming scenes with bodies, body bags and blood should be de-emphasized by the press in consideration of its effects on victims of such criminal incidents.

Editorial comments on crime appeared sparingly in the papers. Considering the fact that editorial comments are the official position of newspapers on policies and issues in the society, the small number of editorial comments on crime in the papers indicate that the papers avoid taking official positions or consider other issues more of national interest than criminalities. With specific reference to ascertaining the editorial policy of the selected newspapers on crime, editors of both papers interviewed revealed that their papers have no official editorial policy on crime, but that they are guided by the newsworthiness of crime stories. Editor of the *Punch* submit,

> We don't have an official policy on crime report per se. But all of us, both the news managers and the correspondents are all guided by the basic principles of journalism.

That of *The Guardian* asserts that:

> There is nothing like a policy on crime reporting. If you are talking about a policy, it means you're restricting the paper to a specialized kind of reporting... As of this moment, we don't have anything like that in The Guardian.

The implication is that crime has to compete for space in the papers like other news items, and also indicates a short shrift attention to crime by the press in spite of its prevalence in the society.

## Glamorizing Crime: Between the Offenders and the Victims

Offenders engaged the attention of the newspapers more than victims as the table 6 shows. Concentration on offenders than the victim, confirms Merenin, (1987) and Dambazau, (1994)'s position that Nigerian newspapers glamorize and celebrate offenders by concentrating too much on them in their news report. The results as shown in Table 6 similarly corroborate Amari's (1999) assertion that newspapers concentrate on offenders by describing them in euphemisms without taking cognizance of the effect of their reports on the victims and on the offenders themselves who sometimes receive tougher sentences from juries and judges because of the way their deed is reported by the press. It is in this vein the media have been accused of promoting support for repressive penalty (Reiner, 2002)

**Table 6: Focus of Crime Reports. Jan 2001 - Dec 2003**

| Focus | *Guardian* | Punch | Jan-Dec 01 Total |
|---|---|---|---|
| | | | |
| Victim | 215 (37%) | 170 (36%) | 385 (37%) |
| Offender | 362 (63%) | 301 (64%) | 663 (63%) |
| Total | 577 | 471 | 1048 |

| Focus | *Guardian* | Punch | Jan-Dec 02 |
|---|---|---|---|
| Victim | 211 (31%) | 235 (31%) | 446 (35%) |
| Offender | 324 (61%) | 501 (69%) | 825 (65%) |
| Total | 535 | 736 | 1271 |

| Focus | *Guardian* | Punch | Jan-Dec 03 |
|---|---|---|---|
| Victim | 154 (41%) | 280 (37%) | 434 (39%) |
| Offender | 224 (59%) | 468 (63%) | 692 (62%) |
| Total | 378 | 748 | 1126 |

However, it could be argued that the two newspapers also glamorize the offenders though they were restrained in their choice of words. The two papers dispensed with euphemisms and sensational headlines in their reports but indirectly 'celebrate' the offenders. This in a way conforms to calls from scholars who advocate reporting crime as a public health issue. Disclosing whom they concentrate more on between the offender and victim in their stories, the reporters disclosed that they try to balance their story by including both the offender and victim while adding that the house style of their papers requires them to do so. The quantitative survey indicates that both parties reflect in the news but in unequal proportion.

The desires of the newspapers to portray offenders in their true light and disclose their identities to members of the public in order for them to be wary and cautious can also be adduced as why the papers concentrated more on offenders than victims.

## Discussion

The results show that crime against persons i.e. rape, murder, assault etc received greater coverage in the papers than drug crimes, local acts and financial crimes, which most often require extensive and thorough investigation. The findings thus confirm the contention of scholars that crimes against person's i.e. violent crimes are reported most by the press. Previous findings (Shelly & Ashkin, 1981; Marsh, 1991; Soothhill & Walby, 1991; Reiner, 2002) have also indicated that crimes against persons command more attention from the press than property offences, and that these usually get reported disproportionately by the press than property offences and crimes in which no violence occurred. The trend also confirms postulations of some researchers (Chiricos et al., 1997; Beckett & Sasson, 2000; Reiner, 2000; Dubois, 2002) that crimes against persons are reported most by the press. The foregoing discussion invariably supports Sandman et al. (1976), contention that the public relishes violent crime stories and is fascinated by it more than routine crime stories of burglaries and crimes in which no violence occurred. The degree of violence could put value in the news as information could be sold only for its value. This could lead to fear of crime among the people, police activities might also increase and young people might join gangs for self-protection (Cohen, 1972; Fishman, 1980). Fear of crime has been perpetuated through publicisation of crime in Nigeria. This is not to discredit such trend but to further assert that violent crime in particular could unfold security threats and fault perceived existence of adequate security by the people.

With respect to the sources of published crime stories, four sources, official sources, victims, offenders and reporters' investigation were identified but official sources was found to be the major source of crime stories available to the press just like the findings of Chibnall, Schlesinger and Amari showed. In spite of sourcing their stories mainly from the police however, the Nigerian press considers the arguments of scholars like Sandman et al. (1976), Chibnall, (1977) and Amari, (1999) which advised against the press being dependent on official sources for crime news because of its adverse effect on both the accused and audience. Sandman et al. (1976) specifically observed that sourcing crime stories from official sources denies the reporter the opportunity of meeting face-to-face with the accused and hearing his/her protestations of innocence while Chibnall, (1977) averred that the practice makes reporters develop a symbiotic relationship with such contacts. Apart from this, crime news could be filtered from the perspective of the official sources. Hence, the public only get to read the 'accredited' crime news which usually portrays the image of the official sources.

Concerning the focus of the crime stories between victims and offenders, the study reveals that although the reporters try to balance the stories by focusing on both victim and offender in their reports, offenders' rank highest in the focus of the crime reports as shown in table 6. Concerning the location of crime stories in the papers, the study shows that crime stories are usually tucked away inside the papers except those which are shocking and outrageous like homicide, assault and rape which find their way to the front pages.

Thus Williams and Dickinson (1993), and Folarin, (1998) viewed that the importance a newspaper attaches to an issue is reflected in the positioning of the news item in the layout and headline display, the prominence given to crime against persons, property and financial crime show that these are the categories of crime Nigerian papers are interested in most and which they feel the public ought to know more about. This lends credence to the findings in table 1 which showed that the Nigerian Press has a bias for violent crimes. The finding corroborates Sasson (1995); Barlow, (1998) and Beckett and Sasson, (2000) findings that most crime stories in newspapers consist primarily of brief accounts of discrete events, with few details and little background material. Reiner (2002) also observed in most media reports that there are usually very few attempts to put the problem of crime into a larger perspective which could bring about the contextual causes and remedies.

On the genre of published crime reports, the study shows that news is featured disproportionately when compared with other genres like features, illustrations, opinion articles and letters in the newspapers. The preponderance of news stories compared to other genres of crime stories in the papers is a testimony to this fact, and the implication, just like Sherizen (1978) advanced, is that it provides citizens with a public awareness of crime based upon an information rich and knowledge poor foundation. Nigerians who are interested in learning about crime from the papers are only treated to examples and incidents with nothing added to their knowledge. One of the recommendations of those who advocate reporting crime as a public health issue is that newspapers provide a balanced perspective that reflects the concerns of the victim and the offender (St. Louis Post Dispatch, 1992) The papers did this although the table shows that the reports were written more from the angle of the offenders but there was no euphemisms like those described by Seymour and Lowrance (1988) as being injurious to the victim.

The study also reveals that the two newspapers selected for the study have no official editorial policy on crime other than seeing it as part of everyday news staple. The amount of editorial comments on crime in the two papers attests to this fact. By and large, the Nigeria print media also creates public awareness about crime. There is tendency to cover crime reports especially violent crimes which could be more fascinating to the public and which could be favourable in media markets. The tendency to focus more on the offenders thereby projecting their dexterity which could create fear in the general public and influence imposition of harsh sentence is also evident.

## Conclusion

One of the findings of this study relates to the fact that the papers concentrated and devoted more space to crime against persons to the detriment of other crime category like drug crime, and financial crime. This is an obvious lapse on the part of the press since these other types of crime are equally important to the public, as they need to be educated and informed about other crime categories in order to save them from becoming victims of drug peddlers and scammers. There is the need for the media to give adequate coverage to all categories of crime other than crimes against persons to guide against sensationalism and in order not to increase fear of crime among the public. With respect to the genre of the crime reports, the papers concentrated on news stories that are mainly brief accounts of events with few details and little background material on the crime incidents. There is the need to discuss causes of crime, its trends and remedies by writing good feature stories on crime in order to educate the public on crime patterns in the society. This will make crime reporting more development oriented and beneficial to both the public and policy makers in Nigeria. Since most reports are just brief accounts and examples of crime incidents, the public and policy makers gain nothing from such reports other than its somewhat morbid entertainment.

The lack of editorial policy on crime by the two newspapers is condemnable. There should be specific crime editorial policy. Crime stories need to be editorially justified and reported within legal and ethical constraints. Since crime and security are of great concern to members of the public, the press ought to have an official viewpoint on it instead of seeing it as just part of items to be included in papers. This will be in line with its agenda-setting role because by giving incisive commentaries on crime, members of the public and consequently, the policy makers would regard it seriously enough to warrant actions on it, thereby reducing its incidence. Official editorial policy would guide and guard the lens through which reporters observe and report crime incidence. This would serve both the interest of the public as well as protect the press by situating their actions within legal context. Similarly, more editorial comments on crime should be published in the newspapers in line with its agenda-setting function, while the media should, as a matter of utmost priority and urgency, have official editorial policy on crime to indicate to the public that they are also concerned about crime and are willing to express and reflect community anxieties over it. This would make the impact of the press felt as it would be fulfilling one of the press' major roles of watchdog. The media distrust of the police, which is the major source of their crime stories, is indicative of the rot in the Nigeria police. The reporter's stand that they still go ahead to interview alleged suspects held by the police shows that the police have lost some basic values. And unlike the findings of other studies, which gave no hint of distrust of the police by reporters as reason why they should double check from the accused, this study has exposed a Nigerian peculiarity that needs further re-examination.

Correspondingly, the Nigerian media, as is being advocated by the Berkeley Media Study group should try to start reporting crime as an epidemic which needs careful handling, rather than just sensationalizing crime stories by focusing on violent crime stories to increase circulation figures. This is not to assert that all crime reports (especially the violent crime) follow sensational pattern but by reporting crime sensibly and responsibly, and by giving equal coverage to all categories of crime, instead of the current practice of reporting mainly violent crimes, the papers would be giving a fairly accurate picture of the crime situation in the country instead of a distorted picture that could heighten fear of crime and actually induce it among the public.

Finally, the press should allow readers more space to express their personal concern over crime by allotting more space to reactions and feedbacks in the form of opinion articles and letters. Ultimately, the media needs to be responsible and objective in crime reporting because of the effects of its activities on the criminal justice system, in order not to trigger off harsh reactions to offenders that at the long run may defeat the purpose of correction by increasing the rate of recidivism. Sensationalism, which induces fear of crime and dramatizes crime incidence, should be eschewed completely.

## References

Amari, J. (1999). Is crime coverage out of balance? *Newswatch* 03/12/1999 Retrieved on 28th December 2007 from www.gannett.com./go/newswatch/99/march/nw0312

Barlow, M. T. (1998). Race and the problem of crime in time and newsweek cover stories, 1946-1995. *Social Justice*, *25*, 149-182.

Beckett, K., & Sasson, T. (2000). *The politics of injustice*. Thousand Oaks: Pine Forge Press.

Chermak, S. M. (1995). *Victims in the news: Crime in American news media*. Boulder: Westview.

Chibnall, S. (1977). *Law-and-Order news*. London: Tavistock.

Chiricos, T., Eschholz, S., & Gertz, N. (1997). Crime news and fear of crime: towards an identification of audience effects. *Social Problems*, *44*(3), 342-357.

CLEEN (2007). Crime statistics in Nigeria. Retrieved on 28th December 2007 from http://www.cleen.org/crime%20statistics%201994-2003_graphics.pdf, accessed on May 1st, 2007.

Cohen, S. (1972). *Folk devils and moral panics*. London: Paladin.

Dambazau, A. B. (1994). *Law and Criminality in Nigeria*. Ibadan: University Press Plc.

Davis, J. (1952). Crime news in Colorado newspapers. *American Journal of Sociology, 52*, 325-330.

Ditton, J., & Duffy, J. (1983). Bias in the newspaper reporting of crime news. *British Journal of Criminology, 23*(2), 159-165.

Dominick, J. (1978). Crime and law enforcement in the mass media. In C. Winick (Ed.), *Deviance and Mass Media* (pp.234-258). Beverly Hills, California: Sage.

Dowler, K. (2003). Media consumption and public attitudes towards crime and justice: The relationship between fear of crime, punitive attitude and perceived police effectiveness. *Journal of Criminal Justice and Popular Culture*, *10*(2), 109-126.

Dubois, J. (2002). *Media coverage of organized crime: Impact on public opinion.* Ottawa: Universite du Quebec.

Ericson, R., Baranek, P., & Chan, J. (1987). *Visualizing deviance.* Milton Keynes: Open University.

Fishman, M. (1981). Police news: Constructing an image of crime. *Urban Life*, *9*(4), 23-29.

Folarin, B. (1998). *Theories of mass communication.* Ibadan: Stirling Horden.

Garofalo, J. (1981). Crime and the mass media: A selective review of research. *Journal of Research in Crime and Delinquency, 18*(2), 319-350.

Graber, D. (1980). *Crime News and the Public.* New York: Praeger.

Hall, S., Critchley, C., Jeferson, T., Clarke, J., & Roberts, B. (1978). *Policing the crisis*. London: Macmillan.

Harris, F. (1932). *Presentation of crime in newspapers.* Minneapolis: Minneapolis Sociological Press.

Kirby, M., Kidd, W., Koubel, F., Barter, J., Hope, T., Kiton, A., Madry, N., Manning, P., & Triggs, K. (1997). *Sociology in perspective.* Oxford: Heinemann Educational.

Lloyd, C., & Walton, P. (1999). Reporting corporate crime. *Corporate Communications: An International Journal*, *4*(1), 43-48.

Lynch, M., Stretesky, P., & Hammond, P. (2001). Media coverage of chemical crimes in Hillsborough County, Florida, 1987-1997. *British Journal of Criminology*, *40*(1), 112-126.

Marsh, H. L., (1991). A comparative analysis of crime coverage in newspapers in the United States and other countries from 1960-1989: A review of the literature. *Journal of Criminal Justice*, *19*(1), 67–80.

Marshall, G. (1996). *Oxford concise dictionary of Sociology.* Oxford: Oxford University Press.

Okunola, R. A. (2002). Crime in Society: Currents and perspectives. In U. C. Isiugo-Abanile, A. N. Isamah & J. O. Adesina (Eds.), *Currents and perspectives in Sociology* (pp.349-366). Ibadan: Malthouse Press Limited.

Regan, P. (1977). *Crime against the elderly: Findings from interviews with Blacks, Mexicans, Americans and Whites.* Lexington: Massachusetts Heath.

Reiner, R. (2001). The rise of virtual vigilantism: Crime reporting since World War II. *Criminal Justice Matters*, *43*, 4 – 5.

Reiner, R., Livingstone, S., & Allen, J. (2000). Casino Culture: Media and crime in a winner-loser society. In K. Stenson & R. Sullivan (Eds.), *Crime, risk and justice* (pp.175-93). Cullompton: Willan.

Reiner, R. (2002). Media made criminality: The representation of crime in the mass media. In M. Maguire, R. Morgan & R. Reiner (Eds.), *The Oxford handbook of Criminology* (pp.302-337). Oxford: Oxford University Press.

Riger, S., Gordon, M., & Lebaily. (1978). Women's fear of crime: From blaming to restricting the victim. *Victimology, 3*(4), 274-285.

Rodney, S. (1992) Sociology. In U. C. Isiugo-Abanile, A. N. Isamah & J. O. Adesina (Eds.), *Currents and perspectives in Sociology* (pp.349-366). Ibadan: Malthouse Press Limited.

Roshier, B., (1973). The selection of crime news by the Press. In S. Cohen & J. Young (Eds.), *The manufacture of news* (pp.40-51). London: Constable.

Sandman, P. M., Rubin, D. M., & Sachsman, D. B. (1976). *Media: An introductory analysis of media of mass communication* (2nd edn) Englewood Cliffs, New Jersey: Prentice Hall, Inc.

Sasson, T., (1995). *Crime Talk: How citizens construct a social problem.* New York: Aldine De Gruyter.

Schlesinger, P., & Tumber, H. (1994). *Reporting crime.* Oxford: Oxford University Press.

Schlesinger, P., Dobash, P., & Murdock, G. (1991). The media politics of crime and criminal justice. *British Journal of Sociology 42*(3), 397-420.

Seymour, A., & Lowrance, L. (1988). *Crime victims and the news media.* Fort Wort: Texas Christian University.

Sheley, J., & Ashkins, C. (1981). Crime, Crime News and Crime views. *Public Opinion Quarterly*, *45*(4), 492-506.

Sherizen, S. (1978). Social creation of crime news: All the news fitted to print. In C. Winick (Ed.), *Deviance and Mass Media* (pp.90-101). Beverly Hills: Cal. Sage.

Smith, S. (1984). Crime in the news. *British Journal of Criminology*, *24*(3), 289-295.

Soola, E. O. (2003) *Coverage of crimes and violence in Nigerian mass media: Matters arising*. Paper presented at the National Conference of African Council for Communication Education, Nigerian Chapter.

Soothill, K., & Walby, S. (1991). *Sex crime in the news.* London: Routledge.

*St. Louis Post-Dispatch.* (1992). Guidelines on privacy issues.

Stevens, J. E. (1998). Reporting crime as epidemic. Retrieved on 28th December 2007 from www.gannett.com/go/newswatch1991march/nwo3/12.

Sundeen, R. & Mathieu, J. (1976). The fear of crime and its consequences among elderly. *The Urban Communities*, *3*(6), 211-219.

Thompson, C., Young, R., & Burns, R. (2000). Representing gangs in the news: Media constructions of criminal gangs. *Sociological Spectrum, 20*(4), 409-432.

U.S. Department of Justice. (1977). *Public opinion about crimes: The attitude of victims and non-victims in selected cities*. Washington D.C: U.S. Government Printing Office.

Westfeldt, W., & Wicker, T. (1998). Indictment: The news media and the criminal justice media. *Newswatch,* 03/12/1999.

Maxfield, M. E. (1984). Fear of crime in England and Wales. London: HMSO.

Williams, P., & Dickinson, J. (1993). Fear of crime: read all about it? The relationship between newspaper crime reporting and fear of crime. *British Journal of Criminology, 33*(1), 33-56.

# PART IV.

# PERSPECTIVES ON CRIME PREVENTION AND VICTIMIZATION

# CHAPTER SIXTEEN

# THE BEST INTEREST OF CRIME VICTIMS: PROTECTION OF RIGHTS AND REMEDIES IN QUEENSLAND, AUSTRALIA

WING HONG CHUI

## Abstract

This chapter provides an overview of the current situation regarding legal protection and services for victims of crime in Australia. While the chapter primarily discusses the main principles of justice for victims under Queensland law, the ideas raised here may have direct relevance to other States in Australia and beyond. The chapter consists of four sections. The first section examines the empirical data about crime victimization in Australia. Several crime victimization surveys were conducted nationally and internationally to overcome the limitations of reported crime statistics. The second section explains the importance of studying the topic of 'victim protection' in Australia and elsewhere. The third section is concerned with various pieces of Queensland legislation that aims at protecting the victim's rights as a witness and as the injured party. It also describes a wide range of formal responses to victims of crime such as crime victim compensation, and legal assistance to the victims and their families. The final section discusses the development of victim services in Australia. It is hoped that this chapter lays the basis for future policy opportunities to improve legal protection and service provisions for victims.

## Introduction

The aim of this chapter is to discuss issues surrounding the protection of victim in the criminal justice system in Queensland, Australia. It attempts to examine victim problems, policies and programmes within the Australian context. As argued by several commentators, victims in general played a minor role in the criminal justice process. They were often used as witnesses to an alleged crime, but they have little involvement in the decision making process as to how offenders should be sentenced (Laub, 1997; Dignan, 2005; Doak, 2005; Tapley, 2005; Williams, 2005). Recognition of victim's rights and the emergence of the victim's voice in Australia did not start until the late 1970s (Cook, David, & Grant, 1999; Israel, 2003). A number of victim advocacy organizations such as child rights groups, anti-rape activists, women's equality network, civil liberties organizations, and law-and-order groups have continued to demand greater support for victims of crime and more recognition of the rights of victims of crime in Australia, North America and elsewhere (Karmen, 1990). These special interest groups are concerned with the ways in which victims have been harmed or otherwise, and how victims can be empowered and assisted. Unsurprisingly, a number of laws were enacted to address the concerns and needs of victims in the 1970s and 1980s. The first Australian compensation scheme for crime victims was set up in New South Wales in 1967 and South Australia was the first Australian state to pass the Victims of Crime Bill in 1985 (Spalek, 2006). The subsequent enactment of victims' right legislation was followed by the development of victim support services and policy from the 1990s.

This chapter is divided into four main sections. The first section describes different ways of measuring the prevailing rate of crime victimization. The second section explains the importance of studying the topic of 'victim protection' by examining the empirical data about crime victimization in Australia. The third section deals with the current legislation that intends to protect the rights of the victim as a witness and as the injured party. It also describes a wide range of initiatives for victims such as compensation schemes and legal support to the victims of crime and their families. The fourth section discusses the development of victim services in Australia. It is beyond the scope of this chapter to discuss these issues across six States and two Territories in Australia, because each has a separate system of administration of justice to victims of crime. To avoid undue complications, this chapter will only discuss the main institutional responses to victims with reference to the State of Queensland. However, given similar principles of justice for victims of crime embodied in law in other jurisdictions, the ideas raised here may have direct relevance to other States in Australia and beyond Australia.

## Measurement of Crime Victimization

In Australia, there are two major sources of statistics on crime and the incidence of victimization which are compiled by the Australian Bureau of Statistics (ABS) on a regular basis. They are the *Recorded Crime* series of reports and the *Crime and Safety* surveys (Grant, David, & Cook, 2002). The former, collect information on all types of recorded crime to the state, and territory state police agencies on a calendar year basis. The latter are direct reports from members of the public about the experiences of crime through Australia-wide household surveys on a regular basis (ABS, 2006). The results generated from these two sources may provide different pictures of crime or victimization statistics given their varied methods of data collection and sets of crime victimization measurement. In this respect, the comparability of these reports or surveys at national level, at state level, or within states at local level, is often lacking (Mayhew, 1995). Despite this, each of these reports provides the Australian criminal justice personnel essential information regarding the level and extent of victimization. For instance, in the latest *Recorded Crime* report, the number of victims recorded by Australian police declined in most offence categories in 2005 when compared to 2004. The number of victims of homicide and related offences decreased by 10%; victims of motor vehicle theft and unlawful entry with intent both decreased by 8%; other theft and kidnapping/abduction both decreased by 5%. In contrast, the number of victims of blackmail/extortion and robbery increased by 6% and 2% respectively. The official data in 2005 indicated that the victimization rate for motor vehicle theft was 397 per 100,000 population; unlawful entry with intent was 1,398 per 100,000 population; homicide and related offences was 4 per 100,000 population; other theft was 2,544 per 100,000 population, and robbery was 83 per 100,000 population (ABS, 2006).

Examples of the *Crime and Safety* surveys at the national level are *General Social Survey*, *National Crime and Safety Survey* and *International Crime Victims Survey* (ABS, 2004). The *General Social Survey* collects information on a wide range of topics such as housing, education, work, family, and crime and safety. The *National Crime and Safety Survey* primarily collects data on safety issues, perceived level of safety, and the incidence of crime reported or unreported to the police. The *Women's Safety Survey* is concerned with personal safety issues amongst females. The *International Crime Victims Survey* (ICVS), conducted by the Australian Institute of Criminology, a federal government agency, is part of an international research project into crime, incidences of victimization, and crime prevention and control (ABS, 2004). These surveys provide the policy-makers and criminal justice practitioners with another perspective to recorded crime reports to understand the issues surrounding law and order. This information can be used to improve the development, implementation and evaluation of criminal justice policies, programmes and services for crime victims.

There are differences in terms of the ultimate objective, sampling method, scope and coverage, and research methodology amongst these four surveys. The following table illustrates that even when data on assault prevalence rates of females aged 18 years and over were amended for comparability on age and sex of victims, the assaults rate for the *National Crime and Safety Survey* were significantly lower than the *General Social Survey*, *Women's Safety Survey* and ICVS rates.

**Table 1: Assault Prevalence Rates, Adjusted only for comparable respondent group (females aged 18 years and over)**

| Offence category | 2002 *General Social Survey* | 2002 *National Crime and Safety Survey* | 1996 *Women's Safety Survey** | 2000 *International Crime Victims Survey* |
|---|---|---|---|---|
| Total population (number) | 7,327,000 | 7,309,200 | 6,880,500 | 6,790,319 |
| Assault victims (number) | 528,000 | 294,000 | 404,400 | 627,635 |
| Assault victims (prevalence) | 7.2% | 4.0% | 5.9% | 9.2% |
| 95% confidence interval | (6.5, 7.9) | (3.7, 4.3) | (5.3, 6.5) | (7.8, 10.6)** |

* Includes all females who experienced an incident involving physical violence by either a male or female perpetrator.

** Confidence intervals used available relative standard errors which were based on full population of persons aged 16 years and over. Therefore, confidence intervals are these figures or greater.

Source: Adapted from ABS, (2004: Table 3)

In addition to the above two sources of victim data at the national level, various criminal justice agencies in each state and territory conducted crime victimization surveys in order to measure the estimated levels of victimization of personal and household offences during the preceding 12 months. One example is the *Queensland Crime Victimization Survey, 2000* (Office of Economic and Statistical Branch, 2001). Its key findings not only discuss the risk factors associated with victims aged 15 years and over, but they further examine the characteristics of crime incidents such as location of offences, use of weapons, whether physically injured, number of offenders, relationship of offender to victim, and what offenders did. What is more, survey respondents were asked whether the experience of victimization were reported to the police. The most common reasons for not reporting personal and household offences were that the crime incident was too trivial, nothing was stolen, and the victim perceived that there was nothing the police could do for victims of crime.

While it is beyond the scope of this chapter to analyze all findings on crime victimization in Australia from the above studies, it is worth highlighting some of the key results from the Australian component of a recent ICVS which may be of great interest to lay readers. In 2004 ICVS, more than half (52 per cent) of Australians had experienced at least one incident of crime in the five years prior to the survey, down from 55 per cent reported in the 2000 ICVS (Johnson, 2005). The 2004 study also indicates that 17 per cent of Australians were victims of crime one year prior to the survey, a drop from 24 per cent in 2000. Between the 2000 and 2004 ICVS study, there was a decline in the crime rates in seven of the nine specific crimes, including assault/threat, personal theft, burglary, attempted burglary, motor vehicle theft, theft from motor vehicle, and bicycle theft; whereas the crime rates for robbery and motorcycle theft remained stable (Johnson, 2005). This downward trend is consistent with the crime statistics collected by police and courts.

## Why Study Crime Victims?

There are a number of reasons for the increasing interest in studying victims of crime in Australia. Firstly, the latest international report prepared by the Organization for Economic Co-operation and Development (OECD) indicates that amongst other developed nations Australia had the highest rate of victimization (see Wright, 2006). Based upon these findings, Wright (2006) further reports that ‘Australia had the highest proportion of victims of assaults, threats and crimes of sexual nature of the OECD’s member nations, the second highest proportion of burglaries, and high rates of robberies, car thefts and thefts from cars'. Whilst acknowledging the fact that measuring crime is a difficult task, these observations in many respects justify an urgent need to address the considerable number of victims being affected by serious crime in Australia.

Secondly, the consequences of various forms of victimization such as sexual assault, domestic violence, child abuse, burglary, and theft have been widely investigated (see, for example, Boles & Patterson, 1997; Alexander, 2002; Grant, David, & Cook, 2002; Goodey, 2005) and point to the importance of putting the victim centre-stage because of the possible emotional, psychological, financial, social, and practical consequences on the victim. There is evidence that the effects associated with the traumatic experience do not diminish quickly after the incident, and 'the elderly, children, women and ethnic minorities' are the most vulnerable group to long-term trauma (Newburn, 1993). Rape is often cited as having a long-lasting effect on the victim (Kilpatrick et al., 1987; Lurigio, Skogan, & Davis, 1990). Newburn (1993) further argues that it is the responsibility of relevant government or non-governmental organizations to understand and respond to the needs of the victim, thereby minimizing the detrimental effects of crime on victims. According to the President's Task Force on Victims of Crime (1982), fundamental needs of victims are: (i) victims must be protected; (ii) the criminal justice system must be responsive to the victim's needs; and (iii) victims should be assisted to overcome the burdens imposed by crime (cited in Boles & Patterson, 1997).

Thirdly, researchers such as Mawby and Walkate (1994) have drawn our attention to studying the 'victim' in a more critical and detailed manner. Critical feminist criminologist, like Lees (1996) point to some of the treatment of victims by the criminal justice system, as damaging and unnecessary. For instance, Lees (1996) found that questioning by police at times could be threatening whereas the legal profession could humiliate and embarrass the victim with aggressive and excessive cross-examination in the British context. This is now commonly termed as 'secondary victimization' (Spalek, 2006). Her observation rehearses the findings reported by Australian studies. The New South Wales Task Force on Services for Victims of Crime (1987) found that about 46 per cent of victims were not satisfied with the way they were treated by the police, and the majority of the respondents complained about the limited availability of support services (also cited in Israel, 2003, p. 352). Eastwood's (2003) study shows that child complainants of sexual abuse in the criminal justice system found the trial process to be an unpleasant experience when it involved cross-examinations, lengthy delays between reporting and trial, and the humiliation of meeting the accused again; and thus the child complainants held the view that it was not worth the trouble. In order to prevent further trauma from being inflicted on the child by the system, a more child-centred policy focus was recommended to encourage reporting of sexual abuse of children. In this respect, the key issue is to identify ways to safeguard the victims from being intimidated and treated with respect and dignity whilst protecting the rights of defendants (Home Office, 2002; Goodey, 2005).

Instead of merely examining the impact on direct victims, the needs of indirect victims who witnessed the incidence of victimization or are affected by the specific crimes against their family members, friends and colleagues should not be overlooked. In a recent study of the impact of female sexual assault on the male spouse, Smith (2005) concludes that a sexual assault disrupts the lives of those who love the direct victim in many ways. Five men in her study disclosed how it had left them with feelings of anger, helplessness, aggression and guilt towards the victim, and they suffered from emotional disorders, health problems, and marital problems. This qualitative study emphasizes the importance of assistance to both survivors and their significant others in assisting them with handling the crisis or trauma.

## Current Legislation

### *Criminal Offence Victims Act, 1995 (Queensland): An Overview*

In this section, an overview of the *Criminal Offence Victims Act,* 1995 is provided to outline the fundamental principles of justice for victims of crime in Queensland. This Act is still enforced and several amendments have been made in subsequent years to make explicit the treatment given to victim by public officials.

#### *Definition of victim*

Section 5 of the Act defines who is a victim: A *victim* is a person who has suffered harm from a violation of the State's criminal laws –

- because a crime is committed that involves violence committed against the person in a direct way; or
- because the person is a member of the immediate family of, or is a dependant of, a victim mentioned in paragraph (a); or

- because the person has directly suffered the harm in intervening to help a victim mentioned in paragraph (a).

*Thirteen principles of justice for victims*

The above definition recognizes the impact of crime on both direct and indirect victims, and the State's responsibility to address the issue. Part 2 of the Act sets out thirteen major principles of justice for victims, and the following summarizes these principles.

- Fair and dignified treatment – A victim should be treated with courtesy, compassion and respect in responsive to age, gender, disability, ethnic or cultural and linguistic differences.
- Access to justice – A victim should not be denied access to the State's system of justice.
- Guidelines to help responses to victims – The guidelines should be made available to public officials in order to guide their conduct when dealing with victims in day-to-day practice.
- Information to be provided to victim about crime prevention methods – Information about how to prevent crime or secure their personal and home safety should be given upon request.
- Privacy of victim to be protected and property returned – In addition to privacy being guaranteed, a victim's property used for evidence should be returned as soon as reasonably possible and the inconvenience caused should be minimized.
- Victim's version of events to be reported as soon as reasonably possible after crime – After the crime happens, a law enforcement officer should make the report of a victim's version of the circumstance as quick as possible.
- Protection from violence and intimidation from accused person – A law enforcement officer should help the victim to have the benefit of the principles such as 'refusal of bail', 'prohibiting publication of information about proceedings', and 'prohibiting publication at large of complainant's identity' whenever appropriate.
- Welfare of victim to be considered – The welfare of the victim should be considered at all stages of investigation and prosecution of a crime.
- Information during sentencing of impact of crime on victim – The victim may give the prosecutor details of the harm inflicted to a victim by the crime, and the prosecutor should inform the sentencing court of these appropriate details.

- Information about investigation and prosecution of offender – A law enforcement officer should keep a victim informed regarding the process of investigations being conducted without jeopardising the investigation, the charges laid for the crime, the name of the person charged, the outcome of any proceedings as well as appeals, and so on. In particular to those victims of violent and sex crime, they should be advised whether the alleged offender has absconded before trial, the date of commencement and length of sentence on the offender, and eligibility dates for the offender to have staged release into the community, parole and final discharge for the sentence of the offence, and so.
- Victim to be advised on role as witness – The prosecution has to explain clearly the trial process and the role victims play as witnesses.
- Information about services – A victim should have access to information about available counselling, welfare, medial and legal assistance, and about victim-offender conferencing services.
- Information about compensation or restitution – A victim should be informed about the right to have access to information about the details of crime victim compensation or restitution for injury. A victim can ask the court to order the offender to pay him or her for the damage caused by the crime.

### *Crime victim compensation*

Part 3 of the Act is concerned about the compensation for personal injury for indictable offences which was introduced in 1995. Criminal Injury Compensation was first introduced in Queensland in 1969. From 1969 up until 17 December 1995, the legislation that governed Criminal Injury Compensation was the *Criminal Code*. In this regard, *Criminal Code* applies to all offences that occurred between 1969 and 17 December 1995 whereas *Criminal Offence Victims Act* applies to all indictable offences that occurred on or after 18 December 1995. An indictable offence is usually tried in the Supreme or District Court after a committal hearing in the Magistrates Court (Department of Justice and Attorney-General, 2004). Section 19 of the Act states the eligibility requirements for the payment of compensation:

- for injury suffered by the applicant caused by a offence committed against the applicant; or
- for the death of someone on whom the applicant was dependant, caused in circumstances constituting murder or manslaughter; or

- for funeral or other expenses from the death of a member of the applicant's family, caused in circumstances constituting murder or manslaughter; or
- for injury suffered when helping a police officer to make an arrest or prevent an office.

In general, there are two types of applicants for Criminal Injury Compensation: court applicants and ex gratia (act of grace or gift) applicants. Court applicants are persons who apply for compensation in the District or Supreme Court. The judge first assesses the injuries an applicant has suffered; the impact of the injuries; and whether he or she has contributed in any way to injuries, and then decides how much an offender has to pay for compensation. Carter (2004) notes that, "the court may also order that stolen property be returned to its owner. There are often practical problems in obtaining the court-ordered compensation from the [offender] and in many cases the police cannot locate the owner of stolen property to return to him or her" (p. 79). Ex gratia applicants are those who apply for payment from the State Government and who have suffered injury when assisting a police officer to arrest an offender, the offender cannot be found or identified, the offender is under 10 years of age or the offender is found to be of unsound mind or not fit to stand trial. It is important to note that the eligibility for the ex gratia application depends on when the offence was committed because that governs which pieces of legislation applies. Cases tried in the Magistrates Court are covered by the *Penalties and Sentences Act,* 1992, and no ex gratia payments are available (Department of Justice and Attorney-General 2004).

## *Victim Impact Statement*

Broadly speaking, there are three ways of allowing victims of crime in Queensland to tell the court how the crime has affected them.[1] They are: prosecutor's submissions, sworn evidence (when victims are called as

---

[1] The Australian Law Reform Commission (2006) comments that there 'are differences between state and territory laws concerning the availability, content, form and use of victim impact statements' (p. 391). Please consult the following legislations for more details: *Criminal Offence Victims Act,* 1995 (Queensland); Crimes *(Sentencing Procedure) Act,* 1999 (New South Wales); *Sentencing Act,* 1991 (Victoria); *Sentencing Act,* 1995 (Western Australia); *Criminal Law (Sentencing) Act,* 1988 (South Australia); *Sentencing Act,* 1997 (Tasmania); *Crimes (Sentencing) Act,* 2005 (Australian Capital Territory); *Sentencing Act,* 1995 (Northern Territory).

witnesses at the sentence hearing) and a victim impact statement (Department of Justice and Attorney-General, 2006a). A victim impact statement is usually a written statement signed, and presented to the court when passing the sentence. As set out in the *Criminal Offence Victims Act,* 1995 the right to submit a victim impact statement is guaranteed, and it is hoped that the victim will have a chance to explain how the crime has impacted upon him or her. More specifically, Department of Justice and Attorney-General (2006a) explicitly suggests that the statement should include accurate and relevant details of any physical injury, emotional harm or other financial loss or damage a victim has suffered as a result of crime. A victim may also wish to attach documents such as receipts, evidence of receiving counselling services, medical reports and psychiatric reports to support the statement. However, in Queensland the judge makes decisions whether it is necessary for the victim to read the statement in court. This is opposed to the current practice in South Australia where the *Victim Impact Statement (Amendment) Act,* 1998 allows victims to read the statement to the sentencing court (Edwards, 2001 cited in Spalek, 2006, p. 105).

The debate over victim participation in the criminal justice process has been continued (Kelly & Erez, 1997; Sanders et al., 2001; Edwards, 2002; Forsterlee et al., 2004). Advocates of victims' rights argue that the involvement of victims not only enables them to covey their feelings and personal experiences to the offender and court but also leads to increased victim satisfaction as well as co-operation with the criminal justice system (Australian Law Reform Commission, 1988). More importantly, a more participatory approach is found to promote psychological healing amongst victims because victims are able to gain a sense of control during the process (Kelly & Erez, 1997). On the other hand, arguments against victim participation in the sentencing process are many, and some examples are: a victim impact statement is too subjective and adds very little to what is not known to the court; the prosecutor may lose control over cases, thereby reducing the certainty and predictability of outcomes; and most victims are vindictive and unforgiving and this may in turn inflate the level of punishment (Erez, 1991). The controversy surrounding the use of a victim impact statement may explain a variation of current practice in different states in Australia (Israel, 2003).

While the *Criminal Offence Victims Act,* 1995 provides guidelines to deal with victims of crime in general, there are specific ordinances which are exclusively relevant to victims of a particular type of offence. In the following three sub-sections an overview of the legal responses to victims of three specific crimes, namely domestic violence, child abuse, and juvenile offending is provided.

### *Legal Response to Victims of Domestic Violence*

Alexander (2002), an accredited Family Law specialist in Victoria, has carefully analyzed the variation of respective statutory provisions in terms of the legislative intent, criminal responsibilities, and enforcement of judgment and orders in relation to domestic violence. She emphasizes the importance of being sensitive and empathetic to the victim's needs when handling victims of domestic violence. A good knowledge of legal remedies and non-legal remedies such as the available support service for medical treatment and accommodation is essential for those who work with the victim in day-to-day practice, such as the police, court personnel, legal practitioners, and community workers (see Chui 2004). One observation Alexander has raised is that the prosecution rate for domestic violence is relatively low due to the lack of co-operation from the victims, and the conspiracy of silence towards spousal violence in the community at large. However, it is often questionable whether criminal law provides adequate protection for the victim by punishing offenders and deterring them from repeating their conduct, and 'securing a criminal conviction is often a very long and difficult process' (Alexander, 2002).

Across different states in Australia, the primary legal measure that aims at protecting the victim in violent family situations is the *Family Law Act,* 1975 of Australia. The Act illustrates its procedure for obtaining a restraining order or an injunction intended to stop further violence against adults or children. The discussion of the statutory provisions such as parenting orders, the relationship between violence and property and spousal maintenance disputes, and the terms of the injunction therein is a practical one. In particular, the discussion of the procedural and enforcement matters under the legislation provides the legal practitioner with a quick reference to family litigation on domestic violence. However, several commentators such as Alexander (2002) believe that the procedures available under the *Family Law Act,* 1975 are not highly recommended in practice, because they are usually 'slow, expensive and not so effective' (p. 75). Under the current legislation, there are a number of possible legal remedies or procedures that exist when dealing with domestic violence cases in different jurisdictions. They include the peace compliant, state court injunctions, compensation for the injuries by way of a civil suit for damages, criminal injuries compensation, and restitution. The peace complaint is a procedure whereby "someone may complain to a magistrate or justice that violence has taken place and the violent party is then requested to enter into a recognisance (an undertaking), with or without sureties (a pledge of money), to keep the peace or be of good behaviour" (Alexander, 2002, p. 77). State court injunctions can be granted mostly in the District or Supreme Court in each State and Territory. The aim of this injunction is to stop criminal or tortuous conduct taking place. As discussed above both compensation and restitution can be sought by victims of domestic violence by way of "a civil suit for damages or an application under relevant criminal injuries legislation" (Alexander, 2002, p. 80).

In Queensland, two other relevant legislations, namely *Domestic Violence (Family Protection) Act,* 1989 and *Peace and Good Behaviour Act,* 1982 govern the domestic protection orders. These pieces of legislation ensure that law enforcement officers and several legal services should provide legal aid, legal representation, counselling and support in relation to a report of domestic violence. Further protection to those victims of rape and sexual assault (including those in a domestic violent situation) is guaranteed in Queensland (see Department of Justice and Attorney-General, 2006b). Special procedures are in place to help victims feel more secure while giving evidence at the committal or the trial. For instance, the court will usually be closed to the public except the jury during the trial. Publishing the personal details such as the home address and place of employment is prohibited. A friend or someone whom the victim trusts will be allowed to be the support person at the trial. The prosecutor may request a screen to be placed between the defendant and the victim, but this is subject to the discretion of the magistrate or judge.

## *Legal Response to Child Victims*

If child victims are called as witnesses, this can pose several challenges for them and to the court (Australian Law Reform Commission and Human Rights and Equal Opportunity Commission, 1997; Davidson, Bifulco, Thomas, & Ramsay 2006; Plotnikoff & Woolfson, 2002; Parker, 2004). Once they are inside the courtroom, children will be surrounded by unfamiliar faces and language that may be seen as strange and intimidating. Child witnesses were often questioned excessively and inappropriately by the lawyer while giving evidence (see, for example, Davidson et al. 2006). In view of this problem, Queensland amended section 21 of the *Evidence* Act, 1997 to refrain lawyers from asking improper questions which are misleading, oppressive, repetitive or intimidating. In spite of this amendment, there is evidence to show that 'children's court experiences continue to be "lessons in injustice, inhumanity and disrespect"' (Kelly, 2002, p. 368, cited in Eastwood, 2003, p. 2). In many respects, children may not be able to comprehend fully the complicated legal procedures and rules at the trial. In Eastwood's (2003) study, several child complainants of sexual abuse said that they would not report sexual abuse again, partly because of the trauma suffered associated with the court process. One of her respondents aged 14 from New South Wales said: *"It makes me feel like it is no good going to court … It is just a waste of time … They don't look after you. They couldn't care less. They are not interested … It is the hardest thing and it ruins your life. You never forget it"* (Eastwood, 2003, p. 2). Her response reflects that some of the abusive practice contravenes some of the provisions of the *United Nations Convention on the Rights of the Child* which protects the rights and dignity of children in court.

To address the effect of secondary victimization on child witnesses, the *Evidence (Protection of Children) Amendment Act,* 2003 that commenced on 5th January 2004, introduced new measures to protect the interests of the child (see O'Sullivan, 2004). The four general principles underpinning the way child witnesses are treated are:

- children to be treated with dignity and respect;
- the distress and trauma suffered by child witnesses to be minimized;
- children are not to be intimidated in cross-examination; and
- proceedings should be resolved as quick as possible (cited in O'Sullivan, 2004, p. 1).

Pre-recording evidence is available for those child witnesses under 16 years of age in Queensland. Its intention is to enable them to give their evidence recorded on videotape prior to the trial and in less stressful circumstances. Cross-examination of these child witnesses will be conducted in a separate hearing in another room where a support person may sit next to the child. It is important to note that 'the pre-recording evidence applies to criminal proceedings where there is a sexual offence or a violence offence (if there is a relationship between the child and the accused, such as being family members; or living in the same house; or if the accused had care/authority over the child on a regular basis) (cited in Department of Justice and Attorney-General, 2006c). Indeed similar arrangements have been made available in jurisdictions such as the New Territory and South Australia where child witnesses can be accompanied by a support person and preliminary hearing can be conducted by audio-visual link (Eastwood, 2003; Israel, 2003).

## *Legal Response to Victims of Juvenile Offending*

Following the passage of the *Children, Young Persons and Their Families Act,* 1989 in New Zealand, youth justice conferencing has been developed in all eight Australian states and territories (Hayes and Daly, 2003). Conferencing emphasizes the use of restorative justice principles, and one of the most important principles is to involve victims, offenders as well as the wider community in the decision making process through formal discussion (Umbreit, 1994; Barton, 2003; Johnstone, 2003; Williams, 2005). In Queensland, as set out in the *Juvenile Justice Act,* 1992, both the police and the court can refer matters they consider appropriate to community conference, for young people aged from 10 to 16 inclusive when they commit the offence. Four conditions should be met: a young person must plead guilty; the victim (if there was a victim) must give consent; a caution is inappropriate, and the matter would have otherwise been sent to court if a referral to conference was not made; and the police officer considers that a referral is more appropriate than starting a proceeding.

In most jurisdictions in Australia, evaluation studies have measured levels of satisfaction among victims and offenders in conferences as an indicator of effectiveness. It is not surprising that high levels of satisfaction with the process and outcomes were found among the participants in the actual conferences because of their greater involvement in the process (Hayes & Daly, 2003; Chui, Kidd, & Cameron, 2005; Chui, 2006). Victims are given ample opportunities to express how they felt as a result of crime and put forward their views and requests for reparation and compensation during the conference. In contrast to the traditional adversarial criminal justice model, the restorative justice model puts the victim at the centre stage and this can be empowering for victims to regain their control and heal from the trauma of the losses (Barton, 2003). Research on restorative justice conferencing evaluates its effectiveness from the participant's perspective. One Australian study conducted by Strang et al. (1999) compared conferences with courts in a randomized controlled study, and found higher reported levels of procedural fairness and sense of fairness from the conference participants than those in cases which go to court. Similar results are reported by Hayes and Daly (2003), and in addition, they found that victims saw the conferencing process as helping them to understand why the offence occurred, and thus they were less fearful of the offender and were better able to move on and put the offence behind them. However, drawing from the British experience, Williams (2005) points out that while the restorative justice programmes have their strengths, victims complained that the agreement reached was not enforced and monitored, thereby questioning whether conferencing does protect them from being victimized.

## Development of Victim Support Services in Queensland, Australia

Whilst the above section describes the establishment of legislation and a variety of legal reforms that aim at protecting and helping crime victims in Queensland. This section intends to highlight various forms of initiatives to help victims of crime recover from loss and injury. Generally speaking, there are two main measures to support victims of crime, namely victim liaison services, and counselling services and support groups.

In Queensland, the Office of the Director of Public Prosecutions has appointed victim liaison officers to help victims of violent and sexual crimes and their close family members until the end of court process. These officers give information to victims involved in the criminal justice process about the progress of their case and when the case will go to the court, and refer them to other organizations for specialized assistance such as legal aid, and support and counselling. It is hoped that the victim is well-informed about the court process with the help also from the legal officer or the Crown prosecutor (Department of Justice and Attorney-General, 2006d). In some circumstances, victims can be referred to the Department of Legal Aid to seek for assistance and legal representation or referral to a private solicitor.

Grant et al. (2003) report that in South Australia a Victims of Crime Liaison (Networking) Committee has held bi-monthly meetings to learn about the government and non-government organizations' projects for victims. These service providers mainly provide victims with counselling services and support groups for victims and their families. Similarly in Queensland, various non-governmental organizations such as Relationships Australia, Brisbane Rape and Incest Survivors Support Centre, Immigrant Women's Support Service, Esther Centre and Crisis Care offer direct counselling services to victims of crime, primarily rape and child abuse survivors (see Legal Aid Queensland, 1997). According to the Women's Infolink (2004), 'counselling can provide information, support, insight, new skills and change' (p.1) and this service is usually at no cost. In addition to counselling services from the professional, support groups are available for the victims of crime to participate in. For instance, the Queensland Homicide Victims' Support Group (QHVSG) (1997) provides support and understanding to victims of homicide. OHVSG provides immediate and on-going support for homicide survivors' state-wide with volunteer support workers reaching out to as many families as possible. By doing so it is hoped that survivors feel a sense of inclusion and normality after expressing their emotion. Furthermore, its peer support services include: initial individualized information packs, telephone and personal support contacts, court support, victim impact assistance, respite and court accommodation, emergency financial relief and counselling assistance, information and referral services, monthly newsletter, annual Memorial Day, and support meeting around the state.

In recent Australian psychological research, Yap and Devilly, (2004) highlighted that social support plays an important role in the protection of victims from the consequences of the stressful and traumatic experience. In particular, when the victim perceives having negative or no social support he or she is likely to be less resilient to the emotional and psychological consequences of their life experiences, and to experience further or repeated victimization. On the contrary, perceived positive social support can function as a mediator in the victimization-distress relationship (Yap & Devilly, 2004, p. 12). It is apparent that a much better co-ordinated service for victims as well as witnesses is urgently required to meet their needs and support them to grow out of the traumatic experience (Andrews, Brewin, & Rose, 2003).

## Conclusion

No one would dispute the fact that victims need to feel supported and protected through legislation and receive appropriate assistance to recover from the effects of crime. Victims want justice to be done in order to punish the criminal and protect the community. In recent years various social and legal reforms have been introduced nationally and implemented to further protect the rights of victims. Admittedly the impact of the legal reforms on victim protection is very difficult to measure and its effectiveness has largely remained unknown. The Canadian experience showed that it is not uncommon for the victims appearing as court witnesses to fear for their safety and being intimidated by the court process, which was especially true for children (see, for example, Bala, Lee, & McNamara, 2001). Recent research conducted in England by Crawford and Bull (2006) suggests that child victims and witnesses and their parents or caregivers benefit from support and preparation to participate in court proceedings. Likewise, based upon a domestic violence and disability local study (Radford, Harne, & Trotter, 2006) undertaken in Teeside in 2005, it was found that the police were reluctant to recognize domestic violence as a crime, and did not provide adequate support to their clients in the judicial system. Though these findings may be based on the subjective perception of the victim or the public, more research should be encouraged to validate this view. In addition, there is empirical evidence that conferencing or mediation should be further expanded to resolve dispute or conflict between the offender and the victim. One example is the youth justice conferencing that has been widely used in different parts of Australia (Chui, Kidd, & Preston, 2005). Victims not only enjoyed listening to the reasons why an offender committed an offence and telling their stories of how their criminal behaviour impacted on their life but also their satisfaction towards their cases being dealt with was very high. These positive findings may have implications for future victim-focused policy and practice.

This is still more to be done to improve the delivery and quality of victim support services. In Queensland, a number of initiatives are devoted to support women and child survivor of crime partly due to limited resources. Karmen (1990) draws our attention to other 'forgotten' groups of victims such as the elderly, victims injured and killed by drink drivers, and victims of hate crimes. Equally the needs and rights of these minority groups of victims should be addressed in a sound and responsible legal system.

## References

Alexander, R. (2002). *Domestic violence in Australia: The legal response* (3rd ed.). Annandale, NSW: Federation Press.

Andrews, B., Brewin, C. R., & Rose, S. (2003). Gender, social support and PTSD in victims of violent crime. *Journal of Traumatic Stress*, *16*(4), 421-427.

Australian Bureau of Statistics (ABS) (2004). *Information paper: Measuring crime victimisation, Australia: The impact of different collection methodologies, 2002*. Canberra, ACT: ABS.

—. (ABS) (2006). *Recorded Crime – Victims, Australia, 2005*. Canberra, ACT: ABS.

Australian Law Reform Commission (1988). *Sentencing* (Report No. 44), Canberra. ACT: Attorney General's Publication Service.

—. (2006). *Same crime, same time: Sentencing of federal offenders* (Australian Law Reform Commission Report No. 103). Sydney, NSW: Australian Law Reform Commission. Retrieved on 22nd May 2008 from http://www.austlii.edu.au/au/other/alrc/publications/reports/103/

Australian Law Reform Commission and Human Rights and Equal Opportunity Commission (1997). *Seen and Heard: Priority for children in the legal process* (Report No. 84). Canberra, ACT: Attorney General's Publication Service.

Bala, N., Lee, J., & McNamara, E. (2001). Children as witness: Understanding their capacities, needs and experiences. *Journal of Social Distress and the Homeless*, *10*(1), 41-68.

Barton, C. K. B. (2003). *Restorative Justice: The empowerment model.* Annandale, NSW: Federation Press.

Boles, A. B., & Patterson, J. C. (1997). *Improving community response to crime victims: An eight-step model for developing protocol.* Thousand Oaks, CA: Sage.

Carter, G. (2004) *Australian Law for the 21st Century*. Ashfield, NSW: Wensleydale.

Chui, W. H. (2004). Book review – Domestic Violence in Australia: The Legal Response (3rd ed.) (Alexander, 2002). *Journal of Family Studies*, *10*(1), 124-125.

Chui, W. H., Kidd, J., & Preston, C. (2005). Treatment of child and juvenile offenders in Queensland, Australia: Alternatives to prosecution. In T. W. Lo, D. Wong, & G. Maxwell (Eds.), *Alternatives to Prosecution: Rehabilitative and Restorative Models of Youth Justice* (pp.171-205). Singapore: Marshall Cavendish Academic.

Chui, W.H. (2006). Young offenders. In W.H. Chui & J. Wilson (Eds.), *Social Work and Human Services Best Practice* (pp.27-55). Annandale, NSW: Federation Press.

Cook, B., David, F., & Grant, A. (1999). *Victim's needs, victim's rights: Policies programs for victims of crime in Australia*. Canberra, ACT: Australian Institute of Criminology.

Crawford, E., & Bull, R. (2006). Child witness support and preparation: Are parents/caregivers ignored? *Child Abuse Review*, *15* (4), 243-256.

Davidson, J., Bifulco, A., Thomas, G., & Ramsay, M. (2006). Child victims of sexual abuse: Children's experience of the investigative process in the criminal justice system. *Practice*, *18*(4), 247-263.

Department of Justice and Attorney-General (2004). *Compensation for victims of crime*, Brisbane, QLD: Department of Justice and Attorney-General. Retrieved on 22nd May 2008 from http://www.justice.qld.gov.au/courts/about/compo.htm#1

—. (2006a). *Making a victim impact statement*, Brisbane, QLD: Department of Justice and Attorney-General. Retrieved on 22nd May 2008 from http://www.justice.qld.gov.au/odpp/L04vis.htm#1

—. (2006b). *More Information for victims of rape and sexual assault*, Brisbane, QLD: Department of Justice and Attorney-General. Retrieved on 22nd May 2008 from http://www.justice.qld.gov.au/odpp/L05victims.htm

—. (2006c). *Children giving evidence via pre-recording: Information for parents*, Brisbane, QLD: Department of Justice and Attorney-General. Retrieved on 22nd May 2008 from http://www.justice.qld.gov.au/odpp/C16childEvidence.htm

—. (2006d). *The work of the office of the director of public prosecutions*, Brisbane, QLD: Department of Justice and Attorney-General. Retrieved on 22nd May 2008 from http://www.justice.qld.gov.au/odpp/C05odpp.htm

Dignan, J. (2005). *Understanding victims and restorative justice*. Berkshire: Open University Press.

Doak, J. (2005). Victims' rights in criminal trials: Prospects for participation. *Journal of Law and Society*, *32* (2), 294-316.

Eastwood, C. (2003). *The experiences of child complainants of sexual abuse in the criminal justice system* (Trends and Issues in Crime and Criminal Justice No. 250), Canberra, ACT: Australian Institute of Criminology.

Edwards, I. (2001). Victim participation in sentencing: The problems of incoherence. *Howard Journal of Criminal Justice*, *40*(1), 39-54.

—. (2002). The place of victims' preferences in the sentencing of "their' offenders. *Criminal Law Review*, September, 689-702.

Erez, E. (1991). *Victim Impacts Statement* (Trends and Issues in Crime and Criminal Justice No. 33), Canberra, ACT: Australian Institute of Criminology.

Forsterlee, L., Fox, G. B., Forsterlee, R., & Ho, R. (2004). The effects of a victim impact statement and gender on juror information processing in a criminal trial: Does the punishment fit the crime? *Australian Psychologist*, *39*(1), 57-67.

Goodey, J. (2005). *Victims and victimology: Research, policy and practice*. Harlow, Essex: Pearson.

Grant, A., David, F., & Cook, B. (2002). Victims of crime. In A. Graycar & P. Grabosky (Eds.), *The Cambridge handbook of Australian criminology* (pp.281-293). Cambridge: Cambridge University Press.

Hayes, H., & Daly, K. (2003). Youth justice conferencing and re-offending. *Justice Quarterly*, *20*(4), 725-764.

Home Office. (2002). *Justice for All*. London: Home Office.

Israel, M. (2003). Victims and criminal justice. In A. Goldsmith, M. Israel & K. Daly (Eds.), *Crime and Justice: An Australian textbook in criminology* (pp.351-370). Pyrmont, NSW: Lawbook Co.
Johnson, H. (2005). *Crime victimisation in Australia: Key results of the 2004 international crime victimisation survey* (Research and Public Policy Series No. 64), Canberra, ACT: Institute of Criminology.
Johnstone, G. (Ed.), (2003). *A restorative justice reader: Texts, sources, context*. Cullompton, Devon: Willan.
Karmen, A. (1990). *Crime victims: An introduction to victimology.* (2nd ed.), Pacific Grove, CA: Brooks/Cole.
Kelly, D. P., & Erez, E. (1997). Victim participation in the criminal justice system. In R. C. Davis, A. J. Lurigio, & W. G. Skogan (Eds.), *Victims of Crime* (2nd ed.) (pp.231-244). Thousand Oaks, CA: Sage.
Kelly, L. (2002). Remembering the point: A feminist perspective on children's evidence. In H. Westcott, G. Davies & R. Bull (Eds.), *Children's Testimony: A handbook of psychological research and forensic practice* (pp.361-376). Chichester: John Wiley & Sons.
Kilpatrick, D. G., Saunders, B. E., Veronen, L. J., Best, C. L., & Von, J. M. (1987). Criminal victimization: Lifetime prevalence, reporting to police, and psychological impact. *Crime and Delinquency*, *33*(4), 379-389.
Laub, J. H. (1999) Patterns of criminal victimization in the United States. In R. C. Davis, A. J. Lurigio & W. G. Skogan (Eds.), *Victims of crime* (2nd ed.) (pp.9-26). Thousand Oaks, CA: Sage.
Lees, S. (1996). *Carnal knowledge: Rape on trials*. London: Hamish Hamilton.
Legal Aid Queensland (1997). *Victims of crime*. Brisbane, QLD: Legal Aid Queensland. Retrieved on 22nd May 2008 from http://www.legalaid.qld.gov.au/search/default.asp?query=victims&catalogButton=entirewww&resultsPerPage=15&submit=Search
Lurigio, A. J., Skogan, W. G., & Davis, R. C. (Eds.), (1990). *Victims of Crime: Problems, Policies, and Programs*. Newbury Park, CA: Sage.
Mawby, R. I., & Walklate, S. (1994). *Critical victimology*. London: Sage.
Mayhew, P. (1995). Some methodological issues in victimization surveys. In Criminal Justice Commission (Ed.), *Crime victims surveys in Australia* (Proceedings of a Conference held at Griffith University 28–29 November 1994). Brisbane, QLD: The Print People.
New South Wales Task Force on Services for Victims of Crime (1987). *Report and recommendations*, Sydney: Attorney-General's Department.
Newburn, T. (1993). *The long-term needs of victims: A review of literature* (Research and Planning Paper 80). London: Home Office.

Office of Economic and Statistical Research (2001). *Queensland crime victimisation survey 2000*. Brisbane, QLD: Queensland Government.
O'Sullivan, H. (2004). Child witnesses: Queensland reforms – An overview. Paper presented at the *Child witnesses – Best practice for courts conference*. Retrieved on 22nd May 2008 from http://www.aija.org.au/child/O'Sullivan.rtf
Parker, K. (2004). Challenges in preparing child witnesses to give evidence in court. Paper presented at the *Child witnesses – Best practice for courts conference*. Retrieved on 22nd May 2008 from http://www.aija.org.au/child/papers.htm
Plotnikoff, J., & Woolfson, R. (2002). What do judges know about young witnesses? In H. Westcott, G. Davies & R. Bull (Eds.), *Children's Testimony: A Handbook of Psychological Research and Forensic Practice* (pp. 295-307). Chichester: John Wiley & Sons.
President's Task Force on Victims of Crime (1982). *Final report*. Washington, DC: Government Printing Office.
Queensland Homicide Victims' Support Group (1997). Homepage of Queensland Homicide Victims' Support Group. Retrieved on 22nd May 2008 from http://qhvsg.org.au/index.html
Radford, J., Harne, L., & Trotter, J. (2006). Disabled women and domestic violence as violent crime. *Practice*, *18*(4), 233-246.
Sanders, A., Coyle, C., Morgan, R., & Cape, E. (2001). Victim impact statements: Don't work, can't work. *Criminal Law Review*, June, 447-458.
Strang, H., Barnes, G., Braithwaite, J., & Sherman, L. (1999). *Experiments in restorative policing: A progress report on the canberra reintegrative shaming experiments (RISE)*. Canberra, ACT: Australian Federal Police and Australian National University. Retrieved on 22nd May 2008 from http://www.aic.gov.au/rjustice/rise/progress/1999.html
Spalek, B. (2006). *Crime victims: Theory, policy and practice*, Basingstoke: Palgrave Macmillan.
Tapley, J. (2005). Improving confidence in criminal justice: Achieving community justice for victims and witnesses. In J. Winstone & F. Pakes (Eds.), *Community Justice: Issues for probation and criminal justice* (pp. 237-256). Cullompton, Devon: Willan.
Umbreit, M. S. (1994). *Victims meet offenders: The impact of restorative justice and mediation*. Monsey, New York: Criminal Justice Press.
Williams, B. (2005). *Victims of crime and community justice*. London: Jessica Kingsley.
Women's Infolink (2004). *Women and counselling: A consumer guide*. Brisbane, QLD: Queensland Government.

Wright, S. (2006). Aussies 'most likely' crime victims. *Courier Mail* (28/03/2006). Retrieved on 22nd May 2008 from http://www.couriermail.news.com.au/story/0,20797,186378895003402,00.html

Yap, M. B. H., & Devilly, G. J. (2004). The role of perceived social support in crime victimization. *Clinical Psychology Review*, *24*(1), 1-14.

## Legislation Cited

*Children, Young Persons and Their Families Act, 1989 (New Zealand)*
*Crimes (Sentencing) Act, 2005 (Australian Capital Territory)*
*Crimes (Sentencing Procedure) Act, 1999 (New South Wales)*
*Criminal Code (Qld)*
*Criminal Law (Sentencing) Act, 1988 (South Australia)*
*Criminal Offence Victims Act, 1995 (Qld)*
*Domestic Violence (Family Protection) Act, 1989 (Qld)*
*Evidence Act, 1997 (Qld)*
*Evidence (Protection of Children) Amendment Act, 2003 (Qld)*
*Family Law Act, 1975 (Commonwealth)*
*Juvenile Justice Act 1992 (Qld)*
*Peace and Good Behaviour Act, 1982 (Qld)*
*Penalties and Sentences Act, 1992 (Qld)*
*Sentencing Act, 1991 (Victoria)*
*Sentencing Act, 1995 (Northern Territory)*
*Sentencing Act, 1995 (Western Australia)*
*Sentencing Act, 1997 (Tasmania)*
*United Nations Convention on the Rights of the Child, 1989*
*Victim Impact Statement (Amendment) Act, 1998 (South Australia)*

# CHAPTER SEVENTEEN

# ANTI-TRAFFICKING INTERVENTIONS IN INDIA: TOWARDS THE EXPLICATION OF AN EMPOWERED CHILD IN TAMIL NADU

P. MADHAVA SOMA SUNDARAM AND M.D. ALLEN SELVA KUMAR

## Abstract

Child protection has become an increasingly serious issue, rising concerns worldwide. Today, child trafficking, has plagued countries worldwide, either as country of origin, as country of transition or as country of destination. Indian States and Union Territories are not an exception. Anti-child trafficking is certainly one of the most difficult tasks due to several reasons. Considering children react differently as victims than adults in these situations, the magnitude of this business is impossible to conclude to. Preventing child trafficking is not the responsibility of one group nor is it the responsibility of the states of origins. In fact, child trafficking can only be prevented if all stakeholders who are affected participate in the combat. The national level, regional level, and state level stakeholders need to work together on an equal basis and understand the work being done at individual levels. This is also true for the different actors within the levels whether it is international organization, government representatives or civil society. Therefore, this chapter looks at some ideas on how child trafficking can be combated in India, based on few empirical studies.

## Introduction

Trafficking of human beings is one of the most lucrative and rapidly growing transnational crimes, which generates billions of rupee equivalents per year. In response to the intensive legal and political efforts to combat drug trafficking, criminal networks involved in the drug trade are increasingly diverting resources to the development of human trafficking networks (Heyzer, 1994; Ruggiero, 1997). Simply put, the 'cost' of buying and selling human beings is not very high, and the risks taken are considerably lower than that of trafficking drugs or arms. All countries, whether trafficking is taking place through, from, into or within their borders, must take immediate measures to end this harmful practice.

## What is Trafficking?

Trafficking was first defined in international law through the United Nations Protocol to prevent, suppress and punish trafficking of human beings, especially women and children supplementing the United Nations Convention against Transnational Organized Crime (2000). Known as the 'Palermo Protocol' or the 'Trafficking Protocol', this is the most widely endorsed definition of trafficking and provides an essential basis for national law reform.

### Definition of Trafficking

a) Trafficking in persons shall mean the recruitment, transportation, transfer, harboring or receipt of persons, by means of threat or use of force or other forms of coercion, of abduction, of fraud, of deception, of the abuse of power or of a position of vulnerability, or of the giving or receiving of payments or benefits to achieve the consent of a person having control over another person, for the purpose of exploitation. Exploitation shall include, at a minimum, the exploitation of the prostitution of others or other forms of sexual exploitation, forced labour or services, slavery or practices similar to slavery, servitude or the removal of organs;
b) The consent of a victim of trafficking in persons to the intended exploitation set forth in subparagraph (a) of this article shall be irrelevant where any of the means set forth in subparagraph (b) have been used;
c) The recruitment, transportation, transfer, harbouring or receipt of a child for the purpose of exploitation shall be considered 'trafficking in persons' even if this does not involve any of the means set forth in subparagraph (a) of this article;
d) 'Child' shall mean any person under eighteen years of age. (United Nations, 2000, p. 2)

The definition clearly states that "threat or use of force or other forms of coercion, of abduction, of fraud, of deception, of the abuse of power or of a position of vulnerability, or of the giving or receiving of payments or benefits to achieve the consent of a person having control over another person" is not required to constitute child trafficking.

The Amendment proposed by the Ministry of Women & Child Development, Government of India, to the Immoral Traffic (Prevention) Act, 1956 will include the definition of the UN Protocol to Prevent, Suppress, and Punish Trafficking in Persons, especially Women and Children.

## Child Trafficking: An Overview

The last decade saw an unprecedented level of international concern over the trafficking of human beings, including awareness on the trafficking and exploitation of children. Today, trafficking of children is recognized as a distinct and egregious violation of children rights comprising one of the worst forms of child labour. It is a growing problem that affects millions of children and families in many countries around the world. Unchecked, trafficking will continue to grow. Combating it, however, will require an intensive, collective effort on many levels. For example, women and children from Nepal and Bangladesh are trafficked to India both because of proximity and high demand in the sex industry. Similarly, in South-East Asia, many children are trafficked into Thailand from Myanmar and Laos.

Trafficking is not a discrete act. In fact, it is a combination or series of events that takes place in a child's home, community, at transit points and at final destinations. It can occur within one country, across national borders or between regions and involves several or more actors. While trafficking patterns vary, it is relatively common for children from rural areas to be trafficked for exploitation in urban centres and for children from poor countries to be trafficked to wealthier neighbouring countries and beyond. Many different actors are involved in the trafficking process, including recruiters, intermediaries, transporters, employers, brothel/inn operators, and even family members. Various means may be used to entrap victims, including persuasion, deception, threats and coercion. Sometimes it is the children themselves or their families who take the initiative to migrate and approach recruiters.

## The Chain of Trafficking: The Dynamics

There are two main parts in the process of child trafficking.

- Firstly, when children are trafficked for different purposes

- Secondly, when children are caught by the police and brought into detention and are then possibly re-integrated.

In the chain of trafficking children the first part is guaranteed but the second is not always necessary as many children are being unaccounted for. The unknown number of children might be twice as high than the known numbers. Globally it is estimated that around million children are being trafficked but the numbers might suggest that there are even 2 million if not more (ILO-IPEC, 2002).

Within the first part of the trafficking chain there are several sub-parts, which make up the actual process of the crime trafficking. They are:

- Recruitment of the children in their places of origin
- Smuggling of the child to the destination
- Exploitation of the child in the places of destination by several means, although numbers already show that 40% of the countries of destination are at the same time countries of transit.

## The Trafficking of Children, Definitions and International Instruments

United Nations has repeatedly discussed the problems of Child Trafficking in its various conventions and has brought an array of instruments to deal with trafficking at a global level. The details of these conventions are:

- The Universal Declaration of Human Rights, 1948.
- Convention for the Suppression of the Traffic in Persons and of the Exploitation of the Prostitution of Others, 1949 (Approved by the General Assembly Resolutions to 317 (IV) on December 2, 1949).
- The Supplementary Convention on the Abolition of Slavery, Slave Trade and Institutions and Practices Similar to Slavery, 1957.
- Declaration on the Elimination of Discrimination against Women, 1967.
- Convention on the Elimination of All forms of Discrimination against Women, 1979 (CEDAW) (Ratified on April 22, 1991).
- UN Convention on the Rights of the Child, 1989 (Ratified, 1990).
- World Conference of Human Rights, 1993.
- International Conference of Population and Development, Copenhagen, 1994.
- World Conference of Women, Beijing, 1995.

- International Covenant on Civil and Political Rights (ICCPR), 1996.
- World Conference on Population Development, Copenhagen, 1996.
- World Congress against Commercial Sexual Exploitation of Children (Draft Declaration), August 29, 1996.
- Joint Action to Further Enhance the Protection of Children or Combat Trafficking in Human Beings, Brussels, 24 February, 1997.
- United Nations Convention against Trans-national Organized Crime and the attached UN Protocol to Prevent, Suppress and Punish Trafficking in Persons, especially Women and Children, 2000.

The International Labour Organization (ILO) has also contributed to the field of trafficking in person through various documents and some of the important ones as given below:

- Weekly Rest (Industry) Convention, 1921 (No. 21).
- Equal Remuneration Convention, 1951 (N0. 100).
- Discrimination (Employment & Occupation) Convention, 1958, (No. 111).
- Minimum Wage Fixing Convention, 1970 (No. 131).
- Minimum Age Convention, 1973 (No. 138).
- Freedom of Association, (No. 98).
- The Tripartite Consultation (International Labour Standards) Convention, 1976 (No. 144).
- Forced Labour Convention, (No. 29).
- Abolition of Forced Labour Convention, (No. 105).
- Prohibition and Immediate Action for the Elimination of the Worst Forms of Child Labour, Geneva, 1999 (No. 182)

Reaching international accord on the scope of a mere definition has been as complex as the issue itself. The older international legal instruments were criticized both for their narrow focus on prostitution and for failing to protect children. Negotiations on the *UN Protocol to Prevent, Suppress and Punish Trafficking in Persons, especially Women and Children (2000)* dwelled extensively on the question of whether there can be trafficking without coercion of the victim. The answer matters because it determines the criminal liability of the perpetrator or, more particularly, whether or not the penalties and measures proposed in the overarching *UN*

*Convention on Transnational Organized Crime* apply to a particular situation.

The Trafficking Instruments have made a very significant contribution to conceptual clarification around the issue of trafficking in human beings. The definition of 'trafficking in persons' in the Protocol clarifies the distinction between trafficking, and migrant smuggling, the latter being the subject of a separate Protocol to the Convention. The essence of a trafficking operation, as opposed to one of smuggling, is the element of deceit or coercion, and that the ultimate purpose is the exploitation of one person by another. Border crossing is not even an essential element of the crime, because it is the international organized crime that is being targeted by the instruments, rather than the individual movements of victims.

In relation to children, namely persons under the age of 18, the Trafficking Protocol considers them victims of trafficking once they were recruited, transported, transferred, harboured or received for the purposes of exploitation. Whereas an adult victim would have to show some form of coercion or deceit to demonstrate that they did not give an informed consent to the operation, and thus qualify as a victim of trafficking, a child does not have to show any such coercive 'means' to vitiate their consent. The consent of a child, or the means to attain such consent, is irrelevant, as long as the overall objective of the operation is the exploitation of the child (Gandhi, 2000). This distinction in the Protocol for children is extremely significant, because it means that not only are young people under the age of 18 entitled to qualify as 'victims', but also that any action in the chain of the movement of a child can be considered as a trafficking operation, and the responsible person can be categorized as a trafficker, where exploitation is the ultimate result. It even means that families and relatives can be traffickers of their own children or other family members, if the child is exploited.

## UN Convention on the Rights of the Child (CRC)

Because trafficking involves serious violations of children's rights, the 1989 *UN Convention on the Rights of the Child* (CRC) is highly relevant and applicable. Although the CRC neither defines "trafficking" nor addresses it as a specific issue, it spells out a clear rights-based approach that serves as an invaluable guide for action to combat trafficking and protect vulnerable children. In dealing with any children's rights issue, the CRC uses a protection framework built on its overarching call for the child to be considered the subject, not object, of rights and of all rights simultaneously. Article 32 of the CRC stipulates the "right of the child to be protected from economic exploitation and from performing any work that is likely to be hazardous or to interfere with the child's education, or to be harmful to the child's health or physical, mental, spiritual, moral or social development". Articles 9, 10 and 11 also have provisions for illicit movement of the child. Article 34 calls on States Parties 'to protect the child from all forms of sexual exploitation and sexual abuse…[including] the inducement of coercion of a child to engage in prostitution or other unlawful sexual practices', and Article 35 aims to protect children from being treated as chattels. The Optional Protocol, which came into effect in October 2001, explicitly relates to the prostitution of and trafficking in children, although it does not attempt to define trafficking.

## UN Protocol to Prevent, Suppress and Punish Trafficking in Persons, Especially Women and Children

The separate *UN Protocol to Prevent, Suppress and Punish Trafficking in Persons, Especially Women and Children* adopted in December 2000 represent a direct attempt at comprehensively defining "trafficking" in international law. Responding to growing organized criminal involvement in trafficking in persons, this Protocol was designed as a tool for combating cross border trafficking through judicial and law enforcement means. It supplements the United Nations Convention against Transnational Organized Crime and emphasizes the creation of effective legal and law enforcement frameworks and responses. These include:

- The criminalizing of traffickers, not victims,
- Protection of victims from re-victimization,
- Sanctioning of individuals and organizations involved in trafficking, and
- Promotion of child-friendly procedures for securing testimony.

The Protocol provides the current internationally accepted definition (provided earlier in this chapter) of trafficking developed in consultation with governments and a wide range of international organizations working in the field of human rights. The Protocol points out that, as far as children (i.e. under 18) are concerned, "recruitment, transportation, transfer, harbouring or receipt of a child for the purpose of exploitation shall be considered 'trafficking in persons' even if this does not involve any of the means set forth in [the definition]". In line with *ILO Worst Forms of Child Labour Convention (182)*, it specifies that "exploitation" shall include "forced labour or services, slavery or practices similar to slavery [or] servitude".

## National Instruments and Constitutional Provisions

The Constitution of India provides several provisions for protection, development and welfare of children. Article 24 prohibits the children's employment in any factory or mine or in any other hazardous occupation. Article 39 (e) and (f) lay down that the State shall direct its policy in such a manner that the tender age of the children is not abused, children are given opportunities to develop in a healthy manner and childhood is protected against exploitation and against moral and material abandonment.

While commercial sexual exploitation remains the predominant form of exploitation of trafficked children, a number of recent studies in Asia and Central and West Africa indicate that children are very often trafficked for other forms of labour exploitation as well. The children trafficked are generally relegated to the '3 D jobs' – Dirty, Difficult and Dangerous jobs. These include domestic service, armed conflict, services (restaurants, bars) and various other hazardous forms of work (factories, agriculture, construction, fishing, begging, etc). It has also been found that exploitation of trafficked children can be progressive, e.g. those trafficked for work in factories, domestic service or restaurants may be later forced into prostitution; or children trafficked for prostitution may be resold more than once.

The trafficking of children is a result of a demand for cheap and malleable labour in general and a demand for young girls and boys by the fast growing commercial sex sector in particular. There are many supply factors that encourage trafficking of children. Among the most prevalent are,, poverty and the desire to earn a living or help support the family, lack of education and schools, political conflict and natural disasters that devastate local economies, cultural attitudes toward children and girls in particular, and inadequate local laws and regulations.

Children are often abducted, trafficked away, and deprived of the promised better future. Cross-border trafficking is distinguished from mere immigrant-smuggling by the degree of coercion, deception and exploitation. Under international law, trafficking is a crime involving the movement of persons and their exploitation. The exploitation can take several different forms: forced labour, prostitution and in some cases forced conscription. According to the International Labor Organization (ILO-IPEC, 2002), for instance, close to 200,000 foreign children were trafficked into Thailand in 1996.

If child exploitation has not been studied much, there exists, however, a large literature on child labour, both theoretical and empirical. The theoretical literature was initiated by the seminal work of Basu and Hoang

Van (1998). Among the contributors are Ranjan (1999, 2001), Basu (1999, 2000), Dessy (2000), Dessy and Pallage (2001, 2002), Dessy and Vencatachellum (2003). The empirical literature was started somewhat earlier, with the works of Grootaert and Kanbur (1995), and Canagarajah and Coulombe (1997). Studies concentrated on the concept and abusive aspects of Child Labour & Child Trafficking (see: Baland, 2000; Behrman, 1999; Dessey, 2002; Barry, 1981; Beiguelman, 1978; Ghosh, 1998; Heyzer et. al., 1994; Ruggiero, 1997)

Apart from the International level, many conventions have been arranged at the regional level to deal with trafficking in persons. Since regional cooperation plays an important role in prevention and investigation of trafficking, Countries in the in the South Asian region have taken the issue seriously and have come up with various conventions. Some of these SAARC conventions are given below.

- The Colombo Resolution on Children, 1992.
- Rawalpindi Resolution on Children of South Asia, August 20-22, 1996.
- Declaration of the Ninth SAARC Summit, Male, 1997.
- Colombo Declaration, Tenth SARRC Summit, 1998.

## Preventing Child Trafficking - International Level

The international community, especially the specialized agencies of the United Nations is involved in formulating international standards for preventing child trafficking. Still, there are some difficulties as child trafficking can be tackled from many different angles. After all, these different aspects include the human rights aspect, the aspect of rights for children, the crime aspect, the health aspect (as many children might be infected with sexually transmitted diseases like AIDS when doing their job), the aspect of forced labour and many others (Alfredsson, 1999; Barry, 1981; Brownlie, 1981). Consequently, there are a number of UN organizations dealing with the issue of trafficking in children. These organizations include:

- UN Office on Drugs and Crime (UNODC)-dealing with the technical aspects of the crime of child trafficking such as drawing up of international legislative standards,
- Commission on Human Rights (CHR)-dealing with the human rights aspects. The Right of the Child Convention falls within this organization,
- International Labour Organization (ILO)-dealing with forced labour and child labour,

- UN Development Program (UNDP)-dealing with the development aspect of the issue, as many children are coming from developing countries and countries with economies in transition. But the UNDP is also working on training manuals for the police,
- World Health Organization (WHO)-dealing with the issue of diseases that children might get when being forced to work as prostitutes,
- UN International Children Fund (UNICEF)-dealing with the issue of children itself.

Keeping this list in mind, it becomes clear that dealing with the issue on the international level is quite diverse. Looking at one of the most important parts of the problem, the UN Convention on Transnational Organized Crime should be emphasized on.

## Preventing Child Trafficking – National Level

At the National level, in India, though there is no exclusive law to deal with Child Trafficking, the existing substantive law, namely, the Indian Penal Code (IPC) has many sections, which focus specific aspects related to child trafficking. The following table gives the details.

**Table 1: IPC Sections that cover some aspects of Child Trafficking**

| IPC Section | Offence |
|---|---|
| Section 361 | Kidnapping from lawful guardianship – enacting of a male less than 16 years of age or a female under 18 years of age, or a person of unsound mind from custody of a lawful guardian without consent of guardian. |
| Section 362 | Abduction – compelling or inducing of a person by force or deceit to go from any place. (Abduction is in relation to any person ) |
| Section 363A | Kidnapping or maiming a minor for purpose of begging. |
| Section 366 A | Inducing of a minor girl under 18 years of age to do any act that may force or seduce her to illicit intercourse with another person. |
| Section 366 B | Importing a girl under 21 years age into India from outside India or from Jammu and Kashmir with the intent that she may be forced or seduced to illicit intercourse with another person. |
| Section 369 | Kidnapping or abducting a child less than 10 years with |

| | |
|---|---|
| | intention to steal from the child. |
| Section 372 | Selling or hiring a person under 18 years of age or purpose of prostitution or illicit intercourse with any person or any unlawful or immoral purpose |
| Section 373 | Buying or hiring a person less than 18 years of age for purpose of prostitution or illicit intercourse with any unlawful or immoral purpose. |
| Section 374 | Unlawfully compelling a person to labour against his/her will. |
| Section 376 | Sexual intercourse by a man with / with out consent of the girl under 16 years of age. |

Within the IPC section, there are other social legislations, which deal with some aspects of child trafficking. Some of these legislations are given below

- The Child Marriage Restraint Act, 1929
- The Immoral Traffic (Prevention) Act, 1956
- The Bonded Labour System (Abolition) Act, 1976
- Child Labour (Prohibition and Regulation) Act, 1986
- The SC/ST (Prevention of Atrocities) Act, 1989
- The Juvenile Justice (Care and Protection of Children) Act, 2000

The Government of India, in its recent initiative, is in the process of amending the Immoral Traffic (Prevention) Act, 1956. Some of the major changes that the Ministry of Women and Child Development, Government of India, are trying to make are:

- A comprehensive definition of trafficking as per the UN instruments.
- Provisions for confiscation of property and assets of traffickers and other related agents
- Provision providing protective mechanisms, immunities and safeguards for the members of voluntary agencies who take initiatives for preventing, trafficking, facilitating rescue or carrying out victim's protection activities to be included in consultation with the Ministry of Law and Justice.
- The words 'his' and 'her' wherever occur in the Act to be substituted by a gender-neutral word for example 'person' so as to cover both sexes.

## International Response Mechanisms vs. National Response Mechanisms

Summarizing the different mechanisms on both the international and national level, the important question is, is it possible to prioritize one over the other or they are important in their own respective ways? The answer to that is simple and complicated at the same time. If it were not necessary to have international and national mechanisms at the same time nobody would pay for them.

Eventually, international mechanisms that come in the form of International Conventions such as the UN Conventions against Transnational Organized Crime are very much essential. Without discussing the issue on the international level countries that fail to react to combating child trafficking might get away to formulize it in a lesser way.

The formulation of international standards and norms in the form of International Conventions gives the countries an opportunity to exchange their experiences. Best practices can be put to good use. From these conventions those countries that are really willing to combat child trafficking are then able to integrate these norms into their national legislations.

International Conventions become ineffective if they are not monitored properly. After all, it is those countries that clearly have a problem with child trafficking that are very often denying that they have one. They might then sign and ratify the International Convention on Transnational Organized Crime but are not really serious about implementing the standards, mentioned in the instruments. For that, it needs monitoring mechanisms. It is certainly not enough, as with many other issues, to hope that countries are always willing to implement conventions voluntarily.

These national authorities are then an essential factor as they are the actual implementers of the international standards. Sometimes, these national actors might not even be aware that they are actually implementing standards that were agreed upon at International Conventions before. Eventually though, they are doing the actual fieldwork. The more local the level gets the more actors are working within the frameworks of the legislations right above them knowing exactly those laws and legislations.

Considering the background and the other issues connected with it in the foregoing paragraphs, it is important to look at the impact of trafficking on children in India.

## Children in Tamil Nadu: A Snap Shot

There are about 227 lakh persons under the age of 19 Years (age as per census classification), in Tamil Nadu. Of this 115.68 lakhs are males and 111.224 lakhs are females. Table 1 shows the data as per the different age groups.

**Table 2.Child population by different age groups**

| Child Population | Males | Females | Total | India |
|---|---|---|---|---|
| 0-4 Years | 26.784 | 25.473 | 52.257 | 1023.780 |
| 5-9 Years | 30.393 | 29.275 | 59.669 | 1112.947 |
| 10-14 Years | 30.728 | 28.394 | 60.124 | 886.918 |
| 15-19 years | 27.775 | 28.082 | 55.856 | 790.349 |
| **Total** | **115.68** | **111.224** | **227.906** | **3813.994** |

Source: Ministry of Women and Child Development
*All Figures are in Lakhs* (100,000)

## Studies in Tamil Nadu on Trafficking

Tamil Nadu covers an area of 130,058 km,[2] and is the eleventh largest State in India. The western and northern regions of the state have lofty hills while the eastern and southern are coastal plains. Tamil Nadu has a coastline of about 1000 km which forms about 18% of the country's coastline (third longest). The major administrative units of the state constitutes 39 Lok Sabha constituencies, 234 Assembly constituencies, 30 districts, 8 municipal corporations, 152 municipalities, 561 town panchayats and 12,618 village panchayats. Tamil Nadu is the sixth most populous state in India with a population of 62,405,679 as of March 1, 2001 (approximately 6.05% of India's population). It is the eleventh most densely populated State in India. In 2001, its population density was 478 persons per square kilometre, having increased from 429 in 1991, significantly higher than the Indian average of 324 persons per square kilometre, approximately 47% of Tamil Nadu's population live in urban areas, one of the highest percentages in India. Tamil Nadu's population grew by 11.19% between 1991 and 2001; the second lowest rate for that period (after Kerala) amongst populous states (States whose population exceeded 20 million in 2001). Its decadal rate of population growth has declined for every decade since 1971, one of only three populous states (along with Kerala and Orissa) to show this trend. While there are some studies on the international trafficking of persons, especially to and from India, there is a paucity of research on these lines within Tamil Nadu. This chapter heavily relies on two researches that concentrated in Tamil Nadu. One was a part of a national level study by Sen and Nair (2004), which collected data from Tamil Nadu, also. The other was a study of rehabilitated victims of trafficking in Tirunelveli district in Tamil Nadu.

The National level study was conducted by Sen and Nair (2004), which analyzed the dimensions of the flow of persons, trafficked in various States in India. The flow also indicated the movement of traffickers. It is seen that maximum percentage of interviewed women and children have been trafficked from the states of Andhra Pradesh (25.9 per cent), Karnataka (15 per cent), West Bengal (12.5 per cent) and Tamil Nadu (12.3 per cent). In most states, intra-state trafficking is a common phenomenon. This is particularly true for a state like Tamil Nadu, where, out of a total of 156 interviewed trafficked victims, 148 (94.8 per cent) had been subjected to intrastate trafficking. Similarly, in Rajasthan, intra-state trafficking is 88.5 per cent, followed by Assam and Meghalaya at 88.4 per cent, Bihar at 80.26 per cent, and Uttar Pradesh at 73.5 per cent.

According to a study (Ambeth Selvi & Soma Sundaram, 2006), as per the version of the traffickers, the districts listed as source areas by the traffickers include Dindugal, Madurai, Trichy and Chengelpet in Tamil Nadu. The traffickers were also, asked to list the places where they supply trafficked women and girls. It is important to note that the demand areas include not only cities but also smaller towns. The places mentioned by the traffickers include Tindivanam, Dindugal, Madurai and Salem in Tamil Nadu.

Sen and Nair (2004) also analyzed the inflow of trafficked women and children into Tamil Nadu. The in-flow chart shows that in most of the states, trafficking within the state is quite high. This is true for states like Andhra Pradesh, Rajasthan, Uttar Pradesh, Assam and Meghalaya, Karnataka, Tamil Nadu, and West Bengal. On the other hand, there are a few exceptions like Delhi and Goa where intra-state trafficking is very minimal, with only 0.4 percentage and 0.6 percentage respectively.

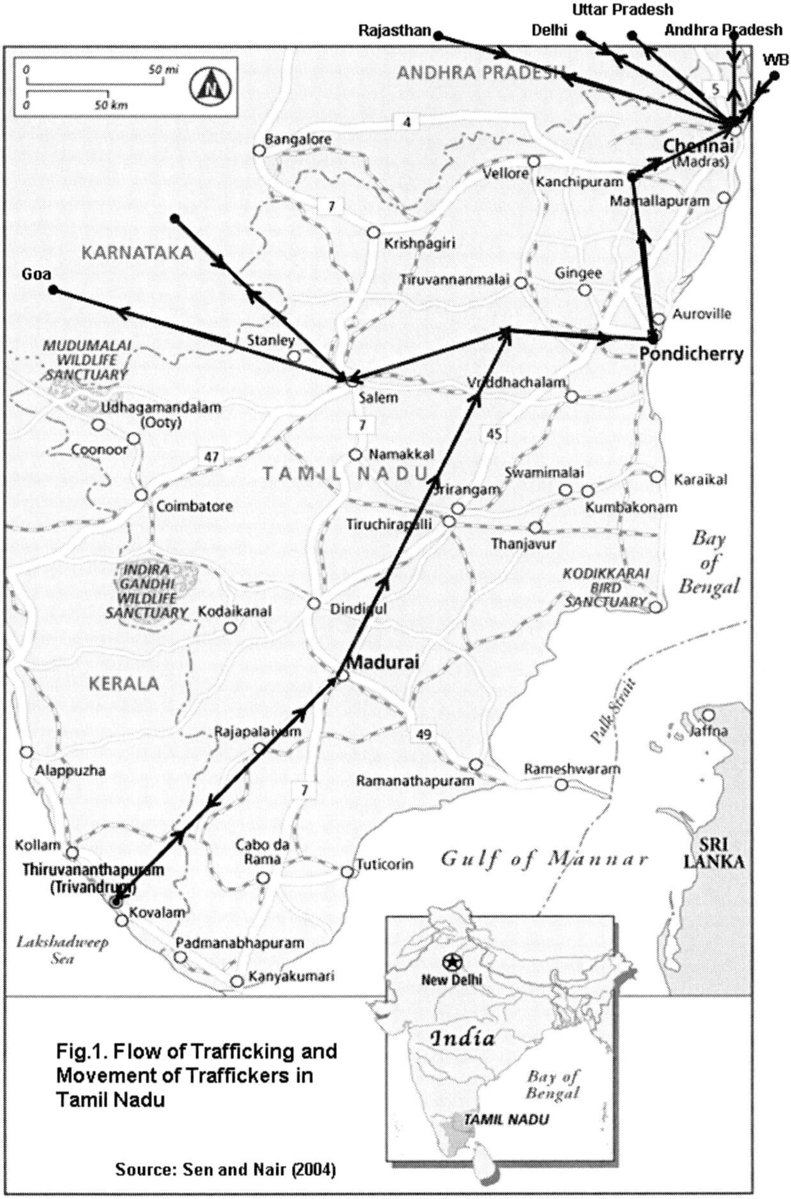


Fig.1. Flow of Trafficking and Movement of Traffickers in Tamil Nadu

Source: Sen and Nair (2004)

**Fig 2. Inflow of Trafficking in Tamil Nadu**

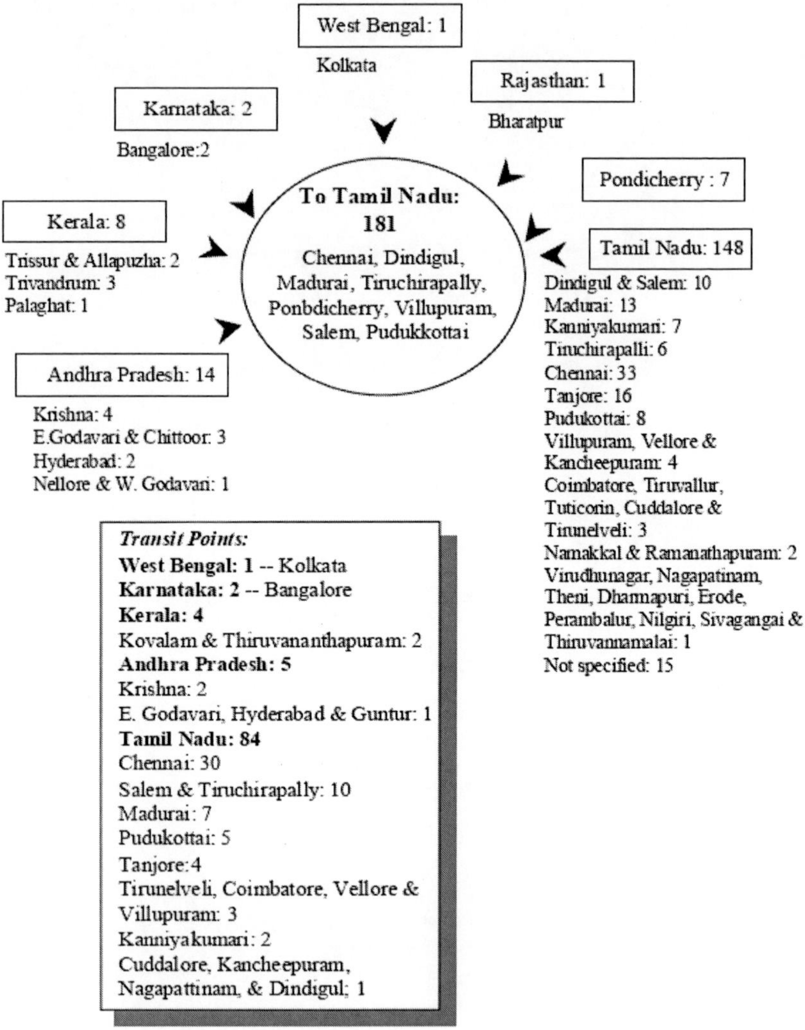


Source: Sen and Nair (2004)

**Fig 3. Trafficking in Tamil Nadu (2001)**

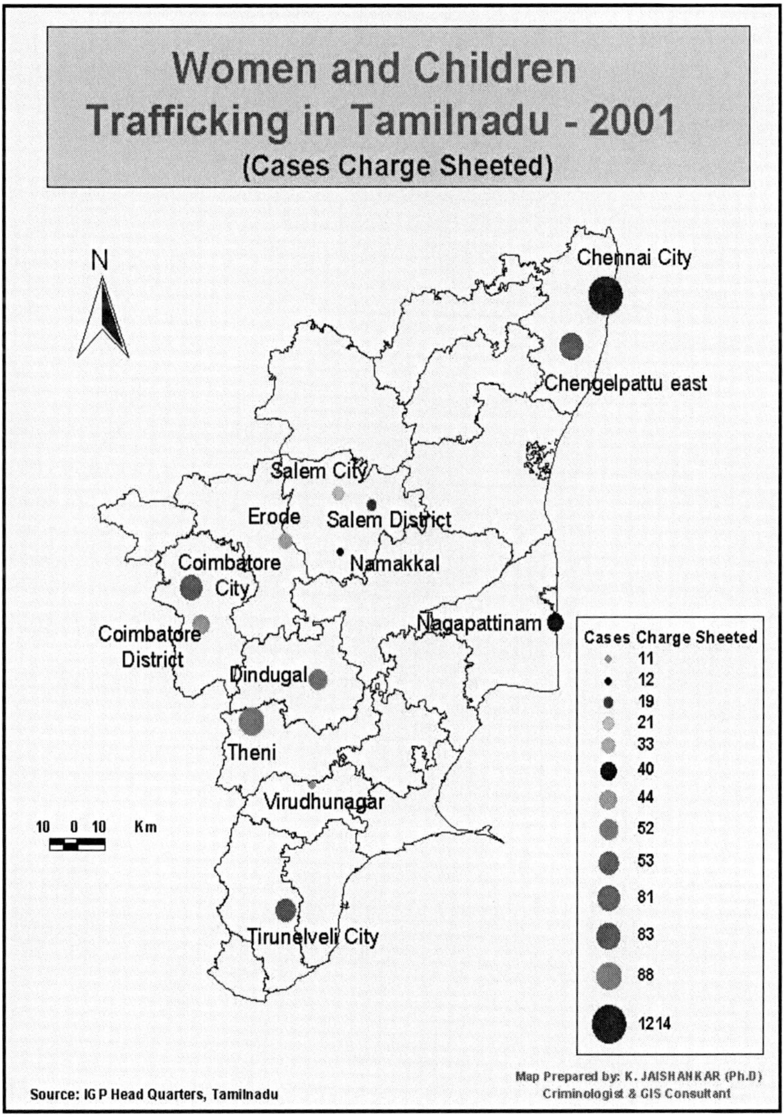

Jaishankar (2002) mapped the available data on women and children in Tamil Nadu. The figure 3 shows the number of cases arrested in Tamil Nadu, for the year 2001, for the offence of trafficking.

In order to get a clearer picture of this kind of re-trafficking, Sen and Nair (2004) further examined and analyzed the state-wise position. Among the 133 respondents who were bailed out by the brothel owners, there was none from Bihar, Assam and Meghalaya; one was from West Bengal, three from Uttar Pradesh, four from Goa, six each from Rajasthan and Delhi, 11 from Karnataka, 13 from Maharashtra, 22 from Tamil Nadu and 67 from Andhra Pradesh. This is a wake-up call for the law enforcement agencies in these states to take extra precautions for prevention of re-trafficking. This study also covered trafficking of male children, and a specific question asked was about the areas from where traffickers recruit male children. Though the majority of the brothel owners did not give proper answers, their responses suggests that the trafficking of male children takes place from Andhra Pradesh, Maharashtra, West Bengal, Tamil Nadu, Kerala, Bihar and also Nepal. To a further question on the reasons for such trafficking, 40.9 per cent attributed it to the vulnerability of the male children due to illiteracy, unemployment and poverty, while 31.8 per cent stated that it was due to the demand for male children in exploitative labour, the rest of the respondents (27.3 per cent) said that monetary gains to the traffickers was the main consideration in the trafficking of male children.

The second study focused on the victims of soft trafficking, who have worked in industries, through the likes of "Suba Mangala Scheme"[1] (Ambeth Selvi & Soma Sundaram, 2006). This study focused on the problems faced by women who were working on these schemes, which is considered as 'soft trafficking'. Figure 3 shows the various problems seen by this study.

---

[1] Subha Mangala (Good marriage) scheme is a variant of the soft trafficking, prevalent in many parts of Tamil Nadu, where girls of marriageable age are taken, with or without consent of the parents, for work in factories in other districts, for a period of 2-3 years. At the end of the period they are sent home with some money, with which they can get married and hence the schemes name. The scheme is also known as "Sumangali" (Married women) scheme in some parts of Tamil Nadu.

**Fig 4. Problems faced by Trafficked Victims**

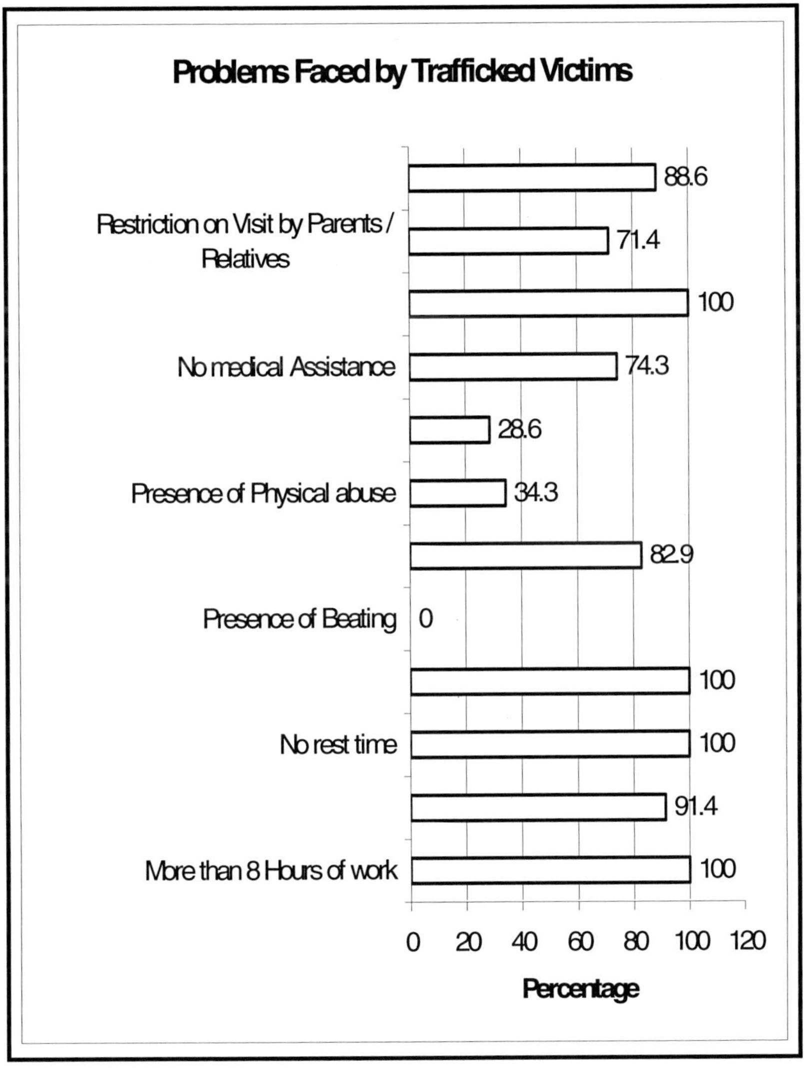


Source: Ambeth Selvi and Soma Sundaram (2006)

The lead author when training village level watchdog committee[2] members, that came under the ambit of the Juvenile Justice Act, 2000, for the Department of Social Defence (DSD), Tamil Nadu, in collaboration with UNICEF, conducted a series of programmes (some 30 programmes), where in, about 1500, members were trained. These programmes were conducted at Cuddalore, Nagapattinam and Nagarkoil, at two levels - basic and advanced. One of the areas of focus in the second-advanced level training was a discussion on Child Trafficking, with an objective of prevention. Some of the issues that were raised are:

- The village level watch dog committee members were aware that children from their villages are taken to work (soft trafficking) in
    - Prawn industries,
    - Fishing,
    - Salt industries etc.,
    - Brick industry
    - Domestic work
    - Agriculture related works
    - Spinning factories
- The children were taken to Melvidalam, Dindigul, Tiruppur, Cochin, Trivandrum, Thuthukudi, Mandapam, and Quilon.
- Instances were reported at Nagapattinam that children were taken to Pondicherry, in the Nagapattinam programme.
- Almost all the members were aware of the "Subamangala scheme", and knew some families that have sent their children to Tiruppur. Some village panchayat heads said that as many as 35 children have been taken.
- Both male and female children are taken.
- The methodology involved is that an agent from these companies comes to the village and recruits 2 – 3 children per village. After 6 months, these children recruit more children and they are taken,

[2] Village level Watch Dog Committees are set up by the Government of Tamil Nadu to supervise the children at the village level. There are about 12000 such committees in Tamil Nadu, and the lead author of this chapter conducted the Training of Trainers (TOT) for the whole State on issues related to Child Rights and one of the components was Child Trafficking. These programmes were conducted in two levels, with funds from UNICEF and UNDP, with the initiative of the DSD, Tamil Nadu.

- They were unable to intervene in this mainly due to the economic condition of the family, which send their children.
- Many of the village panchayat members, who also function in the village level watchdog committees, were not aware that this constitutes child trafficking and they view this as a method of income for poor families.
- Partly due to their lack of awareness and since they were not questioned by anybody earlier, they have not given it a serious thought.

**Table 3. Twelve Strategies for Implementation**

| *No* | *Issues* | *Action Steps Required* |
|---|---|---|
| 1 | Do we have a comprehensive understanding of the problem? If not, how do we build it? | • Monitor, Review, Reform existing policies, programmes, laws, and Rules.<br>• Provide for formulation of nodal and district level coordination committees, with personnel from the connected departments. |
| 2 | • What is the magnitude of trafficking in TN?<br>• Do we have approximate numbers? How do we generate it?<br>• Any studies at State level? Is it sufficient or do we need more studies? | A baseline study with multi centre data would shed light on dynamics of trafficking, will explain the root causes of trafficking. Also, a comparison of the socio-economic conditions of the trafficking affected households and non-affected households is recommended. |
| 3 | Do we have a system that monitors trafficking and traffickers? | • Develop a system of identification, investigation, reporting, follow-up and referral of children at risk within and outside homes/institutional care.<br>• Start monitoring with the supply and demand areas, identified by studies |
| 4 | Is there Boy / Male trafficking? Despite the conventional belief that only girls are trafficked, research elsewhere shows that, there are several instances of boys being trafficked. | More research is needed to understand the process and causes of boy trafficking. |
| 5 | What about "Subamangla | • More inputs on the scheme is |

| No | Issues | Action Steps Required |
|---|---|---|
| | Scheme" offered by some factories/ Companies? Do we need to have closer look at these? | needed<br>• The question of legality/Illegality involved.<br>• If legal, develop minimum standards for boarding, lodging, means of communication with family and for maintaining a non-abusive environment.<br>• Provisions for periodical inspections by the labour and police personnel. |
| 6 | Is the law enforcement at the Police Station level aware of it? Do we require awareness education, as we did for the Juvenile Justice Act, 2000? | Provide for specific capacity building programmes on child trafficking for the law enforcement personnel-during their training and through In service programmes |
| 7 | The identified source areas and demand areas need special programmes on awareness, prevention and rehabilitation schemes.<br>• **Source Areas -** Dindugal, Madurai, Trichy and Chengelpet in Tamil Nadu.<br>• **Demand Areas** - include not only cities but also smaller towns, like Tindivanam, Dindugal, Madurai and Salem (Sen 2006). | • Establish sound information systems regarding trafficking routes and networking of NGOs and other agencies engaged in prevention, rescue and rehabilitation of victims.<br>• Provide for Awareness, Prevention, Referral, and Rehabilitation work in these trafficking prone areas. |
| 8 | How can the State in partnership with community, set up mechanisms for identification, reporting, referral, investigation and follow-up of such acts, while respecting the dignity and privacy of the child? | • Creation of a Child Protection Cell at the DSD, TN for research, planning, and monitoring-at state level.<br>• Develop new schemes suited to TN and work towards convergence of existing schemes. |

| *No* | *Issues* | *Action Steps Required* |
|---|---|---|
| 9 | How can we ensure that all children have a right to be protected against neglect, maltreatment, injury, trafficking, sexual and physical abuse of all kinds, corporal punishment, torture, exploitation, violence and degrading treatment? | • Sensitize Judiciary, medical authorities and Media- during investigation and trial.<br>• Mobilize families, civil society and community to respond to the needs of children in difficult circumstances and help them access protective and developmental services for children.<br>• Provide for appropriate programmes in coordination with the Child Protection Cell, envisaged earlier |
| 10 | How can the State take effective legal action against those committing such violations against children even if they be legal guardians of such children? | Revisit the state rules on JJ Act, 2000 and related state level documents. |
| 11 | What do we have for rescued victims? | Provide for establishment of facilities for shelter, food, clothing, health care, counselling, education, training, skill development, so as to facilitate social and economic rehabilitation of rescued victims. |
| 12 | Do we have a workable mechanism for dealing with our children in other States and Children from neighbouring states | Develop communication with neighbouring states and NGOs to prevent cross-border trafficking of children and facilitate repatriation and rehabilitation of victims. |

## Conclusion

While International organizations like the United Nations have taken Child Trafficking seriously, and developed effective instruments and mechanisms to deal with the problem effectively, a lot needs to be done at the State level. To start with there is a need to monitor, review, reform the existing policies and rules related to child trafficking, especially in context to soft trafficking issues need to be discussed, as fast as possible. Studies have identified the source and destination areas within Tamil Nadu, so the enforcement personnel in these areas need to be empowered on trafficking issues.[3]

Dealing with the rescued victims is a major issue that needs to be addressed. State Protocols to this effect needs to be developed and circularized to the concerned departments. Furthermore awareness needs to be generated at the local level and steps may be taken to develop such mechanisms, in order to deal with the issue. While there are a plethora of laws dealing with different aspects of this issue, creation of a unified procedure or law is the need of the hour.

## References

Alfredsson, G., & Eide, A. (Eds.). (1999). *The universal declaration of human rights: A common standard of achievement.* London: Kluwer.

Ambeth Selvi, A. S., & Madhava Soma Sundaram, P. (2006). A study of rehabilitated victims of child trafficking in Tirunelveli. Paper presented in the 28th All India Criminology Conference, Madurai, February, 16-18.

Baland, J. M., & Robinson, J. A. (2000). Is child labor inefficient? *Journal of Political Economy, 108*(4), 663 - 679.

Barry, K. (1981). *Female Sexual Slavery.* New York: Avon Books.

Basu, K. (2000). The intriguing relation between adult minimum wage and child labour. *The Economic Journal, 110* (March), C50–C61.

—. (1999). Child labor: Cause, consequence, and cure, with remarks on international labor standards. *Journal of Economic Literature, 37*(3), 1083– 1119.

[3] Recently, due to the efforts of the lead author, a sensitization programme for the enforcement personnel from all the districts of Tamil Nadu was conducted by the National Institute Public Cooperation and Child Development (NIPCCD) at the Police Training Academy, Tamil Nadu.

Basu, K., & Van, P. H. (1998). The economics of child labor. *American Economic Review*, *88*(3), 412–427.
Beiguelman, P. (1978). The destruction of modern slavery: A theoretical issue. *Review, 2*(1), 71-80.
Behrman, J. R. (1999). Labor markets in developing countries. In O. Ashenfetler & D. Card (Eds.), *Handbook of Labor Economics,* vol. 3B (pp.2860-2939). Amsterdam: Elsevier Science B.V.
Brownlie, I. (1981). *Basic documents on human rights.* Clarendon Press.
Dessy, S. E. (2000). A defense of compulsory measures against child labor. *Journal of Development Economics*, *62*(1), 261–275.
Dessy, S. E., & Pallage, S. (2002). Why banning the worst forms of child labor would hurt poor countries. Manuscript, UQAM.
Dessy, S., E. & Pallage, S. (2001). Child labor and coordination failures. *Journal of Development Economics*, *65*(2), 469-476.
Dessy, S. E., & Vencatachellum, D. (2003). Cross-country differences in policy response to child labour. *The Canadian Journal of Economics, 36*(1), 1-20.
Ghandhi, P. R. (Ed.), (2000). *Blackstone's international human rights documents.* New York: Blackstone Press.
Ghosh, B. (1998). *Gains from global linkages: Trade in services and movements of people*. London and New York: Macmillan Press and St. Martin Press.
Gomango, S.P. (2001). *Child Labour: A precarious future*. New Delhi: Author Press.
Grootaert, C. & Kanbur, R. (1995). Child labour: An economic perspective. *International Labour Review*, *134*(2), 187–203.
Heyzer, N., Lycklama, A., Nijeholt, G., & Weerakoon, N. (Eds.), (1994). *The trade in domestic workers causes, mechanisms and consequences of international migration.* Kuala Lumpur: Asian and Pacific Development Centre; London and New Jersey: Zed Books.
ILO-IPEC (2002). *Unbearable to the human heart: Child trafficking and action to eliminate it.* Geneva: International Labor Organization.
Jaishankar, K. (2002). Mapping child and women trafficking in India: A case of Tamil Nadu. Paper presented in the showcase session of the Sixth Annual International Crime Mapping Research Conference, Denver, Colorado, United States of America. 8-11, December 2002.
Lalitha, S. (1996). Victimisation of girl- child in the home. *Journal of the Indian Law Institute*, *38*, 1-107.
National Crime Records Bureau (2003). Provisional Figures for 2003, Government of India, New Delhi.

—. (2004). Provisional Figures for 2004, Government of India, New Delhi.

Patel, S. K., & Talati R. C. (2000). Child labour in India: A Multi – dimensional problem. In M. K. Rao. (Ed.), *Exploited children – A comprehensive blueprint for child labour rehabilitation.* New Delhi: Kanishka publications.

Ranjan, P. (2001). Credit constraints and the phenomenon of child labor. *Journal of Development Economics*, *64*(1), 81–102.

—. (1999). An economic analysis of child labor. *Economics Letters*, *64*(1), 99–105.

Ruggiero, V. (1997). Trafficking in human beings: Slaves in contemporary Europe. *International Journal of the Sociology of Law, 25*(3), 231-244.

Sen, S., & Nair, P. M. (2004). A report of trafficking in women and children in India, 2002-2003, NHRC, New Delhi.

United Nations (2000). Protocol to prevent, suppress and punish trafficking in persons, especially women and children, supplementing the United Nations convention against transnational organized crime. Retrieved on May 21, 2008 from http://www.uncjin.org/Documents/Conventions/dcatoc/final_documents_2/convention_%20traff_eng.pdf

## Legislations/Instruments cited

*The Bonded Labour System (Abolition) Act, (1976).*

*Child Labour (Prohibition and Regulation) Act, (1986)*

*The Child Marriage Restraint Act, (1929)*

*The Immoral Traffic (Prevention) Act, (1956)*

*The Indian Penal Code, (1861)*

*The Juvenile Justice (Care and Protection of Children) Act, (2000)*

*The SC/ST (Prevention of Atrocities) Act, (1989)*

*The UN Convention of the Rights of the Child, (1989)*

—. *Protocol to Prevent, Suppress and Punish Trafficking in Persons, Especially Women and Children (2000).*

# CHAPTER EIGHTEEN

# CHILDHOOD BULLYING: A PERVASIVE SOCIAL PROBLEM

MICHAEL L. PITTARO

## Abstract

Bullying has traditionally been perceived by many to be a customary rite of passage that some children encounter, particularly during the child's early middle school years. As such, the behaviour was likely to be dismissed as seemingly harmless normal childhood conduct. The old adage that kids will be kids, particularly as it relates to adolescent males, is a common misperception based on an obvious lack of knowledge often mostly by parents, educators, and community members. Nevertheless, bullying is now recognized as a pervasive social problem that can profoundly influence the psychological well being of the intended victim, and equally important, disrupt the harmonious balance of the typically safe school environment. This chapter presents an exploration into childhood bullying from the social learning and social reaction (labelling) perspectives of deviance.

## Introduction

Although bullying can take place virtually any where or at any time, this chapter will focus predominantly on the bullying that occurs mostly within the school environment, particularly during a child's middle school years (Young, 2004). Bullying has, from a historical perspective, been perceived by many to be a customary rite of passage that many children routinely confront, or at the very minimum witness, during the elementary, middle, and high school years with teasing being the most common, yet most widely misunderstood form of childhood harassment (Whitted & Dupper, 2005). As such, bullying is often dismissed as normal childhood conduct involving the perceived harmless actions of children teasing other children (Whitted & Dupper, 2005). We now realize and have come to accept that victims of bullying may encounter a number of negative psychological, emotional, legal, and social consequences as result of being bullied, most notably delinquency (Agnew, 2005).

Some of the research studies on bullying suggest that nearly half of all children have either witnessed or experienced a bullying incident at least once during the formative school years, with upwards of 30% encountering such tormenting behaviour on a regular, consistent basis (Whitted & Dupper, 2005). Unfortunately, the United States lags behind most European countries where extensive bullying research has been conducted for nearly two decades (Duncan, 1998). In response, the United States has gained a significant foothold in the bullying research arena, especially after the investigation into the shocking American mass school killings at Columbine high school in April of 1999 (Rabrenovic, Goodman-Kaufman, & Levin, 2004).

The most recent research to date, from an international perspective, on bullying has essentially been quantitative in scope and based predominantly on a limited number of self-report studies; therefore, there is a clear and obviously crucial need for international research studies that are more qualitative in scope (Bowles & Lesperance, 2004). In this writer's opinion, qualitative studies would unquestionably yield constructive, practical information that would certainly appeal to scholars, practitioners, parents, teachers, and students alike. Before one can adequately address the problem with complete and utter tenacity, one must fully recognize and understand that childhood bullying is not confined to one particular country or region. Childhood bullying does not have any geographic boundaries nor does is occur within a vacuum. Qualitative research will undoubtedly assist the reader in accepting that the problem exists on a global scale by unearthing the possible causes and manifestations of bullying along with the perceived obscurity as to how one becomes a bully.

Contemporary research findings naturally seem to suggest that the key to successful intervention is to dismantle the all-to-familiar aggressive, antisocial behaviours displayed by the bully, which would, at least in theory, eliminate future bullying behaviours (McConville & Cornell, 2003). Such aggressiveness is believed to be learned and reinforced, in part, by the anticipated reactions of others, including the feedback received from ones peers as well as the bully's targeted victims (McConville & Cornell, 2003). Bullying is, by most people's definition, a negative label notoriously attached to someone who is perceived to be a troublemaker. Therefore, the bully label is universally perceived to be a negative one assigned by society even though the connotation of bullying is not necessarily present. For instance, in India, bullying is prevalent in the name of "ragging," which is prevalent in schools and colleges throughout India (Jaishankar & Shariff, 2008). The bully label is believed to be the impetus or cause of subsequent bullying behaviours in that the bully has now identified with and internalized the behaviour and characteristics linked to the label that has been branded by society (Tannenbaum, 1938).

Therefore, childhood bullying warrants international attention because it is perceived by many to be a pervasive social problem. This chapter has approached the concept of childhood bullying from the criminological perspectives of both social learning theory as well as labelling theory, hereafter referred to as social reaction theory. The basic premise of this chapter is to bring awareness to the global reader that childhood bullying is a multifaceted social issue that warrants widespread awareness as well as early intervention and prevention (Newman-Carlson & Horne, 2004). Since aggression is believed to be predominantly a learned behaviour in accordance with social learning theory, it is likely to be repeated if it is positively reinforced through the reactions and responses of others (Newman-Carlson & Horne, 2004; Spivak, 2003). In rare, but nonetheless memorable events of the recent past, some bullying victims have resorted to violent retaliatory acts of vengeance after being repeatedly ostracized and bullied by ones peers (Spivak, 2003). Consequently, the stress of being bullied could conceivably result in another high school massacre similar to that which occurred at Columbine high school in 1999. Therefore, it is not only the bully who learns such aggressiveness from observing the behaviours of others, but also the victim who has been the targeted recipient, whether real or perceived, of repeated acts of aggressive bullying tactics.

## Prevalence of the Problem

An investigation performed by the United States Secret Service determined that, of the 40 boys involved in the nation's most recent school shootings, the majority were repeatedly bullied by fellow peers (Crothers & Levinson, 2004). Once again, the psychological stress of childhood bullying appears to be the impetus that has led to some of the deadliest school massacres of American history (Crothers & Levinson, 2004). The now infamous Columbine high school mass murder is believed to have originated from years of pent up anger, frustration, shame, and humiliation which eventually erupted into unfathomable vengeance in April of 1999 (Smokowski & Holland-Kopasz, 2005). In response, a growing number of researchers now recognize and accept that bullying is an insidious danger to not only the child but also the school environment and surrounding communities (Smokowski & Holland-Kopasz, 2005; Stancato, 2003).

Sadly, it took the tragic death and injury of dozens of students over the years in America and abroad to capture and hold the attention of parents, educators, students, law enforcement, and most importantly, researchers and policy makers (Smokowski & Holland-Kopasz, 2005). As a result, scholars have expressed an emerging interest in studying bullying behaviours and the potential impact that such behaviours may have on children, educators, the school, and the community at large. Since bullying affects approximately one in three students in the United States, bullying is literally the most rampant form of violence amongst school children, yet its potentially damaging impact on individuals and society is still highly misunderstood and blindly underestimated (Kondrasuk, 2005; Smokowski & Holland-Kopasz, 2005).

Bullying can generally be defined through a wide variety of harassing behaviours that are meant to intimidate or harm another child who is perceived to be weaker, and therefore, unable or unwilling to protect or defend oneself against such tormenting actions (National Youth Violence Prevention Resource Center, 2006). The resulting harm may either be psychological or physical; however, bullying, by most accounts, is more psychological in scope (American Academy of Child & Adolescent Psychiatry, 2001). The bully uses varying degrees of emotional intimidation or acts of physical violence to establish dominance and control over others, even though the victim's actions are, by all accounts, largely unprovoked (Smokowski & Holland-Kopasz, 2005).

In most situations, the bully is often physically or psychologically more powerful than the targeted victim, which reinforces or further establishes the tormentor's dominance, especially when demonstrated in the presence of one's peers (Smokowski & Holland-Kopasz, 2005). In this particular situation, the bully learns early on that physical size can be an effective tool used to control others. Likely, this learned response stems from parents who socialize boys to be overly aggressive and competitive. Competitiveness may be rewarded, even at a young age, for participating in sports or other extracurricular activities that further reinforces the notion that physical stature, competitiveness, and aggression can be successfully used to settle problems.

## Bullying as a Social Problem

According to the National Youth Violence Prevention Resource Center (2006), it is estimated that approximately 30% of all children, which equates to almost six million American students, are involved in bullying as either the bully, the victim, or the victim turned bully. The evidence strongly suggests that bullying, regardless of one's geographic location in society, begins in elementary school, peaks in the sixth grade, and continues to occur frequently, but typically decreases from that point foreword (Rabrenovic, Goodman-Kaufman & Levin, 2004). In fact, children in the sixth grade are four times as likely to be the victim of a bully as those in the 12$^{th}$ grade (Rabrenovic et al., 2004). While bullying is much more common amongst adolescent boys than girls, there has been a notable rise in girls engaging in bullying behaviours (National Youth Violence Prevention Resource Center, 2006). It should also be noted that bullying behaviours are not confined to one particular race, ethnic group, culture, or socioeconomic group, but rather occurs equally amongst all student populations (Crothers & Levinson, 2004).

The research suggests that if bullying is not addressed and resolved in early childhood, the bullying behaviours could conceivably lead to a host of maladaptive behaviours in adulthood social and familial relationships, stemming from the development of negatively impaired social skills established in adolescence (Crothers & Levinson, 2004). Further, if left to fester in early childhood, bullying could conceivably lead to delinquency and adult criminality (Garrity et al., 2004). When compared to non-bullies, bullies are six times as likely to be sentenced for a crime before the bully reaches age 24 (Garrity et al., 2004). This is not meant to imply that all childhood bullies will succumb to a life of delinquency and crime but rather to extend awareness to a problem that could affect a small, yet significant number of individuals whose behaviour may only worsen over time.

A research (Smokowski & Holland-Kopasz, 2005) indicates that most bullying incidents take place where adult supervision is limited with most incidents occurring on the school's playground, in hallways, bathrooms, or other secluded areas where teachers are less likely to be present or frequent (Smokowski & Holland-Kopasz, 2005). As a result, it is estimated that nearly 60,000 American students refrain from going to school each day for fear of being bullied (Rabrenovic, Goodman-Kaufman & Levin, 2004).

A recent report by the National Association of Attorneys General (2000) suggests that bullying is the second major cause of school violence (Berry-Fletcher & Fletcher, 2003). What makes this problem so unique is that bullying is not confined only to the United States but rather extends globally; thereby making bullying an international social problem that, until recently, failed to attract the attention it so desperately deserved, particularly within the United States, which lags behind most European countries in bullying research (Packman et al., 2005). To emphasize the point being made, a recent survey's findings concluded that American children aged 8 to 15 perceived bullying to be considerably more problematic, than, racism or peer pressure to engage in drug use, underage drinking, or premarital sex (Lyznicki, McCaffree, & Robinowitz, 2004).

## Cyber bullying: From the Playground to Cyberspace

It would be remiss not to introduce a growing phenomenon whereby bullies have essentially moved from the school playground to cyberspace. Cyber bullying, like most Internet-related crimes, is a relatively new trend in deviancy, whereby children take full advantage of modern technology to harass and torment a victim in cyberspace (Pendley, 2004). According to Keith and Martin (2005), 91% of adolescents aged 12 to 15 years old as well as 99% of all adolescents aged 16 to 18 utilize the internet on a daily basis. Bullying, via the Internet, is initiated through email, instant messaging, chat rooms, and similar outlets of communication (Pendley, 2004). There is no questioning the fact that today's youth are computer savvy when compared to their parents. Therefore, it is expected that the incidence of cyber bullying will increase significantly over the next few years, thereby creating a completely new and unique social problem similar to that of cyber stalking and other crimes of the Internet for which there is limited information and even far less public policies in place to adequately address intervention and prevention efforts.

### *Cyber Bullying: A Growing International Concern*

An international glimpse into cyber bullying revealed that 13 million children in the United States, aged 6 – 17, are victims of cyber bullying and one-third of all teens and one-sixth of all pre-teens have had threatening or embarrassing statements made about them online (Jaishankar & Shariff, 2008). A 2006 Canadian study noted that half of the students surveyed were identified as bully victims whereas one in four claims to have been cyber bullied (Jaishankar & Shariff, 2008). A British survey of over 500 British 12 to 15 year olds found that one in 10 had experienced cyber bullying, most commonly through threatening emails, exclusion from online conversations, or through the spread of rumours about them on the Internet (Jaishankar & Shariff, 2008).

In a recent Australian study of 120 students in grade eight, one-quarter revealed that they knew someone who had been cyber bullied, and 14 percent stated that they had been the targeted recipient of such bullying, but more importantly, more than half of the students in the study believed that cyber bullying was on the rise (Jaishankar & Shariff, 2008). India has established a "ragging" commission to address what Americans commonly refer to as "hazing," but is considered far more severe (Jaishankar & Shariff, 2008). The list goes on and on, which further emphasizes this writer's point in that both traditional bullying and cyber bullying cross all international borders.

## Criminological Perspectives on Bullying

### *Social Learning Theory*

Children largely learn to abide by and accept society's norms and values through a complex, yet highly integrated socialization process whereby ones family, school, peers, and community have a significant influence on how each child will subsequently act and behave in a social setting. While most learning that takes place through the socialization process is overwhelmingly positive and socially appropriate, children and adults also exposed to and subsequently learn negative behaviours by observing and imitating the destructive behaviours and actions of others, particularly when such learning occurs through the frequent communication and interaction of one's deviant peer groups (Bandura, 1977). Therefore, in its most simplistic form, social learning theories assume that deviance and crime are the result of a convoluted socialization process in which children are particularly susceptible to learning negative behaviours from others and processing such maladaptive behaviours as acceptable and appropriate (Bandura, 1977). This is especially true if such negative behaviours are reinforced through the elicited positive reactions and responses of one's family or peers who outwardly condone and support such bullying behaviours, which supports the controversial subculture of violence theories (McConville & Cornell, 2003). One of the most widely recognized social learning theories and unquestionably one of the most practical to apply and explain bullying behaviours, in this writer's opinion, is that of Albert Bandura (Bandura, 1977).

Bandura (1977) essentially argued that aggression is not necessarily an innate characteristic of human behaviour, but rather a learned behaviour that is internalized by socializing and imitating the behaviours and actions of others, particularly one's parents or peers. Children basically model such aggressive behaviours based on what that child has directly observed within the family or amongst one's peers. If one witnesses a peer or parent acting aggressively, one is likely to mimic or model that behaviour, particularly if the behaviour is perceived to be socially acceptable and appropriate (Bandura, 1977). As such, the response or reaction that the bully receives may be perceived as positive in the bully's estimation and therefore, will likely to be repeated. One must accept that negative attention is attention nonetheless; therefore, any action that elicits a response, whether positive or negative is likely to be repeated according to social learning theory (Bandura, 1977).

Bandura based much of his perception of social learning theory on a vast amount of psychological research that had been conducted on both classical and operant conditioning to date (1977). When applied to childhood bullying, classical conditioning research assumes that learning takes place because of the association of a stimulus with an anticipated response (Bandura, 1977). The stimulus is the bullying behaviour, regardless as to whether it is verbal or physical, and the anticipated response is two-fold in that the bully is receiving a reaction not only from the victim but also from one's peers who have witnessed such behaviours firsthand. Those individuals who have witnessed bullying incidents on school campuses are hereafter referred to as bystanders.

In the case of operant conditioning, the behaviour is likely to be repeated simply because it has been rewarded (Bandura, 1977). The importance of "rewards" was further emphasized in Burgess and Aker's Differential Reinforcement theory (1968), a theory which states that deviant behaviours are more likely to be learned if such behaviours or attitudes are reinforced or rewarded. However, Bandura stressed that rewards are not always necessary for learning to occur (1977). Antisocial behaviour can also be learned through imitation or the modelling of observed behaviours and actions in others (Bandura, 1977). When applied to bullying, the reward is the attention received by the bystanders who witness the bullying incident; however, it may also include tangible rewards such as the unlawful taking of items from the victim without the victim's consent such as money or other material articles. As mentioned, children learn such aggressive behaviours and attitudes by observing such aggressive attitudes and behaviours in others, which could conceivably have a profound psychological influence on the personality and social development of the bully, but far more important is its harmful impact on the victim (Newman-Carlson & Horne, 2004). This clearly explains how one can theoretically evolve from victim to bully in a relatively short period.

### *Social Reaction (Labelling) Theory*

Frank Tannenbaum (1938) was one of the first to introduce labelling theory, which is more commonly referred to as social reaction theory by some contemporary criminologists (Barkan, 2006). Social reaction theory is described as a social process in which the individual, over time, begins to identify with a negative label that has been set by society, such as troublemaker or in this case, bully (Schmalleger, 2006) According to the theory, the individual will continue engaging in deviance or crime once the individual begins to identify with and internalize the negative label that has been branded, and act accordingly (Tannenbaum, 1938). When applied to bullying scenarios, the bully will steadfastly identify with and adopt the negative label given by teachers, students, or parents through a socialization process which, in most cases, will only perpetuates the bullying problem further. Theoretically speaking, the bully will continue to torment and harass other children because the bully has been labelled or tagged as a troublemaker. In other words, the bully identifies with the label and reacts accordingly by assuming that particular identity. The label given by society can be quite powerful and stigmatizing to the individual, particularly if one is an impressionable, attention-seeking child or young adolescent.

The stigmatizing label may even be applied to the victim. Simply stated, some children may learn to identify with the negative label stemming from the hurtful rumours, innuendos, or unfounded accusations initiated by the bully. This behaviour could permanently harm the emotional well-being and social development of the intended victim, particularly if the victim is subjected to repeated exposure to rumours, innuendos, and unfounded accusations (Siegel, 2005). If a child is labelled as a nerd, geek, loser, or any other similar slang term that may be used to describe a child or adolescent who is perceived to be different or unusual. That child may soon learn to identify with and internalize the characteristics of that label which is, by all accounts, a precarious self-fulfilling prophecy (Green, 2006).

### *Social Learning Theory versus Social Reaction Theory*

This chapter has attempted to approach the subject of bullying from the psychosocial perspectives of social learning theory and social reaction (labelling) theory. Both have been successfully applied to explain the process of how one becomes a bully as well as how one falls prey to becoming a victim. However, the application of social learning theory to bullying is far more effective than that of social reaction theory in explaining bullying behaviours and is therefore, the superior choice. Bullying is equated with aggressiveness and aggressive behaviours have been repeatedly linked to deviance and crime in the social learning studies.

Social reaction theory adequately explains the process of how one becomes a bully, but it relies too heavily on the label itself and how one internalizes the label rather than the context in which the behaviours are internalized. Social reaction theory essentially explains how the bullying behaviours continue as a result of being labelled, but the theory does not satisfactorily explain the origin of how one becomes a bully. The theory has also been criticized for failing to adequately explain the secondary deviance process simply because it lacks empirical support showing that secondary deviance causes further deviance in those who have been labelled. Lastly, social reaction theory naturally puts a great deal of emphasis on the label itself; however, there may be individual differences as to how the label is applied. For instance, some bullies are well-liked student athletes who are extremely popular amongst ones peers, yet this group may not be branded as troublemakers based on the positive reputation and status within the community that each has established, especially amongst teachers and school officials. Therefore, the theory does not account for those who engage in bullying behaviours but are never labelled because each is well liked and popular, particularly amongst adults.

Social learning theory, when applied to bullying, emphasizes the importance of communication and socialization in learning bullying behaviours whereas labelling theory does not. Social learning theory essentially relies on the continuous interaction between individuals and society (Schmalleger, 2006). The theory assumes that everyone has the ability to become a bully because aggression is not an innate characteristic, but rather one that is learned by interacting with others in a group process which further facilitates learning. Social learning theory dictates that aggression is learned from observing and imitating aggression in others, including the acquisition of those norms, values, and beliefs held and exhibited by the bully. Therefore, social learning theory is far more helpful in explaining bullying behaviour when compared to social reaction theory, because the theory is more comprehensive in scope. Of course, social learning theory, like any other criminological theory introduced to date, has been met with its fair share of criticism; however, the perceived flaws suggested by the theory's critics are trivial and therefore, pale in comparison to those against social reaction theory.

## Issues on Bullying

### *Characteristics of the Bully*

Like most antisocial behaviours and acts of delinquency, bullying is predominantly linked to males, specifically pre-adolescent boys who use intimidation and aggression to instil fear in the targeted victims. (Smokowski & Holland-Kopasz, 2005). Consequently, childhood peer groups are highly influential in the development and continued maintenance of bullying behaviours, particularly if those behaviours are condoned and supported in a social setting (Lyznicki, McCaffree, & Robinowitz, 2004). Thus, boys are nearly twice as likely to be bullies when compared to girls and consequently, twice as likely to be the victims of bullying, thereby making bullying a predominantly, but not exclusively, a male social problem (Juvonen, 2005).

As inferred, bullying amongst girls does occur, but not as frequently as it does with boys; however, when it does take place, the bullying behaviour is often restricted to verbal taunting through the spreading of hurtful rumours and false sexual innuendos (American Academy of Child & Adolescent Psychiatry, 2001). Unlike adolescent boys, adolescent girls are particularly notorious for inflicting psychological harm without the need to resort to physical violence (Pendley, 2004). Girls are also more likely to shun other girls from participating in school outings, events, or activities by intentionally ostracizing the victim or victims from interacting with the perceived popular peer cliques (Pendley, 2004). While girls tend to primarily target other girls, boys have no true gender preference as to who is victimized and will thereby victimize both girls and boys (National Youth Violence Prevention Resource Center, 2006).

### *Risk Factors for Becoming a Bully*

As one would expect, and the literature seems to agree, most bullies are impulsive, aggressive, destructive, and enjoy controlling and dominating others, all of which are believed to be learned behaviours (Smokowski & Holland-Kopasz, 2005). Those who share these antisocial behavioural characteristics are likely to gravitate toward bullies (Whitted & Dupper, 2005). There is also evidence that bullies have a low tolerance for frustration, are in support of violence to solve problems, and lack empathy toward others (Smokowski & Holland-Kopasz, 2005). Many of the earlier studies suggested that bullies were insecure and lacked self-esteem and self-confidence; however, there are a growing number of studies that dispute those findings claiming that bullies are extremely confident and have high levels of self-esteem (National Youth Violence Prevention Resource Center, 2006).

In other words, some bullies are popular even if only at a superficial level. Some bullies are well-liked students, many of whom are popular athletes, thereby dispelling the myths that bullies are always social outcasts who possess poor academic skills and lack a wide variety of friends (Rabrenovic, Goodman-Kaufman, & Levin, 2004). If this assumption is correct, bullying behaviour is likely to be repeated if the behaviour is reinforced or rewarded. A bully's peers may be a considerable source of support in that many sixth grade males will encourage the bully to continue harassing the victim either because the peers share the bullies feelings or are fearful of the bully (Rabrenovic et al., 2004). Therefore, the bully is perceived to be popular amongst ones peers through a socialization process in which the bully is erroneously labelled as well-liked and accepted but at the same time, intimidating to a large degree (Rabrenovic et al., 2004). The bully label is considered a negative label that is often bestowed by parents, educators, community members, or law enforcement; however, in some cases it is quite the contrary, particularly in regard to what has been described in social reaction theory. As such, the bully label may be welcomed as a positive branding that is often equated with power and dominance, especially amongst ones peers. In other words, a bully label is not always negative in the eyes of today's students.

As a group, bullies frequently engage in other antisocial behaviours at an early age, including, but not limited to, drinking alcohol, smoking tobacco, and experimenting with illicit street drugs (Smokowski & Holland-Kopasz, 2005). Unlike what has already been addressed, some bullies perform poorly in school and, for obvious reasons, express a general dislike for school and anything remotely related to academics (Smokowski & Holland-Kopasz, 2005). As noted, most bullying behaviours decline in late adolescence; however, for some, the behaviour manifests itself well into adulthood and may lead to a host of troublesome problems in one's future personal, intimate, and work-related relationships (Smokowski & Holland-Kopasz, 2005).

## *Family Influence*

The premise of this chapter is to illustrate how bullies, like many others who display deviant behaviours, are the product of their social environment. As such, one's family dynamics has a sizeable influence on the personality development of a bully, particularly for those who are raised in a dysfunctional family environment where aggression is high and overall parental supervision is low (Smokowski & Holland-Kopasz, 2005). Moreover, the absence of a father figure has repeatedly been found in the bullying literature; however, a male's presence in the family structure could also be a contributing factor, particularly if the father openly demonstrates and condones aggressive attitudes and behaviours (Flouri & Buchanan, 2003). In some situations, the male may attempt to dominate other household members through fear and intimidation in which the mother often remains passive and unresponsive to the children's maladjusted plight for attention (Smokowski & Holland-Kopasz, 2005). Hence, children may learn that aggression is normal, acceptable, and encouraged based on what has been observed. Adolescent boys in particular are likely to mimic these observed behaviours, which is precisely in alignment with the key principles of social learning theory.

The child's aggressive and antagonistic behaviours are likely to increase if the caretaker either condones or tolerates bullying behaviours towards one's peers, siblings, or teachers; thereby reinforcing the notion that such behaviours are, in fact, learned (Smokowski & Holland-Kopasz, 2005). If there is discipline in these homes, it is often inconsistent and hostile which further supports the hypothesis that the modelling of aggressive behaviours can have a profound impact on the personality and social development of an individual (Flouri & Buchanan, 2003; Liska & Messner, 1999). This modelling of aggressive behaviour further perpetuates the intergenerational cycle of violence in which learned antisocial behaviours are passed from one generation to the next similar to that identified in the renowned cultural transmission theory.

## *ADHD and Bullying: Is there a Correlation?*

Contemporary research suggests that there is a strong correlation between Attention Deficit Hyperactivity Disorder, hereafter referred to as ADHD, and bullying (Smokowski & Holland-Kopasz, 2005). ADHD is one of the most frequently observed behavioural disorders exhibited in childhood and is negatively characterized by inattention, hyperactivity, and impulsivity (Unnever & Cornell, 2003). As such, the ADHD label is socially perceived to be a negative one that has been repeatedly linked to delinquency and other antisocial behaviours in the research literature (Unnever & Cornell, 2003). According to social reaction theory, the ADHD child may begin to act according to the negative label that has been bestowed to that individual by society. As a result, it has been hypothesized that many children with ADHD are at an increased risk of engaging in bullying because of the behavioural symptoms consistently associated with ADHD, specifically that of impulsivity and attention seeking conduct (Unnever & Cornell, 2003).

Some bullies display other mental abnormalities such as depression and oppositional conduct disorder which, if not addressed, could also lead to a host of problematic behaviours as the child ages (Smokowski & Holland-Koopasz, 2005). In fact, some studies have concluded that bullies are more inclined to exhibit aggressive behaviours, as an adult, toward one's spouse, children, and in some instances, co-workers (Smokowski & Holland-Kopasz, 2005). Theoretically speaking, ADHD could be linked to both social learning theory and social reaction theory in that the child soon learns to identify with the ADHD label and will act accordingly by acting out in socially unacceptable ways to receive attention from others. The child soon learns that acting out elicits a response, albeit a negative one, but a response nonetheless from parents, teachers, and one's peers.

Contrary to popular opinion, bullies often display highly developed social skills because the bully plans and anticipates the projected reactions of the victim while, at the same time, takes precautionary steps to avoid adult detection (Whitted & Dupper, 2005). This behaviour is reinforced and therefore, repeated because of the anticipated tangible rewards as well as the social reinforcement received from one's peers and the anticipatory reactions of the intended victims (Whitted & Dupper, 2005). Therefore, the bully's strategy is both methodical and meticulous.

## *The Negative Consequences of Bullying*

As noted, the overwhelming majority of these young tormentors are elementary and middle school males (Rabrenovic, Goodman-Kaufman, & Levin, 2004). This is also true of the victims in that most victims are males of the same age and grade as the bullies (Rabrenovic et al 2004). Bullying victims tend to be overtly introverted, sensitive, and insecure, making this particular individual more susceptible to being the target of bullying behaviours (Smokowski & Holland-Kopasz, 2005). Bullies often look for these specific character traits when choosing a victim (American Academy of Child & Adolescent Psychiatry, 2001). As mentioned, continuous exposure to bullying can significantly impair one's social and emotional development (American Academy of Child & Adolescent Psychiatry, 2001). Some victims become so distraught, as in the case of the Columbine shooters that the victim will seek revenge by retaliating against the tormentors, which, in turn, creates an explosive, hostile environment for all students (Rabrenovic et al., 2004).

The practical application of social learning theory and social reaction theory are apparent since the victim learns how to be aggressive by observing the behaviours displayed by the tormentor, which is unquestionably a component of social learning theory. Conversely, social reaction theory prescribes that such negative behaviours are likely to be repeated if one identifies with the label given by one's peers. When applied to bullying victims, the victim is often labelled as geek, nerd, or any other socially unacceptable label branded by today's students. The victim may learn to identify with that particular label and subsequently assume that identity. The investigation into the Columbine shootings revealed that *Harris* and *Klebold*, the shooters, chose violence, suicide, and death as an alternative to end the pain and confusion of adolescence (Stancato, 2003). Both were repeatedly teased and bullied by the so-called popular students, which naturally became the targets of Harris and Klebold's monstrous, yet controlled rage (Stancato, 2003). One of the primary problems associated with internalizing anger, frustration, and shame is that some individuals, especially those with low self-esteem and self-confidence, may contemplate suicide to end the relentless emotional pain and suffering of being bullied (Smokowski & Holland-Kopasz, 2005).

Therefore, the evidence suggests that bullying victims who internalize the pain and anger of being victimized could conceivably become the next murder-suicide case if such behaviours are not properly addressed (Berry-Fletcher & Fletcher, 2003). Victims who have been chronically abused by one's peers are at a greater risk of suicide, the third leading cause of death for American Adolescents (Kim et al., 2005). It should be noted that suicide is a complex issue and not necessarily a means to an end for those who have been bullied; however, being bullied does increases one's risk, at least anecdotally (Kim et al., 2005). According to Kim et al., 2005, adolescent females are at a greater risk of suicide in comparison to adolescent males simply because the sexual innuendos and rumours are especially hurtful and relentless amongst adolescent females (2005).

### *Risk Factors for Becoming a Victim*

As mentioned, most bully victims tend to be smaller in stature than the typical bully, and are therefore, easier targets to prey upon, thereby raising the risk of an assault even further (Smokowski & Holland-Kopasz, 2005). However, students who are overweight or possibly even taller than the tormentor may also become the target of bullying, thereby dispelling the notion that bully victims are always smaller in stature than the bully (Unnever & Cornell, 2003). The threat of physical harm is always present; however, most of the harm caused to the victim is emotional, not physical (Packman, 2005). As such, the overwhelming majority of bullying victims are passive, submissive, and non-assertive to the point where each becomes an easy target for the bully to identify, pursue, and eventually taunt (Smokowski & Holland-Kopasz, 2005). Most victims appear to be outwardly timid and reserved; however, children should be taught that cowering or reacting defensively toward a bully may only worsen the situation (Whitted & Dupper, 2005). Slightly more than half of those bullied told a teacher or parent of the bullying incidents but felt that both, teachers and parents alike, did not address the situation properly and may have worsened the situation by inadvertently minimizing the importance of such victimization (Fekkes, Pijpers, & Verloove-Vanhorick, 2005).

### *Bystanders*

According to the National Youth Violence Prevention Resource Center, approximately 88% of America's middle school children have witnessed a bullying incident, yet the overwhelming majority of bystanders chose not to intervene in order to assist the defenceless victim (2006). A bystander has many options in that the bystander could choose to side with the bully, try to help the victim, or choose not to get involved (Fekkes, Pijpers & Verloove-Vanhorick, 2005). Most unfortunately choose not to get involved. To complicate matters further, one's peers can exert substantial pressure into recruiting others to join in on bullying a victim (National Youth Violence Prevention Resource Center, 2006). Failing to join in could conceivably create a situation in which the bystander becomes the next target of the bully (Whitted & Dupper, 2005). Therefore, many will chant and rally in support of the bully for fear of being the next victim if one does not side with the tormentor.

It should be noted that bystanders are susceptible to learning aggressive behaviours if the bystanders choose to side with the bully by encouraging and supporting the bully's behaviour and actions. As a result, bystanders could conceivably adopt the same attitudes, beliefs, and values as the bully simply by observing the response that the bully receives from victimizing another and accepting such taunting behaviours as just (Fekkes, Pijpers, & Verloove-Vanhorick, 2005). Therefore, social learning theory could also be applied to bystanders in addition to bullies and victims.

Unfortunately, many others simply choose not to get involved and turn a blind eye to the harassment. As a result, those who choose not to offer aid, often experience intense feelings of guilt and shame for not assisting or, at the very minimum, reporting the incident to someone who would have intervened on the victim's behalf (National Youth Violence Prevention Resource Center, 2006). Bystanders should be taught that there is an inherent moral and ethical responsibility and obligation to recognize and report a bullying incident to a responsible adult, especially one that was witnessed firsthand (Whitted & Dupper, 2006). The studies suggest that bystanders who intervened on behalf of the victims were highly effective in stopping the behaviour from continuing in the majority of cases (Fekkes Pijpers & Verloove-Vanhorick, 2005).

## Intervention and Policy Recommendations

One of the most widely recognized bullying programs is the Olweus Bullying Prevention Program, a Norwegian program that predominantly concentrates on and advocates for the creation of a positive school environment (Smokowski & Holland-Kopasz, 2005). The program emphasizes zero tolerance for bullies by focusing predominantly on students in the elementary and middle school years where bullying is believed to be especially problematic (Smokowski & Holland-Kopasz, 2005). Further, the program emphasizes the importance of teaching students how to handle various bullying situations and how to get help through teacher or parental involvement (Smokowski & Holland-Kopasz, 2005).

Since bullying is perceived to be a behavioural problem, the bullying program emphasizes the importance of counselling not only for the bully, but also for the victim (Smokowski & Holland-Kopasz, 2005). Assuming that bullying behaviours are, in fact, learned, these behaviours could theoretically be unlearned through counselling and other intervention and prevention strategies. Intervention is absolutely paramount to decreasing the number of victims since a single bully could conceivably have multiple victims (Cole, Cornell & Sheras, 2006). An important aspect of the counselling component of the program is to have the bully accept responsibility for one's actions as well as an emphasis on socialization skills and empathy development, both of which are lacking in most bullies (Smokowski & Holland-Kopasz, 2005).

According to Smokowski and Holland-Kopasz (2005), the most successful intervention programs are those that maintain a zero tolerance rule with immediate and certain punishments for those who choose to engage in bullying, similar to that expressed in deterrence theory (Liska & Messner, 1999; Smokowski & Holland-Kopasz, 2005). The message disseminated to students from school administrators must be clear, concise, and certain that bullying behaviours of any kind are forbidden and therefore, will not be tolerated (Whitted & Dupper, 2005). Bullying is not only confined to students but also extends to teachers and other school officials, each of whom have a moral, ethical, and in some instances, a legal responsibility to intervene on a student's behalf (Whitted & Dupper, 2005).

As mentioned, bullying is not confined solely to school campuses but rather extends into the community; therefore, it is imperative that school officials unite with parents and other community members (Smokowski & Holland-Kopasz, 2005). In fact, the focus should not be solely on changing the behaviour of the individual child, but rather on shifting the attitude and culture of the school in a direction whereby individualism, diversity, and multiculturalism are embraced and celebrated, not feared (Whitted & Dupper, 2005). The main objective of bullying intervention programs should be focused primarily on creating a safe, positive learning environment where students do not have to live in fear simply when walking down the hall, going to the bathroom, or playing on the playground (Smokowski & Holland-Kopasz, 2005). To do so, the prevention program must target not only bullies, but also victims, bystanders, families, teachers, and community members through the implementation of a comprehensive, yet strategic multifaceted program (Whitted & Dupper, 2005). Since all are major stakeholders in the life of a child, each must be empowered to take responsibility and ownership throughout the entire process of assessment, development, implementation, and evaluation of such programs (Whitted & Dupper, 2005).

Without a swift and appropriate intervention plan in place, the bully is likely to encounter serious academic, social, emotional, and legal difficulties; therefore, intervention is absolutely critical to decrease the number of bullies and subsequent number of victims (American Academy of Child & Adolescent Psychiatry, 2001). Since bullying tends to originate in elementary schools, it is imperative that intervention and prevention efforts begin when children are the most impressionable and formidable (Whitted & Dupper, 2005). It may be helpful for school officials to administer a needs assessment plan to raise awareness and determine the extent of bullying within a particular school, especially since most parents and teachers underestimate the prevalence and seriousness of bullying (Whitted & Dupper, 2005).

Creating a positive, healthy, learning environment requires a degree of connectedness amongst those in the school community (Smith & Sandhu, 2004). Students who feel attached to school and the community are less likely to succumb to the typical stress and pressures often associated with adolescence (Smith & Sandhu, 2004). To be truly effective, teachers as well as parents should assist students in developing an understanding and respect for diversity, multiculturalism, and individuality, particularly in the United States.

## References

Agnew, R. (2005). *Juvenile delinquency: Causes and control.* 2nd ed. Los Angeles, CA: Roxbury Publishing.

American Academy of Child and Adolescent Psychiatry. (2001). American Academy of Child and Adolescent Psychiatry. Retrieved June 8, 2006, from http://www.aacap.org/publications/factsFam/80.htm

Barkan, S. E. (2006). *Criminology: A sociological understanding.* 3rd ed. Upper Saddle River, NJ: Prentice Hall.

Berry-Fletcher, A. J., & Fletcher, J. D. (2003). Victims of school violence. In J. M. Sgarzi & J. McDevitt (Eds.), *Victimology: A study of crime victims and their roles* (pp. 238-257). Upper Saddle River, NJ: Prentice Hall.

Bowles, C. L., & Lesperance, L. (2004). Being bullied in adolescence: A phenomenological study. *Guidance and Counselling*, *19*(3), 94-102.

Burgess, R., & Akers, R. (1968). A Differential Association-Reinforcement Theory of Criminal Behaviour. *Social Problems, 14*,128-47.

Cole, J. C., Cornell, D. G., & Sheras, P. (2006). Identification of school bullies by survey methods. *Professional School Counselling, 9*(4), 305-313.

Crothers, L. M., & Levinson, E. M. (2004). Assessment of bullying: A review of methods and instruments. *Journal of Counselling and Development*, *82*(4), 496-503.

Duncan, R. D. (1999). Peer and sibling aggression: An investigation of intra and extra-familial bullying. *Journal of Interpersonal Violence, 14*(8), 871-886.

Fekkes, M., Pijpers, F. I. M., & Verloove-Vanhorick, S. P. (2005). Bullying: Who does what, when, and where? *Health Education Research, 20(1)*, 81-91.

Flouri, E., & Buchanan, A. (2003). The role of mother involvement and father involvement in adolescent bullying behaviour. *Journal of Interpersonal Violence. 18*(6), 634-644.

Garrity, C., Jens, K., Porter, W., Sager, N., & Short-Camilli, C. (2004). Bully-proofing your school. *Reclaiming Children and Youth. 13*(3), 186-189.

Green, F. G. (2006). More deadly than asbestos. Retrieved June 8, 2006, from http://www.keystosaferschools.com/more_deadly_than_asbestos.htm

Jaishankar, K., & Shariff, S. (2008). Cyber bullying: A transnational perspective. In F. Schmalleger & M. Pittaro (Eds.), *Crimes of the Internet* (pp.66 – 83). Upper Saddle River, NJ: Prentice Hall.

Juvonen, J. (2005). Bullying in schools pervasive, disruptive, and serious. Retrieved June 8, 2006, from http://www.rand.org/health/centers/adolescent/bullying.html

Keith, S., & Martin, M. E. (2005). Cyber-bullying: Creating a culture of respect in a cyber world. *Reclaiming Children and Youth, 13*(4), 224-229.

Kim, Y., Koh, Y. J., & Leventhal, B. (2005). School bullying and suicidal risk in Korean middle school. *Pediatrics, 115*(2), 357-363.

Lyznicki, J. M., McCaffree, M. A., & Robinowitz, C. B. (2004).Childhood bullying: Implications for physicians. *American Family Pediatrics, 70*(9), 1723-1728.

McConville, D., & Cornell, D. G. (2003). Aggressive attitudes predict aggressive behaviour in middle school students. *Journal of Emotional and Behavioural Disorders, 11*(3), 179-187.

Meadows, R. J. (2006). *Understanding violence and victimization.* 4th ed. Upper Saddle River, NJ: Prentice Hall.

National Youth Violence Prevention Resource Center, (2006). Bullying. Retrieved June 8, 2006, from http://www.safeyouth.org/scripts/teens/bullying.asp

Newman-Carlson, D., & Horne, A. M. (2004). Bully busters: A psychoeducational intervention for reducing bullying behaviour in middle school students. *Journal of Counselling and Development, 82*(3), 259-268.

Packman, J., Lepkowski, W. J., & Overton, C. C. (2005). We're not gonna take it: A student driven anti-bullying approach. *Education, 125*(4), 546-556.

Rabrenovic, G., Goodman-Kaufman, C., & Levin, J. (2004). School violence: Causes, consequences, and intervention. In S. T. Holmes and R. M. Holmes (Eds.), *Violence: A contemporary reader* (pp.115-132). Upper Saddle River, NJ: Prentice Hall.

Schmalleger, F. (2006). *Criminology today: An integrative introduction.* 4th ed. Upper Saddle River, NJ: Prentice Hall.

Siegel, L. J. (2005). *Criminology: The core.* 2nd ed. Belmont, CA: Thomson Publishing.

Smith, D. C., & Sandhu, D. S. (2004). Toward a positive perspective on violence prevention in schools: Building connections. *Journal of Counselling and Development*, *82*(3), 287-294.

Smokowski, P. R., & Kopasz, K. H. (2005). Bullying in school: An overview of types, effects, family, characteristics, and intervention strategies. *Children and Schools*, *27*(2), 101-110.

Spivak, H. (2003). Bullying: Why all the fuss?. *Pediatrics*, *112*(6), 1421-1422.

Stancato, F. A. (2003). The Columbine tragedy. *Clearing House*, *77*(1), 19-22.

Tannenbaum, F. (1938). *Crime and the community*. New York, NY: Columbian University Press.

Unnever, J. D., & Cornell, D. G. (2003). Bullying, self-control, and ADHD. *Journal of Interpersonal Violence*, *18*(2), 129-147.

Whitted, K. S., & Dupper, D. R. (2005). Best practices for preventing or reducing bullying in schools. *Children and Schools, 27*(3), 167-175.

# CHAPTER NINETEEN

# CRIME SCIENCE AND THE ARMS RACE DYNAMICS OF CRIME PREVENTION

AIDEN SIDEBOTTOM[1]

## Abstract

Traditional criminology has lavished disproportionate attention on the study of criminality at the expense of studying the crime event itself. This tendency has created an orthodoxy in which crime prevention agencies are perceived solely as crime solvers - not crime prevention specialists. In a departure from this mode of thought crime science represents a new approach in which the study of crime and crime prevention predominates. Based on the central assumption that crime is the product of numerous converging factors driven by opportunities existing in the immediate situation, crime science advocates an interdisciplinary approach in which the prevention of crime can benefit from drawing on numerous disciplines typically beyond 'criminological borders'. To this avail the current chapter applies the concepts of numerous fields to further Ekblom's concept of an 'arms race', in which crime prevention is posited as being in a "perpetual struggle to keep up with changing opportunities for crime and adaptable offenders" (1999, p. 27). It will document how the supply of opportunities for crime changes as a product of social and technological development, and outline the benefit of integrating numerous scientific disciplines in the pursuit of crime reduction. The chapter therefore takes the following form: 1) by way of a preface, a brief introduction to crime science; 2) discussion of Ekblom's concept of an arms race, its theoretical underpinnings and wider implications; and 3) how this concept relates to crime prevention.

[1] This author is grateful to the assistance provided as part of the annual University College London, Jill Dando Institute of Crime Science scholarship. Additionally he is indebted to Tamara Walker, Dr. Shane Johnson and an anonymous reviewer for their useful comments on earlier drafts of this chapter.

## Crime Science: An Introduction

The locus of crime causation for traditional criminology has typically focused on internal dispositions and distant forces such as poverty and parenting. This slant is somewhat expected as criminology has long been a sub-discipline of sociology. Though it would be naive to assume such factors do not influence criminal propensity, difficulty arises in translating such theories of criminality into forms of practical and feasible crime prevention. As Smith states, "it is easy to see that happy families tend not to produce criminals. It is hard to see how public policy can decree that family relationships be constructive and positive" (2000, p. 149). Furthermore offender focused theories of criminality fail to sufficiently address the criminal event itself, under-recognizing the manifold variables beyond the offender necessary for crime to occur.

Borne out of this disproportionality emerged crime science which is outcome focused in regards to crime reduction, placing greater emphasis on the criminal event over offender criminality (see Smith & Tilley, 2005). In seeking this objective, it advocates the need to be multidisciplinary and draw upon numerous relevant branches of science in the service of crime reduction (Pease, 2005). Laycock (2004) demonstrates this by way of analogy; medical science seeks to improve the health and well being of individuals and does so through drawing upon numerous fields such as physics and biology to achieve this goal. Similarly crime science seeks to exploit and utilize areas such as design, ecology and physics to aid and improve crime reduction. As Pease states, "there is a range of science contributions which are not currently being mainstreamed in the crime reduction enterprise. Crime reduction would be well served to facilitate trickle-down of military and commercial applications and by having recourse to a wider range of scientific disciplines" (2005, p. 193).

An illustrative case is the work of Shane Johnson and Kate Bowers using epidemiological theory and method to further the understanding and prediction of crime victimisation. Using techniques which assess the communicability of certain contagious diseases (see Johnson et al., 2007), this innovative work provides evidence that crime, in this case burglary and theft from cars, also appear 'communicable' (i.e. the risk of being victimised appears to cluster in space and time). This work is an extension of the important criminological area of repeat victimisation, which states that in keeping with the power law phenomenon[2] (Newman, 2005), a small

---

[2] Power laws (also known as Pareto's law) refer to incidences of scale invariance in which a small minority accounts for a large majority. Power law distributions are remarkably common amongst natural and social sciences. For a comprehensive

proportion of offenders commit a large amount of crime and a small number of victims experience a disproportionate amount of victimisation (Farrell & Pease, 1993; Pease, 1998). In conjunction these spatio-temporal patterns akin to epidemiological phenomenon enables the development of more accurate predictions of when and where such crimes are more likely to occur (see Bowers, Johnson & Pease, 2004; Johnson & Bowers, 2007; Townsley et al., 2003).

It is not just the *tools* but the *methods* of science which can aid crime prevention. Crime science promotes a need and outlines the benefits of 'thinking scientifically' about crime, adopting a data-driven and evidence based approach which tests hypotheses and seeks to emulate the methodological robustness of the natural sciences. This is particularly important in evaluating crime prevention where Ekblom and Pease note that "most evaluations of crime prevention are carried out with little regard for methodological probity" (1995, p. 585). Demonstrating these standards are important given lay understanding of crime is often couched in conventional wisdom and preconceptions which run counter to empirical evidence (see section on crime fallacies in Felson, 2002). Thinking scientifically hence improves the validity and reliability of how crime is evaluated, allowing one to better infer 'what works' in preventing crime (Sherman et al., 1997).

## Goodies and Baddies: A False Dichotomy

A widely held assumption is that perpetrators of crime are 'a breed apart' from non-criminal individuals (Laycock, 2003) – a polarised view challenged by extant evidence. Gabor (1994) provides evidence that *most* individuals over their lifetime commit some form of crime. Home Office research in Britain found 33% of males had committed a criminal act by their 46$^{th}$ birthday, albeit relatively minor and part of a criminal career which was short lived, as indicated in the age-crime curve (Gottfredson & Hirschi, 1990; Campbell, 1995). This suggests that for the most, crime is generally minor and moreover committed by lots of people, what Karstedt and Farrall (2007) call the crimes of everyday life. At the other end of a crime severity continuum lays extreme cases of crime which are both few in occurrence and committed by a small group of offenders. Of course crimes at this pole receive disproportionate media attention and hence a certain degree of social amplification serves to cloud public perception

---

discussion see Newman (2005). Also see Eck, Clarke & Guerette (2007) for an application to crime distribution.

(Cohen, 1987; Pidgeon, Kaseperson, & Slovic, 2003). The important message of such findings however is that viewing *crime* as being committed by aberrant individuals with innate criminal propensities is myopic, and more importantly, does little in terms of broadening our understanding of the crime event and crime prevention. Changing an individuals predisposition is immensely difficult, time consuming and resource exhaustive - even if it were a feasible option for reducing crime, it completely overlooks the fact that behaviour (of which crime essentially is) is far from consistent and varies considerably across situations (Mischel, 1968). A sombre trawl through human history cites numerous examples in which seemingly 'normal' individuals have committed acts of atrocity in situations which seemed conducive or contributory to such abhorrence, the rapes of Nan King and Mylai being cases in point (see Zimbardo, 2007).

What such research and historic incidents suggest is a simple axiom - that behaviour (including crime) is the interaction between an individual and opportunities for behaviour in the situation. Crime science assumes the same is true for crime, crime being the interaction between individuals and opportunities available in the immediate situation; opportunities which are causal factors of crime (Felson & Clarke, 1998). This interactionist perspective of crime is hence ecological, indeed Ekblom and Sidebottom (2007) state all concepts and terms emanating from opportunity theories of crime implicitly possess an 'ecological dimension'. It is warranted to expand on this further as an ecological perspective highlights the reciprocity between person and environment which is needed to understand the concept of opportunity referred to herein. Ekblom and Sidebottom (2007) argue that opportunity by itself is a rather ambiguous term which denotes numerous meanings and as a result risks differential interpretation. The ecological approach is therefore important in firmly securing how one thinks of opportunity, not as an amorphous potentiality but rather as a *function of the situation and persons operating within it* - the open window on the third floor is only an opportunity for crime to the burglar who perceives it, and has a ladder with which to reach it!

## How to Reduce Opportunities for Crime: Situational Crime Prevention

The ecological perspective of crime described above highlights the necessary elements which crime prevention must seek to alter. For practical crime prevention however it is far easier and morally more acceptable to reduce or alter opportunities for crime in the situation, than it is to change human disposition (Laycock, 2004). This is the aim of situational crime prevention (SCP) (Clarke, 1992), which assumes that crime reduction is best served by shifting attention from offender predisposition to environmental features which mediate or facilitate criminal behaviour (Wortley, 2002). It postulates that crime is the product of a multiplicity of causes, of which "offenders are but one element in a crime, probably not even the most important" (Felson, 2002, p. 34). This opportunity centred approach stems from and is grounded in a tripod of criminological theories which highlight the inherent situational nature of crime; these are routine activity theory (Cohen & Felson, 1979), crime pattern theory (Brantingham & Brantingham, 1995) and rational choice theory (Clarke & Cornish, 1986). Though, it is not the intention of the current chapter to provide a comprehensive account of such theories, a brief discussion of each is warranted.

Routine activity theory (Cohen & Felson, 1979) postulates that the criminal event is the direct result of the convergence in space and time of three essential elements: 1) motivated offenders, 2) suitable targets, which can be both animate and inanimate such as the lady walking home or an unlocked car, and finally, 3) an absence of capable guardians, which can refer to police officers or equally passer-bys who by virtue of their presence act as deterrents. Cohen and Felson argue that the coming together of these requisite elements for crime is mediated by their respective daily activities, lifestyles and places which they frequent.

Extending the last point of converging elements meeting in space and time, crime pattern theory emphasises the importance of place in understanding crime and offender mobility (Brantingham & Brantingham, 1995). Crime pattern theory states that individuals possess cognitive maps which contain the spatial information used to navigate through the environment (Kitchen, 1994). Given most people tend to operate between major reference points such as the home or work their spatial awareness in such areas is far greater. Crime pattern theory suggests it is in those areas of heightened spatial awareness in which offenders are more likely to perceive and act upon available opportunities for crime. This postulate of crime pattern theory is supported by extant work into offender mobility, particularly journey to crime research which measures the distance between offender home and offence location. Across numerous countries and crime types it has repeatedly been found that a disproportionate number of crimes occur within a short distance of offenders home, with numbers of crimes decaying as the distance from the offenders' home increases (Baldwin & Bottoms, 1976; Reiss, 1976; Rengert, Piquero, &

Jones, 1999; Rossmo, 2000; Wiles & Costello, 2000; Gandhirajan, Thilagaraj, & Jaishankar, 2003; Chainey & Ratcliffe, 2005).

The third component of SCP is Rational Choice Theory, which assumes that offenders are essentially rational, purposive agents, and when presented with an opportunity for crime conduct a rudimentary form of cost-benefit analysis evaluating the perceived risks, efforts and rewards associated with crime commission (Cornish & Clarke, 1986). When the previously described elements of crime converge in space and time and the offender perceives the commission of such crime as beneficial, the likelihood of crime occurring is high.

SCP is thus a theory-based series of methods which draw upon numerous strands of criminological theory interwoven by the rationale that opportunity is a "root cause" of crime (Felson & Clarke, 1998). Practically SCP is comprised of five major streams that act as a template for situational techniques to reduce crime. These are:

- increasing the effort to commit crime,
- reducing the potential rewards gained through crime,
- making crime riskier to commit,
- reducing any excuses for committing crime, and
- removing potential provocations.

The benefit of this approach is that it alerts crime prevention specialists that crime is influenced by differential opportunities for crime, and that manipulating the situations which avail such opportunities can render a crime reduction effect. Since its inception in the 1970's SCP has amassed over one hundred published case studies in which the introduction of situational measures has brought about a crime reduction effect (Felson et al., 1997; Homel et al., 1997; Webb, 1997; Clarke & Newman, 2005; Wortley & Smallbone, 2006), leading some commentators to claim it is "the fastest-growing form of crime control worldwide" (Clarke, 2005, p. 39).

Discussion of SCP would not be complete without discussing (or perhaps dispelling) the often raised criticism of displacement, which suggests offenders blocked in one way will merely be shunted to other times or places to commit crime (see Reppetto, 1976, Weisburd et al., 2006). Though the potential for displacement must always be entertained, empirical evidence repeatedly indicates that displacement as a result of SCP is neither inevitable nor absolute, and typically produces a net benefit (Hesseling, 1994). Additionally there are potential sources of 'added value' in SCP, such as 1) *diffusion of benefits,* whereby positive effects of a given crime preventive scheme go beyond the spatial area in which it was implemented (Clarke & Weisburd, 1994); and 2) *anticipatory benefits,* the finding of a 'prematurity effect' whereby a drop in crime often antedates the onset of the respective crime prevention scheme (Smith, Clarke, & Pease, 2002).

The purpose of describing crime science and SCP is to highlight that crime is the product of numerous factors converging in space and time. Moreover offender-centric thinking as to the contributory factors of crime is restrictive if one aspires to maximise practical crime prevention. Theoretically by adopting this approach it raises the awareness that crime is a product of the situation and the persons operating within it. Yet situations do not remain constant, and whilst displacement discusses the potential short-term effect of SCP, what of the long-term protracted effects, where situations are changed by innovative and entrepreneurial offenders, crime prevention specialists or wider external forces. It is with these longer term changes that the foregoing article takes its focus, describing the interplay between those seeking to exploit opportunities for crime and those seeking to prevent them; and how these dynamic, interrelated competitions create what Ekblom (1999) terms a crime 'arms race'. At this juncture and in relation to Ekblom's proposal it is important to delineate and clearly define the proposed meaning of the situation and the environment. The situation as referred to in SCP is the immediate spatial and temporal setting in which behaviour (specifically crime) takes place; in an ecological sense the interaction between the individual and situational opportunities for behaviour. Here the environment is a series of situations and refers to the wider backdrop both spatially and temporally. Hence changes in the environment (i.e. social or technological developments) are likely to have a 'downstream effect' on the immediate situation.

## The Arms Race

What do the fox and the thief have in common? The fox is driven by certain basic life essentials, such as respiration, procreation etc. Meeting these needs requires regular sustenance, often in the form of rabbits. Rabbits however aspire to fulfil the same needs whilst seeking to avoid fox predation. In this competition of nature the fox must outwit, outrun or employ any method available to overcome present obstacles and eat the rabbit. The thief seeking to steal a mobile phone may do so for a variety of different reasons and motivations, these withstanding, to complete this task the thief has to overcome certain obstacles such as the carrier of the phone or inbuilt immobilisation systems. Like the running rabbit seeking to thwart or prevent the fox, crime prevention in the tradition of SCP must make the thief's stealing of the mobile phone harder, riskier, and perhaps even impossible.

Nature plays host to myriad evolutionary struggles, within these as one competitor adapts, defined as the ability of a creature to change and become better suited to an environment (Schmitt & Pilcher, 2004), it exerts selection pressure on its competitor which gives rise to counter-adaptation (Dawkins & Krebs, 1979). Continually reciprocated such move, counter-move, counter-counter-move escalate to form an arms race, a co-evolutionary struggle for temporary advantage. Ekblom (1999) cogently argues that crime prevention is enlisted in a similar arms race with innovative offenders, an equally adaptive agent reacting in response to and attempting to circumvent the impinging pressures exerted upon them from crime prevention specialists.

Case studies exist demonstrating numerous co-evolutionary struggles across a multitude of crime types (for a review see Ekblom, 1999). An illustrative example is changes in car theft in the UK in the aftermath of increased proliferation of car immobilisation systems and improved security measures (see Webb, Smith, & Laycock, 2004). Brown (2004) in examining patterns of car theft opined that the abundance of such security mechanisms may be initiating an adaptation on the part of offenders as evidenced in emerging *modus operandi* (MO). Donkin and Wellsmith (2006) for example found a statistically significant increase in recent years of cars stolen using keys acquired from burgling the house of the car owner. Drawing similar conclusions to that of Flood-Page and Taylor (2003) and Copes and Cherbonneau (2006), they argue that offenders in light of the actions of security minded car manufacturers appear to have adapted their skill set to overcome increased car security brought about through technological development.

The wider implications of the above findings are important as they illustrate that the environmental backdrop on which opportunities for crime occur influences those with both licit and illicit intentions - just as increased security on behalf of car manufacturers as a result of improved design and technology has aided the prevention of car theft, so too has it exerted an effect on offenders seeking to overcome such developments. In relation to crime prevention, it is vital to understand and anticipate the potential effect of changes in opportunities for crime, and the dynamics between those seeking to exploit or engineer opportunities to commit crime versus those seeking to prevent them. To achieve this requires an appreciation of the means by which opportunities for crime arise.

## Sources of Opportunity

It has been described herein that opportunities in the immediate situation can be casual factors in crime – but opportunities are transient. Offenders are thus limited by the opportunities which present themselves and the resources they posses with which to act upon them (Ekblom & Tilley, 2000). Walsh provides a fascinating account of the changing face of crime itself, documenting numerous crimes which due to "unintended consequences of economic and social change" (1994, p. 149) have been rendered obsolescent; examples include eavesdropping and ship wrecking. Reflecting these recurrent changes, just as the potential opportunity to commit safe-breaking has substantially lowered in light of more sophisticated safe security (Shover, 1996), the opportunity to commit cyber crime has increased rapidly in recent years as electronic mediums proliferate (Sommer, 2004). The task of crime prevention is therefore to cultivate the ability to forecast, understand and respond accordingly to the changing nature of opportunity. But what of this changing nature?

Within an arms race many of the countermoves by offenders are resultant of spotting and exploiting security weaknesses which exist as by-products brought about through social and technological development (Ekblom, 2005). These are often overlooked by crime prevention specialists. Bouloukos, Farrell, and Laycock (2003) for example, describe in the advent of the Euro currency how criminals seized an overlooked opportunity of counterfeiting a lower valued extant European coin which was virtually indistinguishable from that of a newly introduced Euro. Hence from an incidental shift in monetary coinage emerged an opportunity for crime which crime prevention specialists had not braced themselves for, and subsequently had to retrofit a solution. These wider changes are of course expected as part of societal development and progression, yet they too can provide the tools and targets for future crime. Against these changes the crime prevention arms race, as in most in nature, is often asymmetrical, i.e. the cost to one co-evolving group is far greater than the cost to the other. Dawkins and Krebs' (1979) 'life-dinner principle' between predator and prey accurately captures this differentiation - as in the co-evolution of the fox and the rabbit, one is running for this life, the other for his dinner. For crime prevention the asymmetry is similarly pronounced, crime prevention specialists required to safeguard *all* opportunities for crime, offenders needing only to exploit one (Ekblom, 2005).

Martin Killias relates these wider changes to crime in his concept of breaches, "sudden new opportunities for offending that opened as a result of changes in the technological or social environment" (2006, p. 11). These opening and closing of breaches provide the shifting tapestry on which the arms race takes place, as Laycock warns, "with the rate of change and technological innovation and the globalisation of industry, the opportunities for crime are rising at an unprecedented rate" (2004, p. 39). An example of this confluence of factors is a study by Knutsson and Kuhlhorn (1992). During the late 1960's Sweden saw a huge rise in the crime of cheque forgery which subsequently decreased by 90 per cent after 1971. The authors suggested that such a decline arose due to a change in banking procedure; prior to 1971 any cheque of less than 300 Swedish crowns would be automatically honoured irrespective of customer identification. Upon introducing mandatory identification regardless of the amount of the cheque, such a criminal breach was closed, such a crime became obsolete. Drawing parallels to iatrogenic medical practice however, in which one problem is cured only at the expense of starting another (Marx, 2001), the closing of crime breaches can have unintended consequences. For example, though cheque fraud in Sweden diminished with the advent of compulsory identification, the crime of fraudulent internet transactions began to rise (Mann & Sutton, 1998). It is almost a Faustian bargain that in obtaining new technology one surrenders to the potential creation of new opportunities for offending, and hence the continuance of the arms race.

## When a Flower Opens It Makes No Noise[3]: Recognising Opportunity

It is trite but a truism, that a breach only represents an opportunity for crime if it recognised, and then of course exploited. The breach which goes unnoticed will never be acted upon and thus holds no criminological value. It is noteworthy however to consider how information pertaining to a new or newly recognised opportunities for crime disseminate. Cohen and Machalek (1994) suggest that humans are behavioural strategists whom benefit from, and hence utilise, cultural transmission. Just as ants utilise swarm intelligence[4] to optimise food routes via creating pheromone-laden trails for fellow hungry ants (Bonabeau & Meyer, 2001), humans tend to develop and favour habits and behavioural tactics which confer some form

[3] Taken from Devlin, K. (2002). *The Millennium Problems*. Granta.

[4] Swarm intelligence pertains to the behaviour which emerges from a group of social insects used to develop efficient solutions to difficult problems (Kennedy & Eberhart,2005).

of benefit (Vila, 1994) and do so through the process of knowledge transfer. Offenders are no different. Ekblom (2007, p.51) states crime prevention faces "offending *cultures* where learning can transfer from experts and innovators to followers". This notion of criminal knowledge transfer is well established, prisons have often been labelled as 'universities of crime' where criminal information is shared and offered (Ekblom & Tilley, 2000). In arms race terms this capacity for knowledge transfer is important and suggests that knowledge gleaned by entrepreneurial offenders has the capacity to trickle-down to the offender community at large.

The proposal of knowledge transfer and cultural transmission is captured in the evolutionary theory of *memetics* proposed by Dawkins (1976). The theory of *memetics* suggests that *memes* (ideas or pieces of cultural information) evolve through selection and replicate in a manner analogous to genes through individuals and across generations. This transference can be through a variety of sources, such as word of mouth or electronic mediums like the internet. Memes themselves survives in the 'meme pool' by virtue of their memetic fitness, i.e. being of value to the possessor. Therefore just as genes which confer some form of genetic fitness remain in the gene pool, memes such as the meme for Beethoven's fifth symphony remain in the population through consistent exposure, and its inherent gratification to lovers of classical music.

The application of memetic theory to crime prevention has received little attention (an exception being Ekblom, 1999) despite the current author believing its integration may reap benefits. In relation to crime, "examples of memes are criminal values and subcultures, methods of offending, or of prevention, and the requisite designs, tools and equipment developed by either side" (Ekblom 1999, p. 30). In the proposed arms race the implication of memetics suggests criminals learn and adopt the strategies of others which have been criminogenically productive. The criminal memes to exploit opportunities and breaches therefore propagate and disseminate to an 'always listening' criminal audience. This diffusion of information is further proliferated by mediums such as the internet (Collins & Mansell, 2005) which Mann and Sutton (1998) rather aptly define as the 'open university of crime'. This proposed ability to 'Google' techniques of how to clone phones or make bombs for example changes the nature of offending, drawing the poles of offender sophistication closer together "which may mean a wider circle of offenders acquire 'expert' techniques" (Ekblom, 2005, p. 31).

## Crime Distribution: Endemism vs. Cosmopolitanism

Thinking of crime as a function of opportunity corroborates the repeated finding that crime is not randomly distributed (Eck 1997), but rather clusters in spatial hotspots (Sherman, Gartin, & Buerger, 1989), on certain products (Clarke, 1999) and on repeatedly victimised individuals and places (Pease, 1998; Eck, Clarke, & Guerette, 2007). These capture the inherent ecological nature of crime – interactions between offenders and victims in the immediate situation. Yet the ecological perspective of crime can be extended further to formulise how crime is unevenly distributed and how this may foster the foresight needed to anticipate emergent opportunities for crime.

Few crime types can be defined in ecological terms as endemic, by that it is referred to crime which appears exclusively or is confined to a particular geographic region. Rather, and in keeping with the language of ecology, many crime types are better explained by the concept of cosmopolitan distribution (Hesse et al., 1951), a cosmopolitan species being one which exists over a large geographic range (Bock, 1987). The moray eel is an example of a cosmopolitan species, being found in numerous aquatic areas around the world. Similarly crime types such as burglary or murder are found across myriad societies and geographic regions and could thus be described as cosmopolitan. When referred to in ecology however, the term cosmopolitan distribution is often far narrower in scope, suggesting that although certain species are found in numerous areas throughout the world, they are only found in conditions which are suitable for habitation and in accordance with the given species' requisite needs. These patterns of cosmopolitanism thus relate to the interactionist nature of crime, certain species as with certain crimes being ecologically dependent on certain requisite ingredients, specifically the opportunity for crime itself. From a long-term perspective and in relation to the arms race, it is these changing conditions and commensurate opportunities brought about through societal or technological development which may influence the distribution of crime. It is often viewed as trite to assert that internet fraud only occurred in the advent of the internet, the illegal cloning of phones only emerging once the mobile phone became ubiquitous. But as referred to earlier, crime and its distribution is inherently reflective of wider changes in the environmental backdrop in which opening of breaches can be exploited by the adaptive criminal. As technology 'leapfrogs' extant technology, crime takes different forms.

Can recognition of the distribution of crime, be that endemic or cosmopolitan, aid crime prevention? This can be answered by way of example, in which crime prevention specialists are alert of potential crime threats through anticipating technologies which may transcend their current endemic distribution to that of cosmopolitanism, and how such dispersal may engender new opportunities for crime. Near Field Communications (NFC) is short-range wireless technology often used in mobile phones to increase their utility and system capabilities (see Whitehead et al., 2008). It works through the insertion of a wireless chip which can represent electronic money to be used to purchase items by merely scanning one's mobile phone against appropriately synchronized detectors. The mobile phone thus becomes the possessor's train ticket, car keys and form of identification, making the extant wallet, keys and credit cards potentially redundant. Technology forecasters predict the prevalence of this form of mobile phone technology to grow markedly in future years in line with basic supply and demand laws and the commensurate drop in retail price. Mobile phone theft is already a considerable problem in most mobile phone prevalent societies (Mailley, Whitehead, & Farrell, 2006) with handsets matching all of Clarke's (1995) CRAVED model which describes the attributes which increase a products risk of theft. Adding NFC technology to an already existent 'hot product' can only be viewed as exacerbating their criminogenic value and one can assume such products will be 'tomorrows thief' phone of choice. However at present NFC operating mobiles are only available in limited areas such as Japan and China and thus are endemic in terms of their global distribution. As NFC equipped mobile phones disperse geographically and transfer from endemic to cosmopolitan distribution, related opportunities for crime are likely to become more ubiquitous. Of course this clear-cut change in distribution type is perhaps unrealistic, and social and technological development may be far more random. However the proposed endemic-cosmopolitan distinction is as much a tool of thought as an accurate indicator of geographic dispersal. Recognition of the potential for changes in space and time raises awareness of how geographic dispersal of technology and products effects new opportunities for crime. Equivalently it warns that a lack of consideration of such changes results in crime prevention playing perennial catch up against the adaptive and exploitive offender.

## How Does Crime Prevention Run the Arms Race?

The arms race thesis illustrates that crime is influenced by changing opportunities brought about through numerous external factors. It additionally highlights the reciprocity between offenders and crime prevention specialists seeking to act upon or control the same opportunities, both parties influenced by each other's actions as well as impinging external changes. The arms race thesis however poses a dilemma to crime prevention - if such adaptive change is likely then retroactive interventions may only engender a brief period of grace before the adaptive offender's next counter-move. Indeed the very notion of the adaptable offender bestows an urgency and necessity on crime prevention (Ekblom, 1997). Crime prevention must therefore position itself to be proactive and anticipate the opening of criminal breaches rather than consigning itself to mere reactionary responses. The remainder of this chapter suggests some possible ways this might be achieved.

One area of crime prevention which has yielded promising results in terms of efficacious crime reduction is 'design against crime', which seeks to design security *into* products, services, areas and buildings to maximise their crime preventive potential without sacrificing their aesthetic value nor utility (Ekblom, 2002; Gamman & Hughes, 2003). Examples include the changing from the use of money to pre-pay phone cards immediately ended the crime of stealing cash from phone boxes. Similarly phone companies through extensive product modification virtually eradicated the $800 million dollar a year crime of 'cloning' (Clarke & Newman, 2005). Other examples are more subtle, such as designing bicycle stands in a manner which encourage the locking of *both* wheel and frame to maximise security (see www.bikeoff.org). This approach is hence opportunity-centric, not seeking to bring about a change in the disposition of a potential perpetrator but rather alter the available opportunities for crime through intelligent and creative design. As Ekblom states, "any intervention in the causes of criminal events can, in principle, be improved by explicit and professional attention to design" (2005, p. 206).

Despite convincing evidence of its effectiveness, further work is still needed to empower and incentivise designers and manufacturers to consider proactively the potential for designing out crime as part of the 'standard' design process. Typically manufacturers are somewhat reluctant to do this, especially when in certain cases they may profit from crime (i.e. through sale of items to replace what is stolen) and certainly may perceive any change in process as costly and inconvenient (Clarke & Newman, 2005). The design industry itself is particularly apathetic in regards to their ability to aid crime prevention (Erol et al., 2002). Learmount (2005) found 65% of design firms when questioned believed designing out crime was not within their remit and an issue that received little attention. Encouraging designers and manufacturers to 'think thief' (Gamman & Hughes, 2003) however and alert such stakeholders of their potential roles in reducing crime is therefore important (Clarke & Eck, 2003). As

Learmount eloquently warns, "failure to tackle (product) vulnerability… could bequeath owners, users and society as a whole, a crime legacy of years" (2005 p. 146). To stay ahead of adaptive offenders' crime prevention may find efficacious methods through aiming to reduce criminal opportunity at the 'blue-print' stage in which houses, products and areas are being designed, actively considering potential for offender countermove and aiming to proactively manipulate such vulnerabilities.

The endemism-cosmopolitanism distinction illustrated that crime prevention specialists through awareness of the distribution of technology may be able to initiate bi-lateral transfer of lessons learned in relation to crime and its prevention. However knowledge capture and transfer must move forward as well as lateral and foresight is needed to look at how new technology might impact crime and its prevention. Appreciating the potential effects of such changes offers crime prevention a head start as it were in anticipating future crimes. Of course prediction by its nature is a somewhat inexact science and open to error, in that prediction is more probabilistic than absolute. However horizon scanning is commonplace in certain institutions and should not be derided as mere clairvoyance. The medical community for example invests large amounts of time and money scanning for future outbreaks of diseases, as do stockbrokers and investment companies scouring the markets in hope of finding 'the next big thing'. Furthermore it has been described and repeatedly found that crime is not random (Eck, 1997) and collectively exhibits distinct patterns which can be factored into a prediction model.

For example, in the last decade increased sophistication of global positioning technology has seen in-car satellite navigation systems become increasingly prevalent. Development of such a product could be anticipated through the obvious utility it would offer to drivers and the relative ubiquity of automobiles as a major form of transportation. However when such products were mainstreamed they were not designed without consideration of how to effectively conceal the item once in an automobile, nor were any personalisation systems such as immobilisers designed-in. In other words if a satellite navigation system was present in a car, firstly it would be clearly visible to a would-be offender and secondly, if the offender were to steal it then they or a potential buyer would have no system to overcome in order to use it. The somewhat expected result was a huge spate in theft of such products forcing manufacturers to bolt-on and retrofit added security measures. The moral to the story however is that such 'obvious' opportunities for crime could have been both predicted and prevented at no hindrance to the manufacturer nor the customer. Failure however to 'think thief' resulted in manufacture upheaval, resource usage, and potentially avoidable thefts from cars. Crime prevention must therefore project its arms race into the future, "shortening the cybernetic 'control loop' of 'change-detect-and-respond' as much as we can. Specific threats coming over the horizon can then be assessed and responded to, whether by doing nothing, further monitoring, or acting to develop and deploy preventive measures" (Ekblom, 2002, p. 163).

Scanning technological innovation in an attempt to predict future crime opportunities moves crime prevention away from the limited efficacy of retroactivity. However a potential pitfall is the deluded search for an illusive silver bullet – or panacea for crime (Marx, 2001). Uniformity in crime prevention often has negative consequences. Ashton and colleagues (1998) for example found that the recurrent design of petrol stations increased the risk of crime, relieving offenders of the "responsibility for finding anew at each station where valuable goods were kept and how they were protected" (Pease, 2005, p. 191). Mono-systems such as Microsoft networks are similarly vulnerable given their formulaic security mechanisms. Crime prevention must therefore digest the principles of Pawson and Tilley (1997) and the need for context in crime prevention, i.e. an appreciation that context is paramount in how effective crime prevention measures are. It is somewhat paradoxical that high fidelity copies of successful crime prevention initiatives often fail when implemented elsewhere, this is generally a direct result of under appreciating the various contextual factors such as implementation processes or wider situational differences that contribute to scheme success or failure. Crime prevention itself must hence acquire the ability to adapt and assimilate to the situation where it is to be implemented. Ekblom warns that the arms race dynamics makes "knowledge of what works in crime prevention a wasted asset" (2005, p. 230). Searching for the uniform solution to reducing crime may ultimately come at the cost of overlooking the paramount issue of context, giving rise to larger problems and more long term consequences.

Crime prevention can further apply the principles of nature and evolution which underpin the thesis of offender adaptation. In many of the co-evolutionary struggles which unfold in nature the use of deception or mimicry is employed to improve a species chances of survival. Ekblom (1999) cites the example of insects which possess a 'flag' on their leg that signals to predators' their distastefulness. Yet can crime prevention adopt similar shortcuts? The notion of signalling is already heavily relied upon in crime prevention, one hope the burglar alarm signals to would-be offenders that such a property poses a danger and is not worth the risk of attempting to burgle it. Similarly anti-robbery devices which discharge smoke to blind the criminal is analogous to the ink based defence mechanism of the common squid.[5] The common use of publicity in crime prevention is also similar, Johnson and Bowers (2003) finding that such activity can have a positive impact on crime, as well as the earlier described phenomena of *anticipatory benefit* whereby a reduction in crime precedes the scheme itself. Yet the use of signalling could still be furthered in crime prevention particularly through tapping into the emotions elicited by offenders during crime commission. As Cusson suggests, "one of the major goals of situational crime prevention is instilling fear in any individual contemplating a crime by increasing the risks" (1993, p. 55). Exploiting such fears through tailored publicity for example and incorporating signalling tools as part of an adaptive system of crime prevention may serve to block or reduce possible offender adaptation.

The theory of memetics is a similar field with which crime prevention can make use. As described knowledge transfer is a huge asset to the adaptable offender. Crime prevention must therefore look to "minimize the opportunities for the offender to learn or pass on that learning" (Ekblom, 1999, p. 39), making it more difficult for offenders to access restricted web-based systems for example. Smallbone and Wortley (2000) on applying SCP to sex offences against children drew similar conclusions. They found 19% of offenders claimed to use internet pornography to incite or prime sexual contact with children. Furthermore they concluded that the internet provided a forum or 'meeting of minds' as it were for offenders of this nature. In a proactive manner reducing the opportunity of such cyber connections and removing excuses via imposing mandatory registration will exert pressure on offenders of this sort and may serve to keep crime prevention ahead in the arms race.

In light of the many possible routes of adaptation and prevention, the co-evolutionary struggle between crime prevention and offenders forms what Ekblom terms a complex adaptive system, "a whole ecosystem of adapting, adjusting and calculating agents who react to the policy-maker's or practitioner's attempt to move things in a certain desired direction" (2005, p. 235). Felson (2006) similarly views crime as an ecosystem in which offenders can act both parasitically and symbiotically through feeding off available opportunities which they utilise for crime. Both perspectives illustrate the need to adopt a systemic approach to crime

[5] Biomimetics which studies and imitates the methods, mechanisms and process of the natural world is currently underutilised in crime prevention and may represent a veritable goldmine of potential innovations. See: Bar - Cohen, Y. (2006).

prevention – one which is proactive and aware of the adaptive offender. To attempt to combat adaptation crime prevention specialists must address the multiplicity of causes which contribute to crime as well as appreciate the downstream effect of wider societal changes at the context specific level. Crime prevention has to therefore develop a foresight capability, sensitive to the numerous factors which mediate crime and its prevention, not just via invoking the police but through innovation and seeking crime prevention through numerous sources.

## Conclusion

The aspiration of the present chapter was to highlight that broadening criminological thinking is necessary to optimise effective and practical crime prevention. Integral to this aim is the centrality of opportunity as a casual factor of crime. Yet opportunities for crime change, often by virtue of social and technological advancements. Commensurately these influence both offenders and crime prevention specialists whom are locked in a reciprocal arms race. To run such an arms race crime prevention specialists should seek to integrate the techniques and knowledge from numerous fields and disciplines, and in the tradition of crime science intelligently apply such knowledge in the service of reducing crime. It is hoped that through this application crime prevention can become progressively more proactive, staying ahead of adaptive offenders. Through following this precedence a systemic approach to crime prevention is better placed to anticipate, respond and accordingly adapt to potential opportunities for crime. It is through implementing this approach and developing such strategies that crime prevention can "ensure that the balance is tilted as far as possible, for as much of the time as possible, in favour of prevention specialists" (Ekblom, 1999, p. 47).

## References

Ashton, J., Senior, B., Brown, I., & Pease, K. (1998). Repeat victimisation: Offender accounts. *International Journal of Risk, Security and Crime Prevention*, *3*, 269–80.

Baldwin, J., & Bottoms, A. (1976). *The urban criminal: A study in Sheffield.* London: Tavistock.

Bar - Cohen, Y. (2006). Biomimetics – Using nature to inspire human innovation. *Bioinspiration & Biomimetics*, *1*, 1–12.

Bock, C. E. (1987). Distribution- abundance relationships of some Arizona land-birds: a matter of scale? *Ecology*, *68*, 124–129.

Bonabeau, E., & Meyer, C. (2001). Swarm intelligence: A whole new way to think about business. *Harvard Business Review, May edition. 79*(5), 106-114.

Bouloukos, A., Farrell, G., & Laycock, G. (2003). Transnational organised crime in Europe and North America: Towards a framework for prevention. In K. Aromaa, S. Leppä, S. Nevala, & N. Ollus (Eds.), *Crime and Criminal Justice Systems in Europe and North America 1995-1997,* (pp.176-192). Publications Series no. 40. Helsinki, European Institute for Crime Prevention and Control, affiliated with the United Nations.

Bowers, K. J., Johnson, S. J. & Pease, K. (2004). Prospective hot-spotting: The future of crime mapping? *British Journal of Criminology*, *36*, 1–18.

Brantingham, P. J., & Brantingham. P. L. (1995). Criminality of Place: Crime generators and crime attractors. *European Journal of Criminal Policy and Research, 3*, 5-26.

Brown, R. (2004). The effectiveness of electronic immobilization: Changing patterns of temporary and permanent vehicle theft. In M. G. Maxfield & R. V. Clarke (Eds.), *Understanding and Preventing Car Theft*, Crime Prevention Studies, Vol 17, (pp.101–120). Monsey, NJ: Criminal Justice Press.

Campbell, A. (1995). A few good men: Evolutionary psychology and female adolescent aggression. *Ethology and Sociobioiogy*, *16*, 99-123.

Chainey, S. P., & Ratcliffe, J. H. (2005). *GIS and Crime Mapping*. London: Wiley.

Clarke, R. V. (1992). Introduction. In: R.V. Clarke (Ed.), *Situational Crime Prevention: Successful Case Studies* (pp.3-36). Albany, NY: Harrow and Heston.

—. (1999). *Hot Products: Understanding, anticipating and reducing demand for stolen goods.* (Police Research Series Paper 112). London: Home Office Policing and Reducing Crime Unit.

—. (2005). Seven misconceptions of situational crime prevention. In N. Tilley (Ed.), *Handbook of Crime Prevention and Community Safety* (pp.39–69). Cullompton, UK: Willan Publishing.

Clarke, R. V., & Newman, G. (2005). Modifying criminogenic products – what role for government? In Clarke, R.V & Newman, G. (Eds.), *Designing out crime from products and systems. Crime Prevention Studies. Vol. 18* (pp.7-84). Monsey, NY: Criminal Justice Press and Cullompton: Willan Publishing.

Clarke, R. V., & Weisburd, D. (1994). Diffusion of crime control benefits: observations on the reverse of displacement. In R. V. Clarke (Ed.),

*Crime prevention studies*, vol. 2 (pp.74-84). Monsey, NY: Criminal justice press.

Cohen, S. (1987). *Folk devils and moral panics*. 2nd edition. Oxford: Blackwell.

Cohen, L. E., & Felson, M. (1979). Social change and crime rate trends: A routine activity approach. *American Sociological Review*, *44*, 588-608.

Cohen, L. E. & Machalek, R. (1994). The normalcy of crime: From Durkheim to evolutionary ecology. *Rationality and Society*, *6*, 286-308.

Copes, H., & Cherbonneau, C. (2006). The key to auto theft: Emerging Methods of Auto Theft from the Offenders Perspective. *British Journal of Criminology, 46*(5), 917-934.

Cornish, D., & Clarke, R. (1986). Situational prevention, displacement of crime and rational choice theory. In K. Heal & G. Laycock (Eds.), *Situational Crime Prevention: From Theory into Practice* (pp.1-16). London: Her Majesty's Stationery Office.

Cusson, M. (1993). Situational deterrence: Fear during the criminal event. *Crime Prevention Studies,* 1 (pp.55-68). Monsey, N.Y.: Willow Tree Press.

Dawkins, R. (1976). *The Selfish Gene.* Oxford, UK: Oxford University Press.

Dawkins, R., & Krebs, J. R. (1979). Arms races between and within species. *Proceedings of the royal society of London. Series B, Biological sciences, 205*(1161), 489 – 511.

Devlin, K. (2002). *The Millennium Problems*. Granta: London.

Donkin, S., & Wellsmith, M. (2006). Cars stolen in burglaries: The sandwell experience. *Security Journal*, *19*, 22–32.

Eck, J. E. (1997). Preventing crime at places. In L. Sherman, D. Gottfredson, D. MacKenzie, J. Eck, P. Reuter, & S. Bushway (Eds.), *Preventing Crime: What Works, What Doesnt and Whats Promising*, A report to the United States Congress (pp.1-70). US Department of Justice.

Eck, J. E., Clarke, R. V., & Guerette, R. T. (2007). Risky facilities: Crime concentration in homogenous sets of establishments and facilities. In Farrell et al. (Eds.), *Imagination for crime prevention: Essays in honour of Ken Pease*. Crime Prevention Studies (pp.225–264). Monsey, NY: Criminal justice press

Ekblom, P. (1999). Can we make crime prevention adaptive by learning from other evolutionary struggles? *Studies on Crime and Crime Prevention, 8*, 27-51.

—. (2000). The conjunction of criminal opportunity - A tool for clear, joined-up thinking about community safety and crime reduction. In S. Ballintyne, K. Pease & V. McLaren, (Eds.), *Secure foundations: key issues in crime prevention, crime reduction and community safety*. London: Institute for Public Policy Research

—. (2005). Designing products against crime. In N. Tilley (Ed.), *Handbook of Crime Prevention and Community Safety* (pp.203– 244). Cullompton, UK: Willan Publishing.

—. (2007). Making offenders richer. In G. Farrell, K. Bowers, S. D. Johnson, & M. Townsley (Eds.), *Imagination for crime prevention: Essays in honour of Ken Pease* (pp.41–58). Crime Prevention Studies. Monsey, NY: Criminal justice press.

Ekblom, P., & Tilley, N. (2000). Going equipped: Criminology, situational crime prevention and the resourceful offender. *British Journal of Criminology*, *40*, 376 – 398.

Ekblom, P., & Pease, K. (1995). Evaluating crime prevention. In M. Tonry & D. P. Farrington (Eds.), *Building a Safer Society: Strategic Approaches to Crime Prevention. Crime and Justice* 19 (pp.21–89). Chicago, IL: University of Chicago Press.

Ekblom, P., & Sidebottom, A. (2007). What do you mean, Is it secure? Redesigning language to be fit for the task of assessing the security of domestic and personal electronic goods. *European Journal on Criminal Policy and Research*, vol. 14, pp. 61-87.

Erol, R., Press, M., Cooper, T., & Thomas, M. (2002). Designing out Crime: Raising awareness of crime reduction in the design industry. *Security Journal, 15*(1), 49-62.

Farrell, G., & Pease K. (1993) Once bitten, twice bitten: Repeat victimisation and its implications for crime prevention. *Crime Prevention Unit Series, Paper 46. Police research Group.* London: Home Office

Felson, M. (2002). *Crime and Everyday Life*. Third Edition. Thousand Oaks, CA: Pine Forge Press.

—. (2006). *Crime and Nature*. Sage Publications.

Felson, M., Berends, R., Richardson, B. & Veno, A. (1997). Reducing pub hopping and related crime. In R. Homel (Eds.), *Policing for Prevention: Reducing Crime, Public intoxication and Injury* (pp.115–132), Crime Prevention Studies, 7, Criminal Justice Press, New York.

Felson, M., & Clarke, R. V. (1998). *Opportunity makes the thief.* Crime Detection and Prevention Series, Paper 98. Police Research Group. London: Home Office.

Flood-Page, C. & Taylor, J. (2003). *Crime in England and Wales 2001/2002: Supplementary Volume*. Home Office Statistical Bulletin 1/03. London: Home Office.

Gamman, L., & Hughes, B. (2003). Thinking thief: Designing out misuse, abuse and criminal aesthetics. *Ingenia, 15*. Retrieved on 14th February 2008 from www.raeng.org.uk/news/publications/ingenia/issue15/Gamman.pdf

Gandhirajan, C. K., Thilagaraj, R., & Jaishankar, K. (2003). Journey to Crime: Spatial behaviour of criminal gangs in Chennai City. *The Indian Police Journal, 3*, 13-21, July – September.

Gottfredson, M. R., & Hirschi, T. (1990). *A general theory of crime*. Stanford, CA: Stanford University Press.

Hesse, R., Allee, W. C., & Schmidt, K. P. (1951). *Ecological animal geography*. 2nd edition. Wiley: New York, NY, USA.

Hesseling, R. B. P. (1994). Displacement: A review of the empirical literature. In R. V. Clarke (Ed.), *Crime Prevention Studies* (pp.197–230), *3*. Monsey, NY: Criminal Justice Press.

Homel, R. (1997). Preventing alcohol related injuries. In O'Malley & Sutton, A. (Eds.), *Crime prevention in Australia: Issues in policy and Research (pp.* 217-237*)*. Sydney: Federation Press.

Johnson, S. D., & Bowers, K. J. (2003). *Spreading the Word: The role of publicity in crime prevention*. Home Office Research Findings 213 . London: Home Office.

Johnson, S. D., & Bowers, K. J. (2004). The burglary as clue to the future: the beginnings of prospective hot-Spotting. *European Journal of criminology*, *1*(2), 237-255.

—. (2007) Burglary Prediction: The roles of Theory, Flow and Friction. In G. Farrell, K. Bowers, S. D. Johnson, & M. Townsley (Eds.) *Imagination for crime prevention: Essays in honour of Ken Pease* (pp.203–224). Crime Prevention Studies. Monsey, NY: Criminal justice press.

Johnson, S. D., Bernasco, W., Bowers, K. J., Elffers, H., Ratcliffe, J., Rengert, G., & Townsley, M. T. (2007). Space-Time patterns of burglary: A cross national assessment of residential burglary. *Journal of Quantitative Criminology, 23*(3), 201-219.

Karstedt, S., & Farrall, S. (forthcoming). Crimes of everyday life: Nusiness practices and consumer compliances. *Compliance and Regulatory Journal.*

Kennedy, J., & Eberhart, R. C. (2005). *Swarm Intelligence*. Morgan Kaufmann, San Francisco, CA.

Killias, M. (2006). The opening and closing of breaches: A theory on crime waves, law creation and crime prevention. *European Journal of Criminology*, *3*(1), 11–31.

Kitchen, R. M. (1994) Cognitive maps: what are they and why study them? *Journal of Environmental Psychology, 14,* 1-19.

Knutsson, J. & Kuhlhorn, E. (1992). Macro-measures against crime: The example of check forgeries. In R. V. Clarke (Ed.), *Situational crime prevention, successful case studies* (pp.113-121). Albany, NY: Harrow and Heston.

Laycock, G. (2003). *Launching crime science*. London: JDI. Retrieved on 14th February 2008 from http://www.jdi.ucl.ac.uk/publications/crime_science_series/launching.php

—. (2004). New challenges for law enforcement. *European Journal on Criminal Policy and Research, 10*, 39–53.

Learmount, S. (2005). Promoting design against crime. In R.V. Clarke & G. Newman (Eds.), *Designing out crime from products and systems* (pp.141-178). *Crime Prevention Studies, 18.* Monsey, NY: Criminal Justice Press and Cullompton: Willan Publishing.

Mailley, J., Whitehead. S., & Farrell, G. (2006). Progress and prospects in the prevention of mobile phone theft. *Justice of the Peace, 170*(22), 404-407.

Mann, D., & Sutton, M. (1998). Netcrime: More change in the organisation of thieving. *British Journal of Criminology*, *38*, 201–229.

Marx, G. T. (2001). Technology and social control: The search for the illusive silver bullet. In P. B. Baltes & N. J. Smelser (Eds.), *International encyclopedia of the social and behavioral sciences,* 23, 15506-15512. New York: Elsevier.

Mischel, W. (1968). *Personality and assessment.* New York: Wiley.

Newman, M. E. J. (2005). Power laws, Pareto distributions and Zipf's law. *Contemporary Physics, 46*, 323–351.

Newman, G., & Clarke, R. V. (2002). *Etailing: New opportunities for crime, new opportunities for prevention.* Produced for the Foresight crime prevention panel by the Jill Dando Institute of Crime Science, UCL.

Pawson, R., & Tilley, N. (1997). *Realistic Evaluation.* London, UK: Sage.

Pease, K. (1998) Repeat victimisation: Taking stock. *Crime detection and Prevention Series Paper 90.* London: Home Office.

—. (2005). Science in the service of crime reduction. In N. Tilley (Ed.), *Handbook of crime prevention and community safety* (pp. 173-199). Cullompton: Willan.

Pidgeon, N., Kasperson, R., & Slovic, P (2003). *The Social Amplification of Risk and Risk Communication.* Cambridge: CUP

Reiss, A. J. (1976) *Settling the frontiers of a pioneer in American criminology: Henry McKay.* In J. F. Short, Jr (Eds.), *Delinquency, crime, and society* (pp.64–88). Chicago: Chicago University Press.

Rengert, G. F., Piquero, A. R., & Jones, P. R. (1999) Distance decay re-examined. *Criminology*, 37, 427–445.

Reppetto, T. A. (1976). Crime prevention and the displacement phenomenon. *Crime & Delinquency*, 22, 166 – 177.

Rossmo, D. K. (2000) *Geographic Profiling*. Boca Raton, Florida, USA: CRC Press.

Schmitt, D. V. & Pilcher, J. J. (2004). Evaluating evidence of psychological adaptation. How do we know one when we see one? *Psychological Science*, *15*(10), 643–649.

Sherman, L. W., Gartin, P. R., & Buerger, M. E. (1989) Hot spots of predatory crime: Routine activities and the criminology of place. *Criminology*, *27*(1), 27-55.

Sherman, L., Gottfredson, D., MacKenzie, D., Eck, J., Reuter, P., & Bushway, S. (1998). *Preventing crime: What works, what doesnt, what's promising*. National Institute of Justice, Washington.

Shover, N. (1996). *Great pretenders: Pursuits and careers of persistent thieves*. London: Westview Press/Harper Collins.

Smallbone, S. W., & Wortley, R. K. (2000). *Child sexual abuse in Queensland: Offender characteristics and modus operandi*. Brisbane: Queensland Crime Commission.

Smith, D. J. (2000). Changing situations and changing people. In A. von Hirsch (Ed.), *Ethical and social perspectives on situational crime prevention.* Portland, Oregon: Hart Publishing.

Smith, M. J., Clarke, R. V. & Pease, K. (2002). Anticipatory benefits in crime prevention. In N. Tilley (Ed.), *Analysis for crime prevention. Crime prevention studies* (pp. 71–88), vol. 13. Monsey, NY: Criminal justice press.

Smith, M., & Tilley, N. (Eds.). (2005). *Crime Science, New approaches to preventing and detecting crime.* Crime Science Series, Cullompton: Willan.

Sommer, P. (2004). The future for the policing of cybercrime. *Computer Fraud & Security Bulletin*, Jan, 8-12.

Townsley, M., Homel, R., & Chaseling, J. (2003). Infectious burglaries: A test of the near repeat hypothesis. *British Journal of Criminology*, *43*, 615-633.

Vila, B. J. (1994). A general paradigm for understanding criminal behavior: Extending evolutionary ecological theory. *Criminology, 32*, 501-549.

Walsh, D. (1994). The obsolescence of crime forms. *Crime Prevention Studies 2,* 149-164, Monsey, N.Y: Willow Tree Press.

Webb, B. (1997). Steering column locks and motor vehicle theft: Evaluations from three countries. In R. V. Clarke (Ed.), *Situational crime prevention: Successful case studies* (2nd Ed.). Guilderland, NY: Harrow and Heston.

Webb, B., Smith, M. & Laycock, G. (2004). Designing out vehicle crime through vehicle licensing and registration systems. In M. G. Maxfield & R. V. Clarke (Eds.), *Understanding and Preventing Car Theft* (pp. 67-84), Crime Prevention Studies, Vol 17. Monsey, NJ: Criminal Justice Press.

Weisburd, D., Wyckoff, L., Ready, J., Eck., E. Hinkle, J., & Gajewski, H. (2006). Does crime just move around the corner?: A controlled study of spatial displacement and diffusion of crime control benefits. *Criminology, 44* (3), 549-591.

Whitehead, S., Mailley, J., Storer, I., McCardle, J., Torrens, G. & Farrell, G. (2008). IN SAFE HANDS: A Review of Mobile Phone Anti-theft Designs. *European Journal on Criminal Policy and Research, 14*(1), 39-60.

Wiles, P., & Costello, A. (2000) *The road to nowhere: The evidence for travelling criminals*. Home Office Research Study No. 207).

Wortley, R. K. (1996). Guilt, shame, and situational crime prevention. *Crime Prevention Studies*, 5, 115-132.

—. (2002). *Situational prison control: Crime prevention in correctional institutions*. Cambridge studies in criminology.

Wortley, R. K. & Smallbone, S. W. (2006). Applying situational principles to sex offences against children. In R. K. Wortley & S. W. Smallbone (Eds.), *Situational perspectives on sexual crimes against children* (pp.7-36). New York: Criminal Justice Press.

Zimbardo, P. (2007). *The Lucifer Effect: How good people turn evil.* Rider & Co.

# CHAPTER TWENTY

# INTER-COUNTRY ADOPTION AND HUMAN RIGHTS VIOLATIONS IN INDIA

DEBARATI HALDER AND K. JAISHANKAR

## Abstract

Adoption in India is synonymous with numerous laws and guidelines explaining safer and legal ways to relocate orphans, remanded, or deserted children to their new homes and families. But the issue of transnational or inter-country adoption still cries for attention in matters of both the parents (both biological and foster parents) and the child's violation of rights. Unlike the regular in country adoption laws, very few laws or guidelines have been created to protect the interests of the children, their natural and adoptive parents. It was only after the Public Interest Litigation was filed by Mr. Laxmikant Pandey regarding inter-country adoption rules that the Supreme Court drafted certain guidelines to protect the interest of the children and the parties involved. This led to the formation of the Centre for Adoption. The resource authorities' guidelines are the only available compact guidelines that are regulating the inter-country adoption in India. Questions concerning a safer environment for the adopted child when taken abroad, exploitation, dissertation, discrimination, inheritance rights, and safeguards against illegal trafficking still need to be looked at in depth. In spite of such noble efforts by the law makers as well as the courts, the picture is not very satisfactory. As a result the plight of foreign adoptive parents is also pitiful. Foreign parents are often victimized by unnecessary delays caused by long proceedings which cause unwanted harassment. Sometimes they even become innocent targets of national as well as international political situations. The authors analyse the laws regulating transnational adoption in India, find out the loopholes which encourage various human rights violations in the name of inter-country adoption and suggest some solutions to check the growing violation of human rights involved in this issue.

## Introduction

Inter-country Adoption (ICA), began primarily as an ad hoc humanitarian response to children orphaned by the Second World War, who could not find a family to care for them in their own country However, now it is a complex social phenomenon that has lent itself to serious abuse (Krishnakumar, 2005). Adoption has a three tire meaning, namely:

- Taking up all legal and social duties and responsibilities of a non biological child as the adopter's own child,
- Statutory process of terminating a child's legal rights and duties towards the natural parents (Ghosh, 2006) and
- Replacing the child in the family of foster parents in its foster home.

While in country adoptions in India have become much easier with the already existing Hindu Adoption and Maintenance Act of 1956, Guardianship and Wards Acts of 1890, Juvenile Justice Act of 1986, Juvenile Justice Care and Protection Act of 2000 and 2006 (Amended). Inter-country adoptions still require the establishment of universal laws. The draft guidelines on adoption of Indian children prepared by the Central Adoption Resource Agency (CARA), Ministry of Child and Women Development, can throw little light on the problems of inter-country adoption. In spite of the carefully drafted guidelines, researches, newspaper reports and innovative new coverage's' by media have discovered the existence of a huge amount of child right violation in inter-country adoptions in India. Along with these violations, the parental rights are also being violated in the name of adoption. Numerous red tapes, domestic as well as international formalities, international treaties, human rights laws make anxious adoptive parents opt for illegal ways, such as "buying children" in an attempted "legalized" manner which most often results in risking the safety of both the child as well as the adoptive parents.

This chapter analyses the provisions made by CARA in context to inter-country adoption and finds out the various human rights violations in the name of transnational adoption in India. The chapter concludes with certain suggestions to combat the problem from both legal as well as criminological perspectives.

## Part I. Introduction to CARA guidelines

Considering the need for a regularized body to look after adoption procedures in India the Central Adoption Resource Authority (CARA) was established in 1990 under the aegis of the Ministry of Welfare in pursuance of Cabinet decision dated 9.5.1990. After the CARA became an autonomous society in 1999 the government designated it as the Central Authority on 17.7.2003 to present the Hague Convention on Protection of Children and Cooperation in respect to inter-country Adoption (1993). The guidelines for in country adoption were introduced in 2004 but it took a little longer time to set up the guidelines for inter-country adoption, which was finally drafted in 2006. These guidelines are nothing but a follow up of various directions given by the Supreme Court of India in L.K. Pandey vs. Union of India (WP No 1171 of 1982 and other cases). These guidelines are at par with the Juvenile Justice Care and protection (Amendment) Act, 2006, and are amended and updated from time to time keeping in mind the welfare of such child (CARA, 2008).

The policies regarding trans-national adoption are embedded in Part II, in Para 2.4., Part III, in Para 3.4, Part IV in Para 4.10 and 4.11, Part V in Para 5.4. The procedure for such adoption is depicted in Part VI, Para 6.5. Part II. The CARA guidelines depict in the beginning that it encourages in country adoption rather than inter-country adoption and only where the child finds no suitable home in the country, trans-national adoption would be considered. The next section of the chapter discusses various provisions regarding agencies, suitable child, procedure and the rights that are described in the CARA guidelines.

### *The proper channel*

CARA guidelines repeatedly depict that individual adoption efforts for in country as well as inter-country are not recognized. All adoptions must take place through specialized agencies. The specialized adoption agency shall work under the overall supervision of State Adoption Resource Agency. In absence of such agency in any state, the concerned State Government Department shall carry out all its functions. All Child Care Institutions (CCI) must be registered under the provisions laid down under the Juvenile Justice (Care and Protection of Children) Amendment Act, 2006 as per Section-34 (3).The State Government shall recognize suitable CCI's as specialized adoption agencies under Section 41(4) of the Juvenile Justice Amendment Act, 2006. The specialized adoption agencies can turn into agencies for inter-country adoption only when they have proper infrastructure for normal adoptable children as well as children with special needs, and have quality child care services. In addition to these, they must comply with all the requirements of CARA, such as proper registration, aim and objectives of the agencies, standards of childcare as provided under the JJ Act and also rules framed by Government of India or her respective States. These include proper communication facilities, regular health checkups for the children and many more. These specialized agencies can apply for recognition by CARA through the State Government concerned. Once recognised, the agency becomes a Recognized Indian Placement Agency (RIPA) and is duly recognised by the CARA as the only agency for transnational adoption. CARA shall develop a set of standards or model accreditation criteria for RIPAs as envisaged under the Hague Convention of 29 May 1993 on Protection of Children and Cooperation in respect to inter-country adoption. Until then, as an interim measure, the RIPAs will be treated as accredited agencies for placing Indian children in inter-country adoption.

The specialized adoption agencies look after the rehabilitation of the adoptable children for inter-country adoption from the domestic side. However, a foreign social/child welfare agency/accredited agency desirous of sponsoring applications of foreign adoptive parents for adopting an Indian child can also make an application for authorization to CARA through its central authority/competent authority and the Office of the Indian Diplomatic Mission in that country. Foreign agencies recommended for the purpose by the Indian Diplomatic Mission may be considered by CARA for authorization. No authorization is required for Central Authorities. But such foreign adoption agencies can be recognized only when it is duly registered under the relevant law of the concerned country. Thus, it should be recognized/ licensed by the appropriate authority of that country to undertake inter-country adoption. It also has to be duly accredited by the Competent Authority under the Hague Convention on Inter-country Adoptions, 1993 (wherever applicable). These are:

- It has submitted its memorandum, mission statement, copies of registration status.
- Latest license issued by the concerned Government authority to undertake international adoptions.
- List of board/executive members and list of countries it is working with.
- It should be a child welfare agency with an established standing and must be staffed with qualified social workers who have experience in the field of adoption.

- It should submit the activities of the organization, annual reports for the last 5 years, list of staff with their qualifications and accounts for the last three years.
- Such agencies should run on a non-commercial and non-profit basis and should provide an annual statement on payment made to the Indian agencies.
- It has to give an undertaking that in case of any trouble caused to the child by maltreatment or abuse, it will inform the concerned Child Protection Services/Government Department, Indian Diplomatic Mission, CARA and the concerned RIPA immediately with full details and immediate action will be taken to protect the child.
- Additionally rehabilitation efforts must be communicated to all concerned.
- Finally the head/chief executive of the organisation should be willing to sign a written undertaking to follow the guidelines and to send progress reports as required.

Agencies that would follow the above guidelines would be recognized by CARA for sponsoring applications of foreign prospective adoptive parents. Prospective parents could be NRIs (Non Residential Indians), OCIs (Overseas Citizens of India), PIOs (People of Indian Origin) or international citizens.

### *Who are adoptable for inter-country adoption?*

As per CARA and the Juvenile Justice Care and Protection (Amendment) Act 2006 guidelines, only three types of children are recognized as adoptable. These include children who are orphans and are already under the care of some specialized adoption agency, abandoned and those who are surrendered. In case of an abandoned child below two years, such declaration shall be done within a period of sixty days from the time the child is found. For an abandoned child above two years of age, such a declaration shall be done within the period of four months. In case of a surrendered child, two months reconsideration time shall be given to the biological parent or parents after surrender before declaring the child legally free for adoption.

### *The procedure*

CARA guidelines have given a compact procedure for the inter-country adoption. Let us briefly examine these procedures.

The first step is the registration of the prospective adoptive parents who are desirous of adopting Indian children with the nearest Authorized Foreign Adoption Agencies (AFAA) or Central Authority/Government Department dealing with adoption matters. The applicants should obtain the permission of the competent authority of their country for adopting a child from India wherever required.

In the second step a home study report of the prospective parents should be prepared by a professional social worker of the AFAA or Central Authority/Government Department dealing with adoption matters in their country of habitual residence which should remain valid for 2 years only. Each application should indicate any preferences the PAP(s) might have about the child's age, sex, physical/medical condition, or location within India.

In the third step the AFAA/CA/concerned Government Department of the receiving country shall submit one attested/notarized copy of the adoption application along with the requisite documents directly to CARA for approval. The AFAA/CA/concerned Government Department of the receiving country may indicate their preference of a particular RIPA(s), if any. On approval of the application by the CARA, the adoption case would be opened and a suitable recognized Indian placement agency would be identified by the CARA to meet all the demands of the adoption.

In the fourth step the RIPA shall make every effort to match a child according to the choice given by the PAP(s) and shall forward a copy of the CSR and MER of the matched child to the AFAA/CA/concerned Government Department of the receiving country along with a letter of introduction about the child. This process is commonly called a "referral for adoption". The RIPA shall not transmit this information to the PAP(s) directly. Once the matching information has been received and discussed by the AFAA/CA/concerned Government Department of the receiving country with the PAP(s), the PAP(s) may then visit the child in India.

On acceptance of the child by the PAP(s), the AFAA/CA/concerned Government Department of the receiving country shall send back the original copy of the "referral for adoption" to RIPA, within four weeks of receipt of the referral, along with the following documents: CSR and MER duly signed by PAP(s) as well as notarized/ attested, and power of attorney in favour of the official/social worker of RIPA for filing the case in the court. The AFAA/CA/concerned Government Department of the receiving country shall send a copy of the "referral for adoption" to CARA along with all relevant documents.

In this step the concerned RIPA shall send to CARA the following documents for issuance of the No-Objection Certificate:

- Copy of the CSR and MER duly signed by the PAP(s)
- Release Order from CWC
- Clearance Certificate, where ever required.

After scrutiny of the relevant documents, CARA shall expeditiously issue No objection certificate (NOC) for the placement of a particular child in inter-country adoption, ensuring that due procedures have been followed and the placement is in the best interest of the child. CARA would then mail the copies of the NOC to RIPA, SARA, AFAA/ CA/concerned Government Department of the receiving country following which the concerned Central Authority shall act promptly to conclude an Article 17(c) of the Hague convention on inter-country adoption agreement with CARA and notify the CARA, AFAAs, RIPA and the PAP(s) accordingly. Only after such procedure is completed, a decision to entrust the child to the PAP(s) can be taken.

This step concerns filing of the petition in a competent court with all required documents by the RIPA to get an appropriate order on the placement of the child with the PAP(s) and allowing the child to travel along with the PAP(s) to their country of habitual residence. After the issuance of the court order, the child has to be given required passport and visa to leave for the habitual residence of his/ her adoptive parents. The guidelines clearly mention that the child must be accompanied by the adoptive parents. The adoptive parents are also required to come and stay with the child in India for a minimum one week so that they get a chance to get acquainted with each other.

The last step is the progress reports stage where the AFAA/CA/concerned Government Department of the receiving country shall keep CARA informed about the progress of the placement through half-yearly post placement reports for a period of two years in all such cases where adoptions are finalized in India. Cases where adoptions are finalized in the receiving country, the AFAA/CA/concerned Government Department of the receiving country shall transmit a copy of the adoption order/citizenship certificate to CARA at an early date.

### *Duties of the government in case of abuse of the child*

The Indian diplomatic missions are envisaged with the duty to ensure safeguards of children of Indian origin adopted by foreign parents against neglect, maltreatment, exploitation or abuse. Whenever a report is received on disruption of adoption of an Indian child by a foreign/PIO/NRI/OCI couple, the Embassy should contact the local central authority and other concerned authorities to ensure that the interest of the child is looked after.

A report in this regard shall also be sent to CARA at the earliest. In a disruption case where the child is required to be returned to India, the Embassy may render necessary help and facilitate the repatriation of the child in consultation with the local authorities, agency and CARA.

### *Rights of the adoptive parents and the adopted child*

The CARA guidelines have carefully drafted rights for adopted children and the parents, both adoptive and biological. Such rights include right to a family life, education, health, a dignified life and over all the right to know about their biological parents. The adoptive parents are also offered equal rights, such as right to choose the sex, age of the child, right to know the medical background, biological parents and proper legal procedures from the domestic side.

CARA has also highlighted the rights of the biological parents in beautiful terms. The guidelines have stated in compassionate terms that biological parents should be treated fairly and with respect, they should be encouraged to inform the authorities about the proper birth dates, medical histories and reasons for surrendering the child. Their religious preferences for their child's upbringing are also noted. Unwed mothers are guaranteed secrecy by this guideline as well. Finally biological parents shall not be coerced into making any commitment to an adoption plan prior to the birth of the child. CARA guidelines have also mentioned about the counselling of the child as well as the parents to get adjusted to each other. However, these guidelines fail to protect the interests of the child as well as the parents involved in the inter-country adoption. This is discussed in the next part.

## Part 2. Types of violation of human rights

Adoption is the legal relocation of an abandoned, deserted or dejected child in lawful methods. But right from the period when a child is marked as ready for adoption, he or she and the parents, both biological and adoptive are subjected to various types of violation of human rights in India. At first we would discuss about child right violations and then the parental rights violations.

### *Child trafficking in the guise of transnational adoption*

The biggest threat to the child in inter-country adoption is becoming a victim of child trafficking racket. While for in country adoption, there are strict rules and guidelines prescribed in the Hindu Adoption and Maintenance Act, 1956, Guardian and Wards Act, 1890, the Juvenile Justice Care and Protection, Act (Amended) 2006, India lacks universal law for inter-country adoption. After the domestic procedure for adoption by the foreign adopting parents is over, it becomes more a question of international law and international treaties to look after the well being of the child. Moreover, the lack of awareness regarding the legal procedures for inter-country adoption has given rise to many fake adoption agencies. Children are sold abroad by providing false information about them, falsifying documents, and making use of loopholes in the adoption guidelines prescribed by the Supreme Court. Some agencies also make bargain offers to adoptive parents for the wholesale purchase of babies, while some others seem to blackmail those who refuse to increase the purchase price of babies. International placement agencies collect payment far in excess of the actual adoption costs, sharing a portion of this with the Indian adoption agencies (Krishnakumar, 2005). The lure of easy money tempts agencies to dodge ethical norms. Despite the child maintenance amount and lawyers fees being stipulated, they (adoption agencies) sell the child (in the guise of receiving donations) to foreigners who are desperate to parent (Santhanam, 1999).

Studies have shown that many child racketeers come in disguise as adoptive parents to use the child for different purposes like child prostitution, begging and even organ trade (Dixit, 2001). Frontline, a leading magazine for social causes in its various issues, in 2005, revealed a multi-billion-dollar, countrywide racket in inter-country adoption of children, run by private adoption agencies that exploit the loopholes in the rules. The investigation pointed out that states like Andhra Pradesh and Tamil Nadu have hundreds of adoption agencies who are running child trafficking business successfully. These agencies gain license from the government but use the loopholes in the rules and regulations to sell children under the disguise of lawful adoption.

## *Post adoption negligence*

When the adoption is in country, the voluntary coordination committees, various child rights activists and the adoption agency may have an access to find out the post adoption status of the child in its foster home. In this way, child exploitation, the securities of health and nutrition, mental development of the child can be taken care of. But when the child is given for inter-country adoption, post adoption follow-ups become increasingly difficult. Ramamurthy (The Hindu, Sat, 23rd December,

2003) brought to attention the case of M. Cynthia who was abandoned by her German adoptive parents after five years of adoption. They sent her back to a friend's house in Chennai in September 2000 because of adjustment problems. The adoption agency had no idea that she was back in India or that she had been facing problems with her adoptive parents. They also had no clue that she was being treated as a hired help by the family in Chennai. Such cases point out the fate of children who return to the orphanage again and continue to live a life without any future. Even though CARA guidelines outline the role of the Indian diplomatic missions, foreign accredited agencies and professional social workers in protecting a child from post adoption maltreatment, it has virtually not helped anyone.

### *Post adoption domestic succession*

Even though adoption severs a child from its biological family, in some cases when any relative of the biological family leaves any material property for the adopted child, it becomes a matter of great concern over the domestic as well as private international law. In many cases such succession is swiftly covered up by the other probable heirs on the pretext of “adoption”, while in other cases the domestic government fails to recognize the rights of the successor because he or she is a “non entity” in the mother land after inter-country adoption. The smooth succession for any inter-country adopted child thus remains a Herculean task. Once the testator dies after bequeathing the property in the name of the child who had been given in adoption, the identity of the child has to be proved. In cases where there is a challenge to the succession by other survivors, the procedure becomes even tougher. The country of residence will take the matter as per the laws of domicile and if such succession becomes legally void due to any unfortunate mistake, the adopted child would never be able to claim legal rights of the property and there by has to suffer great financial, physical and emotional agony. Unfortunately India has not entered into any agreement or treaties to solve such succession matters. The British law still rules the courts in such cases. Every adopted child develops a strong inclination to know his/ her roots at some point of time. Such legal turmoil over successions from the biological family may even leave the adoptee in great frustration.

## *Violation of parental rights*

### *Religious discrimination*

Religious discrimination is a border line violation of basic rights for both the parents as well as the child.

Prior to the amendment of Juvenile Justice Care and Protection Act (Amended), 2006, adoption procedures in India were not secular. The Hindus were guided by Hindu Adoption and Maintenance Act, 1956 and the non Hindus including Muslims, Christians, Parsis, were covered by Guardians and Wards Act, 1890. As such the old laws discriminated the needy child as well as their prospective parents. The Hindu Adoption and Maintenance Act, 1956 extends only to the Hindus, which are defined under Section-2 of the Act. Under this Law only Hindus could adopt babies who are raised or sheltered in Hindu homes. Minority castes such as Christians, Muslims or Parsis did not recognize adoption hence the adoptive parents had to remain as guardians to their adopted children as per the Guardian and Wards Act, 1890.

The amended Juvenile Justice Care and Protection Act of 2006 eradicated the problem of racial discrimination to a certain extent. The present Act amended Sec 41 of the previous Act and in Sec 21, Clause (ii), states that the court may allow a child to be given in adoption to a person irrespective of marital status or to parents of same sex, irrespective of the number of living biological sons or daughters, or to childless couples.

Unfortunately, there is no uniform rule regarding inter-country adoption. Hence the adoptive parents from overseas have to become guardians to their adopted children first as per the Guardians and Wards Act, 1890 irrespective of their religion. The adoption finalises only when the country of residence of the adoptive parents grants a final nod for adoption according to their laws. It is indeed tedious for a prospective parent as well as the child to be in the half adopted situation unless the adoptive parents are finally getting the adoption order from the respective country. As per CARA guidelines, in case of surrendered children, the biological parents can put their preferences about the religious upbringing of the child. Ironically this enhances the chances of the child being victimized in his / her adoptive home overseas.

### *Cheating the adoptive parents*

Parental rights violation often also happens when the adoptive parents are done with the adoption procedures and leave for their respective homes. They are often cheated by the law enforcement officers, in context to the viability of inter-country adoption where the country itself may not have been in the convention list, or the adoptive parents do not qualify as per the Indian adoption Act. As a result they become victims of protest by human rights groups. The case of celebrity pop singer Madonna can be cited as a glaring example.

The pop singer had adopted a 13 month old Malawian baby boy, David in 2006 (Oprah.com, 2006).

> When she came back to London with the baby with appropriate court orders within two weeks, all hell broke loose. Controversy started blowing up questioning the legality of the adoption, the intention of the adoption and even the usage of celebrity status of the adoptive parents to "buy the baby" in place of adoption.
>
> Malawi is an African nation, with more than one million orphan children, most of whom are malnourished and AIDS affected. The country did not have any proper law or treaty for inter-country adoption. The domestic adoption procedure requires an 18 month wait before the final adoption. But Madonna and her family were given two weeks temporary custody of the child during their stay in the country by the judge who was handling the adoption case. During the immigration, no one questioned the legality of the adopted boy. When they returned home, questions of illegal adoption procedure stemmed up and various child rights activists demanded that the adoption be revoked. The adoptive parents were in total shock and the child had to suffer great mental agony as their family privacy was invaded by the media and human rights groups. All peace was restored after many international discussions and parliamentary debates and the baby was permanently placed in the celebrity family's care (para. 10).

Such cases leave foreign parents reeling as they are only attempting to give the child a better future. Following the media attention that the Madonna case received many prospective foreign parents have changed their minds on adopting children from less developed countries. One of the primary examples is another celebrity couple, Brad Pitt and Anjelina Jolie who planned to adopt their fourth child from India. But the Madonna adoption controversy made them to change their mind as they didn't want to be put through the same turmoil as the pop star (Staff Reporter, 2006).

### *Cheating the biological parents*

As per Indian laws and regulations, a child can be adopted in two ways:

1. Through the voluntary coordination agencies who put up a list of local adoption agencies and help abandoned, orphan or deserted children find a new home abroad, and,

2. In cases where the biological parents are willing to surrender their children for adoption. A "child relinquishing letter" has to be obtained from the biological parents ensuring and informing them of the child's future security. This gives the biological parents 30 days to reconsider their decision.

In cases where biological parents are present it is often seen that they are cheated or forced to give up their child in lieu of a handful amount of money.

Krishnakumar (2005) has shown typical cases where parents are cheated or forced to give up their new born. This also includes vulnerable mothers from poor families, unwed or single. The pressure may be exerted before birth, or at the maternity clinic/hospital, or in the adoption agency, which may house the mother till delivery. Such pressure is also reinforced by free pre- and post-natal care. For example, a children's home in a Chennai suburban area runs a short-stay home for deserted, destitute and abandoned women. It takes particular interest in rehabilitating unwed mothers who give away their children in adoption. Another way is by falsely informing the mother that her baby was stillborn or died shortly after birth so as to take away the infant. According to the findings of an inquiry conducted by the Delhi government, many agencies operate from within the hospital premises in New Delhi (Krishnakumar, 2005).

There have been many such cases of buying children from the Lambada tribes in Andhra Pradesh (Krishnakumar, 2005). Accepting financial or material rewards from the adoption agency in exchange for children is another way. This seems a common practice amongst some agencies, as is clear from the letters sent to Indian officials by foreign adopters. Another heinous way is offering desperate women financial incentives to conceive a child specifically for adoption abroad and luring them to sell their babies.

## Part 3. Reasons behind violation of human rights in inter-country adoption

The reasons behind the gross violation of human rights in inter-country adoption are mainly, lack of a proper universal law and the existence of weak rules and regulations.

As far as India is concerned, the country lacks a uniform secular law for adoption in general. As has been mentioned in the CARA guidelines, the existing rules and regulations are conglomerations of various Indian Acts, judicial precedents, international treaties and agreements. The main acts influential for drafting CARA guidelines are the Hindu Maintenance

Act,1956, Guardianship and Wards Act 1890, Juvenile Justice Care and Protection (Amendment) Act, 2006. The aims, objectives and principles of the CARA guidelines are reflective of the Supreme Court guidelines in the landmark case of Laxmikant Pandey vs. Union of India [AIR1984 SC469]. Moreover CARA guidelines were taken from the Hague convention on protection of children and cooperation in context to inter-country adoption, 1993. The draftsmen adopted best of all these rules but the guidelines itself became highly inconvenient to follow due to the incompatibility of the basic rules. The following criticisms of the laws and guidelines related to adoption will best explain our reason.

### *The Supreme Court Judgment*

The process of adoption was a well known legal process to fill up the absence of biological children in India since ages. The process got modern legal accreditation with the passage of Hindu Maintenance and Adoption Act, 1956 which still rules any adoption related issues for Indian Hindus. But the inter-country adoption still remained in a confusing state till the Supreme Court's decision in case of Laxmikant Pandey vs. Union of India [AIR1984 SC469].

CARA guidelines were born through the landmark judgment of the Supreme Court in this case. The case was instituted on the basis of a letter addressed to the court by Lawyer Laxmikant Pandey alleging that social organisations and voluntary agencies engaging in the work of offering Indian children to foreign parents are indulging in malpractices. The Supreme Court pointed out all probable minute problems of the inter-country adoption and framed certain rules and principles which were adopted in the CARA guidelines. The Supreme Court pointed out that since there was no statutory enactment in our country then for adoption of a child by foreign parents or laying down the procedures which must be followed in such a case, decision had to be taken by the guidelines provided by the Guardian and Wards Act, 1890, for the purpose of felicitating such an adoption.

### *The Guardianship and Wards Act, 1890*

The biggest draw back of the Guardianship and Wards Act, 1890, is that it does not provide the child the same status as a child born biologically to the family. Unlike a child adopted under the Hindu Adoption and Maintenance Act, 1956, here the child cannot become their own, take their name or inherit their property by right. This act confers only a guardian-ward relationship which exists until the child completes 21 years of age. Foreigners, who seek to adopt an Indian child, do so under this Act to assume legal guardianship of the child, after giving an assurance to the court, that they would legally adopt the child as per the laws of their country, within two years after the arrival of the child in their country (Agrawal & Agrawal, 2007).

### *Juvenile Justice Care and Protection (Amendment) Act, 2006*

It was mainly the Juvenile Justice Care and Protection (Amendment) Act, 2006 which influenced the CARA guidelines. Section 4 of the new Act amended the internal meaning of adoption and states that "adoption" means the process through which the adopted child is permanently separated from biological parents and become the legitimate child of his adoptive parents with all the rights, privileges and responsibilities that are attached to the relationship thereby bringing equality to all the communities adoption procedures in India. Furthermore, the new Act made adoption more child centric, for both in country and inter-country adoption. It amended section 41 of the principal Act in section 21 of the new act and stated that:

- Adoption shall be resorted for the rehabilitation of children who are orphan, abandoned or surrendered through procedures prescribed,
- In keeping with the provisions of the various guidelines for adoption issued from time to time, by the State Government, or the Central Adoption Resource Agency and notified by the Central Government, children may be given in adoption by the court after satisfying investigations have been carried out.
- The State Government shall recognise one or more of its institutions or voluntary organisations in each district as specialised adoption agencies in such manner as required for the placement of orphaned, abandoned *or* surrendered children for adoption in accordance with the guidelines notified under sub-section (3)
- The children's homes and the institutions run by the State Government or voluntary organisations for children in need of care and protection, who are orphan, abandoned or surrendered, shall ensure that these children are declared free for adoption by the Committee. All such cases shall be referred to the adoption agency in that district for placement of such children in adoption in accordance with the guidelines notified under sub-section (3).

The new Act specifies that a child can be adopted by any individual, irrespective of his/her marital status, by parents who wish to adopt a child of same sex irrespective of the number of living biological sons or daughters, or by couples who have no children of their own.

It could be seen that, the Juvenile Justice Care and Protection (Amended) Act), 2006, has made adoption a simpler and universal law than the traditional laws. It ensures a child's right to have a safer future and home, domestic or international. But the law neither mentions the after care procedures of the adopted child nor does it mention anything about the status of the child in inter-country adoptions.

The law is still tricky in case of inter-country adoptions as prospective foreign parents still have to first take the role of guardians and take the child to their country. The process has to be finished there as neither the new law nor any existing law specifically mentions a procedure in cases of overseas adoption. Once the child becomes ready for overseas adoption, the international law needs to recognise Indian adoption procedure and the child is adopted according to the laws of the country of adoptive parents' residence. The child becomes the ultimate sufferer unless the "guardians" turn real parents as per the law of his new residence.

## *CARA guidelines*

While the guidelines had adopted separate procedures for in country adoption and inter-country adoption there are no separate chapters dealing with this issue only. Besides these set of rules most often lack the force of law. Hence the parties never really remain obliged to follow the guidelines or even the Indian law in case the habitual resident belongs to a country which is not a member or has relinquished its membership from the convention.

The CARA guidelines should have included and implemented constitutional provisions of Right to life (Article 21 of Indian Constitution) in a broader and firm manner. The guidelines fail to ensure the health, safety and adjustment of the child after he/she has left India. Furthermore licensing procedure should have shown that the prima facie interest should be child centric and not merely business. The guidelines also do not provide for moral policing system checking each adoption procedure. It should be noted that as the numbers of adoptions increase, the number of regulations followed are lesser. The guidelines should have put a maximum number of adoption procedures a month, by each adoption agency so that social workers, the authorities, and voluntary coordination committees would not be overburdened. Lack of proper control leads to misuse of the power and neglecting the core principals for adoption procedure. Also due to lack of regular checks at the adoption agencies and the manner in which they operate can also lead to many problems.

A series of scandals uncovered in Andhra Pradesh and Tamil Nadu over the past few years have laid bare the inter-country adoption network throughout the country. Since the CARA guidelines mention nothing about any penal actions against unrecognized adoption agencies, child trafficking in the name of inter-country adoption has gotten an easy way out. Thus, it can be seen that CARA guidelines for inter-country adoption has increased legal confusion even more than before.

## Suggestions

Inter-country adoption has to be dealt with great care as it often opens up floodgates of child trafficking, child exploitation, sexual harassment of children and finally may even cause deaths of innocent children due to long and tedious legal procedure. The authors feel certain suggestions may help eradicate such problems. The suggestions are:

- Creation of an Universal Adoption Law
- CARA guidelines should have two chapters separately dealing with in country and inter-country adoptions.
- The guidelines should be given immediate legal status.
- Penal offences must be included in case of any sort of failure by the agencies to comply with the rules and regulations.
- Professional counselling must be done by a team consisting of recognized child psychologists, professional social workers and legal practitioners who are familiar with the international law of the receiving country.
- Neither the CARA guidelines, nor any other laws dealing with inter-country adoption mentions about linguistic help towards the children. Children must be accompanied by a compassionate translator during the meetings with prospective adoptive parents.
- The immigration procedure for the adopted child must be done carefully in order to prevent child trafficking.
- The guidelines must make provisions to monitor the child's growth through unbiased professional social workers of the receiving country and the Indian embassies till he/she reaches adulthood in order to save him/her from any kind of sexual or racial abuse by his/her adoptive family as well the new community.

- Before the adoption case is opened it should be mandatory to check the bilateral relationship of the receiving country with India.
- In case the biological parents demand to know about the prospective adoptive parents, they must be informed thoroughly before surrendering their child.
- In country and inter-country adoption should be treated separately for different legal procedures
- If possible prospective adoptive parents should be given the status of foster parents in India and international treaties should be entered accordingly.
- CARA principles should be made stricter to inspect even minor adoption agencies.
- Licensing procedure for the adoption agencies should be made stricter.
- Awareness programmes should be arranged for the poor, needy women and parents in case both the parents want to give their child up for adoption, to go through the correct legal procedures rather than becoming the victims of touts.
- Arrangements should be made to follow up the well being of the child by CARA for at least 10 years after the inter-country adoption.
- The adoptive parents must be made to inform the Indian agency about the child's well being.

## Conclusion

Inter-country or transnational adoption may become the best option for orphan children to start a fresh life in a new country. But when the country of domicile for these children does not have any proper law to show them their destiny, violation of their rights is very much expected right from the time, they are listed as ready for adoption for overseas. The country desperately needs better laws and guideline for inter-country adoption. The authorities need to ensure thorough checks of every adoption agency to ensure that they are protecting the child's rights as has been provided in the constitution and the Juvenile Justice Care and Protection Act, 2006. Every child has a right to life, home and education. It is essential that the authorities not only make laws to provide safer transnational adoption to the children but also to ensure safety of the child even abroad.

## References

Agrawal, M., & Agrawal, R. (2007). Custody under Hindu, Muslim, Christian and Parsi Law's. Retrieved on 28th May 2008 from http://www.legalserviceindia.com/article/l34-Custody-Laws.html

CARA (2008). Retrieved on 28th May 2008 from http:// www.adoptionindia.nic.in/about_us.htm#

Dixit, R. (2001). Illegal means to adopt continue, Sep 4, 2001, *The Times of India.*

Ghosh, S. S. (2006). *Inter-country adoption, procedure and Supreme Court Guidelines.* Retrieved on 30th May 2008 from http://www.legalservicesindia.com/articles/adopt.htm

Krishnakumar, A. (2005). The adoption market. *Frontline, 22*(11), May 21-June 2, 2005.

Ministry of Women and Child Development. (2004). Central Adoption Resource Agency, Draft guidelines on Adoption of Indian Children without Parental Care.

Oprah.com (2006). Madonna: The adoption controversy. Retrieved on 28th May 2008 from http://www2.oprah.com/tows/slide/200610/20061025/slide_20061025_350_101.jhtml

Ramamurthy, D. (1999). The pains and pleasures: A look at the changing trend on the adoption scene. *Frontline*, *16*(9), April 24 - May 7, 1999.

Santhanam, K. (1999). A matter of choice, Child. February 7, 1999, *The Hindu*, Folio.

Staff Reporter. (Nov 7, 2006). Angelina Jolie and Brad Pitt drop adoption plan. Retrieved on 28th May 2008 from http://www.dancewithshadows.com/society/angelina-jolie-adoption.asp

# PART V.

# TECHNOLOGY AND CRIME: CONTEMPORARY PRACTICES AND CONCERNS

# CHAPTER TWENTY ONE

# HOMELAND SECURITY IN THE UNITED STATES: AN ANALYSIS OF THE UTILIZATION OF NOVEL INFORMATION AND VIRTUAL TECHNOLOGIES

NICOLAS A. VALCIK, CARLOS L.V. AIKEN, XUEMING XU AND MOHAMMED S. ALFARHAN

## Abstract

The purpose of this chapter is to discuss the acquisition of three dimensional Photo-realistic models and technology combined with a software application that can provide data that will create a virtual set of structures cybernetically that could be used for training, crime prevention and homeland security purposes. The world is 3D and mapping and capturing it digitally as realistically and accurately as possible for 3D visualization and analysis is the future. Such results provide information allowing the extraction of quantitative 3D information (position, size, volume, orientation, and attributed characteristics), its integration with other digital information and the possibility of virtually experiencing the result in 3D visualization systems. The location and shape of a feature, a rock cliff, a monument, the outside of a building, the room inside a building, etc. combined accurately with high resolution digital photography as its surface skin, creates a 3D photorealistic model, a virtual model. This chapter will discuss the theory behind existing technology on the potential uses of these types of technologies and how these types of technologies can be combined for Homeland Security use. This chapter will also discuss the pros and cons of using such technology for Homeland Security.

## Introduction

There is a wide variety of methods for computer modelling man made structures or natural terrains for training, and crime scene analysis and crime prevention. These incorporate cameras, laser scanners and other survey devices for data capture. They utilize a variety of photogrammetric methods by itself and also combined with laser scanners with a wide range of accuracy and complexity in use. Such a combination of technology can be used to secure facilities, training for Homeland Security personnel or be used for simulating a hostile combatants' facility. For training purposes this technology could be used to generate an on-line simulator that would put first responders through a series of realistic situations that could have trainees go through a series of decision-making processes that would ultimately have positive or negative outcomes based on the respondent's actions (for e.g. a natural gas line explosion that creates several trauma cases.) Having a realistic training simulator on-line would also allow respondents from any part of the country to train on the same situation in a team oriented fashion. For example if a facility is protected by a federal agency, local law enforcement team and a state law enforcement agency a situation could be generated that would allow all three agencies to jointly train together even though they may be located in vastly different areas. The three dimensional photo realistic technologies would allow the team to see what the structures looked like at 1:1 scale and to any desired accuracy and resolution. The underlying database with the facilities characteristics would allow for the officers to face realistic situations (i.e. hazardous materials located in a room could be "missing" for training purposes). This would allow the officers to train with situations that could actually occur at the facility.

By using such technology, a hostile facility could be generated from information gathered that would allow for personnel to train virtually on the facility without having to actually construct a new physical training centre for the trainees. By constructing a simulator virtually, the team could train in a very cost effective manner and train on a virtual facility that would not require the team to travel to a joint location. The simulator could provide a random amount of choices that would allow for the team to make decisions and overcome different obstacles.

This research discusses two novel products and processes that were developed at The University of Texas at Dallas (UTD) – photorealism and the Logistical Tracking System, or LTS©[1] – and how these new tools, although originally developed for non-related purposes, can be utilized concurrently for training, protection of infrastructure, loss prevention and safety of people in open environments.

Protecting infrastructure and civilians from terrorist or criminal acts has held great importance long before the terrorist acts of 9/11 and the rising influence of Homeland Security in the field of criminology. Hazardous materials inventory control takes on greater significance in the wake of chemical attacks such as the *sarin* gas attacks perpetrated by the *Aum cult* on the subway systems in Tokyo, Japan (Valcik, 2006). A computerized system that accurately inventories all radioactive, chemical or biological materials can prevent organizations such as the Aum cult from obtaining materials for constructing such weapons. It can also prevent such dangerous materials from being lost due to neglect or oversight. In 2003, a Texas Tech University professor alerted officials to the disappearance of vials of *Y. pestis*, a dangerous pathogen; however, due to poor inventory controls, the authorities never determined if the vials actually ever existed or if they had been properly disposed but without any record of their destruction (Valcik, 2006). Should an organization obtain deadly materials despite all due vigilance, the addition of three-dimensional imagery of buildings or tunnels can enable law enforcement and first responders to clearly assess the situation or provide training for future emergencies. The use of three-dimensional imagery of structures can prove useful during acts of violence, such as in the case of a shooting at Case Western Reserve University that resulted in one person being killed and two others injured at the hands of a former employee (Valcik, 2006). Such technology could have informed law enforcement about room capacities, security camera feed and potential hiding places or fortifications for the suspect prior to any attempts to subdue the shooter. These are just a few of examples of how these technologies can become important tools in the field of criminology.

## Development of the Logistical Tracking System

The Logistical Tracking System (LTS) is an Internet-based database housed on a Microsoft SQL Server 2005© that interacts with ESRI's

---

[1] LTS was initially developed by Dr. Nicolas Valcik, Danald Lee, Tarang Sethia and Dr.Patricia Huesca-Dorantes. Five student assistants provided additional programming support for LTS, Rajesh Ahuja, Mohit Nagrath, Shalu Agrawal, Dinikeshwari Nagaraj and Priyanka Datta.

ArcView© and ArcSde© to aid in the collection of information on facility infrastructure. The university already possessed a GIS license through its Bruton Center[2] and its Geoscience department[3] and offered a degree program that utilized Geospatial Information Systems (GIS), thus enabling OSPA to draw upon available tools and expertise to develop the new system.

LTS was developed in 2001 by the Office of Strategic Planning and Analysis at The University of Texas at Dallas to enable accurate state and federal reporting of facilities information at a time when new mandates and requirements exceeded the capabilities of the university's existing facilities data system. It was originally conceived as a facilities inventory system and was responsible only for enabling departments to record building and room characteristics to fulfil state reporting requirements and to report how research facilities were utilized so that indirect research costs (such as utilities and administrative personnel salaries) could be recovered. In time, it was expanded and modified to include other university areas of operation such as Environmental Health and Safety,[4] Physical Plant,[5] Controller's Office,[6] the University Police Department,[7] Telecommunications,[8] and Shipping/Receiving.[9]

LTS was developed because there was no product on the market that was comparable. Separate products exist that could provide services on facility information using CAD (Computer Aided Design) files, that could track hazardous materials, or that could connect security systems together for police use. However, none of these systems could be integrated to

[2] The Bruton Center is located at The University of Texas at Dallas in the School of Social Sciences. http://www.bruton.utdallas.edu.

[3] The Geosciences Department at The University of Texas at Dallas operates in the school of Natural Science and Mathematics.

[4] Environmental Health and Safety at The University of Texas at Dallas. http://www.utdallas.edu/utdgeneral/business/safety/

[5] The Physical Plant is now known as Facilities Management at The University of Texas at Dallas. http://www.utdallas.edu/facilities/

[6] The Controller's Office is officially known as The Office of Finance at The University of Texas at Dallas.
http://www.utdallas.edu/BusinessAffairs/Controller/index.html

[7] The University Police department at The University of Texas at Dallas. http://www.utdallas.edu/utgeneral/business/police/version5/frames.html

[8] Communications and Technical Services at The University of Texas at Dallas. http://www.utdallas.edu/ir/cats/

[9] Central Receiving and Mail Services at The University of Texas at Dallas. http://www.utdallas.edu/utdgeneral/business/procure/departments/receiving/index.html

perform all three functions or allow the end users to extract information from a wide array of sources that would be needed in an emergency. An inventory system can inform first responders of the existence of hazardous materials but not the characteristics of the structure in which they are housed, for example building materials or room capacities. Furthermore, the use of Geographic Information Systems (GIS), typically used for mapping or plotting demographic points, would make LTS even more useful by providing building and room information in a visual format that is easily understood by emergency personnel. However, most companies at the time were offering CAD-based products. GIS enabled LTS to link floor plans to the multiple infrastructures embedded in the campus such as telecommunications, security, water lines, natural gas lines, and electrical lines. The Shipping and Receiving department was using barcodes to track university equipment, so it seemed appropriate to expand the use of barcodes to track hazardous materials and link the materials to owner and location through the floor plans contained in LTS. Changes in the location of a particular item could be automatically updated in LTS once the barcode passed through a reader at a given location.

The expansion of LTS into a comprehensive system changed the way university departments were able to perform their duties by enabling them to collect and manage information that previously was nonexistent or inaccessible. The university police department uses LTS to access security camera information and to inventory secured doors, police calls boxes and first responder information. Since LTS links personnel assignments to facilities, security officers now understand how many personnel might be in a particular location or who is authorized to be in certain facilities after normal business hours. LTS enables police to track students living in university-owned residences so that security can account for residents in times of crisis or for security purposes. The Environmental Health and Safety department now has the ability to track the transportation and storage of hazardous materials, monitor fire alarm panels, provide information on lab inspection/danger levels, maintain an inventory of safety equipment, and collect information on asbestos for each room. Data on hazardous materials, which had been maintained on index cards that were accessible to a few people, were now recorded in LTS, thus linking hazardous materials by location through the digital floor plans and making critical information accessible to first responders in an emergency situation through their wireless pocket PCs (Personal Computers) and tablet PCs. IP (Internet Protocol) addressable security cameras were added to LTS so that security and safety personnel can access images remotely without the need for any middleware to be installed on the user's machine other than a simple browser plug. In 2006, UTD received an Award of Recognition in the Unique or Innovative Category from the National Safety Council – CSHEMA (The Campus Safety and Health and Environmental Management Association) Division for LTS's ability to inventory hazardous materials in a new and innovative manner.[10]

## Virtual Simulators and Three-Dimensional Photorealistic Modeling

Current technology is transitioning toward virtual reality and three-dimensional photorealistic modelling. GIS is currently used by Homeland Security to combat terrorism by allowing law enforcement, first responders and military organizations to utilize modern positioning technology and advanced mapping techniques rather than the paper maps and blue line architectural drawings of the past (Purpura, 2007). Through GIS, law enforcement, first responders and military organizations have a powerful tool to analyze positional data and to compare this against a host of data that can be housed in GIS database tables (Purpura, 2007). This method allows for intelligence to be generated on potential terrorist or criminal activities that can occur in a given location.

Higher education institutions and private industry firms are currently developing virtual reality simulators and other forms of virtual reality modelling. At The University of Missouri – Rolla, a research project has been undertaken to provide training for first responders via virtual reality simulator (The University of Missouri-Rolla, 2007). The training simulator at The University of Missouri-Rolla maintains stations that the respondents use to interact with the simulator when experiencing emergency situations (The University of Missouri-Rolla, 2007). Iowa State University is developing a virtual reality simulator for fire safety and training (Newswise, 2005). Private industry companies such as Barco are marketing virtual reality simulators and training modules for Homeland Security as well (Barco, 2004). Cincinnati recently received a homeland security grant to purchase laptop computers for fire-fighters and develop virtual reality training simulators (Greenemeier, 2004).

---

[10] The National Safety Council – CSHEMA Award of Recognition in the Unique or Innovative category was for Esequiel Barrera – Director of Environmental Health and Safety, The University of Texas at Dallas and Dr. Nicolas A. Valcik – Assistant Director for the Office of Strategic Planning and Analysis, The University of Texas at Dallas.

According to the National Research Council, the use of sensors during times of crisis can be critical during an emergency situation (National Research Council, 2003). However, there are major obstacles in the use of sensors, namely the deployment of sensors in locations where sensors are not present or have been disabled and the gathering and integration of data gathered from sensors for use in a manner that can be easily utilized by first responders or other emergency personnel (National Research Council, 2003). GIS can be utilized in conjunction with sensors to provide more information to first responders so that they can act more efficiently and effectively to a crisis situation (National Research Council, 2003). Companies such as Object Security have already developed three-dimensional software that is integrated with sensors precisely for homeland security purposes (Object Security, 2007).

An ideal virtual reality system should have true, accurate, detailed 3D shapes of objects, such as man-made structures, with true colour provided by photography and perhaps texture preserved onto the actual structures, all globally positioned by satellite positioning. This would require a methodology that could provide the accurate 3D shape and colour in a required detail and accuracy. GIS software does not allow for overhang (an XY position with more than one Z or elevation values) such as roof overhang and has limitations on accuracy and resolution. Methods using GIS–the most common of all the technologies for mapping and often used for model building–are limited in handling true 3D features which are more representative of the real world. Such true 3D models are required for realistic modelling of most features especially man-made ones and this requires methods that work at oblique (sideways) angles, usually from the ground.

The University of Texas at Dallas (UTD) has used and developed various survey and photographic methods to map natural terrain and man-made features such as buildings. In capturing objects such as buildings and urban scenes in 3D accurately from the ground, the methods employed most often are either photography based (photogrammetry) or survey instrument based (Burson, 2000). Haala and Brenner (1999) present the generation of models of buildings with photogrammetry exclusively while Vosselman and Sander Dijkman (2001) describe using Light Detection and Ranging laser scanners or LIDAR. Schulz and Ingensand (2004), Amann et al. (2001), and Baltsavias (1999) compare the two methods. When photogrammetry is taken from the ground at oblique angles they are classified as close range photogrammetry methods. These methods are required when the most detailed and accurate models are needed on the sides, and especially the inside, of buildings. This is specialized photogrammetry and only until recently have such modern softcopy– that is, computer–photogrammetry been developed. This technique utilizes overlapping photography from different angles to generate with the camera characteristics the three-dimensional shape of the target. Convergent photogrammetry, widely recognized as the most geometrically accurate of the photographic methods, creates a 3D geometric model from several single photographs taken from the sides of a target with all photographic perspectives converging at object centre. Sirovision from Australia is an example of this process, a new close range oblique photogrammetric capture technique which has been developed for creating 3D photographic models resulting in clouds of points that are defined by image pixels and their associated triangulated meshes (Haneberg et al., 2006). This works effectively for natural surfaces and has been tested on man made structures.

**Figure 1: Example of Sirovision Capture on Part of a UTD Building**

The process is low cost and fast but can be complicated when applied to complex features like buildings. It is at least a significant complementary method for capturing 3D features.

## Survey Methods

Survey methods would involve positioning points by combining laser based systems for measuring distances and horizontal and vertical optical angle based systems for the locations. When these technologies are integrated these are called total stations, a common survey device. It can then be absolutely referenced when tied with satellite positioning like Global Navigation Satellite Systems such as the US GPS system (Global Positioning System) resulting in a unifying system of locations where every point on the earth can be related with any other.

Reflectorless laser range finding technologies, or LIDAR, capture locations by detecting reflective energy from the target which, when combined with the angle information, can provide location models. The models can be built usually by fitting surfaces to the dense points or building models using CADD (Computed Aided Drafting and Design) based software. These shapes can then be combined with the tremendous colour detail provided by photography. Whereas photogrammetry, by definition, results in photorealistic models, laser mapping requires the texture mapping of photos onto the 3D geometries. This merging of laser mapping and photogrammetry is sometimes called hybrid photogrammetry.

We applied reflectorless total stations to mapping the UTD campus, outlining the different floors of the buildings. When captured from the air by airborne LIDAR and photography, only the roof shape can be mapped (Fig. 2). Therefore, oblique mapping is required to capture more detail, especially with the overhang. Aerial photography and mapping is combined with ground measurements with reflectorless laser total stations and laser rangefinders (Fig. 3-4) and CADD software to build the entire structures including the overhang. An example is the Theater Building at UTD where the outlines were combined with the aerial roof mapping to use GIS and extrude the shape of the buildings (Fig. 5-6). The rooms were also created by extruding the floor plans into walls or by laser mapping. The results have as much detail as is manually defined by the operator.

At UTD some of common methods and some new ones in building 3D models of UTD campus features are demonstrated. UTD survey methods were originally used to map the UTD campus, outlining the different floors of the buildings. When captured from the air by airborne LIDAR and photography only the roof shape can be mapped (Fig. 3), a limitation of data acquired from a vertical angle. Therefore, oblique mapping is required to capture more detail, especially with the overhang. Aerial photography and mapping is combined with ground measurements with lasers (Fig. 4-5). The Theater Building example at UTD outlines was combined with the aerial roof mapping to use GIS (not true 3D) and extrude (extend upwards) the shape of the buildings (Fig. 6-7). The rooms can also be created by extruding the floor plans into walls or by surveying, a better method. A GIS integrated laser method UTD uses can capture 3D data in the field (3DLT) (Alfarhan & Aiken, 2007) and attribute each feature separately accurately and efficiently, building the models of the rooms almost in real time. We have applied this to mapping the interiors of UTD buildings to complement the mapping of the external surfaces (Fig. 8).

Comparisons with the floor plans show certain features which are better defined; however, this method for capturing detail is tedious and time consuming. For capturing the maximum amount of information in 3D, the best method is close range photogrammetry and/or fast laser scanning because this captures everything within the line of sight. At UTD a combination of methods are used: the laser scanning technology best suited to the task for the shape, GPS for the globally accurate position, and the appropriate type of digital cameras. The 3D information can then be measured from the photographically enhanced terrain models where the shape is combined with the colour. The common approach is to paste patterns or photographs onto surfaces. These texture mapping methods are only accurate at the control points and are usually based on rubber sheeting (stretch to fit) techniques.

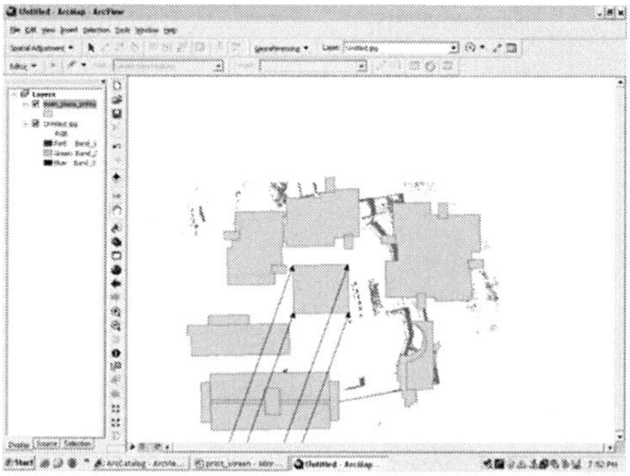

**Figure 2**: ESRI Spatial Adjustment Tool of Theater Roof Position using Outlines of Buildings (Akinfenwa, 2005)

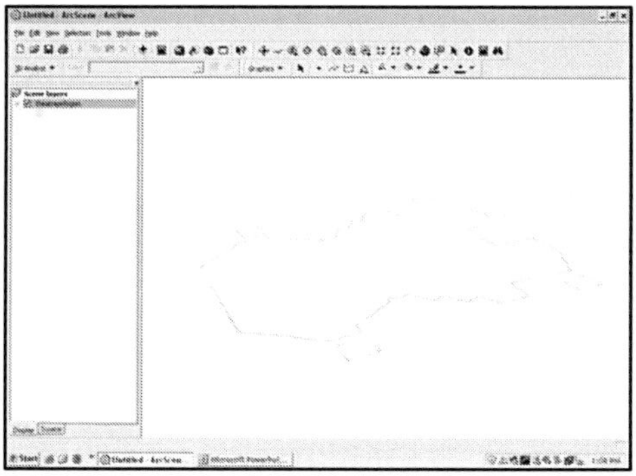

**Figure 3**: Georeferenced UTD Theater Outline Mapped by Reflectorless Total Station of Corner points. Displayed in Arc Scene. (Akinfenwa, 2005)

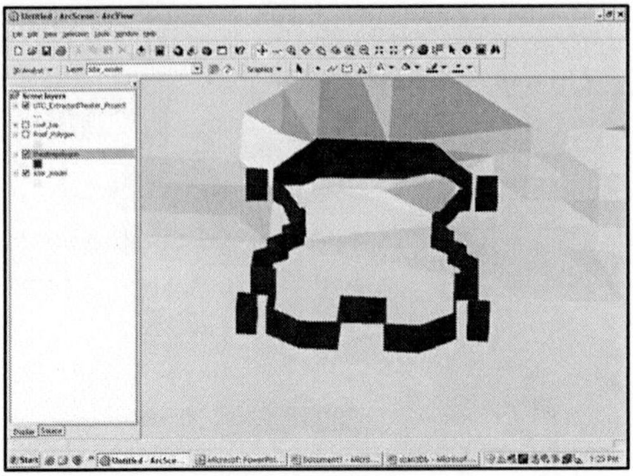

**Figure 4:** Extruding (extending) upward the outline of surveyed building. Background surface of the ground is generated from airborne LIDAR (Akinfenwa, 2005)

**Figure 5:** Extruded roof outline combined with extruded building outline (Akinfenwa, 2005)

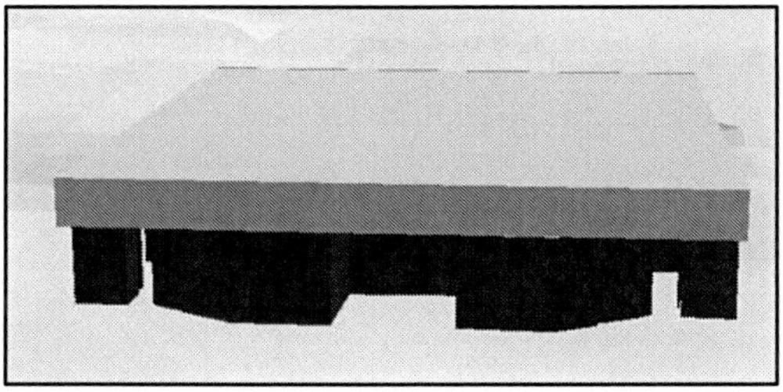

**Figure 6**: Model of theatre by using GIS software (Akinfenwa, 2005)

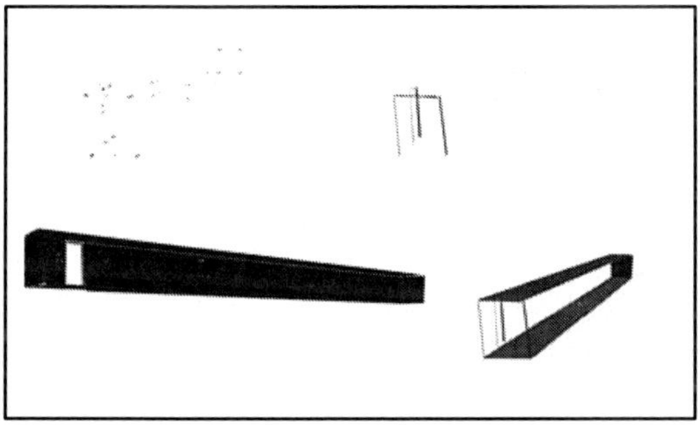

**Figure 7**: Example of Capturing a Hallway by Laser Mapping with 3DLT. Clockwise from Upper Right

## The Best Approach: Combining Laser Scanning With Photography – The 3D Photorealistic Model

The use of fast laser scanners–ground/terrestrial LIDAR or TLS (terrestrial laser (LIDAR) scanning)–that create within seconds "point clouds" at ranges of a few meters to 1-2 kilometres, has exploded into a multitude of applications including homeland security. The point clouds are data sets consisting of millions to hundreds of millions of points. The brightness of the points relates to the reflective characteristics of the target material. These clouds themselves are used for analysis and planning because the points are so dense that they look like surfaces of a solid, although specialized software can extract 3D edges (breaklines), points (break points) and surfaces (Jackson & Bishop, 2005). The point clouds can also be colored by combining them with the photograph (Biber et al., 2004).

This laser scanning technology has the ability to create geospatial data sets through the use of rapid survey techniques to produce precision data which can be interrogated, measured and understood from a threat and vulnerability perspective. Nuclear, biological and chemical (NCB) dispersion, road network vulnerabilities and damage visualization can be provided to first responders so that they can test a vulnerable site to identify and measure actual and potential security weaknesses. Generating photorealistic 3D imagery allows operational planning to be accurately visualized, command and control scenarios to be tested and disaster recovery and contingency plans to be designed and explained. Combining security expertise with science marks a powerful first step toward what can be ultimately done with such data.

The UTD Theater was scanned with a single scan as shown in Figure 8. Examples of merging of a series of these dense point clouds demonstrate the amazing detail provided even in black and white (Figures 9-10). The points here display the intensities of the reflections which are determined by the characteristics of the surfaces being scanned, for example colour, angle, texture and so forth. Surfaces were also created of the building. The building outlines were nearly identical to those of the total station mapping but delineated everything with great detail. A fast laser survey can produce a data cloud which could itself be interrogated by a spectrum of threat software (Persus, 2007). How the local population interacted on the model allows accurate environmental activity to be assessed and planned. The areas' critical vulnerable areas and the environmental patterns need to be accommodated within the solution. A range of sympathetic construction materials as well as the arrangement of appropriate natural obstacles and subtle changes to the areas road scheme could be made. The solution can then be tested as a computer model against recognized threats before a solution is recommended. Such fast scanners are becoming more common in the world and in security applications but are still very new. This is an important technology to be considered.

Scanners are often utilized to capture street scenes (Figure 11) and bridges (Figure 12). These are point clouds, colored by integrated cameras, each using about four scan positions. The extraordinary detail allows continual data mining and extraction as needs change. Please note that even the vegetation has been captured. Scanners that record first and second arrivals can then determine which scan points are vegetation and which are the ground or structure behind it.

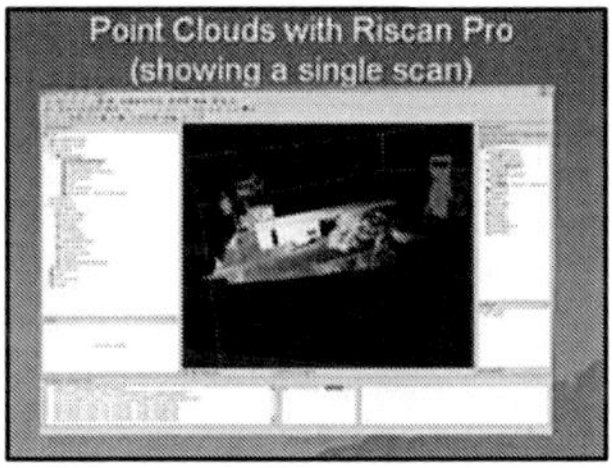


**Figure 8:** From this angle a single scan looks like a solid but actually millions of very closely spaced laser points. (Akinfenwa, 2005)

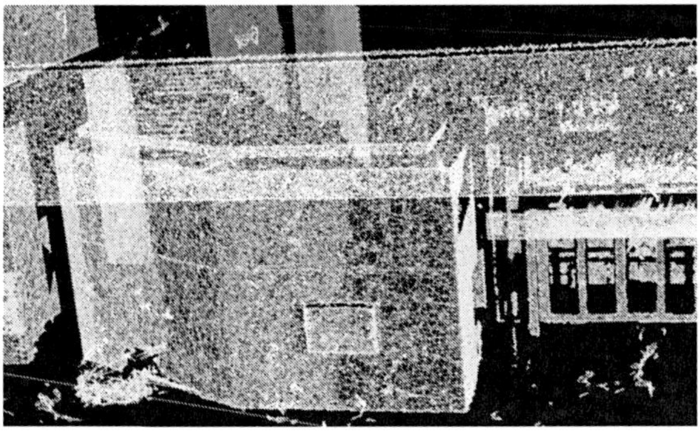

**Figure 9:** 3D view of combined points, a closer view. (Akinfenwa, 2005)

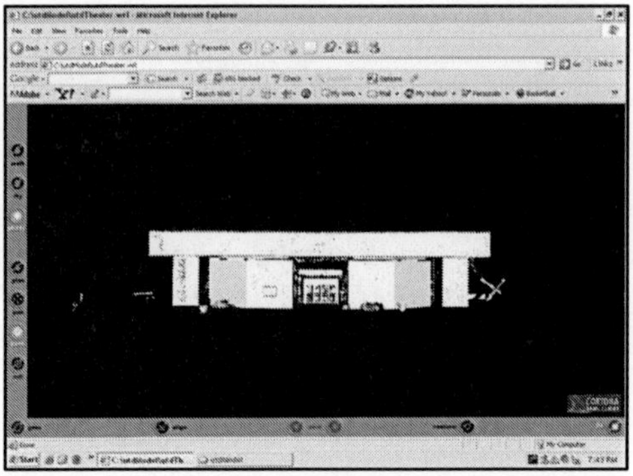

**Figure 10**: A surface fitted to the laser points shown in free Virtual Reality Modeling (VRML) Cortona software. (Akinfenwa, 2005)

**Figure 11**: Street Right of way, Dallas, Texas. Combined colored point cloud, Note amazing detail available for planning and measurement.

**Figure 12**: Bridge. McKinney, Texas Colored Combined Point Clouds

Scanning the interiors and exteriors of buildings produces results that are commonly used for design and maintenance. Figure 13 demonstrates the scanning of the exterior and interior of a building used for a SWAT (Special Weapons and Training) training center. The scanner was wheeled through all the rooms and around the perimeter of the building to map it entirely. The combined point clouds or surface models are used for planning exercises or simulations.

The figure 13 demonstrates the point clouds colour-coded by the scan, the surfaces of the walls and the removal of the outside walls. This is the most common approach to scanning–to integrate and georeference (place a data set in absolute global reference) a point cloud and then selectively extract information using specialized point cloud processing, analysis and extraction software. These scanned "images" can be colored by built-in detectors or cameras attached to the scanner thus producing an image comparable to a true photograph but in reality is a series of colored points. When zoomed into more closely or rotated, the variable distance between the points is obvious and they look less like 3D volumes.

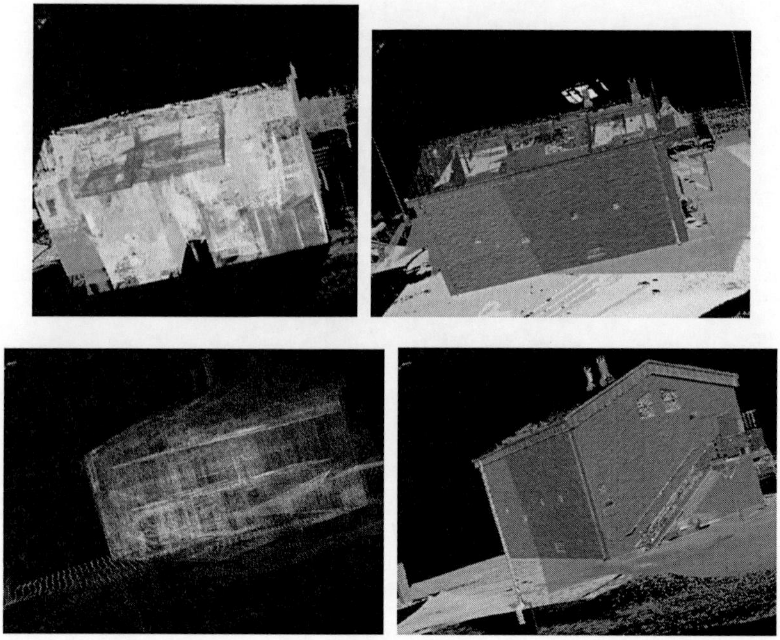

**Figure 13: SWAT Training Building**, (left upper) integrated point cloud (colored by scan site sequence), points mapping external walls removed, (right upper) surfaces fitted to clouds defining walls, (right lower) surface fitting of all interior and exterior walls of entire building.

The results would be useful for planning and analysis to a certain point and line and point extraction but less than adequate for use in virtual visualization applications because as one zooms in closer less information is provided. This situation is quite unlike photorealistic surfaces which provide more information as one zooms in and is only dependent on the resolution of the camera used. We now use fast laser scanners because this enables us to acquire data faster in the field and more accurately at higher resolution. However it is not always obvious in the final 3D photorealistic model what type of laser was used, due to the power of the effect of the detail provided by a photographic skin. Figures 14-19 are tests conducted in 2003 for capturing two crime scenes.

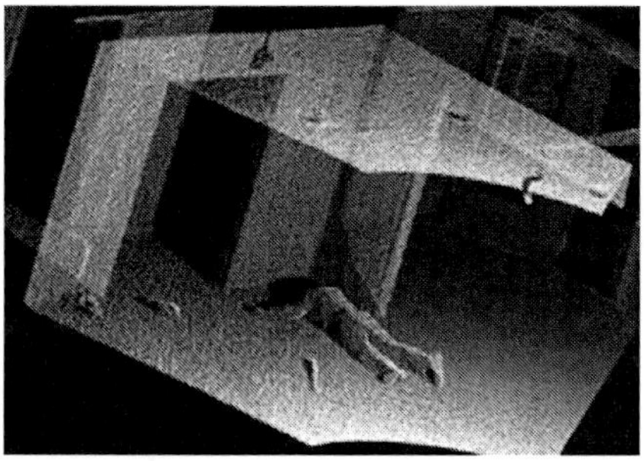

**Figure 14**: Point Cloud, One Scan. Simulated Crime Scene, Real drug dealer's house, Rowlett, Texas, USA

**Figure 15**: Simulated Crime Scene with Surface Fit of Several Scans.

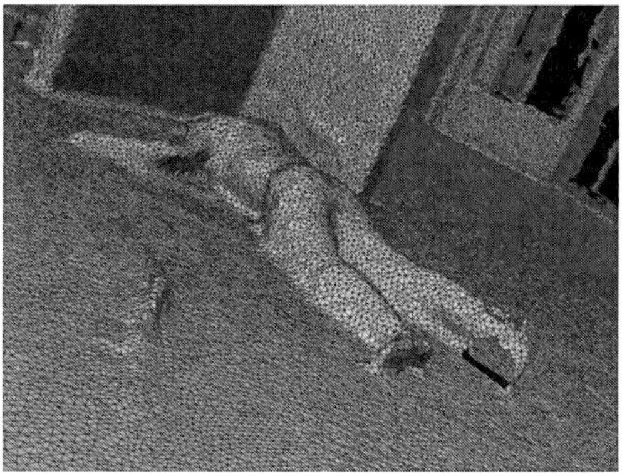

**Figure 16**: Meshed surface fit around body in crime scene.

**Figure 17**: Test setup—Crime Scene, UTD, Texas. Laser scanner and digital camera.

**Figure 18**: UTD Crime Scene combined laser scans and integrated colouring as seen from above the room.

**Figure 19**: UTD Crime Scene. Seen from Inside the Colored Point Cloud

The first is a test of a crime scene setup of an actual crack-cocaine house by a forensics unit of a police force. An officer lay very still on the floor of a UTD room as we mapped the room. Attempts at using meshes for modelling have not proven ideal because of the detail of the data set but could be useful depending on the goals. The second scene was in a UTD building with Dr. Aiken posing as the corpse. Again, a point cloud was created as well as surfaces with great detail.

## Virtual Models

The use of the cloud of points to analyze, model or plan is fast and powerful but is not a real virtual model with the detail and nuances provided by an actual surface enhanced with photographic information. Until recently, the construction of detailed virtual models has not been very efficient or practical. Since 1999, UTD has developed and used a patented method–in collaboration with RealEarthModels LLC (Aiken & Xu, 2003)–to drape oblique photographs onto laser derived digital terrain models thus creating 3D virtual models (Xu et al., 2000). A prototype test conducted in 1999 in the parking lot at the Dallas Bulk Mail Station demonstrated the ability to integrate a surface built by any means (in this case GPS and a total station) with photography taken at anytime by any means, in this case an off the shelf digital camera. The merging of several photos can then be geometrically interpreted by digitizing the contacts and analyzing, in this case the orientations of contacts (strikes and dips).

We have built models at over thirty sites around the world from geologic exposures to buildings, tunnels, monuments and cars by draping hundreds of photographs onto very complicated 3D surfaces up to many kilometres in extent. The source of the terrain data is not relevant; only its detail and accuracy. Our models have been used for virtual fieldtrips for academic groups, scientific associations and companies experienced with simple 3D stereo systems such as a computer monitor, dual projector systems such as a GeoWall (geowall.org), the expensive CAVES (Cave Automatic Visualization Environments—sophisticated immersive visualization systems). Not only can our models be visualized at millimetre resolution and with great accuracy depending on the types of lasers and cameras utilized, they also can be analyzed and measured in 3D with the proper software. We have integrated over 100 photographs and almost 100 laser scans for a location, all correctly related to each other and the terrain model, and ultimately related globally by GPS.

## Applications to Man-Made Structures

The College of Architecture at Texas Tech University in cooperation with Historic American Buildings Survey (HABS) and the National Park Service (NPS) began digitally documenting the Statue of Liberty in order to create, for the first time, complete architectural drawings of the statue's exterior, accurate to 1/4 inch. These scaled drawings will be used to monitor and care for the statue, providing a complete historical documentation. The drawings could also be used to reconstruct an exact, full-scale duplicate of the statue, in the event of any catastrophic loss (Texas Tech, 2007).

As an example the capture and modelling of another type of monument scanning has been applied to the Mt. Rushmore National Monument in South Dakota. In cooperation with the Mt. Rushmore National Monument and National Park Service, REM LLC captured data at distances up to 450 meters and built a model of the monument at a few centimetres accuracy and resolution (Fig. 20-25). As in the case of the Statue of Liberty this was done for the purpose of preservation, maintenance and security planning but by archiving the 3D digital model. As an example of its use in animation, this model was used by CBS Digital for the special effects featured in a television disaster film on CBS TV (CBS, Category 7: End of the World, 2005). The model could be used for close up and distance perspectives in blue screen shots because of the great detail that had been captured.

**Figure 20**: Photograph from Tourist Viewpoint of Mt. Rushmore National Monument, South Dakota, USA.

**Figure 21**: Scanning at Mt. Rushmore National Monument, South Dakota, USA.

**Figure 22**: Three Integrated Scans Colored by Range (blue distant, red nearby).

**Figure 23**: Surface Fit (triangulated mesh) to Scanned Points.

**Figure 24**: One can zoom into the photorealistic model of Mt. Rushmore and see detail never before obvious and it can be observed from different angles.

**Figure 25**: Mt. Rushmore Model was used in a Scene from a CBS TV mini-series Category 7: End of the World (CBS, 2005) for both distant (shown here) and close up blue screen special effects.

Figures 26 through 27 features a location along a railroad cut near the university that is utilized as training site. Because of its proximity to UTD and with its variety of features (cliffs, bridge, power lines, buildings, railroad etc.) UTD has been testing mapping and surveying methods for the last ten years. Scanning of tunnels for engineering applications and lately security is very common especially in Europe. A mountainside east of Salina, Utah along Interstate highway 70 was mapped and modelled (Fig. 28).

A tunnel east of Salina, Utah along a road parallel to Interstate highway 70 provided a fine example of an unlined tunnel (Figure 28). It is unlined with the rock exposed so academics and oil company personnel visit this location frequently to see various geologic features in 3D. It is used for virtual field trips where one can virtually "fly" to the top of the tunnel and examine and measure everything in detail. These were subsequently utilized in visualization CAVES (Thurmond et al., 2006) in universities and companies. The geology was mapped in detail (at centimetres) several years later (Covault, 2006) and then these data added to the photographs to be experienced, an example of the ability of these types of models to be expanded and edited as details change. Academics and oil company personnel visit this location frequently to see three dimensional features such as geology at amazing detail, to centimetre. We "built" this tunnel model to demonstrate the creation of a virtual field trip in this case for use in our classes and therefore for companies where one can virtually "fly" to the top of the tunnel and measure everything in detail.

**Figure 26**: Photorealistic Point Cloud of a railroad cut, Plano, Texas. Note all the background features also mapped by the scanner such as power lines and buildings.

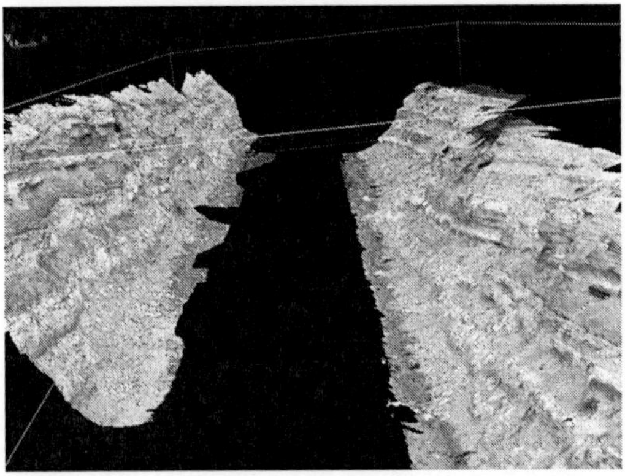

**Figure 27**: Photorealistic Model using surface fitting of terrain on both sides of Railroad Cut.

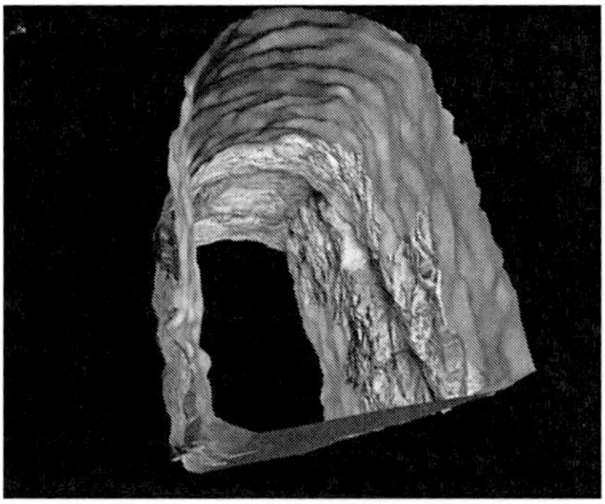

**Figure 28**: Looking inside Model of Salina Tunnel, Utah (Integrated Mountain Side not Shown)

A model was built of the Dallas Rapid Transit (DART) rail tunnel in Dallas, Texas (Figure 29) to monitor existing tunnel conditions and defining baseline measurements upon which all other existing and subsequent measurements and installations can be based. This model can also be used for security planning.

By scanning and photographing this part of the DART tunnel, information could be captured photo realistically for monitoring and management. The surface was used to compare the tunnel design specifications with actual conditions. Leaks (brown) were mapped along the paint markers of other measurements such as GPR (ground penetrating radar). At UTD a variety of methods have been developed and applied toward capturing existing structures in three dimensions geometrically and in some cases capturing the ultimate model photo realistically.

Maintaining a good work flow for these projects can mean the difference between very long project duration and a more reasonable completion time. If point clouds are used, the processing is very fast. If surfaces and regular geometric models are used, then the entire process can become much more time consuming. Figure 30 demonstrates the general workflow to acquire and build a model using scanning and mapping photos onto surfaces with the utilization of GIS and CADD software integrated into the procedures.

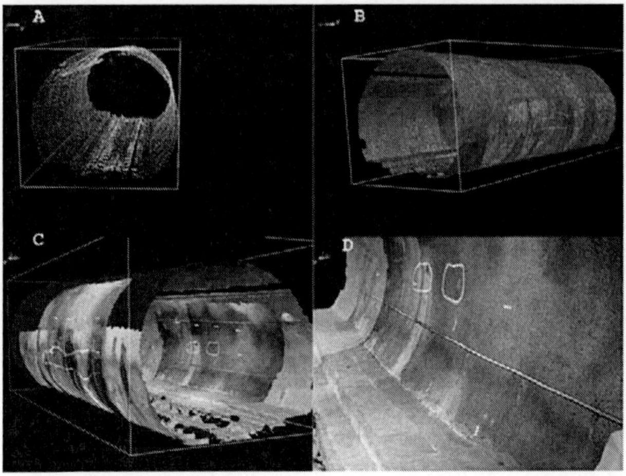


**Figure 29**:
A. The merged Point Cloud of the Dallas Rapid Transit southbound light rail tunnel at Mockingbird Station.
B. The Triangulated Mesh surface fit of the Point Cloud for Modeling.
C. The 3D Photorealistic Model using 14 Photos. The Blue Indicates Areas where Photos were not mapped onto the surface. The Red and White Lines are Locations of Surveys made of the Tunnel Lining Investigating possible problem areas.
D. Close up from Inside the Tunnel.

Projects that took several months to fully process to final model now take us a few days or less. Scanners are becoming less expensive, faster, more accurate and smaller in size. Even photogrammetric methods are becoming more efficient and powerful. All of our experience indicates that a blend of these approaches can be applied to any situation. Currently, our greatest challenge continues to be our capacity to model complex 3D features where meshes may not be appropriate and CADD modelling not very accurate. Stated another way, we must determine what approach can be utilized that can include the photorealistic surfaces.

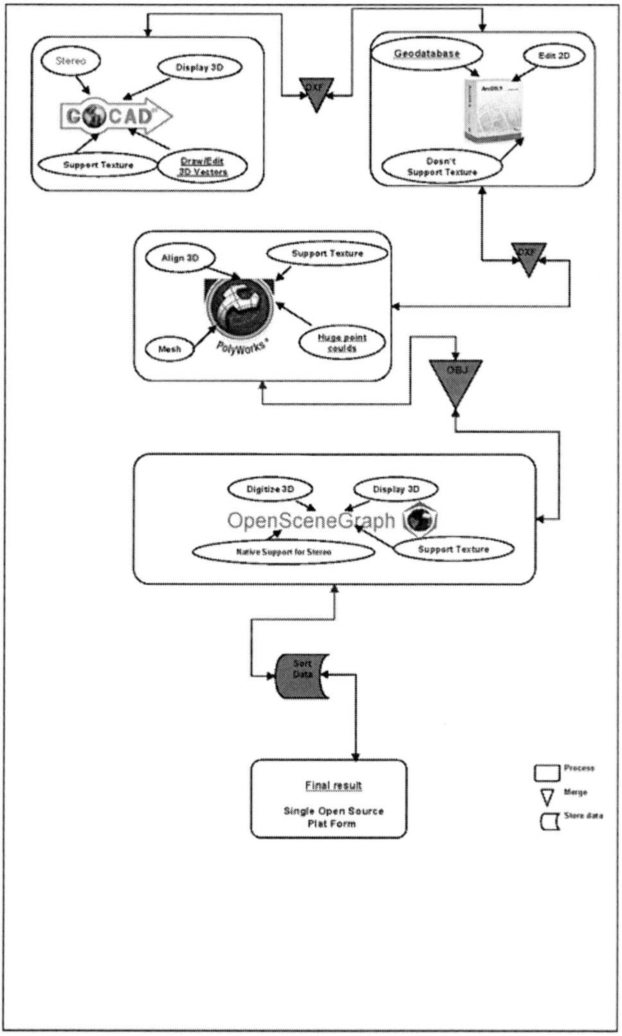


**Figure 30**: Workflow of 3D Photo real Mapping steps (Alfarhan and Aiken, 2007)

## Potential Uses of LTS and Photorealism – Integration of Concepts

One can conclude that a system like LTS has great potential for Homeland Security application. LTS has the ability to track equipment and personnel to specific locations. It can be used to secure a wide variety of facilities and buildings. Restricted or sensitive inventory can be recorded electronically and accessed quickly in times of emergency. The military could use the GIS feature to map down potential enemy facilities and then input information about the facilities through the LTS system. GIS floor plans could be of great assistance in targeting key personnel or locations in a facility with GPS guided munitions. The coordinates that GIS utilizes could also be relayed to a Predator for remote targeting purposes. Photorealism could be used to show operatives what a particular facility would look like in a 3D context both for the interior and exterior of the building. Gathering information on enemy facilities could be gathered through several known methods (i.e. ground penetrating radar, satellite imagery or operatives) to allow for more accurate planning. For training purposes, both LTS and photorealism could be combined with cutting edge gaming technology to project facility information in a 3D format for operatives to pre-plan operational issues that may be encountered in a particular mission (i.e. hostage rescue scenario). With the gaming technology, information on potential combatants and capabilities could be accessed via LTS and projected to scale in a room using photorealism to give the response personnel the most realistic training possibly inside an enemy facility. For example if a facility has three rooms and a corridor a projection would be to scale of such a facility. As the operative went through the facility virtually, the gaming technology would access known threats to the operative that would be stored in LTS (i.e. a guard armed with an AK-74S, 3 hand grenades and a bayonet). The gaming technology would allow for the operative to take actions against the potential threat with the appropriate response. The same type of integrated technology could be used for emergency response situations and prison uses.

New technology such as gaming and advanced graphic technologies can add substantially to both LTS and photorealism. Such technologies can be used for training in a variety of settings and roles. Everything from health care workers to special operations personnel could use such technology to not only train for realistic situations but also train in an economical fashion. Virtual training in a realistic setting would allow training to occur more frequently for personnel since a real environment would not have to be constructed. The number of training personnel could also be reduced and used in limited numbers. The advent of new technology may also lend itself to progress capabilities of tracking tags that could be used to tag HAZMAT and other items. Instead of a barcode to track a container, a smaller tag in the size of a microdot with an active RFID capability could be used. New technology in the form of a new seamless type of projection system could be used to make a scenario not only more realistic but also allow for interaction with the trainee. With the gaming technology, sensors could equip a room that would allow the user to interact with the technology and register correct or incorrect actions for a particular situation. Potential threats could be programmed to "attack" the user which in turn would force the trainee to act in a certain manner.

Vocal interaction could also be developed to not only have the trainee interact with the training simulation but also vocal queries could be used to access data inside LTS. Future development of LTS would also allow for users to interact with the GIS maps of facilities and campuses. Currently GIS maps in LTS are static and only viewable. With advances in PC technology and wireless capability, users could interact with LTS or photorealism with smaller devices that can respond to queries more quickly than ever before. This allows first responders to have more data quickly that will enable first responders to make better decisions. As camera technology improves, so too will the ability for security and emergency personnel to access live feed to determine a particular situation in times of crisis or to further progress a security situation with an organization.

## Conclusion

Current technologies allow for security personnel, emergency response teams, military agencies and other organizations to improve their information collection on facilities, tracking of restricted or sensitive items or personnel, and training personnel for a variety of duties and roles. What we have described in this research is the potential to successfully integrate two existing technologies to progressively improve security and emergency response situations for homeland security uses. As these types of technologies become more widespread, costs will diminish and the ability to implement software solutions and gaming technologies will become a common tool utilized by law enforcement and defence departments across the globe.

## References

Abdel-Salam, M., Xu, X., & Aiken, C. (2003). Web-residing 3d virtual geology for teaching earth sciences for all levels: The virtual fieldtrip. Geological Society of America Annual Meeting, Seattle, Washington, October 2003.

Aiken, C., & Xu, X. (2003). *Method and apparatus for 3D feature mapping.* U.S. Patent No.6, 590,640 Washington D.C.: U.S. Patent and Trademark Office.

Aiken, C., & Xu, X. (2005). Special effects modelling; *category 7: End of the world* , Mt. Rushmore scenes and special effects, CBS TV mini series, Los Angeles, CA (November, 2005).

Aiken, C., Xu, X., & Nuebert, B. (2004). Scanners, digital cameras and 3D models, Texas society of professional surveyors. One Day Short Course, San Antonio, Texas, p.78.

Aiken, C., Xu, X., Thurmond, J., Abdel-Salam, M., Olariu, M., Olariu, C., & Thurmond, A. (2004). 3D laser scanning and virtual photorealistic outcrops: Acquisition, visualization and analysis. Short Course #3, Two Day Short Course, AAPG Convention, p.100.

Akinfenwa, A. A. (2005). Extraction of 3D data by several methods for the building of a 3D model in ARCGIS: Laser Scanning, direct laser rangefinder measurements and Pictometry. MS GIS Project, Geoscience Department, The University of Texas at Dallas.

Alfarhan, M., & Aiken, C. (2007). Real time integration of laser rangefinders and ArcGIS to capture 3D geology features, 17th annual South Central Arc User Group (SCAUG) Conference, April 11th - 13th 2007, in New Orleans, Louisiana.

Alfarhan, M., Aiken, C., & Xu, X., (2006). The use of a laser rangefinder attached to a pocket PC to capture and analyze 3D digital geologic data in the field: A case study – preston railroad cut, Texas. Penrose Conference: "Unlocking 3D Earth Systems - Harnessing New Digital Technologies to Revolutionize Multi-Scale Geologic Models." Durham, UK, September, 2006.

Amann, M. C., Bosch, T., & Lescure, M. (2001). Laser Ranging: A critical review of usual techniques for distance measurement. *Optical Engineering*, *40*(1), 10-19.

Barco. (2004). Global business leaders and government officials to view homeland security and distributed mission operation (DMO) solutions at Barco's 2004 Simulation Technology Expo. Retrieved on 28th January 2008 from http://www.barco.com/VirtualReality/en/pressreleases/show.asp?index=1340

Bellian, J. A., Kerans, C., & Jennette, D. C. (2005). Digital Outcrop Models: Applications of terrestrial scanning Lidar technology in stratigraphic modelling. *Journal of Sedimentary Research*, *75*(2), 166-176.

Burson, E. (2000). *Geospatial data content, analysis and procedural standards for cultural resources site monitoring*. Geomarine report to U.S. Army Corps of Engineers.

Covault, A. H. (2006). Structural architecture and deformation of the salina creek tunnel normal fault. Master's Thesis, Geosciences Department, The University of Texas at Dallas.

Greenemeier, L. (2004). Cincinnati wins federal funds for security: City is the first of four to get portion of $10 million fund to advance emergency preparedness. *InformationWeek*, June 14, 2004. Retrieved on 28th January 2008 from http://www.informationweek.com/story/showArticle.jhtml?articleID=21700448

Haneberg, W. C., Norrish, N. I., & Findley, D. P. (2006). Digital outcrop characterization for 3-D structural mapping and rock slope design along interstate 90 Near Snoqualmie Pass, Washington. Proceedings 57th Annual Highway Geology Symposium, Breckenridge, Colorado, September 27-29, 2006.

McCaffrey, K. J. W., Jones, R. R., Holdsworth, R. E., Wilson, R. W., Clegg, I. P. J., Holliman, N., & Trinks, I., (2005). Unlocking the spatial dimension: Digital technologies and the future of geoscience fieldwork. *Journal of the Geological Society*, *162*, 1–12.

National Research Council. (2003). *Information technology for counter-terrorism: Immediate actions and future possibilities*. Washington D.C.: The National Academies Press.

Newswise. (2005). Fire-Safety Training goes High Tech. Iowa State University, October 24, 2005. Retrieved on 28th January 2008 from http://www.newswise.com/articles/view/515576/

Object Security. (2007). SimulateWorld 4D simulation system - Secure, safe, distributed, flexible. Retrieved on 28th January 2008 from http://www.objectsecurity.com/en-products-simulateworld.html

Olariu, I., Ferguson, J., & Aiken, C. (2006). Outcrop fracture characterization using terrestrial laser scanners, deepwater Jackfork Sandstone at Big Rock Quarry, Arkansas. Penrose Conference: "Unlocking 3D Earth Systems - Harnessing New Digital Technologies to Revolutionize Multi-Scale Geologic Models." Durham, UK. September 2006.

Oldow, J. S., Walker, D. J., Aiken, C., & Xu, X. (2006). Digital acquisition, analysis, and visualization. *The Earth Sciences Eos: Transactions American Geophysical Union*, *87* (35), 351-351.

Pringle, J. K., Howell, J. A., Hodgetts, D., Westerman, A. R., & Hodgson, D.M. (2006). Virtual outcrop models of petroleum reservoir analogues: A Review of the Current State-of-the-Art. *First Break*, *24*, 33-42, March 2006.

Purpura, P. (2007). *Terrorism and homeland security: An introduction with applications*. Boston, MA: Butterworth-Heinemann.

Schulz, T., & Ingensand, H. (2004). Terrestrial laser scanning – investigations and applications for high precision scanning. FIG Working Week, Athens, Greece, May 22-27, 2004.

Thurmond, J., (2006). Five years of 3D outcrop analysis: The past, the present, and the future. Penrose Conference: "Unlocking 3D Earth Systems - Harnessing New Digital Technologies to Revolutionize Multi-Scale Geologic Models." Durham, UK, September 2006.

Thurmond, J., Loseth, T., Rivenaes, J., Martinsen, O., Xu, X., & Aiken, C. (2005). Deep-Water Outcrops of the World. In Nilsen. T., Shew, R., Steffens, G., & Studlick, J.T. (Eds.), *Deep-Water Outcrops of the World Atlas.* Tulsa, OK: American Association of Petroleum Geologists. Special Publication, CD-ROM.

Tuck, D., Xu, X., Thurmond, J., Gillespie, P., Farseth, R., & Aiken, C. (2005). Capturing digital field data to create 3D photorealistic outcrop models of the structure in the lower Jurassic interbedded pelagic limestones and marls of the Lias formation near Kilve, Somerset, England. GSA South Central Sectional Meeting, San Antonio, TX. GSA Abstract with Program 37, No. 3.

The University of Missouri – Rolla, (2007). Research – projects – homeland security, virtual reality and prototyping laboratory, Rolla, Missouri. Retrieved on 28th January 2008 from http://web.umr.edu/~vrpl/proj-fr.htm,

Valcik, N. (2003). Building a space management system. *Midwestern Review of Business and Economics,* 32,16-21, Bureau of Business and Government Research, Midwestern State University, Wichita Falls, Texas.

Valcik, N. (2006). *Regulating the use of biological hazardous materials in universities: Complying with the new federal guidelines.* NY, Lewiston: Edwin Mellen Press.

Wolf, P. R., & Dewitt, B. A. (2000). *Elements of photogrammetry, with applications in GIS*. Boston, MA: McGraw-Hill, Third Edition.

Xu, X. (2000). 3D virtual geology; photorealistic outcrops and their acquisition, visualization and analysis. Unpublished Doctoral Dissertation submitted to The University of Texas at Dallas.

Xu, X., Aiken, C., Thurmond, J., & Nuebert, B. (2004). Beyond point clouds: The future of 3D virtual models. *GeoWorld*, 38-41.

Zeng, X., McMechan, G. A., Bhattacharya, J. P., Aiken, C., Xu, X., Hammon III, W.S., & Corbeanu, R. M. (2005). Geophysical Prospecting: 3-D imaging of a reservoir analog in point bar deposits in the Ferron Sandstone, Utah using Ground-Penetrating Radar. *Geophysical Prospecting, 52*(3), 151–163.

# CHAPTER TWENTY TWO

# CRIMINAL JUSTICE FIREWALLS IN THE UNITED STATES: PROSECUTORIAL DECISION-MAKING IN CYBER AND HIGH-TECH CRIME CASES IN CALIFORNIA

JOHNNY NHAN

## Abstract

Prosecutors are the gatekeepers of the criminal justice system that control the entry and processing of cases. Their selection of cases and subsequent legal actions can affect enforcement priorities. Prosecutorial decisions and case outcomes are often influenced by many factors, such as the complexity of a case. The complexity and abstract nature of cyber cases in particular pose a challenge to prosecutors. This exploratory chapter uses interview data from prosecutors, law enforcement officials, California state emergency services officials, and private industry (motion picture and technology sector) to assess the impact of decision-making factors related to Internet and high-tech crime. This research investigates the impact of technology, law, inter-organizational relationships, funding, and political variables. Initial findings suggest prosecution of high-tech and Internet crime in California remains limited to a small number of specialized prosecutors who face structural and procedural disincentives such as inflexible and weak laws, dependence on collaborators such as law enforcement and private industry, and technological complexity. This has resulted in routine case avoidance and plea bargains which undermine the capacity to enforce and deter high-tech and cyber crime in California.

## Introduction

In the world of computer networks, system administrators set policies that instruct gateway software, or "firewalls," to control the flow of information for a system or network (Tanenbaum, 2003). Similarly, public prosecutors serve as gatekeepers of cases that enter the criminal justice system. Decisions to file cases are based largely on the judgment of prosecutors despite historic controversy calling for more prosecutorial discretionary guidelines and ethical standards[1] (Donovan, 1981; Ma, 2002; Heymann & Petrie, 2001). Legal and extralegal factors often affect the decision-making and procedural processes (Adams & Cutshall, 1987; Gurney, 1985). In addition, prosecutors decide on case procedures and the degree of charges once cases are accepted. Benson, Maakestad, Cullen and Geis (1988) found that in complex corporate crime cases, prosecutorial decisions were influenced by limited resources, alternative remedies, legal and technical difficulties, and political factors. Similarly, complex computer and high-tech crimes pose a significant and fast-growing challenge for prosecutors.

The explosion of computer crimes has been facilitated by the permeation of inexpensive personal computers, exponential growth of digital information, and high-speed computer networks in modern society. This has created new avenues and types of crime that has outstripped traditional forms of social and legal control.[2] A recent security threat report shows that 54% of identity theft related breaches were a result of computer or data storage theft (Turner et al., 2007). Another industry report shows on average, it costs companies $268,000 to inform customers of a security breach, regardless of whether or not any lost data was ever used.[3] The motion picture industry estimate losses from Internet piracy in 2005 at $2.3 billion, costing the U.S. 141,030 potential jobs and $837 million in potential tax revenues (Siwek, 2006).[4] The high cost and

---

[1] The American Bar Association (ABA) Criminal Justice Section Standard 3-1.2 (b) states, "The prosecutor is an administrator of justice, an advocate, and an officer of the court; the prosecutor must exercise sound discretion in the performance of his or her functions." Standard 3-3.1 states, "A prosecutor should not invidiously discriminate against or in favor of any person on the basis of race, religion, sex, sexual preference, or ethnicity in exercising discretion to investigate or to prosecute. A prosecutor should not use other improper considerations in exercising such discretion."
http://www.abanet.org/crimjust/standards/pfunc_blk.html#1.1

[2] While there is no agreed upon definition of computer or "cybercrime," this article will use the term loosely to include all forms of computer and Internet enabled crimes ranging from identity theft to computer network security breaches.

[3] Datagate: The Next Inevitable Corporate Disaster? McAfee and Datamonitor Global Survey on Impact of Data Loss: April 2007. *See*
http://www.mcafee.com/us/local_content/misc/dlp_datagate_research.pdf.

[4] *See* http://www.mpaa.org/piracy_internet.asp

prevalence of computer and high-tech crimes suggests that prosecutors and the criminal justice system are being overwhelmed by increasingly sophisticated malefactors.

This chapter will examine structural and dynamic variables between organizations and actors that influence prosecutorial decision-making processes in high-tech and computer crimes. Three categories will be analyzed: technical issues, legal issues, and relationships with other formal and informal social control agents. First, methods of inquiry will be discussed. Second, the impact of Internet technology will be assessed in comparison with corporate white-collar crime. Next, legal issues focusing on the difficulties of fitting cyber-crimes with the California legal system will be examined. Finally, prosecutorial relationships with major security stakeholders will be analyzed using a nodal governance theoretical framework. This includes law enforcement investigators, corporate bodies, state government, and the public. The goal of this chapter is to assess the variables affecting prosecutorial acceptance of cases, how cyber and high-tech cases are processed, and their impact on the overall capacity of California cyber-security network.

## Methodology

This chapter uses data derived from interviews, observations at state-sponsored and private cyber-security meetings, published literature and survey reports, and relevant documents provided by research participants. Interviews were conducted from 2005 to September, 2007 with individuals from three groups found to be significant in influencing prosecutorial decision-making processes: California state emergency services, specialized law enforcement taskforces, and private industries. These groups are considered security stakeholders due to having representatives in the California High-Tech Task Force Committee. [5] Two representative private industries, the technology sector, consisting of hardware and software companies, and the film industry, were selected for this research based on the nature of their relationships with law enforcement. The general public, a fourth group considered as an important security stakeholder, was not interviewed due to the limited scope of the research. Instead, public perceptions of cyber crimes were derived from the Pew Internet and American Life Project[6] survey data and other Internet sources.

---

[5] *See* http://www.jciac.org/docs/art-HTC.pdf

[6] The Pew Internet and American Life Project surveys American households using random telephone and online surveys on the impact of the Internet.

Limiting the scope of this research to the geographic area of California can be problematic. The borderless Internet environment makes it challenging to confine the unit of analysis geographically. Therefore, primary data collected for the tech sector came from Arizona and Washington in addition to California. To address the problem of assessing prosecutorial decision-making and legal processes in California using data from national sources, stakeholders were defined by parameters in which they function instead of strictly geographic boundaries. For example, some technology companies based in California may have their security staff and operations located in other states. It was appropriate to interview subjects in security positions in Arizona and Washington that performed cyber security functions for companies based in California.

Two members of the California State Office of Emergency Services (OES) were interviewed because of their direct control over budgets and policies related to cyber enforcement.[7] Law enforcement was represented by a sample from each of the five California regional high-tech crimes taskforces, whose members includes federal, state, county, and city law enforcement officers and agents, as well as specialized state and county prosecutors. Private industry was represented by two industries that have had historically contrasting relationships with law enforcement. The technology sector was selected for its direct involvement in Internet security and historic avoidance in soliciting police assistance and reluctance in taking legal action. The film industry was selected for its active partnership with law enforcement and their pursuance of legal actions.

Subjects were selected from a convenience sample of referrals by known contacts in law enforcement and each industry. A large portion of subjects were selected for their membership to the high-tech crimes taskforce steering committee, indicating working relationships with law enforcement. There was at least one specialized prosecutor assigned to each taskforce. It must be noted that while the sample sizes were small, there are relatively few law enforcement agents and prosecutors working specifically in cyber security in California. To increase reliability and validity of answers, many subjects were interviewed multiple times.

The vast majority of interviews were done face-to-face at the subjects' location and lasted between one and two hours. Several interviews (n=5)

---

http://www.pewinternet.org/

[7] While the Governor's Office of Emergency Services is a large, this small sample size directly reflects the limited number of staff working directly with high-tech and computer crimes within their Law Enforcement division that handles statewide emergencies such as natural disaster response.

were conducted over the telephone. Semi-structured questions were asked regarding issues related to cyber-security, enforcement, legal issues, and relationships with other actors in the security field. These questions were modified over time to focus on areas of importance discovered from previous interviews, consistent with the flexible nature of qualitative design (Lofland & Lofland, 1984). Subjects were given the opportunity to express their views and bring forth important issues, yielding very rich answers which gave insight into the cyber security scene, resulting in "emergent" outcomes (Patton, 1990). For example, it was discovered through the course of the interviews that the Sarbanes-Oxley Act[8] had a significant effect on the tech sector in California, a factor that would not have been incorporated into a survey. Despite the flexibility of qualitative research designs, this research remains specific to California's cyber-security enforcement and legal processes and should not be generalized.

In addition to interviews, public state-sponsored steering committee meetings were observed. Quarterly meeting participants included representatives from California state emergency services, taskforces, and various private industries. These meetings serve as an open forum to bring forth and discuss crime trends and policy concerns by all parties.

The purpose of the research is to explore the functional mechanisms of prosecuting high-tech and Internet crimes, an area with minimal previous research. This qualitative method of inquiry was determined to be appropriate for the nature of the information, where specifics of cases and damages involving high profile corporate clients are guarded as sensitive information.

**Table 1:**

| Participant category | Number of respondents |
|---|---|
| Law enforcement/prosecutors | 22 |
| Private industry: | |
| Film industry security | 10 |
| Information technology | 18 |
| State representatives | 2 |
| Total | 52 |

[8] The Sarbanes-Oxley Act of 2002 (Pub. L. No. 107-204, 116 Stat. 745), commonly known as "Sarbox," regulates accounting and internal business reporting processes.

## Prosecution in White-Collar and Complex Crimes

To understand the prosecutorial decision-making process in cyber-cases, it is important to examine prior white-collar crime cases that share many similarities. White-collar crime, a term coined by Sutherland (1939), has evolved to three distinct orientations based on offender status (Sutherland's original orientation), type of offence, and organizational culture (Barnett, 2007). The FBI uses an offence typology of white-collar crime, defined as "...classes of non-violent illegal acts which are characterized by deceit, concealment, or violation of trust and which are not dependent upon the application or threat of physical force or violence. Individuals and organizations commit these acts to obtain money, property, or services; to avoid the payment or loss of money or services; or to secure personal or business advantage" (USDOJ FBI, 1989, p. 3; ibid). This definition of white-collar crime can encompass a broad range of offences and offenders, ranging from embezzlement by corporate CEOs to identity theft performed by lower-class individuals. The wide array of crime types fitting this category gives prosecutors an inherent discretion which is often influenced by contemporary politics (Baker, 2004).

Prosecutorial discretion in white-collar cases is often influenced by anticipated difficulties and rewards (Ayers & Frank, 1987; Benson et al., 1988). An important distinction Sutherland makes between white-collar crime and street crime is that it is not easily detected. White-collar criminal activities are often hidden within normal business activities, making it very difficult to detect, enforce, and present to lay juries (Pontell, Calavita, & Tillman, 1994). For example, fraud investigators found it "virtually impossible" to distinguish between legitimate medical services, non-deliberate errors, and criminal activities in complex medical fraud cases (Jesilow, Pontell, & Geis, 1993). Extensive expertise and investigatory expenses deters prosecutors from pursuing white-collar cases which significantly diminishes maximum criminal justice system capacity (Pontell, 1982, 1984).

To deal with its inherent complex nature, white-collar cases that are prosecuted require extensive collaborative strategies and expertise similar to those used in cyber and high-tech cases. For example, during the 1980s, New York State created several organized crime task forces to investigate corruption and racketeering in the construction industry. The onerous investigation required vast state and federal resources. The Construction Industry Strike Force (CISF), a partnership between law enforcement (Organized Crime Task Force) and the New York County District Attorney's Office, along with the expertise of lawyers, investigators, accountants, and analysts spent two years investigating corruption and racketeering in the school construction program (Goldstock et al., 1990).

Despite intensive collaborative efforts investigating and prosecuting white-collar cases, their complexity may be too difficult for lay jurors to understand. Legal experts explain that complicated accounting practices often confuse jurors' perceptions of harm in comparison to street crimes (Iwata, 2005). Similarly, computer networking technology is very complicated, requiring similar time consuming and resource-intensive investigations in cases that can overwhelm both prosecutors and lay jurors.

## Technical Issues: The Complexity of Distributed Digital Information

Computer networks were developed for the purpose of distributing and exchanging digital information between autonomous computer systems (Tanenbaum, 2003). These networks have evolved into a robust decentralized global "network of networks," or Internet,[9] aided by increasingly inexpensive networked computers and computing devices which have expanded beyond academics and entered into the realm of mainstream business, home, mobile, and social spheres (ibid). Information from any source can now be digitized and distributed globally.

Consequently, information is increasingly being stored digitally at an exponential rate. A 2007 IDC study found that in 2006, 161 exabytes (161 billion gigabytes) of digital information was generated, equivalent to approximately 3 million times the information in all books ever written (Gantz et al., 2007). This figure is expected to grow six-fold from 2006 to 2010 as digital mediums are rapidly integrating into daily life activities.

This large amount of digital information conceived from multiple sources makes cases difficult and time consuming for prosecutors who are bound by evidentiary guidelines and the linear flow of the American legal system. One county prosecutor explains the daunting task of preparing cyber cases:

> That's how many documents you're going to have for exhibits and you have to figure out each of those comes from where?[sic] You have eBay, you have the [Internet Service Provider], you have Yahoo! and then you have people who committed the crime and used someone's credit card

[9] The Internet, or World Wide Web, is a distributed system running Internet Protocol (IP) software that is designed to transport datagrams in hierarchical layers (Tanenbaum, 2003).

> when they went in to Target. Now you have the Target video and it all comes to you in different fashions...some come on CD or DVD with a proprietary program that doesn't work on our equipment...What am I going to need to authenticate this to get the foundation to introduce this at trial? You don't want everything. You want to go to trial as succinct and comprehensible for the juror as possible.

Consequently, the overwhelming amount of work to process complex information gives prosecutors incentive to plea bargain or avoid cases altogether. The same county prosecutor explains, "A lot of [prosecutors] don't want to get involved with 'computer stuff' and so they shy away from it...probably 75% of prosecutors shy away from anything to do with computers." One federal prosecutor describes the amount of data as simply "staggering."[10] Likewise, many prosecutors tend to avoid overwhelming white-collar medical fraud cases full of obscure esoteric medical knowledge and jargon (Jesilow, Pontell, & Geis, 1993).

## *Borders*

Fitting the borderless "abstract" Internet to a geographically-oriented legal system is another prosecutorial and policing challenge (Huey, 2002). The potential large scale of cyber crime and lack of a localized crime scene is problematic for the current capacity of law enforcement forensics (Brenner, 2007). It can be argued that the Internet is not completely "borderless" and free from social control since server and routing locations are based in physical spaces (Herbert, 2000). However, conflict occurs when geopolitical factors arise from differences in law and victim location. One computer security expert expressed his frustration, stating, "Until international law uniformly [deals with cybercrime], there's no deterrence." Domestically, Internet crimes are especially problematic for non-federal law enforcement agencies and prosecutors. The possibility of multiple victims across different jurisdictions creates confusion. One investigator explains:

> If I'm [the victim] in California and you're in Georgia, if you steal [from me] in Georgia, where is the crime committed? Because the fact is every pinpoint that [the data] touches is a crime scene. You have to go to each location and generate a report. It is hugely inefficient. It's burdensome on the cop and the victim. The jurisdictional problem is huge.

---

[10] Unpublished interview data from Megan Scafiddi, 2007, University of California, Irvine.

In cases where the targets of attacks are computer systems, the victim and jurisdiction are even more difficult to decipher. Victim location is often obscured by digital evidence spread over several jurisdictions. One county prosecutor explains:

> You have an ISP whose server is in Texas or Missouri or some place, and [at] some point somebody interferes and diverts your business someplace else, whether it's a pharming[11] deal or phishing[12] scam or intrusion. The question is where did the crime take place? California is a forward place, they give you venue where the defendant is where the crime occurred where any one incidence where the crime is related or where the victim lives or works. [But in other parts of the country,] the guy goes to the police and [the police tell him], 'you know what, your crime occurred in Texas.' No, no, no. People get bounced around like that all the time because nobody will handle their case.

The two-tiered court system also complicates jurisdictional matters. Federal courts are not immune to this problem, where sensitive jurisdictional issues arise with international cases. For example, the inadequacy of laws against cyber crimes in the Philippines makes prosecution very difficult (Brenner, 2001). One state prosecutor explains, "When law enforcement goes out of the country, you have to deal with the State Department and protocols that no one knows of, that can run afoul."

In addition, many computer savvy criminals and groups use elaborate organization structures and actively deploy sophisticated counter-forensics technology to mask illegal activities, further complicating investigations and prosecution. Similar to corporate crime, where energy giant Enron and accounting firm Arthur Andersen performed complicated faulty audits to hide misconduct (Coffee, 2002) cyber criminals are increasingly using group organization structure to hide illegal activities.

### *Structural and Technological Buffers*

Online criminal groups have become increasingly organized to circumvent apprehension and prosecution. Many law enforcement investigators and prosecutors who were interviewed cite the high payoffs and relatively low risk of cybercrime as an incentive for organized crime

---

[11] Pharming is an attack on a website that redirects traffic from one website to another.

[12] Phishing is a scam performed by manipulating someone(s) to act using misinformation, such as an imposter email from a legitimate bank petitioning for private information.

groups. One federal prosecutor believes "there's a very direct link to large scale commercial piracy and organized crime," adding, "There are Russian and Asian organized crime groups that specialize in this."[13]

Copyrighted digital media and software are illegally distributed through "darknets," hierarchical private peer-to-peer piracy networks run by exclusive core groups (Biddle et al., 2002). The Motion Picture Association of America (MPAA) describes the exponential momentum of this distribution chain as an "avalanche" of data to tens of millions of peer-to-peer file-sharers.[14] A small number of top members profit while insulating themselves from prosecution. Organized criminals further distance themselves by exploiting talented youths and operating overseas in countries with lax laws.[15] One film industry Internet security expert explains, "Organized crime pulls the strings and all the minions follow." One taskforce supervisor expresses the frustration in apprehending lesser criminals, stating, "We only catch the easy ones, the smart ones buffer themselves with lots of layers."

Advanced technology is used to further insulate crime groups from apprehension and prosecution. "Botnets," or large distributed networks of infected computer systems, are often remotely controlled by criminals and groups to obtain personal information or attack systems. According to one network security expert, "[Botnets] are a major threat which serve as a middleman, making it *very* difficult to find out who's in charge." These cutting-edge crimes are problematic in fitting with legal definitions and punishment.

## Legal Issues: Making Old Laws Fit New Crimes

Computer crimes have outpaced legal controls in the United States, forcing prosecutors to fit existing laws in order to charge criminals. This becomes problematic when certain activities on the Internet do not fit traditional crime definitions. According to one county prosecutor, "It's a way that you have to sort of stretch to figure out how to make all these laws apply when they're designed for other things," adding, "They work but there's not a statute that deals with a particular behavior." The

[13] Ibid footnote 10.
[14] The Pyramid of Internet Piracy. Retrieved from http://mpaa.org/pyramid_of_piracy.pdf
[15] For example, the offices of The Pirate Bay, a popular Internet peer-to-peer torrent index site, was raided by Swedish police in 2006 and shut down for several days before returning to service in the Netherlands at full capacity and its administrators mocking law enforcement (Norton, 2006).

prosecutor gives an example of a case where an individual created an account on a social networking site using the identity of someone else without permission. He explains:

> What was unlawful? Is it identity theft? Does it fall under a statute? What did he do that's unlawful? Posting people's picture isn't unlawful. Using their name is not necessarily unlawful, but in this case, he stole the material digitally [and] posted it [which] violated 502c1 scheme to deceive, but that's kind of stretching it. It fits, but you have to work hard to get there. It's legitimate, but other than that, there's no other way to pursue this criminally.

Industry experts share these same sentiments. According to one film industry Internet security expert, "[prosecutors] are still using old laws to convict criminals that don't reflect the true nature of the crime and lump everything," adding, "The problem lies where the charge does not reflect the true nature of the crime and doesn't differentiate a smaller middle user or distributor to a large-scale manufacturing operator." One computer security expert explains the problem stems from a disjuncture between lawmakers and practitioners, stating, "Non-technical people are drafting laws and not involving enough technical people." Making unique varieties of cybercrime fit is even more difficult considering laws are inconsistent from state to state.[16] This translates into a lack of interest in pursuing legal remedies and highlights the need for more flexible and punitive laws.

## *e-Laws*

Most laws and legal provisions specifically designed for the Internet environment allow for some flexibility but can marginalize electronic crimes. The Digital Millennium Copyright Act (DMCA)[17] is heavily used by computer software and entertainment media industries to combat piracy. It contains provisions dealing specifically with circumventing security and anti-piracy technologies, not just illegal distribution. More importantly, the DMCA makes cybercrime a criminal offence, despite falling under civil U.S. Copyright Law.[18] Although this law tailors to computer and high-tech crimes, one Internet security expert argues, "[We] must take the 'e' away from everything. It's not 'e-Crime,' it's just crime. The patterns are the same, the motives are the same." This marginalization is consistent with findings that show that prosecutors belonging to

---

[16] Susan W. Brenner "The Challenge of Cybercrime" Case 'n Point Newsletter v. 6. URL: http://ceb.com/newsletterv6/criminal_Law.htm retrieved on June 30, 2007.

specialized units are generally considered less important and prestigious than those of mainstream felonies such as robbery, rape, and homicide (Heymann & Petrie, 2001).

Another ramification of marginalizing computer crimes is the severe lack of funding by policymakers. According to one California state emergency services coordinator, computer crimes have to compete against traditional street crimes for budgetary consideration. She explains the frustration in public recognition of the impact of victimization from cybercrime reflected by inadequate funding, stating, "You have funds for crimes against women and they get funding, but based on ID theft, that's devastating [also]. But since it's not violent, it doesn't qualify." The result of under-funding has meant extremely large caseloads for prosecutors.

Similar to white-collar crime investigations of financial institutions where large caseloads exerts pressure on prosecutors (Pontell, Calavita, & Tillman, 1994), cyber cases have also yielded an overwhelming amount of cases in an area of constant change that outpaces legal developments. One county prosecutor explains cybercrime "is not one of these oddball things you see from time to time," adding, "It's representative of a developing area of crime that we haven't seen and poses interesting dilemmas as to how to categorize it as a crime, how to investigate it appropriately and also, how to punish it." Light penalties are a result of marginalizing cybercrime, resulting in compromised prosecutorial strategies.

### *Laws with no teeth*

With the focus on violent crimes, computer crime cases are undermined by the weak penalties for cyber cases, giving prosecutors incentive to plea bargain cases. For example, California Penal Code 502,[19] governing computer crimes related to unlawful access, modification, and destruction of computer systems and networks, defines imprisonment of up to three years or a fine of up to $10,000. Realistically, however, time of imprisonment is systematically reduced or even bypassed. One investigator explains, "It's not unusual when suspects get probation for up to five times," adding, "No one has time to deal with them." One ramification of weak laws is the lack of deterrence on cyber malefactors. One federal agent assigned to a taskforce compares cyber with traditional street crimes with harsher penalties, stating, the cyber criminal typically gets

---

[17] The Digital Millennium Copyright Act of 1998. Pub. L. No. 105-304, 112 Stat. 2860 (Oct. 28, 1998).

[18] Title 17, U.S. Code. See http://www.copyright.gov/circs/circ1.html

[19] *See* http://calwater.ca.gov/cpc502.shtml

> ...two [years of] imprisonment or probation. Afterwards, the cyber-criminal has to pay a few thousand dollars as a fine but still has a lot of money left over from the crime, which is worth it. There's almost an incentive to commit a large crime.

In a similar example in a white-collar crime case in the 1980s, a paving contractor was only fined $75,000 without restitution after pleading guilty to defrauding New York City agencies $342,000 (Goldstocket al., 1990). A county prosecutor explains the situation, stating, "The problem is when you get a case where you know the most that will happen is the guy is going to get a probation and minimal time and most you can do is 3 months, you don't have much bargaining room." Consequently, prosecutorial strategies are based around these light penalties.

## Winning at a Price: Free Zones and Discount Justice

The culmination of technical complexity, jurisdiction overlap, extensive evidence preparation, inflexible laws, and light penalties gives prosecutors incentive to plea bargain or avoid cases altogether. With heavy caseloads, certain monetary thresholds are often required for cases to be filed. For example, due to the heavy volume of reported crime, the Internet Crime Complaint Center (IC3) typically sets a $5,000 felony threshold for Internet crimes investigations.[20] Consequently, Internet malefactors have adapted by using strategies referred to as "spread the pain," where crimes are committed under the investigatory thresholds across multiple jurisdictions.[21] One county prosecutor explains:

> What happens is you start to make a free zone and everyone realizes it's like drugs and the federal government – unless it's a certain dollar amount or certain quantity, they're not going to touch it. If it's in an area where we don't get to it, and [federal prosecutors] don't get to it, it's like this is where we're free to operate.

---

[20] Violations of section U.S.C. 1030(a) (2) Fraud and related activity in connection with computers are misdemeanors. 18 U.S.C. § 1030(c)(2)(A). Obtaining information worth less than $5,000 is a misdemeanor, unless committed after a conviction of another offense under section 1030. 18 U.S.C. §c)(2)(C). Prosecuting Computer Crimes Manual. Published by the Office of Legal Education for United States Attorneys.

[21] Microsoft Corporation Response to Federal Identity Theft Task Force Request for Comments. January 19, 2007. Retrieved on the World Wide Web on June 30, 2007. URL: http://www.idtheft.gov/comments/142.pdf

To handle the large volume of cases efficiently, plea bargaining becomes the primary strategy. One county prosecutor explains his strategy in most cases:

> It's going to be a very very expensive trial, but in the front end, we charge it completely heavy, so [the defendant] is looking at 30-40 counts. So here's the deal, we're gonna offer you to plead to 2 counts and probation with 6 months in jail. Now that's a steal. We give you a discount at this stage because we don't want to do the extra work.

A similar strategy is used in complex white-collar crime cases, where "prosecutors may hit defendants with many counts, hoping a few will stick" (Iwata, 2005). In the face of strong evidence, according to the prosecutor, 80-90% of defendants accept plea bargains, claiming, "If you round off numbers, we always win." However, a consequence of this strategy of successful plea bargaining is a systematic exclusion of certain types of cases. The prosecutor explains, *"Weaker cases go by the wayside,"* adding, *"So by the time you get the cases that go to trial, you get either the really tough cases or the easy cases."* The end result is a system that has a minimal deterrence and ultimately undermines the establishment of a robust security network. Nevertheless, prosecutors represent only one stakeholder in this security network. Without the help of collaborators, such as law enforcement and private industry, prosecutorial effectiveness could be significantly weakened.

## Creating Partnerships: A Nodal Governance Theoretical Model in a Risk Society

Cyber crime, whether defined as a new crime-type or simply new medium for existing crime, will continue to increase until offset by formal and legal controls. It represents a societal risk in the information age that must be managed (Ericson & Haggerty, 1997). Police have adapted by shifting from a model of exclusive coercive control to a hegemonic model of risk management and by becoming "experts" or "knowledge workers" utilizing technologies and strategies to combat cyber crime. A key to this strategy is outsourcing policing duties with "risk professions and their forms of expert knowledge" (ibid). As a result, security outcomes are co-produced through external public and private relationships with stakeholders (Dupont, 2006).

Security is managed through a decentralized interconnection of nodes, or stakeholder entities (Shearing & Wood, 2003; Burris, Drahos & Shearing, 2004). Similar to a computer network, nodes are interconnected through a web of formal and informal isometric relationships (Drahos, 2004). These processes of managing information in an information society are essential to understanding and enabling power and equality for citizens across geographic boundaries (Castells, 1996). When this nodal governance model is applied, prosecutorial capacity is affected by key stakeholders, namely, law enforcement, private businesses, and the public.

### *Law Enforcement*

The biggest potential impact of prosecutorial effectiveness comes from prosecutorial relationships with law enforcement. The efficiency and effectiveness of the criminal justice system to sanction crime can be severely bottlenecked by overloaded or weak links (Pontell, 1982, 1984; Pontel, Calavita, & Tillman, 1994). Bad or negligent evidence collection can produce evidence admissibility problems in court. The ephemeral and changing nature of digital evidence requires extra attention while preserving privacy (Brenner & Frederiksen, 2002; Kerr, 2005). A knowledge divide between law enforcement personnel and computer forensic investigators further aggravate this problem. Digital evidence, such as a personal computer at a crime scene that is inadvertently browsed by an officer, can be rendered inadmissible in court. One taskforce supervisor explains, it is "important for time logging and preventing the defense from accusations of tampering."

To ensure the integrity of evidentiary guidelines by law enforcement, several prosecutors are embedded within each high-tech crimes taskforce in California. This strong nodal relationship increases prosecutorial efficiency and invaluable experience and knowledge with cyber cases. One taskforce county prosecutor explains, "If you've never prepared one of these [cyber] cases for trial, you'll never be prepared for the overwhelming amount of work you have to do for the documents and physical evidence."

### *Industry*

Another security stakeholder that can significantly affect prosecutorial capacity is private industries. In general, industries with parallel goals have stronger relationships and mutually desirable outcomes. The film industry, for example, seeking to incapacitate copyright infringers, has working relationships with both law enforcement and prosecutors. According to one film industry security manager, "the partnership is really good, especially since a lot of the management is [also] former law enforcement. This builds instant trust and rapport." Co-produced outcomes by way of strong partnerships make prosecutions more effective, even leading to proactive enforcement.

Industries with divergent desirable outcomes often have weak nodal relationships that can significantly reduce prosecutorial capacity. The technology sector has historically been reluctant to take legal action, citing potential negative publicity.[22] However, closer analysis reveals structural points of conflict between business models and prosecutorial priorities. One county prosecutor explains that many cases do not come to fruition simply because they are considered part of routine business activities. He explains a case of patent infringement:

> You can bet your bottom dollar that company A, which was the original victim, is negotiating with the Chinese company and before we get through with the case, they're going to reach and agreement that's going to license these things because it's all about money…That severely undermines criminal prosecution, a lot of people think this is not a crime, this is business.

Another investigator gives an example:

> In ID theft cases, companies reimburse the victims, so the victim becomes the credit card companies, and the credit card companies don't want to do anything so the whole thing is a wash. They absorb the loss as a cost of business. In the end, it's property crime [and] nobody got hurt.

These corporate actions designed to benefit consumers serve to further mask the consequences of victimization in cyber crimes. Consequently, cyber crimes do not evoke the type of fear associated with street crimes, resulting in little incentive for members of the public to participate as security stakeholders.

### *The Public*

The prosecutorial apathy towards computer crimes can be attributed in part to public attitudes towards computer crimes. While the public can be considered the largest stakeholder in computer security by volume of

---

[22] According to a CSI/FBI computer security survey, 48% of respondents cited potential negative publicity of weak security as reason for not engaging the law enforcement and legal community after a computer intrusion (Gordon, Loeb, Lucyshyn & Richardson, 2006)

potential victims and perpetrators, structural incentives by businesses often negates liability and victimization. One prosecutor explains a credit card theft victim disincentive to pursue legal action:

> The credit card company contacts the victim [and] says, 'Well if you want to, you contact the prosecutor.' Most people, they say, 'Do I have to pay for this?' No, of course not...you were defrauded...Why should I call the prosecutor? Well they're going to want you come out, leave your job, you get paid $12 a day, you get to stay in a funky Holiday Inn and basically be uncomfortable. You get flown back, you miss work. What if I don't call? Well nothing will happen, so maybe 10% of the people will call us.

Another taskforce investigator echoes this opinion, stating, "[The public doesn't] care until it affects them." Moreover, when companies are victimized by file-sharers, legal action can create hostile relationships which further undermines the development of a robust security network.

## Conclusion

It has been shown that the rapid development of complex network technology combined with the abstract nature of cyberspace has outstripped laws, resulting in prosecutorial strategies resorting to plea bargaining or avoidance altogether. This is consistent with legal research of white-collar crime, which shows that complex cases involving financial data take significantly more resources and expertise. According to findings by the Committee of Law and Society, prosecutorial discretion is an area in need of research (Heymann & Petrie, 2001). This article has explored this issue using empirical data to try to understand the structural underpinnings that influence, or even dictate, prosecutorial decision-making processes in complex cyber cases. Beyond the scope of this research, much remains to be explored, including more in-depth political pressures and incentive structures for prosecutors. Moreover, defensive strategies, an important factor in determining prosecutorial strategies and case outcomes, were not examined in this article. Currently, prosecutors enjoy high conviction rates, allowing for high rates of plea bargaining. However, as defensive strategies develop, this may change.

Another limitation of this exploratory study includes a small sample size in each category. However, it must be noted that reflective of general sentiments of high-tech and computer crimes, there are very few specialized investigators and prosecutors relative to street crimes. In addition, more emphasis on federal law enforcement efforts should be explored, as well as expanding the scope of this research beyond

California. In-depth case studies combined with statistical analysis of cases can give more insight into prosecutorial tendencies and better identify variables and their significance.

Policy-wise, the key to ameliorating cybercrime may lie in sharing responsibility and developing a security network consisting of partnerships between security stakeholders. It has been shown that key actors can influence enforcement and prosecutorial decisions. The stronger the inter-nodal relationships, the more effective co-produced outcomes can be. The strength of relationships is dependent upon structural and cultural factors, along with the compatibility of desired outcomes. An information disjuncture between nodes can result in the unwillingness of certain industries to utilize legal resources and remedies. This is further complicated by the ramifications of enforcement unique to Internet crime, such as company fear of poor public reputation in relation to weak security, making the establishment of nodal relationships with certain industries difficult (Gordon et al., 2006). Moreover, aggressive legal actions can trigger backlashes in public perceptions as experienced by the film and music industry, and even more prolific hacker attacks, as experienced by the tech sector.

As mentioned, the current strategy by the state and private industries to deal with high-tech crimes in California is similar to collaborative taskforce strategies employed for white-collar crime. However, the long term solution is to move beyond the niche of a taskforce and integrate into the mainstream by removing the "e" from e-crimes and building a network of defensible spaces using collective efficacy in crime control. Without a major change in public and political attitudes, laws and funding will remain severely inadequate, resulting in prosecutorial compromises that create "free zones" and discounted justice that serve to only worsen the problem.

## References

Adams, K., & Cutshall, C. R. (1987). Refusing to prosecute minor offenses: The relative influence of legal and extralegal factors. *Justice Quarterly*, *4*(4), 595-609.

Ayers Jr. K. A., & Frank, J. (1987). Deciding to prosecute white-collar crime: A national survey of state attorneys general. *Justice Quarterly* *3*(4), 425-439.

Baker, J. S. (2004). The Sociological origins of "White-Collar Crime." The Heritage Foundation Legal Memorandum, (14). Retrieved September 25, 2007 from http://www.heritage.org/Research/LegalIssues/upload/70073_1.pdf.

Barnett, C. (2007). The measurement of white collar crime using uniform crime reporting (UCR) Data. U.S. Department of Justice Federal Bureau of Investigation Criminal Justice Information Services (CJIS) Division Report. Retrieved September 25, 2007 from http://www.fbi.gov/ucr/whitecollarforweb.pdf.

Benson, M. L., Maakestad, W. J., Cullen, F. T., & Geis, G. (1988). District attorneys and corporate crime: Surveying the prosecutorial gatekeepers. *Criminology*, 26(3), 505-518.

Biddle, P., England, P., Peinado, M., & Willman, B. (2002). The darknet and the future of content distribution. *2002 ACM Workshop on Digital Rights Management* presented at The Wyndham City Center Washington, D.C., November 18, 2002.

Brenner, S. W. (2001). Cybercrime investigation and prosecution: The role of penal and procedural law. *E-Law: Murdoch University Electronic Journal of Law*, *8*(2). Retrieved on 5th May 2008 from http://www.murdoch.edu.au/elaw/issues/v8n2/brenner82.txt

—. (2007). Private-Public sector cooperation in combating cybercrime: In search of a model. *Journal of International Commercial Law and Technology*, *2*(2).

Brenner, S. W., & Frederiksen, B. A. (2002). Computer searches and seizures: Some unresolved issues. *Michigan Telecommunications and Technology Law Review*, *8*(39), 39-114.

Burris, S., Drahos, P., & Shearing, C. (2004). Nodal Governance. *Australian Journal of Legal Philosophy, 30*(2), 30-58.

Castells, M. (1996). *The information age: Economy, society and culture, vol. I: The rise of the network society.* 2nd Ed. Maiden, MA: Blackwell Publishers Inc.

Coffee, J. C. (2002, July 30). Understanding Enron: It's about the gatekeepers, stupid. *Columbia Law & Economics.* Working Paper No. 207.

Donovan, L. (1981). Justice department's prosecution guidelines of little value to state and local prosecutors. *The Journal of Criminal Law and Criminology*, *3*(72), 995-992.

Drahos, P. (2004). Intellectual property and pharmaceutical markets: A nodal governance approach. *Temple Law Review*, 77, 401-424.

Dupont, B. (2006). Power struggles in the field of security: implications for democratic transformation. In J. Wood & B. Dupont (Eds.), *Democracy, Society and the Governance of Security* (pp.86-110). New York: Cambridge University Press.

Ericson, R. V. & Haggerty, K. D. (1997). *Policing the Risk Society*. Toronto: University of Toronto Press.

Foley, L., Foley, J., Hoffman, S. K., McGinley, T. G., Barney, K., Nelson, C., Pontell, H. N., & Tosouni, A. (2005). Identity Theft: The Aftermath 2004. Identity Theft Resource Center. Retrieved June 25, 2007, from http://www.idtheftcenter.org/artman2/uploads/1/The_Aftermath_2004_1.pdf

Gantz, J. F., Reinsel, D., Chute, C., Schlichting, W., McArthur, J., Minton, S., Xheneti, I., Toncheva, A., & Manfrediz, A. (2007). The expanding digital universe: A forecast of worldwide information growth through 2010. IDC white paper sponsored by EMC. Retrieved June 9, 2007, from http://www.emc.com/about/destination/digital_universe/

Goldstock, R., Marcus, M., Thatcher II, T. D., & Jacobs, J. B. (1990). *Corruption and racketeering in the New York City construction industry: Final report to governor Mario Cuomo from the New York state organized crime task force*. New York: New York University Press.

Gordon, L. A., Loeb, M. P., Lucyshyn, W., & Richardson, R. (2006). 2006 CSI/FBI Computer Crime and Security Survey. *Computer Security Journal*, 22(3).

Gurney, J. N. (1985). Factors influencing the decision to prosecute economic crime. *Criminology, 23*(4), 609-628.

Herbert, S. K. (2000). Zoning Cyberspace. *Studies in Law, Politics, and Society*, *20*(2), 101-123.

Heymann, P., & Petrie, C. (2001). *What's changing in prosecution?: Report of a Workshop*. Washington D.C.: National Academies Press.

Huey, L. J. (2002). Policing the abstract: Some observations on policing cyberspace. *Canadian Journal of Criminology*, *44*(3), 243-255.

Iwata, E. (2005). White-Collar Crime Cases Prove Difficult to Prosecute. USA Today. Retrieved September 26, 2007 from http://www.usatoday.com/money/industries/health/2005-06-28-white-collar-usat_x.htm.

Jesilow, P., Pontell, H. N., & Geis, G. (1993). *Prescription for Profit: How doctors defraud Medicaid.* Los Angeles: University of California Press.

Kerr, O. S. (2005). Digital Evidence and the New Procedure. *Columbia Law Review*, *105*(279), 79-318.

Lofland, J., & Lofland, L. H. (1984). *Analyzing social settings*. Belmont, CA: Wadsworth Publishing Company, Inc.

Ma, Y. (2002). Prosecutorial Discretion and Plea Bargaining in the United States, France, Germany, and Italy: A comparative perspective. *International Criminal Justice Review, 12*(2002), 22-52.

Norton, Q. (2006). Pirate Bay Bloodied but Unbowed. *Wired.* Retrieved June 12, 2007 from http://www.wired.com/science/discoveries/news/2006/06/71089

Patton, M. Q. (1990). *Qualitative Evaluation and Research Methods* (2nd ed.). Newbury Park, CA: Sage Publications, Inc.

Pontell, H. N. (1982). System capacity and criminal justice: Theoretical and substantive considerations. In H. E. Pepinsky (Ed.), *Rethinking Criminology* (pp.131-143). Beverly Hills: Sage Publications.

—. (1984). *A capacity to punish: The ecology of crime and punishment.* Bloomington: Indiana University Press.

Pontell, H. N., Calavita, K., & Tillman, R. (1994). Corporate crime and criminal justice system capacity: Government response to financial institution fraud. *Justice Quarterly*, *11*(3), 383-410.

Shearing, C., & Wood, J. (2003). Nodal Governance, Democracy, and the New 'Denizens'. *Journal of Law and Society*, *30*(3), 400-419.

Siwek, S. E. (2006). The true cost of motion picture piracy to the U.S. economy. Institute for Policy Innovation Policy Report #186. Retrieved September 19, 2007 from http://www.ipi.org/ipi%5CIPIPublications.nsf/PublicationLookupFullTextPDF/293C69E7D5055FA4862571F800168459/$File/CostOfPiracy.pdf?OpenElement

Sutherland, E. H. (1939). White-Collar Criminality. *American Sociological Review*, *5*(1), 1-12.

—. (1948). *White-Collar Crime*. New York: Dryden Press.

Tanenbaum, A. S. (2003). *Computer Networks 4th edition.* New Jersey: Prentice Hall.

Turner, D. et al., (2007). Symantec Internet Security Threat Report: Trends for January-June 07. (12). Retrieved September 19, 2007 from http://eval.symantec.com/mktginfo/enterprise/white_papers/ent-whitepaper_internet_security_threat_report_xii_09_2007.en-us.pdf

U.S. Department of Justice, Federal Bureau of Investigation (1989). White Collar Crime: A Report to the Public. Washington, D.C.: Government Printing Office.

# CHAPTER TWENTY THREE

# JURISDICTIONAL AND DEFINITIONAL ISSUES OF CYBER-STALKING

LYNNE ROBERTS

## Abstract

Cyber-stalking; the active stalking of another individual, group or organisation in 'cyberspace' using information and communication technologies; is an emerging form of criminal activity that crosses national and jurisdictional boundaries. This chapter provides an international perspective on cyber-stalking, examining the types and prevalence of cyber-stalking. Cyber-stalking is an interpersonal crime that challenges notions of the requirement for physical proximity for harm to occur. Victims and perpetrators of cyber-stalking may be geographically separated, creating additional difficulties in the investigation and prosecution of cyber-stalkers for crimes that transcend national and jurisdictional boundaries. Effective law enforcement and legal responses to cyber-stalking are dependent upon the formulation of laws, that recognise both the harms that can result from cyber-stalking and the cross-jurisdictional nature of the crime. These laws need to be supported through co-operation between jurisdictions and the continued training of law enforcement and legal officers to increase their technological sophistication and understanding of cyber-stalking behaviours.

## Introduction

Cyber-crime is emerging as a major international criminological issue. Networked computers provide the media for new types (or variations on old types) of criminal activity to emerge. Cyber-stalking is one such crime enabled by the Internet. In contrast to many 'property' (financial) crimes enabled by the Internet, cyber-stalking represents a crime 'against the person'. This raises new issues for criminology and criminal justice in terms of the 'harms' that can be committed against a person in the absence of the physical presence of the offender. Yet relatively little research has been conducted into cyber-stalking (See Bocij, 2003b; Bocij & Sutton, 2004) to date. In a recent editorial J. Reid Meloy, a prominent stalking researcher, articulated one of the key future questions for stalking research as "What is the nature of cyber-stalking … ?" (Meloy, 2007, p. 6).

This chapter provides an overview of the current state of knowledge on cyber-stalking. It begins with a brief overview of what is known about stalking.[1] Building on this knowledge, the concept of cyber-stalking is explored. Developing typologies of cyber-stalking and current estimates of the prevalence of cyber-stalking are provided. Possible relationships between cyber-stalking and off-line stalking are examined to shed light on whether cyber-stalking is simply an extension of off-line stalking behaviours or whether it is a new form of deviant/criminal behaviour.

The chapter ends with an examination of the difficulties in investigating and prosecuting cyber-stalkers. Cyber-stalking is a crime that transcends national and jurisdictional boundaries. Victims and perpetrators of cyber-stalking may be geographically separated by physical borders (for example, residing in different countries) when the offences occur. This is problematic for investigating the crime, in determining the jurisdiction in which alleged offences have taken place and in which charges may be filed. Legal definitions of stalking (and cyber-stalking) and applicable sentences vary across jurisdictions, if indeed they exist, further muddying the water.

## Stalking

Stalking[2] refers to repeated unwanted intrusive behaviours that result in the victim experiencing fear, physical or psychological harm or emotional distress (Finch, 2001). While the range of possible behaviours included in the stalking spectrum is wide, eight clusters of stalking behaviours have been identified across studies: hyper-intimacy, mediated contacts, interactional contacts, surveillance, invasion, harassment and intimidation,

---

[1] In this chapter the term 'stalking' is used to refer to all types of stalking behaviours. The terms 'cyber-stalking' and 'off-line stalking' are used specifically to refer to computer-mediated stalking behaviours and stalking behaviours that are not computer-mediated respectively.

[2] In this chapter the term 'stalking' is used to refer to all types of stalking behaviours. The terms 'cyber-stalking' and 'off-line stalking' are used specifically to refer to computer-mediated stalking behaviours and stalking behaviours that are not computer-mediated respectively.

coercion and threat and aggression (Cupach & Spitzberg, 2004, cited in Spitzberg & Cupach, 2007).

Stalking behaviour has been recorded in early Roman texts through to contemporary literature. Over time, conceptions of possible victims of stalking has widened from 'celebrities' and other public figures to include women harassed by ex-partners and finally to any individual who is subject to repeated intrusive pursuit that causes fear (Finch, 2001; Mullen & Pathe, 2002; Sheridan & Davies, 2004).

Changing conceptions of victims are also reflected in changing conceptions of stalking motivations. 'Celebrity' stalkers were largely seen to have erotomania or morbid infatuations with their victims. With the broadening of victims definitions, stalkers are now seen to vary in their motivations and in their mental state (Mullen & Pathe, 2002). Indeed, Kamphius and Emmelkamp (2000) caution that "stalking describes a behavioural problem, not a psychiatric diagnosis per se" (p. 208).

Spitzberg and Cupach (2007) outlined two theoretical frameworks within which stalking behaviours can be understood. First, viewed within an attachment framework, stalkers may exhibit an anxious or pre-occupied attachment style. Second, relational goal pursuit theory posits that individuals who associate the relationship with the victim with the meeting of their higher order goals (e.g. happiness and self-worth) may ruminate and experience negative affect when the relationship is thwarted, potentially motivating ongoing pursuit of the relationship.

More than twenty typologies of stalking have been proposed in the academic literature with three common underlying dimensions: the type of the underlying disorder (physiological, psychological or both), the type and context of the original relationship, and the primary motivation of the stalker (Spitzberg & Cupach, 2007). The profusion of typologies suggests that further research is required in this area. As Kamphius and Emmelkamp (2000) commented:

> There is a clear need to derive a consensus on a typology of stalkers, with associated diagnostic criteria. At present there is no evidence that one proposed typology is superior to another. The typology eventually agreed upon should have clear implications for treatment (p. 207).

## *Stalking prevalence*

Most research into stalking has been based on clinical samples of victims or forensic samples of offenders. In order to determine the prevalence of stalking, community samples are required. However, even prevalence estimates from community studies may be impacted by the definitions of stalking and thresholds used (e.g. the minimum amount of time over which stalking behaviours must persist, the minimum number of episodes required and whether it is a requirement that the behaviours evoke fear; Mullen & Pathe, 2002). Community-based surveys conducted in westernised countries report varying rates of stalking victimisation. In Australia, the 2005 Personal Safety Survey (Australian Bureau of Statistics, 2006) reported 19% of women and 9.1% of men reported ever being stalked (threshold of two or more incidents). In the United Kingdom, the 2004/5 British Crime Survey indicated that 23% of females and 15% of males have been stalked (Finney 2006; using threshold of two or more incidents). In a postal survey of a German city (Dressing, Kuehner, and Gass, 2005) 11.6% of adult respondents reported ever being stalking (using stricter threshold requirements of a minimum 2 weeks duration, more than one form of intrusive behaviour and the behaviour must have provoked fear).

Based on a meta-analysis of 175 stalking studies, Spitzberg and Cupach (2007) identified that females are significantly more likely to be stalked than males, estimating that 60-80% of victims are females. The majority (79%) of stalkers are known to their victim and are commonly (49%) previous romantic partners. Almost a third (32%) of stalking cases results in physical violence (12% sexual violence).

## *Effects of stalking*

Victims may experience difficulty in knowing when intrusive relationship 'pursuit' behaviours become persistent stalking. Based on an empirical examination of an epidemiological study of stalking in the Australian community, Purcell, Pathe and Mullen (2004a) judged that intrusive behaviours that persist for longer than two weeks meet the threshold for persistent stalking. In almost half (45%) of the cases intrusive behaviours ceased within two weeks. Of the remaining cases, the median length of stalking was six months. There were no raised levels of psychiatric morbidity for victims of brief harassment (less than two weeks) but significantly elevated levels for those exposed to longer periods of harassment.

Spitzberg and Cupach (2007) identified three levels of stalking effects: first, second and third order effects. First order effects are the impacts on the victim and may include impacts on the individual's affective health (fear, anxiety, shame, loss, suicidal ideation, depression, sleep disturbances, impaired psychological well-being) social health (decreased trust, increased alienation and isolation, restricted social activities), resource health (additional security measures, absenteeism from work), cognitive health (maladaptive beliefs, attributions of self-blame, personality adaptation), physical health (physical and sexual violence) or resilience. Stalking may also result in behavioural or general disturbance (Dressing, Kuehner, & Gass, 2005; Kamphuis, Emmelkamp, & Bartak, 2003; McEwen, Mullen, & Purcell, 2007; Purcell, Pathe, & Mullen, 2002; Spitzberg & Cupach, 2007). It is victims who are exposed to protracted periods of stalking who experience the highest rates of psychiatric morbidity, irrespective of the nature of the prior relationship with the perpetrator and the recency of victimisation (Purcell, Pathe, & Mullen, 2005). The ongoing experience of vulnerability may create more psychological distress than an actual physical assault (McEwen et al., 2007). However, Dressing and colleagues (2006) note that while serious individual consequences are reported to result from stalking, the cross-sectional design of most stalking studies do not enable causal interpretations to be made (i.e. Is psychiatric morbidity a vulnerability factor or a consequence of being stalked?). Second order effects are impacts on the individual's social and institutional networks. Third order effects are direct impacts on network members themselves. For example, network members may themselves be stalked by the perpetrator (Spitzberg & Cupach, 2007).

## *Stalking legislation*

Stalking behaviour has progressively been criminalised since the initial stalking legislation was passed in September 1990 in California. This was driven by the 'star stalking' and murder of actress Rebecca Schaeffer by a fan (Mullen & Pathe, 2002). Since this first legislation stalking laws have been introduced into most westernized countries including the United States (49 states by end of 1993), Canada (1993), Australia (all states and territories between 1993 and 1995), United Kingdom (1997) and New Zealand (Purcell, Pathe, & Mullen, 2004b).

While there is a lack of uniformity in anti-stalking legislation across jurisdictions, laws typically contain three essential elements. First, laws specify that the offending behaviour(s) must be repeated, with a minimum contact requirement often specified as two or more occasions. Second, laws typically require that the offender either intends, or could be expected to know, that their conduct would cause mental or physical harm to the victim. The third element is that the victim must experience physical harm or emotional distress or fear for their safety (Purcell et al., 2004b). The 'reasonable person' standard may be employed to ensure that conviction is not based solely on an individual victim's vulnerabilities. Dennison and Thomson (2005) argue in favour of conservative stalking laws claiming that both the victim's experience of fear or harm and the perpetrator's intent to cause fear or harm should be subject to the reasonable person standard.

The absence of traditional criminal intent requirements in some legislation makes stalking a 'victim-defined crime' (Mullen & Pathe, 2002; Purcell et al., 2004b). Repeated inappropriate socially inept behaviours, where each behaviour individually may be legal, taken together may be defined as criminal based on the reaction of the victim. Prior to the introduction of specific stalking legislation, only incidents that on their own met the definition of a criminal offence could be prosecuted, often restricting prosecutions to incidents of physical assault or property damage (Purcell et al., 2004b).

## Cyber-stalking

Cyber-stalking refers to stalking activities conducted in 'cyberspace' using information and communication technologies. Cyber-stalkers may utilise a range of tools and virtual environments including email, chat rooms, bulletin boards, newsgroups, instant messaging and key-logging Trojans. In their study of New York Police Department cyber-stalking cases, D'Ovidio and Doyle (2003) reported the most commonly used methods of cyber-stalking were email (79%) and instant messages (13%). The four main types of cyber-stalking activities reported in a survey were threats, harm to reputation (cyber-smearing), damage to data or equipment and attempts to access confidential information and computer monitoring (Bocij, 2003b; Bocij & Sutton, 2004; Pittaro, 2008).

As with stalking in general, there is no consistently used definition of cyber-stalking in the literature. It should be noted however that the term cyber-stalking is itself not accepted universally. For example, Bahm (2003) argues in favour of the terminology 'the use of technology to stalk' in order to cover current and future forms of technology that can be used in stalking.

Two general typologies of cyber-stalking have been proposed. Ogilvie (2000) developed a typology of cyber-stalking that broadly characterises cyber-stalking according to the media used. Email cyber-stalking (the 'private' dimension) includes unsolicited emails, viruses and spamming. Internet cyber-stalking (the 'public' dimension) includes posting false information, personal information or pictures of the victim on the Internet and slander. Computer cyber-stalking includes the embedding of Trojans (used to log keystrokes or provide remote control of the computer) and unauthorised access to the victims computer. Spence-Diehl (2003) described a typology of cyber-stalking based on the degree of overlap with offline stalking. This typology consists of three categories: cyber-stalking restricted to cyberspace; cyber-stalking that begins in cyberspace but transitions to off-line stalking; and cyber-stalking as one method of stalking utilised in conjunction with other methods of off-line stalking. The two typologies, while developed separately from each other, can be used in conjunction with each other to describe both the relationship with off-line stalking and the type of media used. Each of the categories of stalking proposed by Spence-Diehl can utilise any, or a combination, of the media categories described by Ogilvie.

Other specific categories of cyber-stalking have been proposed. Bocij and McFarlane (2003a) describe third party cyber-stalking as a type of stalking by proxy where the perpetrator incites others to engage in harassing activities on his/her behalf. This may include activities such as placing false advertisements on the Internet using the victim's contact details. Adam (2002) describes the 'pay-off' for third-party cyber-stalkers in terms of "...the original perpetrator becomes a voyeur, someone who invades and transgresses by watching and looking. This further reinforces the power that the perpetrator has over the victim" (p. 137).

Third party cyber-stalking would appear to be a sub-category of Olgilvie's (2000) Internet cyber-stalking category. Involving third parties in stalking activities is not restricted to cyberspace. Stalking by proxy occurs off-line when the stalker engages others to communicate with, track or contact their victim. The forms this may take include the hiring of private detectives to monitor the victim's movements, ordering or cancelling goods and services, and enlisting the help of friends, family and acquaintances (Mullen, Pathe, & Purcell, 2000).

Bocij (2003a) proposed a typology of corporate cyber-stalking based upon whether the organisation is the stalker or the victim and the reasons for the stalking behaviour. This typology includes three categories of individuals stalking organisations (motivations of revenge, financial gain and ideological), two categories of organisations stalking individuals (where the organisation is an unknowing accomplice of a stalking employee, and for financial profit) and one of organisations stalking other organisations for competitive reasons. This typology does not fit neatly into more traditional conceptualisations of stalking, where the focus is on the repeated unwanted behaviour of one individual resulting in mental harm, physical harm or emotional distress to another individual. It moves the focus from interpersonal relationships to corporate relationships with its partial focus on financial and competitive gain.

## *Cyber-Stalking Prevalence*

Most surveys of stalking do not allow the disaggregation of cyber-stalking from other stalking behaviours. Typically telephone calls, mail and electronic communication are combined into a single category (e.g. ABS, 2006). In addition, most stalking surveys do not ask questions about other types of cyber-stalking activities such as the use of Trojans and cyber-smearing. Research to date that provides some indication of the prevalence of cyber-stalking is reviewed below.

Some studies of general stalking have included limited measures of cyber-stalking. Prevalence studies of college students have reported that between a half and a third of college students who report being stalked, report emailing as part of the stalking behaviours (Alexy, Burgess, Baker, & Smoyak, 2005; Fisher, Cullen, & Turner, 2000). In a study based on the examination of records of 1005 North American stalkers Mohandie, Meloy, McGowan and Williams (2006) reported that a quarter of stalkers used mediated contacts such as letters, packages and email, with only one in twenty using cyberspace as the most frequent form of contact. Other surveys have focussed on cyber-harassment. Surveys of college students have found that between one in ten and a third of students report at least one form of online harassment (Finn, 2004; Spitzberg & Hoobler, 2002). Bocij and colleagues (Bocij, 2003b; Bocij & Sutton, 2004) used snowball sampling to obtain a survey sample of 169 Internet users. The results indicated that one in five met the criteria of repeated perpetration dependent upon ICT by one offender that caused distress to the victim. However, the sampling method utilised means that a non-representative sample was obtained.

To date, research specifically addressing cyber-stalking has not included community population-based surveys, limiting the generalisability of research findings. The exact prevalence of cyber-stalking and the percentage of general stalking episodes that contain cyber-stalking elements is still to be determined. As Spitzberg and Hoobler (2002) commented, previous estimates of the proportion of stalking cases that include cyber-stalking elements "represent little more than guesswork and extrapolation" (p. 76).

## Relationship between cyber-stalking and off-line stalking

A currently contentious issue in the cyber-stalking literature is whether cyber-stalking is best conceptualised as a new form of deviant/criminal behaviour or as an extension of off-line stalking behaviours.

Bocij and colleagues (Bocij & McFarlane, 2003; Bocij & McFarlane, 2003a, b) argue that it is a fallacy to assume that cyber-stalking is simply an extension of stalking. They describe cyber-stalking in terms of a new form of deviant behaviour exploiting new forms of information and communication technologies. In support of their argument they note that cyber-stalkers can pursue victims in other locations without need for physical or geographic proximity and may never have seen (in person or in photograph) or know any personal details (such as the age, gender, or ethnicity) of their victims. Some cyber-stalkers restrict their stalking activities to the Internet and some forms of stalking behaviours such as third party stalking are easier to encourage on-line. Cyber-stalkers can create multiple identities to aid in their stalking activities (Pittaro, 2008). Further, they argue that motivations for cyber-stalking can vary from those of stalking and include corporate cyber-stalking for political, profit or competitive advantage. They also point to the distinction between stalking and cyber-stalking made by the public, press and governments.

Alternatively, cyber-stalking behaviours may be viewed as falling broadly within existing conceptualisations of stalking, with information and communication technologies providing new tools or methods for a stalker to use. Central to definitions of both cyber-stalking and stalking are that persistent unwanted behaviours cause distress to victims. Cyber-stalking activities aimed at engaging the victim (such as repeated emails and instant messages) fit neatly within the 'mediated contacts' cluster of general stalking behaviours (Spitzberg & Cupach, 2007) and are analogous to off-line behaviours of repeated and unwanted phone-calls, letters and parcels. Other behaviours such as cyber-surveillance using trojans fall within the surveillance cluster.

The conceptualisation of cyber-stalking as a form of general stalking is also supported by the 'cross-over' between cyber-stalking and off-line stalking. As suggested by Spence-Diehl's (2003) typology of cyber-stalking, while some individuals will restrict their stalking behaviours to cyberspace, others may begin by cyber-stalking their victim but transition to off-line stalking of their victim over time. Others may utilise cyber-stalking in conjunction with off-line stalking.

Cyber-stalking exhibits a marked degree of similarity with other forms of stalking. Rather than a new crime, cyber-stalking represents an old crime modified to take advantage of the affordances of the electronic environment. Over time as Internet use is 'normalised' there are likely to be less distinctions made between stalking and cyber-stalking. While some stalkers will exclusively use off-line or on-line methods of stalking, the majority are likely to use elements of both.

### *How does 'cyberspace' facilitate stalking activities?*

The widespread adoption of the Internet provides individuals with unprecedented access to information about other individuals. The Internet, as a tool for stalking, can be used by stalkers to obtain information about current or potential stalking victims. This may include both information placed in the public domain by the individual (e.g. a personal web page) and information placed on-line without the knowledge or consent of the individual and over which the individual has no control. Identifying information typically available through search engines includes work place details, addresses, telephone numbers and organisations or groups to which an individual may belong. This publicly available information obtainable through searching the Internet may be supplemented through the use of paid on-line information broker search agencies (Tavani, 2005). For example, Docusearch.com offers a 'comprehensive background dossier' for $59 that is based on searches of proprietary databases.

Stalkers may use the information obtained from both public and commercial sources on the Internet to aid in stalking their victims off-line. In a well-documented case Amy Boyer, aged 20, was stalked and murdered by Liam Youens. Search facilities, including Docusearch, were used by Youens to obtain information on where Boyer lived and worked and her vehicle details. Youens developed two web-sites. The first presented personal information about Boyer, including a picture of her. The second described in explicit detail Youen's plans to murder Boyer (Tavani, 2002; Tavani & Grodzinsky, 2002).

The Internet provides a wide range of opportunities for individuals to interact with other people that they might otherwise never meet. This expands the available 'pool' of victims. McGrath and Casey (2002) caution that this may result in increased stalking of 'strangers'. Preliminary research supports this supposition, with more than four out of ten survey respondents in one study not knowing the identity of their cyber-stalker (Bocij, 2003b; Bocij & Sutton, 2004).

Individuals with even limited technological sophistication can engage in the on-line surveillance of (potential) victims. They may engage in 'pre-surveillance' through lurking in chat rooms, and may use applications such as 'finger' to determine when a targeted victim is online (Casey, 2004). In addition to providing the stalker with more information about the victim, the surveillance may feed voyeuristic fantasies and increase perceptions of power over the victim. This on-line surveillance is less likely to be detected than physical surveillance (McGrath & Casey, 2002).

Many individuals develop a range of relationships on-line ranging from acquaintances to friends and romantic partners (McKenna, Green, and Gleason, 2002; Parks & Floyd, 1996; Parks & Roberts, 1998; Wolak, Mitchell, and Finkelhor, 2002), experience a sense of community within virtual communities (Roberts, Smith, and Pollock, 2006) and give and receive emotional support (Whitty, 2002). However, interactions on-line predominantly occur in text. The reduced sensory information available in text-based interactions may facilitate fantasy development, transference and a false sense of intimacy (Finn & Banach, 2000; McGrath & Casey, 2002; Meloy, 1998).

In addition, it is easier to misrepresent one-self on-line than in face-to-face interactions and the likelihood of detection of this deception is reduced. Individuals are more likely to misrepresent themselves in online than offline romances, particularly in relation to age and physical attributes (Cornwell & Lundgren, 2001). The rapid expansion and increasing acceptance of on-line dating services may provide a fertile field for the development of one-sided obsessive relationships where individuals engage in deceptive impression management in order to facilitate early attraction (Spitzberg & Cupach forthcoming). In a survey of female customers of three Internet dating sites, 15.7% reported experiencing on-line verbal abuse, 26.9% obscene emails and 8.2% threatening emails (Jerin & Dolinsky, 2001).

Cyber-stalkers can use technological means to provide a level of anonymity to their stalking behaviours. Anonymous email re-mailers and web-browsing services can be used to strip identifying information from messages. Stalkers can hide their identity through the use of anonymous and forged emails (Casey, 2004). The anonymity provided may reduce social inhibitions, restraints on behaviour and accountability for actions (Bocij & McFarlane, 2003a; D'Ovidio & Doyle, 2003; McGrath & Casey, 2002). The ability to disguise ownership of messages and to destroy evidence combined with the absence of capable guardianship of the Internet means there are limited deterrents to cyber-stalking behaviours online (Bocij & McFarlane, 2003a). However, not all cyber-stalkers are technologically sophisticated and some are unaware of measures to keep their communications anonymous (McGrath & Casey, 2002).

## *Cyber-stalking perpetrators*

Limited information is known about cyber-stalkers. Research based on cases that have been criminally investigated suggests that cyber-stalkers are predominantly young males who are well-educated and technologically sophisticated (D'Ovidio & Doyle, 2003; Lucks, 2004) – matching the profile of early adopters of the Internet. While a preliminary typology of cyber-stalkers has been proposed (McFarlane & Bocij, 2003) this was based on a sample of only 24 cyber-stalkers. The studies conducted to date into cyber-stalking perpetrators are limited by their small sample sizes and being drawn from specific populations. As such, the results are best seen as preliminary and may not be generalisable to all cyber-stalkers.

## *Cyber-stalking Victims*

As with perpetrators, limited research has been conducted into the characteristics of victims of cyber-stalking. D'Ovidio and Doyle (2003) examined the characteristics of cyber-stalking victims from 171 closed cases investigated by Computer Investigation and Technology Unit of the New York Police Department. Just over half (52%) of victims were female, a third (35%) were male and the remainder were organisations (8% educational institutions, 5% private corporations and 1% public sector agencies).

Cyber-stalkers may seek 'victims of opportunity', targeting inexperienced Internet users through services such as AOL (Casey, 2004). Novice users report more threats than experienced users (Bocij, 2003b; Bocij & Sutton, 2004). More competent computer-mediated communication users may be less likely than inexperienced user to become the victims of cyber-stalking (Spitzberg, 2006) and experience harassment as less distressful (Bocij, 2003b; Bocij & Sutton, 2004).

Limited research has detailed the harms experienced by victims of cyber-stalking. In the absence of physical harm and the physical presence of the offender, it is likely that the ongoing threat and experience of vulnerability will create psychological distress. There are no guarantees that an on-line stalker will not, at some stage, transition to stalking their victim(s) off-line. In addition, the harm caused by cyber-smearing (e.g. placing false information about an individual on the Internet) may be greater than harm caused off-line due to the persistence of records on-line and the increased potential audience (Bocij & McFarlane, 2003b).

The Internet presents a 'double-edged sword' for stalking victims (Spence-Diehl, 2003). While information and communication technologies provide tools for stalkers to use in stalking their victims, they can also provide the means of information, communication and support for victims and helping professionals. On-line organisations such as WHO@ (Working to Halt Online Abuse: www.haltabuse.org) and Cyberangels (http://www.cyberangels.org/) provide advice and support to cyber-stalking victims.

Working from a feminist perspective, Adam (2002) recommends victims 'reappropriate the gaze' by investigating and tracking their cyber-stalkers online, with the aim of stripping their anonymity. From a different perspective, Bocij (2005) has argued that victims of cyber-stalking may in turn victimize others, and become 'reactive stalkers' themselves. Further research is clearly required into the consequences of stalking victims attempting to take matters into their own hands rather than relying on legal and professional help.

## Legislation and criminal investigation

Laws criminalising cyber-stalking provide a form of protection and method of address for victims. Downing (2005) provided three general principles for drafting cyber-crime laws that are of direct relevance to cyber-stalking. First, there needs to be consistency in legislation between cyber and off-line behaviours, so that conduct is criminalized uniformly whether or not the conduct is facilitated by a computer network. Second, laws should be drafted without reference to any specific technology to ensure they do not become quickly outdated. Third, laws need to enable prosecution of offenders across jurisdictions.

The introduction or amendment of legislation to cover cyber-stalking behaviours has been rapid in westernised countries. At the time of writing, forty four states in the US had stalking and/or harassment legislation that was explicitly inclusive of electronic communication (see http://www.ncsl.org/programs/lis/cip/stalk99.htm). In Australia, some states have, or are in the process of, amending legislation to include cyber-stalking (see, for example, the *Crimes (Stalking) Act 2003* in Victoria). In the United Kingdom, cyber-stalking behaviours are being prosecuted under the *Protection from Harassment Act, 1997* (see Seenan, 1999 for details of the first successfully prosecuted case). This rapid adoption of cyber-stalking legislation has led one researcher to comment that "cyber-stalking is well on its way to being criminalized before being empirically examined" (Spence-Diehl, 2003, p. 6).

However, the amending of legislation to incorporate cyber-stalking behaviours is far from universal across the world. Cyber-stalking may still be regarded in many jurisdictions as constituting a 'social harm' rather than a criminal offence (Joseph, 2003). Even where legislation exists, it may be problematic to successfully prosecute cyber-stalking as it is difficult to establish a 'credible threat' if a direct threat has not been made or if the stalker and victim live in different jurisdictions. Similarly, Meloy (1998) argued that cyber-stalking alone is unlikely to be prosecuted, but that cyber-stalking in conjunction with other means of pursuit may be.

The criminal investigation of stalking/cyber-stalking poses problems for police as, unlike most crimes, stalking consists of repeated individual behaviours that individually may not constitute criminal offences. Other difficulties facing police are that stalking may be perceived by some as part of a relationship, there is no unique profile of stalkers and it is difficult to predict which stalkers will become violent. Further, police investigations may need to cover multiple jurisdictions (National Centre for Victims of Crime, 2004).

In order to convince authorities to investigate or prosecute cyber-stalking, the onus is often on the victim to produce evidence. Victims of cyber-stalking may find this easier to comply with than victims stalked off-line as electronic communication (e.g. chat room discussions) can be logged and threatening emails saved, providing a form of objective data (Deirmenjian, 1999).

Difficulties in investigating cyber-stalking arise in identifying the stalker when they have taken steps to ensure the anonymity of their communications (Joseph, 2003). Cyber-stalkers frequently have greater technical ability than victims and law enforcement agents (Aggarwal, Burmester, Henry, Kermes, & Mulholland, 2005). Police may also have difficulty in obtaining information from Internet Service Providers. For example, D'Ovidio and Doyle (2003) noted that in 18% of New York Police Department cyber-stalking cases examined the police were unable to access required records in order to arrest the cyber-stalking suspect.

The need for both law enforcement staff and prosecutors to increase their technical ability and understanding of computer-related crimes has been recognised. In the US, specialized cyber-crime units have been established within or across government departments in addition to FBI computer crime squads. Computer crime prosecutors are employed within each US Attorney's office (Joseph, 2003).

Computer solutions have been developed to aid in the investigation and prosecution of cyber-stalking. For example, the Predator and Prey Alert (PAPA) system, consisting of integrated software and hardware modules, can be utilized to capture, record and verify evidence for use in prosecution. It consists of a sessional recorder, a victim module, an agent module and a dispatcher. The system operates by capturing information received by the victim. This can be supplemented by the law enforcement agent remotely shadowing ongoing interactions with the investigator able to take control of the victim's desktop if required (Aggarwal et al., 2005; Aggarwal, Henry, Kermes, & Mulholland, 2005).

Not all cyber-stalking involves perpetrators and victims from the same jurisdiction. Where victims and perpetrators are located in different jurisdictions investigation and prosecution may be hampered by differences in statutory definitions of stalking. Some jurisdictions may deny or ignore extradition requests (D'Ovidio & Doyle, 2003).

There is a lack of clarity over what constitutes jurisdiction in cyberspace. As Brenner and Koops (2004) ask: "is it the place of the act, the country of residence of the perpetrator, the location of the effect, or the nationality of the owner of the computer that is under attack? Or all of these at once?" (p. 3). Cyber-crime jurisdictional clauses differ significantly across states and countries. The 'reasonableness standard' suggests that the exercise of jurisdiction requires a close connection with the crime, but this leaves the potential for both negative and positive jurisdiction conflicts. Negative jurisdiction conflicts occur when no jurisdiction claims jurisdiction over a cyber-crime. Positive jurisdiction conflicts occur when more than one jurisdiction claims jurisdiction over the one cyber-crime. While the reasonableness standard dictates the jurisdiction with the closest connection to the crime has priority in prosecuting, it may be difficult to determine who has precedence of jurisdictional claims (Brenner & Koops, 2004).

Jurisdictional issues in relation to cyber-stalking are being tested in the courts. An Australian example (cited in Smith, Grabosky, & Urbas, 2004, p. 52) detailed how a Victorian Magistrate initially dismissed the case of a Melbourne resident who stalked a Canadian actress on the grounds of lack of jurisdiction (based on the harm occurring in Canada rather than Melbourne). At appeal by the Director of Public Prosecution, the Supreme Court determined that although the harm occurred outside of Australia, the criminal conduct was committed within Victoria and the case was therefore within jurisdiction.

While jurisdictional issues result in difficulties in investigating and prosecuting cyber-stalking, these problems are not specific to cyber-stalking but occur with other types of cyber-crime and cross-border crime (D'Ovidio & Doyles, 2003; Smith, Grabosky, & Urbas, 2004).

## Conclusion and Future Directions

This chapter has presented an overview of cyber-stalking as a form of stalking that takes advantage of the affordances of the electronic environment. There is a need to extend the boundaries of our perceptions of stalking to include current conceptions of cyber-stalking and future methods of stalking that may arise as the proliferation of new information and communication technologies continues. This inclusive approach demands research into the dynamics between on- and off-line stalking and into the prevalence, incidence, duration and effects of stalking conducted within electronic environments.

Cyber-stalking is an interpersonal crime that challenges notions of the requirement for physical proximity for harm to occur. Effective law enforcement and legal responses to cyber-stalking are dependent firstly upon the formulation of laws that recognise both the harms that can result from cyber-stalking and the cross-jurisdictional nature of the crime. These laws need to be supported through co-operation between jurisdictions and the continued training of law enforcement and legal officers to increase their technological sophistication and understanding of cyber-stalking behaviours.

## References

Adam, A. (2002). Cyberstalking and Internet pornography: Gender and the gaze. *Ethics and Information Technology, 4*, 133-142.

Aggarwal, S., Burmester, M., Henry, P., Kermes, L., & Mulholland, J. (2005). Anti-Cyberstalking: The Predator and Prey Alert (PAPA) System. *Proceedings of the first international workshop on systematic approaches to digital forensic engineering, (SADFE '05)*, 195-205.

Aggarwal, S., Henry, P., Kermes, L., & Mulholland, J. (2005). Evidence handling in proactive cyberstalking investigations: The PAPA approach. *Proceedings of the first international workshop on systematic approaches to digital forensic engineering, (SADFE '05)*, 165- 176.

Alexy, E. M., Burgess, A. W., Baker, T., & Smoyak, S. A. (2005). Perceptions of cyberstalking among college students. *Brief Treatment and Crisis Intervention, 5*(3), 279-289.

Australian Bureau of Statistics. (2006). *Personal safety survey Australia: 2005 (Reissue).* Canberra: Commonwealth of Australia.

Bahm, T. (2003). Eliminating "cyber-confusion". *Stalking Resource Centre Newsletter, 3*(2), 2. Retrieved April 15, 2007 from http://www.ncvc.org/src/AGP.Net/Components/DocumentViewer/Download.aspxnz?DocumentID=33500

Bocij, P. (2003a). Corporate cyberstalking: An invitation to build theory. *First Monday, 7*(11). Retrieved April 15, 2007 from http://firstmonday.org/issues/issue7_11/bocij/index.html.

—. (2003b). Victims of cyberstalking: An exploratory study of harassment perpetrated via the Internet. *First Monday, 8*(10). Retrieved April 15, 2007 from http://firstmonday.org/issues/issue8_10/bocij/index.html

—. (2005). Reactive stalking: A new perspective on victimisation. *The British Journal of Forensic Practice, 7*, 23-34.

Bocij, P., Bocij, H., & McFarlane, L. (2003). Cyberstalking: A case study of serial harassment in the UK. *The British Journal of Forensic Practice, 5*(2), 25-32.

Bocij, P., & McFarlane, L. (2003a). Cyberstalking: The technology of hate. *The Police Journal, 76*, 204-221.

Bocij, P., & McFarlane, L. (2003b). Seven fallacies about cyberstalking. *Prison Service Journal, 149*, 37-42.

Bocij, P., & Sutton, M. (2004). Victims of cyberstalking: Piloting a web-based survey method and examining tentative findings. *Journal of Society and Information, 1*(2). Retrieved April 15, 2007 from http://josi.spaceless.com/.

Brenner, S W., & Koops, B-J. (2004). Approaches to cybercrime jurisdiction. *Journal of High Technology Law, 15*(1), 1-46.

Casey, E. (2004). *Digital evidence and computer crime: Forensic science, computers and the Internet* (2nd ed). London: Elsevier Academic Press.

Cornwell, B., & Lundgren, D. C. (2001). Love on the Internet: Involvement and misrepresentation in romantic relationships in cyberspace vs. realspace. *Computers in Human Behavior, 17*, 197-211.

D'Ovidio, R., & Doyle, J. (2003). A study on cyberstalking: Understanding investigative hurdles. *FBI Law Enforcement Bulletin, 72*(3), 10-17.

Deirmenjian, J. M. (1999). Stalking in cyberspace. *Journal of American Academy of Psychiatry and Law, 27*(3), 407-413.

Dennison, S. M., & Thomson, D. M. (2005). Criticisms or plaudits for stalking laws? What psycholegal research tells us about proscribing stalking. *Psychology, Public Policy & Law, 11*(3), 384-406.

Downing, R. W. (2005). Shoring up the weakest link: What lawmakers around the world need to consider in developing comprehensive laws to combat cybercrime. *Columbia Journal of Transnational Law, 43*, 705- 762

Dressing, H., Kuehner, C., & Gass, P. (2005). Lifetime prevalence and impact of stalking in a European population. *British Journal of Psychiatry, 187*, 168-172.

Finch, E. (2001). *The criminalization of stalking: Constructing the problem and evaluating the solution.* London: Cavendish.

Finn, J. (2004). A survey of online harassment at a university campus. *Journal of Interpersonal Violence, 19*(4), 468-483.

Finn, J., & Banach, M. (2000). Victimization online: The down side of seeking human services for women on the Internet. *CyberPsychology & Behavior, 3*(2), 243-254.

Finney, A. (2006) *Domestic violence, sexual assault and stalking: Findings from the 2004/05 British Crime Survey.* Home Office Online Report 12/06. London: Home Office. Retrieved April 15, 2007 from http://www.homeoffice.gov.uk/rds/pdfs06/rdsolr1206.pdf

Fisher, B. S., Cullen, F. T., & Turner, M. G. (2000). *The sexual victimization of college women.* National Institute of Justice and Bureau of Justice Statistics Research Report: NCJ 182369. Retrieved April 15, 2007 from http://www.ncjrs.gov/pdffiles1/nij/182369.pdf

Jerin, R., & Dolinsky, B. (2001). You've got mail! You don't want it: Cyber-victimization and on-line dating. *Journal of Criminal Justice and Popular Culture*, 9(1). Retrieved April 15, 2007 from http://www.albany.edu/scj/jcjpc/vol9is1/jerin.html

Joseph, J. (2003). Cyberstalking: An international perspective. In J. Yewkes (Ed.), *Dot.cons: Crime, deviance and identity on the Internet* (pp. 105-125). Cullompton: Willan.

Kamphius, J. H., & Emmelkamp, P. M. G. (2000). Stalking — A contemporary challenge for forensic and clinical psychiatry. *British Journal of Psychiatry, 176*, 206-209.

Kamphius, J. H., Emmelkamp, P. M. G., & Bartak, A. (2003). Individual differences in post-traumatic stress following post-intimate stalking: Stalking severity and psychosocial variables. *British Journal of Clinical Psychology, 42*, 145-156.

Lucks, B. D. (2004). *Cyberstalking: Identifying and examining electronic crime in cyberspace.* Unpublished doctoral dissertation, Alliant International University, San Diego, CA.

McEwan, T., Mullen, P. E., & Purcell, R. (2007). Identifying risk factors in stalking: A review of current research. *International Journal of Law and Psychiatry, 30*, 1-9.

McFarlane, L., & Bocij, P. (2003). An Exploration of predatory behaviour in cyberspace: Towards a typology of cyberstalkers. *First Monday, 8-9*. Retrieved April 15, 2007 from http://www.firstmonday.org/issues/issue8_9/mcfarlane/index.html

McGrath, M. G., & Casey, E. (2002). Forensic psychiatry and the Internet: Practical perspectives on sexual predators and obsessional harassers in cyberspace. *Journal of the American Academy of Psychiatry and the Law, 30(1),* 81-94.

McKenna, K. Y. A., Green, A. S., & Gleason, M. E. J. (2002). Relationship formation on the internet: What's the big attraction? *Journal of Social Issues, 58*(1), 9-31.

Meloy, J. R. (1998). The psychology of stalking. In J. R. Meloy (Ed.), *The psychology of stalking: Clinical and forensic perspectives* (pp.1-23). San Diego: Academic Press.

—. (2007). Stalking: The state of the science. *Criminal Behaviour & Mental Health, 17*, 1-7.

Mohandie, K., Meloy, R., McGowan, M. G., & Williams, J. (2006). The RECON typology of stalking: Reliability and validity based upon a large sample of North American stalkers. *Journal of Forensic Sciences, 51*, 147-155.

Mullen, P., Pathe, M., & Purcell, R. (2000). Stalkers and their victims. Cambridge: Cambridge University Press.

Mullen, P. E., & Pathe, M. (2002). Stalking. In M. Tonry (Ed.), *Crime and Justice: A review of research, Volume 29* (pp.273-318). Chicago: University of Chicago Press.

National Centre for Victims of Crime (2004). *Stalking. Problem-oriented guides for police problem-specific guides Series No 22.* US Department of Justice. Retrieved April 15, 2007 from http://www.cops.usdoj.gov/mime/open.pdf?Item=1042.

Ogilvie, E. (2000). Cyberstalking. *Trends & issues in crime and criminal justice, No 166*. Canberra: Australian Institute of Criminology.

Parks, M. R., & Floyd, K. (1996). Making friends in cyberspace. *Journal of Communication, 46*, 80-97.

Parks, M. R., & Roberts, L. D. (1998). 'Making MOOsic': The development of personal relationships on-line and a comparison to their off-line counterparts. *Journal of Social & Personal Relationships, 15,* 517-537.

Pittaro, M. L. (2007). Cyber stalking: An analysis of online harassment and intimidation. *International Journal of Cyber Criminology, 1*(2), 180–197. Retrieved September 1, 2008, from http://ccrimejournal.brinkster.net/pittaroijccvol1is2.htm

Purcell, R., Pathe, M., & Mullen, P. E. (2002). The prevalence and nature of stalking in the Australian community. *Australian and New Zealand Journal of Psychiatry, 36*, 114-120.

Purcell, R., Pathe, M., & Mullen, P. E. (2004a). Editorial: When do repeated intrusions become stalking? *The Journal of Forensic Psychiatry & Psychology, 15*(4), 571-583.

Purcell, R., Pathe, M., & Mullen, P. E. (2004b). Stalking: Defining and prosecuting a new category of offending. *International Journal of Law and Psychiatry, 27*, 157-169.

Purcell, R., Pathe, M., & Mullen, P. E. (2005). Association between stalking victimization and psychiatric morbidity in a random community sample. *British Journal of Psychiatry, 187*, 416-420.

Roberts, L. D., Smith, L. M., & Pollock, C. M. (2006). Psychological sense of community in virtual communities. In S. Dasgupta (Ed.), *Encyclopaedia of virtual communities and technologies* (pp. 390-396). Hershey, PA: Idea Group Inc.

Seenan, G. (1999, October 16). Three months' jail for internet stalker. *The Guardian* (p. 9).

Sheridan, L., & Davies, G. (2004). Stalking and harassment. In J. R. Adler (Ed.), *Forensic psychology: Concepts, debates and practice* (pp. 197-211). Cullompton: Willan.

Smith, R. G., Grabosky, P., & Urbas, G. (2004). *Cyber criminals on trial.* Cambridge: Cambridge University Press.

Spence-Diehl, E. (2003). Stalking and technology: The double-edged sword. *Journal of Technology in Human Services, 22*(1), 5-18.

Spitzberg, B. H. (2006). Preliminary development of a model and measure of computer-mediated communication (CMC) competence. *Journal of Computer-Mediated Communication, 11*, 629-666.

Spitzberg, B. H., & Cupach, W. R. (forthcoming 2007). Cyber-stalking as (mis)matchmaking. In M. T. Whitty, A. Baker, & J. Inman (Eds.), *Online matchmaking* (pp.127-146). Basingstoke: Palgrave Macmillan.

Spitzberg, B. H., & Cupach, W. R. (2007). The state of the art of stalking: Taking stock of the emerging literature. *Aggression and Violent Behavior, 12*, 64-86.

Spitzberg, B. H., & Hoobler, G. (2002). Cyberstalking and the technologies of interpersonal terrorism. *New Media & Society, 4*(1), 71-92.

Tavani, H. T. (2002). The uniqueness debate in computer ethics: What exactly is at issues, and why does it matter? *Ethics and Information Technology, 4*, 37-54.

—. (2005). Search engines, personal information and the problem of privacy in public. *International Review of Information Ethics, 3*, 39-45.

Tavani, H. T., & Grodzinsky, F. S. (2002). Cyberstalking, personal privacy, and moral responsibility. *Ethics and Information Technology, 4*, 123-132.

Whitty, M. T. (2002). Liar, liar! An examination of how open, supportive and honest people are in chat rooms. *Computers in Human Behavior, 18*, 343-352.

Wolak, J., Mitchell, K. J., & Finkelhor, D. (2002). Close online relationships in a national sample of adolescents. *Adolescence, 37*(47), 441-455.

# CHAPTER TWENTY FOUR

# REVEALING PATTERNS IN CRIMINAL BEHAVIOUR: A CASE-STUDY OF DATA MINING IN POLICE OPERATIONS IN TURKEY

FATIH OZGUL, JULIAN BONDY
AND HAKAN AKSOY

## Abstract

In this 'real world' case study of a police operation in Turkey, the utility and value of applying data mining techniques in the identification and interdiction of organised crime syndicates is explored. This case study demonstrates the effectiveness of a Crime Graph Algorithm (CGA) within the context of the evolution that has taken place with organised crime and terrorist organisations. Increasingly in many of these criminal organisations the traditional hierarchical structures have given way to more dynamic, fluid and opportunistic groupings that require increasing sophisticated techniques to uncover their scope and membership. This case study indicates that criminal justice agencies are able to respond effectively to these new challenges but that new tactics and new skill sets may need to be considered in future police resource planning. While their pre-existing infrastructure and procedures for collecting information and their increasing use of computers to facilitate their operations means many police agencies are well placed to take advantage of these techniques it is also the case that police managers will need to 'complete the circle' in ensuring they have the human resources and skill sets to increase the efficacy of their activities. This chapter illustrates some of the techniques now available to extract and reveal patterns and associations. It demonstrates that the application of a Crime Graph Algorithm (CGA) can reveal previously undetected criminal associations and how these relate to broader understandings in criminology and organisational theory.

## Introduction

This chapter demonstrates the utility and value in applying data matching techniques in criminal justice. Pattern matching which has been traditionally associated with information sciences is increasing being used in a broad range of disciplines. Criminal justice agencies, with their pre-existing infrastructure and procedures for collecting information, and their increasing use of computers to facilitate their operations are well placed to take advantage of these techniques to extract patterns in criminal behaviour from police and other justice agency data sets and increase the efficacy of their activities.

This chapter uses a recent police operation in Turkey to illustrate some of the techniques now available to extract and reveal patterns and associations. It demonstrates that the application of a Crime Graph Algorithm (CGA) that was developed and trialled in Bursa, Turkey can reveal previously undetected criminal associations.

Based on initial findings of CGA; thirty-four offenders were considered to be in a single offender group of which seven of them were highly networked ruling members. After *Operation Cash* was launched in 2006, Turkish national police arrested the seven detected ruling members, and disrupted a previously unknown criminal network consisting of twenty members of which three whom had never been previously identified or arrested. Turkish police arrested seventeen people, recovered worth U.S. $200,000 of stolen goods, and cash worth U.S. $180,000.

Increasingly complex and technologically savvy criminal activity requires that law enforcement agencies respond in kind if they are to fulfil their organisational goals. The successful road-testing of a CGA and the resultant police operation illustrates one way in which police can shift from a reactive crime-reporting model to a pro-active crime prevention model. The successful application of emergent and innovative techniques to detect and interdict in the activities of criminal organisations demonstrates that that the sophistication of the policing model can be as important as the more traditional approaches to detecting and frustrating organised crime.

## Background

Link analysis and group detection is a newly emerging research area that is at the intersection of link analysis, hypertext and web mining, graph mining (Cook & Holder, 2000) and social network analysis (SNA) (Scott, 2004). Graph mining and social network analysis (SNA) in particular attracted attention from a wide audience in police investigation and intelligence (Getoor, 2004), (Badia et al., 2005). As a result of this attention, the police and intelligence agencies realized the knowledge about offender networks and detecting covert networks are important to crime investigation (Senator, 2005). Group detection refers to the discovery of underlying organisational structure that relates selected individuals with each other, in broader context; it refers to the discovery of underlying structure relating instances of any type of entity among themselves (Marcus et al., 2007).

### *Data mining, network analysis and crime investigation*

While the understanding of, and capacity to counter, organised crime has developed significantly in recent decades, these insights and enhanced response strategies have been hampered because the criminologists and law enforcement agencies that have focused on this area of serious crime have not employed valuable analytical and conceptual methods that have been used effectively in other settings. Similarly, while law enforcement agencies have been collecting and employing large databases in their crime detection, prevention and investigation strategies, these have tended to rely upon traditional forms of analysis such as association analysis, classification and prediction, cluster analysis, and outlier analysis to identify patterns. While a number of researchers (Hobbs, 1995; Jackson et al., 1996) advocate an ethnographic approach to investigating criminal networks the dilemma has been that these forms of study are often too demanding to be used on a large-scale basis. At the same time law enforcement databases while usually containing rich geographic and other data are often poor in their relational content. However, these approaches are not mutually incompatible and when used in combination reduce their individual deficiencies.

The social network field has identified many approaches for finding primary groups in networks (Fershtman, 1997; Freeman, 1992; Richards, 1995; Seidman & Foster, 1978). Gest, Moody and Rulison (2007) argue that these approaches can be divided into those that identify precise graph theory features and those that interrogate the graph to identify a solution iteratively. Many graph-centric methods for finding primary groups confront difficulties where data are messy; this in turn leads to projects that are not robust to the kinds of data that analysts typically encounter. These methods also often identify groups with significant overlap. An alternative approach has been to identify groups based on a search and clustering processes. For example, using algorithms that attempt to generate clusters with relatively high in-group density. These algorithms vary significantly. Much of the research on group detection algorithms has been to identify ways to catalyse or accelerate these types of searches, with some very sophisticated pattern recognition techniques being most popular (Fershtman, 1997). While these have been successful in small group settings, these iterative techniques can be very time-consuming on large networks. Recent studies have attempted to identify search processes either directly on graphs (Guimera & Amaral, 2005) or through summary statistics generated by the network structure (Moody, 2001) and thereby overcome earlier difficulties with very large network analysis. Another line of enquiry has been to adopt a statistical modelling approach, using guided search algorithms based on a tie probability model (Frank, 1995). These models work on the understanding that groups should focus on connections, so the probability of a connection between each node is a function of a parameter on the group partition and that these nodes are shuffled across partitions until the parameter is maximized.

This chapter argues that SNA provides additional insights and greater explanatory power than existing criminological approaches like patron-client, enterprise and organisational theories by highlighting and centralizing the implicit belief held by each theory – that human relationships are the foundation of human society. Not only are these relationships central, they are not randomly generated. Instead these relationships are often highly specialised and are likely to include members with specialised contact possibilities, who act as channels for transmission across the totality of contact and connection possibilities and who traverse various networks. For example, in a social network there will be individuals who link to other groups through occupational specialisation or geographic location. This understanding of the fundamental role of social relations as an organising principle for understanding complex and fluid social groups and the recognition of ways in which people are linked together clearly has application for understanding organised criminal activity.

This recognition of the importance of individuals who, by virtue of their specialised occupational or locational attributes, act as the conduits between criminal groupings has been particularly relevant in criminological analyses. This is because while many of these individuals have been previously identified because of their specialisation they had not necessarily been identified as significant nodes within and between networks.

SNA has a number of additional features that are clearly aligned and offer high utility in criminal investigations into organised criminal activity and more broadly in crime prevention strategies. These attributes include:

- The systematic and deliberative focus on the relations and inter-linkages within and external to members of the group and other units of analysis.
- Through its focus on the interlinkages and content between the units of analysis, social network analysis foregrounds the interdependency and reduces a priori theorizing regarding the linkages and relations between the units of analysis, in this case members of organised crime groups.
- The concentration on co-dependency, interactions and interlinkages encourages the investigator away from individual units of analysis, and in criminal investigation away from individual deficit models, and towards broader understandings of social relations.
- The systematic and deliberative focus on the relations and inter-linkages within and external to members of the group and other units of analysis
- The concentration on co-dependency, interactions and interlinkages encourages the investigator away from individual units of analysis, and in criminal investigations, away from individual deficit models and towards broader understandings of social relations.

Since discovery of an underlying organisational structure from crime data leads the investigation to terrorist cells or organised crime groups, detecting covert networks are important to crime investigation. Detecting an offender group or even a part of group (subgroup) is also important and valuable. A subgroup can be extended with other members with the help of domain experts. An experienced police officer usually knows the associates of well-known offenders, so he can decide which subgroups should be united to constitute the whole group. Another outcome of offender group detection is considered to be pre-emptive strike or crime prevention. For example a drug-dealing network prepares all required vehicles and people for transaction where all members are in the process of getting prepared. Such cases can be prevented with offender group detection before it happens. A further advantage of group detection is acting in a group of offenders to commit a crime is regarded as an aggravating factor for a heavier punishment in many country's laws. For instance, Turkish Crime Code extends six years imprisonment for group leader and one year imprisonment for group members in addition to the substantive penalty. Specific software like Analyst Notebook (2007), and Sentient Data Detective (2007) provide some visual spatio-temporal representations of offender groups in graphs, but they lack automated group detection functionality.

In this chapter, we acknowledge the following contributions for offender group detection;

- We identify and discuss converting arrest data to graph format where there is no standardised way of doing this. We suggest the choice of representation for edges and nodes must follow the rules in SNA where one-mode or two-mode social networks representation are now standard (section 3).
- We explain precisely how to use police arrest data to look for possible offender groups (section 4). Surprisingly this has not been explained precisely before.
- We show how we can apply filters to graph data in order to adhere to countries' criminal law requirements (section 6).
- We show that ruling members, not new recruits, are likely to be detected, but "big brother" of network is unlikely to be detected (section 7).

## Group Detection

Group detection approach primarily refers to the discovery of underlying organisational structures that associate selected individuals to each other based on density-based cluster algorithms from the social network theory. This task is defined and different methods applied in data mining, in social network analysis, and in graph theory. For example, Getoor and Diehl (2005) state group detection aims clustering of object nodes in a graph into groups that share common characteristics. But to some extent, subgraph discovery does the same job for finding interesting or common patterns in a graph. On the other hand social network analysis tries to detect cohesive subgroups among which there are relatively strong, direct, intense, frequent, or positive ties (Wasserman & Faust, 1994). Graph matching (Cook & Holder, 2007) methods are also recommended for group detection tasks. There are also many specific dyadic and group detection models. Among them, Adibi et al., (2004, 2005) propose KOJAK group finder which first positions possible groups, then expands these groups using knowledge-based reasoning techniques and then adding more candidates relying on observed interactions that shows possible associations. Kubica et al., (2002, 2003) first proposes a generative model for multi-type link generation, called collaborative graph model (cGraph) and introduce a scalable group discovery algorithm called k-groups, which is similar to k-means algorithm. When we focus on offender group detection, the most remarkable works in this field are CrimeNet Explorer, which is developed by Xu et al. (2005), and Terrorist Modus Operandi Detection System (TMODS), which is developed by 21$^{st}$ Century Technologies (Moy, 2005).

### *CrimeNet Explorer*

Xu et al. (2005) defined a framework for automated network analysis and visualization. Using COPLINK connect and COPLINK detect (Chen et al., 2002) structure to obtain link data from text, CrimeNet Explorer used an Reciprocal Nearest Neighbour (RNN) based clustering algorithm to find out links between offenders, as well as discovery of previously unknown groups. CrimeNet Explorer framework includes four stages: network creation, network partition, structural analysis, and network visualization. CrimeNet Explorer uses concept space approach for network creation, RNN-based hierarchical clustering algorithm for group detection; social network analysis based structural analysis, and multi dimensional scaling for network visualisation. CrimeNet Explorer is the first model to solve offender group discovery problem and its success comes from the powerful functionality of overall COPLINK structure. On the other hand, since CrimeNet Explorer was evaluated by university students for its visualization, structural analysis capabilities, and its group detection functionality, the operationally actionable outputs of CrimeNet Explorer has not been proved in real-time police investigations.

### *Terrorist Modus Operandi Detection System (TMODS)*

TMODS, which is developed by 21$^{st}$ Century Technologies (Marcus et al., 2007), automates the tasks of searching for and analysing instances of particular threatening activity patterns. With TMODS, the analyst can define an attributed relational graph to represent the pattern of threatening activity he or she is looking for. TMODS then automates the search for that threat pattern through an input graph representing the large volume of observed data. TMODS pinpoints the subset of data that match the threat pattern defined by the analyst thereby transforming a manual search into an efficient automated graph matching tool. User defined threatening activity or pattern graph can be produced with possible terrorist network ontology and this can be matched against observed activity graph. At the end, human analyst views matches that are highlighted against the input graph. TMODS is mature and powerful distributed java software that has been under development since October 2001 (Marcus et al., 2007). But it needs a pattern graph and an analyst to run the system. Like a supervised learning algorithm, TMODS tries to tailor the results according to pre-defined threatening activity. Another possible drawback is graphs used in TMODS are multi-mode and can be disadvantageous for further analysis. Multi-mode graph means that nodes in multi-mode graphs are more than two types of entities. A person, a building, an event, a vehicle are all represented as nodes; when for instance we want to detect key players in multi-mode graph, a building can be detected as key player, not a person. This can be a cause of confusion. To overcome this confusion the definition of a one-mode (friendship) social network should be used rather than representing all entities as nodes.

## Offender Group Representation

Wasserman and Faust (1994, p. 35) states that the modes of a network as the number of sets of entities on which structural variables are measured. One-mode (friendship) networks, the predominate type of network, study just a single set of actors while two-mode (affiliation) networks focus on two sets of actors, or one set of actors and one set of events. One could ever consider (three and higher) mode networks but rarely have social network methods has been designed for such complicated data structures. According to this definition it is better to represent actors (offenders) as nodes and events (crimes) as edges in one-mode (friendship) social networks. Thereby other social network analysis solutions can be used on one-mode (friendship) networks such as for friendship identification, finding key actors, and social network analysis based group detection algorithms.

## Police Arrest Data

We recommend looking for common characteristics of offenders in police arrest data. Do they commit the crime together? Are they committing similar offences in similar locations? Have any of these offenders been convicted of offences with others? This information can be obtained from a relational database table, text-based arrest reports, and /or CCTV footage.

In *Operation Cash* we obtained this information from Bursa Police Arrest Data where the table included the fields for: P_ID (person id), C_ID (crime reference number), BRANCH (police branch that deals with),

CRT_ID (Crime type it belongs to), CR (Name of the offence), MOT_ID (Modus Operandi it belongs to), MO (name of the modus operandi), D (date stamp), DIS (district), NG (neighbourhood), and NG_ID (neighbourhood number).

## Crime Graph Algorithm (CGA)

Crime Graph Algorithm is developed for detecting possible offender groups as exhibited in Figure 1. The source of link information is gathered from police arrest records where a link table; consisting of From (From Offender), To (To offender), and W (how many times this offender pair caught together by the police) is produced with an inner join SQL query.

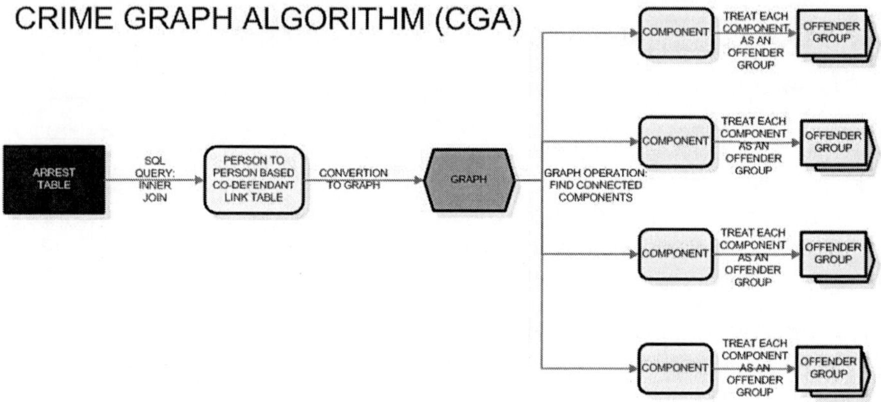


**Figure 1. Crime Graph Algorithm**

Inner join query result, which we call co-defendant link table, then converted to graph where nodes represent offenders, edges represent crimes committed together using offender group representation exhibited in section 3. Number of times caught together is counted to be used for edge weight (W). At this point a subgraph detection operation is needed; various social network analysis algorithms such as k-clique, k-core (Wasserman et al., 1994) can be used for this purpose. We used strongly connected components (SCC) algorithm in *Operation Cash* because it is scalable and gives concrete results. SCC algorithm is defined as (Cormen et al., 2001) a directed graph strongly connected if for every pair of vertices U and V in a graph there is a path from U to V and a path from V to U. The strongly connected components of a directed graph are its maximal strongly connected subgraphs.

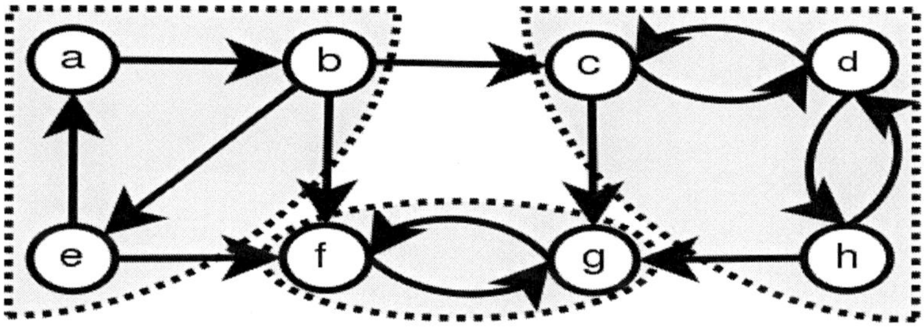


**Figure 2.** This figure shows graph with its strongly connected components marked

In a graph generated from an arrest table where there are at least couple of hundred thousand of crimes (edges) and thousands of offender (nodes) that make scalability and performance issues very important. Additionally every component represents a unique offender group because one offender can only belong to one group thereby concrete a result of group membership is obtained.

## Filtering for Legal Requirements

Turkish Crime Code requires that an criminal organisation (offender group) must consist at least of three members, and two members in an offender group must have been convicted together for committing the same crime at least two times (Turkish Crime Code, Article Number:261). According to this definition, where edge weight is W and number of members is N;

$W_{group} >= 2$, $N_{group} >= 3$

is the threshold to constitute a criminal organisation. This requirement can be different in different countries but it is essential to create a filter for a legally accepted criminal organisation.

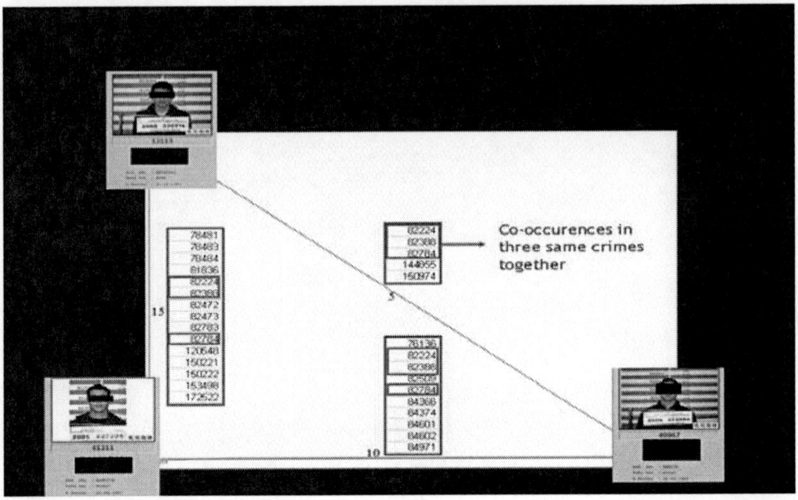


**Figure 3.** This triad of thieves committed various crimes together. The person in the top left has committed 15 crimes together (W=15) with the person in the left bottom and 5 crimes together (W=5) with the person in the right bottom. The person on the left bottom has also committed 10 crimes together (W=10) with the person on the right bottom. Overall, these three persons have committed 3 crimes together as a group which is shown in crime reference numbers 82224, 82388, and 80784 highlighted in red boxes.

## Operation Cash

Offender group detection action is started with preparation of Bursa Police arrest data. Initial data pre-processing and data cleaning are done in cooperation with Bursa Police Department on more than 300,000 crimes and 6000 offenders. Starting from 1994 to 2007, arrest data included all offenders with a unique person-id number. This uniqueness allowed us to track all offenders' activities. We had opportunity to find out an offender's history over time with all his/her crimes had committed. We produced first the link table, and then converted it to a massive graph; at the end all components in the graph are obtained with SCC. Accepting that even two offenders caught by the police is enough to be a component, total number of components were 33004 (199,728 crimes; with an average of 6.05 crimes per component). When $W_{group}$ threshold is put to 2, number of components is dropped to 4488 (15,482 crimes; with an average of 3.45

crimes per group). When $N_{group}$ threshold is put to 3, number of offender groups, which is aligned to the Turkish Criminal Law definition, the number of components is reduced to 1416. Recalling the fact that these groups included many offenders who committed various types of crimes from theft to violence, from gangs to terrorists; we only focused on active theft groups who committed crimes in the last five years. As a result, 63 theft groups are detected and these findings were introduced to the police experts for further examination. According to police experts, our findings were very valuable but insufficient in themselves to prosecute. There was however agreement to further investigate the identified group members, if appropriate, to gather further evidence, and if confirmed to prosecute these cases for arrest and charges being laid. A decision was reached to test the effectiveness of this technique by randomly selecting one from the 63 of these identified potential crime groups. After this decision, a judicial warrant was obtained for electronic surveillance and telephone interception of all of the members of selected group for ten weeks. Our findings for this theft group are exhibited in figure 4 as offenders by person-id numbers, and with degrees of members in brackets. The degree is a metric in social network analysis that is count of incoming and outgoing links for an actor (Wasserman et al., 1994). High degree values for an actor suggest that actor is likely to be a key player in the network.

After this electronic surveillance, which verified who was who in the network, and provided sufficient evidence from the police managers perspectives for successful prosecution, *Operation Cash* was launched. By the end of this operation, police had arrested 17 people, recovered worth US$ 200,000 of stolen jewellery, PCs, laptops and mobile phones, and seized cash to the value of US$ 180,000.

The evidence that was obtained post-Judicial warrant and subsequent interviews with the people arrested demonstrated that the ruling members had been correctly identified using Crime Graph Algorithm. *Operation Cash* which set out to confirm the value of this investigative tool ultimately broke a serious organised crime syndicate consisting of 21 members of which three (AB, MRK, and SE) had never been identified or arrested by the police so their names were not available in the database. This operation also managed to get four ruling members (12113, 38594, 41211, and 277801). These four leaders included the chief of gun-jewellers thieves (12113), a skilled expert thief who specialised in electronic goods (277801), the chief of electronic goods thieves (38594), and chief of car and gadget supplier for the network (41211). Interestingly, "big brother" of the network (220868) has only two records in police database. His leadership position is identified after interviews with suspects and cross-examination of these statements and the surveillance records.

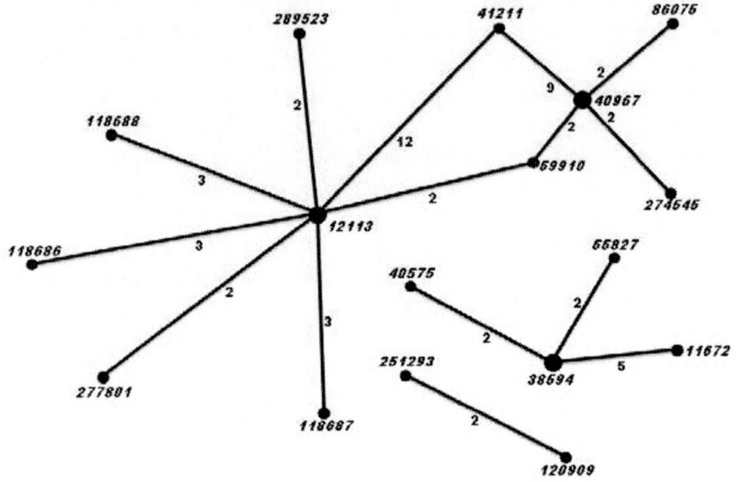


**Figure 4.** As filtering is applied in order to meet Turkish Criminal Code requirement, the theft group, consisting of 17 offenders with degrees in brackets: 12113(**54**), 41211(**42**),40967(**32**), 38594(**18**), 11672(**10**), 59910(**10**),118686(**6**),118687(**6**),118688(**6**),40575(**4**),55827(**4**), 86075(**4**), 120909(**4**),251293(**4**),274545(**4**),277801(**4**), 289523(**4**)

*Operation Cash* has attracted wide attention and positive feedback in local and national newspapers across Turkey (Zaman, Olay, and PolisHaber, 2006). The police commissioner of Bursa city stated that *Operation Cash* was the most successful operation among all operations by Bursa Police in 2006.

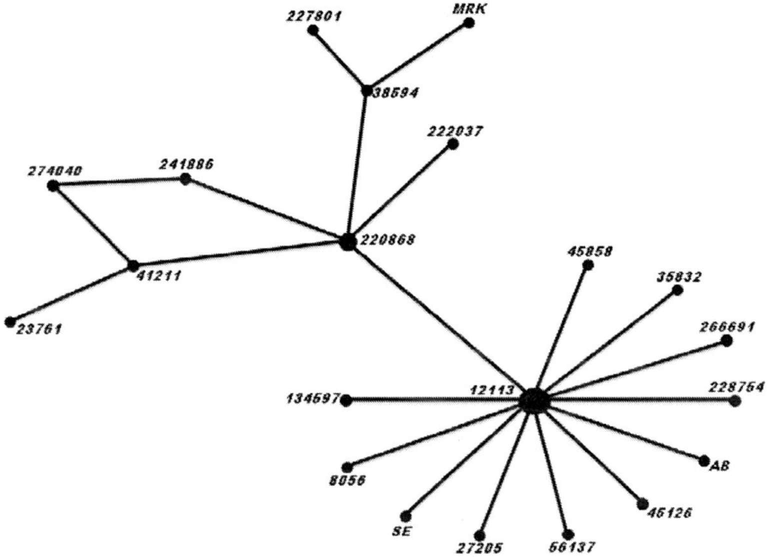


**Figure 5.** Theft network after verification of evidences. 12113(**24**),38594(**6**),41211(**6**), 241886(**4**),274040(**4**), 8056(**2**), 23761(**2**), 27205(**2**), 35832(**2**),45126(**2**),45858(**2**),56137(**2**), 143597(**2**),220868(**2**), 222037(**2**), 228754(**2**), 266691(**2**), 277801(**2**), AB(**2**), MRK(**2**), SE(**2**)

## Conclusion

It has been shown that co-defendant information in police arrest data is beneficial for the police to detect ruling members of offender groups. It has been also shown that detecting an underlying criminal network is possible with link mining and group detection techniques.

The CGA has been successful for partly detection of offender groups. Domain expertise is still needed for complete detection of groups. Other specific project-based conclusions reached in discussion with police and domain experts include a range of specific findings that mesh neatly with other relevant established research and theory.

An example of this connectedness between the specifics of this case study wider understanding can be seen in the fact that in this instance many of the group members came from the same extended family grouping (e.g. small-aged pick pocketing group). How far this case-specific conclusion can be applied can not is unknown; however, this finding accords with other research that connects offenders with family structure, family function and family membership. Similarly the case specific finding that group members likely to cooperate and come together for required skills to commit crimes.(e.g. theft from offices group, theft from residences group, fraud group, violence group) again parallels the broader literature regarding organisational structures and effectiveness (see Georgopoulos & Tannenbaum (1957), Pugh, Hickson, Hinings & Turner, 1968). It is also worth noting however, that studies into the structures of organised crime conclude that they tend to be much more fluid than non-crime organisations and that that their patterns of affiliation and influence were more important in than formal structures and specialisations (Williams, 2001).

Other case study specific findings include a clustering effect whereby group members were high likely to be from the same age group and peer group. They were also highly likely to have come from the same home cities and towns, they were likely to live in the same areas, likely to operate in the same areas and work in the same industries (e.g. scrap dealer auto theft group). Again these findings are not incongruent with wider criminological research that emphasise the significance of the leveraging effect of clusters of risk factors (Catalano & Hawkins, 1996).

Perhaps, in addition to demonstrating the capacity and effectiveness in 'real world' policing of CGA, this case study also supports the growing recognition that organised crime operates through dynamic and fluid networks in place of the formalised hierarchies of earlier generations of crime organisations. While these networks have a more elusive character, they still create patterns that can be, in a cost effective and sustainable manner, decoded so enabling successful law enforcement interdiction.

## References

Adibi, J., Pantel, P., Grobelnik, M., & Mladenic, D. (2005). KDD-2005 Workshop report link discovery issues, approaches and application (LinkKDD-2005). *SIGKDD Explorations, 7*(2), 123-125.

Adibi, J., & Chalupsky, H. (2004). The KOJAK Group Finder Connecting the dots via integrated knowledge based and statistical reasoning, *IAAI.*

Analyst Notebook, i2 Analyst Notebook (2007) i2 Ltd. Retrieved on 31 July 2007 from http//www.i2.co.uk/

Badia, A., & Kantardzic, M. (2005). Graph building as a mining activity finding link in the small. In Proceedings of the *Eleventh ACM SIGKDD International Conference on Knowledge Discovery and Data Mining, LinkKDD 2005 Workshop* Chicago, IL.

Catalano, R. F., & Hawkins, J. D. (1996). The social development model: A theory of antisocial behavior. In J. D. Hawkins (Ed.), *Delinquency and crime current theories* (pp. 149-197). New York: Cambridge University Press.

Chen, H., Chung, W., Xu. J., Wang, G., Qin, Y., & Chau, M. (2004). Crime data mining a general framework and some examples. *Computer, 37*(4) 50-56.

Chen, H., J. Schroeder, H. R. V., Ridgeway, L., Atabakhsh, H., & Gupta, H., et al. (2002). COPLINK Connect information and knowledge management for law Enforcement. *Decision Support Systems*, *34*, 271-285.

Coles, N. (2001). It's not what you know - it's who you know that counts: Analysing serious crime groups as social networks. *British Journal of Criminology, 41*(4), 580-594.

Cook, D. J., & Holder, L. B. (2000). Graph-Based data mining, *IEEE Intelligent Systems, 15*(2), 32-41

—. (2007). *Graph mining*, Wiley-Interscience, Hoboken, New Jersey: John Wiley Sons, Inc.

Cormen, T. H., Leiserson, C. E., Rivest, R. L., & Stein, C. (2001). *Introduction to algorithms*. Second Edition. MIT Press and McGraw-Hill.

Edwards, A., & Gill, P. (Eds.) (2003). *Transnational organised crime: Perspectives on global security*. London UK: Routledge.

Georgopoulos B. S., & Tannenbaum, A. S. (1957). A study of organizational effectiveness. *American Sociological Review, 22*(5), 534-540.

Getoor, L., & Diehl, C. P. (2005). Link Mining: A Survey, *SIGKDD Explorations, 7*(2), 3–12

Getoor, L., (2004). Link mining: A new data mining challenge *SIGKDD. Explorations, 5*(1), 84-89.

Guest, S. D., Moody, J., Kelly, L., & Rulison K. L. (2007). Density or distinction? The roles of data structure and group detection methods in describing adolescent peer groups. *Journal of Social Structure, 8*(1). Retrieved on 31 July 2007 from http//www.cmu.edu/joss/content/articles/volindex.html

Hobbs, D. (1995). *Bad business*. Oxford, UK: Oxford University Press.

Jackson, J. L., Herbrinck, J. C., & Jansen, R. (1996). Examining criminal organisations possible methodologies, *Transnational Organised Crime, 2*(4), 83-105.

Kubica, J., Moore, A., Cohn, D., & Schneider, J. (2003). cGraph: A fast graph-based method for link analysis and queries. *IJCAI 2003 Text Mining and Link Analysis Workshop.*

Kubica, J., Moore, A., Schneider, J., & Yang, Y. (2002). Stochastic link and group detection. *18th National Conference on Artificial Intelligence*, AAAI Press/ MIT Press.

Marcus, S. M., Moy, M. & Coffman, T. (2007). Social network analysis. In D. J. Cook & L. B. Holder (Eds.), *Mining graph data* (pp. 443-468). John Wiley & Sons, Inc.

McIllwain, J. C. (1999). Organized crime: A social network approach. *Crime, Law & Social Change, 32*, 301–323.

Moy, M. (2005). *Using TMODS to run the best friends group detection algorithm.* 21st Century Technologies Internal Publication.

Olay. (2006). Technological tracking to criminal groups. *Bursa Local Newspaper,* 19th December 2006., Retrieved on 31 July 2007 from http//www2.olay.com.tr/blocks/haberoku.php?id=5990&cins=Spot%20Bursa>.

PolisHaber. (2006). Operation 'Cash' By Police. Retrieved on 31 July 2007 from http//www.polis.web.tr/article_view.php?aid=3666

Pugh, D. S., Hickson, D. J., Hinings C. R. & Turner, C. (1968). Dimensions of organization structure. *Administrative Science Quarterly*, *13*(1), 65-105.

Scott, J. (2004). *Social network analysis: A handbook.* London, UK: Sage Publications.

Senator, T.E. (2005). Link mining applications progress and challenges. *SIGKDD Explorations*, *7*(2) 76–83.

Sentient Data Detective. (2007). Sentient Information Systems. Retrieved on 31 July 2007 from http//www.www.sentient.nl

Wasserman, S., & Faust, K. (1994). *Social network Analysis: Methods and applications.* New York: Cambridge University Press.

Williams, P. (2001). Transnational Criminal Networks. In J. Arquilla & D. Ronfeldt (Eds.), *Networks and netwars: The future of terror, crime, and militancy* (pp.61-97). California: Rand Corporation.

Xu, J. J., & Chen, H. (2005). CrimeNet Explorer: A Framework for Criminal Network Knowledge Discovery. *ACM Transactions on Information Systems,* 23(2), 201-226.

Zaman. (2006). Police tracked down 63 crime groups with new technology help. National Newspaper, 9th January 2007, Retrieved on 31 July 2007, from http//www.zaman.com.tr/webapp-tr/haber.do?haberno=437444

# CHAPTER TWENTY FIVE

# CYBER BULLYING AMONG SCHOOL STUDENTS IN INDIA[1]

K. JAISHANKAR AND DEBARATI HALDER

## Abstract

In the 21st Century even a school student (read an intelligent adolescent) considers Internet and mobile phones as indispensable part of his daily existence. The usage of modern technologies such as Internet and mobile phones has increased the prevalence of bullying by school and college students. Bullying and cyber bullying are rampant in Indian society among school children and young adults. However, neither the parents, nor the teachers, nor the government policy makers are much aware of the human rights violations that happen as a result of cyber bullying. Hence, cyber bullying has continued to be an unknown term in the Indian scenario. This chapter provides a profile of cyber bullying among school students in India.

## Introduction

In India, the incidences of bullying in the institutions can be traced back to the mythological period of Mahabharata.[2] Young Karna,[3] who was

---

[1] Forms a part of the project report of the lead author. Jaishankar, K. (2008). *Cyber bullying in India: A research report on developing profile, reviews and policy guidelines.* Tirunelveli: Department of Criminology and Criminal Justice, Manonmaniam Sundaranar University.

[2] The Mahābhārata is one of the two major Sanskrit epics of ancient India, the other being the Rāmāyana.

[3] Karna is one of the central figures in Hindu epic Mahabharata. He was the first son of Kunti, and was thus half brother to the Pandavas, and the eldest of them. Although Duryodhana of the Kauravas appointed him as king of Anga, his role in the legend far exceeds the importance of a king. He fought for the Kauravas in the great battle at Kurukshetra and died. Source: Wikipedia

the adopted son of a chariot driver, was bullied by the Pandavas[4] when he wanted to take part in an armoury show. Similarly, Pandavas were also several times teased, bullied and physically hit by their Kaurava[5] cousins during the martial training, under Guru Dronacharya.[6] Hence it can be deducted that school bullying is not a new phenomena in India. School bullying has till date existed and continues to be a part of learning in Indian schools.

Even though school bullying or college bullying is prevalent by the name of *ragging,*[7] the connotation of bullying is not present in the Indian context. In spite of new laws regarding ragging in schools and colleges, bullying per se has not been condoned. School bullying is inclusive of verbal bullying and physical abuse by the stronger school children to their weaker class mates or school mates. The term "physical abuse" for school bullying can be understood in its broader terms. It may amount to simple patting, slapping, and simple hurt to even grievous attack like murder.

In comparison to developed countries the gravity of the problem of school bullying has been less understood in India. Indian schools,[8] has

---

[4] In the Hindu epic Mahābhārata, the Pandava (or Pandawa) brothers are the five acknowledged sons of Pandu , by his two wives Kunti and Madri. Their names are Yudhishtira, Bhima, Arjuna, Nakula and Sahadeva. All five brothers were married to one woman, Draupadi. Together, they fought and prevailed in a war against the party of their cousins the Kauravas, the climax of which was the Battle of Kurukshetra. Source: Wikipedia

[5] The Kauravas are descendants from Kuru, a legendary king of north India, who were the opponent of Pandavas in the Mahabharata. The term Kaurava in broad sense includes the pandavas also, who were also the posterity of the same clan. But in commoner and narrower meaning the term refers to the children of king Dhritarastra, as it is the elder family line of that of King Kuru and Pandu`s sons or Pandavas are excluded. The Kauravas represent the material or evil forces, who drove the Pandavas from their territory.

[6] In the epic Mahābhārata, Drona or Dronacharya is the royal guru to the Kauravas and the Pandavas. He was a master of advanced military arts. Source: Wikipedia

[7]Ragging includes teasing, bullying, usage of abusive words; physical harm including hitting, kicking, inflicting grievous harm and mental torture which may even lead the victim to death or total mental imbalance.

[8] School education in India is a two-tier system, the first ten years covering general education followed by two years of senior secondary education. Primary education is divided into two stages: the first five years constitute the primary stage (Standards I-V) and the next three years, the upper primary stage or middle school (Standards VI-VIII).Secondary education usually lasts between two and four years. After two years, pupils who have completed ten years of education (Standard X) take the Secondary School Certificate. Pupils then enter higher secondary schools or Junior Colleges and complete a further two years of education (Standards XI

witnessed such bullying incidents and it is accepted as a common behaviour of school students. Unfortunately, in India, parents and even teachers fail to understand the graveness of school bullying. Most of the bullying incidences are mediated by the teachers and die down within a short gap. At most the case of school bullying is settled by the parents or elders or in some other cases it may be reported to the teachers, and they take steps like warning the bully with serious consequences. Very rarely they are reported outside the immediate family of the victim and the traumatized victim is labelled as a poor student who lacks the power to stand up for himself.

While bullying by adults is considered a serious infringement of constitutional right, namely, right to lead a dignified life and may also be punishable under the penal laws attracting provisions relating to defamation, school bullying is a much neglected issue in India. Bullying in the schools by the classmates is considered as a very normal behaviour of childhood. The perpetrator is treated as "spoilt child", "arrogant" and even "funny" when he constantly makes fun of others on their physical appearance or response to the teacher or other friends, but never "hostile".

The reason behind bullying is believed to be mainly the exposure of the children to the violence, bullying, dirty jokes etc in the television shows. It is further believed that economics disparities and home environment also plays a major role in making the child a perpetrator. In some cases the bullies are hero worshipped and are encouraged to venture more in continuing the game of "bossing over" over the comparatively shy or weak children. However, the victim who often becomes withdrawn or traumatized is always considered as "introvert', "coward", "shy" or "mentally disturbed" child. Bullying makes the bullied victims withdrawn or even revenge takers.

Majority of schools in India, declare their school norms in the student's handbook which highlights discipline, punctuality, cleanliness and proper dress code. A student can be "expelled" from the school due to "bad behaviour" or in consequence of "bad academic report". The term "bad behaviour", may grossly include, class bunking, mischievous activities like repeatedly avoiding the home works or given assignments, smoking or

---

and XII). Courses focus on university preparation. Public examinations are held at the end of Standard IX either by individual states or by Central Boards and lead to the award of the Higher Secondary School Certificate (also called All India Senior School Certificate or Indian School Certificate or Pre-University Course).Vocational education is offered in two years at Higher and Technical Schools and lead to the Certificate of Vocational Education (CVE). Most graduates enter employment.

drinking alcohol inside the school premises, showing disrespect to the teachers and school staffs and in some extreme cases, fighting with classmates causing severe physical harm. Even so, expulsion from the schools due to bad behaviour is again very rare in comparison to that of bad academic reports. However, bullying or cyber bullying does not appear as any kind of offence in these handbooks.

Much has been talked about the reasons of bullying, mental state of the children who are being bullied and even the need of school counselling. But nowhere the necessities to create an anti bullying law or uniform school policies are mentioned. As a result the problem of school bullying had grown to a dangerous extent.

## *Ragging: The alternative term for bullying?*

The dangers of school bullying were first noted by the Raghavan Committee,[9] which was constituted to prevent ragging in educational institutions. The committee had included schools narrowly to its definition of educational institutes' while discussing and defining ragging. The committee understood that ragging starts from the very base i.e., from the schools and residential hostels in the form of bullying. The residential hostels for the children who are about to write the school leaving exams are particularly vulnerable as the sexual abuse, physical harassment and verbal teasing becomes a standard norm for the hostel life for these children. However, even though this committee discusses about school bullying as the birth point of ragging, it does not discuss any preventive measures for such school incidences.

Ragging can be called as the offspring of school bullying. In comparison to school bullying cases, ragging reports are more in number and policy guidelines are being made to prevent ragging in India. According to a Supreme Court judgement in India, ragging is:

> Any disorderly conduct whether by words spoken or written or by an act which the effect of teasing, treating or handling with rudeness any other student, Indulging in rowdy or undisciplined activities which causes or Is likely to cause annoyance, hardship or psychological harm or to raise fear

[9] The Ministry of Human Resources Development (MHRD), following a directive by the Supreme court, appointed a seven member panel headed by ex-CBI director Dr. R. K. Raghavan to recommend anti-ragging measures. The Raghavan Committee report, submitted to the court in May 2007, includes a proposal to include ragging as a special section under the Indian Penal Code.

> or apprehension thereof in a fresher or a junior student or asking the students to do any act or perform something which such student will not do in the ordinary course and which has the effect of causing or generating a sense of shame or embarrassment so as to adversely affect the physique or psyche of a fresher or a junior student.

Counsellors and psychologists had shown that the perpetrators of ragging may have been either severely bullied by others in school and at home, or may have got into this habit of bullying since their school days. Since there is no law or school policy guidelines to curb bullying in the Indian schools, the perpetrators after coming to the college become more vigorous in their act. Strict school environment and dispute resolutions by the elders and teachers are almost nil in higher educational institutes and campuses. It becomes more open and the feelings of maturity and independence help the young adults to act and behave the way they wish. Nevertheless, mostly college students are over 18 and hence when they commit any nuisance by the name of ragging, they are immediately held under the Indian Penal laws.

After an overwhelming response to stop ragging in the educational institutes, many state governments came up to enact ragging prevention laws. The final death nail to the ragging activities was the recommendations of Raghavan Committee, which minutely analyzed various aspects of ragging, reasons of ragging and the responsibility of educational institutes in the prevention of ragging.

## Bullying and School Shoot outs: Cases and Recent Trends

Bullying is rampant in Indian schools and has already started gaining the needed recognition from the teachers, educationists, medical and health professionals and parents as well. The Times of India (2005) reported some cases of school vandalism which amounted to simple bullying or teasing words in some elite schools in Calcutta (Banerjee, 2005). Banerjee (2005) reported that bullying is rampant even in schools like South point or the Heritage school which are known as the most elite schools of the country. Sehggal (2004) in a newspaper report (The Tribune, para 2) revealed that “about 20 to 30 per cent of children are regularly involved in incidents of bullying, either as bullies or as victims.” Sehggal (2004) emphasized that it is not only boys but even the girls are also perpetrators. Truly, school bullying not only gives rise to mentality of ragging in higher educational institutions, it also changes a child into a hard core criminal, which is evident by the following examples.

- India's first school shooting took place in early December, 2007, in an elite school named Euro International school at Gurgaon (near New Delhi) where *Abhishek Tyagi,* a VIII class student was shot from point blank range by two of his school mates. This incidence was a planned murder provoked by bullying of the victim. The Gurgaon Police Commissioner *Mohinder Lal* said that "the two boys allegedly killed *Abhishek Tyagi* as he was physically stronger than both and been beating them up for the past two months, and the two carried a grouse against *Abhishek* as he used to *"tease them"* at every opportunity so the decided to take *"revenge"* (TOI, Dec, 2007).
- It is quite similar to the previous school shoot out case in Gurgaon. On 3rd January, 2008 a student of VIIIth standard was shot dead by an Xth standard student in Chorbari village, Satna district of Madhya Pradesh. They both had heated arguments and bullied each other. The elder student had shot the junior in a spate of anger (Staff Correspondent, The Hindu, Jan, 04, 2008).
- It occurred in Bangalore, where a school student shot two students of class 10 with an airgun near the school premises. The victims suffered minor injuries. The perpetrator was found to be a brilliant student and he was upset at being bullied by the victims (Special Correspondent, The Hindu, Feb, 03, 2008).
- The most recent case of school shooting occurred near Ghaziabad. A 12th standard student was shot dead by two of his classmates at an inter college near Ghaziabad inside the inter college at Metnara village in this district. The offender wanted to take revenge on the victim as he had eve teased the former's sister (Kumar, 17, February, 2008).

## School Bullying and Information Technology

With no law to prevent bullying among school students and easy accessibility of Internet and cell phones equipped with all the modern devices, school bullying has taken to cyber bullying now-a-days. The trend of sending bullying messages and dirty jokes to rival groups in the class and eventually to children of rival schools has become a new fashion in India. "Certain paranoia over Internet usage (and the resulting free speech it brings along with it) has gripped India. This is affecting students from participating in meeting places on the Internet like Orkut as well as writing blogs" (Nita, 2007, para 1). Lack of uniform school policy guidelines, lack of anti-bullying law and weak Information Technology act has made the situation even more serious.

*If u think they r hot...Well, let me tell u they're not They're ugly, they're fat, they look like ratz!!!! Even alienz look better dan dat!!!!!* This was an email sent out by the 10th standard class students of a respected Mumbai school, about the students of a rival school. While this may seem to be more of a playful prank than a serious offence, it is only the beginning of a trend that can escalate into a serious problem. In this case the teachers intervened and the problem was eventually resolved. In India, younger kids are discovering the power of the Internet, and cyber bullying has already started trapping them in its insidious Web (Kapoor, 2003).

In India, the growth of cyber bullying has been silent, but rampant. It was only in the 1990's children got free access to Internet either at home or in the Internet parlours and schools. Even though the schools had restricted their usage of Internet solely for academic purposes, cyber cafes and personal computers are hugely used by children for bullying others by "pranks", "dirty jokes", "sexual remarks". The problem of cyber bullying came into highlight only in 2006 when elite school boys of Mumbai used the social network Orkut to bully their Principal (Chaturvedi, 2007).

In continuation of that incident, many children of elite schools started using Internet to vent out their bitter feelings against teachers/individuals. The problem became graver with the reporting of the murder case of *Adnan Patriwala*, a 16 year old student from Mumbai region who was kidnapped and murdered allegedly as a result of cyber hatred by his own friends (Indiatime.com, 2007). This case becomes very significant as it was the first cyber bullying case in India, which lead to murder of a school student. The perpetrators in this case are under trial now, but there are no provisions in the Indian IT Act to deal the case. So, the case has been coupled with Indian Penal Code and Juvenile Justice Act.

## Cyber-bullying: Definitions and Conceptualization

There is no dearth of definitions of Cyber bullying. It is defined by various scholars. Bill Belsey (2005), defined cyber bullying as

> Cyber bullying involves the use of information and communication technologies to support deliberate, repeated, and hostile behaviour by an individual or group, that is intended to harm others (para 1).

Shariff (2005) defines cyber bullying as:

> Cyber bullying consists of covert, psychological bullying, conveyed through the electronic mediums such as cell-phones, web-logs and web-sites, on-line chat rooms, 'MUD' rooms (multi-user domains where individuals take on different characters) and Xangas (on-line personal profiles where some adolescents create lists of people they do not like) (p. 468).

According to Nancy Willard, Director for the Center for Safe and Responsible Internet Use, cyber bullying is a speech that is "defamatory, constitutes bullying, harassment, or discrimination, discloses personal information, or contains offensive, vulgar or derogatory comments" (Willard, 2003, p. 66). The numerous tactics students can employ to cyber-bully can include flaming (sending derogatory messages to a person(s), harassing and denigrating (put-downs), masquerading, outing and excluding (Willard, n.d.).

Patchin and Hinduja (2006) define cyber bullying as "willful and repeated harm inflicted through the medium of electronic text" (p. 152). "Cyber bullying can be defined as an aggressive, intentional act carried out by a group or individual, using electronic forms of contact, repeatedly and over time against a victim who can not easily defend him or herself " (Smith et al., 2004, p. 6). Cyber bullying can take many forms, and for this chapter the concept of 'cyber bullying' is subdivided (Smith et al., 2004, p. 6) into 7 sub-categories:

- Text message bullying
- Picture/Video clip bullying (via mobile phone cameras)
- Phone call bullying (via mobile phone)
- Email bullying
- Chat-room bullying
- Bullying through instant messaging
- Bullying via websites.

These sub-categories were chosen because 'cyber bullying' is a very broad term, and the sub-categories would help to get a better understanding of the range of cyber bullying and the forms which were most prevalent (Jaishankar & Shariff, 2008).

There are various international definitions for cyber bullying. An Indian definition in these lines is

> Cyber Bullying is abuse/harassment by teasing or insulting, victim's body shape, intellect, family back ground, dress sense, mother tongue, place of origin, attitude, race, caste, class, name calling, using modern telecommunication networks such as mobile phones (SMS/MMS) and

Internet (Chat rooms, emails, notice boards and groups) (Jaishankar, 2008, p. 13).

## *The medium*

It is found out that cyber bullying can happen in two circumstances:

(a) Firstly, when the perpetrator wants to air his grievances, hatred and anger and

(b) Secondly, when the perpetrator wants to make simple fun of his fellow classmates, juniors or unknown net friends.

In both the cases the medium is either the cell phone or the Internet. While simple text messages or photo messages are used for cell phone bullying, the Internet users use the social networking websites like the Orkut, Face book etc for sending bullying, teasing and obscene messages to their chosen victims.

## *Types of cyber bullying*

The perpetrators of cyber bullying tend to target their victims both directly and indirectly, irrespective of the age, sex, language and religion of the victim. Yet, cyber bullying can be divided in to two basic types based on age group of perpetrators, (i) by the school children in the age group of 8 to 16, and (ii) by adolescents/young adults in the age group of 16 to 20 and above. Below we have analyzed the two types broadly:

### *Cyber bullying by the children in the age group of 8 to 16*

It is found that majority of the school children who are using Internet as a hobby, tend to target their teachers to bully or tease, defame, in order to vent out their anger, depression or hatred. The Internet has become a popular medium for such kinds of mischief. Such acts are committed by groups of students who are generally in the age group of 12 to 16. A fine example of such type of cyber bullying was recently reported in Mumbai, where, some students of a school in Mumbai who were agitated with the teachers started a net community to express their grievances against teachers. They had posted obscene and derogatory remarks about the teachers (Chaturvedi, 2007). Another kind of cyber bullying includes sending teasing remarks to fellow classmates or students of other schools or community and this is done irrespective of their sex or language. Such remarks may point at their physical appearance, their social status or their educational qualifications. In this type of cyber bullying the age group of the perpetrators and the victims remain nearly the same.

There are some rare reported cases where school children had abused girls by obscene words. While many schools don't allow usage of cell phones inside the campus by the students, it is seen that, children who are in the age group of 14 to 16, send obscene messages to girls. In most of these cases, when the incident is reported, the child is counselled by the parents or the school teachers in the same manner when he/she does some mischief in the school. Unfortunately, the parents or the teachers don't feel that such incident is an abuse/harassment/crime.

### *Cyber bullying by adolescents/young adults in the age group of 16 to 20*

Most of the adolescents/young adults in the age group of 16 to 20 use Internet as a hobby apart from using it for education purposes. As per the Juvenile Justice (Amended) Act 2005, children of the age group of 18-20 are called young adults[10] as they are neither children nor full adult. Such persons are either finishing their schools or are fresher in their colleges. In most reported cases of cyber bullying by young adults; teasing, harassment, stalking and even murder as a result of the Internet friendship are found to be common.

One of the major forms of cyber harassment reported by people belonging to such age group is cyber stalking. Girls of the same age group or even elder women are often trapped and harassed. They are sent obscene messages and are even made subjects of cyber pornography, without their knowledge. In such cases both Internet and cell phones are used as mediums. Predominantly, the perpetrators victimize their own girl friends, who have been their fellow classmates or their female colleagues who have just finished their studies and joined jobs as trainees. Gradually, the perpetrator becomes more courageous to harass unknown women whom he may meet directly or in social networking sites like the Orkut or the Face book or he may just trace out randomly.

The case of a fake profile of Delhi school girl in Orkut, reported some months back, is a good example of such crime (techshout.com, 2007). In this case, a fake profile of a school girl was created under the title "sex teacher" by some boys who wanted to take revenge on the girl. The parents of the girl found out the truth when they started receiving

---

[10] According to the Juvenile justice amended Act 2005 "children between the age group of 18 and 20 are called young adults"; however, persons below the age of 18 are called Child.

telephone calls asking for the victim. The victim had undergone tremendous mental trauma and her academics were hampered.

The other form of cyber crime is harassing the victim regularly. In such case both men and women become targets. They are bullied, teased, sent obscene messages, defamed and are even threatened to certain extent. The victim may be known or may be unknown to the perpetrator. Mostly such crimes are committed by senior school students and the victims are either their fellow classmates or junior students. The motive may be pure fun or the expression of hatred, anger or frustration.

While both the above types of cyber bullying are to some extent addressed by the existing Information Technology Act,[11], Special Relief Act 1963, Tort Law[12] and the cases of cyber bullying which are aggressive and severe in nature, remain evasive. Such serious cases of cyber bullying emerge, when students of a particular class target a teacher or a school management or in cases of college students, a senior faculty or the college administration by defaming remarks, bullying or make derogatory comic pictures and posts the comments in the Internet for public viewing. Cyber police cells are now getting equipped to control cyber crimes like cyber stalking, cyber harassment and sexual harassment using the Internet. But the perpetrators of cyber bullying remain completely untouched by the law as well as the law enforcement authority.

### *Reasons behind cyber bullying*

- The perpetrator wants to air his hatred, anger or frustration towards a particular person or group of persons.

---

[11] Section 67 of the Information Technology Act: Publishing of information which is obscene in electronic form. - Whoever publishes or transmits or causes to be published in the electronic form, any material which is lascivious or appeal to the prurient interest or if its effect is such as to tend to deprave and corrupt persons who are likely, having regard to all relevant circumstances, to read, see or hear the matter contained or embodied in it, shall be punished on first conviction with imprisonment of either description for a term which may extend to five years and with fine which may extend to one lakh rupees and in the event of a second or subsequent conviction with imprisonment of either description for a term which may extend to ten years and also with fine which may extend to two lakh rupees.

[12] "In case if the identity of the cyber bully is known, then the victim could also seek for injunction and damages from a civil Court under existing Specific Relief Act 1963 as also under the existing Tort law of the country" (Pavan Duggal, cited in Ramasubramanian, 2007, para 21)

- The target could have been unavailable personally and the perpetrator may leave the derogatory remarks in his/her absence to vent out his/her anger.
- Bullying one person through the Internet may be fun for children who are restricted to use bullying words either at home or in the schools.
- Children are not watched over when they use the Internet. Hence, they could bully or tease others freely through the net which is impossible in real life.
- When the perpetrator is a young adult or an adult, cyber bullying may be done to sexually harass women, as an anonymous person.
- Verbal harassment of persons through the Internet or the cell phones seems to be much safer than real life crime as the perpetrator can easily hide his identity.

## Cases of Cyber bullying in India

### *The MMS case*

One of the earliest cases of cyber bullying happened in Delhi in 2004. A 17 year old boy student from Delhi Public school, a prestigious school, captured video clippings of his amorous activities with his girl classmate and circulated through multi-media service (MMS) on cell phones to his friends. The clippings later reached other children of different schools. Even though both the students were expelled from the school, the boy joined some other school while the girl left the country (Indianinfo.com 2004).

### *Bullying teachers – Hirandani School case*

Bullying teachers through the Internet is most common among the cyber bullying cases in India One such case was highlighted when some students of Hiranandani Foundation School, Powai, posted derogatory remarks on the new Principal and some teachers. The comments were posted on the school's community sub-group on the highly popular social networking site, orkut (Staff reporter, Planet Powai.com, 2007).

### *Bullying teachers –Scottish School case*

The other famous case of cyber bullying is the Bombay Scottish school bullying. Angered over a few things, one of the students, started a discussion, *"All those who hate DPN"* (DPN here are the initials of the principal D.P.N. Prasad). Many students seem to have a grouse against the authorities and the post flourished with quite uncharitable comments. The school authorities noticed and the students were made to apologize and delete their offensive posts (Chaturvedi, 2007).

### *Creation of fake profile*

In the case of fake profile of a Delhi school girl the mischief mongers have posted obscene photographs and contact details of a school girl of south Delhi. They had displayed her home address and telephone numbers on the profile, using suggestive names like 'sex teacher' for her. Two strangers visited the girl's house and asked whether she is available for 'sex' and also the girl started receiving telephonic calls of sexy nature. The cyber cell of Delhi police registered a case under the IT act (Rediff.com, 2007).

### *Taking revenge through Internet*

The Air Force Balbharati School case is a landmark case of cyber bullying for revenge. A student of the Air Force Balbharati School, Delhi, was teased by all his classmates for having a "pockmarked face". The student was fed up with teasing and bullies and finally found a unique way to take revenge. He scanned photographs of his classmates and teachers, morphed them with nude photographs and put them up on a website that he uploaded on to a free web hosting service. It was only after the father of one of the class girls, who was featured on the website, objected and lodged a complaint with the police, the matter came to limelight (Joshi, 2003).

### *Cyber bullying, kidnapping and murder*

A Mumbai teenager named Adnan Patrawala, son of a businessman was trapped on Orkut and later he was murdered. It was revealed that he came in contact with Angel, a profile created by someone by utilizing the name of a girl. Scrapbooks of Adnan and Angel revealed that they were continuously talking to each other. According to scrapbooks, Angel was continuously insisting Adnan to meet her, but Adnan wanted Angel's photograph first, which was never sent by her. Finally, Adnan replied that he wanted to meet her, and he left his home on the same day to meet the Angel. The next day, Adnan's parents got a call from his mobile itself and the person on the other side told them that they had abducted Adnan, and they wanted Rupees two crores (Twenty million) as ransom. Even Adnan talked with his parents and told them that he was fine.

Earlier Adnan's parents believed that it was a prank but after few hours next call came, this time the abductors said strongly that they were not joking and demanded Rupees two crores (Twenty million). After getting the call, Adnan's parents registered a case of abduction in the nearby police station; eventually, the police started the investigation. Immediately, after that the boy was found murdered some where in Mumbai. The police investigated the case and held three persons in the age group of 17 to 19 years and they were virtual net friends of Adnan whom he never met in real life. Various online discussions, blogs and even on line condolence messages which were shown in the Orkut profile of Adnan Patrawala revealed that the deceased himself was a bully (Alam, 2007). He used severe abusive languages and "dirty jokes" to his friends to get the status of "rich young hero". The influence of such bullying is also not waved out for the motives behind his murder.

## Issues of Cyber Bullying in India

### *Ragging and cyber bullying*

Even though it is a common belief that ragging takes place only in colleges and universities towards the freshers, it has been noticed that ragging does exist in schools. A new student to the class may be ragged in the same manner as any other ragging happens in the colleges with the freshers. Again ragging is very common among out going senior students towards their juniors. The victims are harassed both verbally and physically. However, the difference between ragging in the schools and ragging in the colleges lies in the graveness of the incidents. The victim may even die as a result of the physical and mental torture meted out to him, in college ragging. There are numerous cases where college ragging has made innocent fresher a mental patient and thereby ruined his career as well as all prospects of life.

Residential hostels of public schools are also reported to have ragging incidents. While several laws have been passed to prevent ragging in the educational institutions, it has in a way excluded schools from the definition of "education institutes". Unfortunately, the law makers are oblivious that the habits of bullying, teasing, aggressiveness, sexually coloured remarks, slowly turn a child into a perpetrator of crimes like ragging, sexual harassment or even a psychopath. In India there are no school policy guidelines to combat the incidents of ragging, bullying, and teasing among the students.

By the advent of new laws, now ragging has become a punishable offence.[13] Hence the students have eventually chosen Internet and cell phones to find out new ways of ragging or harassing the juniors. Young adults who are students of colleges are often found harassing girls with derogatory remarks or stalking for fun. Experimenting with the information technology is a new found hobby for rich younger generation in India and some of the students commit serious cyber crimes like hacking one's email id, cyber stalking, cyber defamation, or even cyber fraud. While all other cyber crimes have become punishable by the cyber law, cyber bullying, cyber teasing or even cyber ragging has not been defined properly by the cyber law. Hence the offender never gets punished on account of loopholes of law and continues enjoying a heroic status among his friends.

### *Impact of aggressive behaviour on cyber usage*

School aggressiveness, vandalism, group fighting, and school shootouts are newly cropping up in Indian schools. Child psychologists opine that such aggressiveness may be the result of parental pressure for doing well in studies, internal jealousy, partiality practiced by teachers towards a group of selected students and even in some cases television programmes and violent action movies (Raj, 2006). Such impact is very much visible in the usage of Information technology among children in India. School children often use the Internet to convey defaming messages to their opposite groups, competitor schools or even to their teachers who have tried to dominate over them in various ways.

Previously, before the growth of Internet or the cell phones, only verbal bullying was very common among school students. It still exists and neither the teacher nor the parents look upon it as a serious crime even though verbal bullying may gradually turn a child into a habitual perpetrator of bullying or cyber bullying. With the advent of information technology, aggressive verbal bullying could be easily sent to the target

---

[13] The West Bengal Prohibition of Ragging in Educational Institutions Act, 2000 (W.B. Act XIII of, 2000) provides that "Ragging" means the doing of any act which causes, or is likely to cause any physical, psychological or physiological harm of apprehension or shame or embarrassment to a student, and includes–(a) teasing or abusing of playing Practical joke on, or causing hurt to any student. or (b) asking a student to do any act, or perform anything, which he/she would not, in the ordinary course, be willing to do or perform.

without any immediate effect. Of late it has been seen that students of higher class have started using the Internet to play kidnapping games with their friend's parents. The case of Adnan, a student who was found murdered by his own Orkut friends reflects the same (India Time, 2007).

### *Sexual harassment, eve teasing and cyber bullying*

In India, numerous laws have come up to define and deal with sexual harassment. Sexual harassment can be verbal, or physical, direct or indirect. It can happen to any one, be it a school girl, a college student, a working woman or even an elderly woman. Rarely there are reported cases about sexual exploitation of men. Hence in general, sexual harassment and/or eve teasing[14] implies harassment of women only. Women's rights against being sexually exploited were first legally established in the case, Vishaka vs. State of Rajasthan.[15] The Supreme Court in this case laid

---

[14] The term eve-teasing is used to refer to "sexual harassment of women in public places such as the streets, public transportation, parks, beaches, and cinema halls. This type of public harassment by a lone man or gangs of men includes verbal assaults such as making passes or unwelcome sexual jokes; nonverbal assaults such as showing obscene gestures, winking, whistling, and staring; and physical assaults such as pinching, fondling, and rubbing against women in public places". In addition, in several instances eve-teasing has been followed by more violent assaults such as rape and murder. Eve-teasing is first officially defined by the government of New Delhi in 1984 as: When a man by words either spoken or by signs and/or by visible representation or by gesture does any act in public space, or signs, recites or utters any indecent words or song or ballad in any public place to the annoyance of any women. Eve teasing, however, is not a legal category. In the Indian Penal Code, the word 'eve-teasing' does not exist. However, victims of eve teasing could take recourse to certain sections of the IPC such as 292, 294, 298 (A&B), 354 and 509

[15] Vishaka is a group of social activists and NGO's who went to the court with the aim of preventing sexual harassment of working women in all work places by filling a vacuum in the existing legislation. The immediate cause for bringing the case was the acquittal of the offender in a criminal case brought on behalf of a social worker of the ministry of the Ministry of Health of the Government of Rajasthan, who had been subjected to a brutal gang rape in a village in that State. In line with other gender sensitive decisions, the court recognized that sexual harassment is a clear violation of the Constitution [Article. 14 (sexual non discrimination), 19(1) (g) (pursuance of an occupation), 21 (life and liberty) and 42 (just and humane working conditions], and merits an effective alternative remedy under Article 32. Recognizing that existing Indian laws had not adequately protected women from workplace-related sexual harassment, the court issued

down certain guidelines for workplace safety of women. Gradually such guidelines on the lines of the vishaka's case were formulated in the educational institutes including schools and colleges. However, even though the guidelines are being used in colleges and educational institutes, in practice, they are not yet invoked properly for the school students. There are numerous case reports of sexual harassment of young students, either by their teachers or senior students. Sexually abused children are left traumatized, and they may even refuse to go to school or talk to friends. Various children-rights campaigns have started creating awareness regarding the sexual harassment cases but the responses are still very poor.

Even though a few cases have been reported about direct sexual harassment of children and young women by fellow classmates, the upcoming rate of harassment through obscene messages, dirty voice mails via cell phones and sending of derogatory remarks in one's personal mail box as well as social networking websites are mind boggling. But such cases are not treated as seriously by law as the cases of direct sexual harassments of adults are treated. One such case was reported recently in a daily newspaper in India where aggrieved by the broken engagement a post graduate student's profile was created by her ex-boy friend in an obscene manner in Orkut. Her phone numbers and address details were given, and she was disturbed by unwanted people at her home. She contacted the Bilaspur Police station, but they refused to help her. Then she contacted the Calcutta police cyber cell. Even though the case was not under their jurisdiction, the Calcutta cyber cell promised to assist the victim. Even so, no FIR[16] was lodged. This incident shows that, on account of lack of proper law and misunderstanding of the existing law, even the police become helpless to assist the victims of cyber bullying (Sen, 2006).

---

guidelines on the prevention of sexual harassment in the work place, and explained that they would be judicially enforceable until suitable legislation is enacted. The Guidelines define sexual harassment, and outline the duty of employers to prevent, punish and remedy sexual harassment.

[16] First Information Report (FIR) is a written document prepared by the police when they receive information about the commission of a cognizable offence (A cognizable offence is one in which the police may arrest a person without warrant and grave in nature). It is a report of information that reaches the police first in point of time and that is why it is called the First Information Report. It is generally a complaint lodged with the police by the victim of a cognizable offence or by someone on his/her behalf. Anyone can report the commission of a cognizable offence either orally or written.

## Conclusion

The cases discussed in this chapter reveal an astonishing fact, i.e., almost all the cases of cyber bullying in India involving the school children had happened in 2006 -2007 period. These crimes which began as a mild prank in the form of teasing or defamation in 2006 have gone to the level of murdering a person (Adnan) in 2007. Almost all the cyber bullying cases have gone unreported and the police never took any serious note of these incidents. The children are at the most, warned severely by their principals or suspended from their respective schools. However, such warning failed to create general awareness about the risks of cyber bullying. The children are mostly arrested under the Economic wings and not on the grounds of defamation. The Information technology Act (even though it has some provisions on cyber defamation) has not been used effectively by the police in these cases. The common provision which has been applied to all of them is section 67 of IT act dealing with obscene publication. It was only with Adnan's case that an offence was registered under the Indian Penal Code.

The above mentioned cases reveal the lack of school policy guidelines, law on cyber bullying and weak Information Technology Act, which had paved the way for the increasing rate of cyber bullying incidences among the children within a year.

## References

Alam, M. M. (2007, August 21). Orkut brought death for Adnan. Retrieved December 12, 2007, from www.merinews.com/catFull.jsp?articleID=126031

Banerjee, S. (2005, February 15). Dadas in school? *The Times of India, Calcutta edition*. Retrieved December 12, 2007, from http://www1.timesofindia.indiatimes.com/articleshow/1022116.cms

Belsey, B. (2005). Cyber bullying definition. Retrieved on 15th February 2007 from http://www.cyber bullying.ca

Chaturvedi, S. (2007, March 15). When tradition ends at 256 kbps. Retrieved December 22, 2007, from www.ciol.com/content/news/2007/107031517.asp

Indianinfo.com (2004, December 19). DPS student involved in MMS case arrested in Delhi. Retrieved December 22, 2007, from http://news.indiainfo.com/2004/12/19/1912mmscase.html

Indiatime.com. (2007). Adnan Patriwala, cool dude from Orkut. It's India Time. Retrieved December 25, 2007, from www.indiatime.com/2007/08/21/adnan-patrawala-coool-dude-from-orkut/

Jaishankar K., & Shariff S. (2008). Cyber bullying: A transnational perspective. In F. Schmallager, & M. Pittaro (Eds.), *Crimes of the Internet* (pp. 66-83). Upper Saddle River, NJ: Prentice Hall.

Jaishankar, K. (2008). *Cyber bullying in India: A research report on developing profile, reviews and policy guidelines.* Tirunelveli: Department of Criminology and Criminal Justice, Manonmaniam Sundaranar University.

Joshi, M. S. (2004). Full guide on cyber crimes in India. Retrieved December 25, 2007, from http://www.indiaforensic.com/compcrime.htm

Kapoor, G. (2003, May, 26). School Spats: Fights, squabbles and school rivalries take a nasty turn online. *Rediff.com.* Retrieved December 25, 2007, http://www.rediff.com/netguide/features.htm

Kumar, A. (2008, February, 17). Another school shootout, 12th Std student killed. *Mynews.in.* Retrieved February 24, 2008, from http://mynews.in/fullstory.aspx?passfrom=enterprisestory&storyid=2377

Limber, S. P., & Small, M. A. (2003). State laws and policies to address bullying in schools. *School Psychology Review, 32*, 445-455.

Nita. (2007, March, 20). Free speech in the internet is making school and college principals jittery. Retrieved March 22, 2008, from http://nitawriter.wordpress.com/2007/03/20/ban-on-internet/

Patchin, J. W., & Hinduja, S. (2006). Bullies move beyond the schoolyard: A preliminary look at cyber bullying, *Youth Violence and Juvenile Justice*, *4*(2), 148-169.

Ramasubramanian, P. (2007, December, 10). India lacking laws to curb cyber bullying. CyberMedia India Online Ltd. Retrieved March 22, 2008, from http://www.ciol.com/content/101207102065.aspx

Raj, M.S. (2006, March, 19). *Mental health, emotional landmines.* Retrieved March 15, 2008, from http://www.thehindu.com/thehindu/mag/2006/03/19/stories

Rediff.com. (2007, February, 6). *Fake orkut profile of school girl posted.* (Feb 2007). Retrieved December 23, 2007 from www.rediff.com/news/2007/feb/06orkut.htm

Sehggal. M. (2004, February). *Bullying rampant in school says study. The Tribune*, Chandigarh edition. Retrieved December 23, 2007, from www.tribuneindia.com/2004/20040224/edu.htm

Sen, S. (2006, September, 05). *Jilted lovers misuse net to avenge insult.* Retrieved December 23, 2007 from http://economictimes.indiatimes.com/articleshow/1958517.cms

Shariff, S. (2005). Cyber-dilemmas in the new millennium. *McGill Journal of Education, 40*(3), 467-487.

Smith, P., Mahdavi, J., Carvalho, M., & Tippett, N. (2004). *An investigation into cyberbullying, its forms, awareness and impact, and the relationship between age and gender in cyberbullying*. A report to the Anti Bullying alliance. Unit for School and Family Studies, Goldsmiths College, University of London. Retrieved February 15, 2007, from http://www.antibullyingalliance.org.uk/downloads/pdf/cyberbullyingreportfinal230106_000.pdf

Special correspondent, The Hindu. (2008, February, 3). Two boys injured as schoolmate shoots at them with airgun. *The Hindu*, online edition, Retrieved February 24, 2008, from www.hindu.com/2008/02/03/stories/2008020359790800.htm

Staff correspondent, The Hindu. (2008, January, 4). Student shot dead by senior in Satna. *The Hindu*, Tamil Nadu edition, Madurai. Retrieved January 25, 2008, from www.hinduonnet.com/2008/01/04/stories/2008010461580100.htm

Staff reporter, Planetpowai.com. (2007, March). HFS Suspended Six Students for Derogatory Comments on 'Orkut'. Retrieved December 22, 2007 from www.planetpowai.com/news/2503200704.htm

Techshout.com (2007, February). Fake Orkut profile of Delhi School girl posted as "Sex teacher". Retrieved December 22, 2007, from www.techshout.com/internet/2007/09/fake-orkut-profile-of-delhi-schoolgirl-as-sex-teacher-posted/

The Times of India. (2007, December).'Yes, I killed Abhishek'. *The Times of India,* Delhi Edition. Retrieved on January 25, 2008, from http://timesofindia.indiatimes.com/Yes_I_killed_Abhishek/articleshow/2617934.cms

Willard, N. (2003). Off-campus, harmful online student speech. *Journal of School Violence.* 1(2), 65-93.

—. (n.d.). Retrieved September 2005 from: http://www.cyberbully.org.

# PART VI.

# GLOBALIZATION AND CRIME: ISSUES OF POLITICS, PRISONS, AND TERRORISM

# CHAPTER TWENTY SIX

# PRIVACY OR PUBLICITY: MEDIA COVERAGE AND JUVENILE PROCEEDINGS IN THE UNITED STATES

PATRICK WEBB

## Abstract

This investigation presents arguments which support and oppose the media coverage of juvenile proceedings. Various aspects such as confidentiality and public safety are identified as viable explanations. In an attempt to remedy this debate, a proposal is offered which suggests a combined approach.

## Introduction

Since the mid-1990s, United States have established more punitive measures in terms of dealing with young offenders, sometimes punishing them as adults even while the cases remain in juvenile court. Juvenile justice systems have increasingly introduced and perpetuated adult concepts of accountability, retribution and public safety, and placed less importance on helping youth in trouble with the law (Gibeaut, 1999). According to research conducted by Marsha Levick, a lawyer with the Juvenile Law Center in Philadelphia, indicates that by 1997, juvenile proceedings were beginning to look a lot more like the adult system. Juvenile offenders were getting tougher, more adult-style punishments were imposed and the old privacy protections were eroding. In keeping with the trend of increasing punitiveness, juvenile proceedings were open to the public and sometimes to the news media in 30 states. More than 40 states allowed the public *release* of the juvenile's name, address and photograph. Nearly every state disclosed the juvenile court records to other public agencies, such as schools, and allowed courts to consider prior juvenile records for adult sentencing. Thirty-nine states required juveniles to register as sex offenders (Gibeaut, 1999).

In terms of disclosure and juveniles, what does our present 'punitive' trend indicate? Could it be that the privacy protections which were initially established to protect the juveniles from the publicity are under attack in the name of public interest? What are the arguments which support and oppose the use of media coverage in juvenile proceedings? This investigation will discuss the complexities and positions associated with the media coverage of juveniles in the United States. In terms of selection criteria, the following information that was selected and examined will cover the past twenty years of legal, sociological, and criminal justice literature. In particular, this investigation will examine various explanations that support and oppose the media coverage of juvenile proceedings. In addition, we will also identify various measures which include the conditional uses of the media in relation to juvenile proceedings.

## Arguments against Media Coverage

### *The history of the juvenile courts and confidentiality*

From a historical standpoint the juvenile justice system was created to protect the best interests of juveniles (Ainsworth, 1991). The goal of the juvenile court, under this philosophy, was guidance and rehabilitation rather than determination of guilt or innocence and imposition of punishment. This philosophy was reflected in a 1923 policy statement by the children's bureau of the federal government, which declared that there should be no publicity within in a juvenile court proceeding. The hearings should be private, with no people present other than those directly concerned in the case at hand (Hughes, 1997). Since the early days of the juvenile courts, anonymity had been one of the hallmarks of the juvenile justice process. The juvenile court system's efforts to protect youthful errors form the full gaze of the public and bury them in the graveyard of the forgotten past seemed crucial to the successful rehabilitation of juvenile offenders (Bauers, 1993; San Bernardino County Department of Public Social Services v. Superior Court, 1991). Early architects of juvenile court feared that without confidentiality, the public would brand a child as a criminal and reject him for his behaviour, making a healthy readjustment to society difficult (*Smith v. Daily Mail Publishing Company,* 1979). To the contrary, as we examine the current research literature regarding confidentiality within the juvenile justice system, we see a prevailing trend which desires to diminish such an important and viable attribute within the system.

### *Minimal punishment and conventional opportunities*

Many of the arguments in favour of confidentiality are predicated upon a theory of minimal punishment and rehabilitation. From a philosophical perspective, the juvenile justice system is based, in part, on the notion that punishment should be minimized (Hughes, 1997). To this end, the act of publishing an offender's name was criticized because its effect, some claimed, was to punish the juvenile (Kfoury, 1991). In fact, the primary notion which established the juvenile justice system was based on protection and treatment of the youth, not retribution and punishment as with the adult system.

In addition, adverse publicity might create future disabilities for youth by limiting employment and educational opportunities (Hughes, 1997). Studies suggest that media coverage of juvenile hearings would disrupt the youngster's chance at rehabilitation, would damage the youth's self-esteem, disrupt the youth's family and affect the youth's relationship with peers, teachers, and even with the community (Davis, 2000; Henning, 2004; Mclatchey, 1999).

Studies reveal that public records may impede a child's prospects for future employment (Funk, 1996). When choosing among applicants, employers are less likely to select those with a criminal or juvenile record. Even employers who do not automatically exclude applicants with a record are unlikely to place ex-offenders in positions of power, trust, and authority, thereby limiting the delinquent child's prospects for career advancement and economic stability (Nelson, 1998). Without confidentiality protections, ex-offenders carry the deviant label through each phase of their lives, lack meaningful opportunities for rehabilitation, and never earn full re-entry and status in the community (Doe v. Webster, 1979). Where crimes are especially serious and public outrage is particularly great, the risk of long-enduring stigma may be even greater (United States v. Three Juveniles, 1995). Advocates who worry about the impact of stigma thus argue that juvenile records should remain confidential so that children will have a second chance at job opportunities and community standing (Doe v. Webster, 1979).

### *Disruption of relationships among family members*

Advocates of confidentiality also worry that publicity will embarrass family members and cause or exacerbate tension and resentment within the family (Kfoury, 1991b). The stigma of a child's conduct marks the parent and other significant caretakers as well as the child. Some family members may be embarrassed simply by the child's involvement in the system; others may have their own privacy interests at stake.

Due to the fact that a child's family is so integrally involved in the rehabilitation of delinquent juveniles, many juvenile court records include confidential psychiatric and psychological information about the child's parents or siblings (In re Sheldon, 1990). Thus some family members will have an independent interest in maintaining the confidentiality of juvenile records.

Studies indicate that when records are public and parents are embarrassed, tensions in the home may emerge, breaking down support systems necessary for effective rehabilitation or depriving the child of adequate support and supervision (Gilbert et al., 2001). Family disputes even may cause parents to force a child out of the home. Children without a stable home structure or strong family ties have limited prospects for rehabilitation and are likely to re-offend (Nelson, 1998). Publicity, or the threat of it, has played a decisive role in a number of recent high-profile cases here in New York and elsewhere, and the fallout from it has inflicted long-term damage on many clients. From the outset of such cases, even those that ultimately are tried behind closed doors, reporters and camera people invade the lives of the accused children, their families and the crime victims. To begin with, young people who have been arrested in a publicity case are often forced to participate in what is commonly referred to as a *perp walk* in which law enforcement officials parade them into the courthouse for arraignment after notifying the press of their intention to do so. The resultant bevy of cameras and reporters is unnerving; as one juvenile defender recently stated, "What I dislike is the camera people always needing another head shot of Philip every time he's led away in chains . . . and the reporters calling out: "Did you do it, Philip? Do you have anything to say, Philip?" That was the damage that hurt Phil, having the probing cameras in his face (Woodruff, 1998, A2).

## *Public humiliation and labelling*

Publicity of juvenile court hearings may also result in the child facing public ridicule and thereby lose standing and reputation in the community (Thompson v. Barnes, 1972). Recent news reports, lawsuits, and anecdotal information from across the country provide evidence of children who feel perpetually stigmatized by their juvenile record. In one Connecticut case, the police notified a school, as required by state law, that one of its students had been arrested for possession of marijuana, resulting in the student's expulsion (Packer v. Board. of Education of Thomaston, 1998).

The state supreme court subsequently ruled that the expulsion was improper, as possession of marijuana off campus did not "markedly interrupt or severely impede the day-to-day operation of a school" (Pell 2000, p. 879). A year after the court's decision, the child's family reported to the media that they still felt "branded" and were making plans to move from the town where they had lived for nearly thirty years (Seymour, 1999, p. 1). Students stigmatized in this way are likely to experience long-term emotional and social consequences (Joiner, 2004).

Proponents of confidentiality argue that publicity undermines rehabilitation and results in labelling the youth which is paramount to their self-esteem. Studies reveal that media scrutiny undermines the process of repentance and rehabilitation, which remains a central purpose of the juvenile system (Kintzinger, 1980; Cohen, 1999). In 1977, a team of clinical psychologists determined that publicity had a number of detrimental effects on juvenile offenders. It "placed additional stress on the juvenile during a difficult period of adjustment in the community, and it interfered with his adjustment at various points when he or she was otherwise proceeding adequately", as well as threatening his long term prospects for employment and a crime-free adulthood (Cohen, 1999, p. 50).

The effects of media coverage, especially in regards to pre-trial publicity, are also felt in the detention centre for many juveniles. When a group of state officials toured the secure juvenile detention centre in New York recently, a buzz went up among them when they spotted the familiar face of a fifteen-year-old girl. She had been charged with murder in a high-profile case nearly one year earlier, had been widely photographed, and so was instantly recognizable. One member of the group later described acutely the girl's obvious discomfort at having her identity so obvious to these strangers, and the clear distance she put between herself and the other detainees (Cohen, 1999).

A vast amount of information has been written about how "labelling" affects youngsters and why confidentiality had been an important part of the rehabilitation process. In fact, societal reactions to juveniles who have been labelled may be negative and may in turn cause a person to be isolated and that, in turn, could lead to even more deviant behaviour (Mahoney, 1974). Labelling theory as a whole centres on the premise that another person's perceptions of you can control your behaviour. Under that theory, someone adjudicated a delinquent who has not been made public would be less likely to resort to negative behaviour than a juvenile whose status as a delinquent has been publicized (Louis, 1984; Laubenstein, 1995). Proponents of juvenile offender anonymity argue that electronic media coverage of a juvenile court trial would permanently stigmatize the juvenile offender, hinder the development of socially acceptable behaviour, and perhaps even confer celebrity status upon the juvenile, spurring him or her to engage in future delinquent behaviour (Kfoury, 1991). Regardless of the outcome of the case, the youth will be stigmatized as a criminal in her neighbourhood, school or community centre, and so far less likely to turn to these support systems for guidance. For young people who were considered "at risk" before their arrest, this can be devastating and itself lead to future delinquent activity (Cohen, 1999, p. 51).

Fears about the harmful impact of stigma on children have persisted well after the inception of juvenile courts. Confidentiality advocates continue to fear that authority figures and even peers who learn about a child's delinquent conduct forever will view the child as deviant and consciously or subconsciously treat the child differently, expecting the worst (Kelly, 1977). Children who experience the shame and humiliation of labelling, advocates of confidentiality argue, also may develop a poor self-image (Kfoury, 1991b). In addition they may be socialized into a life of delinquency by responding and acting according to external perceptions and expectations (Zober, 1981). Rejection by adults also may breed resentment and cause the child to develop negative attitudes toward authority figures. In the long run, stigma may damage the child's positive relationships with classmates, teachers, and other school personnel (Kelly, 1977). In addition this experience may prevent him from adequately reassimilating into society, encouraging further delinquent behaviour (Nelson, 1998).

### *Celebrity status and the adversarial nature*

Research indicates that supporters of confidentiality claim that the juvenile offender might be pleased with the negative media attention he or she receives, thus becoming a repeat offender (Louis, 1984; Laubenstein 1995). By the same token, that attention might have an impact on the other juveniles who also commit crimes in the hopes they, too, would receive similar kind of publicity or approval of their peers (Laubenstein, 1995). Due to the fact that sentencing in the juvenile court (and to some extent, the sentencing of juveniles tried as adults) continues to be based in part on treatment and rehabilitation concerns, pre-sentence reports contain highly sensitive and private information about young people and their families. Intimate facts about child abuse, sexual orientation, substance abuse, HIV status, domestic violence, parent-child conflict, mental illness, learning disabilities, and criminal histories are routinely discussed in sentencing hearings. When these facts are revealed, the damage often cannot be undone (Cohen, 1999).

Most states have focused on the potentially harmful effects of publicity on a juvenile offender and have enacted closure policies for their juvenile courts. In fact, one court refused a juvenile's request for an open hearing, not only because of the possible deleterious effects on the juvenile's rehabilitation, but also because opening the proceeding might convey to the "immature respondent an impression of celebrity rather than solemnity" (In re Robert, 1981, p. 986). In a similar vein, others warned that media should not identify juveniles because that only perpetuates the public's already "flawed perception" of today's youth (Laubenstein, 1995, p. 1904).

Finally, advocates of confidentiality claim that open juvenile proceedings interfere with informal relationships between judges and juveniles. They believe that open courts would turn the hearing into adversarial proceedings, thus reducing the paternalistic role of the state in juvenile care (Hughes, 1997). Numerous studies indicate that pre-trial publicity usually leads to more conservative decision making on the part of probation officers, prosecutors, and judges. The entire system is sensitive to the enormous political impact of media coverage, leading to a "better safe than sorry" attitude (Cohen, 1999, p. 50).

## Arguments for Media Coverage

### *Public education and accountability*

Confidentiality laws for juvenile records were created to protect the identities of juvenile offenders, but the effect of these laws far exceeds this intended scope. Those who oppose confidentiality argue that such laws inhibit full and accurate reporting on the juvenile justice system (Greenebaum, 1993). Increased access to juvenile records would produce two benefits: (1) the public would become more educated about the juvenile justice system, and (2) the system would become more accountable (Oddo, 1998).

As the juvenile justice system changed from within, so did the public's perception of juvenile offenders. Instead of believing that courts should take juveniles by the hand and guide them toward rehabilitation, many in modern society view juvenile crime as a growing problem that calls for "get tough" measures (Aron & Hurley, 1998, p. 11). In addition, modern society is less inclined to protect the confidentiality of juvenile offenders at the expense of the public's right to be informed about juvenile crime and the manner in which the system handles wrongdoers (Oddo, 1998). A 1998 California poll showed that the voting public believed that the courts should not keep records of juveniles who commit serious crimes confidential. The survey concluded that the public feels that courts make too many decisions regarding juvenile crime behind closed doors (The Quill, 1998). Despite the public's call for greater access to information about juvenile cases, most states do not allow media access to juvenile records except in certain circumstances (Smith et al., 1980). For example, most states only allow access to juvenile records involving violent and repeat offenders (Mclatchey, 1999).

### *Perception, public interest and the media*

Due to the perception that violent juvenile crime is on the rise, the public is demanding harsher treatment of juvenile offenders. Public perceptions of juvenile crime are based almost exclusively on media coverage of juvenile incidents. The media usually focuses only on the most violent juvenile offenders – those who commit murder, rape, and robbery and are subsequently transferred to adult court. The media's focus on violent crime is driven by the sensational nature of violent offences and the availability of access to information once the juvenile is transferred to the adult court (Cohen, 1999).

Public interest is also considered a valid argument for the support of media coverage of juvenile proceedings. Due to the increased amount of juvenile crime, public interest and awareness has intensified resulting in a demand for more exposure. In addition, the recent trend in which juveniles are being tried as adults also supports the need for such coverage. It has also been suggested that the slow pace of reform in the juvenile courts is the result of insufficient publicity (Hughes, 1997).

Due to the media's focus on violent crime, public perception of the juvenile justice system primarily reflects the idea that juveniles who commit crimes are no different than adults who commit crimes (Aron & Hurley, 1998). The public is not truly aware of the complexity involved in the processing of juvenile offenders within the juvenile justice system. The public is unable to call for changes other than harsher treatment of juvenile offenders because it is not fully aware of other aspects of the juvenile system that deserve attention (Martin, 1997). If the media were allowed greater access to information about the juvenile justice system, the public would be better informed and could better assess the system and its shortcomings (Mclatchey, 1999).

### *Victim's rights movement and the inconsistency of the labelling theory*

The rise of the victims' rights movement also has had an effect on the public's tolerance of and response to juvenile crime. In an effort to secure victims greater access to and influence in the criminal and juvenile justice systems, victims' rights advocates have fought for the right to attend and participate in delinquency proceedings (Mason, 2000). Subsequently, a number of states have amended their state constitutions to recognize the rights of victims of adult and juvenile crime (Henning, 2004). A number of states have amended state constitutions to recognize the rights of victims of adult and juvenile crime. Other states have adopted statutory amendments that explicitly grant victims the right to attend and participate in various stages of juvenile delinquency proceedings. Victims' rights advocates hope that granting victims greater access to and participation in the proceedings will help the system better accommodate the needs and concerns of those harmed by crime (Beck et al., 2003).

Despite the abundance of literature associated with the negative "labelling' effects related to the media-coverage of juveniles, research examining labelling has produced inconsistent results. In addition, scholars have not actually measured how someone who has officially been adjudicated as a delinquent might be affected by the resulting publicity. Part of the problem stems from the difficulty measuring self-esteem, which makes it difficult to determine if a juvenile has been harmed by having his name released.

According to Oklahoma Publishing Company v. District Court (1977), the Supreme Court ruled that once the media has been admitted into a juvenile proceeding, they could not be prevented from revealing information about the case. Therefore, those who argue for media coverage of juvenile proceedings maintain that confidentiality does not really exist. They argue that the identities of the juveniles will ultimately be released. In fact, some of those same advocates would argue, the fear of embarrassing oneself or one's family would actually serve as a deterrent. With openness in the juvenile justice process, a community can also see that the process is working, and can perhaps force the process to become more effective. Research indicates that the public has a safety interest in guarding against juvenile delinquents in addition to judicial abuse and systemic malfunction associated with closed proceedings (Davis, 2000; Cohen, 1999; Oestreicher, 2001).

### *Constitutional Measures*

Oestreicher (2001) argues that both the Fourteenth Amendment and the Sixth Amendment support the use of media coverage in juvenile proceedings. The implication of such reveals that the due process clause incorporates that the press First Amendment claim and the juvenile's Sixth Amendment claim against the state-enacted presumptive closure statutes are, structurally, Fourteenth Amendment claims. For example, free speech carries with it some freedom to listen. Therefore, the First Amendment prohibits the government from summarily closing courtroom doors which had long been open to the public at the time that the First Amendment was adopted. In addition, the Supreme Court has emphatically and repeatedly affirmed that juvenile "commitment is a deprivation of liberty. It is incarceration against one's will, whether it is called 'criminal' or 'civil.'" The question presented, therefore, is whether those states presumptively closing delinquency proceedings from the public and press have deprived youth's liberty without due process—that is without "fundamental fairness" (Oestreicher, 2001, p. 228).

### *Due Process and First Amendment Challenges*

Despite continued support among many child advocates, the presumption of confidentiality has undergone at least two significant waves of attack since its inception. The first came in conjunction with what some have called the due process movement in juvenile court (Scott & Grisso, 1997). In the 1960s, a new set of reformers began to challenge the absence of due process in juvenile proceedings (Butts & Mears, 2001). They argued that public access to the courtroom and public scrutiny of the juvenile process may improve the integrity of the courts by providing a check on corrupt practices such as racism or ineffective assistance of counsel (Martin, 1995).

The Supreme Court began responding to these complaints in In re Gault, the first in a series of cases that conferred specific due process rights on children in juvenile proceedings. (Breed v. Jones, 1975). In Gault, the Court decided that, although the guarantees of due process assured juveniles the right to counsel, the right to timely notice of charges, the opportunity to confront witnesses, and the right against self-incrimination, due process did not prohibit states from conducting confidential juvenile proceedings. (Packer v. Board of Education of Thomaston, 1998). While expressing great concern about the failure of juvenile courts to observe fundamental requirements of due process, the

Court explicitly noted that many aspects of the juvenile court process still were valued and should remain unencumbered by constitutional restraints (Kelly, 1977).

Among those valued aspects were efforts to save juveniles from the stigma associated with the "criminal" label, decisions not to disqualify juvenile offenders from civil service, and policies that "hide" or protect juvenile records from the public eye (Nelson, 1998, p. 1101). In addition, although there was early evidence of evolving scepticism about the viability of rehabilitation and increasing support for juvenile accountability (Blum, 1996). The belief in rehabilitation was not rejected in the due process era, and youth still were viewed as less mature and less deserving of punishment than adults (Slobogin, 1999). Even when the Court expressed fear that children were getting "the worst of both worlds" because they received neither the promised rehabilitation from juvenile court nor the procedural rights of adult defendants, the Court ultimately concluded that principles of due process do not prevent states from providing and improving upon provisions for the confidentiality of court and law enforcement records that relate to juveniles (Kent v. United States, 1966, p.556; Packard v. Board of Education of Thomaston, 1998).

In 1971 the Court again commented briefly on the issue of juvenile confidentiality in McKeiver v. Pennsylvania, when it decided whether due process guarantees juveniles a right to trial by jury (McKeiver v. Pennsylvania, 1971). In concluding that a jury trial is not constitutionally required for juveniles, the Court expressed concerns that jury trials might adversely affect the juvenile justice system with publicity, unnecessary delay, formality, and adversarial proceedings. Thus, in both Gault and McKeiver, the Court recognized the value of confidentiality to juvenile court and initially left the states to decide whether and to what extent confidentiality would be preserved.

The Court, however, was forced to revisit the issue in a second series of cases involving asserted limitations on state efforts to preserve confidentiality. This time, the Court determined that, although states have a legitimate interest in preserving a juvenile offender's anonymity, this interest in confidentiality will be outweighed when it interferes with another's fundamental rights, such as a criminal defendant's Sixth Amendment right to confront witnesses at trial or the media's right to access or publish lawfully obtained information. First, in Davis v. Alaska, the Court reversed a trial court's order precluding a criminal defendant from cross-examining the key government witness, a juvenile offender. The defendant had intended to show bias arising from the witness's probationary status after a juvenile adjudication. The Court found that the defendant's rights outweighed the state's interest in preserving the offender's anonymity (Davis v. Alaska, 1974).

A series of three First Amendment cases decided between 1977 and 1982 placed more significant restrictions on the states' interest in maintaining juvenile confidentiality. In those cases the Court made clear that the media cannot be prohibited from publishing information, even about sensitive juvenile matters, when media representatives obtained that information while lawfully present at a juvenile proceeding (Globe Newspaper Co. v. Superior Court ,1982). However, because the Court did not rule on the constitutional validity of any state statute that denied the media access to juvenile court proceedings or records in the first place, none of these cases undercut the fundamental baseline of confidentiality for juvenile offenders that existed in most of the states.

### *Public Safety and the Perceived Failure of Juvenile Rehabilitation*

The second major attack on the presumption of confidentiality in juvenile court began in the late 1980s and early 1990s, when concerns about deteriorating public safety and the need for accountability became rampant (Melli, 1996). Preserving confidentiality has become less popular, as it appears to frustrate society's increasing desire to hold delinquents accountable for their actions (Rossum, 1995). As long as the public perceives that crime is increasing, citizens will demand greater accountability and responsibility from offenders. Public access to the justice system may satisfy "prophylactic" needs of the public, especially in serious cases, by tempering community outrage and providing "an outlet for community concern, hostility, and emotion" (Reporters Comm. for Freedom of the Press, 1999). By granting public access, government leaders can respond to public fear by showing how, in their assessment, the system effectively responds to juvenile crime (Martin, 1995).

Proponents of eroding confidentiality also argue that juvenile records should be available to law enforcement officials who can anticipate crime and protect the community from those most likely to commit crimes in the future (Funk, 1996). Some advocates go further and argue that citizens, neighbours, and teachers have a right to "fair warning" about children or adolescents who pose a danger to others (Blum, 1996, p. 349). Similarly, some argue that employers are entitled to information contained in juvenile records when selecting employees, as they seek to avoid personal loss from theft or violence and escape liability that might arise under an employer's common law duty to provide a safe work environment (Funk,

1996). Employers can try to avoid these losses by declining applicants with juvenile and criminal records.

In response to concerns about the impact of stigma, advocates of public records argue that any stigma associated with disclosing juvenile records is beneficial because it serves as an additional deterrent to the undesirable delinquent conduct (Blum, 1996). Under this theory, a child will abstain from criminal conduct in order to avoid embarrassment to himself and his family and to keep from jeopardizing future opportunities (Blum, 1996). Furthermore, where publicity has not been an effective deterrent and juveniles subsequently reoffend as adults, advocates maintain that judges in criminal court need delinquency records so that sentencing adequately will respond to the danger a defendant poses to safety in the community. This argument also reflects the retributive theory that an adult with a juvenile record deserves more punishment than an adult with no juvenile record (Funk, 1996).

National perceptions of high and rising crime have generated a great deal of public pressure for state legislatures to get tough on juvenile crime (Scott & Grisso, 1997). Responding to this perceived increase in serious crime by children, policymakers have begun to question early assumptions about the differences between children and adults (Butts & Mears, 2001). Many have rejected the notion that children are less culpable and less blameworthy than adults and have argued instead that young offenders of today are actually quite savvy and sophisticated. A much less idealized view of adolescence now accompanies increasing scepticism about the likelihood of rehabilitation. Given current views that children are indistinguishable from adult criminals, policymakers now often argue that children who engage in adult-like criminal behaviour should be punished like adults (Scott & Grisso, 1997). Some constituents are ready to abandon the rehabilitative philosophy altogether and have called upon policymakers either to do away with juvenile court in its entirety or to strip the court of its rehabilitative features, such as individualized "sentencing" and confidentiality (Blum, 1996, p. 349). These proponents argue that juveniles are not and cannot be rehabilitated, either because previous attempts have failed or because some juveniles are fundamentally hard-wired for criminal conduct (Lipsey, 1999).

Legislatures have responded to these public demands by introducing accountability and punishment into juvenile court and have begun to treat rehabilitation as a secondary objective (Sheffer, 1995). Some states even revised juvenile court purpose clauses in the 1980s to reflect a shift away from rehabilitation and toward public safety, punishment, and individual accountability (Feld, 1988). States now may be willing to provide therapeutic and rehabilitative services to children only to the extent that such services appear compatible with the safety of the community. Other manifestations of the public safety attack are the use of mandatory minimum sentences in juvenile court, the imposition of penalties that mirror those used in adult court, and the increased transfer of juveniles to adult criminal court (Lipsey, 1999).

Confidentiality has been especially hard hit by the public safety and accountability movement. As the rehabilitative philosophy of juvenile court falls away, confidentiality loses its place. While almost every state still has some statutory provision for the confidentiality of juvenile hearings and records, the majority of states now grant multiple exceptions to the general rule. In many states, these exceptions eviscerate the rule. Beginning in the 1990s, a number of states abandoned presumptive closure statutes entirely and opened juvenile proceedings to the public (Oestreicher, 2001).

Confidentiality also has been eroded in more indirect ways. In a number of states, sex offender registration laws now include juveniles on state registries; law enforcement databases include DNA profiles of juvenile offenders; juvenile drug courts and other specialty courts regularly share information with other public and private agencies; interagency collaboratives facilitate the exchange of juvenile records among law enforcement officials, schools, and public housing authorities; and some states now permit or even require law enforcement personnel to notify schools when students have been arrested (Haller, 2001).

At the beginning of the twenty-first century, the public safety agenda continues to drive the debate on confidentiality and rehabilitation. Therefore, current discussions generally reflect both a utilitarian desire to improve public safety through threatened publicity and severe public consequences, and a retributive desire to punish young offenders with sanctions that approximate those for adults in criminal courts (Scott & Grisso, 1997). Public safety advocates expect that eroding juvenile confidentiality will deter crime, reduce recidivism, and empower the public to protect itself from known offenders. It is not at all clear, however, that publicity and punishment will generate these desired improvements in public safety, nor does it appear that rehabilitation has forever failed as a viable response to juvenile crime.

## Conclusion

Studies reveal the existence of measures which advocate a conditional or qualified form of public and press access to juvenile proceedings as a means to serve the needs of the children by focusing public attention on abuses and deficiencies within the juvenile justice system. Many of the measures incorporate the policy of allowing the press access to juvenile hearings-which might include the privilege to watch and report, with the condition that no names be disclosed at the proceeding. Various studies argue that public access should be extended not only to juvenile delinquency hearings, in which they are accused of being perpetrators of crimes, but also to juvenile dependency hearings, in which children are thought to be victims of abuse or neglect (Hughes, 1997).

In terms of juvenile records, Mclatchey (1999) argues that allowing media access to confidential juvenile records on the condition that the media not reveal identifying information represents the best solution to the media access problem. Conditional access would allow a reporter to investigate many aspects of the juvenile justice system without interfering with the state's efforts to rehabilitate juvenile offenders. To this end, conditional access to juvenile records strikes a balance between rehabilitation of the juvenile and public awareness. Conditional access to juvenile records does not threaten the confidentiality of a juvenile offender because the condition restricts the media from disclosing the juvenile's identity. Access to juvenile records is a privilege, and reporters who abuse the privilege of conditional access could face contempt charges or other sanctions (Mclatchey, 1999). To this end, similar measures are being considered that deal with the conditional (qualified) notion of media-coverage of juvenile proceedings.

The current law of United States governing the right of access to juvenile proceedings primarily makes the decision of whether to grant media access to a particular proceeding one for the presiding judge to resolve at his discretion. However, the purposes and goals driving the enactments of right-of-access statutes evidence the legislature's intent to limit this discretion. To further the goals of these statutes, a presiding judge should grant access only in cases where it is absolutely clear either that no harm will result to the juvenile from the media's presence and subsequent coverage of the proceedings, or that publicity is necessary to prevent a greater harm to the general public. Publicity is detrimental both to the juvenile's prospects for rehabilitation, and to society's chances of reforming young people before they become adult offenders. In contrast, media access serves no benefit which cannot be supplied by other means. Accordingly, the presiding judge in a juvenile courtroom should always use this statutorily-conferred discretion to bar the media from entering the courtroom unless it is absolutely necessary to serve a compelling state interest (Laubenstein, 1995).

If it is possible for one to predict in what direction the juvenile justice system is travelling in terms of allowing media-coverage of juvenile proceedings, one could argue either position with a myriad of supporting explanations. When considering the current overall trend in the juvenile justice system which embraces a "conservative approach within a rehabilitative context", it appears that whatever the decision will be – rest assured, it will be televised.

## References

Ainsworth, J. (1991). Re-imaging childhood and reconstructing the legal order: The case for abolishing the juvenile court. *North Carolina Law Review*, *69*, 1083.

Aron, C., & Hurley, C. (1998). Juvenile justice at the crossroads. *June Champion*, 22, 11.

Bauers, S. (1993, August 15). Fighting to lift veil on child welfare. *Philadelphia Inquirer*, p. E1.

Blum, A. (1996). Disclosing the identities of juvenile felons: Introducing accountability to juvenile justice. *Loyola University Chicago Law Journal*, *27*, 349, 370.

Beck, E., Blackwell, B., Leonard, P., & Mears, M. (2003). Seeking sanctuary: Interviews with family members of capital defendants. *Cornell Law Review*, *88*, 382, 387-390.

Butts, J., & Mears, D. (2001). Reviving juvenile justice in a get-tough era. *Youth & Society*, *33*, 169, 171.

Cohen, L. (1999). Kids, courts, and cameras: New challenges for juvenile defenders. *Law Review Association of the Quinnipiac College School of Law*, *18*(2), 48-52.

Davis, C. (2000). How Iowa editors are using law expanding access to names of juveniles. *Newspaper Research Journal*, *21*(4), 38-49.

Feld, B. (1988). The juvenile court meets the principle of offense: Punishment, treatment, and the difference it makes. *Boston University Law Review*, *68*, 821, 843-845.

Funk, T. (1996). A mere youthful indiscretion? Reexamining the policy of expunging juvenile delinquency records. *University of Michigan Journal of Law Reform*, *29*, 885, 926-27.

Gibeaut, J. (1999). A jury question. *American Bar Association*, *2*(1), 79-81.

Gilbert, J., Grimm, R., & Parnham, J. (2001). Applying therapeutic principles to a family-focused juvenile justice model. *Alabama Law Review*, *52*(1153), 1-55.

Greenebaum, S. (1993). Conditional access to juvenile court proceedings: A prior restraint or a viable solution? *Washington University Journal of Urban & Contemporary Law, 44*, 135-136.

Haller, R. (2001).The innocence protection act: Why federal measures requiring post-conviction DNA testing and preservation of evidence are needed in order to reduce the risk of wrongful executions. *New York Law School Journal of Human Rights*, *18*, 101, 104.

Henning, K. (2004). Eroding confidentiality in delinquency proceedings: Should schools and public housing authorities be notified? *New York University Law Review, 22*(2), 98-112.

Hughes, T. (1997). Opening the doors to juvenile court: Is there an emerging right of public access? *Communications and the Law*, *19*(1), 1-50.

Joiner, W. (2004). *One strike and you're out of school.* Retrieved July 31, 2006 from http://www.salon.com/mwt/feature/2004/02/02/zero_tolerance/index.html

Kelly, D. (1977). Labelling and the consequences of wearing a delinquent label in a school setting. *Education*, *97*, 371, 372-73.

Kintzinger, A. (1980). Freedom of the press vs. juvenile anonymity: A conflict between constitutional priorities and rehabilitation. *Iowa Law Review*, *65*, 1471, 1484.

Kfoury, P. (1991). *Children before the court: Reflections on legal issues affecting minors, 2nd ed.* Salem, NH: Butterworth Legal Publishers.

—. (1991b). Confidentiality and the juvenile offender. *New England Journal on Criminal and Civil Confinement*, 55, 56.

Laubenstein, K. (1995). Media access to juvenile justice: Should freedom of the press be limited to promote rehabilitation of youthful offenders? *Temple Law Review*, 1897, 1904-1905.

Lipsey, M. (1999). Can rehabilitative programs reduce the recidivism of juvenile offenders? An inquiry into the effectiveness of practical programs. *Virginia Journal of Social Policy & Law, 6*, 611.

Louis, A. (1984). Media access to juvenile courts. *Journalism Quarterly,* 751, 753.

Mahoney, A. (1974). The effect of labelling upon youths in the juvenile justice system: A review of the evidence. *Law and Society Review*, 583-584.

Martin, G. (1995). Open the doors: A judicial call to end confidentiality in delinquency proceedings. *New England Journal on Criminal & Civil Confinement*, 21, 393, 400-401.

—. (1997). *Judicial access to information critical to the juvenile court process and to preserving the juvenile justice system. National conference on juvenile justice records: Appropriate criminal and non-criminal justice uses*. U.S. Department of Justice Office of Justice Programs Bureau of Justice Statistics. Retrieved July 31, 2006 from www.ojp.usdoj.gov/bjs/pub/ascii/ncjjr.txt

Mason, L. (October 4, 2000). A law for victims of juvenile crime: Bill would ensure statewide enforcement of rights. *Legal Intelligencer*, S1.

Mclatchey, S. (1999). Media access to juvenile records: In search of a solution. *Georgia State University Law Review*, *20*(4), 148-162.

Melli, M. (1996). Juvenile justice reform in context. *Wisconsin Law Review*, 375, 390-391.

Nelson, K. (1998). The release of juvenile records under Wisconsin's juvenile justice code: A new system of false promises. *Marquette Law Review*, 81, 1101-02.

Oddo, D. (1998). Removing confidentiality protections and the "get tough" rhetoric: What has gone wrong with the juvenile justice system? *Boston College Third World Law Journal, 18*, 105, 107-08; 119-121.

Oestreicher, S. (2001). Toward fundamental fairness in the kangaroo courtroom: The due process case against statutes presumptively closing juvenile proceedings. *Vanderbilt Law Review, 26*(3), 214-247.

Pell, C. (2000). Pre-offense monitoring of potential juvenile offenders: An examination of the Los Angeles county probation department's novel solution to the interrelated problems of truancy and crime. *Southern California Law Review*, *73*, 879- 880.

Free information, public says. (1998, October, November). *The Quill*, p.12.

Combating Juvenile Crime. (1998, February 21) *The Salt Lake Tribute*, p. A10.

Rossum, R. (1995). Holding juveniles accountable: Reforming America's juvenile injustice system. *Pepperdine Law Review*, *22*, 907, 918-920, 925-926.

Reporters Communicate for Freedom of the Press, Access to Juvenile Courts (1999). Retrieved July 28, 2006 from http://www.rcfp.org/juvcts/index.html

Scott, E. & Grisso, T. (1997). The evolution of adolescence: A developmental perspective on juvenile justice reform. *Journal of Criminal Law & Criminology*, *88*, 137, 141-144.

Seymour, L. (1999, February 15). Schools targeting off-campus crimes. *The Los Angeles Times, Metro Desk*, p.1.

Sheffer, J. (1995). Serious and habitual juvenile offender statutes: Reconciling punishment and rehabilitation within the juvenile justice system. *Vanderbilt Law Review*, *48*, 479, 485-86.

Slobogin, C. C. (1999). Treating kids right: Deconstructing and reconstructing the amenability to treatment concept. *Journal of Contemporary Legal Issues*, *10*, 299-333.

Smith, C. et al. (1980). A National Assessment of Serious Juvenile Crime and the Juvenile Justice System: The Need for a Rational Response, Volume III: Legislation, Jurisdiction, Program Interventions, and Confidentiality of Juvenile Record 229, U.S. Dep't of Justice.

Woodruff, C. (1998, February 17). Pitcher debate shifts to court openness. *Schenectady Daily Gazette*, A2.

Zober, E. (1981). The socialization of adolescents into juvenile delinquency, *Adolescence*, 16, 321, 328.

## Cases Cited

Kent v. United States, 383 U.S. 541, 556 (1966).

Breed v. Jones, 421 U.S. 519, 540-41 (1975).

Davis v. Alaska, 415 U.S. 308, (1974).

Globe Newspaper Co. v. Superior Court, 457 U.S. 596 (1982).

Joe v. Webster, 606 F.2d 1226, 1234-36 (D.C. Cir. 1979).

McKeiver v. Pennsylvania, 403 U.S. 528, 545-51 (1971).

Packer v. Bd. of Educ. of Thomaston, 717 A.2d 117, 121-22 (Conn. 1998).

In re Robert M. (1981), 109 Misc 2d 427, 439 NYS2d 986, 989.

In re Sheldon G., 583 A.2d 112, 121-22 (Conn. 1990).

San Bernardino County Dep't of Pub. Social Servs. v. Superior Court. (1991). 283 Cal. Rptr. 332, 340 (Ct. App. 1991).

Smith v. Daily Mail Publ'g Co., 443 U.S. 97, 107-08 (1979).

Thompson v. Barnes, 200 N.W.2d 921, 926 (Minn. 1972).

United States v. Three Juveniles, 61 F.3d 86, 93 n.7 (1st Cir. 1995).

# CHAPTER TWENTY SEVEN

# REFLECTIONS ON TERRORISM IN CHINA

KAM C. WONG


## Abstract

This research investigated an old political problem in a new cultural context: what is the idea of terrorism in China? Specifically, this research posed two inter-related research questions in search of an understanding of terrorism on Chinese soil: how did China conceive of terrorism in the imperial past? What is China's conception of terrorism in the communist present?


## I. Introduction

Terrorism is an age old political phenomenon; as old as civilization itself. In the West, Greek historian Xenophon (cir. 431 – 350 BC) employed terror to intimidate the enemy. Roman emperors, such as Tiberius and Caligula, used terror to induce fear in the ruled (Unknown (n.d.). In the East, Chin Shih Huang (259 - 210 BC), the first Emperor of China, resorted to terror to secure his empire (Zhu, 1994: 93).

Terrorism becomes a global phenomenon, international problem and public concern only in the twentieth century, with the rise of the Irish Republican Army in the West and formation of Palestinian Liberation Army in the Middle-East. Finally, 9/11 made terrorism a household name and international menace (White House, 2001).

To date, there is no consensus over the meaning and causation to terrorism (Schmidt and Youngman compiled 109 different academic definitions, and found that they share some common features (Schmidt, A.P. et al. (1998). The idea of terrorism is often associated with: violence, force (in 83.5% of the definitions); political (65%); fear, terror (51%); threats (47%); psychological effects, anticipated reactions (41.5%); victims not target of violence (37.5%); intentional, planned, systematic, organized (32%); methods, strategy, tactics (30.5%) (Schmidt et al., 1981).

This chapter investigated into the idea of terrorism in China. It asks one simple question: is there an indigenous notion of terrorism in China (Tao, 2002). Specifically, how did China conceive of terrorism in the past? What is the idea of terrorism in contemporary China?

This chapter is organized in the follow way. After this brief "Introduction," section II provides for a brief review of literature on terrorism in China. The review informs that there is very little research into the conceptual origin and intellectual history of terrorism in China, Section III "Terrorism in Imperial China" makes the case that while Western notion of "terrorism" has no counterpart in China's past, China has treated subversive activities most severely, as challenging to "heavenly mandate" ("tianming") and disruption of "cosmic order" ("dao"). Section IV: "Terrorism in Communist China" explores PRC's (People Republic of China) thinking about terrorism since 1949. It finds that PRC understanding of terrorism exhibits a remarkable continuity with the past. Terrorist acts are considered a kind of counter-revolutionary crimes; Mao called it "antagonistic contradiction." The last section, Section V: "Conclusion" offers a reflection on what have been learned.

## II. Literature review

A key word search (China, terrorism) of criminal justice electronic search engines[1] turned up three relevant items (Anonymous, 2002; Mabrey 2005; Wang, 2003).

In 2002, an anonymous author wrote about the up surge of terrorism in Xinjiang, China after 9/11:

> Chinese police in the capital of the far western region of Xinjiang arrested 166 violent terrorists and other criminals in a crackdown on crime. The arrests were made between Sep 20 and Nov 30 in a three-month push to crack cases in the predominantly Muslim region" (Anonymous, 2002).

The next year, John Z Wang published an article describing terrorism in Xinjiang, China in more details:

> The Eastern Turkistan Islamic Movement (ETIM) was designated a terrorist organization by Afghanistan, Kyrgyzstan, China, the United States, and the United Nations in 2002. However, no systematic studies

[1] ProQuest (October 25, 2005) - Criminal Justice data set. A confirmation with a web search of Wilson Web with keywords: China, terrorism yield 130 items, only 1 is a peer reviewed article related to China terrorism (Wang, 2003). A renewed search on March 25, 2008, found nothing of interest.

have been published on the new terrorist organization in Xinjiang, China. Using a case-study approach and interviews, this article attempts to provide information in terms of its historical evolution, related religious and ethnic issues, organizational agenda, activities, and role in the current international terrorist network. This article argues that better international cooperation and the improvement of social and religious policies will help curtail activities of the ETIM (Wang, 2003).

Finally, in 2005, Mabrey confirmed the obvious – China was no longer insulated from terrorism, especially from separatists' attacks at high profile international events:

> The People's Republic of China has been well-insulated from the threat of terrorism, with less than 300 official terrorism-related casualties recorded in the last 10 years. However, the rise of religious separatist extremism in western China and China's role as host of the 2008 Summer Olympics in Beijing are making counter-terrorism a new priority for the Chinese security forces (Wang, 2003).

A key word electronic search (China, terrorism) of political science – Asian studies journals turned up 566 articles.[2] Very few of them are directly related to terrorism in China. A detailed examination of these literature shows that the term "terrorism" started to appear with some frequency at the end of 19th century and beginning of the 20th century, a time of great social turmoil (Perry,1984) and political upheaval for China Perkins, 1989). The subject matter of terrorism was brought up in relationship with dynastic rebellion, e.g., 1911 revolution (Wong, 1977), domestic strives, e.g., banditry (Tiedemann, 1982) and warlords (Lary, 1966), civil wars, e.g., e.g., KMT vs. CCP (Boorman & Boorman, 1966), anti-foreignism, struggles, e.g., Boxer rebellion, (Perry, 1984), and external wars, e.g., war of resistant against Japan (Thaxton, 1977, p. 55).

More recently, research in terrorism has shifted to exploring domestic unrests, e.g., Xinjiang separatist movement (Tanner, 2004), international terrorism, i.e., multilateral cooperation to fight terrorism (Lampton & Ewing, 2003), and global human rights issues, i.e., how fighting terrorism raises human rights issues (Hoffman, 2004).

Finally, a key word (China, terrorism) search of legal journals search[3] turned up 256 articles of interest.[4] A careful examination of this corpus of

---

[2] Project Muse Political Science Journals (October 5, 2005). A follow up search on March 25, 2008 JSTOR - Political Science Journals uncover 3100 items with key phrases terrorism in China or Chinese terrorism. None of them are relevant to our inquiry, i.e., idea of terrorism in China.

[4] Lexis Nexis Academic Universe (October 7, 2005). Updated March 25, 2008.

legal writings turned up two articles that discussed in some length to the recent development of terrorism in China. Both articles were written by Matthew D. Moneyhon, a law student then (2002 - 2003). Both of them were devoted to the reporting of political development in Xinjiang, and with it the necessity to touch upon separatists' terrorist activities.

In one article, Moneyhon discussed terrorism in the context of independence and succession movement in Xinjiang. He observed that notwithstanding violence acts and terrorism activities by Xinjiang separatists - terrorists, the only political settlement that was acceptable to China would be Constitutional "autonomy," not separate statehood (Moneyhon, 2002).

In another article Moneyhon observed that the PRC has been using economic development as a means to incorporate Xinjiang within its political fold:

> Viewed within the context of China's evolving minority policy, Go West looks more like the latest incarnation of Beijing's strategy to integrate and assimilate ethnic minorities into the fabric of greater China, than it does a serious economic development and poverty alleviation plan (Moneyhon, 2003, Conclusion).

All the above studies adopted a conventional (Western) definition of terrorism in discussing terrorism in China.

If we were to investigate terrorism in China indigenously, we need to broaden the scope and deepen our research. Instead of looking at "terrorism" as an established conceptual category, we need to look at "terrorism" in context of Chinese history, culture and society (Price, 1997). For example, how armed groups and secretly societies challenging the government were dealt with in imperial China (Perry, 1980; Tong, 1991). This search strategy turned out to be much more fruitful and far more instructive.

Banditry[5] was a serious social qua political problem in China. Banditry took on political character when they directly or indirectly challenged state authority. For example, in a May 1468 edict, the emperor wrote indignantly about the open challenge to his rule by roaming armed bandits:

> Recently banditry in and around the capital has become rampant. Openly riding their horses in gangs of several dozen, at night they set fires,

---

Search function adjusted to China and terrorism appearing within same paragraph.

[5] Bandits were variously called *dao* and *zei*, see *Hanyu dacidian*, Vol. 7, pp. 1431-32 and vol. 10, p. 183 respectively.

> brandish their weapons, and plunder residents' goods. During the day, [they] intercept the carts of those people who pass by, seizing their donkeys and mules. They even go so far as to take people's lives. Even though there are intendants charged with apprehending bandits, imperial soldiers from the warden's offices of the five wards, and patrolmen, they do not really try to capture the bandits; so that now they are totally unrestrained by fear and act outrageously (Robinson, 2000, p. 529).

Bandits or rebel groups in China resembled modern day terrorists in purpose, constitution, organization, and methods. They were oppressed by the government. They were anti-establishment, e.g., disrespectful of local gentry. They were against the government, e.g., disregard local magistrate. They sought social justice and political change by violent means, e.g., redistribution of wealth. They used terror tactics to induce fear, e.g., making travelling in the country side unsafe. [6] They were well organized, e.g., charismatic leadership with loyal followings.

In imperial China, at the turn of the 20th century, secret societies conspired to undermine government authority, with the use of violence and terror (Ownby, 1996, 2001). The most famous one was the Triad Society (or "Triads"). The Triads was first formed to "resist Qing, and return to Ming" ("fan Qing, fu Ming"). In order to avoid capture they turned underground (Chesneaux 1971). Much like modern day terrorists, they established elaborate rituals and rules to bind them together as an effective rebel group. They have no qualms in using terror to achieve their objective, e.g., torturing of informants (Ownby, 1996).

By conventional standard, secret societies were consummate terrorist groups.[7] Indeed, they were enlisted by both Dr. Sun to sabotage the Qing dynasty (DeKorne, 1934) and used by Chairman Mao to subvert the Nationalist government (Schram, 1966).

This literature search instructs there is very little serious research into terrorism in China, either as a domestic problem or as a domesticated concept.

To look at terrorism as a domestic problem is to recognize terrorism as a socially constructed experience (Berger & Luckmann, 1996, p. 51-55, 59-61). This cautions against taking for granted how (Chinese) people

---

[6] In 1400s the bandits in China build up a reputation of ruthlessness to effectual their exploits. For example, the "whistling arrow bandits" (*xiangmazei*, commonly abbreviated to *xiangma*) attached bells to their mounts or using whistling arrows when they raided (Robinson 2000, p. 529). This recalls the pirates in the 17th century who used flags to announce their presence. This induced fear in the seafarers. In so doing, they could achieve their piracy without a fight (http://www.kipar.org/piratical-resources/pirate-flags.html).

think, feel, and act towards terrorism. To investigate terrorism as a domesticated idea is to research into how terrorism, as an imported idea, is given meaning anew in contemporary China.

Chinese "terrorism" research to date has not seen fit to question the appropriateness of adopting conventional (Western) idea of terrorism to understand associative terrorism experience in China.

## III. Terrorism in Imperial China

As observed above, terrorism is an imported idea. As imported idea it is rootless and ill fitting (Hu, 2001, Literature Review). In order to discover terrorism in China, we need to understand China's view on gratuitous violence and idea of cosmic order (or "dao"). In imperial China, all forms of violence were frowned upon as immoral and dysfunctional (Puett, 1998). Violence was considered alien to human nature and disruptive of the cosmic order ("luan").

This is contra distinctive from Hobbes who assumed that the nature of man is self-interested and barbaric and the nature is chaotic and disorderly (Hobbes, 1666, esp. Chapters XIII to XXIV) In "Luxing", it was said that people are born to peace only to have disorder imposed on them by evil doers. As a result the five punishments were established (*Book of History,* 1996, p. 264 – 280) ("Minister Lu on Punishment").

The use of violence to challenge the Emperor, destabilizes the state, harm the citizens, and disrupt social order is considered a gravest offence (Turner, 1993). The Emperor has an affirmative duty to restore the cosmic order ("tianming") and in accordance with rule of nature ("dao") (van der Valk, 1983). Conducts seeking to undermine the authority of the Emperor, for e.g., individual assassination or collective uprising, were strictly prohibited, resolutely deterred and severely punished (Puett, 1998, p. 438-440). This is particularly the case with barbarian rulers, e.g., Northern Wei (386 – 534), Liao (916 – 1125), Jurchen Chin (1115 – 1231), Yuan (1271 – 1368) and Qing (1644 – 1911) dynasties. For example, as alien rulers from a lesser (barbaric) culture, the Chin emperor has to walk on thin ice to come to terms with China's high culture and Confucius officialdoms. The Juren emperors have resorted to violence and terror to bring Chinese (Han) officials to their knee, e.g., in one case eight officials were executed and 34 were banished for engaging in factional activities (Tao, 1970).

In imperial China, political criminality (*zhengzhi fenzui*) was violence directed against the Emperor, inducing fear and causing "chaos" (*luan*). Emperors were fearful of secretive oppositions and unpredictable threats. Emperor of Sung, Taizhong was reported to have said:

> If there is no external threat (*waiyou*), the state must have internal trouble (*neihuan*). External threats are only at the border and can be protected against. However those who are treacherous (*jianxie*) have no form, as internal threats, they are much to be feared! The emperor should always pay attention and be aware of this possibility (Zhu , 1994, p. 446).[8]

The author *Shiji*, Au Yangxiu, has equated external threat by barbarians as those afflicting the skins and internal attacks by the hoodlums and traitors (terrorists) as those are corrupting the internal organs (*fuxin zhi huan*[9]) (Zhu, 1994, p. 446). Throughout the centuries, Chinese emperors have spared no effort to prevent such internal threats:

> During the *Qin* dynasty, those who committed political crimes (*zhengzi fanzui*) against the emperor was punished at the minimum with death, most of them were punished with purging the clan. According to historical account, those who engaged in "wei luan"[10] (creating disorder) and "wei ni" (creating dissent)[11] are often torn apart by vehicles, before death they are subjected to "five punishment," [12] then "yi san zu" (termination of three clan[13]), "mei qizong" (extermination of the ancestor), this often implicates thousands of households and tens of thousands of people. People who engaged in crimes of slandering (*feibang*) and heresy *(yaoyan)* against the emperor must be punished with the heaviest penalty. Even those who disclosed the where about of the emperor must be severely punished with death (Zhu, 1994, p. 93)

---

[9] Literally, "disease in one's vital organ, i.e., serious hidden trouble. *The Pinyin Chinese-English Dictionary* (Hong Kong: Commercial Press, 1979) 766L.

[10] "Luan" literally means public disorder or loss of control as a state of affair, both of which implicates the emperor's capacity and legitimacy to rule. *Hangyu Dacidian* (Shanghai: Hangyu Dacidian, 1994), Vol. 1:797R.

[11] "Ni" liberally means contrary, here being contrary to order and regulation. *Hangyu Dacidian* (Shanghai: Hangyu Dacidian, 1994), Vol. 10:823R.

[12] "Wu xing" are the five chief forms of punishment, in ancient China, being tattooing of the face, cutting off the nose, cutting off the feet, castration, and decapitation. *The Pinyin Chinese-English Dictionary* (Hong Kong: Commercial Press, 1979) 731R. "Wuxing" is a serious punishment not only because they are painful but also because they are humiliating to the person and loss of face to the family. In the text of Xiaojing. Kaizhong Mingyi" ("Filial piety. Making clear the principle in the beginning") it is said: "Shenti fafu, shou zhi fulwu, bugan huishang, yao zhi shi ya" ("The body and its associates parts (hair and skin), is given by the parents, dare not harm, this is the beginning of filial piety.") In essence the body is a family trust. This conception of "body politics" is to have grave implications on Chinese social control strategy and policy.

[13] The three clans being the offender's family, his mother and wife.

Through the centuries, violence against the Emperor took many forms, e.g., from regal assassination to civil uprising to destruction of royal temples, and comes from many quarters, e.g., from deprived citizens to disaffected public to disillusioned intellectuals (Esherick, 1983).

However, in rare circumstances the use of violence against the Emperor, might be justified, e.g., "guan bi min fan" (people rebel as a result of oppressive officials) (Wakeman, 1977). Thus, while official history might condemn individual assassins and collective violence, unofficial history often laud such acts as heroics, necessary and functional in disposing a tyrant, in venting grievances, and in doing heaven's justice (Yen, 1934). The issue of benevolence vs. malevolence "terror" was rarely discussed in official history of the time, but alive and well in Chinese culture *Tiedemann* 1984, p. 395).

As to response to political violence, as early as the Spring and Autumn (*Chunqiu* 770-475 BC) and Warring States (*Zhan guo,* 475-221 BC) periods, there specialized violence suppression officials called "jin bu shi" ("violence suppression officials"). They functioned very much like the anti-terrorists units today. Recent research shows Emperors took extensive precautions to protect against assassinations. The imperial security system at the capital consisted of body guards and palace patrol. They performed protective duties much like that of the secret service today (Dray-Novey 1993). The comprehensive *baojia* system of the Qin dynasty and the elaborate spy system during the Sung era kept the emperor well informed of any plots against outside the palace gate (Chen 1995). Finally, the extensive KMT spy system and secretive CCP *zhongyan deke* ("Special Central Bureau") were terrorist and anti-terrorist units (Wakeman, 1992).

After this brief discussion of political violent in imperial China, we need to attend to three challenging intellectual issues.

First, can "terrorism" be perpetrated by the state in China? In China, there is no such thing as state sponsored terrorism.

The right of the Emperor to use force is unlimited. From antiquity, the utility and legitimacy of the state to use violence to suppress violence – from punishment to warfare - has never been questioned, and in fact considered a duty of a sage emperor.

> Moreover, if you use war to get rid of war, even war is acceptable; if you use killing to get rid of killing, even killing is acceptable; if you use punishment to get rid of (the need for) punishment, even punishing is acceptable (Shangjunshu, Huace) (Cheng, 1988, p. 284).

The issue was whether the violence used was proper in usage in purpose and degree. It is important to note that Chinese considered state sponsored violence (or organized violence) as a continuum to be deployed in response to challenges to authority or disruption of order. Emperor and officials were cautioned against arbitrary, gratuitous, and excessive use of violence. There were no fix "cruel and unusual" idea or inflexible "an eye for an eye" rule. For example, Shangyang, putative father of legalist school, has proposed the use of heavy punishment for minor offence in order to hold off bigger harm to come.

Second, can terrorism be perpetrated by "pure" speech alone?

In imperial China, intellectuals were a privileged class. They held a lot of soft – moral, reasoning - power. The power of the pen and impact of the words were most formidable. Through out history brace intellectuals and outspoken scholars provide the only effective check and balance on the Emperor. By the same token, intellectuals were viewed with much suspicion. As a result, speech was strictly controlled and words were meticulously vetted. Qi Huangdi burned all the books, while Qing Emperors prosecuted people for speech crime. To the Emperors dissenting intellectuals with a pen were as dangerous as a terrorists with a gun (Kessler, 1971).

> The court, ever so sensitive to slights and expression of hostility to Manchu rule, decided to deal harshly with offenders. The purported author, Chuang T'ing-lung, was dead, and so his father was arrested and thrown into a Peking jail, where he later died. When the case was closed in 1663, the father's and son's body was disinterred and mutilated, their families were bound over to Manchus as slaves, and their possessions were confiscated. A similar fate lay in store for all the scholars involved in preparing the history, the printer, and even some of the purchasers. Altogether seventy men were executed (Kessler, 1971).

Third, whether all violent challenges to state authority were deemed to be "terrorist" in nature?

In China, the Emperor ruled his empire and governs his citizens by and through the family. The family head assumes the role and function of an Emperor at home. Philip Kuhn has called this as "third realm" (Huang, 1993). This author has described the family as "more or less government" (Wong, 1998). They amounted to the same thing: the Emperor has cooped local community to rule themselves. Any challenge to the head of the family is a challenge to the Emperor. Assault on or threat to the family power structure is considered every bit as serious as challenging the state authority, e.g., it is considered the ten most serious crimes.[14] By this logic,

[14] Geoffrey MacCormack, "On the Pre-Tang Development of the Law of 'Treason': moufan , dani and pan," (The three most heinous crimes, called abominable, in the

terrorist acts are not only those that threatened the state – Emperor but also those who intimidated the clan - family - heads. Any disobedience to parents were severely dealt with by state law, family rules and social norms, and made an absolute offence.

## IV. Terrorism in Communist China

The use of "terror" as a political instrumentality was never questioned by the Communist Party. Ever since the formation of the Communist Party (CPP) in 1920s, CCP members were both perpetrators and recipients of political terrors. KMT (Kuomintang or Chinese Nationalist Party) used terror tactics to purge the ranks of CCP. CCP resorted to terrorism – assassination and bombing – to intimidate KMT officials and destabilize the KMT government. More recently, the cultural revolution recalls white terror of the French revolution and "strike-hard" campaign qualifies as state sponsored terrorism, in theory and practice.

According to the official and authoritative PRC "police encyclopaedia," the *Gongan baike quanshu*, counter-revolutionary crime (*fan geming zui*) is defined as: "Conduct which harmed the People's Republic of China with the purpose of over-throwing people's proletarian dictatorship and socialist system" (*Gongan baike quanshu,* 2000, 350R). This comes close to being terrorism.

The PRC Criminal Law (1979) provides in Article 90 that "Conduct which is harmful to the People's Republic of China and done with the purpose of over-throwing the proletarian dictatorship and socialist system are all counter-revolutionary crimes." Counter-revolutionary crimes include crime involving: (1) inciting people to resist and harm the implementation of state law and order and (2) use counter-revolutionary slogans, pamphlets and other means to incite others to over-throw the proletarian dictatorship and socialist system (The PRC Criminal Law (1979) Article 102)

What constitutes counter-revolutionary crime however it not too clear, An exhaustive review of prior and existing counter-revolutionary laws, regulations, and directives does not tell us is what constitute a counter-revolutionary crime beyond the fact it refers to speech or act which is as

---

Han Code were plotting rebellion (moufan), sedition (dani) and rebellion (pan). *Buxiao* ('lack of filial piety') made the list of ten most abominable crime.) http://jalh.ku.edu/article/maccormack2005.pdf

intended or in effect was harmful to the state's political order or challenge the established government.[15]

---

[15] See for example "Zhongguo Renmin Zhengzhi Xieshang Huiyi Gongtong Ganlin (The Chinese People's Political Consultative Conference Common Program) (promulgated on September 29, 1949) Article 7; PRC Constitution (promulgated on September 20, 1954) Article 19; Zhengwuyuan, Zuigao Renmin Fayuan, "Guanyu Zhenya Fangeming Huodong de Zhishi" (Government Administrative Council and Supreme People's Court "Directive on the Suppression of Counter-revolutionaries") (promulgated on July 23, 1950); Zhonghua Renmin Gongheguo Zhenzhi Fangemin Tiao Li (PRC Punishment of Counter-revolutionary Regulations) (promulgated on Feb. 20, 1951), Article 2.; Zhongyang Sifabu "Guanyu Eba, Guanfei, Bufa Dizhu Ruhe Shiyong Zhenzhi Fangemin Tiaoli Pifu" (Party Central Judicial Department "Reply Regarding How to Apply Punishment of Counter-revolutionary Regulations to Local Tyrant, Habitual Criminals, and Illegal Landlord") (promulgated in 1951); Zhongyang Xiren Xiaozu "Guanyu Fangeming-fenzi he Qita Huaifenzi de Jieshi ji Chuli de Zhengce Jiexian de Zanxing Guiding" (Party Central Party of Ten Committee Temporary Regulations Regarding Policy and Limits on Explaining and Handling of Counter-revolutionary Elements and Other Bad Elements (promulgated March 3, 1956); Zhongyang Xiren Xiaozu "Guanyu Fangeming-fenzi he Qita Huaifenzi de Jieshi ji Chuli de Zhengce Jiexian de Zanxing Guiding" (Party Central Party of Ten Committee "Temporary Regulations Regarding Policy and Limits on Explaining and Handling of Counter-revolutionary Elements and Other Bad Elements") (promulgated March 3, 1956); Zhonggong Zhongyang Xiren Xiaozu Dui "Guanyu Fangeming-fenzi he Qita Huaifenzi de Jieshi ji Chuli de Zhengce Jiexian de Zanxing Guiding" de Buchong (Communist Party Central Party of Ten Committee "Supplement to Temporary Regulations Regarding Policy and Limits on Explaining and Handling of Counter-revolutionary Elements and Other Bad Elements (promulgated June 24, 1957) (Counter-revolutionary damages mean causing damage with counter-revolutionary intent and purpose); Renmin Gongan Pianweihui Guanyu Zhongyang Xiren Xiaozu "Guanyu Fangeming-fenzi he Qita Huaifenzi de Jieshi ji Chuli de Zhengce Jiexian de Zanxing Guiding" de Buchong Jieshi Zhong Yixie Wenti de Jieda (PRC Organizing Committee "Answers to Certain Questions on Supplementary Explanation Regarding Temporary Regulations Regarding Policy and Limits on Explaining and Handling of Counter-revolutionary Elements and Other Bad Elements") (promulgated 1957) (Contemporary counter-revolutionary elements means people who spread reactionary pamphlets with counter-revolutionary intent); Zhongyang Xiren Xiaozu "Guanyu Putong Fangemin Fenzi ji Qita Fandong Fenzi de Jieshi" (Committee of Ten from Party Central "Explanation Regarding Common Counter-revolutionary Elements and Other Reactionary Elements") (November 1957) (Counter-revolutionary elements are people who insist upon their reactionary class viewpoint); Zhongyang Zhengfa Xiaozu "Guanyu Xinde Fangeming Fanzui Xingwei de Jiexian" (Party Central Political-legal Committee "Regarding the classification of Counter-revolutionary Elements" (1962) (People who are merely critical of the party or government

A careful reading of the legal literature and case studies (*Xingshifanzui anli congshu* 1990) confirms that counter-revolutionary crimes are "intent" (in China "purpose")[16] more so than a "conduct"[17] and "result" crime.[18] Thus, for the same harmful conduct, e.g., personal or property damage, the existence of counter-revolutionary purpose (*mudi*)[19] separates the distinction between crime vs. non-crime (*zui yu fei zui*[20]).[21] In Chinese

---

policy or implementation are not counter-revolutionary.) (Zuigao Renmin Jianchayuan, 1990, pp. 269-331)

[16] A "purpose" (*mudi*) crime is one which punishes people for motive and purpose. It is similar to common law basic intent vs. ulterior intent distinction, e.g., burglary – breaking and entering of other's premises at night with the intent committing a felony therein.

[17] A "conduct" (*xingwei*) crime is one which punishes certain conduct, irrespective of result intended, e.g., perjury.

[18] A "result"(*houguo*) crime is one which punished result, e.g., murder. However, the war separating "intent" and "result" crime is not as firm and insular as it might first appear. This is so far two reasons. First, since intention cannot be judged by once action, and action is most evident with its impact and consequences. The "result" of the action speaks to the intent of the actor, both as direct as well as circumstantial evidence. Direct because one is charge with the natural consequence of ones act. Word is not more than action. Circumstantial, because how might ones intent be explained given certain action. Words speak louder than words. Second, even if one does not intent ones action, the result of the act is all the same. People are responsible of serious harm to society, a reckless type of attribution of responsibility.

[19] The PRC criminal law jurisprudence does not draw a clear distinction between intent (*yitu* or *zuiyi*), purpose *(mudi*) and motive (*dongji*) in the finding of guilt and imposing of punishment. It is embraced by the term "*fanzui zhuguan*" (subjective mental condiction (xinli zhuangkuang). Editorial Committee, *Faguan shouce* (Judges handbook) (Sangxi: Shangxi renmin chubanshe, 1995), p. 51. PRC legal scholars do draw a analytical distinction between "*fanzui mudi*" (criminal purpose) and "*fanzui donji*" in that "dongji" is *mudi* is precipitated by *dongji*. *Ibid.* p. 55. In common law jurisdiction, only intent is the mental state (*mens rea*) that needs to be proven. Intent is usually defined as "knowingly" and "purposely." Motive is considered as irrelevant as a legal principle or immaterial as evidentiary proof. However, increasingly and by statue, motive is being considered as important in the Anglo-American jurisprudence, e.g., hate crime with racial animus.

[20] The "*zui yu fei zui*" is an analytical, rhetorical and instructional device to highlight the main differences between one crime vs. another, especially as interpreted and applied. This is usually done by comparing two similar cases along critical dimensions, in counter-revolutionary crimes the issue of intent.

[21] Editorial committee, *Zhongguo gongan baike quanshu* (China police encyclopedia) (Jilin: Jilin Chubanshe, 1989), p. 351L. "*Fen ge ming mudi*" (counter-revolutionary purpose or intent) is defined as: "With the purpose of

criminal law jurisprudence, harmful conduct is used to demonstrate and prove the existence of counter-revolutionary motive (*dongji*) and purpose (*mudi*).[22]

For purposes of terrorism crime analysis, counter-revolutionary crime covers *more* and *less* than conventional terrorist conducts.

*Counter-revolutionary crime is more than terrorist conduct.* Whereas all terrorist acts are counter-revolutionary act, not all counter-revolutionary acts are terrorist act. The reason is a simple one, Counter-revolutionary crime covers violence as well as non-violent subversive acts, e.g., distribution of promotional materials supporting the overturn of CPC is certainly a non-violence counter-revolutionary offence.

However, as applied, most if not all counter-revolutionary crimes in China are covered as terrorist conduct. First, in order to prosecute under counter-revolutionary law there must be serious harm to social, political and economic order. In such cases, the conduct being prosecuted is more likely to be disruptive, threatening, violent or harmful ones.[23] Second, proving a counter-revolutionary crime requires the demonstration of "harmful" purpose and intent. In most cases only violent conduct is likely to be prosecuted and convicted.[24] In fact, a comprehensive review of pertinent PRC Criminal Law provisions covering counter-revolutionary crimes show that most of them require the use of force to bring about damage to property, disruption of services, and harmful to people.

*Counter-revolutionary crime is less than terrorist conduct.* Counter-revolutionary crime may also cover *less* than conventional terrorist conduct. Counter-revolutionary requires the proof of a counter-revolutionary purpose. Not all terrorist acts are perpetrated with requisite counter-revolutionary purpose. Take the case of hostage taking in order to

---

overthrowing people's proletarian dictatorship and socialist system, is an important element constituting counter-revolutionary crime, is a distinction between counter-revolutionary crime, counter-revolutionary and other crime."

22 Editorial committee, *Zhongguo gongan baike quanshu* (China police encyclopedia) (Jilin: Jilin Chubanshe, 1989), p. 351L. "*Fen ge ming mudi*" (counter-revolutionary purpose or intent) is defined as: "We can ascertain the purpose of perpetrator can by looking at the counter-revolutionary conduct and effect in practice."

23 Editorial Committee, *Faguan shouce* (Judges handbook) (Shangxi: Shangxi renmin chubanshe, 1995), p. 75.

24 Editorial committee, *Zhongguo gongan baike quanshu* (China police encyclopedia) (Jinlin: Jilin Chubanshe, 1989), p. 351L. "*Fen ge ming mudi*" (counter-revolutionary purpose or intent) is defined as: "We can ascertain the purpose of perpetrator can by looking at the counter-revolutionary conduct and effect in practice."

force the PRC government to purge corruption. This is clearly a terrorist act. It is however not clear it is a counter-revolutionary crime. Thus, only SOME but not violent acts are deemed to be carried out against the state.[25]

Doctrinally, the most authoritative statement on the nature and treatment of political violence – from revolution to terrorism – can be found in an essay written by Mao '*On the Correct Handling of Contradictions among the People*' (Johnson 1968, pp. 435-440). The intellectual foundation of the "on contradiction" doctrine was that of Hegel's dialectics. The doctrine has been applied to justified government draconian anti-crime measures at the expense of human rights concerns (Clarke & Feinerman, 1995).

In "On Contradiction" Mao taught that there are two kinds of contradictions (conflicts), one within the ranks of the people and the other between the people and the class enemy. The former being non-antagonistic (and personal) can be resolved peacefully, i.e., through education and with punishment, the later as antagonist (structural) conflicts cannot be resolved amicably without resort to force, i.e., war. Terrorism belongs to the second type of contradiction.

## V. Conclusion

This chapter began with an observation that the effort to treat terrorism as a uniform set of human experiences and a universal conceptual category ill serves the purpose of academic research and understanding terrorism (Reimann, 2002). In order to understand terrorism in China on its own terms there is a need to investigate "terrorism" (like activities) in local context and with indigenous perspective; in practical terms, how "terrorism" originated and developed in (imperial) China? This entails the study of history, culture and above all else philosophy and in the case of China, Confucius ideas and ideal; specifically, how China viewed order, violence and control?

This investigation shows that Western concept of terrorism was not able to adequately capture the essence and characteristics of "terrorism" like "political violence" in historical China. The Western idea of "terrorism"

---

[25] In order for one to survive this argument, one can adopt a broader and more inclusive definition of counter-revolutionary crime in arguing that anytime *violence* is used *contrary to law* in order to change state policy and practices, it is deemed to be ipso facto counter-revolution in effect. This argument stretches counter-revolutionary acts to include violent conduct seeking to change policy and practices that are themselves illegal, improper and otherwise disapproved by the PRC.

included more, e.g., state terrorism, and less, e.g., clan violence. It also accentuates some aspects, e.g., terror on innocence, at the expense of others, e.g. terror to family.

Some of the inadequacies of conventional terrorism label in capturing China experience are summarized below:

First, as an agriculture society, China sought order, stability and continuity, and above all else harmony (Wright, 1953, pp. 31-34). Thus, Confucius ethics taught that conflicts are to be avoided and violence, condemned (Wall & Blum, 1999). The former is a precursor of the second. The second is a consequence of the first. Both have a tendency of disturbing established social relationships ("wunlun")[26]and if left unchecked rupture ("luan") pre-ordained cosmic order ("dao"), which takes years to established and still more time to rehabilitate.

Thousands of years of Confucius education was successful in fostering a culture, creating a custom and developing a personality that equate conflicts as "bad" and violence as "evil", at a cognitive and emotive level. Thus, people were taught to avoid conflicts at all cost, even if they were in the right. Violence was found to be objectionable, however it was manifested (threat vs. force), whoever it was directed again (emperor, officials, parents, peers); whatever the impact (physical injury vs. psychological harm). There were few attempts to discriminate one type of conflict and violence from another. There was very effort to avoid conflict and suppress violence, individually, collectively and nationally. The focus is on maintaining peace and order, not discriminating causes (of disorder), e.g., for judging the state of "cosmic order" (Hsu, 1970) and entitlement to "mandate of heaven". Thus, Emperor and officials were equally to be blamed for natural disasters as with human upheaval. In the ultimate analysis, terrorism is not the focus of Emperor's concern, disturbance of the peace.

Second, like all other countries, East and West, past and present, political violence, of which "terrorism" is a species, did exist in China and in abundance, e.g., assassination, banditry (Tiedemann, 1982), secret society activities (Chesneaux, 1971) and peasant rebellion (Perry, 1980). These violent acts were found to be particularly odious because they were secretly organized and openly challenging the emperor's authority and legitimacy. To a Confucius scholar, they were acts of disloyalty and signs of chaos ("luan"); both were affronts to the Emperor's mandate to rule. Here again, it matters not how political violence was perpetrated, e.g.,

[26] The five relationships ("wulun") are ruler-subject, father-son, husband-wife, elder brother-younger brother, and friend-friend.

slandering vs. assassinating vs. rebellion. What matters was that the Emperor's authority must be re-established, "luan" quelled and mandate from heaven restored. The act that is punished in not violent per se, but the acts of insubordination and disloyalty, which challenges not only the Emperor's safety but the people's order of things.

Third, terrorism is the instrumental use and strategic employment of threat, violence or terror to achieve political – regime change or policy reform – objectives. Terrorism, as instrumental use of violence, has no place in Chinese ethical and jurisprudential thought. (1) The instrumental use of violence is frowned upon, thus treated as barbaric and animalistic, i.e., Chinese ethics has no principles of end justifying means.[27] The use of violence means to achieve political ends, make the perpetrator as morally apprehensible as the oppressive government. (2) The strategic use of violence will likely fail. The way to reform government and change policy is through adherence to Confucius ethic and with the use of moral reasoning. It starts with appealing to higher moral principles and ends with setting a good personal example. Fighting violence with violence is not recommended, and not likely to succeed or prevail. People were taught not to bend to raw power but succumb to sound reasons. Here again, people are punished not for violence but its instrumental use; more broadly abdication of reason and forfeiture of morality. When rationality and morality is gone, a country is not governable and communal living is not possible.

Fourth, one of the characteristics of terrorism is the indiscriminate killing of innocent people to promote fear and terror. This would not happen in imperial China for two reasons, one philosophical, the other practical. (1) Philosophically, killing indiscriminately or terrorizing innocent people was *ipso facto* not reasonable and just (*hu he qing li*), however noble the cause, i.e., against "qing" and "li" in China (Fan, 1992). (2) Practically, China was a non-democratic (autocratic) country (Wittfogel, 1970). There was no point in attacking civilians, since they

[27] One possibility is to argue that Confucianism is not a set of ethic principles as much as it is a set of rules for practical reason to deal with life contingencies. *Zhang Rulun,*" Chapter VIII. Is an Ethics of Economic Activity Possible?" In Yu Xuanmeng, Lu Xiaohe, Liu Fangtong, Zhang Rulun & Georges Enderle (Eds.) *Economic Ethics and Chinese Culture* - Chinese Philosophical Studies, XIV ("For Confucius, *jen* is an all-encompassing ethical ideal… It is an existential goal which one must attempt to achieve for oneself through one's own self-cultivation. All the "worldly goods" are totally subordinate to the higher goal of *jen*. But this does not mean that people can do anything to achieve this goal.")
http://www.crvp.org/book/Series03/III-14/contents.htm

have no say over the conduct of the Emperor. Nor would the emperor yield in the face of such terrorizing acts, for three reasons. It is morally wrong to negotiate on matters of principle. It is morally wrong for the learned and educated ("zhunzi") to make concession to the uneducated ("xiaoren").[28] It is also unimaginable for the emperor – parent to negotiate with citizens – subordinate.

Fifth, there was no state terrorism in paternalistic China (Ling, 1994). In accordance with Confucius teachings the state is build upon a family model. The relationship between emperor/officers and citizens/charges was, and still is, that exist between father and sons. Sons have to show respect and demonstrate loyalty to familial authority figures, from parents to officials to emperor. The family authority figures have a moral duty to take care of the best interest of the children, e.g., food, shelter and education. Thus when citizens challenge the state – from dissenting to resisting to rebelling – the state has the authority and duty to react in a most violent manner. This is not considered as state terrorism. This is viewed as state performing its moral duty. If the citizens misbehaved they can hardly blame the state for acting "violently" against their misconduct, seeking a return to the right path or "dao". The whole purpose of suppressing violence, terrorism included, is to fortify an authority structure passed down by Confucius. Terrorism is not the objective on control, disruption of "dao" is.

Sixth, the concept of terrorism was also not able to make allowance for good "political violence". The only proper course of act and effective measure by the oppressed people against the abusive state was to engage in *righteous* political resistance, from assassination to rebellion, in a *last ditch effort* to return the country to the heavenly way. The aim was never to overthrow the Emperor but to return the throne to proper "heavenly" authority. View in this light, the "terrorism" act that challenges the Emperor resulting is brought on by the Emperor. In order for such resistance be recognized as legitimate, the resisters must be righteous in its cause and proper with means. Conversely, violence used to press the rulers to conform to the cosmic order and return to heavenly (benevolent) rule is deemed as understandable, justifiable and necessary (Crowell, 1983). Years later, Mao has justified such grassroots - peasant rebellions as examples of class wars; present day freedom fighters not terrorists. In the ultimate analysis, the use of violence for or against the Emperor in China

[28] The gentleman and based people lived in two distinctive world, separated by a great divide. The gentleman is regulated by principles of "li" and "ren". The based people are moved by consideration of "li" (utility) and compelled by punishment ("xing").

must be evaluated against a fix moral universe and universal ethical percepts, espoused by Confucian and enshrined within Confucian teachings.

To conclude and re-iterate, since the beginning of the Republic (1949 to 1959) and up through the economic reform period (1979 – now), the pre-occupation of the communist leadership has been with assuring security (to defend "mandate from heaven") and achieving stability (to maintain "cosmic order"). Conceptually, terrorism, as we come to know it in the West, did not gain a foothold in the leadership's thinking.

"Terrorism" as threats to political security and social stability were treated just like any other destabilizing acts, i.e., treated as contradictions between the people and enemy of the state. Conversely, all political dissent and social unrest having the potential to disrupt Party rule is considered as "terrorists" like. As observed, this indiscriminate way of thinking about political-social "violence" is traceable to China's past where the emperor ruled absolutely and resolutely with mandate from heaven in maintaining a cosmic order, against ALL challenges.

## References

Anonymous. (2002). 166 terrorists nabbed. *Crime & Justice International. 18*(59), 16.

Berger, P. L., & Luckmann, T. (1996). *The social construction of reality: A treatise its the sociology of knowledge*. Garden City, New York: Anchor Books.

*Book of History* (Shangshu) (1996). Henan Chubanshe.

Boorman, H. L., & Boorman, S. A. (1966). Chinese communist insurgent warfare, 1935-49. *Political Science Quarterly*, *81*(2), 171-195.

Chen, C. C. (1975). The Japanese adaptation of the Pao-Chia system in Taiwan, 1895-1945. *The Journal of Asian Studies*, *34*(2), 391-416.

Cheng, L. S. (1988) *Shangyang and his school of thought* (Shangyang ji qi Xuepei) Taiwan, Taiwan Xuesheng shuju.

Chesneaux, J. (1971). *Secret societies in china in the nineteenth and twentieth centuries*, tr. Gillian Nettle. Ann Arbor: University of Michigan Press.

Clarke, D. C., & Feinerman, J. V. (1995). Antagonistic contradictions: Criminal law and human rights in China. *The China Quarterly*, 141, 135-154.

Crowell, W. (1983) Social unrest and rebellion in Jiangnan during the six dynasties. *Modern China, 9*(3), 319-354.

DeKorne, J. C. (1934). Sun Yat-Sen and the secret societies. *Pacific*

*Affairs*, *7*(4), 425-433 (1934).
Dray-Novey, A. (1993). Spatial order and Police in imperial Beijing. *The Journal of Asian Studies, 52*(4), 885-922.
Editorial committee. (2000). *Zhongguo gongan da baike quanshu* (China police large encyclopedia) (Two volumes) Jinlin: Jilin Chubanshe.
Esherick, J. (1983). Symposium on peasant rebellions: Some introductory comments, *Modern China*, *9*(3), 275-284
Fan, Z., & Xin, X. (1992). *Qing Li Fa Yu Zhong Guo Ren* (Compassion, reason, law and the Chinese people). Beijing: Zhongguo renmin daixue chubanshe.
Hobbes, T. (1660). *Leviathan.* Retrieved on 28th August 2008 from http://www.earlymoderntexts.com/pdfbig/hobbebig.pdf
Hoffman, P. (2004). Human rights and terrorism. *Human Rights Quarterly*, *26*(4), 932-955.
Hsu, D. L. (1970). Crime and cosmic order. *Harvard Journal of Asiatic Studies*, *30*, 111 – 125.
Huang, P. (1993). Public sphere/civil society in China? The third realm between state and society, *Modern China*, *19*(2), 216 – 240.
Hu, L. H. (Ed.) (2001). *Contemporary terrorism and response* (Dangdai shijia kongbu zhuyi yu duice) Beijing: Dongfang Chubanshe.
Johnson, C. (1968). The third generation of guerrilla warfare. *Asian Survey*, *8*(6), 435-447.
Kessler, L. D. (1971). Chinese scholars and the early Manchu state. *Harvard Journal of Asiatic Studies*, *31*, 179-200.
Lampton, D. M., & Ewing, R. D. (2003). *The U.S.-China relationship facing international security crises: Three case studies in post-9/11 bilateral relation.* Washington, D.C.: Nixon Center.
Lary, D. (1966). Warlord Studies. *Modern China, 6*(4), 439-470.
Ling, L. H. M. (1994). Rationalizations for state violence in Chinese politics: The hegemony of parental governance. *Journal of Peace Research*, *31*(4), 393-405
Mabrey, D. (2005). Counterterrorism efforts in China. *Crime & Justice International*, *20*(84), 29.
Mao, (August 1937). On contradiction. Retrieved on July 28, 2006 from http://www.marxists.org/reference/archive/mao/selected-works/volume-1/mswv1_17.htm
Moneyhon, M. (2002). Recent development: Controlling Xinjiang: autonomy on China's new frontier. *Asian-Pacific Law and Policy Journal, 3*(4).

—. (2003). China's great western development project in Xinjiang: Economic palliative, Or political Trojan horse? *Denver Journal of International Law and Policy, 31*, 491.

Ownby, D. (2001). Recent Chinese scholarship on the history of Chinese secret societies. *Late Imperial China, 22*(1), 139-158.

—. (1996). *Brotherhoods and secret societies in early Qing China: The formation of a tradition*. CA, Stanford: Stanford University Press.

Perkins, P. (1939). The failure of civil control in occupied China. *Pacific Affairs*, *12*(2), 149-156.

Perry, E. J. (1984). Collective violence in China, 1880-1980. *Theory and Society*, *13*(3), 427-454.

Perry, E. (1980) *Rebellion and revolution in North China, 1845-1945.* CA, Stanford: Stanford University Press.

Price Jr., H. E. (1977). The strategy and tactics of revolutionary Terrorism. *Comparative Studies in Society and History, 19*(1), 52 – 66.

Puett, M. (1998) Sages, ministers, and rebels: Narratives from early China concerning the initial creation of the state. *Harvard Journal of Asiatic Studies*, *58*(2), 425-479.

Mathias, R. M. (2002). The progress and failure of comparative law in the second half of the twentieth century. *American Journal of Comparative Law, 50*, 671, 689 - 690.

Robinson, D. M. (2000). Banditry and the subversion of state authority in China: The capital region during the middle Ming Period (1450-1525), *Journal of Social History, 33*(3), 527-563, 529.

Schmid, A. P., & Jongman, A. J. (1981). *Political Terrorism: A Research Guide to Concepts, Theories, Data Bases and Literature.* Amsterdam: Royal Netherlands Academy of Arts and Sciences Social Science Research Center (SWIDOC) and New York: Transaction Books.

Schram, S. R. (1966). Mao Tse-tung and secret societies. *The China Quarterly*, *27*, 1-13.

Tanner, M. S. (2004). China rethinks unrest. *The Washington Quarterly, 27*(3), 137-156.

Tao, A. L. (2002). Need to clearly recognize terrorism with Chinese Characteristic (Xuyao yingqing juyou Zhongguo tesi de gongbu zhuyi) Retrieved July 28, 2006 from http://www3.nbnet.nb.ca/stao/sles143.htm

Tao, J. S. (1970). The influence of Jurchen rule on Chinese political institutions. *The Journal of Asian Studies*, *30*(1), 121-130.

Thaxton, R. (1977). On peasant revolution and national resistance: Toward a theory of peasant mobilization and revolutionary war with special reference to modern China. *World Politics*, *30*(1), 24-57.

Tiedemann, G. R. (1982). The persistence of banditry: North China plain. *Modern China*, *8*(4), 395-433.

Tong, J. (1991). *Disorder under heaven: Collective violence in the Ming dynasty.* CA, Stanford: Stanford University Press.

Turner, K. (1993). War, punishment, and the law of nature in early Chinese concepts of the state. *Harvard Journal of Asiatic Studies, 53*(2), 285-324.

Unknown (n.d.). History of terrorism. Retrieved July 28, 2006 from http://www.terrorismfiles.org/encyclopaedia/history_of_terrorism.html

van der Valk, M. H. (1983). The revolution in Chinese legal thought. *Pacific Affairs*, *11*(1), 66-80.

Wakeman, Jr., F. (1992). American police advisers and the nationalist Chinese secret service, 1930-1937. *Modern China, 18*(2), 107-137.

—. (1977) Rebellion and revolution: The study of popular movements in Chinese history. *The Journal of Asian Studies*, *36* (2), 201-237.

Wall, J. & Blum, M. (1999). Community mediation in China. *The Journal of Conflict Resolution*, *35*(1), 3 – 20

Wang, J. Z. (2003). Eastern Turkistan Islamic Movement: A case study of a new terrorist organization in China. *International Journal of Offender Therapy and Comparative Criminology*, *47*(5), 568.

White House (2001). The global war on terrorism: The First 100 Days White House. Retrieved July 28, 2006 from http://www.whitehouse.gov/news/releases/2001/12/100dayreport.html

Wittfogel, K. (1970). *Oriental Despotism.*

Wong, K. C. (1998). Black's theory on the behavior of law revisited II: A restatement of Black's concept of law. *International Journal of the Sociology of Law, 26*(1), 75–119.

Wong, Y-T. (1977). Popular unrest and the 1911 Revolution in Jiangsu. *Modern China*, *3*(3),321-344.

Wright, A. F. (1953). Struggle vs. harmony: Symbols of competing values in modern China. *World Politics*, *6*(1), 31 – 44.

Zuigao Renmin Jianchayuan (1990). *Xingshifanzui Anli Conshu (Fangeminzui)* (Book on Criminal Cases) (Counter-revolutionary Crimes) Beijing: Zhongguo Jiancha Chubanshe.

# CHAPTER TWENTY EIGHT

# TERRORISM: TECHNOLOGY, RELIGION AND GLOBALIZATION

EMILIO C. VIANO

## Abstract

This chapter provides a comprehensive overview of the history and development of terrorism as it is understood at this time. It also strives to address why one can speak of a "new" terrorism today. In particular, it analyzes the impact that new technologies, globalization, worldwide news media, and religious fundamentalism have on new forms and expressions of terrorism. It also identifies new areas for research and work and in particular it covers the role that social scientists and criminologists can play in the analysis, investigation and prevention of terrorism.

## Introduction

Terrorism is definitely an interdisciplinary topic. To understand, address, combat and prevent it, it requires the insights and contributions of history, political science, social science, philosophy, religion, psychology, sociology, finance, strategic studies, international relations, criminal justice, crime prevention and control, public safety, warfare, counterterrorism theory and practice, anthropology, languages and cultural studies. History, the social sciences, political science, and psychology are especially useful in understanding the origins, reasons, justifications, motivations, and changes in the meaning and definition of terrorism. For example, recent times have seen the emergence of terrorism which is not ideological in a political sense. It is instead inspired by religious fundamentalism and ethnic-separatist elements. Terrorists may be loners like the Unabomber (*Theodore Kaczynski*) in the United States or people working in cells, small groups or bigger coalitions. They do not answer to and are not dependent on any government; they function across national borders; and they use advanced technology and receive funding practically anywhere in the world. Contemporary terrorists are not worried about limiting casualties. On the contrary, religious terrorists like Al-Qaeda prefer large numbers of casualties.

Current terrorism takes great advantage of ease and speed of travel, advanced communications, constantly improving technology, fast, silent and anonymous financial transactions, and scientific and technological breakthroughs that greatly facilitate its mission. Most of all, the "new" terrorism has a global dimension that would not have been possible just 30-40 years ago. There is no question that globalization has greatly facilitated the activities of terrorism while it is also one of its root causes along with religious extremism. Theories to explain the appearance, growth and expansion of terrorism need the input of diverse scholarly and scientific approaches to help us understand the complex matrix of social, cultural, economic, religious, psychological, political and strategic variables behind the phenomenon (Sharif, 1995; Ross, 1999).

The interest of the social sciences in terrorism dates back to the analysis by political sociologists of anarchism, revolutionary movements, and insurgencies. Sociologists focusing on social change have also dedicated considerable space to the topic. Marxist and leftist sociologists did address issues related to terrorism too but in the context of liberation movements. The analysis and development of the area expanded particularly in the 1970s spurred by the growth of the phenomenon in the Middle East, related especially to the Palestinian-Israeli conflict; in Europe, particularly in Germany, Spain, the United Kingdom (Northern Ireland), and Italy; and in various Latin American countries. In South America especially, theologians and other reformers involved in the liberation theology movement and the struggle for social and political change in the hemisphere also contributed to the field. Industrial society and its future work on the phenomenon was no doubt influenced and coloured by political currents like Marxism and other left-leaning approaches, which stressed themes related to the struggle of the oppressed against subjugation and exploitation by colonialism and capitalism. On the opposite side of the spectrum, the centre and centre-right perspectives emphasized instead the darker, criminal or anti-democratic side of terrorist activities. Sociology has provided the conceptual approaches, theories and tools to analyze, understand, and explain terrorism as a social phenomenon and to formulate remedial and preventative interventions.

The rich literature on crime, deviance and the administration of justice that expanded progressively in quantity, quality and insightfulness from the 1970s on, first in the United States and then in Europe and elsewhere, helped to stimulate interest in the phenomenon and provided the analytical tools and conceptual framework needed to approach the phenomenon. For instance, one can easily understand how differently terrorism is seen by conflict theory versus functionalism. Conflict theory sees it as an expression and manifestation of the struggle for power, control, and access to resources that universally characterize social life and as a reaction to exploitation and oppression by the subjugated in society who must resort to this type of stealthy and covert violence to compensate for the inequality in military and political power monopolized by the oppressors in control. Functionalism will instead underline how terrorism represents an aberration and a dysfunction in social life, a manifestation of a disease-like condition that can and must be cured or eliminated by a well planned intervention meant to eradicate it as a dysfunction and to restore order and a healthy condition.

## The History of Terrorism

Terrorism, in the most generally accepted use of the word, is basically and fundamentally political. It is also very much about power: pursuing power, acquiring power, and using power to cause political change. Consequently, terrorism is also violence or, just as importantly, the threat of violence utilized and aimed in the pursuit of or in the service of a political objective.

The word "terrorism" initially became popular during the French Revolution when it did have a pro-governmental, "positive" connotation. The "regime de la terreur" of 1793-94, from which the English word originates, was established as a means to impose and consolidate power during the transient anarchical time of disorder and unrest that followed the revolution of 1789, as it often happens after revolutions. Thus, instead of meaning an anti-government operation, like it does today, the regime de la terreur was actually a government tool used by the recently established revolutionary state. It was meant to consolidate and firm up the power of the new government by intimidating, terrifying and eliminating counter-revolutionaries, political opponents and any other dissidents that the new regime judged to be "enemies of the people."

The liberal use of the guillotine in a very public spectacle at Place de la Concorde in Paris and elsewhere throughout France sent a very powerful message to everyone who might even just think of opposing the revolution or wanted the return of the previous regime. At that time and quite ironically, terror was connected with the ideals of virtue and democracy. Robespierre, the main figure of this period of terror in France, asserted that virtue is the result of a popular government at peace but that at a time of revolution or unrest virtue must ally itself with terror in order for democracy to survive and overcome any threat. He expressed his approach in his famous statement: "Virtue, without which terror is evil; terror, without which virtue is helpless; terror is nothing but justice: prompt, severe and inflexible. Therefore it emanates from virtue."

Like modern terrorism, the French regime of terror was neither random nor indiscriminate. It was organized, deliberate and systematic. Secondly, its goal and main justification was the creation of a new and better society instead of the previous corrupt and undemocratic political system. The indiscriminate use of the guillotine by Robespierre and the perception that anyone was fair game finally moved the National Assembly's diverse currents to unify in rejecting him and his close collaborators and send them to the same fate: execution by beheading. At this point, terrorism became equated with abuse of office and power with "criminal" implications (Hoffman, 1998). Less than a year after the execution of Robespierre, the word "terrorism" was popularized in English by Edmund Burke in his polemic tract against the French revolution where he wrote about "thousands of those Hell hounds called Terrorists…. let loose on the people" (Hoffman, 1998, para. 14)

One of the major outcomes of the French revolution was the growing rejection of absolute monarchical systems that claimed to derive their authority directly from God and therefore to be entitled to a divine right to rule without constraints or limits. It did also inspire the overall political awakening of Europe. Independence and nationalist movements flourished and succeeded in creating modern nation states in some parts of Europe, like in the case of Germany and Italy. At the same time dramatic socio-economic changes were taking place as a consequence of massive industrialization, particularly in England and Germany. The alienation and exploitation of workers by 19th century capitalism provided the fertile ground for the sprouting and growing of new "universalist" ideologies. The most important ones are socialism and eventually communism.

During this period of intense change in Europe the concept of terrorism was expanded and elaborated on. For example, an Italian revolutionary, Carlo Pisacane, who forsook his nobility status to lead an ill-fated rebellion against the Bourbon monarchy in Southern Italy, developed the idea of "propaganda by deed" which has exerted considerable influence on revolutionaries, insurgents and terrorists ever since. Pisacane wrote that "The propaganda of the idea is an illusion. Ideas result from deeds, not the latter from the former. The people will not be free when they are educated. They will be educated when they are free." Pisacane argued that violence is needed not only to attract attention to the cause or to generate publicity but to inform, educate, and in the end get the masses behind the revolution. Pamphlets, wall posters or gatherings will never effectively substitute for the didactic value of violence.

One of the most notable groups to put Pisacane's theory into practice was probably the Narodnaya Volya (People's Will or, also, People's Freedom), a small group of Russian proponents of constitutional government in Russia started in 1878 to limit the unconstrained power of the tsar. Because the Russian impoverished and illiterate masses were apathetic, fearful and alienated, the group resorted to spectacular violent acts to attract attention to its cause and to demonstrate that the tsarist government was not invulnerable and omnipotent. Narodnaya Volya refined the "propaganda by deed" approach by avoiding mass casualties and focusing instead on specific targets selected for their special association and support of the tyrannical and corrupt tsarist regime and for their symbolic value like the tsar himself, principal members of the royal family, and senior government officials. At times, well prepared attacks on the royals were on purpose not carried out in order to adhere to the principle that "not one drop of superfluous blood" should be spilled. Ironically, the success of the group in assassinating tsar Alexander II on March 1, 1881 led to its complete suppression. One of the conspirators who failed in his attempt and was captured gave the government ample information on the leadership, plotters and safe houses of Narodnaya Volya. Arrests, quick convictions, and sentences of death or imprisonment in Siberia, promptly carried out, eliminated the organization.

The message of Pisacane and of Narodnaya Volya deeply impacted the growing anarchist movement. An anarchist conference in London in 1881 endorsed the killing of the tsar and supported the idea of tyrannicide as a means for achieving revolutionary change. At that conference, an "Anarchist International" or "Black International" was also established, at least on paper. This, real or not, spurred the growth of the mythology of a global revolution in the offing and of related fears and suspicions. Following the assassination of President McKinley in 1901 by a young Hungarian refugee, the U.S. Congress quickly approved legislation barring anyone who did not believe in or rejected organized government from entering the country. From 1887 until the end of the 1920s anarchists succeeded in a series of political assassinations and several well-publicized bombings but had little impact on the domestic or international politics of the countries involved. Well ahead of today's "information revolution," the anarchists made widely available manuals of "how to" or "do it yourself" bombs and other violent acts.

During the last two decades of the 1800s, increasing unrest and liberation movements troubled the decaying Ottoman (Istanbul) and Hapsburg (Vienna) empires. Notably, the Armenians undertook a violent campaign against the Ottoman empire in eastern Turkey. Their goal was to eliminate Ottoman rule on their nation, publicize their cause, and attract sympathy and support. Unfortunately, their quest for freedom and autonomy brought upon them the first recognized holocaust of the 20$^{th}$ century. An estimated one million Armenians were slaughtered by Turkey. At the same time, in what are today Greece, Bulgaria and Serbia, the Inner Macedonian Revolutionary Organization also tried to win independence from the Ottomans. The Macedonians did not succeed in obtaining their independence at that time and their revolutionary organization eventually degenerated into an organized crime group composed of thugs and political assassins.

A similar movement in Bosnia made up mostly of young Bosnian Serbs, "Mlada Bosnia" or "Young Bosnia," was very committed to the establishment of a Southern Slav political entity and approved of assassination as a tool to achieve its objective. This eventually led to the assassination of Archduke Franz Ferdinand on June 28, 1914 and eventually to the outbreak of World War I. The Young Bosnians' activities and assassination plots were supported by other underground Serbian nationalist organizations. Among them was the pan-Serbian nationalist "Narodna Obrana" ("People's Defense or National Defense"), eventually also called the "Black Hand," with close ties to the Serbian military and government. There is still debate and controversy over the exact role of the Serbian military and government in manipulating, training and supplying the Young Bosnians, including the Archduke's killer, and then over their belated attempt to stop the Archduke's assassination. Regardless, one can consider this an early and prime example of "state sponsored" terrorism.

By the 1930s "terrorism" did not mean so much revolutionary movements and violence against governments or empires but rather the politics and practices of mass oppression and repression utilized by dictatorships and their leaders against their own citizenry. In other words, it meant again, like at the end of the terror regime in France, governmental abuse of power as it was taking place especially in Nazi Germany, Fascist Italy and the Stalinist Soviet Union. Mussolini in Italy and Hitler in Germany did reach power depending in great part on "the street," that is on gangs of black or brown-shirted supporters, often thugs, that were free to harass, beat and discourage any opponent or dissident and expose them and other scapegoats to public condemnation and victimization. This type of "terror" became an integral part of Fascist and Nazi governance, carried out at the whim of and in total obedience to the ruling party which claimed for itself absolute control and domination of the country and its people. Total compliance was guaranteed through various violent measures including fear, coercion, political violence, street attacks, and the widespread persecution of Jews, Gypsies, homosexuals, and religious figures and others who protested.

At the head of the Soviet Union, Stalin learned from Hitler how to transform a political party, the Communist Party, into an instrument totally submitted to his will and the state's law enforcement, military and intelligence agencies into servile tools of repression, coercion and oppression. Unlike Germany, Italy and other countries (e.g., Spain), Stalin did not have to brawl his way to the top. In the 1930s the Communist Party was firmly in control in the Soviet Union. Thus, Stalin's repressive purges, mass exiles, mass forced labour, mass transportation to Siberia and gulags were planned and viciously carried out as a progressive conspiracy to seize total power and completely silence any dissent through state terrorism.

There is no question that similar forms of state-planned, imposed or directed violence have taken place and are still taking place in various parts of the world. It has been a well known aspect of right of centre military dictatorships in Latin America, Europe, Asia and Africa, especially in Chile, Argentina (Buchanan, 1987; Cox, 1983), Brasil in South America; Greece, Spain and Portugal in Europe; various African countries; and The Philippines, Indonesia, Burma and Pakistan in Asia. It has even affected elected governments in the 1980s in, for instance, El Salvador, Guatemala, Nicaragua, Colombia and Peru and today, Zimbabwe, Uzbekistan, Egypt and others in the Middle East. The Cultural Revolution in the People's Republic of China in the 1960s under Chairman Mao is an example of state terrorism on the left. The use of violence and intimidation by those already in power against their own people is generally called "terror" to distinguish it from "terrorism" which is violence carried out by non-state entities (Moxon-Browne, 1994).

The meaning of terrorism changed once more after World War II. It reclaimed the revolutionary reputation with which it is associated today. At that time, in the late 1940s, 1950s and even 1960s, it was connected with the uprisings by indigenous populations in various parts of the world -- Africa, Asia, the Middle East -- to expel European colonial powers from their countries. At times they involved long guerrilla wars or terrorism. Well known examples are Algeria, Cyprus, Israel, Kenya and Vietnam. Many nationalistic rebellions took the form of guerrilla war. The

Cuban revolution of 1956 became a model for left-wing ideologues as a struggle against capitalist powers. Thus, while it did not create guerrilla warfare, it popularized it throughout the world. What the ideologues did was to move beyond the structure of the guerrilla war and create an underpinning theory. While guerrilla war became and still is the preferred method of fighting for revolution in Latin America, only the Sandinistas, among guerrilla movements, succeeded in overthrowing the established government in Nicaragua in 1979.

Because these movements were perceived internationally as a struggle for liberation, de-colonization and self-determination, thanks in part to adroit public relations campaigns by the insurgents and their supporters in the First World, the term "freedom fighter" became increasingly used to describe them. This was also part of the Cold War's psychological and political warfare between the Soviet Union and its supporters, which praised the insurgents fighting against capitalism, and the United States and Western European countries which resisted them, for instance in The Philippines and Puerto Rico in the case of the United States. Thus, for example, the United States in the 1980s called the guerrillas in El Salvador, Guatemala and Honduras "terrorists" because of their leftwing leanings and invested considerable military and counter-insurgency resources to defeat them. At the same time, it considered the Mujahedins fighting the Soviet occupation in Afghanistan "freedom fighters" and provided them with ample assistance, training and arms. Several Third World and communist-block countries used this way of describing insurgency and rebellion, stating that any armed struggle against Western colonialism was not terrorism but fighting for freedom. This view was possibly most famously expounded by the chairman of the Palestine Liberation Organization (PLO), *Yasser Arafat*, when he spoke before the United Nations General Assembly in 1974. He stated that the main difference between the revolutionary and the terrorist is to be found in the reason why each fights. "For whoever stands by a just cause and fights for the freedom and liberation of his land from the invaders, the settlers, and the colonists, cannot possibly be called terrorist" (Arafat, 1974, para. 48).

At the end of the 1960s and in the 1970s, terrorism was still viewed within a revolutionary framework even though it expanded to encompass nationalist and ethnic separatist groups beyond a colonial or neo-colonial context and also radical and ideologically driven organizations. In particular, ethnic minorities seeking independence or autonomy used terrorism, and still do in some cases, not only to inflict casualties and serious damage to the dominant group but also to attract international attention, sympathy and aid. Among them were, and still are in some cases, the Palestinian Liberation Organization (PLO), the Quebec, Canada's separatist group Front de Libération du Québec (Front for the Liberation of Quebec, FLQ), the Basque ETA (Euskadi ta Askatasuna or Freedom for the Basque Homeland), a South Moluccan group seeking independence from Indonesia and striking out in The Netherlands, the PKK (Kurdistan Workers' Party) (Criss, 1995), the Irish Republican Army (IRA) which renounced the armed struggle in 2005 (Bell, 1996) and others. The American intervention in Vietnam and the perception that there were congenital social and economic disparities in the modern, capitalistic, and liberal state justified the evolution of several left-wing political extremist groups, like radical student organizations and various Marxist, Leninist or Maoist movements in Europe, the United States and Latin America, into terrorist entities. The late 1960s saw major student's upheavals in Western Europe and the United States that had in some case terrorist overtones and rhetoric (Wilkinson, 1994).

Recently, the term "terrorism" has been utilized to describe broader, less narrow phenomena. In the early 1980s, terrorism was considered a planned and calculated strategy to destabilize the Western world as part of a vast global conspiracy. Claire Sterling (1986) in her book *The Terror Network* described apparently isolated terrorist events committed by different groups around the globe as in reality connected elements of a massive secret plan, supervised by the Soviet Union and implemented by its Warsaw Pact client countries, to annihilate the free world. The attempt on the life of Pope John Paul II that severely wounded him was seen as part of this master plan. It was committed by a Turk as the reported proxy of the Bulgarian secret service acting on instructions by Moscow. The Cold War atmosphere at the time made this theory very appealing, particularly to receptive American and some European governments.

The communist conspiracy was eventually overshadowed in the mid-1980s when a series of suicide bombings aimed mostly at American diplomatic and military targets in the Middle East abruptly called attention to the growing menace of state-sponsored terrorism. Several renegade foreign governments like Iran, Iraq, Libya and Syria were suspected and accused of being actively involved in sponsoring or commissioning terrorist acts. The major episodes of this state-sponsored or supported terror during the 1980s were the bombings of the Marines barracks in Lebanon in 1983 attributed to Hizbollah ("The Party of God", also "Islamic Jihad") supported by Iran and Syria and of the Pan American flight 103 over Scotland on December 21, 1988 in which 250 passengers and crew, mostly Americans, were killed. In 1991 two Libyan agents were charged with the killing and the government of Colonel al-Qaddafi was widely believed to have been involved. Sanctions were imposed by the United Nations on Libya in 1992. The sanctions were suspended in 1999 when Libya handed over the suspects for trial. A Scottish court that actually met in The Netherlands convicted one of the accused and acquitted the other. The sanctions were lifted in 2003 after Libya took responsibility for the bombing and agreed to a $2.7 billion settlement that also included compensation for the bombing of a French UTA (Union des Transports Aériens) airplane over Niger in 1989.

In the early 1990s, the meaning and use of the term "terrorism" were once more twisted by the appearance of two new expressions: narco-terrorism and the "grey area phenomenon." Narco-terrorism was initially linked to an overall communist and Soviet plot to sabotage Western society. It presumably involved the use of drug trafficking to support and implement the objectives of certain governments and terrorist organizations like the Soviet Union, Cuba, Bulgaria, and Nicaragua, among others. The emphasis on this supposed type of narco-terrorism diverted attention from a truly emerging trend: the alliance of completely criminal, violent and economically driven organizations with terrorist and guerrilla entities using violence not only for the advancement of their business activities but also for specifically political ends. One of the best known examples of this was the growing power and influence of the Colombian cocaine cartels with their close alliance with left-wing terrorist groups in Colombia and Peru and their repeated efforts to undermine Colombia's elections and the governments of that country. The CIA was also alleged to have engaged in some form of drug trafficking mostly directed at minority communities in Southern California to finance arms deals for the "freedom fighters" it supported against the Sandinista regime in Nicaragua (Brown & Merrill, 1995).

In the 1990s terrorism was also placed by some analysts into the "grey area phenomenon," possibly stressing the difficulty to clearly pinpoint where terrorism is and what it is. Basically, this approach reflects the growing fluidity and chameleon-like changeability of sub-national conflict in the post-Cold War era. Terrorism in this sense represents threats to the stability of nation states by non-state actors and violence impacting large regions of the world or major urban areas where the central government has lost its influence and control to new half-political, half-criminal groups. It also covers different types of conflicts that do not fit well into traditionally recognized concepts of war as the fighting between clearly marked armed forces of two or more recognized countries. It involves instead irregular forces as one or more of the combatants. The shift here is clearly towards non-state conflict. Consequently, one could say that terrorism is simply a manifestation of violence in a particular time period and thus it evolves and manifests itself in different ways. In a sense, terrorism is always changing and new (Yonah & Latter, 1990). It must be kept in mind that terrorism also existed and thrived in Europe and in North America. In the United States in particular, the most notorious example is the Oklahoma City bombing carried out in 1995 by people following a strong rightwing ideology (Baumel, 1999; Smith, 1994; Stern, 1996; Walter, 1995; Corcoran, 1995; Coates, 1987).

## The New Terrorism

The United States and the world, particularly the Western world, were awakened to the existence of a new form of terrorism based in the Middle East by a series of events that ultimately culminated in the September 11, 2001 catastrophic attacks in New York and Washington D.C. Since then the names of Osama Bin-Laden and Al-Qaeda have become universally known and immediately connected with a violent struggle against the United States and Western interests based in the Middle East but with an international reach and a strong religious dimension (Stern, 2002).

The "new" terrorism has greater potential to cause damage to the United States, the West, and many other countries, including some in the Muslim world. The dangerousness of the new terrorism stems in particular from its being built around loosely linked cells that do not depend on a single leader or state sponsor. It is transnational, borderless, and carried out by non-state actors. If one were to compare the "new" and the "old" terrorism, one would emphasize the following differences:

- The new terrorism is more violent. In the old model, terrorists wanted mostly attention, not mass casualties. Presently, they want both.
- The most dangerous terrorists today are transnational non-state actors who operate at the global level and want to inflict damage and even destroy not just the West but all secular state systems, including the Islamic ones.

Previous terrorist organizations had mostly local agendas and aspirations. Today's terrorism is global in reach and has strategic objectives. Its members are transnational, non-state actors whose allegiance goes to a cause, not a particular state or political entity. This presents considerable challenges to governments attempting to respond and combat terrorism. In the diplomatic, economic and military areas they operate on state to state level and have difficulty effectively addressing a challenge posed by a non-state actor. A state reacting to a real or perceived threat wants to know whom to threaten with force, whom to negotiate with, and whom to sanction. The new terrorism makes this practically impossible.

The new terrorism is much better financed than its predecessors who depended mostly on the respective state sponsor to fund their activities. Contemporary terrorists can access income generated from legal and illegal sources and are not accountable to state sponsors or others. Al Qaeda for example is often mentioned as a rich, multinational organization with many sources of income. Reportedly, it has investments and secret accounts worldwide, several in Western countries. This wealth can be used to buy entry and safe haven in certain countries; to subcontract certain missions to local organizations that know best the terrain; and to compensate the families of terrorists killed in action.

Contemporary terrorists are much better trained in the conduct of war than those in the past who often were amateurs using home-made explosives and old weapons. Many terrorist operatives are reputed to be well trained in military, special operations and intelligence functions.

Current terrorists are more impenetrable than previous groups. The loose, but networked, cellular structure of Al Qaeda and similar terrorist organizations of today are especially hard to penetrate, particularly for bureaucratic and hierarchical security organizations like those of the United States and other Western countries. In particular, Western intelligence's reliance on technical means of intelligence collection and relative neglect of intelligence gathering by on-the-ground human agents make it quite difficult to identify, locate, and infiltrate this type of cell-like decentralized organization. It is normally composed by many cells whose members are unknown to one another, have never met in one place together, and utilize strict communication discipline. Religious and highly motivated extremists are also difficult to entrap using money, entertainment and sex. They cannot be so easily bought, bribed or blackmailed. The large reward offered by the United States for the capture of Osama Bin Laden is to date still uncollected. This demonstrates the special challenges that Western intelligence is faced with in trying to address the threat posed by contemporary terrorist organizations with a religious component.

The reputed availability of weapons of mass destruction greatly raised the bar on the threat posed by today's terrorists and the potential damage that they can inflict. In the past the major concern was about small arms; explosives, particularly Semtex or plastique; rocket-propelled grenades; and once in a while, the shoulder-fired anti-aircraft missile. While these weapons continue to be used, these days a major concern is about nuclear, radiological, chemical and biological weapons, all potentially catastrophic. Reportedly, covert suppliers of these weapons of mass destruction (WMD) are numerous, originating mostly from Russia and Eastern European countries once under the control of the Soviet Union (Gavel, 2002).

## Terrorism and New Technologies

Significant changes in the terrorists' methods include the utilization of new technologies, the deployment of terrorists across international frontiers, and changes in the origins of support. Information technologies used by terrorists include the internet, cellular phones, instant messaging and real time photographic and filming capabilities. This has amplified the global reach of several terrorist organizations. To date, however, there has not yet been a major cyber-terrorist attack. However, hacking has been utilized. Internet sites have been under attack; websites have been hijacked or defaced; there have been cases of denial of service, automated email bombings, and also web sit-ins. Management and administrative functions of terrorist organizations; coordinating operations; recruiting possible members; improving communications between members; attracting people sympathetic to the cause; collecting, managing and transferring funds; and spreading the group's message and philosophy have been greatly facilitated by the impressive technological advances in global information. There is no doubt that this has facilitated the tasks of the terrorists and allowed them to greatly expand the range and speed of their activities. In particular the synchronization of terrorist attacks, like those of September 11, 2001 and those on various U.S. embassies in East Africa in 1998, was made possible by contemporary information technology.

Different groups like *Aum Shinrikyo*, the Popular Front for the Liberation of Palestine, Israel's *Kahane Chai*, Peru's Shining Path, the Kurdistan's Workers Party and others all operate and maintain user-friendly website, often also in English or with English sections. The internet is very beneficial to terrorist groups just like it is to legitimate groups, trade, and commerce. Methods utilized through the internet are sending encrypted messages, embedding invisible graphic codes using steganography (Denning, 2001), sending death threats through the internet, and hiring hackers to gather intelligence and penetrate websites and servers.

Globalization and the establishment of regional trading zones like the European Union, Mercosur, NAFTA and others have made it easier for terrorists to expand their activities internationally across borders that often today do not exist any more in an operational sense. Thus, it is not only legitimate commerce and trade that gain from the abolition of border controls. Criminals, organized crime, drug trafficking and terrorists also see their work made easier and their movements less easily detected. This has facilitated the territorial expansion of terrorist groups, the establishment of cells abroad, free movement across vast regions of the world in the planning and execution of terrorist activities. It has also been easier for terrorists to avoid detection, being stopped or captured. If they are arrested, the international nature of their activities also complicates their prosecution because of the complexities of extradition treaties and procedures.

Thanks to technological innovations and easing of financial operations worldwide, terrorists are also expanding their net in assembling financial resources to fund their operations. While Al-Qaeda is reputed to be one of the best financed terrorist networks, the number of groups supported by global financing networks is large. It is reported that *Aum Shinrikyo*, Hamas, Hezbollah, the IRA (O'Day, 1994), the Tamil Tigers and others benefit from a vast network of funding sources. These sources may include legal enterprises like non-profit and charitable organizations whose illegal activities may constitute only a small percentage of overall fund-raising activities and which may be unknown to donors; legal companies, like Bin Laden's group of construction companies, diverting legal funds to illegal activities; and illegal enterprises like drug production, trafficking, and smuggling; bank robberies, fraud, kidnappings, extortion. Websites have also been used to raise funds (CSIS, 1998).

The smooth movement of terrorists' financial resources is illustrated, for example, by the reported movement of gold and U.S. currency across the border between Afghanistan and Pakistan as U.S. and allied military forces were rooting out the Taliban. Once the gold and currency arrived in Pakistan, they were swiftly transferred to the informal *hawala* or *hundi* banking system to other Middle Eastern countries. There it was converted into gold bullion and dispersed around the world. Additionally, terrorist funds have been converted into other prized commodities like diamonds in Sierra Leone and the Congo, and tanzanite in Tanzania. In general terrorist groups, whose assets may be a small fraction of the total amount of funds moved daily by organized transnational crime groups, use a variety of vehicles for the transfer of money, from couriers transporting money to using traditional banks, Islamic banks, money changing enterprises, and informal exchanges like the *hawala* or *hundi* systems.

In conclusion, terrorist groups are able to use the same ways of communication, coordination, and cooperation as other international organizations like states, multinationals, non-governmental organizations, and individuals. There is no question that what is good for international commerce and communications is also good for international terrorism (White, 2002).

## Terrorism in the Contemporary World Scene

Samuel Huntington (1996) outlined a theory of conflict for the 21st century. He states that different historical periods have been dominated by particular types of conflict. After the collapse of the Soviet Union in 1991, the United States is the world's only superpower. The struggles that may threaten world peace will no longer focus on nationalism or ideology. Most conflicts will be the result of volatile regions where cultural confrontations threaten to spread violence and one of the major factors defining culture is religion. In Huntington's opinion, international peace will be especially threatened in "torn countries," where more than one civilization exists within a single area. The Balkans, where violent ethnic and religious strife and ethnic cleansing took place in the 1990s, is a classic example of Huntington's thesis which stresses the links between religion and terrorism. Each culture or civilization has its religious zealots that try to impose their values and views on everyone else. Each religion has its literal believers who have deeply absorbed its symbols and myths and linked them to ethnic and nationalistic aims.

According to Huntington's thesis, terrorism is emerging and will probably continue to find supporters among violent, true believers in areas of conflict. The implications for the United States are clear: first, it will be targeted by religious zealots from different cultural backgrounds because they believe that the United States has wrongly intervened in their societies and has violated their religious norms. Western Europe and Japan will be targeted as well. Second, since the United States routinely welcomes immigrants from all types of civilizations, there is within it a growing potential for religious strife. While the United States is not a "torn" country, it does provide a battleground for zealots of different religions who want to change or punish America with violence and for right wing extremists who violently object to the increasing diversity of the country and forcefully oppose those who tolerate it and the government that makes it possible. The 1995 Oklahoma City bombing is a clear example of the latter. Religious terrorism and violent extremism will persist as problems for America and Western-style countries both at home and abroad.

Experts like Bruce Hoffman (1998) and Walter Laqueur (1996, 1997, 1998) state that we are not only witnessing a strong resurgence and expansion of terrorist groups motivated by religion but that the situation is made much more dangerous by the fact that religious terrorists behave differently than ethnic and nationalistic terrorists. The reason is that they are not constrained by the same factors that may inhibit other types of terrorists. In Hoffman's view, religious terrorists differ from political terrorists in many ways. "Holy terror" represents a value system that is opposite to "secular terror." Secular terrorists function within the dominant political and cultural reality. After all, they want to win, to defeat the political system that is oppressing them. While they may want to destroy a certain political structure, they also want to replace it with their own. Religious or "holy" terrorists are under no such constraint. For them the world is a battlefield between the forces of good and evil, light and darkness. Winning is not understood in political terms. The enemy must be completely destroyed. For political terrorists, killing is the outcome of an operation. For holy terrorists, killing is a sacramental act. Killing is the goal of their operation. For Islamic terrorism, for example, the purpose of terrorism is to kill the enemies of God or to convert them to Islam (Rapoport, 1989).

No doubt, most Islamic theologians and believers would strongly disagree with such statements and be offended by the use of the expression "Islamic terror." However, what it is being referred to here are fundamentalist and violent extremists that can exist in any religion. They change a religion based on peace and justice into one of intolerance and hatred. Violent extremism can be Islamic, Jewish, Christian or other religions' terrorism (Sargent, 1994). The last three decades of the 20$^{th}$ century saw for example the formation of the Sikh Dal Khalsa and the Dashmesh organizations in the Punjab region of India, in 1978 and 1982 respectively; the emergence of the Shiite Hezbollah in Lebanon with Iranian patronage; the beginnings of militant Sunni organizations like Hamas and Islamic Jihad linked to the start of the Palestinian intifada in 1987; and of Aum Shinrikyo in Japan the same year.

## Terrorism and Globalization

The root causes of the appearance and growth of religious terrorism can be found in the accelerated disappearance of traditional forms of social and cultural cohesion within and between societies under the apparently unstoppable impact of globalization, along with the historical legacy and current reality of political repression, economic disparities and social change in today's world. This has heightened and deepened the sense of fragility, instability and unpredictability that many feel for different reasons in various parts of the world. Presently, the scale, amount and intensity of religious terrorism, rather unprecedented in militancy and activity, indicate the depth of perception that those particular faiths and the communities linked to them stand at a critical survival juncture and that extreme measures must be taken to ensure that they continue existing.

The perceived corruption of indigenous customs, religions, languages, economies, entertainment and so on are blamed on an international system that is frequently associated with American culture and values. The resulting distortions in local communities that result from being exposed to the global marketplace of ideas, goods and values are more frequently blamed on the U.S. led modernization. Christopher Coker (2002) aptly observes that while globalization is reducing the propensity for instrumental violence, that is violence between states and communities, it is increasing the incentives for expressive violence that is violence that is ritualistic, symbolic and communicative. The current international terrorism is more and more frequently rooted in a deeply felt need to assert identity or meaning against the advancing forces of homogeneity, particularly on the part of those cultures that are threatened by or are left behind by the secular atmosphere created by Western-led globalization.

According to a report published by the United Nations Development Program, one of the regions with the biggest deficit in terms of human development – the Arab world – is also the epicentre of the world's most menacing religiously driven terrorism. There is substantial political discontent in the disenfranchised areas of the region of the world that feel bypassed by the promises of globalization, particularly greater freedom, economic prosperity, and access to education, training and knowledge. As a result there are dashed expectations, increasing resentment of the hegemonic and often corrupt governments often supported by the United States, and a desire to strike at the overpowering forces of modernization and globalization. There is also a desire to change the course of U.S. policy in the Middle East and Persian Gulf, particularly as it impacts the Israel-Palestinian conflict. Given the enormous military power of the United States, the preferred course of action is not direct confrontation but rather the asymmetrical response that is terrorism.

The United States is a preferred target first of all because of its involvement in the politics and conflicts of various regions of the world and secondly because it is perceived to be the primary moving force behind globalization. Thus, today it is not possible to analyze terrorism without taking into consideration globalization. Both are tightly interwoven forces that impact and characterize global security in the 21st century. The main concern is whether or not terrorism will be able to disrupt the promise of a better life for millions of people. Globalization is not an inevitable, linear development that cannot be stopped. Terrorism could severely disrupt it. At the same time terrorism derives substantial benefits and its operations are greatly facilitated by the very globalization against which it fights.

Thus one could say that terrorism is a by-product of larger historical shifts in the worldwide distribution of all types of power, economic, military, political, ideological and cultural. At the same time, this power in all its different forms is also the leading force behind globalization. It is understandable that during times of major upheaval and change, those in particular who are not benefiting from the various changes and find them alien and threatening will look for alternative ways to understand and control their environments. Assuming that current trends will continue, global disparities and inequalities will continue to grow and so will the availability of information and capability to quickly connect through the world. Thus we can anticipate that the reasons for and the sources of terrorism will not only continue to exist but will grow and expand. At the same time terrorists will have continued access to more powerful technologies, more territory, more targets, more ways to recruit members, and more exploitable sources of discontent and rage than before. Thus, the current threat posed by terrorism is the product of the collision of different elements: maximum Western power, particularly that of the United States; globalization, driven mostly by Western interests; and the fundamentalist reaction to these trends impacting centuries-old ways of life in different parts of the world (Barber, 1991).

A serious problem is that the response of the West to terrorism is inadequate, superficial, and unlikely to dampen or mitigate any of the long term trends already mentioned above. The benign intentions of the mostly and increasingly secular West do not necessarily appear benign at all to those who are marginalized by globalization. To frustrated people in the Arab and Muslim world, and elsewhere as well, the strict following of fundamentalist religious doctrines and practices may appear to be a rational response to the perceived when their own governments are offering no alternative solution or approach. This is not meant to justify the terrorists' actions. However, it underlines the reality that small groups of dedicated terrorists could not survive and operate for a long time without the widespread support of the larger population or at least its threat posed by Western secular forces through globalization, particularly passive acceptance. It is at this level of operation that possibly effective interventions by the West should begin and focus. It is the broader, enabling environment that must be studied and addressed and not just the specific terrorist movement and its cells (Kupperman, 1979, 1984).

Terrorism is a complicated phenomenon. While at times short-term military action may be necessary and useful, it is also necessary to study it through an in-depth, long-term, high-level analysis. Moreover panoply of long-term policy instruments should be used to change the international environment that makes it possible for terrorist networks to be born and rapidly grow into formidable organizations (Howard, 2002). There is no question that the more effective policy tools are probably the non-military ones like intelligence, public diplomacy, strengthened cooperation with allies, up-to-date international conventions and treaties, political reform leading to genuine democratization and the uprooting of corrupt and uncaring regimes, and economic assistance (Burton, 1976; Campbell, 1997; Cobban, 1984).

## Secular, Religious and Fundamentalist Terrorism

Religious terrorism takes theological issues out of context and twists them to justify the violence and the terror. Precisely because they take actions out of context, religious terrorists are not subject to social limitations on violence. Therefore, they kill indiscriminately, feeling justified because they are killing the enemies of their deity. Religious beliefs are a very useful, powerful and ready-made source for justifying terrorism because it can sanctify the terrorist and deify the terrorism. To be "deified" means that the act of terrorism itself is made sacred and holy. The religious terrorists are no longer working only for mortals. They are on a mission from God (Kibble, 1996).

There is another difference between secular and religious terrorists. Political terrorism is also theatre aimed at influencing a wider audience to spread a message and obtain support. Thus, targets must be carefully chosen and there are some limits to what one can do. On the other hand, religious terrorists are working only for their god. Thus, they need no wider audience or social approval and have no reason to constrain themselves. Juergensmeyer (1992, 1999) describes the conditions that must exist for terrorists to reach these conclusions. Believers must identify with a god and believe that they are participating in a struggle to change the course of history and achieve a new relationship between good and evil. They demonize the enemy linking it to ultimate evil. When they think that the struggle has reached a critical stage, violence may be approved and terrorism may result. The right combination of these elements and beliefs can produce a fanatical terrorist.

In general a "normal" religious person will feel justified and righteous when acting in the name of the deity. This is so whether the cause is love or war and it is not limited to socially illegitimate forms of violence. True-believing terrorists actually mimic and exaggerate mainstream social patterns and beliefs. They use the established, social paths and models of religion and ideology to justify their actions (Pearlestein, 1992; Oliverio, 2001).

Fundamentalist terrorism in the 21st century is perceived as being based mostly in the Middle East and/or in Islamic countries. The roots of Middle Eastern terrorism are complex but can be reduced to four major areas: questions on the political control of Palestine or the Israeli-Palestinian conflict (Nusse, 2000); on who should rule the Arab world or intra-Arab rivalries and struggles; on the relations between the two main branches of Islam, Sunnis and Shiites; and on how to eliminate and expel Western colonialism and imperialism and create again a pan-Arab "Caliphate" or realm of Islam. Terrorism originating in this area is especially driven by anti-Western feelings because of the historical colonial domination and exploitation of the region. France and especially Great Britain dominated the region or attempted to for centuries. The Soviet Union also made forays attempting to gain a warm water port and counteract the other two colonial countries' influence. The United States has also played an increasingly dominant role in the region linked to the exploitation of its energy resources and at times in direct or indirect confrontation with the other Western colonial powers and the Soviets. The rejection of Western presence and influence is connected with the colonial experience and also with the deeply held feeling that this entire region should be an exclusive Islamic realm. The presence of American troops in Saudi Arabia or elsewhere in the region has been perceived as not only an indication of colonial ambitions but also as sacrilegious, a modern version of the medieval crusades. The ideology of Al Qaeda and of other groups inspired or associated with it stresses both themes – anti-colonialism or "anti-crusaders" and the reestablishment of the "Caliphate" - as a justification for their terrorist activities (Gurr, 1993; Hoffman, 1998; Howard, 2001, 2002; Johnson, 1997).

## Terrorism, Guerrilla and Crime

Terrorism is commonly confused or equated with guerrilla activities. This is because guerrilla frequently employ the same techniques –

assassinations, kidnapping, bombing of public places, hostage taking – for the same reasons as the terrorists would, to intimidate or coerce, thus impacting behaviour through fear. Additionally, both are frequently undistinguishable from non-combatants. However, there are considerable differences between the two groups. Firstly, guerrilla generally refers to a numerically larger group of individuals who act as a military unit, attack military forces or the police, seize and hold territory, if only for a few hours, and at the same time control a defined geographical area and its population.

Terrorists are also frequently confused or equated with common violent criminals. While it is true that criminals, like terrorists, utilize violence to achieve a specific goal and while the violent acts themselves may be similar (e.g., kidnapping, shooting, arson), the purpose or motive are not. The criminal is driven first and foremost by personal greed and the desire for personal gain and does not necessarily intend for his act to have long lasting consequences or to cause psychological repercussions beyond the act itself. While the use of violence by the criminal does often terrorize the victim, it is meant to force and ensure quick compliance with his demands, rather than to make a political statement. Most importantly, the criminal is not attempting to influence or impact public opinion; s/he just wants to get the money or the goods and escape detection and arrest (Turvey et al., 1999).

On the contrary, the terrorist's basic aim is to ultimately subvert and change the system, something that the violent criminal is not interested in. The terrorist is fundamentally an altruist and believes that he is serving a good cause with the goal of achieving a greater good for a larger number of people that he and his group claim to represent. It is important here to note that identifying with a cause is not sufficient to make someone a terrorist. One can be an extremist but not a terrorist, unless and until he acts violently. The terrorist is basically a violent intellectual ready and committed to use force in the realization of his goals (Perdue, 1988).

The terrorist is also different from the lone assassin whose goal is often quite personal and egocentric. John Hinckley, who tried to kill and did wound President Ronald Reagan, was trying to impress the actress Jodie Foster. There was no political motivation or ideology behind his actions. His was purely a personal quest. Also, one person cannot claim to constitute a terrorist group. Thus, while Sirhan did assassinate Senator Robert Kennedy to protest the United States' Middle East policy favouring Israel against the Palestinians, he acted on his own and did not belong to any organized group.

Terrorism is definitely political in its objectives and motives; violent or threatening violence; meant to have wide and deep psychological repercussions beyond the particular victim or target; committed by an organization with a command hierarchy that can be identified or a cell configuration that permits conspiratorial activities; and carried out by a sub-national group or non-state body. Thus, terrorism can be defined as the deliberate generation, instillation and exploitation of fear into a competing group, or party or government or public opinion through violence or the threat of violence with the goal of introducing political change (Noble, 1999).

## The Definition of Terrorism

The statutory definition that the United States government uses to track and keep statistics on terrorism is: "premeditated, politically motivated violence perpetrated against non-combatant targets by sub national groups or clandestine agents, usually intended to influence an audience" [22 U.S.C. 2656f (d)].

By this definition, terrorism has several elements:

- Premeditation. There must be an intent and a prior decision to commit an act that entails this type of violence.
- Political motivation, thus eliminating criminal violence for monetary gain or personal revenge. Of course criminal violence can have political repercussions as it generates more and more fear of crime. And, on the other hand, terror is often connected with criminal activities but its goal is serving a greater good.
- Attacking people who cannot defend themselves or respond in kind.
- Planned and carried out by a group. There is debate whether or not there can be a case of "individual" terrorism. The place and the role of clandestine agents and sub national groups is a delicate issue because at times governments, including the United States, have utilized both. This has sometimes meant the use of force which has generated civilian casualties.

Another area of criticism of the definition is that it does not include the threat of violence which some consider terrorism as well. The blurriness of the definitional lines reminds us that terrorism is only one form of behaviour along a continuum of possible political behaviours of people who strongly oppose their political situation and conditions and want to change them.

When debating definitions, it is essential to remember that terrorism is first and foremost a method rather than a group of enemies or the objectives they want to realize; and that it is cantered on what people do rather than who they are and what they are attempting to achieve. Thus, counterterrorism could be considered not so much a war against evildoers, but rather an attempt to civilize the way in which a heated political contest is waged.

## New Areas of Inquiry

There is no question that, after September 11, 2001 in the United States, March 11, 2004 in Spain and July, 2005 in England, interest and research in the topic has grown exponentially and in countless areas. One of them is the mindset of the terrorists and the tactics they use in their quest for power and, ultimately, political and social change. Although terrorists bank on the efficacy of violence in achieving change, their actions are not random, crazed or capricious acts, killing or maiming for the sake of it, as politicians attempting to justify their policies and huge expenses in the "war against terrorism" maintain they are. On the contrary their actions are carefully planned and conservatively executed. Innocent and harmless people get caught in the middle just as they are in acts of war by various armed forces. Both the military and the terrorists claim that they are performing carefully targeted acts, "precision bombing" in U.S. military parlance, to gain an advantage, and for the terrorists in particular, recognition and publicity. Recently there have been increases in the utilization of violence. Possibly due to the "CNN effect," that is the need to attract worldwide media coverage for maximum impact, terrorists have been engaging in more dramatic and destructively lethal deeds to garner the same amount of attention that a less violent and bloody action would have obtained in the past. In a world saturated with violence and aggression by the media, entertainment, movies, video games and sports like football, hockey, boxing, etc., terrorists seem to have understood that to get and hold a jaded public's attention, they must increase the level and drama of their actions (Miller, 1982).

Another element that is impacting terrorism's organizational and operational dynamics is the internet and information age. The rise and expansion of network forms of organization is a central outcome of the continuing information revolution. The speed of communications, the facility of sharing and diffusing information, the ease and instantaneity of transferring funds worldwide have changed many aspects of contemporary life, including terrorism's conduct and modes of operation. This permits the creation of organizations with multiple, dispersed leaders and private sources of funding. The reasons, motives and rationales of the terrorists may not have changed but their modus operandi certainly has. What the information and internet age have made possible are flatter, less hierarchical, very flexible and localized structures and networks of power with centripetal dynamics fuelled by intense and easy communications and exchanges (Picard, 1993).

Terrorism is evolving. Terrorists' shift toward looser, less hierarchical organizational structures and their growing use of advanced communications technologies for command, control and coordination, will further empower small terrorist groups and individuals. While most of the governmental efforts and public concern, anxiety and attention are focused on preventing and foiling traditional violent terrorist acts, the next 9.11 might very well be an act of cyber-terrorism or massive *netwar*, disabling regional, national or even international computer driven systems that control practically every aspect of our lives, private, public, security, military and commercial (Pollit, 2001; Whine, 1999). The content of information and the conduits of information infrastructures very likely will become the new targets. In this area, the destructive power of terrorism will be exponentially greater than it has been in the past, even if it had been able to use "weapons of mass destruction." The crushing preponderance of U.S. conventional and atomic power may motivate some state and non-state adversaries to preferentially choose this type of terror as an asymmetric response. The implications are clearly significant. For instance, there could be a move away from episodic, dramatic and bloody acts of violence towards a more prolonged and sustained warfare. New planning and "what if" scenarios are needed to prepare for this potentially devastating form of attack. It is also true of course that the frequency and extent to which terrorist organizations use information infrastructures to carry out their activities may also make them more vulnerable to detection and destruction by counterterrorist entities (Rubin, 1999).

As for religious terrorism, the perceived and widespread uncertainty and unpredictability in the world due to globalization and the search for a new world order create a fertile ground for the creation and development of religious terrorist groups, with religious conviction functioning as a firm anchor in today's quicksand-like environment. These groups perceive an opportunity to shape history and the world in line with their divine duty, cause and mission. It is essential that we understand the inner logic of these groups and the dynamics that produce terrorism in order to weaken their breeding ground and sap their strength. Right now it is doubtful that the U.S. government and other Western governments are adequately prepared and ready to meet this challenge (Juergensmeyer, 1999).

Other areas needing much more research continue to be nationalistic and ethnic terrorism, violent extremism in the United States, technological terrorism and weapons of mass destruction, changing group structures and the metamorphosis of terrorism, the origins of Middle Eastern terrorism, and terrorism and the media (Zanni, 1999).

Public policy concerns need to be addressed as well. Thus, another area of inquiry involves the counter-terrorist measures themselves and the impact that they are having on a free and open society like the United States and other democratic countries. The frenzy and the hysteria that followed the 9/11 attacks in the United States and the protracted war against terrorism that is consuming vast resources and political capital all around the world have made the spiralling upward of anti-terrorism measures practically unstoppable. The reasoning often used to muzzle dissent is that if any elected politician, journalist, academic or plain citizen is against counterterrorism measures, s/he must then be for terrorism. A few days after 9/11, who in the United States could be against the Patriot Act? A democratic government often responds to a real or perceived terrorist threat by introducing temporary measures that greatly limit civil and political liberties. This approach makes it easier to justify harsh measures because their sunset provision is reassuring, lulls people into complacency and provides the needed cover for politicians to vote for their passage.

The problem is that it is normally very difficult to repeal such laws once they have been adopted. Since they often authorize and envision large expenditures of funds, for example, interest groups are quickly formed to take advantage of these opportunities and to ensure that they continue to exist and be funded. This in turn supports vast bureaucracies, organizations, police and military expansion, newly created entities and the like. One only has to think of the massive corporate earnings and employment that airport screening and security operations have spawned to realize how difficult it would be to dismantle or reduce them. In the wake of 9/11, population movement control, transportation security, the protection of infrastructures deemed vital, the introduction of a system of threat warnings, and immigration and border control measures were quickly introduced. The *de facto* adoption of a national identity card, in the form of a federally standardized driver's license, was approved. Moreover, the federal government has engaged in widespread detention and interrogation; introduced new surveillance tools, in turn often also adopted by state and local governments; instituted new financial regulations, controls, and rewards; modified the administration of justice system; and promoted greater information sharing among law enforcement and intelligence agencies, a policy enshrined in the eventual creation of an intelligence "tzar" in the country. The U.S. government basically approached the aftermath of 9/11 with the popular assumption that 9/11 happened because something major in the American system of national defence and homeland security was broken and had to be fixed. The growing tendency to want a completely risk-free life and society in a world dominated by science and technology which promise and deliver a constantly increased control of daily life and death situations, provided vast popular support for this approach (Labeviere, 2000).

An international "war on terrorism" was also declared and pressure was placed on the worldwide community of states and international organizations to support United States' policies, measures and intervention without question and to adopt or reinforce similar legislative measures to combat "terrorism." Authoritarian regimes were quick to understand that they could use the cover of the fight against terrorism to legitimate suppressing dissent and opposition political activities. There is no question that the civil and human rights of citizens and non-citizens were greatly reduced and at times violated in the process. This is a fertile field for investigation, analysis, inquiry and affirmation of democratic values for the social scientist (Merari, 1985).

## The Role of and the Opportunities for Social Scientists and Criminologists

The lack of a comprehensive strategy to address terrorism based on a deep-rooted, well grounded comprehension of the history, patterns, motivations, and types of terrorism reflects the lack of understanding of terrorism in the academic community. Some academics consider terrorism a too policy-oriented area to be worthy of serious research interest. Since terrorism is a multi-disciplinary topic of study it depends on the interaction and collaboration of a number of disciplines that are not used to working together, like psychology, sociology, international relations, theology, economics, criminology, anthropology, history, law, and political science.

In the United States most of the work on terrorism is being conducted in policy-oriented research institutes or think tanks. Their work is often limited or narrowly construed to fit the narrow interests and short time frames of the government contracts that fund it. Some of this research is quite good but does not often reach the academic community. Those graduate students who wish to study terrorism find themselves in a serious predicament. Stating a major interest in terrorism and related issues virtually guarantees being excluded from consideration for most academic positions.

Thus, academia is no more strategically oriented, visionary and creative than the government. There is an urgent need for multidisciplinary collaboration that also includes law enforcement, intelligence, and finance. What is most needed is a concerted effort to move beyond the episodic interest in this phenomenon and instead develop, plan and fund a long-term research and policy-development agenda.

The sociologist in general and the political sociologist in particular as scholars and citizens in a free world have a major role to play in researching the impact of anti-terrorism measures, go beyond their stated goals and expose the insidious threat that they pose to democracy, human freedom and individual rights. Sociologists who focus on mass movements, group-think and mob reactions can also find considerable material in the aftermath of 9/11. Racial and ethnic stereotyping, discrimination and hatred have also reared their ugly heads as a consequence of terrorist attacks originating in the Arab world.

Additionally the repercussions of the "war on terrorism" on international human rights and humanitarian laws provide a fertile ground for research and analysis by the sociologist of law. The creation of the "enemy combatant" label to facilitate weakening the Geneva Conventions on the treatment of prisoners of war; the mistreatment and torture of prisoners held at Guantanamo Bay, Cuba; the Bagram base in Afghanistan; and Abu Ghraib prison in Iraq, among others, also remind the social scientist of the fragility that the veneer of culture and civilization have over human nature and its aggressive and violent instincts and of the ease with which groups can be first debased and demonized and then mistreated and abused.

There is no question that the social sciences have a major contribution to make to the analysis, understanding, prevention and policy-making relative to terrorism. Given the unavoidable political nature of labelling certain actions as terrorist, the sociologist must remain vigilant, adhere to the highest professional standards, and maintain his/her independence of thought, analysis and vision. The large amounts of money that governments are making available to defeat terrorism could corrupt the social scientist's work and make him/her at times, wittingly or unwittingly, a tool for repression, conformity, and unbridled state power. Howard Becker's insistent question and critical challenge, "Sociology for Whom?" should remind us of the danger of falling into political, partisan work in favour of the elites and forgetting the prophetic nature of our profession.

## References


Arafat, Y. (1974). Speech by Yasser Arafat at the United Nations General Assembly, New York. 13, November 1974. Retrieved on October 5, 2005 from http://www.mideastweb.org/arafat_at_un.htm

Alexander, Y., & Richard L. (1990). *Terrorism and the media: Dilemmas for government, journalists and the public*. Riverside NJ: Brassey's.

Barber, B. R. (1991). *Jihad v. McWorld: How globalism and tribalism are redesigning the world.* New York: Ballantine Books.

Baumel, J. T. (1999). Kahane in America: An Exercise in Right Wing Urban Terror. *Studies in Conflict and Terrorism*, *22*, 311-329.

Bell, J. B. (1996). Ireland: The long end game. *Studies in Conflict and Terrorism*, *21*, 5-28.

Brown, D. J., & Robert M. (1995). *Violent persuasions: The politics and imagery of terrorism.* Seattle: Bay Press.

Buchanan, P. C., (1987). The varied faces of domination, state terror, economic policy and social response during the Argentinean 'Proceso', 1976-1981. *American Journal of Political Science*, *31*,336-380.

Burton, A. (1976). *Urban terrorism.* New York: Free Press.

Campbell, J., & Bill M. (1997). *The power of myth.* New York: Doubleday.

Coates, J. (1987). *Armed and dangerous: The rise of the survivalist right.* New York: Hill & Wong.

Cobban, H. (1984). *The Palestine liberation organization: People, power and politics.* Cambridge: Cambridge University Press.

Coker, C. (2002). *Globalization and insecurity in the 21st century: NATO and the management of risk.* Adelphi paper 345. London: International Institute for Strategic Studies.

Corcoran, J. (1995). *Bitter harvest: The birth of paramilitary terrorism in the heartland.* New York: Penguin.

Cox, R. (1983). Total Terrorism: Argentina, 1969-1979. In M. Crenshaw (Ed.), *Terrorism, legitimacy and power: The consequences of political violence* (pp.124-142). Middletown CT: Wesleyan University Press.

Criss, N. B. (1995). The nature of PKK terrorism in Turkey. *Studies in Conflict and Terrorism*, *18*, 17-38.

CSIS Global Organized Crime Project. (1998). *Cybercrime, cyberterrorism, cyberwarfare: Avoiding an electronic waterloo.* Washington DC: Center for Strategic and International Studies.

Denning, D. (2000). Cyberterrorism. Testimony before the U.S. House Committee on Armed Services, Special Oversight Panel on Terrorism, 107th Congress, 1st session, May 23, 2001. Retrieved on October 5, 2005 from http://www.cs.georgetown.edu/Denning/infosec/cyberterror.html

Gavel, D. (2002). Can Nuclear Weapons be put beyond the reach of Terrorists? *Kennedy School of Government Bulletin*, Autumn.

Gurr, T. R. (1993). *Minorities at risk: A global view of ethnopolitical conflicts*. Washington DC: U.S. Institute for Peace.

Hoffman, B. (1998). *Inside terrorism.* New York: Columbia University Press. Chapter 1. Retrieved on October 5, 2005 from http://www.nytimes.com/books/first/h/hoffman-terrorism.html

Howard, M. (2002). What's in a Name: How to fight terrorism. *Foreign Affairs*, *81*, January-February 43-59.

Howard, R., & Reid L. S. (Eds.). (2002).*Terrorism and counterterrorism: Understanding the new security environment*. New York: Columbia University Press.

Huntington, S. (1996). *The clash of civilizations and the remaking of world order*. New York: Simon & Schuster.

Johnson, J. T. (1997). The holy war idea in Western and Islamic traditions. University Park PA: Penn State University Press.

Juergensmeyer, M. (Ed.) (1992). *Violence and the sacred in the modern world.* London: Frank Cass.

Juergensmeyer, M. (1999). *Terror in the mind of god: The global rise of religious violence.* Berkeley CA: University California Press

Kibble, D. G. (1996). The threat of militant Islam: A fundamental reappraisal. *Studies in Conflict and Terrorism*, *19*, 353-364

Kupperman, R., & Trent, D. (1979). *Terrorism: Threat, reality, response.* Stanford CA: Hoover Institution Press.

—. (1984). Government response to mass destruction threats. In A. Merari (Ed.), *Terrorism & combating terrorism* (pp.157-162). Lanham MD: University Press of America.

Labeviere, R. (2000). *Dollars for terror: The United States and Islam.* New York: Algora Publishing.

Laqueur, W. (1976). *Guerrilla: A historical and critical study.* Boston MA: Little, Brown.

—. (1997). Postmodern terrorism. *Foreign Affairs*, *75*(5), Sept.-Oct. 23-46.

—. (1998). *The new terrorism: Fanaticism and the arms of mass destruction.* New York: Oxford University Press.

Merari, A. (Ed.). (1985). *On terrorism and combating terrorism.* Lanham MD: University of America Press.
Miller, A. (1982). *Terrorism, the media and the law.* New York: Transnational.
Moxon-Browne, E. (Ed.). (1994). *European terrorism.* New York: Hall.
Noble, K. (1999). *Tabernacle of hate: Why they bombed Oklahoma city.* Ontario: Voyager Publishing.
Nusse, A. (2000). *Muslim Palestine: The ideology of Islam. London:* Harwood Academic Publications.
O'Day, A. (Ed.). (1994). *Dimensions of Irish terrorism.* New York: Hall.
Oliverio, A. (2001). *The state of terror.* Albany: State University of New York Press.
Pearlestein, R. M. (1992). *The mind of the political terrorist.* Wilmington DE: SR Books.
Perdue, W. D. (1988). *Terrorism and the state: A critique of domination through fear.* New York: Praeger.
Picard, R. G. (1993). *Media portrayals of terrorism: Functions and meaning of news coverage.* Ames IA: Iowa State University Press.
Pollit, M. M. (2001). Cyberterrorism: Fact or fantasy? Retrieved on October 5, 2008 from http://cs.georgetown.edu/~denning/infosec/pollit.html.
Rapoport, D. C. (Ed.), (1989). *Inside terrorist organizations.* New York: Columbia University Press.
Ross, J. I. (1999). Beyond the conceptualization of terrorism: A psychological-structural model of the causes of this activity. In C. Summers & E. Markusen (Eds.), *Collective violence: Harmful behavior in groups and governments* (pp.169-192). Lanham, MD: Rowman & Littlefield Publishers.
Rubin, B. M. (1991). *Terrorism and state politics.* New York: St. Martin's Press.
Sargent, L. T. (Ed.) (1994). *Extremism in America.* New York: New York University Press.
Sharif, I. (1995). *The success of political terrorist events: An analysis of terrorist tactics and victim characteristics, 1968-1977.* Lanham MD: University Press of America.
Smith, B. (1994). *Terrorism in America: Pipe bombs and pipe dreams.* Albany NY: State University of New York Press.
Sterling, C. (1986). *The terror network.* New York: Holt, Rinehart and Winston.
Stern, J. (2002). *The ultimate terrorists.* Cambridge, MA: Harvard University Press.

Stern, K. (1996). *A force upon the plains: The American militia movement and the politics of hate*. New York: Simon & Schuster.

Turvey, B. E., Diana T., & Jerry C. W. (Eds.). (1999). *Criminal profiling: An introduction to behavioral evidence analysis*. San Diego: Academic Press.

Walter, J. (1995). *Every knee shall bow: The truth and tragedy of ruby ridge and the randy weaver family*. New York: Harper Collins.

Whine, M. (1999). *Cyberspace: A new medium for communication, command, and control by extremists*. Institute for Counterterrorism. Retrieved on October 5, 2008 from http://www.ict.org.il.

White, J. R. (2002). *Terrorism*. Belmont CA: Wadsworth Thomson.

Wilkinson, P. (1994). *Terrorism: British perspective*. New York: Hall.

Zanni, M. (1999). Middle Eastern terrorism and netward. *Studies in Conflict and Terrorism*, 22, 247-256.

# CHAPTER TWENTY NINE

# NATIVE AMERICAN INDIAN TRIBAL COMMUNITY AND TERTIARY POWER

JULIE C. ABRIL

## Abstract

There is little literature concerned with the negotiation of power in traditional tribal communities located within the United States. Even fewer literature using sound social scientific methodology exist that addresses empirically how modern Native American Indians have had power taken from them, given back to them, and how it has been transformed to incorporate both traditional and modern elements. That is, it is rarely discussed how traditional tribal power has become a hybrid of both traditional and tertiary powers. In this chapter, it is hypothesized that such a transformation has occurred. Effects of fluidity of power in modern yet traditional tribal societies have not been adequately documented. Using the Southern Ute Indian Tribe as an example, the author employ a variety of concepts to answer the question of how power is implemented and negotiated in a traditional yet modern tribal society.

## Introduction

Historically, a Chief and a small group of sub-Chiefs governed the Southern Ute Indian Tribe. Chiefs could be chosen by a number of methods. They could either inherit their position from a deceased family member. If the current Chief no longer desired the position, he could select a successor. A Chief could also earn the position through achievements in battles and wars. In most cases, the position of Chief was an earned position either by a single deed or an accumulation of deeds. If the current Chief was killed in a fight then the slayer could take the position. The tribal membership in such a case might agree either formally or in spirit that the new Chief had the power to lead the tribe. Responsibilities of the Chief were many and usually involved making the final decision on tribal directives, such as with whom the tribe should engage in battle or where a new camp might be located. The power to make these decisions was implicit and supported by the membership (personal interviews with tribal members).

Chiefs were also responsible for tribal law enforcement. For example, the Chief would rely upon the tribe's Medicine Person (spiritual leader) to inform him if a cultural law had been broken. An example of a cultural legal violation would be if a certain type of animal, e.g., a white buffalo, was killed. The Medicine Person would inform the Chief of what the spiritual ramifications to the tribe were in response to such a violation and then recommend an appropriate punishment. The Medicine Person would then go about doing the necessary spiritual activities to rectify the harm caused by the violation. The Chief would then direct the appropriate sub-Chief (in the case of tribal punishment, it would be the War sub-Chief) to carry out the punishment. We can see remnants of this practice today in the modern Tribal Code which provides for advisors on tribal custom to be allowed to participate in legal matters before the Court as they relate to cultural custom and norms.

The power to direct punishment of wrongdoers also rested with the Chief. The most severe punishment imposed on a tribal member would have been banishment. Death sentences were not used in the history of the tribe. When the author spoke to a Tribal Official, she told her why capital punishment was never used and why banishment was the most severe sanction. She said that anyone could be strong enough to survive a "lashing" (whipping) or other type of physical punishment except capital punishment. Banishment involved harm to one's pride. Pride, in this tribal community, was intimately related to one's family and social standing. If one's pride had been harmed by ridicule and/or banishment then the harm could be irrevocable during a person's lifetime. Moreover, this harm can be transmitted from one generation to the next. We see evidence of this today as some families have derogatory reputations that are the result of transgressions by members who lived many generations ago. The power to condemn entire families because of transgressions of generations past may or may not be restricted to the Southern Ute Indians but it certainly separates the way they perceive the world and exert their collective power from the way non-Indians do. (For more in-depth discussions of the tribe's organization and history, see Ellis, 1989; Smith, 1990; Quintana, 2004; Pettit, 1990; Decker 2004; FitzPatrick, 2000; Jefferson, Roberts, & Thompson, 1972).

## Tertiary agents in a tribal community

Tertiary agencies in a modern tribal community include the police and court. These agencies perform duties that were traditionally carried out by the tribal council and by a small system of Sub-Chiefs and spiritual leaders. Some of these duties include the following:

- Punishment for offences against the tribe, monitoring of community behaviour, and other methods of social control were once the responsibility of the War Sub-Chief. The tribal police now regulate community behaviour and apprehend offenders, while the tribal court determines punishment for social law breaking.
- The tribe's spiritual leaders, usually the Medicine People, traditionally dealt with violations of tribal values and beliefs, such as killing a white buffalo. The tribal court now adjudicates matters involving desecration of Indian cultural icons.
- Spiritual matters, such as communication with Indian spirits, were traditionally the responsibility of both the spiritual leaders and certain participants in the tribe's ceremonies. Today, tribal police are often called upon to respond to certain tribal spiritual matters.
- Cultural matters were once the sole responsibility of the Tribal Council. Today, the tribal police, courts, or their designees (such as the cultural preservation officers) are responsible for the regulation of these affairs.
- The ultimate power within the tribal community has always rested with the Tribal Council. Today, certain judicial powers (such as the power to impose punishments for criminal offences) rest with the tribal court.

The above are only a few examples of where power in the tribal community has historically been vested with the Southern Ute Indians. Table 1 illustrates how various types of social matters that occur in the tribal community have moved from the jurisdiction of traditional to modern agents of tertiary power as a result of evolving community expectations and differential criteria imposed by the federal government and tribal law. Within the Southern Ute Tribe, the community demands both legal protections afforded by modern agencies and their agents as well as incorporation of traditional methods of social control.

**Table 1: Changes from Traditional to Modern Agents of Social Control in the Southern Ute Indian Tribal Community**

| Social Matter | Traditional Agents of Social Control | Modern Agents of Social Control |
|---|---|---|
| Crime and Deviance | Tribal Chief, War Sub-Chief, Medicine People | Police and Court |
| Spirit Entities and Spiritual Matters | Medicine People | Police who are tribal members and Medicine People |
| Juvenile Matters (e.g. delinquency) | Tribal Elders | Police Juvenile Officer and Probation Officer |
| Disrespect of Tribal Elders | Tribal Council and Elders | Police Juvenile Officer, Juvenile Court and Probation Officer |

## The tribal council, police, and court

Only recently have studies of negotiation of legal powers between Indians and the Anglo American-based judicial institutions located on Indian reservations emerged in the socio-legal literature. For instance, Richland (2005, p. 235) investigates how Hopi Indian traditions and linguistics are incorporated into modern tribal court proceedings. Negotiation of legal powers between the tribal community and its police and court has led to a mandate stating that traditional modes of legal processes must be included in modern tribal proceedings, in particular in the Hopi communities, in those cases involving property disputes. Indeed, Hopi law requires that the court gives "more weight" to the "customs, traditions, and culture of the Hopi tribe." Richland further discusses how the Hopi courts adjust their actions to the values of the tribal community. He reports that, "... for the Hopi, knowledge of tradition-whether sacred or secular-is often intimately tied to the legitimate authority of the possessor and is an essential element of that person's efficacy in the world ..." Personal power used in the Hopi court extends to those powers used by some tribal members to evoke a supernatural presence or power from which more personal power is then derived. Richland reports that popqwat (witches/sorcerers) who possess these supernatural powers often use them to manipulate judicial proceedings. As illustrated by Richland's observations and analyses of the Hopi tribal court, negotiation of tertiary power is not only customary but is integral to the functioning of the court. Policing, too, is subject to similar negotiations.

Jesilow and Parsons (2001, pp. 164-165), in their review of the main models of policing structures used in the United States, reported that early American police agencies received their power from the community and that " ... a hundred years ago, police had to negotiate with the populations they patrolled." Jesilow and Parsons add:

> the police needed the support of the community in order to perform their job. Accordingly, officers' decisions fit within the prevailing ideology that they probably shared. To do otherwise would be to risk losing community support...Officers gained respect by upholding local standards and expectations (pp. 164-165, also see Haller, 1976; Miller, 1973).

The same occurs today. Community members must willingly accept the power to negotiate and not have it be forced upon them. Police behaviour and enforcement of laws are also controlled by the community. Citing Dodson (1955), Jesilow and Parsons (2001, p. 170) note, "... laws which are selected are those which the power structure in the community wants enforced." Police maintain order only with the consent of the community. When police are not responsive or are perceived to deviate from their assigned roles which are based on the community's expectations, pressure is placed on the tribal council which then pressures the police department to conform. The power to exert pressure as a means to get the police to conform to the community's expectations is held in abeyance until the time that the tribal community determines that such power requires re-negotiation. These times are often during periods of great change in the tribal community, such as when leadership has changed or as the police modernize their ideology and subsequent responses to community deviance. Tribal membership, thus, provides an opportunity for the individual to negotiate with the police (see Jesilow,

Meyer, & Namazzi, 1995). The public likely will be more open to the police if it senses the officers' value its input and addresses community concerns (Jesilow & Parsons, 2001). The previous literatures provide a foundation for the work here as scant empirically-based ideas have been written on power fluidity occurring on reservations, with the exception of early studies by Wilkins (1987) and Shattuck and Norgren (1991). Most work on this matter relates to either power resurgences among individual or like tribal groups (see e.g. Champagne, 1989) or hypothesized changes that 'should' come as a result of social movements (such as those to revitalize Indian ethnic identities).

## The tribal council

As complexities of tribal societies grow the type of power remaining may be perceived as a result of changing community expectations and transference of obligations from one institution(s) to another and growth of specializations, as Durkheim suggested it would. After negotiations with the federal government, the Southern Ute Indian tribe accepted the tenets of the Wheeler-Howard Act. The tribal council was then formally recognized as the governing body of the tribe. Prior to this Act, the tribe was federally recognized as part of the Brunot Agreement of 1874. The tribe was then given back jurisdiction over many matters occurring within the boundaries of the reservation (see also Ute Indians vs. United States, 330 U.S. 476 (1947)) as is described in the text below that appears in the Tribal Code:

> The Southern Ute Indian Tribe has jurisdiction over all territory within the exterior boundaries of the reservation as established in the Brunot Agreement which was ratified by the United States Congress on April 29, 1874, and as added thereto by Presidential Proclamation and Executive Order. (Southern Ute Tribal Code, Title 1 General Provisions, § 1-1-107 Territorial Jurisdiction)

The most significant changes experienced by the Southern Ute Tribe that resulted from the Wheeler-Howard Act was in (a) the appointment of tribal leadership, (b) the titles of tribal leaders, and (c) the formalized structure of government and its agencies. Power and authority to govern were again legitimated in the new constitution of the tribe, as the Indian Reorganization Act (IRA) required the ratification of such by the membership. The tribe accepted the dictates of the new law because if it did not do so, it might jeopardize its standing with Congress and the President.

The council has a new responsibility not only to negotiate power between itself and the membership but to conform to the competing demands of federal and state law and modernity. An example of this occurred during the Sun Dance (the most sacred of ceremonies). Emergency medical personnel were stationed near the ceremonial grounds. A Ute man reported, "... like at the Sun Dance and Bear Dance...years ago you could walk a little out of town and actually feel the drums on the ground, not anymore. Last year, they (the council) had EMT's (emergency medical personnel) waiting outside the Sun Dance grounds in case someone passed out. That's not right! In the Sun Dance you're supposed to pass out to receive your spiritual dream." The council is in a situation where they must preserve and protect the cultural heritage of the tribe but must also abide by state and federal rules regarding public health and safety. We can see that outside governmental interference with tribal cultural and spiritual activities has a negative impact on the tribe. The Indians felt that "the council is adopting too many outside laws and we're losing our sovereignty." While others demand that elements of the historical government be retained for the tribes' survival.

Another example of where the tribal council is required to acquiesce to state dictates was when the council signed a declaration with the state of Colorado to allow the state to review the criminal records of council members. The result was a perceived infringement on tribal sovereignty to self-govern with officials selected by the community. It was reported by a subject that "It was right after they (tribal council) just signed that declaration with the state of Colorado to let go of their (tribally held criminal) records down here, and each one of their (three council members) records got surfaced down here and was reported to the state. They had priors. If they never had signed that declaration, they (the state) would have never known they had priors and they would have all been treated fairly. Now, the state rule is we can't have leaders who have illnesses (alcoholism)."

Finally, the council is making decisions about eligibility requirements for membership that follows federal policy but is perceived to be deleterious to the tribe. One example is related to the rules regarding the blood quantum requirement. Conflicting comments such as the following were common:

> They're enrolling kids that just got a little bit of Indian in them. That's messed up! I can't even enrol my kids and they're half Ute! I'm full Ute. The only thing is ... they're spread out. This one here (subject pointed to his seven year old son standing next to him) is Southern Ute, Ute

> Mountain, and Northern Ute but they don't recognize him. They should recognize him. They tend to be dropping the blood quantum down to 1/8th.
>
> Council decided that they don't want to lower the blood quantum to become a tribal member. They don't realize that what they're doing is that they are slowing going to be the cause of (the demise of the tribe) and that there's not going to be a Southern Ute tribe anymore because there are not going to be any tribal members. It's been a quarter for some time now but they've tried to lower it lower but the tribal members they won't. Take our grandchildren (for example) they couldn't be enrolled. There are only a little over 1,000 tribal members who are enrolled… who are voters and eligible to vote. Someday the federal government is gonna' come out and say "In order for you to be a sovereign governing tribe, you've got to have a certain amount of eligible voters." If they say 2,000 (as the minimum number of voter's required to sustain a recognized tribe) automatically this tribe would lose out. The land will all go back to the federal government because there won't be enough. (Bring it down) at least to a 16th. The federal government recognizes up to a 32nd…… that would continue the tribe because there are not that many full-blooded tribal members left in the tribe. This happened in other tribes. It happened to the Mountain Ute tribe and it's going to happen here … you used to be able to count on them (council members)… before if you were a tribal member or if you had Indian blood, you could talk to them about anything. Not anymore."

These comments indicate the council, which has been given power by the membership, must shift its focus from them and onto matters often viewed as more important, such as investing for the future of the entire tribe. It was often reported by subjects that the council's focus on other business ventures, governmental obligations, and their attenuate priorities are not adequately explained to the rest of the membership. This leaves many in the community feeling modern tribal council power exists only to be disbursed on unexplained "whims" of council members. One subject responded, "they're the ones who's supposed to take care of the tribal people."

To be effective the council must have the support of the community and this is another area where power is negotiated. There is conflicting evidence about how much the community actually supports the tribal council. For example, when the author asked a man what he thought about the council, he said, "I think the tribal council is more business oriented and 'forget the tribal members' … let's invest in this and that … I think they [the tribal council] need[s] to focus back on the tribal membership." The survey data suggests that the Indians were split in their view of the tribal council, thus possibly negating the more positive interview data.

As the tribal council must answer to the membership, power to create new tribal law is shared with the membership. Enrolled members often vote on many initiatives and a majority rules. Sharing power originates from the historical origins of the tribe. This is done because the tribal council must free itself of extra burdens in order to be effective leaders of the tribe especially when they must interact with federal or state governments. The most important reason tertiary power is given over to the police and court is because both the tribal council and the community feel that certain functions are better addresses by specially-trained agency personnel. Many Utes felt the police and court are the appropriate agencies to respond to and adjudicate legal matters. Many other subjects reported that they would seek out help from the council if they needed support for matters they perceived were not being adequately addressed by either the police or court. For example, many stated the following of they were not satisfied with the police or court, "I'd go to the council. I'd get satisfied" because "they can get things done." This is because the council is perceived to "have more power than anybody," and many Indians felt that "it's their job to make others do their job."

When asked who should respond to problems occurring in the neighbourhood, most responded, "the police." As a result, the tribal council gives powers to the police and court to adjudicate not only legal issues but cultural and spiritual matters as well. Competing demands placed on the tribal government from the community and state and federal authorities has forced the tribal council to morph into a hybrid of tripartite political power within the community.

## The tribal police

Power in this tribal society has experienced a three-stage shift; from traditional to tertiary to a hybrid form of power that has both traditional and tertiary elements. The following data suggests that this includes the police. Here the powers and responsibilities of the tribal police are discussed. It is important to examine the police carefully because often they are the only contact with government and thus representative of power and authority most people encounter. To be effective the police must be responsive to community concerns.

Tribal police deal with the standard policing issues but also must respond to cultural and spiritual matters; matters once the jurisdiction of the tribal council or spiritual leaders. Cultural duties of the police might include responding to spirit entities that are part of the spiritual foundation of this tribal group. When the author asked one woman why she would call the police she responded, "If something weird or evil is going on. I mean, Skin Walkers, they're all over the place! And they (the police) can't do anything about them! [Question: What's a Skin Walker?] "It's a shape shifter (an Indian spirit). Those poor little people (the spirits of the Skin Walkers) have to be like this. They can't face you in broad daylight. (When the Skin Walkers are around) I tell my daughter to go get the police … (Skin Walkers are) the old Spanish people who used to be alive." This suggests that at least some tribal members believe the police should respond to cultural matters. Other subjects reported that they expect the police to be involved in such matters. Several reported that they (Southern Ute Police Department) often help with the Walk of the Warriors ceremony and other cultural events and that this is satisfactory, "the police will just be there talking to tribal members," many reported.

The police must address Indian cultural and spiritual problems because most subjects reported that it would be them to whom they would turn if anything were wrong in the community. Indians, however, will not simply grant the police power. There needs to be an implicit agreement (such as being a tribal member or Indian known by many to be just and fair) for the membership to know that the police are deserving of power. Similar to the tribal council, the police must have the support of the community in order to be effective. If the police are not perceived by the community to be satisfactory then it becomes difficult for the police to be effective crime fighters and peace keepers.

Many reported a negative perception of the police who held office during the previous administration. As a result, the tribal council removed all but a handful of police personnel from the department and replaced those with a new Chief of Police and officers who are members of the tribe. Members now rely on the police due, in part, to the positive efforts of the new administration and the new Chief of Police. As one subject reported that he would use the police "because they do a good job, not like before." Indeed, when asked to whom subjects would turn if there were problems in their neighbourhood, many replied, "The police because they say that they're there to serve and to protect … if that's their job then they should be able to carry that job out," and "probably the tribal police. Because it's the police who you depend on … who you call and who will go out there in the middle of the night." Several subjects reported that the manner which the police treat them is what makes the community respect the power that has been vested in them by the community. It was common to hear comments such as, "They treat me nice. The tribal police do really respect me. I love that about them." The new positive perception of the police is also evidenced by the community's interactions with the police when the officers are responding to calls for service. Many reported they talk to the police on a regular basis during the officers' routine patrols.

Several subjects reported satisfaction with how the police respond to them. One woman reported, "My worst contact was when a police officer came … when my father passed away. They came to the door and they consoled me that he had passed on." [Was it on tribal land?] "Yes." [Can you describe the behaviour of the police?] "He was very nice and sympathetic." Others made comments such as "they make me feel comfortable," "they all treat us with respect, they have never disrespected us," "they let us know what's going one," and "they're more concerned for the people than the law."

Satisfaction with the police, however, is different from the community willingly giving power over to them. The police must perform their customary duties or the community will respond. Evidence of this is found in the comments made by one man who said "if the police don't do their job, I'd go to the tribal court and a file suit." Most people viewed the police' authority has been given to them by the community. Such comments were common: "they're the authority, they're supposed to be there" and "you have to go through the chain of command, you just can't go right to the top (the tribal council)." Yet, when the police do not respond adequately to community concerns, tribal members reported that they are comfortable going to the next level of authority as expressed by one man, "We put you (the police) in charge of these matters. Go do it. If you don't, we'll get someone else to do it, either the council or the tribal court." Thus, the police must respond to community expectations that are conveyed either implicitly or explicitly such as in the case were a woman reported receiving a traffic ticket. The woman who had received a citation for speeding from a tribal police officer said, "I told him, you know this is the rez?" in an effort to convey the message to the officer that he should not have broken the negotiated agreement between the community and the police to enforce a law against an action that some members do not perceive as harmful.[1]

Finally, intruders such as "white people" into Southern Ute spiritual activities were once addressed by the participants in the ceremonies such as the ceremonial warriors. Today, the tribal police are expected to respond to such cultural invasions. This is clearly an area where cultural and spiritual practices that were traditionally the domain of specific tribal members are now the responsibility of the police. This is, again, done to

---

[1] This view is not held by the majority of reservation residents. The tribal council has since been taking aggressive measures to control this behavior.

free other agencies and the community of the added burden of responding to such matters. In a sense, transferring jurisdiction and, ultimately, power over cultural and legal matters to other agencies might simply be viewed by the community as delegation of tasks. As a result of this shift in cultural responsibility, power is negotiated and moved from the community to tertiary mechanisms of social control such as the police.

## The tribal court

The tribal court is viewed as a main source of legitimate power in the community, second only to the tribal council. Indeed, the Chief Justice of the tribal court answers directly to the tribal Chairman. Like the police, the tribal court must often adjudicate matters traditionally under the umbrella of the duties of the tribal council, or the spiritual leaders. For example, the court must address family matters such as supervision of wards of the court, child custody matters, and marital concerns. Common comments regarding why they would go to court included, "to get custody of my daughter" or "I had to go to court for the kids (when they were in trouble)" or "Just for the kids. I go for them." Historically, the council or the Chief would decide with whom a child must reside in cases of abandonment or death of the parents. Today, the court and its officers must place and be responsible for the well being of children in need of supervision. One subject reported that the court had a profound effect on him during which the same worked diligently to keep a family intact as is tribal custom,

> [What was your most memorable experience with the tribal court?] "Well, this memory will never go away for me. We adopted my brother's boy and come to find out he was, had to be on medication and was pretty bad off. It got into my family in here where it almost made me and my wife break up. So, I had to go to court for him. I had to give him up though which is one of the things, you know, it got to me. It was like losing one of my own kids. I couldn't save him, I tried. Nobody else wanted him. I tried for four years and it totally changed my life.

Historically, during the Bear Dance (an annual ceremony) a woman was allowed to drop her current mate for a new one. Now, the tribal court adjudicates unsatisfactory marital arrangements. As several subjects reported, the Bear Dance provided an opportunity for women to take affirmative actions to rid themselves of a mate. Some subjects reported the following:

> The Bear Dance … has its own history in where a man would go with a woman and then he'd stay with her for however long he wanted to stay

> with her but she had the right to throw him away. They would live with her parents. Everything that he had was hers. When she didn't want him anymore, she'd go look for another husband during the Bear Dance.

Participation in the modernized Bear Dance celebration increases solidarity among the Southern Utes and reinforces their collective identity. Yet, the ridding of a mate is now left to the tribal court with the potential to negatively effect the solidarity of the tribal community by taking away a function of the entire tribe and placing it with a specialized agent. It also serves to relieve the community of certain burdens so that it may be free to exercise individual and collective agendas. Negotiation of power to delegate and to accept obligations is the same as Durkheim's (1933) idea that states as societies mature and become more complex community matters are shifted to specialized agents. These developed in response to growing societal complexity and the community's desire to rid itself of matters beyond the scope of its expertise.

For the court to have legitimate power, however, it must be perceived by the community to be fair and impartial. There is evidence of this in the comments of the study subjects such as the following: "I think the tribal court is real fair. What I like about the tribal court and the people that work there were that they explained things to you. Regular, everyday people don't know a lot of things about court life, law-wise or like about the statutes that have here on the reservation. And I think the tribal court is good to explain these things to you;" "The court was OK. I'm glad they had that Teen Court. It teaches kids to feel what it's like to be in court;" and "They even helped me out and they made me understand what the other papers were for and they helped my brother. He [the officer] explained to him what he should write (in the court filings)."

Many subjects also reported satisfaction with the Chief Justice of the tribal court. This might also be attributed to the fact that the Chief Justice is also an enrolled member of the tribe. Comments about the Chief Justice include "The woman … I've known her all my life. She's pretty fair" and "I think she's alright." Comments about the other two tribal court judges include: "they're fair," "I think they're pretty fair," and "they're very fair." It was reported that the judges take unusual steps to connect with the people who come before them. One tribal police officer told the story of his experience with a judge during a trial for assault. He said, "The guy I arrested for assault told the judge he didn't know what assault meant so how could he be guilty. The judge then picked up a pen and threw it in my direction and said, "That's assault!"

To the pleasure of the community the court takes unique steps to reflect the values of the tribe. Several commented that the court offers the tribal-sponsored detoxification services to members as opposed to sending them to services provided by the Indian Health Service, which are negatively perceived. This practice is one element that helped lead to the transformation of power on this reservation. Punishments are also perceived to be fair and a reflection of the influence of the community. As one subject reported he received "a big fine of $500 and that he "liked the attitude of the judge" indicating that the court takes into consideration community social and economic conditions.

The court relies on both formal and informal Indian law to negotiate power between it and the membership. This is done when the court uses the Tribal Code (which is voted for by the adult membership) which gives the court power to use tribal members who are familiar with the cultural norms and values to participate in court matters (see earlier citation from the Tribal Code). The power given to the court through the Code expedites legal matters and reflects the evolving norms and values of the tribe. In doing so, power is negotiated between the membership and the court for the overall benefit of the membership.

## Causes of the Power Shift

In this discussion, negotiation is not explicit, i.e., where both parties sit down to negotiate the terms of the agreement regarding each other's power and authority. Negotiation is implied, and sometimes explicated, through either affirmative or negative responses to community expectations from the authorities. To a lesser extent, power is negotiated between community members and modern institutions of social control when the later are used to respond to matters once thought to be out of the jurisdiction of formalized entities such as the police and court as was previously discussed. This idea is further discussed in this section about the causes of the power shift.

Tribal agents of social control have competing demands placed on them that require: (a) they employ traditional methods of responding to deviance in the manner the community desires, and (b) to uphold federal expectations for tribal law enforcement personnel. Two examples of this include; (a) the woman who told her daughter to "go get the police" because she saw a Skin Walker; and (b) when the police are called upon to regulate behaviours of tribal members during spiritual ceremonies such as the Sun Dance and the Walk of the Warriors. Conversely, while the community desires traditional responses to deviance such must conform to federal law. An example of this includes a story told to me by several tribal members. They reported that recently, there had been a murder of a female member on the reservation. They further reported that many people within the tribe know who the murderer is because some "saw him in dreams" and other culture-specific methods of knowledge creation. Yet, the police cannot respond to this type of evidence because it is not likely to be upheld as a legitimate basis for probable cause to arrest the offender. The police are then forced to design methods of investigation to address both parties' expectations in a manner that is agreeable to each side thus creating a hybrid of power. Several other factors appear to be associated with the creation of a hybrid of authoritative power that now exists within this tribe.

Changes in the paradigms of many members caused by social changes that are the result of advancements in society were reported by the subjects to be a source of conflict among the younger and older generations. Intergenerational conflict is evidenced through statements made by the subjects about the differing desires for the tribal authorities. Subjects reported that the "Elders hang onto old ideas" and that "they want to keep it like it was a long time ago … that's just not possible" conflict with statements made by others that the younger generation "don't even know the language" and that "we need to prepare the children so, hopefully, the tribe can prosper."

Television, the internet, and the encroachment of non-Indians into tribal society were cited by many as a source of conflict and pressure to mould a different type of jurisdiction. One man said about his son "my little one wants what he sees on TV." The desire to "have what everybody else has" combined with the attitude among tribal members that "we were taught to adapt and to survive" pressures the members to demand an alternative type of response to deviance. Pressure to change how tertiary power is used is coming from tribal members both individually and as a group. The push is not new as many tribes have been advocating change since Congress and the President have given some powers back to tribes to regulate their internal affairs as a result of decisions by the USSC, such as the sole authority in making the decision on who is a member of their tribe (see, Santa Clara Pueblo vs. Martinez, 436 U.S. 49 (1978)).

Community expectations have also been moulded by their perceptions of authoritative institutions that may have developed as a result of viewing televised accounts of similarly-situated communities. The "why can't we have that, too?" mentality psychologically penetrates first the individual tribal members and then the tribal community as a whole. Champagne (1989, p. 8) called this type of impact "cultural-normative interpenetration" and occurs when "members of indigenous societies [become] aware of alternate world views, political organizations, religions, and social mores."

Technology facilitates acculturation of tribal members into modern society and has contributed substantially to transformation of authoritative power. Modernization via technologically advanced devices such as computers with advanced Internet communication devices such as web cams and e-mail, satellite televisions, cellular phones, and electronic games (all have been found in virtually all members' homes) have made their way into the tribe' reality. Contact with outsiders, specifically the influx of a large number of Euro-Americans who have found the natural surroundings to be desirable locations to build their "dream homes," has forced a form of modern-acculturation-by-association-due-to-globalization to occur in this tribal community and an associated shift in power. Finally, the large number of tribal members who have returned from urban areas to live on the reservation have brought with them the norms, values, and beliefs of the dominant society and then expect such imported perceptions of vested power to be initiated with a culturally-specific overture into tertiary mechanisms of social control situated within the reservation. Evidence of this is found in the perceptions tribal members have about the police being responsible for responding to community problems. "It's their job!" and "they're paid to do it" attitudes express the community desire to have the type of law enforcement found elsewhere.

Historically, the tribe had its own governmental structure. As society and its perceptions of Indians improve (e.g. "it's cool to live with the Indians"), the tribe is re-empowered to demand a re-negotiation of its authority within its jurisdiction. External demands from state and federal authorities (such as signing the compact with the state of Colorado to release information about the criminal histories of the tribe's elected officials) coupled with the resurgence of Indian social power as evidenced by the growth of Indian political institutions such as the National Congress of American Indians in non-Indian society pressures changes to the former power structure. Modern Indians now *demand* modernized power structures. Traditional Indians *expect* tribal traditions and customs to remain. The fusion of these dual yet competing expectations forced the development of the new tripartite hybrid of authoritative power that exists today within the reservation boundaries.

Beginning in 1934 with passage of the Wheeler-Howard Act, the government requires that many federally-recognized American Indian tribes adopt and maintain a democratically-elected government. Most of these tribes have responded by imitating the European-based government found today in the United States. While not required by federal law, most tribes have governments that have executive, legislative, and judicial branches and associated offices which operate with the same ideology found in the larger American society. The Southern Ute Indian tribe has one such government that also infuses culturally-specific attributes into as many areas as possible, including its laws and institutions of social control. One author has implied the change in the Southern Ute governmental power structure may have been a result of "routine conflict" (Champagne, 1989 p. 3). He argues the impact of the "geopolitical environment, world system, and cultural-normative interpenetration" (5) are three separate types of contact that may result from interaction with a super power structure. Champagne further argues that these are also three levels of analyses that should be conducted as a result of such contact.

Our understanding of the fluidity of power from traditional to legal and then to a hybrid of traditional and legal power can further our knowledge of how power operates in traditional societies which are under dual governance. Champagne (1989, p. 13-14) is on target again when he begins his main arguments with the idea that "the variation in institutional change depends on the conditions of the geopolitical environment, the types of markets available, the degree of interpenetration of Western culture and normative order, the continuity of subsistence economy, the degree and form of social and political solidarity, the configuration of societal differentiation, and the world view and major cultural orientations of the society." Champagne's work may be well suited to help us to better understand why power in traditional tribal societies is fluid. The special circumstances and nature of traditional tribal societies may be unique in their transference of power in modalities that are not likely to be mimicked in the larger, more complex American society.

## Conclusion

Power in Southern Ute Indian community traditionally has been vested in the tribal council and its agents such as the system of sub-chiefs. The council, with its power legitimated both formally and informally along with the implicit authority of the majority of the membership and the explicit authority granted to it by Congressional power, has vested certain tertiary powers in the police, court, and its various modern agents. The power of the tribal police and court is again reinforced by the membership when it abides by and accepts the directives and judgments of these agents. When members continue to use these agents they explicitly acknowledge the power codified in the Tribal Code. Such powers are used to adjudicate cultural and spiritual matters that were once the domain of the designated spiritual or tribal leaders. The tribal community accepts this situation because both the police and the court have earned the trust and confidence of the tribal community. It is accepted because the community generally accepts the judgments of the tribal council. It also accepts the reality that the tribe is evolving and must delegate certain functions to agencies or agents with specialized skills in order for it to be a well-functioning democratically powerful society.

## References


Brunot Agreement of April 29th, 1874 (United States Statutes at Large), 43rd Congress (1873).

Champagne, D. (1989). *American Indian societies: Strategies and conditions of political and cultural survival: cultural survival report 32*. Cambridge: Cultural Survival, Inc.

Decker, P. R. (2004). *"The Utes must go!" American expansion and the removal of a people*. Colorado: Fulcrum Publishing.

Dodson, D. (1955). Speech delivered at Michigan State University. Reported in the Proceedings of the Institute on Police-Community Relations, (May 15-20, 1955). The School of Police Administration and Public Safety, Michigan State University, East Lansing. Cited in Niederhoffer, A. (1969). *Behind the shield: The Police in Urban Society*. New York: Anchor Books.

Durkheim, E. (1933). *The Division of Labor in Society* (English Trans.). New York: Free Press.

Ellis, R. N. (1989). *The Ute Legacy*. Colorado: Southern Ute Cultural Center: Colorado.

FitzPatrick, V. (2000). *Red Twilight: The last free days of the Ute Indians*. Colorado: Yellow Cat Publishing.

Haller, M. H. (1976). Chicago cops: 1890-1925. *Law and Society Review, 10*(2), 303-323.

Jefferson, J., Roberts, W. D., & Thompson, G. C. (1972). *The Southern Utes: A Tribal History*. Colorado: Southern Ute Tribe.

Jesilow, P., & Parsons, D. (2001). Community policing as peacemaking. *Policing and Society, 10*, 163-182.

Jesilow, P., Meyer, J., & Namazzi, N. (1995). Public attitudes towards the police. *American Journal of Police, 19*(2), 67-88.

Miller, W. (1973). *Cops and Bobbies: Police authority in New York and London, 1830-1870*. Chicago: The University of Chicago Press.

Pettit, J. (1990). *Utes: The mountain people*. Colorado: Johnson Books.

Quintana, F. L. (2004). *Ordeal of change: The Southern Utes and their neighbors*. New York: Altamira Press.

Richland, J. B. (2005). What are you going to do with the village's knowledge? Talking tradition, talking law in Hopi tribal court. *Law & Society Review*, *32*(9), 235-272.
Shattuck, P. T., & Norgren, J. (1991). *Partial justice: Federal Indian law in a liberal constitutional system.* Oxford: Berg Publishers, Inc.
Smith, P. D. (1990). *Ouray, Chief of the Utes: The fascinating story of Colorado's most famous and controversial Indian chief.* Colorado: Wayfinder Press.
Wilkins, D. E. (1987). *Dine' Bibeehaz'Âanii: A Handbook of Navajo Government.* Tsaile, Arizona: Navajo Community College press.

## Cases cited

Santa Clara Pueblo vs. Martinez, 436 U.S. 49 (1978).
Ute Indians vs. United States, 330 U.S. 169 (1947).
Wheeler-Howard Act of June 18th, 1934 (also known as the Indian Reorganization Act or IRA).
25 U.S.C.A. 461-479 (1934), 48 Stat. 984 (1934).

# CHAPTER THIRTY

# THE EVOLUTION AND SOCIAL DYNAMICS OF PRISONS IN NIGERIA

IKUTEYIJO LANRE OLUSEGUN
AND AGUNBIADE OJO MELVIN

## Abstract

The prison system in Nigeria is currently undergoing some reforms and this is an attestation that the system is changing some of its philosophies. However, to what extent these changes will go and the likely success or otherwise of this endeavour depends on the readiness of the political will to implement the principles of the reforms. This chapter traces the evolution of prisons in Nigeria, examining the social dynamics involved in the transition from the British-inherited system, which still dominates the prison philosophy in Nigeria, to the current reforms influenced by the global events in criminal justice system. Some health challenges faced by prisoners, which include substance abuse, mental illness and communicable diseases in prisons, are also examined. Improved prisoner-officer relationship, which is part of the outcome of this reform, is also examined and it is concluded that the social structures exert pressure on the effectiveness and efficiency of the roles of prison officers either as reform or punitive agents. Lastly, the chapter examines the state of women prisoners in Nigeria, more so those who give birth in prisons. The chapter concluded that though the prison system in Nigeria is evolving from the retributive to the rehabilitative philosophy of penology, it requires a strong political will to attain the desired change.

## Introduction

The idea behind the setting up of prison in any community is usually either to keep offenders, who are under trials prior to the determination of their cases or to incarcerate convicted offenders. In any case, the offender is denied freedom to movement, association and some other fundamental human rights until liberty is regained either after serving the jail term or on being released on the prerogative of an authorized person. However, over the years, the prison as a system has been shaped by different ideologies, which determined, to a great extent the various operations of the system. For many years, when the idea of a prison began, the philosophy was more of punishment and retribution rather than the rehabilitation of the offender. However, with time the idea of a rehabilitative system began to evolve and many societies started tending towards the idea of rehabilitation and reformation.

In Nigeria, the prison system is also currently undergoing some reforms and this is an attestation to the fact that the system is changing some of its philosophies. However, to what extent these changes will go and the likely success or otherwise of this endeavour depends on the readiness of the political class and prison authorities to enforce the principles of the reforms. This chapter traces the evolution of modern prison in Nigeria, examining the social dynamics involved in the transition from the British-inherited system, which still dominates the prison philosophy in Nigeria, to the current reforms influenced by the global events in criminal justice system around the world and prison health in Nigeria.

## The Origin of Prisons in Nigeria

Globally, the establishment of the prison as a correctional institution dates back to many centuries. In fact, it could be very difficult trying to pinpoint the establishment of prisons to a particular time. This is simply because crime, which leads to imprisonment, is as old as man. Several authors have also noted that what is today known, as the "prison" did not begin with that intention. For instance, Rothman (cited in Alemika, 1987, Enuku, 2001) observed that prison began all over the world not as ultimate institutions for punishment and correction but it was initially meant for the custody of persons caught up in the criminal justice system awaiting trials or the execution of their punishment, which could be, for example, whipping, banishment or death depending on the seriousness of the crime committed.

The prison assumed a custodial role until the mid 19$^{th}$ century when it changed to the institution for enforcing punishment, penitence and correction of the offender (Enuku, 2001). Morris and Rothman, (1995) observed that prisons are common in many societies and prisons constitute a vital part of the criminal justice system. Spierenburg, (1998) argued that in the Dutch Republic, prisons and workhouses were established to lock up beggars and vagrants; while Carney (1979), traced the antecedents of the prison to many historical influences ranging from religion, architecture, philosophy as well as social custom. He further linked the antecedents or forerunners of the prison to institutions like the house of correction in Britain whose philosophy was to force inmates (mostly beggars, vagabonds and vagrant children) to perform hard and unpleasant labour. Such labour was meant to serve as deterrent to crime and convert idle drifters to lives of hard work and discipline. Some popular houses of correction in Europe include the one established at Amsterdam in 1596 and at Ghent, Belgium in 1773 (Carney, 1979).

The antecedents of prison in the pre-colonial Nigerian era have been traced to the Ogboni Cults among the Yorubas and the Ewedos among the people of Benin Kingdom (Elias, 1968). Also, Awe, (cited in Rotimi, 1982) opined that in Nigeria, certain places of detention were in existence before the arrival of the British. He gave the example of the Tivs and the Fulanis of the Northern region, who had designated buildings used as prisons. However, prisons were not as popular in the Eastern parts of the country as Meek, (cited in Rotimi, 1982) observed. More so, Achebe, (1958) in his epic novel, "Things Fall Apart", noted that slaves and criminals were usually kept in custody of the king or a mighty warrior. The prisoners were usually put to death either in form of ritual or outright execution as in the case of Ikemefuna, the slave boy who was put in care of Okonkwo, a notable warrior in the village. Ebbe, (1990) also noted that pre-colonial Nigeria did not employ prisons as penalties. Punishment took the form of fines, mutilation, castration excommunication, lynching, and dedication to the gods, in which case the offender becomes "untouchable".

Prison administration as it were in modern sense was first introduced by the British administration. The first prison in Nigeria was established in 1872 and was located on Broad Street in Lagos (Ebbe, 1990; Enuku, 2001; Rotimi, 1982, p. 74). Later on, prisons were established in other parts of the country, for example, Calabar, Onitsha, Benin City, Sapele, and Degema. (Rotimi, ibid.). In fact, by 1960, Ebbe (ibid.) noted that there was a prison in every provincial headquarters in Nigeria. Presently, Kirikiri is the largest prison complex and has both maximum and medium security branches (Rotimi, 1982; Ebbe, 1982; Igbinovia, 1984; Iwarime-Jaja, 1989).

The Nigerian Prison Service is headed by the Comptroller-General of prisons who is appointed by the President of Nigeria with the approval of the Public Service Commission. The system is currently under the Ministry of Internal Affairs and the present Nigerian prison system is modelled after the British system (Rotimi, 1982; Ebbe, 1990). Though there are certain innovations, which the British system has introduced over the years but which may seem impracticable presently in Nigeria due to certain structural reasons. Some of these reforms include the introduction of alternatives to imprisonment such as provision for probation, where an offender is allowed to serve other punishment under the supervision of the community in lieu of imprisonment. This is usually the case when the offender is either a "first time" offender or a minor. Another alternative is the parole system where a convicted prisoner who has shown signs of penitence and responsive to rehabilitative measures in the prison system is granted freedom on condition that he/she will not commit the offence which brought him/her to prison initially. Other alternatives to imprisonment are mentioned later in the chapter.

Since Nigeria inherited the present prison system from Britain, a brief look at the Prison experience in Britain as well as the much-celebrated reformation of the British prison system by Alexander Maconochie is the next stop point.

## Maconoche's Experience in Britain

In the epoch prior to 1840, the British prison system was characterised by cruelty and the abuse of prisoners common in the prison system of most developing nations today. The advent of Alexander Maconochie to the helms of affairs in March 1840 marked the beginning of a paradigm shift in the penal policy of Norfolk Island, a prison settlement in Britain. He had assumed duties as commandant of the penal settlement at Norfolk Island and applied his penal principles, which stated that:

> as cruelty debases both the victim and society, punishment should not be vindictive but should aim at the reform of the convict to observe social constraints, and a convict's imprisonment should consist of task, not time sentences, with release depending on the performance of a measurable amount of labour (Barry, 1958, p. 58).

In Maconochie's time cruel punishments and degrading conditions in prisons were reduced, and there was respect for convicts' sense of dignity. This respite however did not last as Maconochie was removed from office in 1843, but then a lasting impression had already been made by the reformer of note. Maconochie left a legacy that was to become a model for the treatment of prisoners in the western world. (Barry, ibid; Schuler, 2002). Similarly, just as the penal systems in England and later on in America have evolved over the years, so also has the system in some parts of the world. Let's now talk about the changing penal philosophies in Nigeria.

## Changing Philosophies of the Prisons in Nigeria

The society's reaction to crime and criminals is dynamic. Several years ago, crime and criminals were viewed as diabolical manifestation. Then the attitudes of the society towards prisoners were often based on an attempt to protect the society from the prisoner. These attitudes invariably had profound impact on the lives of prisoners as they were considered as getting too many benefits and receiving too little penalties. At that time, the society also treated criminals like devils; the need for a prison to hold criminals was not the primary concern of the society. Scholars are of the opinion that the reaction a particular society puts up against criminals and criminal behaviour reflects the society's level of development.

Over the years, penal philosophies have changed from retribution and deterrence to rehabilitation and reformation. Churchill, (cited in Carney, 1979) observed that the mood and temper of the public with regards to the treatment of crime and criminals is one of the unfailing tests of civilization. Mandela, (1994) also noted that the litmus test of a nation's development is not just in the ways its elite citizens are treated but how the seemingly "unimportant" people (like prisoners) are treated. Moreover, Rotimi, (1983), noted that the prison system of any society reflects the penal policy, philosophy and sentiments expressed by that particular society. The transformation from retribution and deterrence to rehabilitation and reformation has concomitantly led to a radical break with outdated prison traditions and modifications in the functions and training of prison personnel (Carney, 1979). Prison staff in many developed countries of the world now recognizes that they are not just mere guards, whose sole task is to deprive people of their liberty instead, they have to combine a custodial role with educational and reformative roles (Coyle, 2002). The direct implication of this is the unassailable fact that the society is now changing their perception of the prisoner from an insignificant member of the society who must be left to die gradually of neglect and harsh treatment, to an individual with certain inalienable rights. Thanks to global events in criminal justice, the prison authorities are now aware that the prisoner should be reformed to re-enter the society as a better citizen. Other major highlights of the changing prison philosophies include:

- The incorporation of counselling programmes within the facility, which allow offenders deal with the addictions and behaviours that brought them to prison and refrain from returning to the same lifestyle upon release, thereby helping them break the cycle of incarceration and reduce recidivism.

- The availability of life skills and educational classes to inmates to help them deal with the needs and stress of everyday life, and to seek gainful employment upon release, thus becoming productive members of the society.
- The prison philosophy, which sees prisoners as redeemable, therefore equipping them with abilities to deal with everyday activities rather than as incorrigible elements injurious to the society.

However, since the society's reaction to crime cannot be divorced from the programmes available in prisons as well as the role of prison officers in the implementation of such programmes, prison officers should be trained to be caregivers and reformers, a far cry from their traditional role of being taskmasters, who consistently ensured strict compliance with outdated prison principles.

Finally, one important aim of the changing philosophies of the penal system is to allow for a programme, which would permit the prisoners to be abreast with developments outside the prison walls, and not allowing them to be stagnant while the outside world is developing. This ideation is represented in current alternatives to imprisonment like the "open air" prison system, where offenders are not totally secluded from the "outside world" but are allowed "controlled access" to the "outside world", borstal homes, which are meant for the rehabilitation of minor offenders, house arrest, electronic tagging, and community service among others. However, to what extent prisoners in Nigeria enjoy the associated benefits of the ideology of reformation and rehabilitation in relation to prisons condition and prisoners' health is discussed in the following sub-themes.

## Prison Health and Health Challenges of Prisoners

Health remains one of the most serious casualties consequent on the poverty, social exclusion, marginalisation and lack of sustainable development in Africa (NEPAD Health Strategy, 2004, p. 4); as such a discourse on Prisons health cannot be divulged from the social interactions obtainable within the paradigm on which a society's prison system operates. Prisoners most times are from the poorest sectors of the society and as a result suffer from inequitable access to health care services. Prisons being places with concentrations of poor people, overcrowding and poor food; it is therefore not surprising to find neglect of health and hygiene leading to infections and diseases. Basically, the society has an obligation towards prisons' health for two reasons. First, the prisoners do not enjoy the kind of access to medical expertise that free citizens have. Their incarceration places limitations on such access, no physician of choice, no second options, and few if any specialists. Secondly, because of the conditions of their incarceration, inmates are exposed to more health hazards than free citizens. Being in prison generally exacerbates prisoners' health problems (de Viggiani, 2007). More so, incarcerating any one especially the vulnerable groups such as drug users and those with mental illness has serious health and social implications (The Lancet, 2005). Prisoners therefore, suffer from a double handicap. The myriad challenges facing prisoners in Nigeria and governments' inability in providing quality and equitable access to health care services have not only placed prisoners but also 'free individuals' at different axis of the health care production spectrum. While the gross inadequacy of modern health facilities and inadequacies of physicians have attracted governments' attention (NEPAD Health Strategy, 2004, p. 6), the same cannot be said about the welfare of the prisoners. The average prisoner is usually on a higher web of susceptibility to more health problems than the 'free'. Often, Prisoners bring a range of health problems to prison and are also at risk from a number of health problems while in prison (Watson, Anne, & Hostick, 2004). A review of the literature by Watson et al, (ibid) shows a range of health issues among prisoners to be the following: Mental health; Substance abuse and Communicable diseases. The reality of these health problems have also been confirmed by some studies in Nigeria (Adesanya, Ohaeri, Ogunlesi, Adamson, & Odejide, 1997; Agbahowe, Ohaeri, Ogunlesi, & Osahon, 1998). Hence, our next dialogue on prisons health will be on these issues.

## Mental Health of Prisoners

Health represents a key input to human productivity. According to the World Health Organisation (WHO), health is a state of complete physical, mental and social well-being and not merely the absence of disease or infirmity (2001, p. 1). From this definition, mental health represents a crucial aspect of what constitutes a healthy individual. Attaining a perfect health as projected by the above definition may be difficult. However, for the purpose of conceptualisation, the WHO (2001a, p. 1) proposed mental health as a state of well-being in which the individual realises his or her own abilities, can cope with the normal stress of life, can work productively and fruitfully, and is able to make a contribution to his or her community. The desire to achieve a healthy society as described in the above definition does not exclude prisoners, since they are also members of the larger society. However in practice, some minor elements of retribution and general deterrence philosophy still operate in the care for prisoners with mental health problems in the Nigerian prison. Inmates suffering from this problem are at times perceived to be suffering as a result of their past evil deeds. Such perception evolves from the larger social system's conception of the disease aetiology and the search for solution. The retributive and deterrence rationale for punishment and prisons does not provide the necessary framework for the promotion of mental health in prisons. In principle, retributive and deterrence model considers it necessary to use the criminal as an "example to himself/herself and others". By subjecting prisoners to harsh conditions, authorities hope to convince them to avoid future criminal behaviour and to exemplify for others the rewards for avoiding such behaviour; in other words, the fear of punishment will win over whatever pleasure the illegal activity might bring. Despite recent emulation of rehabilitation and reformation ideology in the Nigerian penal system, many of the colonial inheritance are still maintained in the nation's penal codes and prisons administration. Although it may not be appropriate to lay the total blame on the colonial masters, it would be necessary to emphasis here that class relations in the light of political economy of the Nigerian state have also provided supportive roles in the maintenance of the status quo and failure to drastically reform Nigerian prisons in the face of the myriad of problems facing prisons administration in Nigeria.

Referrals to modern psychiatric hospitals have been the usual practice in meeting the mental health needs of prisoners in Nigeria; however, a more culturally compatible option - a community based model fashioned inline with the socio-cultural realities of the people would be better. The effectiveness of such model in meeting the increasing mental health challenges of the generality has been confirmed at the 'Aro' psychiatric hospital (Ogedenge, 1986). However, it may be difficult applying the 'Aro' mental hospital model as a panacea; as factors such as urbanisation, finance among other factors may serve as hindrances. Other alternatives could be the introduction of open- air prisons strategy as this may be favourable in promoting the general health of the prisoners. However, this will only materialise with the necessary political support. Again other options such as engaging prisoners in sporting activities and skills acquisition may be beneficial to the prisoners as well as the prison staff. While sporting facilities are grossly lacking in many Nigerian prisons;

skills acquisition programmes have been in operation, but more needs to be done in this direction especially by the three tiers of government.

In the final analysis, empirical studies on mental health issues in Nigerian remains crucial in providing the empirical base on which prisons reform in Nigeria could be achieved. An appraisal of the mental health policy in Nigeria by Odebiyi (1998) revealed a generally poor attitude from the government and other stakeholders towards the mentally ill. Again, those in prisons are worse off as they are left out of the policy. The policy has not lived up to expectations in meeting the challenges of caring for the mentally ill in the society and the prisons. Another worrisome problem among prisoners in Nigeria is the increasing prevalence of substance abuse. The increasing rates of substance abuse among prisoners have further made the search for solutions to prisoners' problems more complex. A full adoption and implementation of rehabilitation and reformation ideologies may likely change the situation as this will also affect prison staff orientation and equip the system with professionals that could better manage the complex problem facing the prison system including the problem of substance abuse among prisoners. In line to restore professionalism in the Nigerian prison service, an upward review of the minimum educational qualification any officer should possess has just been initiated. Such efforts may lead to improvement in staff quality as well as the success of prison reforms. However, attracting, developing and retaining quality staff would also necessitate an upward review of the remuneration package of prison staff. Poor remuneration of public employees by the government has caused series of industrial unrest in Nigeria over the years and preference for private employments even among health caregivers.

## Substance Abuse Problem among Nigerian Prison Population

Substance abuse is at times used as a synonym for *drug abuse*, *drug addiction*, and chemical dependency, but our discussions here will be based on the use of substances in a manner outside socio-cultural conventions. The use of illegal drugs was recognised as a major category of health problems among prisoners by the WHO (1999). Substance abuse is common in prisons and very common among those committed to prisons (Watson et al., 2004). Effort to explore the varieties of drugs being abused by prisoners in Nigeria was documented could be seen in Adesanya et al. (ibid). Findings from the study revealed a high prevalence of substance abuse among prisoners. Cannabis was reported to be a commonly abused substance. The readily availability of Cannabis in the surrounding communities of prison yard and the cheap cost of the drug compared with other drugs were proposed as reasons for the free flow of the substance among inmates (Adesanya, et al., ibid). Most prisoners being poor receive less significant attention, while those with better economic status are treated with preference by the prison staff. Enuku (2001) narrated his unfair treatment in the hands of prison staff in one Nigeria prison. While he was denied access to books in the prison where he was, a colleague of his incarcerated for a similar offence and serving in a different but similar prison status was allowed access. If the economic background of prisoners could influence access to items like books, how much more access to cannabis by the influential prisoners? Though there are no enough evidences to support the role of prison staff in the free flow of cannabis in Nigerian prisons, but this cannot be ruled out based on the high level of corruption in Nigeria- a problem currently being rigorously addressed by the present government. Controlling substances like cannabis in Nigeria has been a general problem for sometime. Attempts have been made by the government in discouraging and prohibiting the farming and sale of cannabis among other hard drugs, but much could not be said to have been achieved in this regard. Many local farmers producing the substance have been caught one time or the other and tried; yet cannabis still remains readily available to their consumers in many Nigerian communities (Wannenburg, 2005). It should be emphasized here again that many of the prisoners that are psychotic abusers may have been in the act even before their incarceration. This may be in addition to the predisposition powers of psychological and social-cultural factors.

Programmes and policies have been initiated and implemented to reducing the trafficking and use of hard drugs in Nigeria. Have these efforts yielded fruitful results? The question of how far has the Nigerian society gone in addressing the problem of substance abuse in the society may not be fully explored here. Attempts by the government to curb the wide spread and trafficking of hard drugs led to the promulgation of the National Drug Law Enforcement Agency (NDLEA) by Decree 48 of 1989. This agency has been in the vanguard of the crusade discouraging trafficking and use of hard drugs in Nigeria. A level of achievement could be said to have been realised especially in the arrest and prosecution of offenders by the agency. One would still expect more from this agency especially when their activities are juxtaposed along side of a sister agency the National Agency for Food, Drug Administration and Control (NAFDAC) created by Decree 15 of 1993. The high prevalence of cannabis use among prison population is worrisome; an observation earlier made by Rotimi (1982). Although certain social structural factors may have inhibited the efficiency and effectiveness of this government agency; the issue of substance abuse in Nigerian prisons calls for urgent attention. Efforts have been made towards alleviating the problem of substance abuse among prisoners; but this has also been met with several problems. Although most of the programmes and policies towards readdressing the problem of substance abuse have been institutionally fashioned and predetermined by professionals, agencies and other stakeholders, much consideration has not been extended to the sufferers who also are "thinking beings" and at the same time are the ones going through the experience. In addition, some of the socio-economic challenges that promoted the business of Drug trafficking in Nigeria in the 80s are still present. Thus controlling substance abuse using punitive measures like those within the prison wall and NDLEA would not solve the problem until the socio-economic factors promoting the business of hard drugs at the grass roots among farmers and the larger society are adequately addressed. Hence, a continuation in the use of institutional paradigm in addressing prisoners' challenges may not yield much result as the critical stakeholders-the inmates involved are mostly isolated; thus, still reflecting society's fear of placing and ascribing positive social values to prisoners. This again questions the reformation of prisoners outside a participatory paradigm which considers inputs and prisoners initiatives as important variables in prison reforms. Though there are moves by the present democratic government to reform the economy and which has started yielding some benefits, but there are still gross economic inequalities especially among the civil servants and political office holders.

The adoption and utilisation of participatory perspective in prison system reforms may be more fruitful in achieving more, than using the prevailing paradigm of predetermination of prison problems and solution by the 'experts'. For instance, Hucklesby and Wilkinson (2001) reported that mandatory drug testing as a rehabilitation programme for prisoners has reduced substance abuse in some circumstances, but it also leads to the use of harder drugs. Hence, addressing the problem of substance abuse within the existing framework of prisons administration in Nigeria would be problematic. The focusing of prison reforms on Institution and prison staff with little or no attention on the prisoners again reflects a dominant orientation of elites and the larger society on who prisoners are; factors predisposing individuals to criminal acts; reasons for substance abuse and proffering potential answers to prison problems. The increasing disease burden in developing nations, Nigeria inclusive has not left the prisons population out coupled with the neglect of prisons conditions which has made prisons suitable abode for communicable diseases.

## Communicable Diseases among Prison Population

The reality of HIV/AIDS in Africa and Nigeria in particular is no longer controversial. Various studies have shown the increasing prevalence of sexually transmitted diseases in Nigeria (Ogunbanjo, 1989; Aboyeji & Nwabuisi, 2003; Dehne & Riedner, 2005). While HIV/AIDS seems to be attracting much attention than other communicable diseases, this does not negate the presence of other infections among the prison population. Available empirical evidence on communicable diseases among prison population revealed sexually transmitted infections including HIV/AIDS as the leading diseases (Okochi, Oladepo, & Ademola, 1999; Panchaud, Woog, Singh, Darroch, & Bankole, 2002). An estimate in a report by Potts and Black (cited in Watson, ibid) indicts the prevalence rate of sexually transmitted infection including HIV/AIDS among prisoners, to be 20 times greater than that of the general population. Sexually transmitted infection in prison has become global and thus commands some level of attention. The spatial arrangement of prisons and the involvement of some prisoners in risky sexual behaviour amongst other factors have placed today's Nigerian prisoners in a complex web of susceptibility to various communicable diseases. A study by Okochi et al. (ibid) on sexually transmitted infections (STIs) among prisoners in Agodi Ibadan, Nigeria, revealed that inmates' males and females engage in risky sexual behaviours which may further aggravate the spread of HIV/AIDS and other STIs in prisons. Prisons in Nigeria like in some other cultures have become overcrowded (Enuku, 2001). Providing an explanation for this development requires a complex model as prison crowding is also embedded in a complex network of social structures and social relationships. So also are the solutions to prison overcrowding which has somewhat become a global phenomenon (Bolduc, 1985). Generally, many of those in prisons are under trails or detenus, as such reducing overcrowding in Nigerian prisons may require speeding up the judiciary process and respect for fundamental rights at all levels. Part-time judges may also be employed in this regard to increase the numerical strength of the judges.

Another critical communicable disease among prisoners is tuberculosis. Tuberculosis (TB) has been ranked $9^{th}$ leading global health problem (United Nations Development Programme, 2006). Many studies have confirmed the favourable nature of prisons conditions to the spread of TB.

High mortality and drug resistance rate have also been confirmed by these studies (Reyes & Coninx, 1997; Coninix, Mathieu, Debacker, Mirzoev, Ismaelov, de Haller, & Meddings, 1999). Are these issues been considered as a public health problem in Nigeria? As discussed above, health problems in Nigeria over the years have been addressed from class based approach. While the elites and the affluent in the society have adequate access to modern health care services most poor and less privileged are most times left on their own to survive. The prisoners class ranks the most disadvantaged in this interaction. Thus, the adoption of open-air prison would be economical in meeting the sexual needs and reducing the associated problems with risky sexual behaviour. It may also minimise the further spread of TB among other communicable diseases. Open-air prison would be of tremendous benefit to the prisoners and prison staff in general. For the prisoners, it not only enhance their process of re-entry after regaining freedom; it will also improve their total health; allow more access to their spouse or sexual partner as the case may be; and also improve their level of awareness of critical developments within the larger society.

## The Prison Staff –Prisoners Interaction

In Parsonian analysis of the social system, roles are defined within the social structures in which individual actors operate (Parson, 1962). As such, Prison Staff are simultaneously members of the larger social system and also occupy specific positions that are considered functional to the achievement of prison functions. These roles also change in relation to the prison philosophy obtainable within the prevailing political economy and other social forces. The social system through the socialization process indoctrinates the various prison staff and prisoners into various roles that are based on the societal and institutional expectations attached to their positions. While one may not deny the influence of behavioural or psychological traits on the staff and prisoners' perception and actual performance of roles, the social structures (economic, political, and religious, among others) exert pressure on the effectiveness and efficiency or none performance of these roles. The interaction outcomes between prison staff and prisoner remain critical to the overall objective of the prison system

Expounding on the prison staff –prisoner interaction, Liebling (2006) argued that prison staff understood that order in prisons might depend on developing good relationship with or 'being nice' to prisoners. Taking a humane approach by prison staff will assist prisoners psychologically in dealing with the mental trauma within the four walls of a prison. In practice, 'being nice with or to prisoners is a relative concept. While consensus may be difficult in this regard, making modern prisons humane may not be too difficult when the necessary ideology and political support becomes readily available as could be seen in Maconoche's experience earlier discussed. Under the ongoing prison reforms in Nigeria prison staffs are being trained to appreciate and respect prisoner's rights. This may take some time. Presently the inhumane condition of Nigerian prisons, which is similar to, prisons condition in some other developing nations, calls for a radical approach towards making the Nigerian prison humane.

Theoretically, the Prison staff role within a deterrence model is to represent and communicate the social norms and values to the prisoner in order to control their deviance. As new entrants into the prison system, staff and prisoners are indoctrinated into the different norms and values that guide their interactions. As new recruits in the prison system, prisoners are ordered to surrender all that identified them as responsible adults, allocated a prison uniform and number and are addressed only by surname. The roles attached to prison staff and prisoners positions are subsequently displayed in the power sharing and creation of social outcomes in prison system. Though the prison manuals recognise the rights of prisoners; however in practice representing and acting such beliefs by prison staff will depend on their level of private and public compliance to such provisions.

In practice, the interaction between prison staff and inmates to a large extent differ from what the ideal relationship as defined by the prison system. Liebling (ibid) argued that prison life is really all about relationships. Moral and emotional climates can be easily identified by the keen observer. Although there are variations in the expressions and outcomes obtainable, however, treating a person fairly signifies that they are of value. On the contrary, disrespect denies a person's validity, causing not only righteous indignation and deviance-two relatively health emotions for the individual-but could also result in distress and unresolved shame.

The plausibility of having human prison condition in Nigeria may take more years to achieve based on internal; and external hindrances to the prison sub-system. There is a strong interference on the nature of the interaction between prison staff and inmates and other agencies of the government saddled with the responsibilities of maintaining law and order in the society. Most times some of the factors affecting the prison system could be better appreciated by locating it within the larger social system. In a recent interview, the Comptroller General of the Nigerian Prisons

Service lamented a situation where inmates dictate how the prison is governed, describing it as far from ideal. He further reacted to the public criticisms that the Nigerian prison has lost touch of its mandate of keeping suspects and convicts in safe custody and accepted the complexity of the problems of the Nigerian Prisons Service citing the mandate to keep suspects in secure custody as a major shortcoming of the prison system (Daily Sun, August, 7, 2006). The deplorable condition of the Nigerian prisons has attracted prisoners' reactions which have manifested in increased number of jail breaks in recent times. The phenomenon of jail breaks by prisoners in Nigerian calls for more concrete efforts towards making the Nigerian prison system humane. Making Nigerian prisons humane may start from giving dilapidating prisons a face lift. Many of the existing prisons were structures built several years ago and need to be line with the increasing rate of prison population recently put at 40,444 (Centre for prison studies, 2005).

While prison population has increased, prison facilities have remained unimproved until recently when some forms of refurbishment started taking place and may take some years before many of the existing prisons across the six geopolitical zones in Nigeria could be reached. Although the current prison policy and practice in Nigeria gives a rather pessimistic outlook in relation to the adoption and implementation of humane prison administration policies as contained in the United Nations (1999) Minimum Standard for the Treatment of Offenders. This is currently in practice in some parts of the world especially in Europe and North America (Enuku, 2001). The adoption and implementation of this form of policy in Nigeria, requires necessary political will and a new orientation to prisons on the part of those in charge of prison administration in Nigeria. A temporary remedy which may also serve as a check on the compliance of prison staff to minimum standards for treating offenders may be the provision of feedback boxes in every cell. This should be completely beyond the access of prison staff. An external body such as Human rights organisations could be in charge of the feedback boxes. The continuous implementation of 'one-sided approach' towards addressing prison problems will not be sufficient in realising the fruits of prison reforms. Hence, efforts should be towards a participatory philosophy that would entertain contributions from prisoners, ex-convicts among other stake holders in reforming prison system.

## Women Prisoners and their Children

A disproportionate number of women are wasting away in non-rehabilitative institutions that perpetuate rather than correct criminal behaviours. Female offenders represent a rapid proportion of the ever-increasing prison population. While statistical information on this category of prisoners abounds, limited research efforts have been directed towards exploring the experiences of incarcerated women (Williams & Schulte-Day, 2006). Obviously women prisoners are separate category from their male counterparts. While prisoners generally are confronted with series of health related problems, women prisoners are unique in terms of experiences and apart from the socio-cultural and biological factors that separates their reality from that of their male counterparts. The experiences of pregnant women in prisons for instance are further demarcated from other prisoners'. Being in prison creates a unique and complex set of problems for pregnant women and their children and families. Pregnant women in prison also lack social support from friends and family. They are most times single and from poor socio-economic background (Williams & Schulte-Day, 2006).

In spite of the above background, prevailing prisons condition in Nigeria seems to be blind to the peculiarities of women prisoners especially the pregnant ones among them (Hensley & Tewksbury, 2002; Okochi, et al., ibid). What about the children of incarcerated parents? Children whose parents have been arrested and incarcerated face unique difficulties. Many have experienced the trauma of sudden separation from their sole caregiver, and most are vulnerable to feelings of fear, anxiety, anger, sadness, depression and guilt (Seymour, cited in Wear, 2000). Generally separation is more harmful when the child is young (McGowan & Blumenthal, cited in Sherman, 2005). The incarceration of children with their mothers especially when young also reflects the total war on prisoners and those associated with them.

Although things seem to be a bit better than the pre-colonial and colonial periods of prisons in Nigeria; however, much could not be said to have been achieved in terms of promoting female prisoners health in Nigeria, as separation of females from their male counterparts has been the major consideration given to female prisoners. Many at times, married female prisoners are denied access to their husbands and children and those nursing their children may be kept along side their children in the prison yard which is unfavourable to the psychological growth and development of such children. Again, the use of open-air prison approach may come into play as an alternative, while female prisoners especially the nursing mothers among them could attract special preference in terms of the minimum number of hour they would be allowed to spend outside. This will not only benefit the prisoners but could also have psychological impacts on their families as they may see it as a hope of regaining freedom one day. In the final analysis, a global view of women and children in prisons across cultures still reflects the parochial attitude of the society towards prisoners needs irrespective of prisoners' gender.

## Conclusion and Recommendations

The global developments in penal philosophy indeed call for a shift in penal principles from punishment and retribution to reformation and rehabilitation. In line with this, it is therefore recommended that philosophy underlining the prison system in Nigeria reflect the current trend in the global scene. Many of the developed communities have also devised other alternatives to imprisonment. Since prison congestion is a problem across the globe, many alternatives have been devised in lieu of imprisonment. Some of these include probation, parole, electronic tagging, and fines, among others. Prison staff should be trained on the effective use of these alternatives. Some of these may require that prison staff go for tailored courses (on-the job training and off the job training) to enable them operate more effectively or a review of the training curriculum of prison staff to incorporate the techniques reflecting the reformative and rehabilitative philosophy. It may also require that the prison structures be re-engineered to entertain such innovations like making the system compliant to modern information technology.

The institutionalization of psychiatric department in the prison system should also be replaced with or community psychiatric care. The effectiveness of this type of care has been confirmed in a study by Ogedengbe (1986). If this is introduced into prison health it will make it more reflective of the shift in philosophy. Prisoners' mental heath should be considered important; since some of them may regain their freedom someday and go back to the society. Also the idea of public private partnership (PPP) that is thriving in other sectors can be introduced to the prison management in Nigeria. A shift in philosophy is necessary to enable Nigeria maintain her pride of place in the comity of nations.

In the final analysis, future empirical studies especially from a participatory paradigm will be necessary in the search for holistic solutions to the challenges faced by the Nigerian prison system. Pilot prisons fashioned along rehabilitation and reformation ideology could be tested in some communities before it becomes a national policy. It is hoped that if these ideas are implemented and backed up by the political will, the Nigerian prison system will not only be reflecting the reformative and rehabilitative penal philosophy, it will also serve as a crucial break from anachronistic penal philosophy from which many developing and developed nations of the world are breaking.

## References

Aboyeji A. P., & Nwabuisi C. (2003). Prevalence of sexually transmitted diseases among pregnant women in Ilorin, Nigeria. *Journal of Obstetrics & Gynaecology*, 2003 - Taylor & Francis Abstract. Retrieved March 2, 2007 from http://taylorandfrancis.metapress.com/content/mf8t2cpemxwl25uf/.

Achebe, C. (1958). *Things fall apart.* London: Heinemann Educational books Limited.

Adesanya, A., Ohaeri, U. J., Ogunlesi, A. A., Taiwo, & Odejide, A. (1997). Psychoactive substance abuse among inmates of a Nigerian prison population. *Drug and Alcohol Dependence, 47*, 39-44.

Agbahowe, S. A., Ohaeri, J. U., Ogunlesi, A. O., & Osahon, R., (1998). Prevalence of psychiatric morbidity among convicted inmates in a Nigerian prison community. *East African Medical Journal*, *75*, 1.

Alemika, E. E. O., (1983). The smoke screen: Rhetoric and reality of penal incarceration in Nigeria. *International Journal of Comparative and Applied Criminal Justice*, *1*, 137-149.

Barry, J. V. (1958). *Alexander Maconochie of Norfolk Island.* Melbourne: Oxford University Press.

Bolduc, A., (1985). *Jail crowding*. The Annals of the American Academy. Retrieved on January 12, 2007 from http://www.jstor.org.

Carney, L. P. (1979). *Introduction to correctional science.* Dallas, McGraw- Hill Inc. U.S.A.

Center for the Right to Health. (2003). HIV/AIDS and Human Rights in Nigeria. Background Paper for HIV/AIDS Policy Review in Nigeria.

Coninx, R., Mathieu, C., Debacker, M., Mirzoev, F., Ismaelov, A., de Haller, R., & Meddings, D. R. (1999). First-line tuberculosis therapy and drug-resistant Mycobacterium tuberculosis in prisons. *The Lancet*, 353, 969–973.

Coyle, A. (2002). *A human rights approach to prison management handbook for prison staff.* International Centre for Prison Studies York Road London United Kingdom.

Daily Sun (August 7, 2006). Shocking prison inmates dictates how prison is governed. Retrieved December 11, 2006 from http://www.sunnewsonline.com/webpages/news/abujareports/2006/aug/07/abujaroport-07-08-2006-001.htm.

De V. N. (2007). Unhealthy prisons: exploring structural determinants of Prison health. *Sociology of Health and Illness*, *29*, 1,115-135.

Dehne K., & Riedner, G. (2005). Sexually transmitted infections among adolescent. Retrieved March, 2, 2007, from http://www.who.int/reproductive-health/publications/stis_among_adolescents/stis_among_adolescents_adequate_health_services.pdf.

Ebbe, O. N. I. (1982). *Crime in Nigeria: an analysis of characteristics of offenders incarcerated in Nigerian prisons*. Ann Arbor: University Microfilms International.

—. (1990). *World Fact book of Criminal Justice, Nigeria*. State University of New York, Brockport.

Enuku, U. E. (2001). Humanizing the Nigerian prison through literacy education: Echoes from afar. *The Journal of Correctional Education*, *52*, 18-22.

Fazel, S., & Danesh, J. (2002). Serious mental disorder in 23,000 prisoners: A systematic review of 62 surveys. *The Lancet*, 359,545-550. Retrieved March 8, 2007, from http://www.thelancet.com.

Hensley, C., & Tewksbury, R. (2002). Inmate to Inmate Prison Sexuality. Abstract. Retrieved March 16, 2007, from http://tva.sagepub.com/cgi/content/abstract/3/3/226.

Hilton, N. Z., & Simmons, J. L. (2001). The influence of actuarial risk assessment in clinical judgements and tribunal decisions about mentally disordered offenders in maximum security. *Law and Human Behaviour*, *25*,393-408.

Hoptman, M. J., Yates, K. F., Patalinjug, M. B., Wack, R. C. M., & Convit, A. (1999). Clinical prediction of assaultive behaviour among male psychiatric patients at a maximum-security forensic facility. *Psychiatric Services*, 50, 1462–1466.

Hucklesby, A., & Wilkinson, C., (2001). Drug misuse in prisons: Some comments on the prison service drug strategy. *The Howard Journal,* 40, 347–363.

Igbinovia, P. E. (1988). Nigeria. World Encyclopedia of Police Forces and Penal Systems. G. T. Kurian. (Ed.) (New York: Facts on File).

International Centre for Prison Studies. (2005). Prison brief for Nigeria. Retrieved January 05, 2007, from http://www.kcl.ac.uk/depsta/rel/icps/worldbrief/africa_records.php?code=38.

Iwarime, J. D. (1989). Corrections in Nigeria: A system of reform. *Criminal Justice International*, *5*, 5, 13-19.

Liebling A. U. K. (2006). Prisons in transition. *International Journal of Law and Psychiatry*. *29*(5), 422-430.

Mandela, N. (1994). *Long Walk to Freedom*. London. Little Brown, UK.

Morris, N., & Rothman, D. J. (1995). *The Oxford History of the Prison: The Practice of Punishment in Western Society*. Oxford: Oxford University Press.

Odebiyi, A. (1998). *Appraisal of the mental health care policy in Nigeria*. Ibadan: Development Policy Centre.

Ogedengbe, R. O. (1986). Post-hospital adjustment of former mentally disturbed patients: A case study of discharged patients in two psychiatric centres in Abeokuta. M.Sc. Thesis (unpublished) Obafemi Awolowo University, Ile-Ife, Nigeria.

—. (1989). Sexually transmitted diseases in Nigeria: A review of the present situation. *West African Journal of Medicine*. Abstract. Retrieved March 2, 2007, from http://www.ncbi.nlm.nih.gov/.

Okochi, C. A., Oladepo, O., & Ajuwon, A. J. (1999). Knowledge about AIDS and sexual behaviours of inmates of agodi prison in Ibadan, Nigeria. *International Quarterly of Community Health Education, 19*, 4.

Panchaud, C., Woog, V., Singh, S., Darroch, J. E., & Bankole, A. (2002). Issues in measuring HIV prevalence: The case of Nigeria. *African Journal of Reproductive Health*, *6*, 3, 11-29.

Parsons, T. (1962). *The Social Theories of Talcott Parsons. A critical examination by Black Max*. Englewood Cliffs, N.J. : Prentice-hall, Inc.

Reyes, H., & Coninx, R. (1997). Pitfalls of tuberculosis programmes in prisons. *BMJ*, *315*, 1447-1450 (29 November). Retrieved February 7, 2007 from http://www.bmj.com/cgi/content/full/315/7120/1447.

Rotimi, A. (1982). Prison administration in modern Nigeria. *International Journal of Comparative and Applied Criminal Justice*, 9, 1, 73-83.

Rotimi, A. R. (1983). Penal policy, the public, and implications for prison administration in Nigeria. *Federal Probation*, September, 62-71.

Schuler, P. (2002). Law professor offers story of British naval captain and penal colony he supervised as parable for today's prison system. *The University of Chicago Chronicle*, 21, 13, 11.

Sherman, A. (2005). Children of prisoners. Retrieved March 16, 2007 from www.crocus.georgetown.edu/reports/bbr_children_of_prisoners.pdf .

The Lancet, Editorial (2005). Prison health: a threat or an opportunity. 366, July 2. Retrieved December 20, 2006, from http://www.thelancet.com.

The New Partnership for Africa's Development. (NEPAD) Health Strategy. (2004). Retrieved on, December 2o, 2004, from http://www.afro.who.int/dsd/nepad_health_strategy.pdf.

United Nations. (1999). Standard Minimum Rules for the Treatment of Prisoners: Annex 11-7. Retrieved March 3, 2007, from http://www.arts.mcgill.ca/programs/polisci/faculty/rexb/unsco-ruleoflaw/a11-7.html.

United Nations Development Programme. (2006). Human Development Report. Retrieved March 17, 2007, from http://hdr.undp.org/hdr2006/statistics/indicators/86.html.

Wannenburg, G. (2005). Organised crime in West Africa. *African Security Review* 14, 4. Retrieved March 20, 2007, from http://www.iss.org.za/pubs/ASR/14No4/F1.pdf.

Watson R., Stimpson, A., & Hostick. (2004). Prison health care: A review of Literature. *International journal of Nursing Studies, 41*, 119-128.

Wear S. C. (2000). Children of incarcerated parents. Retrieved March 16, 2007 from http://www.library.ca.gov/crb/00/notes/v7n2.pdf.

WHO (2001). *Basic documents 43rd Edition*. Geneva, World Health Organisation: 1.

—. (2001a). *Strengthening mental health promotion*. Geneva: World Health Organisation (Fact sheet, No.220).

—. (1999). *Health in Prisons project*. Geneva: World Health Organisation.

Williams, Li., & Schulte-Day, S. (2006). Pregnant in prison-The incarcerated woman's experience: A preliminary descriptive study. *Journal of Correctional Healthcare*, *12*(2), 78-88.

# About The Editor

**K. Jaishankar** (PhD) is an Assistant Professor (Senior) in the Department of Criminology and Criminal Justice, Manonmaniam Sundaranar University, Tirunelveli, Tamil Nadu, India. He is the founding Editor-in-Chief of the International Journal of Cyber Criminology and Editor-in-Chief of the International Journal of Criminal Justice Sciences. He is recently awarded the prestigious Commonwealth Academic Staff Fellowship, 2009-10 tenable at UK, University of Leeds. He is a Co-Investigator of an International grant funded by Social Science and Humanities Research Council of Canada to develop a profile of cyber-bullying, inform the current policy vacuum, and develop guidelines to help schools address cyber-bullying. He is a member of the UNODC (United Nations office of Drugs and Crime, Vienna, Austria) Core group of Experts on Identity related crime. Among the recent books he has written/ edited are: *Cyber Bullying: Profile and Policy Guidelines* (DOCCJ, Manonmaniam Sundaranar University, India, 2009), *Trends and Issues of Victimology* (Cambridge Scholars Publishing, UK, 2008), and *Crime Victims and Justice: An Introduction to Restorative Principles* (Serial Publications: New Delhi, 2008). He is the proponent of the *"Space Transition Theory of cyber crimes"* and it has appeared as a Chapter in F. Schmallager, & M. Pittaro (Eds.), *Crimes of the Internet.* Upper Saddle River, NJ: Prentice Hall. His articles have appeared in journals such as, *Punishment & Society, Journal of Contemporary Criminal Justice, Problèmes Politiques Et Sociaux, Journal of Law & Religion, Occasional series in Criminal Justice and International Studies* and others. His areas of Academic Competence are Cyber Criminology, Victimology, Crime mapping, GIS, Communal violence, Theoretical Criminology, Policing, and Crime prevention. Email:
drjaishankar@gmail.com URL: http://www.drjaishankar.co.nr

# CONTRIBUTORS

**Julie C. Abril** is an Assistant Professor, Sociology and Criminal Justice, Eastern New Mexico University, USA and Independent Contractor/Consultant; Executive Counsellor (Term, 2007 - 2009), Division of People of Color and Crime, American Society of Criminology. She received her PhD from the University of California, Irvine in the interdisciplinary Department of Criminology, Law and Society in 2005. She has published peer-reviewed work in the areas of violent victimization, identity, collective efficacy, women in prison, and community safety, cultural crime. She is primarily focused on issues facing modern Native American Indians and DNA genetic data collection. She has received research funds from the United States Department of Justice, National Institute of Justice and the United States Department of Health and Human Services, National Institutes of Health, as well as from a variety of other sources. In 2006, Dr. Abril received a National Research Service Award from the USDH&HS/NIH for her work on violent victimization occurring within one Indian tribal community. She has received many other awards and honours, including the ASC Minority Fellowship in 1998. As a public servant, she served in the White House during the William Jefferson Clinton Administration, the Santa Clara County Superior Court (CA), was an elected member of the Board of Directors of the American Indian Center of Santa Clara Valley (CA), as well as holding numerous other law related volunteer positions. Currently, Dr. Abril is an expert consultant on crime, violence and justice in Indian Country to the U.S. Department of Justice, Office of Justice Programs, National Institute of Justice and is a consultant to several federally-recognized American Indian tribal governments on matters of crime and community safety. Dr. Abril can be contacted at julie.abril@yahoo.com

**Okunola, Rasheed Akanji** obtained MSc and PhD in Criminology and Penology from University of Ibadan, Nigeria, where he has lectured for several years. He has reputation for research and teaching. He is a consultant to many organizations and his papers have appeared in many reputable journals both local and international. He has research interests Criminology, Penology, Mass Media and Popular culture.

**Hakan Aksoy** is a chief inspector and crime analysis expert at Turkish National Police (TNP). His expertise are in the fields of crime mapping and social network analysis. Hakan Aksoy graduated from National Police Academy in 1997. He has authored many articles on crime analysis. He pioneered the use of crime maps at Bursa Police Department in Turkey. He worked for Bursa Police Information Processing Unit for more than ten years. He initiated the usage of crime analysis tools such as creation of interlinked crime databases, integrating demographic data to hard and soft forensic data, using GPS, GIS technologies and crime maps. He is also a tutor for crime analysis trainings at TNP. Hakan can be contacted at aksoy975@yahoo.com

**Mohammed Saad Alfarhan** received a Master of Science in Geosciences (2003) and Master of Science in Geospatial Information Sciences (GIS) (2008) from The University of Texas at Dallas, USA. During Master of Science coursework, Mr. Alfarhan created a new software module for ArcGIS using Visual Basic Language to develop stand alone software that can predict the seed dispersal of three different species for an area during 250 years in order to know which species will extinct and which will be dominant. After completion of his Master of Science degree in 2003, he joined King Abdulaziz City for Science and Technology, Natural Resources and Environment Research Institute, Saudi Arabia. Mr. Alfarhan was responsible for the Geospatial Information Unit. Mr. Alfarhan joined The University of Texas at Dallas, USA, as PhD student in May 2005 in Geosciences with his research focusing on what he considers is a new paradigm in mapping natural features (but also applicable to manmade). Mr. Alfarhan articles have appeared in *Forest Ecology and Management*, and *Geosphere e-Journal*.

**Carlos L. V. Aiken** received his MS in geology from the University of Washington in 1970 and his PhD in Geological Sciences (geophysics) from the University of Arizona in 1976. He is presently a Full Professor at University of Texas at Dallas (UTD) (since 1978) and has taught at Texas Christian University 1975-1978. He was involved in the development of the geographic information systems program at UTD and the MS degree program in Geographic Information Sciences, and the PhD program in Geospatial Sciences with the School of Social Sciences. He has taught courses in GPS surveying, ground LIDAR and GIS. For the last 10 years his interest has been in GIS applications to geosciences, use of lasers for mapping man made and natural features, and has taught several short courses on using lasers, GPS and GIS at professional scientific meetings.

He has mapped and studied many areas in the world including China, Europe, Greenland, New Zealand, Mexico, Central and South America and Canada and has a patent and a screen credit. He has published over 100 papers and maps and is funded by the National Science Foundation for building virtual models for use in undergraduate teaching and another to build a national centre for use of laser scanners and virtual modelling in academia.

**Julian Bondy** is Associate Professor and Director Learning and Teaching in the School of Global Studies, Social Science and Planning at RMIT University, Australia. He oversees all teaching and learning activity across both sectors (Vocational Training and Higher Education) and all fund sources. He is responsible for development of a school wide policy and strategy developed to reflect University and Portfolio strategic directions in relation to teaching and learning. Previously, Dr. Bondy was the Manager of Criminal Justice Programs at RMIT. This position entailed financial, staffing, operational and strategic responsibilities associated with the delivery of criminal justice degree programs at RMIT. In the last fifteen years he has been involved in a wide range research and consultancy activities with and for the Victorian Department of Justice, the Victoria Police, overseas law enforcement agencies and Corrections Victoria. Dr. Bondy can be contacted at julian.bondy@rmit.edu.au

**Rosie Campbell** is a sociologist and who has over 16 years experience of applied social research. Rosie was a founder member of the UK Network of Sex Work Projects (UK NSWP) and was a Chair of the UK NSWP works with sex work projects throughout the UK. Rosie is currently Project-Co-ordinator for Armistead Street and Portside, sex work outreach and support projects in Merseyside, within the Armistead Centre, Liverpool Primary Care Trust. Rosie has carried out applied policy research and consultation on sex work, since 1995. She was part of the research team at; Loughborough, Staffordshire and Strathclyde Universities, who carried out the Joseph Rowntree Foundation funded, multi sited study "From Conflict to Coexistence: Living and Working in Areas of Street Sex Work" (2006), Polity Press. She has been involved in the development of good practice guidance for service interventions for sex workers and the provision of policy advice to authorities developing policies related to sex work at a local, regional and national level. Rosie has published widely on sex work and has presented her work at a wide range of national and international conferences. She has co-edited a book "Sex Work Now" (Willan, 2006).

**Liz Campbell** is lecturer in law in the University of Aberdeen, UK, since 2007. Prior to this, Liz worked as a part-time lecturer and tutor in University College Cork, where she undertook doctoral research on *"Responding to Organised Crime in Ireland: Reconstituting the Criminal Process"*. During the course of her PhD, Liz was a Government of Ireland scholar and received funding from the Irish Research Council for the Humanities and Social Sciences. Liz's main teaching interests are criminology and criminal law and her research relates to various aspects of criminal justice. Her publications have appeared in *Hibernian Law Journal, Irish Criminal Law Journal, Journal of Criminal Law, International Journal of Evidence and Proof,* and *Irish Law Times*. Liz has presented papers based on her research at national and international conferences, including the North-South Irish Criminology Conferences, International Conference on Law and Society in the 21st Century, Socio-Legal Studies Association Annual Conferences and Society of Legal Scholars Conferences. Dr. Liz can be contacted at:
liz.campbell@abdn.ac.uk

**Wing Hong Chui** is an Associate Professor in the Department of Social Work and Social Administration at the University of Hong Kong, and Adjunct Senior Lecturer in the School of Social Science at the University of Queensland, Australia. His main research and teaching interests revolve around criminal justice, criminology, youth justice, and social work practice with offenders. He is the co-editor of *Moving Probation Forward: Evidence, Arguments and Practice* (Pearson Education 2003), *Experiences of Transnational Chinese Migrants in the Asia-Pacific* (Nova Science Publishers, 2006), *Social Work and Human Services Best Practice* (Federation Press, 2006), *Research Methods for Law* (Edinburgh University Press, 2007) and *Understanding Criminal Justice in Hong Kong* (Willan, 2008). He is the Associate Editor of the *International Journal of Offender Therapy and Comparative Criminology* (Sage) and the Managing Editor and Book Review Editor of *Asian Journal of Criminology* (Springer). Dr. Chui can be contacted at:
ericchui@cuhk.edu.hk

**Arnon Edelstein** is a lecturer in the institute of criminology in the Hebrew university of Jerusalem as well as in some colleges in Southern Israel. His main interest is in immigration and crime among second generation immigrants to Israel. His researches focus on suicidal behaviours, substance use and juvenile delinquency among Ethiopian and former Russian youth in Israel. In the last years he works with the national anti-drug authority and the government department of absorption, including five major researches on various topics concerning the absorption of immigrant youth in Israel. Dr. Edelstein developed an integrative theoretical model to explain anti social behaviours among immigrant youth and uses it in his empirical researches as well as in various articles he wrote on these subjects. His second area of interest is in criminal career and multiple murders. In this field he had published a unique book concerning the theoretical concept of criminal career and seriality in crime (Ben Gurion University press). Dr. Edelstein can be contacted at: arnone@mscc.huji.ac.il

**Curtis Fogel** is a PhD candidate in the Department of Sociology at the University of Calgary in Canada. His doctoral research explores the experiences of Canadian gridiron football players with violence, hazing and performance-enhancing drug use, and the way in which these acts are viewed and institutionally handled by football administrators. He has published several articles on criminological topics pertaining to the female strip trade in North America, as well as to the use and abuse of cannabis by graduate students and professionals in Canada. His research interests include: deviance and conventionalized crime in Canadian sport, intersections between legitimate and illegitimate or underground institutions, substance use and abuse, consensual crime, and legislating morality in the virtual world. Mr. Fogel can be contacted at: cafogel@ucalgary.ca

**Lincoln J. Fry** received Ph.D's from the University of Southern California (Sociology) and Mississippi State University (Counselor Education), USA. For the past ten years he has been Grants Administrator for the State Attorney's Office, Florida's Fifteenth Judicial Circuit. He has held academic appointments at California Lutheran University, Howard University, and Nova Southeastern University. He was visiting professor at Stockholm University and Mississippi State University. He held research appointments at the Social Science Research Institute (University of Southern California) and Camarillo Neuropsychiatric Institute (University of California at Los Angeles). He has over fifty publications, journal articles, book chapters and a co-edited reader. His articles have appeared in journals such as *Social Forces, Social Problems, British Journal of Criminology, Criminology, Journal of Health and Social Behavior, the Sociological Quarterly* and others. His current research interests are international criminology, domestic violence and human trafficking. Dr. Fry can be reached at lincolnfry@bellsouth.net

**Gilbert Geis** is Professor Emeritus, Department of Criminology, Law and Society, University of California, Irvine. He received his Ph.D. in sociology from the University of Wisconsin and has been president of the American Society of Criminology and recipient of its Edwin H. Sutherland Award for research achievements. Other recognition has come from the National Association of Certified Fraud Examiners (Donald Cressey Award), the American Justice Institute (Richard A. McGee Award), the Western Society of Criminology (Paul Tappan Award), and the National Organization for Victim/Witness Protection (Stephen Schafer Award). His most recent books are *Criminal Justice and Moral Issues* (Oxford University Press, 2006) and *White-Collar and Corporate Crime* (Prentice Hall, 2007). Professor Geis can be reached at ggeis@uci.edu

**Debarati Halder** is an advocate and legal scholar. She is presently engaged as an Internet safety advocate with Working to halt online Abuse (WHOA), USA, besides looking after her own cases dealing with cyber crimes, as well as other civil suits. Earlier, she was a Research Assistant in the International Project on Cyber Bullying (funded by SSHRC, Canada) at the Department of Criminology and Criminal Justice, Manonmaniam Sundaranar University, Tirunelveli, India. She received her LLB from the University of Calcutta and Master's degree in International and Constitutional Law from the University of Madras. Her work has appeared in scholarly journals, including the *Journal of Law and Religion, Murdoch University E-Journal of Law, ERCES online quarterly review, TMC Academic Journal (Singapore) and Indian Journal of Criminology & Criminalistics* and edited volumes, *Crimes of the Internet, Trends and Issues of Victimology* etc., Debarati's research interests include Constitutional law, International Law, Victim Rights, Cyber Crimes and Laws. E-mail: debaratihalder@gmail.com URL: www.debaratihalder.co.nr

**Keith D. Harries** is a Professor of Geography and Environmental Systems at the University of Maryland, Baltimore County, since 1985 and was department chair during 1985-95. He was formerly professor of geography at Oklahoma State University. He is the author of a dozen books, most on criminal justice topics, including Geography of Crime and Justice (New York: McGraw-Hill, 1974), Crime and the Environment (Springfield: Charles C. Thomas, 1980), Serious Violence (Springfield: Charles C. Thomas, 2nd ed., 1997), Geography of Execution: The Capital Punishment Quagmire in America (Lanham: Rowman & Littlefield, 1997), and Mapping Crime: Principle & Practice (Washington D.C.: U.S. Department of Justice, 1999). His recent research has focused on analysis of neighborhoods where very high and very low crime densities are found adjacent to each other in order to determine the relevant environmental determinants of these conditions. He serves on the editorial boards of the Journal of Quantitative Criminology and International Journal of Criminal Justice Sciences. He has served as external examiner for Ph.D. students at University of Madras and elsewhere. Prof. Keith Harries holds degrees of B.Sc. (Econ), London School of Economics, M.A. & Ph.D., University of California, Los Angeles. Professor Harries can be reached at: harries@umbc.edu

**Sergio Herzog** is a Senior Lecturer at the Institute of Criminology, at the Faculty of Law, in the Hebrew University of Jerusalem, Israel. He received his bachelor's degree in psychology and his Ph.D. in criminology (direct track) from the Hebrew University in Jerusalem. His research interests lie in the areas of criminology, criminal justice systems and social psychology. He has published many articles in journals such as *Police Quarterly, Policing: An International Journal of Police Strategies and Management, Journal of Criminal Justice, Policing and Society, Law & Policy, Police Practice and Research: An International Journal, British Journal of Criminology, International Journal of Comparative and Applied Criminal Justice, Deviant Behavior, International Journal of Comparative Criminology, Journal of Criminal Law and Criminology, International Journal of the Sociology of Law, Journal of Interpersonal Violence, Crime & Delinquency, Crime, Law and Social Change, Homicide Studies, Feminist Criminology, Sex Roles, Law & Society Review,* and *Crime & Delinquency.* Dr. Herzog can be reached at: sherzog@mscc.huji.ac.il

**Amzat, Jimoh** is writing-up his doctoral thesis at the University of Ibadan, Nigeria. He graduated at Usmanu Danfodiyo University (BSc in Sociology) and University of Ibadan (MSc in Sociology) both in Nigeria. He has published in major areas of Sociology in reputable journals. His major areas of interest include Health Sociology, Criminology, Development Studies and Social Problems. He is currently a lecturer at Usmanu Danfodiyo University, Nigeria. Amzat can be contacted at: greatjoa@yahoo.co.uk

**Lee Michael Johnson** is Assistant Professor of Criminology at the University of West Georgia, USA. He received his Ph.D. in Sociology from Iowa State University in 2001. He earned a B.A. in Sociology and Psychology with a Concentration in Social Work with Young People from

Saint Ambrose University in Davenport, IA and an A.A. in Social Work from Scott Community College in Bettendorf, IA. Mike's research and writing interests are in juvenile delinquency, prevention, and intervention as well as victimization and alternative corrections. His background includes work with behaviour-disordered and delinquent youth in residential treatment, including creative and recreational activities. He has published on the topics of art in corrections, criminal justice system involvement and youth crime, victim blaming, and criminal victimization and depression. His teaching areas include juvenile delinquency, victimology, crime and social inequality, family violence, criminological theory, criminal justice, and social problems. Dr. Johnson can be contacted at:
ljohnson@westga.edu

**Abodunrin, Akintayo Julius** is a PhD candidate in Media and Criminal Justice System at the University of Ibadan, Nigeria, where he obtained his BSc and MSc in Sociology. He is currently Art and Culture reporter with the Nigerian Tribune (a national daily in Nigeria). He was nominated for national media award in 2007. He hopes to combine his career in journalism with research in Criminology.

**M. D. Allen Selva Kumar** is an ICSSR (Indian Council for Social Sciences Research) Research Fellow in the Department of Criminology and Criminal Justice, Manonmaniam Sundaranar University, Tirunelveli, India. He is presently pursuing his PhD work in the area of Child Sexual Abuse. He holds a Master's degree in Criminology and Criminal Justice Science from Manonmaniam Sundaranar University, Tirunelveli, India.

**Despina Kyprianou** holds a PhD from LSE (University of London), an MPhil from the Institute of Criminology (University of Cambridge) and an LLB from the University of Thessaloniki (Greece). She is the recipient of numerous academic scholarships and awards, including the Commonwealth Commission Scholarship, the IKY scholarship in Law from the Cyprus State Scholarship Foundation, the A.G. Leventis Foundation Research Grant and the Cambridge Commonwealth Trust Bursary. Her research has been funded by the British Council, the Cyprus Government, the European Commission, and the London School of Economics and Political Science. She is the author of 'The *Role of the Cyprus Attorney General's Office in Prosecutions: Rhetoric, Ideology and Practice*' (Springer) and has published several reports and papers in academic and professional journals. Dr. Kyprianou is the Co-editor of the *Cyprus and European Law Review*. She is also a Member of the European

Society of Criminology, the British Society of Criminology, the Socio-Legal Studies Association (UK), and the Centre for Crime & Justice Studies, King's College and a Fellow of the Cambridge Commonwealth Society. She is also a practising advocate and a lecturer at the Police Academy of Cyprus. In 2006, she was appointed by the President of the Republic of Cyprus as a Member of the Independent Police Complaint Commission and in 2007 she was elected Vice-president of the Commission. In 2007, she was also appointed as a special counsellor to the Attorney General of the Republic of Cyprus. Her research interests are in Criminal Justice, Philosophy of Punishment, Juvenile Justice, Policing and Criminal Procedure with a particular emphasis on Criminal Prosecutions. Dr. Despina can be reached at Dkyprianou@law.gov.cy, kyprianoud@yahoo.com

**Avraham Levi** received his doctorate in psychology from Columbia University, USA in 1972. He has taught at Haifa University, the Hebrew University, Ben Gurion University, and the Institute of Technology at Cholon, and also conducted research in The Henrietta Szold Institute, the Canadian- Wizo Research Institute, the Israeli Army, and the Israeli Police, receiving the award of the Minister of Internal Security for R&D. He continues to conduct research and write while on pension from the police, as well as serve as an expert witness for the Israeli Public Defenders. Dr. Levi can be contacted at avmlevi@netivison.net.il

**Agunbiade Ojo Melvin** is currently a Lecturer in the Department of Sociology and Anthropology, Obafemi Awolowo University, Ile-Ife, Nigeria. He has a Master of Science in Medical Sociology from the same University. He is presently on his PhD programme. His areas of research interest are in Mental Health, Sexual health, Traditional Medicine, Reproductive Health, Sociological theory, and Social Research Methods. E-mail: ojomelvin@yahoo.com

**Tumpa Mukherjee** has completed post graduation in Sociology from University of Calcutta, India. Currently she is working as a part time lecturer in the Department of Sociology at the Scottish Church College and is pursuing her PhD studies at Jadavpur University, Kolkata. She specializes in policing studies with special reference to Community Policing and has presented a paper at the 7th Annual Conference of Asian Association of Police Studies (AAPS) in Bangkok, Thailand, September 2006. Her articles have been published in refereed journals, daily newspapers such as The Telegraph and The Hindustan Times. As a citizen journalist her articles have been published at merinews.com. Her book

*'Community Policing in India: A Sociological Perspective'* has been published by Progressive Publisher in the year 2006. Her forthcoming publication includes an article 'Twilight years in India' which is to be published in the book '12 Geriatres En' (12 Angry Geriatricians) by Fayard, Paris, later this year. She is also co-editing a book on Prisons with Dr. K. Jaishankar, Manonmaniam Sundaranar University. Ms. Mukherjee can be contacted at tumpamukherjee@hotmail.com

**Johnny Nhan** is an Assistant Professor of Criminal Justice at Texas Christian University and a Doctoral Candidate in the Department of Criminology, Law, School of Social Ecology University of California, Irvine, California. His research interests include all areas of Internet crime, focusing particularly on governance, social control, and relations between law enforcement and private industry. He has written on Internet piracy and policing the Internet. He is currently exploring federal policing efforts in network intrusions and hacking. Johnny can be contacted at jnhan@uci.edu

**Ikuteyijo Lanre Olusegun** had his MSc degree in Sociology and Anthropology from the Obafemi Awolowo University, Ile-Ife, Nigeria, where he lectures. His area of specialization is criminology and criminal justice system. He also has interest in other areas like penology, urbanization, reproductive health and migration.

**Fatih Ozgul** is a member of Istanbul Police, Turkey. He is an expert on crime analysis, especially, spatio-temporal analysis of crime, link analysis and offender group detection using Artificial Intelligence and Social Network Analysis. He is also a final year Ph.D. student at Sunderland University's Computing Science Department. He has a master's degree on Geographical Information Systems from Newcastle University. He graduated from Turkish National Police Academy in 1997 and serving as a mid-rank police chief at Istanbul Police. He is the author of a range of policing publications and conference proceedings on crime analysis. Ozgul can be contacted at fatih.ozgul@sund.ac.uk

**Jeevan Ballav Panda** is an Advocate, currently working as a Legal Associate at Khaitan & Co. Kolkata, India. He has recently completed his five years BA LLB (Hons.) from Hidayatullah National Law University, Raipur (Chhattisgarh) with Honours in Intellectual Property Rights and Environmental Law. His areas of interest include- Litigation, ADR, IPR, Criminal Law and Environmental Law. He also has more than a dozen publications to his name in some of the reputed national journals as well as international journals. He is a peer reviewer of International Journal of Criminal Justice Sciences. Mr. Jeevan can be contacted at: jbpanda@gmail.com

**Henry N. Pontell** is professor of criminology, law and society in the School of Social Ecology, and of sociology in the School of Social Sciences at the University of California, Irvine. He received his Ph.D. in sociology from Stony Brook University in 1979. His academic work has spanned such topics as social deviance, punishment and deterrence, crime seriousness, health care fraud, international financial fraud, white-collar and corporate crime, cyber crime, and identity theft. He has testified before the U.S. Senate on financial fraud, has worked closely with numerous government agencies including the FBI and the U.S. Secret Service, and has had his research on white-collar crime highlighted in the national and international media. He has served as president of the Western Society of Criminology and as vice president of the American Society of Criminology and has been elected a fellow of both organizations. In 2001, he received the Donald R. Cressey Award from the Association of Certified Fraud Examiners, for major lifetime contributions to fraud investigation, detection, and deterrence, and the Albert J. Reiss, Jr. Distinguished Scholarship Award from the American Sociological Association. He has held visiting appointments at the Australian National University, the University of Melbourne, the University of Macau, the University of Virginia, and Waseda University in Tokyo, Japan. His most recent books include: *Profit Without Honor: White Collar Crime and the Looting of America* (4th Edition, Prentice Hall, 2007), and the *International Handbook of White-Collar and Corporate Crime* (Springer, 2007). He is editor of the *Masters Series in Criminology* (Prentice Hall). Professor Pontell can be reached at hnpontel@uci.edu

**Michael Pittaro** is the Executive Director of the Council on Alcohol and Drug Abuse in Allentown, Pennsylvania, USA and an adjunct professor with Cedar Crest College's (Allentown, Pennsylvania) criminal justice department. Earlier, Pittaro was the Chair of the Legal Studies Department at Lehigh Valley College, Pennsylvania. He is the author of several publications, including US's first and only criminal justice quick study reference guide, and has been the honoured recipient of several awards for his teaching style and practice. Pittaro is co-editor of *Crimes of the Internet* (Prentice Hall, 2008) and a member of the International Editorial Advisory Board of the *International Journal of Criminal Justice Sciences.*

Pittaro has nearly 20 years of professional criminal justice field experience. He holds a master's degree in public administration and a bachelor's degree in criminal justice from Kutztown University, and he is currently pursuing a PhD in criminal justice from Capella University. Mr. Pittaro can be contacted at crimeNjustice@RCN.com

**Lynne Roberts** is a lecturer in the School of Psychology at Curtin University of Technology in Western Australia. Lynne has conducted both quantitative and qualitative research in and about virtual communities. Based on this research she has published on social interaction, relationship formation, sense of community, gender-switching and ethical research in virtual environments. Earlier, Lynne worked at the Crime Research Centre at the University of Western Australia and during this period she generated interest in cyber-crime and cyber-victimisation. Her other research interests include research and evaluation methodologies, public attitudes to crime and justice, and ethics. Dr. Lynne can be contacted at:
Lynne.Roberts@Curtin.edu.au

**Natti Ronel** is a senior lecturer at the Department of Criminology, Bar Ilan University, Ramat Gan, Israel. He previously served as the Researcher-in-Chief of the interdisciplinary Center for Children and Youth Studies in Tel Aviv University. He is also a licensed clinical criminologist who holds private practice with criminal population, youth and adults who exhibit addiction, violence and/or victimization. Natti leads continuous training courses for Criminal Justice and Victim Assistance professionals and he is a recurring faculty member of the annual postgraduate course of "Victimology, victim assistance, and criminal justice" in the Inter University Centre, Dubrovnik, where he lectures on therapy for recovering victims. His various writings reflect both his clinical and academic experience in criminology. He has a special focus on the spiritual aspect of criminology and victimology - its values and impact upon individuals and communities: spiritual based intervention and recovery, moral transformation, forgiveness and spiritual intelligence. Natti is the proponent of a new criminological theory "The Criminal Spin". He is a member of the World Society of Victimology, the Israeli Society of Criminology (board member) and the Israeli Council for Criminology. He has co-edited a book, *Trends and Issues in Victimology* (Cambridge Scholars Publishing, UK, 2008). Natti is married happily with two grown children and live in Jaffa – the Jewish–Arabic part of Tel Aviv, Israel. Dr. Ronel can be contacted at roneln@mail.biu.ac.il; nattir@gmail.com

**Teela Sanders** is a senior lecturer in the School of Sociology and Social Policy at the University of Leeds, UK. Sitting on the borders of criminology and sociology, Teela explores the inter-relationship between human sexuality and socio-legal structures. Her main research interests have been in the UK sex industry examining the social organisation of sex work, regulation regimes and men who buy sex. She has published research findings in journals such as *Sociology, Urban Studies*, the *Sociology of Health and Illness, Critical Social Policy, Sexualities, Gender, Work and Organization*, and *British Journal of Sociology.* She has published on the indoor sex markets, *Sex Work: A Risky Business'* (Willan, 2005) which was short listed for the Philip Abrahms prize, and also *Paying for Pleasure: Men Who Buy Sex* (Willan, 2008). Teela is a Board Member of the UK Network of Sex Work Projects, and has been the Chair of the women's charity, Genesis, in Leeds. Dr. Teela can be contacted at t.l.m.sanders@leeds.ac.uk

**Aiden Sidebottom** is a research assistant at the Jill Dando Institute of Crime Science, University College London, UK. His research interests include applying evolutionary and psychological theory to crime, especially situational crime prevention and design against crime. Winner of the annual UCL Jill Dando Institute scholarship, Aiden holds a master's degree in crime science from University College London and a bachelor's degree in applied psychology from the University of Durham. He has recently edited a special edition of a journal concerned with environmental criminology and crime analysis. Dr. Aiden can be contacted at: a.sidebottom@ucl.ac.uk

**Robert Smith** is a Research Fellow at the Charles P. Skene Centre for Entrepreneurship at Aberdeen Business School, The Robert Gordon University, Aberdeen, UK. Robert studied for his M.A (1997) at Aberdeen University and his PhD by research at the Robert Gordon University, Aberdeen (2006) whilst working full time as a police officer. Robert has completed 25 years police service as a constable in a variety of roles. Robert's PhD thesis *"Understanding the entrepreneur as socially constructed"* sought to understand the social construction of entrepreneurship using a verstehen based approach which included semiotic analysis. Robert's research interests are eclectic but include – social constructionism, rural entrepreneurship, family business, entrepreneurial policing, criminal entrepreneurship and entrepreneurial crime. Dr. Robert can be contacted at r.smith-a@rgu.ac.uk

**P. Madhava Soma Sundaram (Madhavan)** is the Reader and Head of the Department of Criminology and Criminal Justice, Manonmaniam Sundaranar University, Tirunelveli, India. Madhavan holds Masters' degree in criminology and PhD in criminology from the University of Madras. His doctorate work is in the field of victimology, focusing on fear of crime. Dr. Madhavan has authored two books in Tamil, several project reports and many papers, chapters in books, editorials, book reviews, in journals and magazines. He is a co-editor of *Crime Victims and Justice: An Introduction to Restorative Principles* (Serials Publications: New Delhi, 2008). He is the founding Editor-in-Chief of "Crime and Justice Perspective" – the official organ of the Criminal Justice Forum (CJF), India and the founding editor of the International Journal of Criminal Justice Sciences. He is a member of the Editorial Advisory Board of the International Journal of Cyber Criminology. In recognition of his contribution in the growth of criminology in India, Madhavan was conferred the title of 'Fellow of Indian Society of Criminology' (FISC) by the Indian Society of criminology (ISC) for 2001 and Prof. S.S. Srivastava Award for excellence in teaching and research in criminology for 2009. His areas of specialization are juvenile justice, victimology, child protection and social defense. Dr. Madhavan can be contacted at: drmadhava@gmail.com

**Nicolas A. Valcik** is Associate Director of the Office of Strategic Planning and Analysis and Clinical Lecturer for the Department of Public Affairs at The University of Texas at Dallas, USA. He teaches undergraduate and graduate level courses in organizational behaviour, emergency management and human resource management. He is the author of *Regulating the Use of Biological Hazardous Materials in Universities: Complying with the New Federal Guidelines* (Edwin Mellen Press, 2006), *Empowering Data Usage: Extracting Data from Mainframe Applications Using Job Control Language, FOCUS, ACCESS and SAS* (BookSurge Publishing, 2004), and *The Fifth Dimension: Strategic Planning and Practical Aspects for Higher Education and the Public Sector* (Global Book Publisher, 2003). He is an editor of *Space: The Final Frontier for Institutional Research: New Directions for Institutional Research, No. 135* (Jossey-Bass, 2007). He is project team leader and chief designer of the Logistical Tracking System, a software application designed to manage university facilities and track hazardous materials. He has presented his research on a variety of topics including facilities management, hazardous material safety, strategic planning, and Texas stalking laws at various conferences held by the Association for Institutional Research (national and regional conferences), Campus Safety Health and Environmental Management Association, and the Academy of Criminal Justice and Science. He has previously held positions with the city manager's office in McKinney, Texas, the City of Duncanville, Texas - Economic Development Corporation, and Nortel Networks. Dr. Valcik can be contacted at nvalcik@utdallas.edu

**Emilio C. Viano** is a Professor in the School of Public Affairs, American University and also adjunct professor in the Washington College of Law, Washington D.C. USA. He has earned degrees in anthropology, sociology, and law. He has published over 30 edited/authored books and over 120 scholarly articles. He is frequently asked to advise national and international organizations like the United Nations, Council of Europe, the Organization of American States and others. He has been invited to lecture at many universities worldwide and has organized several international meetings and conferences. Most recently he organized the Transnational Crime section of the 2008 World Congress of Criminology in Barcelona, Spain. Professor Viano is member of the Board of Directors of the International Society of Criminology (Paris) and substitute member of the Board of Directors of the International Association of Penal Law (Paris). He serves on several editorial boards of journals and publishing houses and on the board of various non-profit organizations. He is frequently asked to provide analysis and comments on international media like CNN, BBC, Voice of America and many other media outlets, especially in the USA, Latin America and Europe. Professor Viano's scholarly and professional work has been recognized with prizes, diplomas and awards by various academic and scholarly organizations worldwide. He has received multiple Fulbright awards as well. Professor Viano can be contacted at eviano@american.edu

**Kam C. Wong** is the Chair/Associate Professor, Department of Criminal Justice, Xavier University, Ohio, USA and Visiting Professor of Law, City University of Hong Kong, School of Law. He earned his law degree from Indiana University (Bloomington) and Ph.D. in criminal justice at SUNY - Albany. His areas of expertise are: Comparative policing: PRC vs. U.S.A. China policing, Hong Kong policing People's Republic of China criminal law and criminal process, Homeland Security – USA PATRIOT Act. Dr. Wong was formerly an Inspector of Police with the Hong Kong Police and was awarded the Commissioner's High Commendation. Professor Wong was the former Director of Chinese Laws Program at Chinese University of Hong Kong. He served as the vice-president (1999 to 2000) and vice-chair (2000 to 2002) to Hong Kong Society of Criminology. He is currently an Associate Fellow of Centre for Criminology, Hong Kong University. He is an organizer and founding member of Asian Association of Police Studies, of which he was the vice-President (2001-2) and President (2002-3). Dr. Wong was an editor with the Journal of Crime and Delinquency and Managing Editor for Police Practice and Research: An International Journal. He was the Editor-in-Chief, Occasional Paper Series, Chinese Law Program. He is currently on the Editorial Boards of *International Journal of Comparative Criminology; Asian Policing, Police Practice and Research, Open Journal of Law, Open Journal of Sociology and International Journal of Criminal Justice Sciences*. He has published 75 articles, chapters and books. The most recent ones being: *The Impact of USA Patriot Act on American Society: An Evidence Based Assessment* (N.Y.: Nova Science Publication, 2007): *The Making of USA Patriot Act: Legislation, Implementation, Impact* (Beijing: China Law Press, 2008); *Policing with Chinese Characteristics* (Peter Lang, 2008) (Forthcoming). Dr. Wong can be contacted at wongk1@xavier.edu

**Patrick Webb** is currently an Assistant Professor in the Department of Criminal Justice, University of Houston – Downtown, USA. Earlier he was a Lecturer in the Department of Sociology, Social Work and Criminal Justice at Lamar University in Beaumont, Texas. He completed his Ph.D. from the College of Juvenile Justice and Psychology at Prairie View A&M University. Dr. Webb's areas of professional interest include juvenile justice/delinquency, child psychology and development, marriage and family relations, and research methods. His works have appeared in *Youth Violence and Juvenile Justice*, *American Corrections Association*, *Journal of Ethnicity in Criminal Justice, Doctoral Forum, International Journal of Criminal Justice Sciences* and *Critical Criminology*. Dr. Webb can be reached at PatrickWebb@hotmail.com

**Xueming Xu** received his B.S. at Nanjing University, M.S. at Chinese Academy of Sciences, and Ph.D. from the University of Texas at Dallas, USA. He has more than seven years experience in GIS and GPS, including projects to build dozens of GIS databases and maps of regions around the world. Applying his training in computer science, Dr. Xu designed and wrote the software that has made digital data acquisition successful, and he developed the algorithms and programming that form the basis of 3-D photorealistic mapping. Dr. Xu has patented his unique process for 3-D, photorealistic modelling and continues to develop enhancements to his technique. He currently works for Real Earth Models, a company that specializes in creating 3-D, digital, photorealistic models.

# SUBJECT INDEX

**D**

## R



## S



## T